Reassessing Legal Humanism and its Claims

EDINBURGH STUDIES IN LAW

Volumes in the series:

Elspeth Reid and David L Carey Miller (eds), *A Mixed Legal System in Transition: T B Smith and the Progress of Scots Law* (2005)

Hector MacQueen and Reinhard Zimmermann (eds), *European Contract Law: Scots and South African Perspectives* (2006)

John W Cairns and Paul du Plessis (eds), *Beyond Dogmatics: Law and Society in the Roman World* (2007)

William M Gordon, *Roman Law, Scots Law and Legal History* (2007)

Kenneth G C Reid, Marius J de Waal and Reinhard Zimmermann (eds), *Exploring the Law of Succession: Studies National, Historical and Comparative* (2007)

Vernon Valentine Palmer and Elspeth Christie Reid (eds), *Mixed Jurisdictions Compared: Private Law in Louisiana and Scotland* (2009)

John W Cairns and Paul J du Plessis (eds), *The Creation of the* Ius Commune*: From* Casus *to* Regula (2010)

James Chalmers, Lindsay Farmer and Fiona Leverick (eds), *Essays in Criminal Law in Honour of Sir Gerald Gordon* (2010)

Elaine E Sutherland, Kay E Goodall, Gavin F M Little and Fraser P Davidson (eds), *Law Making and the Scottish Parliament* (2011)

Neil Walker (ed), *MacCormick's Scotland* (2012)

Eric Descheemaeker (ed), *The Consequences of Possession* (2014)

Remus Valsan (ed), *Trusts and Patrimonies* (2015)

John W Cairns, *Law, Lawyers, and Humanism: Selected Essays on the History of Scots Law, Vol 1* (2015)

John W Cairns, *Enlightenment, Legal Education, and Critique: Selected Essays on the History of Scots Law, Vol 2* (2015)

Paul J du Plessis and John W Cairns (eds), *Reassessing Legal Humanism and its Claims:* Petere Fontes*?* (2016)

www.euppublishing.com/series/esil

EDINBURGH STUDIES IN LAW
VOLUME 15

Reassessing Legal Humanism and its Claims

Petere Fontes?

Edited by
Paul J du Plessis and John W Cairns

EDINBURGH
University Press

[D]ie Eule der Minerva beginnt erst mit der einbrechenden Dämmerung ihren Flug. – G W F Hegel, *Grundlinien der Philosophie des Rechts* (1821) Vorrede.

Edinburgh University Press Ltd
13 InfirmaryStreet
Edinburgh EH1 1LT
www.euppublishing.com

First published in hardback by Edinburgh University Press 2016

Typeset in New Caledonia by
Servis Filmsetting Ltd, Stockport,
and printed and bound in Great Britain by
CPI Group (UK) Ltd, Croydon CR0 4YY

A CIP record for this book is available from the British Library

ISBN 978 1 4744 0885 1 (hardback)
ISBN 978 1 3995 7192 0 (paperback)
ISBN 978 1 4744 0886 8 (webready PDF)
ISBN 978 1 4744 0887 5 (epub)

Contents

Preface

The papers collected in this volume were originally delivered on 7–8 June 2013 at a conference organised by the Centre for Legal History of the University of Edinburgh, School of Law. As part of the celebration of 303 years of continuous teaching of Civil Law (*ius civile*) in the University of Edinburgh, the Centre for Legal History hosted an expert symposium on legal humanism, addressing the topic from a variety of perspectives. The symposium challenged and debated the common conceptualisation of legal humanism.

A traditional view of European legal history will often start – after discussion of the early medieval codes – with the rediscovery and teaching of the *Corpus Iuris Civilis* in medieval Italy. It then sets out this history as a progression of schools of jurists, working through Glossators, Commentators, Humanists, Natural Lawyers and Codifiers, with the enactment of the BGB almost as the end of history. It is also traditionally linked to a geographical progression – almost a *translatio studii* – from Italy, to France, to the Netherlands, to Germany. This is not a convincing narrative as scholars have increasingly realised over the past three decades. What of the influence of Pothier? What of the French Code? What of Spanish, Portuguese and Italian scholarship? What of England?

Legal humanism presents particularly difficult issues of understanding. Lesaffer's recent subtle study of European legal history brings home the problems and contingencies of the traditional narrative when he has to use the term "moderate humanism" to deal with the historical realities with which he is faced. The participants examined a whole variety of aspects of what is usually considered under the rubric "legal humanism", covering the "philological" work on the Digest, humanist jurists and political thought, humanists and the legacy of Byzantium, humanists and *formulae,* libraries, humanism and English law, and the humanist legacy as understood in the eighteenth century, and the extent to which legal humanism was and is a meaningful classification other than for a small group of specialist writers. In this respect, the traditional distinctions between the *mos gallicus* and *mos italicus* were considered, as well as the significance in this context of the *usus modernus*. Sources, pedagogy, the working methods of scholars, and the book-collecting habits of lawyers were all considered and debated. This volume is the result of those deliberations.

The conference of June 2013 was the third mini-conference of those planned by the Centre for Legal History on a roughly four-year cycle. The previous conference, in 2008, led to the publication of John W. Cairns and Paul J. du Plessis (eds), *The Creation of the* Ius Commune*: From* Casus *to* Regula (2010) [Edinburgh Studies in Law VII]. This publication promised (at viii) that "The third-mini conference will be devoted to humanism and law." The publication of this volume fulfils that promise. The fourth mini-conference will be devoted to the *usus modernus pandectarum*.

This volume, and the conference that preceded it, would not have been possible without the generous financial support of the Edinburgh Legal Education Trust and the School of Law, University of Edinburgh. The editors of this volume wish to thank both for their support. The School of Law, Research Office provided invaluable assistance in the organising of this conference. Finally, the editors of this volume wish to thank the Editorial Board of the Edinburgh Studies in Law in general and the series editor, Professor Elspeth Reid for accepting this volume.

JWC
PdP
Old College, Edinburgh
April 2015

A Note on Names and Book Titles

The chapters collected in this volume refer to a large number of jurists from the sixteenth to eighteenth centuries. As was the convention of the early modern period, many of these jurists were known by the Latinised versions of their names and surnames in addition to their names and surnames in the vernacular languages of early modern Europe. To assist the reader in traversing this issue, every effort has been made to verify both the vernacular and Latinised versions of the names of jurists using the library catalogues of the British Library. Similarly, for book titles in Latin and their editions, the Universal Short Title Catalogue has been used to verify titles and editions. We have not attempted to standardise names across the volume as to do so would interfere too much with the individual chapters. Instead, we have provided guidance throughout where names might create confusion. This volume, like the others in this series, follows the citation style of the *Edinburgh Law Review*. Since this style of citation is somewhat minimalist, especially in relation to bibliographic information regarding publisher and place of publication of books, this information has been retained in the text and in footnotes in relation to books from the early modern period where such information is central to the point being made.

List of Contributors

JOHN W CAIRNS, Edinburgh
PAUL J DU PLESSIS, Edinburgh
ALAIN WIJFFELS, Leiden, Leuven, Lille, Louvain-la-Neuve
DOUGLAS J OSLER, Frankfurt-am-Main
GUIDO ROSSI, Edinburgh
XAVIER PRÉVOST, Bordeaux
SUSAN LONGFIELD KARR, Cincinnati
WIM DECOCK, Leuven
MARTINE J VAN ITTERSUM, Dundee
BERNARD STOLTE, Groningen
ÉVA JAKAB, Szeged
JASMIN HEPBURN, Edinburgh
DAVID IBBETSON, Cambridge
IAN MACLEAN, Oxford
KAREN G BASTON, Edinburgh

List of Abbreviations

§	paragraph
a o	among others
AD	Anno Domini
ad	on/concerning
adv	*adversus*
art	article
axiom	*axioma*
B	Basilica
b	Year of birth
Bd	volume
cap	*caput*
c	*circa*
C	Codex of Justinian
cf	compare
ch	chapter
col/s	column/s
comm	commentary
cons	*consilia*
contr	*controversia*
CCSL	Corpus Christianorum – Series Latina
D	Digest
disp	*disputatio*
dub	*dubitatio*
ed	editor
ed pr	*editio princeps*
edn	edition
eds	editors
e.g.	for example
eod	the same
esp	especially
f/fol/s	folio/folios
ff	on the following pages
Fn	footnote

fr	fragment
Gl	gloss
ibid/ibidem	in the same place
idem	the same
i.e.	that is
in verb	on the phrase
inv	invoice
IRMAE	*Ius Romanum Medii Aevii*
l	*lex*
let	*lettera*
lib	book
loc cit	*locus citatus*
MS	Manuscript
Mt	Matthew
n/nn	note/notes
necnon	also
NLS	National Library of Scotland
No	number
num	*numero*
par/paras	paragraph/paragraphs
passim	throughout
pt	part
q/quaest	*quaestio*
r	*recto*
rep	reprint
resp	*responsum*
rev	revised
sec	section
sig	sign
rub	rubric
t/tom	tome
tit	title
TLS	Times Literary Supplement
transl	translated
USCT	Universal Short Title Catalogue
ult	final
v	*verso*
vide	see
viz	*videlicet*

VOC	Dutch East India Company
vol	volume
X	*Liber Extra*

Introduction

John W Cairns

William Forbes (1668/1671–1745) neatly expressed a view of what we now know as legal humanism in his "Great Body of the Law of Scotland" when he wrote:

> Andreas Alciat a Milaneze was the first who united the study of the law with polite learning and the knowledge of antiquities. Many learned men who by their elaborate writings afford much light to the Roman law, have copied after him. But James Cujace, born at Tholause, acquired and discovered so complete a knowledge of it that he has surpassed all that went before him and is a true guide to those that came after him.[1]

Forbes was educated in arts, probably at the University of St Andrews, and probably also in law, in the latter possibly at the University of Leiden in the Low Countries. In 1696, he was admitted as an advocate of the Scots bar. Between 1703 and 1714, he published a number of works on Scots law. He enjoyed the patronage of the powerful family of Dalrymple of Stair, and in 1713 he was appointed as the first Professor of Civil Law in the University of Glasgow.[2] The issue of legal humanism and its values was important for Forbes, since he thought that Roman law was authoritative in Scotland.[3] If he had in fact been educated in law at the University of Leiden or indeed any other university in the Netherlands (as seems likely), he would have been quite extensively exposed to Dutch legal humanism or elegant jurisprudence, whether or not he had studied with a luminary such as Gerard Noodt (1647–1725).[4] But no matter, Forbes was repeating a com-

1 W Forbes, "A Great Body of the Law of Scotland Containing the Harmony thereof with, and Differences from the Civil and Feudal Laws" Glasgow University Library (GUL) MS Gen 1246, 17.

2 J W Cairns, "The Origins of the Glasgow Law School: The Professors of Civil Law, 1714–61" in P Birks (ed), *The Life of the Law: Proceedings of the Tenth British Legal History Conference, Oxford 1991* (1993) 151 at 158–174. The best survey of Forbes' work is A Herd, "The Authority of the Civil Law in 18th Century Scotland: The Approach of William Forbes, Advocate and Professor" unpublished LLM dissertation, University of Edinburgh (2013).

3 Herd (n 2) 85.

4 G C J J van den Bergh, *The Life and Work of Gerard Noodt (1647–1725): Dutch Legal Scholarship between Humanism and Enlightenment* (1988), G C J J van den Bergh, *Die hollän-*

monplace of his age: polite or elegant learning in Roman law began with Andrea Alciato (1492–1550), who was the first to link the study of Roman law with that of letters and, in particular, with the study of history; Jacques Cujas (1522–1590) from Toulouse was the supreme scholar of the movement. Indeed, in the lemmatic commentary Forbes composed on Justinian's Institutes, he described Cujas as "incomparabilis".[5] It is worth noting that those now known as legal humanists were in the past seen to constitute the *schola Cuiaciana*;[6] it is also telling that two great Dutch elegant scholars, Noodt and Anton Schulting, could each be described as the "Dutch Cujas".[7]

Forbes also cited the radical Protestant Humanist, François Hotman (1524–1590), as well as Hubrecht van Giffen (Hubertus Gyphanus) (1534–1604), lawyer and philologist, who had studied with Cujas, and the humanistically oriented Leiden professor, Antonius Matthaeus III (1635–1710).[8] Further research would be needed to examine properly Forbes' attitude to legal humanism; but one suspects he was writing what any educated Scots advocate of his day would write: and some very clearly embraced what they understood to be the "elegant" approach.[9] But, since Forbes is best known for his writings on Scots law, this in itself raises many questions about our understanding of legal humanism as an intellectual movement, if indeed it may be described as such.

Legal humanism is usually depicted as part of a typical, if varying from author to author, grand narrative of European legal history, conceived of as a succession of schools of jurists. The story is familiar: the study of law revived in Bologna with Irnerius and his followers who constituted the school of Glossators, the apogee of whose work was the *glossa ordinaria* of Accursius; after a trip north of the Alps to the school of Orléans, the story contin-

dische elegante Schule: Ein Betrag zur Geschichte von Humanismus und Rechtswissenschaft in den Niederlanden 1500–1800 (2002) 193–195.

5 GUL MS Gen 1256, 5.

6 J S Brunquellus, *Historia iuris Romano-Germanici a primis reipublicae Romanae atque Germanicae initiis ad nostra usque tempora ex suis fontibus deducta et in usum auditorii adornata*, editio altera (1730) 371–385.

7 On Schulting as the Dutch Cujas, see van den Bergh, *Life and Work* (n 4) 19; on Noodt as the Dutch Cujas, see C P Sherman, *Roman Law in the Modern World* (1917) I 256.

8 GUL MS Gen 1256 (n 5) 5.

9 For example, C Binning, *Disputatio juridica, de usufructu & quemadmodum quis utatur fruatur* (1698), containing Binning's theses for admission as an advocate, is chock-full of citations considered to be typically humanist. See further, K G Baston and J W Cairns, "An elegant legal education: the Studies of Charles Binning, a Scottish pupil of Cornelis van Eck" (2015) 83 *Tijdschrift voor Rechtsgeschiedenis/Legal History Review* 179.

ues with the Commentators or *Konsiliatoren*, whose leaders were Bartolus and Baldus; next come the legal humanists, who, inspired by Renaissance values, attempted through philological and historical research to recapture the original Roman law, but whose historicising emphasised the connectedness of Roman law to Roman society, thereby rendering Roman law a purely historical study. This meant that "practical" lawyers carried on using the Bartolist method, now known as the *mos italicus*, in opposition to the Humanist method described as the *mos gallicus*, because legal humanism had supposedly most flourished in France.[10] This view of the humanists is very eloquently expressed, for example, by Peter Stein, who claims that the humanists "came to question whether it was really appropriate to try to apply Roman law at all to contemporary problems", and that the humanists were unintentionally "undermining the authority of Roman law".[11] Julian Franklin, however, goes so far as to say some of the French humanists made an attack on the authority of Roman law.[12]

Following the humanists, the story becomes somewhat messier and more varied. The narrative has to encompass secular natural law (sometimes by way of the School of Salamanca or the neo-Bartolists or the neo-Scholastics), the *usus modernus pandectarum* and Roman-Dutch law, and rationalism, all leading to nineteenth-century Pandektenrecht or positivism and conceptualism more generally. It also has to work in the varying codification movements. A major part of the problem scholars face in dealing with what they see as the "post-humanist" development of legal history in Europe is trying to fit into this schema an account of the rise of national legal systems. Further, some scholars focus on studies of Roman law, seeing a movement of the elegant approach from France to the Dutch Republic to the German lands of the Historical School.[13]

In recent years, this approach has been very much associated with the work of Franz Wieacker, which has been translated into English and thereby gained a world-wide audience. It has of course an earlier origin. But Wieacker's book, and its picture of European legal history, has been promoted by the phenomenal success of the work of Reinhard Zimmermann

10 J Gordley, *The Jurists: A Critical History* (2013) 28–127 gives a rich and complex account.

11 P Stein, "Justinian's compilation: classical legacy and legal source" (1993) 8 *Tulane European and Civil Law Forum* 1 at 9.

12 J Franklin, *Jean Bodin and the Sixteenth-Century Revolution in the Methodology of Law and History* (1963) 36–58.

13 F Wieacker, *History of Private Law in Europe with Particular Reference to Germany*, 2nd edn, transl by Tony Weir (1995), Gordley (n 10) 128–274.

who has remarked that "the intellectual framework established by Wieacker is, by and large, still authoritative today".[14] To some extent it underlies, for example, the successful British textbook of Olivia Robinson, David Fergus and Bill Gordon, and the brief but elegant account of European legal history written by Peter Stein.[15] One can even identify it in the somewhat different approach taken by Randall Lesaffer.[16]

Of course, sifting through considerable amounts of material requires historians to sort it out somehow for exposition, and if they are dealing with any kind of *longue durée* (if not necessarily in Braudel's sense), dividing history into periods is a necessary aspect of writing on Clio's open scroll. Further, it is not as if the traditional grand narrative is evident nonsense; and it does provide a framework for research. But it is, at the very least, questionable and in need of greater nuance. Thus, to give one example, Forbes' attitude and the strongly humanistic content of the libraries of practising Scots lawyers such as Charles Areskine and Duncan Forbes of Culloden suggest that any modern narrative that views humanism as a primarily sixteenth-century French movement that was then superseded, is doubtful.[17] Forbes does not even hint that the *jurisprudentia elegantior* of the *schola Cuiaciana* constituted some kind of dead end, turning in Roman law into pure legal history. Scots lawyers of Forbes' generation were aware that some scholars of Roman law were more focused on *jurisprudentia cultior* than others (one student at Leiden described Noodt as more of a critic than a lawyer);[18] but they simply did not express the type of broad claim made by Stein and others.

Forbes' claim that legal humanism started with Alciatus, and that the (humanistic) study of Roman law was perfected by Cujas, whose works provided a guide to all later scholars, certainly anticipates the standard recent or modern scholarship. One clear idea is that legal humanism was something new – the joining of law with history and philology in a reaction against the

14 R Zimmermann, *The Law of Obligations: Roman Foundations of the Civilian Tradition* (1996) x.

15 O F Robinson, T D Fergus and W M Gordon, *European Legal History*, 3rd edn (2000); P Stein, *Roman Law in European History* (1999).

16 R Lesaffer, *European Legal History*, transl by J Arriens (2009).

17 National Library of Scotland, MS 3283 contains Areskine's library catalogue; *A catalogue of curious and valuable books; being chiefly the library of the Right Hon. Duncan Forbes of Culloden, Esq; late Lord President of Session: which will begin to be sold by auction, on Monday the 12th of December 1748* (1748). This first is discussed in K G Baston, "The Library of Charles Areskine (1680–1763): Scottish lawyers and book collecting, 1700–1760" unpublished PhD thesis, University of Edinburgh (2012), accessed at *https://www.era.lib.ed.ac.uk/handle/1842/6417*.

18 J W Cairns, "Alexander Cunningham's proposed edition of the Digest: an episode in the history of the Dutch elegant school of Roman law (Part II)" (2001) 69 *Tijdschrift voor Rechtsgeschiedenis* 307 at 315.

medieval scholarship in Roman law associated with the Gloss and the work of Bartolus and Baldus. This certainly was the propaganda: one can trace it in Brunquellus' *Historia iuris Romano-Germanici*.[19]

Scholars of Forbes' generation tended to ignore the great medieval jurists. It was only with the work of Maurus Sarti in the later eighteenth century that the work of the jurists of the High Middle Ages started to get significant attention.[20] F C von Savigny drew on the work of Sarti to write his *Geschichte des römischen Rechts im Mittelalter*, and the main structure of the modern narrative of European legal history starts to fall into place.[21] One can then start to view it as predominantly German – story: Savigny is concerned to rebuild German legal science after the defeat of Napoleon, just as Wieacker and Koschaker were again after the defeat of Nazism.[22] If this is obviously more than simply a German story, in recent years, such traditional grand narratives of European legal history have begun to be questioned (compare our previous volume, *Casus* to *Regula*).[23] The nature and legacy of legal humanism is particularly important in this respect, as it casts a long shadow over much of European legal history and is generally seen as one of the pivotal movements in the development of European law; it is also seen as fundamental in the development of political thought and historical writing more generally.[24] It therefore deserves closer critical scrutiny.

Despite some path-breaking work, such as that by Douglas Osler,[25] who has been critical of the traditional narratives surrounding legal humanism, the view that the *mos gallicus* became purely academic (the term being used in the modern pejorative sense) has nonetheless become so deeply entrenched in most modern works on European legal history that it is almost entirely unexamined; it has been accepted with such blind faith that few

19 Brunquellus (n 6) 342–388.

20 M Sarti, *De Claris archigymnasii Bononiensis professoribus a saeculo XI usque ad saeculum XIV* (completed and ed by M Fattorini) (1769–1772).

21 E Andersen, *The Renaissance of Legal Science after the Middle Ages: The German Historical School no Bird Phoenix* (1974) 5–9.

22 T Duve, "German legal history: national traditions and transnational perspectives" (2014) 22 *Rechtsgeschichte* 16 at 25, P Koschaker, *Europa und das römische Recht* (1947). The first edition of Wieacker was published in 1952.

23 See, e.g., J W Cairns and P J du Plessis, *The Creation of the* Ius Commune*: From* Casus *to* Regula (2010).

24 Franklin (n 12); D R Kelley, *Foundations of Modern Historical Scholarship: Language, Law and History in the French Renaissance* (1970).

25 D J Osler, "Budaeus and Roman law" (1985) 13 *Ius Commune* 195, D J Osler, "The myth of European legal history" (1997) 16 *Rechtshistorisches Journal* 393, D J Osler, "Images of legal humanism" (2001) 9 *Surfaces* 101, accessed at *http://www.pum.umontreal.ca/revues/surfaces/vol9/osler.htm*

modern scholars have followed the legal humanist credo of *petere fontes* to test the accuracy of the claim, beyond alluding to a particular reading of the *Antitribonian* of Hotman.[26] The consequence is that scholars who have accepted the traditional view have used it to substantiate larger claims about the "death" of Roman law, the separation between a supposed golden age of a pan-European, medieval *ius commune* and the fragmented reception of Roman law into the nation states of Europe, and the relevance of "dogmatic" Roman law as opposed to the "antiquarian" Roman law associated with the humanists. To some extent, one can also suspect the projecting back of a false modern dichotomy between the "academic" and the "practical". This volume therefore sets out to interrogate the orthodox views regarding legal humanism and its legacy.

Our fundamental starting point is that legal humanism, as a pan-European movement, can only really be understood within the context of the political, intellectual and social conditions of the period. In this volume, a number of key themes will be brought to the fore by the authors of the various chapters. These include the working methods of the legal humanists and an assessment as to whether jurists of the period were mainly engaged in "irrelevant" philological analyses of Roman legal texts that did not have any impact on legal practice. The second theme to be explored is the relationship between the *mos italicus* of Northern Italy and the *mos gallicus* of Southern France. Since the legal humanist movement is strongly associated with the universities of France and is generally assumed to have been an offshoot of the medieval Italian *mos italicus*, an investigation into the relationship between these two movements will provide an external perspective on the legal humanist movement. The third theme to be explored in this volume relates to issue of printing and the book trade. Legal humanism is closely associated with textual criticism and the dissemination of texts. Through an analysis of the book trade, issues surrounding the spread of humanist learning and its use and legal practice will be explored.

The success of the German Historical School and of Pandectism (though both deserve their own historical interrogation), the existence of the Dutch elegant school (and its relationship with Roman-Dutch law) as well as the attitudes of the humanists themselves demonstrate just how implausible has always been the view that humanism sounded the "death knell" of Roman law as a "living law". If this is so, then the argument that this new understanding of Roman law as "antiquarian" and historically contingent set the

26 Franklin (n 12) 46–58.

scene for the development of the "*usus modernus*" and secular natural law, is also open to interrogation. But the research in this volume challenges this view, demonstrating that matters were much more complex than a simple conflict between *mos gallicus* and *mos italicus*. No one could ignore the textual and historical work of the humanists. The evidence suggests that it was indeed not ignored, and that it continued to have an impact thereafter.

PART I
DEFINING LEGAL HUMANISM

1 *Antiqui et Recentiores*: Alberico Gentili – Beyond *Mos Italicus* and Legal Humanism

Alain Wijffels

A. INTRODUCTION
B. LEGAL HUMANISM: A CONVENTIONAL AND CONTROVERSIAL HISTORIOGRAPHICAL CATEGORY
C. ALBERICO GENTILI: A CIVIL LAWYER'S COMMITMENT TO SCHOLARSHIP, PUBLIC GOVERNANCE AND INTERNATIONAL RELATIONS
D. *DE ARMIS ROMANIS*
   (1) Structure
   (2) Methods of argumentation
   (3) Legal arguments
   (4) Legal analogies
   (5) The central theme: just wars and good governance through laws
   (6) Public governance: no "Celestial Jerusalem"
E. CONCLUSIONS

A. INTRODUCTION

Legal humanism is a recurrent, and therefore apparently well-established category in many textbooks on legal history. For many generations it has been a distinct topic that has inspired a substantial body of scholarly literature. Especially (but not only) for the sixteenth century, it is a more or less conventional (and convenient) term used for pigeonholing any particular author or work in a broader context of doctrinal currents. Consensus among scholars about the defining features of legal humanism remains nonetheless relative. One may probably recognise a degree of consensus on some characteristics, authors and works, which are all widely accepted as representative of legal humanism, but beyond a perhaps comparatively small core of those characteristics, authors and works – if Agustín and Cujas are not acknowledged as legal humanists, who will be? – legal historians vary and disagree – sometimes about details, sometimes about more fundamental issues – when it comes to labelling a jurist, a law book or a legal reasoning as expressing legal humanism. In the present contribution, I shall confine myself to both a very general and a fairly restrictive definition of legal humanism, which, moreover, does not even provide me with a sufficiently precise tool for establishing, within flexible parameters, what may or may not be regarded as an expression of legal humanism. The purpose of that definition is merely to provide a provisional backdrop for a more specific case study, which will be focused on Alberico Gentili's *De armis romanis*. In recent decades, Gentilian studies have produced a considerable amount of scholarly publications, produced fresh materials and perspectives, and undergone different shifts in their various interpretations. The blunt tool of my non-comprehensive definition of legal humanism may at least contribute to raising some issues about any assessment of Gentili's writings.

B. LEGAL HUMANISM: A CONVENTIONAL AND CONTROVERSIAL HISTORIOGRAPHICAL CATEGORY

Any reference to "legal humanism" fits into a larger historical narrative. The broader context of that narrative is intended as a description, and at the same time an interpretation, of Western legal thinking at a more general level than the *Dogmengeschichte* of specific areas or institutions of the law. Legal humanism is not primarily a matter of substantive law, but it refers to a methodology and an underlying legal theory that underpins any system of positive law. Typically, and taking its cue partly from polemical writings during the transition of the Middle Ages to Early Modern Times (epochs which, as historiographical categories, are related to those of "Renaissance" and "humanism" – and are just as much controversial), the staging of legal humanism in the historian's narrative allows a differentiation with earlier forms of legal thinking, usually described as Scholasticism, Bartolism, *mos italicus* or various other terms.[1] Chronologically, in that narrative, legal humanism is thrust into the limelight towards the beginning of the sixteenth century, although, inevitably, Italian historiography has put forward

1 For a recent example of (legal) humanism as a set notion and reference in legal history, cf the entry "Humanism" by A Mazzacane in S N Katz (ed), *The Oxford International Encyclopedia of Legal History*, vol 3 (2009) 188–193.

legitimate claims to anticipate the narrative by at least a century.[2] That same narrative tends to highlight, for the sixteenth century, a stark confrontation between the traditional late-medieval legal methods (to which I shall refer as *mos italicus*, although it should be understood that it was very much a mainstream approach among civil and canon lawyers throughout the Latin West) and the new school, often dubbed as *mos gallicus* (but that I shall here refer to, perhaps somewhat inconsistently, as legal humanism). When, how and why the confrontation between the two approaches may eventually have come to an end is far less developed, or at least with a much lesser degree of agreement, in that traditional legal-historical narrative. The manichaeism opposing both approaches is sometimes sustained even when it is acknowledged that some jurists were trying to hold a middle ground between the more radical agenda of legal humanism or the determinedly conservative positions of the "Bartolists". Another aspect of that traditional narrative is that it often tends (reflecting a widespread bias in Western culture, not least among scholars until about the last third of the twentieth century) to favour the ancient Greek-Latin foundations attributed to Western civilisation. As a result, that bias has more or less explicitly been transposed to the sixteenth-century intellectual battleground, entailing in general a clearly more positive assessment of legal humanists than their *mos italicus* counterparts. That traditional narrative has now for several decades come under fire. The categories of *mos italicus* and legal humanism have not been jettisoned, but it has become more fashionable to emphasise that, beyond the controversies, many authors were endeavouring to combine essential elements of both approaches. The rejection of too absolute a dichotomy between the two approaches produces, however, a new challenge, as it has to be shown that, contrary to the positions which emphasised the deep blue water which was supposed to divide both camps, the divide could be bridged, and that the approaches were not necessarily altogether incompatible.

My own experience sits somewhat uncomfortably with the category of legal humanism understood either according to the traditional narrative, or according to the more recent and oecumenical historiographical trend. The discomfort probably derives from the fact that, for the sixteenth century, my vantage point has mainly been legal practice in (higher) courts. Whether in the Low Countries, France, Germany or England, advocates' arguments or academic consultations submitted during legal proceedings have been almost

2 D Maffei, *Gli inizi dell'umanesimo giuridico* (1956) has been the main reference on that score in legal-historical literature during most of the second half of the twentieth century.

exclusively dominated – at least in the source-material which has been available to me – by traditional *mos italicus* learning. Even in those few cases where a minimum quantum of interest from a legal practitioner for legal humanism could be surmised, his written opinions in court would almost always remain entrenched in traditional learning.[3] Was there any sixteenth-century court which would stand out in forensic practice, somehow in the same way as Bourges is perceived to stand out among contemporary law schools? It seems unlikely, and if it were the case, it is still striking that sixteenth-century practice-orientated legal literature (*consilia*, *decisiones* . . .) appears to confirm that, on the whole,[4] Western legal practice remained very little affected, either by the polemics between legal humanists and followers of the *mos italicus* (an observation which mitigates the relevance of the traditional narrative), or in any significant way by the legal humanists' works and approaches (which raises questions about how widespread among legal professionals the willingness was, to trouble themselves with legal-humanistic learning). In any case, a life-long research into various courts' records until the beginning of the seventeenth century has continuously exposed me to a vast array of traditional legal scholarship – whether produced by late-medieval authors or sixteenth-century authors – but only rarely to scholarship associated with legal humanism.[5] A few inroads into later (viz late-seventeenth-century and

3 Compare P Stein, "Thomas Legge, A Sixteenth-Century English Civilian and his Books", in J A Ankum, J E Spruit, F B J Wubbe (eds), *Satura Roberto Feenstra sexagesimum quintum annum aetatis complenti ab alumnis collegis amicis oblata* (1985) 545–556, remarking upon Thomas Legge's (1535–1607) collection of law books that its owner would use humanistic authorities such as Alciato and Zasius for discussing antiquarian questions, but would mainly rely on *mos italicus* authorities in order to discuss contemporary civil law issues. Stein's analysis of Legge's collection was not unlike many other Cambridge private and institutional law collections: A Wijffels, "Law books in Cambridge libraries, 1500–1640" (1993) 10 *Transactions of the Cambridge Bibliographical Society* 359, idem, "Law Books at Cambridge, 1500–1640", in P Birks (ed), *The Life of the Law, Proceedings of the Tenth British Legal History Conference, Oxford 1991* (1993) 59.

4 In spite of exceptions, see for example the intriguing collection by Angelus a Sancto Ioanne (so far an unidentified author), *Consiliorum opus, Ad Senatum Mechliniensem*, which is added to his *Antiparadoxorum Iuris Civilis, adversus aevi nostri Colophonem D. Andream Alciatum Monomachia, Paradoxis expedita ad Cardinales* (Antverpiae, Ex Officina Aegiolii Coppenii Diest., 1563). See also X Prévost, *Jacques Cujas (1522–1590). Le droit à l'épreuve de l'Humanisme*, Thèse de doctorat en droit (histoire du droit) (2012). See also Prévost elsewhere in this volume.

5 For a few examples of such comparatively rare occurrences I have come across: A Wijffels, *Qui millies allegatur, Les allégations du droit savant dans les dossiers du Grand Conseil de Malines (causes septentrionales, ca. 1460–1580)*, [*Rechtshistorische Studies*, XI] (1985) [necnon in *Verzamelen en bewerken van de jurisprudentie van de Grote Raad*, Nieuwe Reeks, X], Amsterdam, Werkgroep Grote Raad, (1985)], 318 (W van Dyemen), 333 (L de Lucenne), although neither of those advocates can be said to have written forensic opinions which were outspoken humanistic (on the latter, see also A Wijffels, "Loys de Lucenne, avocat au Grand

eighteenth-century) legal practice have confirmed the decline of the *mos italicus* authorities and methods among practitioners, but not their (belated) systematic replacement by legal-humanistic works and methods. My itinerary through a few European courts has led me to observe the demise of the quasi-monopoly of the traditional Italian learning in favour of a more systematic approach to legal reasoning by subject matter, which I am wont to refer to as the "early-modern method" (a phrase directly inspired by that of *usus modernus*), which then became, and seemingly remained, the "mainstream" approach by legal practitioners until the end of the *Ancien Régime*.

That experience probably explains my restrictive understanding of legal humanism, which has remained a largely vacant category within the boundaries of my own research on legal practice. Along conventional lines, I would then understand legal humanism as an offshoot of fifteenth-century and early sixteenth-century humanism in the sense of a fundamental challenge to the prevailing public governance of its time, its supporting institutions and handling of cultural values and references. The challenge was directed towards establishing an alternative model of governance for the polity, which would "pick up the thread" of classical Antiquity.[6] (I am leaving out here the religious side of this issue, although the criticism of public governance obviously also affected the Church and its underlying ecclesiology. The religious issue cannot be addressed without reference to the discussions about reform within the Roman-Catholic Church, and of course the Reformation. All that affected the standing and jurisdiction of canon law, but less so the bulk of non-ecclesiastical Roman law learning.) The need to purge the classical texts of medieval accretions and corruptions required therefore in the first place a new discipline of historical and philological criticism, applied to the sources of Roman and Greek Antiquity. Both the primary interest for a new foundation of public governance and the relevance of legal texts

Conseil de Malines. La quiétude privée d'une bibliothèque, l'embarras public d'une liaison dangereuse" in (2000) 40 *Publication du Centre Européen d'Etudes Bourguignonnes* 129). See also R Sprenger and A Wijffels, "De *actio quanti minoris* in de praktijk van het Rijkskamergerecht ca. 1535. Uit de aantekeningen van Viglius van Aytta", in D Lambrecht (ed), *Lopend rechtshistorisch onderzoek. Handelingen van het tiende Belgisch-Nederlands rechtshistorisch colloquium* [*Iuris Scripta Historica*, III] (1990) 127. Even in the sixteenth-century *registres des plaidoiries* of the Parliament of Paris, I only came across a memorandum which presented humanistic features, either as a more literary style, or at the service of policy considerations (e.g. historical arguments intended to deny the applicability of particular papal decretals in France, especially those incorporated in the *Liber Sextus*) in very few cases.

6 My own – relative – understanding of legal humanism is set out in broad terms in my textbook used for freshers in Louvain-la-Neuve : *Introduction historique au droit. France – Allemagne – Angleterre*, Paris, Presses Universitaires de France [Coll. Thémis – Droit], 2nd edn (2014).

for acquiring information on a wide range of social, economic, and political features of ancient Rome, resulted fairly quickly in the humanists' concern to establish an adequate textual version of Justinian's compilation – by far the most important *corpus* of legal texts available at the time. That is the preliminary part of the conventional narrative on legal humanism: the scholarly work of historical and philological criticism that gradually transformed the outlook of (the printed versions of) the *Corpus Iuris Civilis* during the sixteenth century. The importance of H E Troje's contributions to that aspect of legal humanism during the 1970s and later on is a reminder of how underdeveloped the history of legal humanism had remained until a generation ago.[7] The following part of the narrative brings legal humanism even more strongly within the ambit of legal history. Because of the lack of independently preserved pre-Justinianic texts outside Justinian's own compilation, at least prior to the fourth and fifth centuries, those compilations only expressed imperfectly the matrix of the polity and culture humanists were seeking in Antiquity. For those who were not satisfied with the textual tradition inherited from Tribonian's travails, the ideal was to reach the "classical" Roman law. Because that stage of Roman law could only be incompletely and imperfectly reconstructed through the historical and philological criticism of Justinian's compilation, a more conceptual approach was required, viz the attempt to re-enact that classical stage of development of Roman law not only through specific positive rules, but also through its way of reasoning, including the concepts and principles which would give sufficient consistency to the whole. However, the attempts at such a re-enactment were always bound to be even more controversial than textual criticism, and even more affected by a scholar's pre-conceptions about law and justice, and by his ideology of the better *polis* which humanism was meant to secure. In other words, in that second stage of legal thinking, the scholar had greater leeway in deciding how to articulate his reconstruction of classical Roman law, and, unless he wished to restrict his work to a more narrow historical approach, in incorporating policy considerations.

Keeping with the narrative's thread by stating that legal humanism did

7 See, especially, his most influential publications: first, his contribution to the *Handbuch*: H E Troje, "Die Literatur des gemeinen Rechts unter dem Einfluss des Humanismus", in H Coing (ed), *Handbuch der Quellen und Literatur der neueren europäischen Privatrechtsgeschichte*, Bd II, *Neuere Zeit (1500–1800)*, *Das Zeitalter des gemeinen Rechts*, 1 Teilband, *Wissenschaft* (1977) 615–795, idem, *Graeca leguntur. Die Aneignung des byzantinischen Rechts und die Entstehung eines humanistischen Corpus iuris civilis in der Jurisprudenz des 16. Jahrhunderts* [*Forschungen zur neueren Privatrechtsgeschichte*, Bd 18] (1971).

not succeed in replacing the Italian method among legal practitioners, and also failed to gain the upper hand in the law faculties, while instead, both *in foris et in scholis*, it was the "early-modern method" which became the mainstream approach in the *ius commune*, presents some advantages.[8] It offers a *prima facie* explanation for the growing fragmentation within the *ius commune* literature and it reflects the long-term changes that can be observed in printed law books from the second half of the sixteenth century onwards.[9] More importantly, it takes on the history of the *ius commune* as a continuing reshaping of Roman law materials according to new developments in Western scholarly thinking, facilitating comparisons between the early modern civil law literatures produced in different jurisdictions. It thus avoids the gap caused by the unfinished storyline of civil law scholarship during the last centuries of the *Ancien Régime*. The early modern approach did not represent an abrupt break from the *mos italicus* and legal humanism, because the *usus modernus* ensured that the heritage of many doctrines of the former was preserved, while it also incorporated the major corrections and insights of the latter. On the other hand, such a narrative remains too simple and fails to integrate properly several loose ends. For example, it does not provide a sufficient explanation for the purpose and influence of the ongoing current of antiquarian legal scholarship during the seventeenth and eighteenth centuries. And it does not lend itself easily to include the commitment of many humanistic lawyers to studies of the particular laws (as was the case with many sixteenth-century French jurists who worked on

8 Conversely, I have over the years taken advantage of that narrative in order to have a convenient framework in which I could discuss various aspects of early modern civil law developments: e.g. "European Private Law: A New Software-Package for an Out-dated Operating System?", in M Van Hoecke and F Ost (eds), *The Harmonization of European Private Law* (2000) 101–116, "Qu'est-ce que le *ius commune*?", in A Supiot (ed), *Tisser le lien social* (2004) 131, "Early-modern Scholarship on International Law", in A Orakhelashvili (ed), *Research Handbook on the Theory and History of International Law* (2011) 23, "Le *ius commune* européen: mythe ou référentiel indifférencié des discours sur la formation d'un droit européen?", in B Bernabé and O Camy (eds), *Les mythes de fondation et l'Europe, Actes du colloque international de Dijon 18 et 19 novembre 2010*, Dijon, Éditions Universitaires de Dijon [Collection *Institutions*] (2013) 87, "Législation et science du droit: l'Édit perpétuel de 1611 entre *mos italicus* et *usus modernus*", in G Martyn (ed), *Recht en wet tijdens het ancien régime – Le droit et la loi pendant l'Ancien Régime* [Studia 141], Brussel – Bruxelles, Algemeen Rijksarchief – Archives Générales du Royaume (2014), 129.

9 I have developed that point in my review of D J Osler, *Jurisprudence of the Baroque. A Census of Seventeenth Century Italian Legal Imprints*, 3 vols, I : A-G, II : H-S, III : T-Z, Sources [Bibliographica Iuridica 4–6 ; Studien zur europäischen Rechtsgeschichte, Veröffentlichungen des Max-Planck-Instituts für europäische Rechtsgeschichte Frankfurt am Main, Bde 235–237] (Frankfurt am Main, Vittorio Klostermann, 2009), LV+848 p, XXIX+831 p, XXIX+735 p (ill), 2012 (80) *Tijdschrift voor Rechtsgeschiedenis/Revue d'Histoire du Droit* 229.

customs and statute law).[10] Such features can be understood and explained in the context of legal humanism in a broader sense than at the starting point of the narrative that has here been summarily described, but inevitably at the price of blurring some of its distinctive core features.

So far for the general background. The present contribution's aim is not, however, to draw a global and fully consistent picture of legal humanism in relation to other legal methods which played a role in early modern times, but to argue that, in many cases, some of the characteristic features of legal humanism were routinely maintained and continued to be developed within the prevailing new model of the *usus modernus*. Alberico Gentili's work provides a strong case for putting forward that argument. As a jurist, he stood at the crossroads of civil law scholarship during the transition between the sixteenth and seventeenth centuries. His legal education was steeped in the *mos italicus* (literally, too, as an alumnus of the law faculty in Perugia),[11] and, although at an early stage he expressed a critical judgement on legal humanism,[12] his work at Oxford shows a willingness and ability to adopt features resulting sometimes in writings which may appear closer to the humanist agenda than to any attachment to traditional scholarship. Nevertheless, most of his work was geared towards the more systematic approach that would become an essential feature of early modern legal methods. Because of his position in England, Gentili did not attempt (as the contemporary regius professor of civil law in Cambridge, John Cowell, did)[13] to elaborate on the other main feature of *usus modernus*, namely a substantive merger of civil law and particular law (which would have required a

10 The latter can be explained, I think, by highlighting the commitment of sixteenth-century French humanists for modernising and improving public governance in the French polity (as I argue in my *Introduction historique au droit* (n 6) 220).

11 F Treggiari, "Alberico Gentili alumnus", in F Treggiari (ed), *Alberico Gentili, la tradizione giuridica perugina e la fondazione del diritto internazionale* [*Atti dell'Incontro di studio (Perugia, 10 ottobre 2008)*], (2010) 7.

12 Often quoted in this context are his *Laudes Academiae Perusinae et Oxoniensis*, ed pr 1605, nowadays more readily available through the edition by G Ermini (ed and transl), *Lodi delle Accademie di Perugia e di Oxford, Testo latino con versione italiana e note*, (1968), but mostly the early work: *De iuris interpretibus dialogi sex* (1582) (reprint Turin, 1937), followed by *Lectionum et epistolarum quae ad ius civile pertinent libri IV*, (1583) [1584]. On Gentili's attachment to traditional legal learning during the early 1580s, and the violent reactions this provoked from Jean Hotman and his English network at court and in Oxford, see now the exceptionally documented article by G Minnucci, "Jean Hotman, Alberico Gentili, e i circoli umanistici inglesi alla fine del XVI secolo", in F Liotta (ed), *Studi di storia del diritto medioevale e moderno*, vol 3 (2014) 203. Minnucci's study appears to confirm the long-held view that over the years, Gentili changed his views on the advantages of incorporating philological and historical learning in legal discourse.

13 J Cowell, *Institutiones iuris Anglicani ad methodum et seriem Institutionum imperialium compositae & digestae* (1605).

substantial knowledge of the English common law).[14] Both in areas of civil law and, more famously, of the law of nations, Gentili's work nonetheless displays the progress of a jurist whose scholarship was reaching beyond the traditional Italian learning and the original sixteenth-century approaches of legal humanism.[15] In recent times, that transitional aspect of Gentili's scholarship has produced diverging assessments of his methods.

C. ALBERICO GENTILI: A CIVIL LAWYER'S COMMITMENT TO SCHOLARSHIP, PUBLIC GOVERNANCE AND INTERNATIONAL RELATIONS

Ever since Erskine Holland's lecture on Alberico Gentili's work,[16] that work has benefited from a sustained scholarly interest. For a long time, that interest was essentially focused on Gentili's contributions to the law of nations, in particular his books on ambassadors, on the law of war and on maritime warfare, which were reprinted and translated in the series of "Classics" of international law. During the latter part of the twentieth century and until the commemorations of 2008 (on the quatercentenary of Gentili's death), especially through the efforts of the *Centro Internazionale di Studi Gentiliani* (CISG) in Gentili's birthplace San Ginesio, research on Gentili has intensified and diversified.[17] Because of the background of some of

14 On a few other attempts at elaborating an English *usus modernus*: A Wijffels, "Civil Law v. Common Law? John Cowell, Thomas Wood and William Jones: The Elusive English *Usus Modernus*", in J Ockeley *et al* (eds), *Recht in Geschiedenis, Een bundel bijdragen over rechtsgeschiedenis van de Middeleeuwen tot de hedendaagse tijd aangeboden aan prof.dr. Fernand Vanhemelryck* (2005), 501–516, in general: H Coing, "Das Schrifttum der englischen Civilians und die kontinentale Rechtsliteratur in der Zeit zwischen 1550 und 1800" (1975) 5 *Ius Commune* 1, see also A Watson, "Justinian's Institutes and Some English Counterparts", in P G Stein and A D E Lewis (eds), *Studies in Justinian's Institutes in Memory of J A C Thomas* (1983) 181, K Luig, "The institutes of national law in the seventeenth and eighteenth centuries" (1972) 17 *Juridical Review* 193.

15 G Minnucci, *Alberico Gentili tra mos italicus e mos gallicus. L'inedito commentario Ad Legem Juliam de adulteriis* (2002).

16 Th. Erskine Holland, *A valedictory retrospect (1874–1910): being a lecture delivered at All Souls College, June 17, 1910* (1910), G Minnucci, *Alberico Gentili tra mos italicus e mos gallicus* (n 15) and, by the same author, *Alberico Gentili iuris interpres della prima età moderna* (2011).

17 See in particular the proceedings of the San Ginesio conferences: *Alberico Gentili giurista intellettuale globale.* Atti del Convegno, 25 Settembre 1983 (1988), *Alberico Gentili e la dottrina della guerra giusta nella prospettiva di oggi.* Atti del Convegno, III Giornata Gentiliana, 17 Settembre 1988 (1991), *Il diritto della guerra e della pace di Alberico Gentili.* Atti del Convegno, IV Giornata Gentiliana, 21 Settembre 1991 (1995), *Azione umanitaria ed intervento umanitario. Il parere del Comitato Internazionale della Croce Rossa – pensiero umanitario e intervento in Gentili.* Atti del Convegno, VI Giornata Gentiliana, 17 Settembre 1994 (1998), *Alberico Gentili consiliatore.* Atti del Convegno, V Giornata Gentiliana, 19 Settembre 1992,

the main participants, the historical contributions to Gentilian studies have come mainly from two different scholarly approaches: on the one hand, historians of political thought,[18] and, on the other hand, legal historians. Both approaches have substantially enriched our understanding of Gentili's work. Gentili has now acquired a much more specific profile in the history of political thinking, in particular in the history of the theories of international relations, and, among legal historians, interest in his work is no longer confined to the history of international law, because his studies on topics of both private law and public law have been perceived as providing a better understanding of his more famous contributions to the law of nations.[19] The fast pace of publications during the last quarter of a century has not always ensured that all those new perspectives could be adequately integrated in a consistent picture of Gentili's contributions to legal scholarship, to a theory of public governance and to the foundations of international relations.

In the area of legal history, not only has Gentili's work received much greater attention beyond the law of nations (in particular through several

a cura di A Wijffels (1999), *Alberico Gentili nel quarto centenario del "De Iure Belli"*. Atti del Convegno, VIII Giornata Gentiliana, 26–27–28 Novembre 1998 (2000), *Alberico Gentili e il mondo extraeuropeo*. Atti del Convegno, VII Giornata Gentiliana, 20 Settembre 1997, a cura di B Kingsbury (2001), *Alberico Gentili. Politica e religione nell'età delle guerre di religione*. Atti del Convegno, II Giornata Gentiliana, 17 Maggio 1987, a cura di D Panizza (2002), *Alberico Gentili. La soluzione pacifica delle controversie internazionali*. Atti del Convegno, IX Giornata Gentiliana, 29–30 Settembre 2000 (2003), *Alberico Gentili. L'ordine internazionale in un mondo a più civiltà*. Atti del Convegno, X Giornata Gentiliana, 20–21 Settembre 2002 (2004), *Alberico Gentili. L'uso della forza nel diritto internazionale*. Atti del Convegno, XI Giornata Gentiliana, 17–18 settembre 2004 (2006), *Alberico Gentili. La salvaguardia dei beni culturali nel diritto internazionale*. Atti del Convegno, XII Giornata Gentiliana, 22–23 settembre 2006 (2008), *"Ius Gentium Ius Communicationis Ius Belli". Alberico Gentili e gli orizzonti della modernità*. Atti del Convegno di Macerata in occasione delle Celebrazioni del Quarto Centenario della morte di Alberico Gentili (1552–1608), Macerata 6–7 dicembre 2007 (2009), Atti dei Convegni nel Quarto Centenario della morte (Vol II), San Ginesio. 11–12–13 settembre 2008, Oxford e Londra, 5–6 giugno 2008, Napoli "L'Orientale", 6 novembre 2007 (2010), Atti dei Convegni nel Quarto Centenario della morte (Vol III), *Inaugurazione del Centenario Gentiliano* San Ginesio, 13–14 gennaio 2008, *Le Marche al tempo di Alberico Gentili: religione, politica, cultura* San Ginesio, 13–14 giugno 2009 (2012).

18 Pioneering work has been achieved in this respect by D Panizza, *Alberico Gentili, giurista ideologo nell'Inghilterra elisabettiana* (1982) and his many contributions in most of the proceedings of the Centro at San Ginesio (mentioned *supra*). For recent studies on Gentili by Panizza (with further references to his intermediate publications), see *Atti dei Convegni nel Quarto Centenario della morte* (Vol II) (n 17) 491–513, 557–586, 641–656, and idem, "Alberico Gentili's *De armis Romanis*: The Roman Model of the Just Empire", in B Kingsbury and B Straumann (eds), *The Roman Foundations of the Law of Nations: Alberico Gentili and the Justice of Empire* (2010) 53.

19 For an excellent survey of the older and more recent legal-historical literature on Alberico Gentili, see the introductory chapters of G Minnucci, *Alberico Gentili tra mos italicus e mos gallicus* (n 15) 1–10 and 11–36.

studies by G Minnucci),[20] but the assessment of his work according to the old dichotomy of *mos italicus* and legal humanism has been largely overcome. By now, legal-historical interest in Gentili's work, apart from the usual attention for his doctrines on specific issues, tends to explain how and why that work combines argumentative methods, authorities and stylistic registers reflecting both the *mos italicus*, legal humanism and the emerging *usus modernus*.[21]

While legal historians have succeeded in shedding the crippling antinomy between *mos italicus* and legal humanism as a *summa divisio* for assessing Gentili's scholarship, an antinomy somewhat reminiscent of those categories has entered with fresh vigour the discussions among historians of political thought. A catalyst in that development was R. Tuck's book on *The Rights of War and Peace* (1999),[22] in which the author sought to investigate the relationship between the development of theories of international relations and international law, on the one hand, and the establishment of liberal political theories, on the other. Tuck's book concentrates almost exclusively on early modern developments. The first chapter of the book is entitled "Humanism" and is largely articulated around the work of Gentili, while the second chapter is intended as an antithetical demonstration of (according to the title given to that chapter:) "Scholasticism". At the beginning of that second chapter, the reader is warned that after the previous pages on Gentili, he will be introduced "to a completely different view of war, put forward in a different literary genre". That antithetical narrative of the first two chapters is then followed by a chapter on Grotius. Tuck's use of the brand-name "humanism" to encapsulate his reading of Gentili, together with the contrasting label of Scholasticism, has since then often been referred to by several other scholars working on Gentili,[23] although alternative, perhaps

20 See (e.g.) on canon law: "Alberico Gentili: un protestante alle prese con il *Corpus Iuris Canonici*", in *Alberico Gentili. La salvaguardia dei beni culturali nel diritto internazionale. Atti del Convegno, XII Giornata Gentiliana, 22–23 settembre 2006* (n 17) 185–211, in particular on matrimonial law: "La nuova metodologia di Alberico Gentili nel I Libro del '*De nuptiis*' (1601)", in *Alberico Gentili. L'uso della forza nel diritto internazionale. Atti del Convegno, XI Giornata Gentiliana, 17–18 settembre 2004* (n 17) 399–431, on criminal law: *Alberico Gentili tra mos italicus e mos gallicus* (n 15).

21 G Minnucci, *Alberico Gentili tra mos italicus e mos gallicus. L'inedito commentario ad Legem Juliam de adulteriis* (n 15) 7–8.

22 R Tuck, *The Rights of War and Peace, Political Thought and the International Order From Grotius to Kant* (1999).

23 For a recent example: D Panizza, "Alberico Gentili's *De Iure Belli*, The Humanist Foundations of a Project of International Order", in *Atti dei Convegni nel Quarto Centenario della morte* (Vol II) (n 17) 557–586.

less pregnant, designations[24] have been proposed to further the debate on the perceived opposition. However, Tuck's distinction has been subject to criticism,[25] partly because it has been remarked that on many important issues of the law of nations, opinions of sixteenth- and early-seventeenth-century writers do not follow any clear-cut distinction between a "humanist" and a "Scholastic" approach.[26] In that debate, the legal dimension of Gentili's work has often been neglected or marginalised. While legal historians tend to read Gentili's writings above all as the scholarly works of a jurist, some scholars on the history of political thought sometimes tend to view Gentili primarily as a political thinker, to whom legal learning was, at best, of secondary relevance.

In Gentili's work, whether his purpose was mainly scholarly or mainly pedagogical, a variety of registers are discernible. When writing in a primarily legal register, the style and argumentative mode combine typically traditional learning and humanistic features. The very endeavour to reconcile the various approaches implies that Gentili was not adhering to the sometimes fashionable rejection of the old learning as a matter of principle. In his writings, reflecting his private annotations as a reader, he appears to judge any opinion, whether by a late-medieval or by a recent, humanistic-committed, author, without any apparent prejudice, but on its own merits, or at any rate according to his own standards.[27] In other works, the reliance on legal authorities and principles is much more limited, and the historical-oratorical register more prominent. *De iure belli* is arguably an example of what is essentially a legal treatise, in which Gentili mainly argues along the lines of

24 In his book *The Rights of War and Peace* (n 22), Tuck himself suggests that the terms "humanism" and "Scholasticism" might be better replaced by "oratorical" and "theological".

25 B Kingsbury and B Straumann, "Introduction: The Roman Foundations of the Law of Nations", in B Kingsbury and B Straumann (eds), *The Roman Foundations of the Law of Nations: Alberico Gentili and the Justice of Empire* (n 18) 1 at 3 and passim (referring in particular to various contributions in the same volume: "Diego Panizza argues for the Scholastic-humanist distinction as an important and useful one, whereas Noel Malcolm and Benjamin Straumann are among those who contest it"); see also 10 on D Lupher's contribution.

26 In addition, one should not forget that "Scholasticism" could refer to both medieval scholastic methods and to the early modern "second Scholastics", on which several contributions in relation to Gentili were published in M Ferronato and L Bianchin (eds), *Silete Theologi in munere alieno. Alberico Gentili e la Seconda Scolastica. Atti del Convegno Internazionale Padova, 20–22 novembre 2008*, s.l. (2011), see especially the contributions by C Zendri and G Marchetto on Gentili's sources (respectively 45–64 and 65–82).

27 A Wijffels, "De la lecture à l'écriture: les notes de lecture d'Alberico Gentili et leur remploi dans la rédaction de son oeuvre doctrinale", in L Giavarini (ed), *L'écriture des juristes XVIe–XVIIIe siècle* (2010) 93–109; idem, "From Perugia to Oxford: Past and Present of Political Paradigms", in F Treggiari (ed), *Alberico Gentili. La tradizione giuridica perugina e la fondazione del diritto internazionale* [*Atti dell'Incontro di studio (Perugia, 10 ottobre 2008)*], (2010) 57–78.

both traditional and more modern legal reasoning, and includes a degree of humanistic learning. In his *De legationibus*, on the other hand, legal expertise is seemingly overshadowed by the oratorical-historical register.

The shift of the medieval liberal arts to the early modern *studia humanitatis* focusing on classical literature, history and moral philosophy, as the key areas relevant to a new model of public governance (in addition to Christian values, all secularising trends notwithstanding), is reflected in Gentili's work, though always founded also on a civil law education. Gentili himself appears to have developed, throughout the years, a greater awareness or concern for the issue of the civil lawyer's place in public governance. Perhaps – but this is, at this stage of our knowledge about Gentili's thought, no more than an hypothesis – his growing interest in (legal-)humanistic studies over the same years was at least partly inspired by the realisation that humanistic expertise had become indispensable in the education and training of civil lawyers aspiring at serving the early modern polity.[28]

D. *DE ARMIS ROMANIS*

De armis Romanis was first published in 1599.[29] An earlier version of its first part, however, was published at Oxford in 1590 under the title *De iniustitia*

28 In previous contributions, where I emphasised Gentili's increasing interest in the importance of legal expertise for public governance, I have not made that hypothetical link with humanistic studies. That would require a better insight into the development of Gentili's thought through his successive works (as G Minnucci has demonstrated over the past years), but also through other sources, such as his reading-notes (for the latter, however, it is sometimes difficult to determine the date of his notes). On Gentili's later publications relevant to public governance (apart from the law of nations), see my arguments in: "Alberico Gentili e il rinnovamento del diritto pubblico nella tradizione dello *ius commune*", in *Alberico Gentili (San Ginesio 1552 – Londra 1608)* (n 17) 519–556, "Le disputazioni di Alberico Gentili sul Diritto Pubblico", in *Alberico Gentili. La salvaguardia dei beni culturali nel diritto internazionale* (n 17) 247–256, "Assolutismo politico e diritto di resistenza: la *disputatio* gentiliana '*De vi civium in Regem semper iniusta*'", in *Alberico Gentili, L'uso della forza nel diritto internazionale* (n 17) 433–457, *Appendice*, 459–496, "Alberico Gentili e i fondamenti storico-concettuali del diritto comune europeo", in *Alberico Gentili nel Quarto Centenario del "De Iure Belli". Atti del Convegno VIII Giornata Gentiliana* (n 17) 173–205, "Intervento'", 251–258, for an earlier example in Gentili's career: "Une disputation d'Alberico Gentili sur le droit du souverain de disposer de son royaume et des biens de ses sujets (1587)", in J Krynen and M Stolleis (eds), *Science politique et droit public dans les facultés de droit européennes (XIIIe–XVIIIe siècle)* [*Studien zur europäischen Rechtsgeschichte, Veröffentlichungen des Max-Planck-Instituts für europäische Rechtsgeschichte Frankfurt am Main,* 229] (2008), 469–484.

29 D Panizza, "Alberico Gentili's *De armis Romanis*: The Roman Model of the Just Empire", in B Kingsbury and B Straumann (eds), *The Roman Foundations of the Law of Nations* (n 18) 53–84, esp Fn 1 at 53–54 on the various editions. I refer hereafter constantly to the new annotated edition with an English translation, which is based on: Albericus Gentilis, *De armis Romanis Libri duo*, Hanoviae, Apud Guilielmum Antonium, 1599, in B Kingsbury and B Straumann (eds), D

bellica Romanorum actio.[30] In the dedicatory epistle of that 1590 edition, addressed to Robert Devereux, Earl of Essex (to whom the edition of 1599 was also dedicated)[31], Gentili stated that the defence of the Romans (which is the central thesis of the second part in the 1599 edition) was ready for publication. It seems therefore that from the start, the format of a disputation of two antithetic arguments had been envisaged and possibly even worked out. There is no compelling explanation why it took Gentili almost another ten years to have the full version with the two parts published.[32]

(1) Structure

The structure of *De armis Romanis* is typically that of a *disputatio* following a detailed *pro et contra* plan. In the first part ("book"), arguments are presented in order to establish that the wars of the ancient Romans were based on unjust causes and led to Rome's tyrannical rule. The second part ("book") consists of counter-arguments and a rebuttal of the arguments produced in the first part, so as to demonstrate that the Roman wars had a just cause and led to commendable imperial rule. As in other Gentilian disputations, the counter-arguments are developed in parallel. In each part, the first chapter deals with issues of historical evidence and methods. From chapter 2 to 11, each chapter follows roughly a chronological sequence (proclaiming to reflect the successive "ages" of ancient Roman history, from Romulus to the Caesars).[33] The wars under the monarchy and the Republic provide the bulk of the arguments on both sides (chapters 2 to 10). In part II, each chapter deals exactly with the same period and arguments as those dealt with in the corresponding chapter of part I. However, part II is much more elaborate than part I.[34] In both parts, the penultimate chapter focuses on a comparison between Roman military glory and Alexander the Great's feats. Finally, the

Lupher (transl), *Alberico Gentili, The Wars of the Romans. A Critical Edition and Translation of De armis Romanis* (2011).

30 Albericus Gentilis, *De iniustitia bellica Romanorum actio*, Oxonii, Excudebat Iosephus Barnesius, 1590.

31 On Gentili's relations with Essex: A Gajda, *The Earl of Essex and Late Elizabethan Political Culture* (2012) passim, pointing out that Essex actually read *De iure belli*, 76; see also 92–93.

32 D Panizza, "Alberico Gentili's *De armis Romanis*: The Roman Model of the Just Empire" (n 18) 56–57, puts the publication in the context of the attacks Gentili was experiencing from the "Puritan party", and of his support to the Earl of Essex and the "War party" at court.

33 The reference to the "ages" of Rome is repeated on several occasions throughout the book: e.g. at the end of part I, ch 3, part I, ch 10, and part II, ch 3.

34 In the 2011 edition, part I covers (Latin text and English translation), 8 to 119 (c 56 pages); part II, 120 to 355 (c 117 pages).

thirteenth and last chapter of part I is entitled "The Tyranny of the Romans", while the last chapter of part II tackles the corresponding issues under the title "The Good Fortune of the Roman Empire".

The arrangement is similar, albeit here worked out on a wider scale, to that of other works by Gentili, where the reader is first given arguments for a specific thesis, then followed by arguments for the opposite thesis, and then perhaps by counter-arguments directed against each of the first batch of arguments (and usually in the same sequence).[35] In *De armis*, the arguments in favour of the Romans' justification are conflated with the counter-arguments of the arguments expressed in part I. Combined with the convention, sometimes expressed in the civil law tradition and usually applied by Gentili himself in other works, according to which the better thesis, or at least the thesis defended by the author, comes after the arguments opposed to the opinion or interests he is defending, the arrangement would therefore *prima facie* imply that Gentili himself favoured the general argument set out in part II. The more prolific part II may also be perceived, if only because the argument is twice as long, to present a stronger case in favour of Roman justice and imperial rule.

The division into arguments, followed by opposite arguments and a rebuttal of the first series of arguments was in late-medieval legal literature a specific offshoot of the Scholastic *sic et non* method. It was commonly applied in legal practice, and the abundant *consilia* literature – which appealed to Gentili – contains many examples of arguments following that same scheme. It was also a common device for structuring academic debates, and was included in the training of law students.

However, in the case of *De armis*, there is a strong case for retracing the

35 See, for example, the public law disputations of 1605: A Wijffels, "Alberico Gentili e i fondamenti storico concettuali del diritto comune europeo, *Alberico Gentili nel quarto centenario del 'De Iure Belli'*". Atti del Convegno, VIII Giornata Gentiliana, 26–27–28 Novembre 1998 (2000) 173 at 191, idem, "Le disputazioni di Alberico Gentili sul Diritto Pubblico", in *Alberico Gentili. La salvaguardia dei beni culturali nel diritto internazionale*. Atti del Convegno, XII Giornata Gentiliana, 22–23 settembre 2006 (n 17) 247 at 254–256, in particular the disputation on the Anglo-Scottish union: idem, "Alberico Gentili e l'unione anglo-scozzese: alla ricerca di una nuova matrice per il discorso politico", in *Alberico Gentili, La soluzione pacifica delle controversie internazionali*. Atti del Convegno, IX Giornata Gentiliana, 29–30 Settembre 2000 (n 17) 159–200, Fn 4, 162–164, the disputation on the subjects' duty of obedience towards their legitimate ruler: idem, "Assolutismo politico e diritto di resistenza: la disputatio gentiliana *'De vi civium in Regem semper iniusta'*", in *Alberico Gentili. L'uso della forza nel diritto internazionale*. Atti del Convegno, XI Giornata Gentiliana, 17–18 settembre 2004 (n 17) 433 at 440–447, idem, "Une disputation d'Alberico Gentili sur le droit du souverain de disposer de son royaume et des biens de ses sujets (1587)", in J Krynen and M Stolleis (eds), *Science politique et droit public dans les facultés de droit européennes (XIIIe–XVIIIe siècle)* [*Studien zur europäischen Rechtsgeschichte, Veröffentlichungen des Max-Planck-Instituts für europäische Rechtsgeschichte Frankfurt am Main,* 229], (n 28) 469–484.

format of the book also to a more ancient and classical model. Gentili's book has been convincingly linked to a famous argument put forward in 155 BC by the Greek sceptic philosopher Carneades while staying in Rome during an embassy on behalf of Athens.[36] Carneades, whose reasoning was directed at questioning man's capacity to establish any absolute truth, was invited to discuss Roman justice. It is reported that, during the first session, he made a speech in support of the intrinsic virtues of Roman justice; the following day, during a new session, he is reported to have refuted the arguments of the day before and thus undermined the claims to any absolute validity of justice, only attributing it a relative purpose in the order of society. Carneades is only briefly referred to in passing in *De armis*, but the overall similarity of the format of the debate and of the topic of the argument is striking. So are also the differences: whereas Carneades' twofold argumentation seems to lead the audience to *aporia*, or at least to no more than a relative truth, Gentili, by inversing the order of arguments so that the argument in favour of injustice is followed and rebutted by an argument in favour of the justice of the Romans' wars and imperial government, may be thought to achieve the opposite effect of Carneades' exercise. Moreover, whereas Carneades' arguments may have been aimed at a more philosophical concept of justice, Gentili's discussion looked into a historical construction of the Roman empire and the concept of justice it addressed was directly linked to the doctrine of a just war.

(2) Methods of argumentation

A degree of dramatic effect is achieved by attributing each part of the work to a named character: "Picenus", i.e. someone from Gentili's native region, in Book I, and a "Roman" in Book II. On several occasions, the register of the debate takes a personal turn, as when Romanus berates his opponent *ad hominem*. Both characters claim a legal training, which seems appropriate as Picenus is acting as a "prosecutor" or "accuser", while Romanus acts for the "defence". As the title of the 1590 edition suggests, the argument is presented as an "actio", in the sense that both protagonists are at times acting as if they were defending a case before a court, following (up to a point) the rules and principles of a trial.[37]

36 D Lupher, "The *De armis Romanis* and the *Exemplum* of Roman Imperialism", in B Kingsbury and B Straumann, *The Roman Foundations of the Law of Nations* (n 18) 85 at 97–98.

37 The *actio* was more generally also the term used for a form of academic argument, e.g. Gentili's previous *Legalium comitiorum Oxoniensium actio Francisco Bevanno doctore [docturae] dignitatem suscipiente*, London, Excudebat Iohannes Wolfius, 1585.

Chapter 1 (both in part I and part II) enhances the quasi-legal setting of the debate by discussing as a preliminary the issue of evidence. It is a theme which is recurrent throughout the whole book. Since the central theme of the debate appears to be the assessment of the ancient Roman empire, the historical evidence is essential. The main source-material, however, does not consist of primary documentary or other material evidence, but of "histories", mainly from ancient (but not always contemporary) authors.[38] However, as in his other works, Gentili also adduces other ancient sources, in particular literary, including poetic, texts.[39] In both chapters 1, the discussion on methods deals primarily with the narratives of ancient historians. Both orators seem to consider that these historians should be subjected to the standards applied to "witnesses", and Picenus's chapter 1 is partly aimed, as in legal proceedings, at challenging the credibility or admissibility of several of those witnesses, whereas Romanus endeavours (as counsel were trained to do during a trial, during the stage of the so-called "*salvationes*")[40] to assert the same witnesses' reliability. From the start, Picenus here emphasises (comparing the wholesale rejection of a document which has been found to contain a forgery with the fate reserved for an historian who has been found to be undependable on a particular issue)[41] the need to apply a lawyer's expertise as a form of historical criticism. Romanus, on the other hand, while asserting the numerical and qualitative prevalence of

38 A systematic study of Gentili's use of (ancient) historiography is still wanting. All the more valuable is therefore the short article by K Hoekstra, "A Source of War. Gentili, Thucydides, and the Justification of Pre-emption", in *Alberico Gentili. La salvaguardia dei beni culturali nel diritto internazionale* (n 17) 113–128 (which could be complemented with an analysis of Gentili's brief reading notes on Thucydides).

39 On the importance of (ancient) poets as "authorities" in (legal) argumentation, see the fundamental contribution by C N Warren, "Gentili, the Poets, and the Laws of War", in B Kingsbury and B Straumann (eds), *The Roman Foundations of the Law of Nations* (n 18) 146–162. Warren's study is essential for understanding what can be understood by "humanism" with relation to Alberico Gentili, including the latter's "legalistic reading" of ancient poets (155), and the "nexus of literary criticism, moral philosophy, law and humanist *imitatio*" which Warren demonstrates through the works of T Tasso, the Gentili brothers and Philip Sidney (158 ff); see also J W Binns, "Diritto e poesia nell'opera di Alberico Gentili", in *Atti dei Convegni nel Quarto Centenario della morte* (vol II) (n 17) 175–188.

40 R C van Caenegem, "History of European Civil Procedure", in *International Encyclopedia of Comparative Law*, vol. XVI Civil Procedure, ch 2, (1973) 16 (i.e. when a party argued against his opponent's challenge of the witnesses the former had produced); W Litewski, *Der römisch-kanonische Zivilprozeß nach den älteren ordines iudiciarii* (1999), vol 2, 383, I de Damhouder, *Practycke in civile saecken* [. . .], 's-Gravenhage, By de Weduwe, ende Erfgenamen van wijlen Hillebrant Iacobsz. van Wouw, 1626, reprint Ghent, 1999, 506–508 (ch 188).

41 *De armis Romanis* (2011 edn) 12 (with references to *consilia* by Alciato, and to Gratianus' *Concordia*, D 9, c 7, mistakenly identified as a reference to Augustine in the 2011 edn); the counter-argument is to be found on 125.

the "witnesses" on his side of the argument, also points to a difference: "Dicerem, esse testes, qui iudicantes audiantur, et quibus historici similiores sint, quam aliis. Sed omnino eadem ratio non est testium, et historicorum".[42] Yet, Romanus is willing to play the game, and while he rejects the suggestion that more recent historians may be more reliable, because they are more detached than the ancient historians, that is for him a reason to adduce as many ancient testimonies in support of his case as possible. In any event, the format of the disputation requires inevitably that both parties can meet their arguments through a sufficiently homogenous register, and that appears to be the case. In the 1590 dedicatory letter, Gentili had called attention to the distinction between facts and opinions.[43] The assessment of facts, in so far as they were commonly accepted by the ancient authors, was in his view easier than the assessment of the authors' opinions.[44] When facts are fairly uncontroversial, and at any rate mostly beyond our capacity to be questioned, they can hardly be as such reassessed. Conversely, opinions (i.e. interpretations) of historical facts are more readily open to fresh and critical (re)assessments. The point is taken up more at length by Picenus in his first chapter.[45] It seems that in *De armis Romanis*, most facts (i.e. the events of Roman military and imperial history) are common ground: what opposes the two argumentations is the assessment of those facts, an assessment which is properly judgmental, viz whether the Roman military conquests and rule over the vanquished adversaries are to be declared "just" or "unjust".

The formal structure of *De armis* may, as already mentioned, indicate that Gentili intended to present the general argument of Book II as the more persuasive. It seems a rather jejune approach to speculate whether or not that was also Gentili's substantive position on the issue. If one considers his general aim, it is clear that the argument in favour of the justifications of a war is as such more strategic and opportunistic than the opposite argu-

42 *De armis Romanis* (2011 edn) 126–128.

43 The Letter has been included as an Appendix to the 2011 edn of *De armis Romanis* 357–361 (with an English translation). On the distinction between facts and opinions: *De armis Romanis* 14; in the 1590 Epistle: 358–360.

44 *Epistle* (1590), loc cit, 358: "Est nobis in censendis narrationibus maior, quam in diiudicandis sententiis difficultas", 360: "Hoc in sententiis scriptorum expendendis non contigit: nam eodem sumus nos loco atque illi, aut etiam meliori, qui studio partium non imbuti, et saeculis succedentibus magis instructi ad iudicandum accedimus" (see also the quote from Picenus' argument in the following note).

45 *De armis Romanis* (2011 edn) 14: " . . . quod cum eodem nos, atque illi fuerint, simus loco, aut etiam meliori, qui studio partium non imbuti, et seculis succedentibus magis instructi, artibusque nonnullis rei isti necessariis subornati fortasse magis, accedimus ad iudicandum: et nobis esse oportet facultatem disputandi, et, quae illis fuit, censendi, etiam contra illos".

ment. In *De armis*, Gentili shows that, in the same register, the civil lawyer is well prepared and intellectually equipped to argue that an opponent is waging an unjust war. Such an argument, however, would mainly be useful to a ruler while the war was being waged. Once the war is over, it will be of little avail to the defeated party, while the interest of the victor, in exacting the terms of the peace or benefiting from the *post bellum* status, will be to argue that his was a just war.[46] What matters most to a ruler is therefore to be in a position to argue that his opponent has been waging an unjust war, to refute any accusations of conducting an unjust war levelled at himself, and, if the opponent at the end of the war has not been altogether defeated and destroyed, that his own fight was nevertheless a just war. Gentili's twofold argumentation can therefore be seen to reflect the versatility of the civil lawyer's argumentative skills, but also emphasising his capacity to justify a ruler's war. The format of the two opposite argumentations was not incompatible with Gentili's shift to an approach in which both belligerents could – at least as long as the outcome remained uncertain – qualify as waging a just war.

(3) Legal arguments

Throughout *De armis,* both advocates use legal arguments and refer regularly to legal authorities.[47] The authorities are drawn from the *corpora iuris*, mainly the Digest and the Code, to a lesser extent the Institutes, Novels, feudal law and canon law. The legal authors who are cited occur largely in both parts, which confirms that both advocates rely on the same modes of legal argument and that they belong to a common legal tradition. Because Book II is more than twice as long as Book I, Romanus' range of authorities is somewhat larger than that of Picenus, but the differences remain limited. In both parts, *consilia* provide a large part of the legal literature quoted; both advocates also refer to civil law commentaries, mostly from late-medieval authors. Both, in the same way as Gentili himself in his

46 I leave here aside the issue, often associated with Gentili, of the war waged for a just cause (at least, subjectively) on both sides. It was a greater challenge for the jurist to assert his expertise in the politically more sensitive area of the debate on just war, which figures prominently through the historical *exempla* in *De armis Romanis*.

47 The importance of legal arguments, which tends to be overlooked or underrated by historians of political theories, may be gauged from the following, non-comprehensive list (references are to the *De armis Romanis* 2011 edn): Bk I, 10, 11, 24, 26, 28, 46, 50, 52, 54, 56, 62, 70, 72, 74, 76, 78, 80, 86, 88, 90, 94, 96, 110, 112, Bk II, 120, 122, 124, 126, 128, 134, 136, 138, 144, 146, 150, 160, 162, 166, 168, 172, 184, 186, 198, 208, 210, 212, 218, 220, 224 ("iure, inquam, ut de iure disputatio nostra est"), 230, 240, 244, 246, 250, 256, 258, 260, 266, 268, 272, 278, 284, 286, 290, 296, 298, 300, 306, 324, 332, 338, 344, 348, 350, 352, 354.

writings and teaching,[48] cite *antiquiores* and *recentiores* as valid authorities. In other words, neither Picenus nor Romanus shows a predominant bias either towards *mos italicus* doctrines or legal humanism. Thus, in both parts, the *consilia* by Alciato and Cefali are quoted more frequently than the other *consiliatores*: Baldus, Francesco Corti jr, T Deciani, F Decio, M A Eugeni, Alessandro Tartagni. A few other civil law commentaries by Alciato and Baldus are quoted by both. Picenus quotes Cujas on feudal law, Romanus the same on the Digest. Another feudal commentary mentioned by Picenus is that by Andrea da Isernia. Romanus, whose longer argument refers to a few more authors, including older authorities such as the Accursian gloss, Bartolus, G del Maino, and more recent authors – a o legal humanists – such as B de Ayala, P Ayrault, L Bayf, G Claro, D Covarruvias, G Fornier, D de Soto. Romanus also refers to a work by Gentili's brother Scipio, and both advocates refer to (different works by) Bodin.

Perhaps the preferences of the two advocates may diverge when it comes to assessing ancient (or more recent) non-legal authors, but, as regards the legal authorities, both display a largely shared legal culture combining late-medieval and early modern legal literature. The arguments in favour of either central thesis, viz the justice or the injustice of the Roman military and imperial conquests, are not determined by a bias either for the late-medieval, "Scholastic" legal methods, or for legal humanism.

(4) Legal analogies

Legal analogies are a distinctive form of legal argument. They occupied a specific place in the Italian method, but they survived (albeit in a more restrained form) the demise of that method and continued to be part (until the present-day)[49] of legal reasoning. In the *mos italicus*, however, the importance of legal analogies was enhanced by the absence of any systematisation of the law by subject matter, hence of any clear boundaries circumscribing the applicable rules and concepts of substantive law to a specific "area" of the law.[50] The use of analogies in legal reasoning may also have been

48 A Wijffels, "Alberico Gentili's Oxford Lectures on Contracts", in J Hallebeek, M Schermaier, R Fiori, E Metzger and J-P Coriat (eds), *Inter cives necnon peregrinos. Essays in honour of Boudewijn Sirks* (2014) 785.

49 T Viehweg, *Topik und Jurisprudenz. Ein Beitrag zur rechtswissenschaftlichen Grundlagenforschung* (1974[5]).

50 H Coing, *Europäisches Privatrecht*, Bd I, *Älteres Gemeines Recht (1500 bis 1800)* (1985) esp 15–25.

supported by a more general countenance in late-medieval scholarship, not least in theological studies, of "allegorical" reasoning and arguments.[51] Late-medieval legal practice shows how all-pervading legal analogies were among university-trained lawyers. The Zeeland jurist Nicolaus Everardus (1462–1532), who, after studying and teaching at Louvain, had a long and distinguished career as a judge, and who was eventually appointed president of the provincial court of Holland and later president of the Supreme Court (Great Council) in Mechlin, published in 1516 a small treatise which became a European bestseller during the sixteenth century: *Loci argumentorum legales*, also known as *Topica* (ed pr 1516).[52] The treatise consists of chapters each dealing with a type of argument, the application of which in legal arguments and reasoning is then explained and illustrated through many references to (late-medieval) civil and canon law literature. Some of those arguments are conventional general logical arguments (e.g. *A simili, A contrario sensu,* etc), but several chapters deal with specifically legal arguments, in particular – but not exclusively – analogies, such as: *A civilibus ad criminalia, A servo ad monachum, A delictis ad contractus, A feudo ad emphytheusim*, etc. Everardus was the first to deal in such a systematic way, or on such a scale, with analogical legal arguments. However, his approach, against the backdrop of legal practice in his days at the courts in the Low Countries (and elsewhere) consisted more in bringing forward in a formal way such analogies, rather than establishing their validity in legal or forensic reasoning. At the same time, formalising in such a way a manner of argumentation which had been so extensively implied entailed the possibility of restricting the use of analogies, since now Everardus was not only exposing

51 J Schröder, *Rechts als Wissenschaft. Geschichte der juristischen Methode vom Humanismus bis zur historischen Schule (1500–1800)* (2001) esp 42–45.

52 O M D F Vervaart, *Studies over Nicolaas Everaerts (1462–1532) en zijn Topica*, (1994), including an analysis of Everardus' work and the best survey of the *Topica*'s editions. It provides a much more balanced view of Everardus than R Dekkers, *Het humanisme en de rechtswetenschap in de Nederlanden*, (1938) 1–36, where Everardus is the subject of the first chapter of a series of portraits of legal humanists from the Low Countries (followed by Viglius, Mudaeus, Reyvardus, and Wesembecius). Drawing Everardus as the first legal humanist in the Netherlands seems somewhat artificial – one cannot escape the suspicion that Dekkers may have tried a little too hard to find a Dutch-Belgian contemporary to supplement the italico-gallico-germanico "triumvirate" of Alciato, Bodin and Zasius (A Wijffels, "*Iudicium* time" (1984) 3 *Rechtshistorisches Journal* 169). More recently, a comparatively biased (in favour of legal humanistic scholarship), though for the later periods solidly argued, monograph is that by G C J J van den Bergh, *Die holländische elegante Schule. Ein Beitrag zur Geschichte von Humanismus und Rechtswissenschaft in den Niederlanden 1500–1800*, (2002) (on Everardus 73–74). Everardus' supposed commitment to legal humanism was probably often assumed, in the older literature, on the strength of his acquaintance with Erasmus.

the potential of legal analogies but also the parameters within which they were deemed acceptable. As legal methods shifted and were subjected to new conventions, it is not surprising that the *genre* of the *Loci* or *Topica* could still inspire legal authors, even when the context of legal argumentation which had prevailed in Everardus' time was on the wane or had become outdated. Barely a generation after Everardus, Johannes Oldendorp's *Topicorum legalium . . . traditio* (ed pr 1551) already illustrates how the approach could be updated while expunging late-medieval scholarship.

Gentili's attachment to the *mos italicus* is partly expressed through his occasionally extensive reliance on legal analogies. Even during the last years of his life, such analogies came up in his work. Perhaps one of the most striking examples is chapter 6 of Book I of his *Hispanica Advocatio*, in which the issue "An hostem captum liceat ducere per territorium alienum" is largely dealt with through an analogy (for which Gentili relied heavily on traditional authors *utriusque iuris*) with a prisoner being taken through ecclesiastical land (such as a cemetery) and who at that stage claims the benefit of asylum.[53]

De armis Romanis includes several examples, among the legal arguments of both protagonists, of legal analogies.[54] Their appearance throughout the two parts of the book is evidence that such arguments, although they tend to echo Gentili's *mos italicus* background, are not incompatible with the prevailing legal-humanistic register of *De armis*. The fact that both Picenus and Romanus use such analogies is also evidence that both advocates apply essentially the same registers of legal reasoning. Some analogies are more strongly reminiscent of the medieval *ius commune* tradition, such as Romanus's argument in chapter 3, which compares the status of Alba after the city has been abolished and absorbed by the Roman state with the position of a *pater familias* who is adopted,[55] or the position of chapels and benefices of a church which has been taken over by another church.[56] In chapter 6, the same Romanus, discussing the importance of taking into account the quality and powers of the official with whom a treaty is made, refers to the Roman law rules on a contract made by a guardian or a ward without the required assistance or authority.[57]

Perhaps the most significant examples of analogies are those that are

53 Albericus Gentilis, *Hispanicae Advocationis Libri Duo*, Amstelredami, Apud Joannem Ravesteinium, 1661 (reprint New York, 1921; reprint Buffalo, NY, 1995), Book I, chs 5–7.

54 *De armis Romanis* (2011 edn), (e.g.) part I, 46, 54, 74, 78–80, part II, 172, 208, 218, 224, 256, 266, 268, 282, 330.

55 *De armis Romanis* (2011 edn) 172.

56 Ibidem.

57 *De armis Romanis* (2011 edn) 208.

discussed by both advocates in their respective parallel chapters. The first such example occurs in the parallel chapters 7, which discuss the Samnite wars. The central analogy here, originally applied by Picenus, relates to the Romans' decision to protect (and incorporate) the defeated Campani against their Samnite allies: Picenus refers to the well-known principle of a hunter's right to a prey he has wounded but which is still fleeing from him.[58] Romanus, in his refutation of Picenus' criticism of the Roman policy towards the Samnites, counters the analogy of the wounded animal, referring to Baldus, G del Maino and Alciato. However, the counter-argument proposed by Romanus is apparently not directed at the analogy as such, but at the authority of an established legal rule and of an alleged customary rule to the contrary backed by a dissenting authorial opinion.[59] Because Picenus had relied on an interpretation of Trebatius' opinion proposed by Cujas in his feudal commentary, this is an opportunity for Romanus to challenge Cujas' authority – whatever the latter's qualities – in comparison to the ancient (and official) authorities.[60] Thus the analogy is dismissed, but Romanus shifts the issue to one of legal authorities, where both the status of the authority and the underlying reason of the principle are decisive – neither a Scholastic argument *ab auctoritate* nor a humanistic historical argument.

A second example is offered in the parallel chapters 9, on the Greek and Syrian wars. Picenus argued that because Perseus of Macedon had repented from having broken the treaty with the Romans, it was the Romans' breach of the treaty that put them in the wrong. He then refers to the case of D.24.2.7: when someone files for divorce and retracts his petition, but the other party has accepted the petition, the marriage is nonetheless dissolved due to the latter's

58 *De armis Romanis* (2011 edn) 54–58, with several references to the Digest, J Cujas (see *infra*), T Decianus, J Cephalus, Baldus.

59 *De armis Romanis* (2011 edn) 218–226.

60 *De armis Romanis* (2011 edn) 220: ". . . Magnus sit Galliae iurisconsultus Cuiacius : et Gallia causidicos doceat facunda Britannos. Non tamen magnus est ille iurisconsultus : certe non adeo magnus, qui et sedeat inter Romanos iurisconsultos, ac Caesares, inter Trebatios, Caios, Iustinianos, Fridericos : et iudicet quasi Pythius Apollo absque verbo uno addito, quo sententia abs se lata pro parte numeri minoris, minoris auctoritatis, minoris dignitatis, hic est pro Trebatio, et Friderico, vel tenuiter subornetur"; the passage should be read as the antithesis to Picenus' argument (ibidem, 54): "Feram vulneratam intercipi vulneranti ab alio non oportere, Trebatius iurisconsultus admonuit: cuius et opinio probata a Friderico Caesare: et moribus adfirmata, atque recepta est" 41.1.5.1 and Cujas' commentary *De feudis* (I have used the edn: J Cuiacius, *Opera ad Parisiensem Fabrotianam editionem diligentissime exacta auctiora atque emendatoria in Tomus XI distributa*, Augustae Taurinorum – Parisiis, 1874, T VIII, *In libros quinque feudorum*, Lib I, Tit 1, s v *Si quis de manso*, col 604), referring to Trebatius and the emperor Frederick I, through Rahewin of Freising's *Gesta Friderici imperatoris*.

acceptance.[61] Romanus replied that the case of divorce was not relevant: he quotes the same text of the Digest more extensively, chides his opponent for relying on a truncated quotation, but then sets out his version of the historical events, arguing that Perseus' response to the Senate and his offer of reparation had been inadequate.[62] It is not so much the inadequacy of the analogy that is denied, but rather the construction of the historical facts to which the underlying principle is said to be applicable, which appears to be controversial.

(5) The central theme: just wars and good governance through laws

As Alberico Gentili's career in England proceeded, one can recognise through his work an increased concern for promoting the place of civil lawyers in the polity. In England, that was an uphill task, but Gentili's commitment was consistent with the late-medieval and sixteenth-century civil law tradition in Italy and, even in his days, in several continental countries – in particular in the Holy Roman Empire, about which he was well informed through his brother at Altdorf. In Gentili's time, civil lawyers seemed to face new prospects: the early modern bureaucracies were in need of skilled civil servants; both in Protestant and in Roman-Catholic polities,[63] the province of the clergy and theologians in matters of state tended to be restricted; and political theory as a distinct discipline, emerging outside the often stifling environment of established university scholarship, was still dependent on the traditional disciplines for which the faculties of divinity, arts and law enjoyed in theory a monopoly. The possibility of ensuring a central position for civil lawyers in public governance (which could look back on a long tradition during the Second Middle Ages) seemed therefore very strong. Gentili's challenge was to demonstrate that university-educated civil lawyers were proficient in the different skills expected from a professional body expected to advise the early modern sovereign on effective and just public governance – the tradition of the *buon governo* or *gutes Regiment*.[64] His best-known and

61 *De armis Romanis* (2011 edn) 80.

62 *De armis Romanis* (2011 edn) 268.

63 See, however, the contrasting prospects of early modern civil lawyers in France and Germany, discussed by M Koskenniemi, "International Law and *raison d'état*: Rethinking the Prehistory of International Law", in B Kingsbury and B Straumann (eds), *The Roman Foundations of the Law of Nations* (n 18) 297.

64 A Wijffels, "Van *buon governo* naar *public governance*. Juristen en openbaar bestuur in de Westerse rechtstraditie", in *Ars Aequi, juridisch maandblad* (Oct 2013) 776, idem, "Justitie en

most innovative works, on international law, were a powerful and convincing demonstration of the unique expertise civil lawyers could provide on key issues of foreign policy: diplomacy, war and warfare, treaty-making.[65] However, the merely technical legal skills – or what was perceived to be mostly technical legal expertise – would not have been sufficient to secure the place of the jurist in the inner circles of political deliberation. For that purpose, the councillor also had to display a command of how to articulate the values, virtues and principles associated in the post-medieval era with good governance. In spite of secularising tendencies, a grasp of essential religious principles (whether Protestant or Roman-Catholic) was still required, but the humanist agenda had much strengthened the relevance of properly understanding the historical heritage of the Biblical and, especially, of the classical (Greek-Roman) ancient world. Those were the values and insights that were expected from the model courtier (Castiglione) or from the "perfect ambassador" (the topic of numerous works in the sixteenth and seventeenth centuries). Similarly, Gentili's work was aimed at building the image of the civil lawyer as a model councillor, but, in order to achieve that purpose, his civil lawyer had to add new layers of expertise to the traditional profile of the lawyer steeped in *mos italicus* learning: the legal-humanistic learning had to be integrated, which in turn required a thorough acquaintance with ancient literature, including political and historical writings and their assessment and controversial reassessments by contemporary historical, literary and philological scholarship. How demanding that task was can be seen through the hundreds of pages of Gentili's handwritten notes made during his readings, which included both traditional legal works, recent works associated with new forms of legal learning (including legal humanism), and a great variety of ancient works of contemporary studies of the ancient world.[66] The result of that reading is then reflected in his own writings, both targeting a scholarly or wider audience, and in his more pedagogical writings addressed to (law) students.[67] Throughout Gentili's different

behoorlijk bestuur. Hans Vredeman de Vries' schilderijen in het stadhuis van Danzig (Gdańsk)" (2011) 13 *Pro Memorie* 103.

65 R Lesaffer, "Alberico Gentili's *ius post bellum* and Early Modern Peace Treaties", in B Kingsbury and B Straumann (eds), *The Roman Foundations of the Law of Nations* (n 18) 210, A Wijffels, "La diversité des acteurs dans le *ius post bellum* selon la doctrine antérieure à Grotius", in S Kotovtchikhine, J-P Pancracio and A Wijffels (eds), *Les acteurs de la guerre* (2010) 81.

66 A Wijffels, "De la lecture à l'écriture: les notes de lecture d'Alberico Gentili et leur remploi dans la rédaction de son œuvre doctrinale" (n 27), idem, "From Perugia to Oxford: Past and Present of Political Paradigms" (n 27).

67 See, e.g., A. Gentili's *Lectionis Virgilianae Variae Liber*, Hanau, Apud Guilielmum Antonium, 1603.

works on disparate topics, the author's continuing concern is always the making of a new type of *iuris interpres*, who would qualify as an indispensable figure at the heart of public governance.[68]

Those general remarks also apply to *De armis Romanis*. On the one hand, it offers a very different perspective on issues related to war and warfare than *De iure belli* (or its preliminary version of the 1580s). Moreover, the register and style are quite different. Whereas *De iure belli* is written along the format of a conventional legal treatise (although espousing the newly evolving features of the systematic early modern methods), *De armis Romanis* addresses a non-specialist audience of policy makers. The point is, however, that *De armis* is unmistakeably written by a jurist, who uses his legal expertise – but also much more – in order to develop a register of extensive literary and historical learning drawn mainly from ancient Rome in order to discuss the legitimacy or illegitimacy of numerous and different situations of foreign policy and war. Significantly, in both parts of the work, the argumentation culminates in a characterisation of the resulting public (*in casu*: imperial) governance. The ultimate standard of that apex is the role of law and justice in that imperial governance.

The antithetical structure of *De armis* reflects a traditional dichotomy in the representation of public governance, of which, in Italy, the frescoes by A Lorenzetti at the Palazzo Pubblico in Siena are one of the most famous examples. The *buon governo* is characterised by its reliance on virtues, the *malgoverno* is branded as tyranny with its reliance on vices.[69] That is exactly the contrasting picture given in *De armis*. At the beginning, Picenus sets out to expose the vices that were in his view the hallmark of Roman imperial rule: "Sed fraus, perfidia, avaritia, audacia, crudelitas, illud nobis imperium peperunt".[70] At the very end of the second part, Rome's (bygone)

68 G Minnucci, *Alberico Gentili iuris interpres della prima età moderna* (2011) 178: "L'idea gentiliana del giurisperito formulata nel *De nuptiis*, a differenza di quella espressa nei *Dialogi*, non è più quella di un puro e semplice esegeta del *Corpus* normativo, o di colui che per interpretare i *Libri legales* abbisogna esclusivamente di quanto la giurisprudenza ha elaborato su quei testi (il che viene ora dal lui considerato un *usus corruptus disciplinae nostrae*), ma di un intellettuale che, alla luce delle più ampie conoscenze, si pone come *sacerdos iustitiae.*"

69 Among the vast literature on Lorenzetti's frescoes of good and evil governance, see Q Skinner, "Ambrogio Lorenzetti and the Portrayal of Virtuous Government", and, by the same, "Ambrogio Lorenzetti and the Power and Glory of Republics", both now in *Vision of Politics*, II, *Renaissance Virtues* (2002) 39–92 and 93–117, see also M L Meoni, *Utopia e realtà nel buon governo di Ambrogio Lorenzetti. Tipologie formali nella rappresentazione dell'agire dell'uomo. Un'analisi antropologica* (2001), C Frugoni (a cura di), *Pietro e Ambrogio Lorenzetti*, (2010); and for a brief survey of various interpretations: A Riklin, *Ambrogio Lorenzetti's politische Summe* (1996).

70 *De armis Romanis* (2011 edn) 16 – an accusation echoed in similar terms in Picenus' last chapter: "Atque haec virtus vestra est: quae virtutes omnes in se complectitur, avaritiam, abiectionem,

imperial governance is supported by a council of virtues: "... pietatem, liberalitatem, fidem, magnanimitatem, pacem, securitatem, aequanimitatem Romanam suspirant, et imperium Romanum: cui iusto, aequo, bono subductos se lamentantur". The last sentence echoes the jurist's expertise in the *ars boni et aequi*, while a quote from Jordanes' *Romana* encapsulates Romanus' entire argument in the formula: "Armis iustis quaesitum, legibus iustis conservatum",[71] confirming thereby that the whole point of the argument on the Romans' just wars was that they established throughout their conquered territories the justice of the *ius post-bellum*.

(6) Public governance: no "Celestial Jerusalem"

Another reason why it does not make too much sense to identify Gentili's position wholesale with the argumentation of Romanus, is the consciously schematic arrangement of abundant and complex historical material. Apart from a few nuances and feigned concessions, the format of the disputation results overall in an artificial black and white dichotomy, as if *all* the wars of the Romans over a period of more than half a millennium had been either just or unjust. Both a jurist and an historian would, were they not pressed to represent a special interest in the debate, differentiate from one occurrence to another. In contrast, the purpose of *De armis* is a display of quasi-forensic and historical methods of argumentation in the political arena, in particular on matters of foreign policy and international relations. The purpose of Gentili is to show, *pace* the *politiques*, the ideal qualification of the *interpres iuris* for working out such an argumentation. For the reasons stated, the civil lawyer's skills at the service of the ruler will prove more useful in the long-term for establishing the lawfulness of his

perfidiam, ceteras virtutes vestras ..." (118), a passage in which those vices converge in the Romans' "luck" (*Fortuna*), which was instrumental in their injustice – an accusation which, moreover, is contrasted with the concept of good governance of a City.

71 *De armis Romanis* (2011 edn) 354, with a reference to Jordanes' *Romana*. Following the tradition of contrasting good and bad governance by associating the former with justice, the latter with injustice, and with, respectively, virtues and vices (see the previous note), Gentili ends Romanus' advocacy of the justice of Roman imperial governance by referring to virtues which for centuries (both in works on moral philosophy and in pictural representations of good and bad governance) had been put forward as necessary auxiliaries of good public governance: despite the differences in political regimes, laws, rites and languages which followed the demise of the Roman Empire, people still look back, says Gentili, on the virtues of their system, viz "... et unitatem scissam animorum deplorant omnes: pietatem, liberalitatem, fidem, magnanimitatem, pacem, securitatem, aequanimitatem Romanam suspirant, et imperium Romanum: cui iusto, aequo, bono subductos se lamentantur" – an explicit juxtaposition of the ideal of good governance and the definition of justice inherited from the Roman legal tradition.

prince's war than for arguing the injustice of the war waged by the latter's adversary.

In chapter 9, Romanus tackles an argument of Picenus who had accused the Romans of having protected brigands and pirates, or even of having committed themselves acts of robbery and piracy.[72] Romanus' reply to that accusation is complex, denying on the one hand that such acts were regarded as legitimate (by the authorities Picenus and himself could adduce), yet allowing on the other hand – both for the past and the present – a degree of tolerance: "Et fuit tamen, et nunc est aliqua latrocinandi licentia", although the arguments which then follow immediately seem to refer (though not explicitly) to practices of the law of nations such as privateering and more generally the right of booty, or at least situations where the adversary is formally regarded as an enemy in the sense of the law of war: "Sed an hostium depraedari res neque licet?"[73] Romanus' line of defence and counter-attack on this issue is, however, preceded by a brief remark in which the advocate admits that, although he is prepared to argue solely on the strength of the Romans' virtues, that does not imply that even the Roman governance was at all times perfect, or able to enforce entirely the virtues of good governance: "An tu putas, caelestem aliquam Hierusalem a nobis isthic defendi?" If Rome's governance imposed itself throughout its empire, it was because it was comparatively, i.e. relatively, superior to that of other cities and states: ". . . et non comparatione aliarum, quae unquam fierint, dicere, virtute civitatem meam propagasse imperium suum in orbem terrarum?"[74]

E. CONCLUSIONS

In a recent comment on the development of the humanities (in the Western tradition), Noel Malcolm reflected on:

> the abandonment of traditional humanism, which had been driven by the desire to master and practice the ideal norms of classical thought and art. Much more needs to be said about this fundamental shift. The process of change seems to have involved scholars who studied the ancient world so intensively because they thought it contained norms to be followed, acquiring such detailed knowledge and contextualizing and historicizing it so thoroughly that a sense of historical distance began to take over, so that the material became an object of

72 *De armis Romanis* (2011 edn) 74.

73 Both quotes from *De armis Romanis* (2011 edn) 258. That would fit with Gentili's insistence, before and after the quotations, that such practices may be allowed in so far as they do not infringe upon the "public law".

74 Both quotes from *De armis Romanis* (2011 edn) 258.

study in its own right, not a means towards the end of extracting precepts or ideals.[75]

In that respect, too, Gentili may appear as a transitional figure, because the humanistic component in his work would still qualify as what Malcolm describes as "traditional humanism". If, on the other hand, Gentili's reader is never presented with an historical argument merely for the sake of making an historical point, it was mainly because, in Gentili's approach, history inevitably contributed to an argument which was bound to be normative, whether strictly for underpinning a legal norm, or at least a norm of public governance.

The shift of emphasis from *De iure belli* (whether in its earlier version[76] or in the 1598 edition) to *De armis Romanis* is to some extent one from *ius in bello* to *ius ad bellum*. The shift explains why the register of *De iure belli* is in many respects more legal, because the *ius in bello* is – apart from the issues of military priorities and strategies – essentially perceived as a matter to be dealt with by lawyers. The *ius ad bellum*, on the other hand, touches upon the *arcana imperii* and therefore to high politics. These require a different register, where legal arguments need to be transcended by the whole range of values that underpin, in the Western medieval and early modern tradition, the policies of public governance. Those values were drawn from Biblical and Christian sources, but, especially in a work focusing on the history of Rome until the end of the Republic, mostly from ancient Roman and Greek authors, or later authors dealing with Roman history and classical studies. As the last parallel chapters in both parts of *De armis Romanis* make clear, the ultimate purpose of Gentili is not only a discussion of just and unjust warfare (and, more generally, foreign policy and diplomacy), but a discussion of the merits of imperial (and imperialistic) governance. The format of the debate allows Gentili to let learned lawyers play a central part in the discussion, but, much more than in *De iure belli*, the argument requires a display of expertise which goes far beyond legal expertise – even though, without that expertise, the argumentation would not have the same professional outlook. The historical material, because of Gentili's agenda in support of civil law scholarship and of the civil lawyers' place in the polity's governance, thus never becomes, in Malcolm's words, "an object of study in its own right", for it

75 N Malcolm, "Masters of what? "[review of: R Bod, *A New History of the Humanities. The Search for Principles and Patterns from Antiquity to the Present*, transl L Richards], *Times Literary Supplement* 6 June 2014, 3–4, quotation at 4.

76 *De iure belli commentationes tres*, London, Apud Iohannem Wolfium, 1589 (started in separate instalments through different imprints in 1588–9).

always has a practical political aim. The original intentions of humanism and even legal humanism may not have been the reinforcement of the position of lawyers in society (and certainly not of the prevailing model of lawyers still steeped in the Italian methods around 1500), but, by the end of the sixteenth century, the general ideal of a better governance was not necessarily deemed to be incompatible with a strengthening of learned lawyers in the polity's administration, providing these lawyers had become sufficiently proficient in the learning and methods derived from the original humanistic agenda.

Yet, the question raised at the beginning of the chapter, in the context of the historiographical tendency of emphasising a degree of convergence between the *mos italicus* and legal humanism, remains unsettled. Any approach, as in Gentili's work, which attempted to combine the old learning and humanistic methods was bound to face the difficulty of maintaining categories of thinking – such as legal reasoning cutting across substantially heterogeneous subject matter – which could not be reconciled with the humanist commitment to consider the historical categories of Roman law. Moreover, the notion of sovereignty, which developed in early modern times, transformed the medieval legal concepts of ordinary and extraordinary power, very much at the expense of the culture of rule of law which had impregnated medieval legal learning.[77] Perhaps Gentili's disposition towards a degree of legal proto-positivism and systematisation, which contributed to the establishment of the early modern paradigm of legal methods, can be seen, at that stage of the development of legal thinking, as an attempt to emancipate legal methods both from the incompatible constraints of the double legacy of late-medieval Scholastic methods and from the original ambitions of early modern humanism.

77 I have started developing that view in a different context (viz the inadequacy of *mos italicus* learning in late-sixteenth century arguments in forensic and diplomatic practice, e.g. "International Trade Disputes and *ius commune*: Legal Arguments on the 'Gdańsk Issue' during the Hanseatic Embassy to London in 1553", in A Cordes und S Dauchy (eds), *Eine Grenze in Bewegung: Öffentliche und private Justiz im Handels- und Seerecht. Une frontière mouvante: Justice privée et justice publique en matières commerciales et maritimes* [Schriften des Historischen Kollegs 81] (2013) 65–89, "Early-Modern *Consilia* and *Decisiones* in the Low Countries: the Lost Legacy of the *mos italicus*", in P Maffei and G M Varanini (eds), *Honos alit artes. Studi per il settantesimo compleanno di Mario Ascheri* (2014), vol 1, 125.

2 Humanist Philology and the Text of Justinian's Digest

Douglas J Osler

A. INTRODUCTION

It is an axiom of European legal history that the advent of humanist philology led to a more accurate text of Justinian's Digest, which finally came to be liberated from the accumulated errors of the preceding centuries of darkness and ignorance. This, indeed, is the message broadcast on the title-pages of the sixteenth-century editions, and in a sense it has been repeated ever since. But what exactly is this humanist philology, and what kind of purged, emended, pristine, accurate texts of the Digest did it produce?

The first half of the sixteenth century confronts us with Erasmus' famous triumvirate of Alciatus, Budaeus and Zasius, but as in other triumvirates, one figure soon faded into the background, while another emerged as the clear front-runner. So it is Andreas Alciatus who has gone down in legal history as the first jurist to introduce the philological method into the study of Roman law. From his earliest work, the Annotations on the *Tres Libri* of the Code, published in 1515,[1] to the final two books of the *Parerga*, published in 1554,[2] four years after his death, much of Alciatus' scholarly effort was directed towards textual criticism of the Roman legal sources. An investigation of the influence of this work on the Digest text may conveniently be subsumed under two questions. First, what is the character of the philological work

1 *In tres posteriores Codicis Iustiniani [libros] annotationes, in quibus obiter quam plurima aliorum authorum loca explanantur. Eiusdem opusculum quo Graecae dictiones fere ubique in Digestis restituuntur* (1515).
2 *Παρέργων iuris libri duo ultimi, XI videlicet et XII . . .* (1554).

which Alciatus delivered into the hands of the sixteenth-century humanist editors of the Digest? And, secondly, how did these editors set about using this material in producing their texts?

B. THE CHARACTER OF ALCIATUS' PHILOLOGICAL WORK

Despite the flood of sixteenth-century editions of the *Corpus Iuris Civilis* flowing year after year from the printing houses of Paris and Lyon, the scope of our enquiry turns out to be surprisingly limited – limited, in fact, to three humanist editions published in the 1520s. The work of Alciatus which is particularly relevant to our enquiry is therefore the collection he published at Milan in 1518.[3] Within this collection two works are specifically concerned with the textual criticism of the Digest, namely the *Dispunctiones* in four books, and the latter of the two books of the *Praetermissa*. The predominant theme of both is that which was to bear particular fruit in Digest editions, namely the restoration of the Greek passages to the Digest. The two hundred or so words, phrases and passages in Greek found in the Latin Digest were all lacking in contemporary editions – the single words and phrases having dropped out altogether, while the longer passages had been translated into a Latin version by the twelfth century. Alciatus was following in a long humanist tradition, going back at least to Lorenzo Valla, when he sought to rediscover the original Greek readings, but no one before had done so on such a scale, or, more importantly, had been able to treat the longer passages, the ones of real legal significance. These are discussed for the first time in the *Dispunctiones*, where they occupy about half its chapters.

How did it come about that Alciatus was the first to offer this Greek material some fifty years after the first printing of the Digest? The answer to this question involves us in a complex tale of political power, subterfuge, two untimely deaths, an ancient manuscript and a Dominican monastery – not in this case the stuff of romantic fiction, however, since the main characters are lawyers and professors; their deaths, predictably enough, entirely natural; and behind the story nothing more exciting than a manuscript of Roman law. That manuscript, the famous sixth-century Florentine manuscript of the Digest, contained all the Greek passages in pristine condition. Yet that was of no great assistance, for in the Renaissance it was kept under lock and key in the Palazzo Vecchio, and no scholar was permitted access. To this

3 *Paradoxorum ad Pratum lib. VI. Dispunctionum IIII. In treis lib. Cod. III. De eo quod interest I. Praetermissorum II. Declamatio una* (1518).

rule there was one exception. Due to his personal friendship with Lorenzo de' Medici, Angelo Poliziano, the greatest scholar of the fifteenth century, was able to work with the manuscript at his leisure. In the summer of 1490 Politian executed one of his famous collations, confronting the manuscript against a contemporary printed edition, altering the latter's text to conform to the readings of the manuscript. Such collations were effectively a means of making a copy of a manuscript, but doing so much more rapidly than copying the whole text word for word. What Politian had in mind for this enormous labour we shall never know, for he died four years later, having published virtually nothing.

The next link in the chain is the Bolognese jurist, Ludovico Bolognini. Some time around the year 1500 the three-volume Digest edition containing Politian's collation came into his hands. Bolognini caused large sections of this collation to be copied into his notebooks, one of which contains a list of almost all the Greek passages. But again the curse of the Florentine struck, for Bolognini died in 1508, once more having published nothing. At this point Alciatus enters the story. Bolognini's notebooks were left to the Dominican friars of Bologna, and it was in their library that they were seen by Alciatus at some point between the years 1515 and 1518. This story is essential to an understanding of Alciatus' work, and indeed of the whole course of Digest editing up to the edition of Torelli of 1553.[4] It is no exaggeration to say that access to this source is the inspiration of Alciatus' *Dispunctiones*; the report of the Greek passages in this work derive directly from Bolognini's notebooks.

What Alciatus' *Dispunctiones* offered to the sixteenth-century editors, therefore, was very simply an indirect channel to the Florentine manuscript to which they otherwise had no means of access. The obvious question, then, is how reliable is Alciatus' work for this purpose? And the answer is: extremely unreliable. The work in fact represents a thoroughly contaminated document. This contamination springs from three sources.

The first source of contamination derives from his primary material, Bolognini. As we have seen, Bolognini was dependent on the collation of Politian. We hear a lot about the accuracy of Politian's collations, to which we may assent, provided it is realised that the word is being used in a relative sense. Politian did not quite live up to the exacting standards which he set himself, let alone those of modern scholarship, but his errors generally relate to mere orthographical details which other humanists did not even bother to

4 *Digestorum seu Pandectarum libri quinquaginta, ex Florentinis Pandectis repraesentati* (1553).

record; only a handful are serious enough to affect a reading. On the whole, then, we can say that Politian's collation is a relatively sincere representation of the manuscript. But the same cannot be said for Bolognini's notebooks. Certainly, for the most part they contain transcriptions of Politian's reading of the Florentine. But somehow, and for reasons which remain obscure, a significant number of textual conjectures have become intermingled in this mass of material. These conjectures have no identifying mark in the notebooks, but are wholly indistinguishable and inextricable from the mass of readings of the Florentine. Anyone working with this source would naturally believe that all the Greek passages were the sincere readings of the Florentine.

This, then, is the first source of contamination in the *Dispunctiones*. Clearly it is due to the unique circumstances surrounding the inaccessibility of the Florentine manuscript and the vagaries of its humanist copies. But this would not have mattered so much were it not for the second source of contamination, namely the reckless inaccuracy in the citation of sources which was endemic to humanist philology. Note, first of all, that no one reading the *Dispunctiones* in 1518 could have guessed the true origin of the material it presents. All the discussion in the preface of the work is of the wealth of manuscript sources on which it is based. Alciatus writes:[5]

> I would never have dared to make changes in the text without the greatest trepidation, even if I could adduce the most convincing reasons, until I knew I was able to corroborate my annotations with very good manuscripts. And so, when I had collated numerous manuscripts, and had also been able to read the Florentine manuscript, albeit fleetingly, I decided to bring together a few of the more important of many observations in a small book.

This is immediately followed in the introduction to Book 1 by the detailed description of a particular *volumen antiquissimum* which he tells us he himself owned, to which we shall return. There are thus three distinct categories of manuscript mentioned: the Florentine, Alciatus' personal manuscript, and the *plura exemplaria* which he had collated. How does Alciatus cite this mass of manuscript material – can we, for example, at least keep the three categories distinct? The answer to that question will be sufficiently clear from the single statistic that in over half of the sixty-six Greek restorations

5 "Non sine summa trepidatione quicquam innovare ausus fui, etiam si certissimis fere rationibus adducerer, donec emendatissimis quoque codicibus nostras annotationes comprobari posse cognovissem; cum igitur et plura a nobis collata exemplaria fuissent, cum item Etruscorum Pandectas obiter ceu per transennam legere mihi datum esset, decrevi pauculas aliquas de multis insigniores tamen in codicillum observationes redigere" (p 64r).

in the work there is no mention of any source whatsoever. Moreover, when Alciatus does cite a manuscript source, it is often by means of some such anonymous formulation as *antiqui codices*. To which of the three categories should we refer such a citation? Lest we might naively believe there to be a definite answer to this question, we should note that sometimes *antiqui codices* are explicitly differentiated from the Florentine, as in the phrase, *ex quibusdam antiquis codicibus et ex Etrusco volumine* (II.18), while on other occasions they are clearly to be identified, as when he writes in one section (II.11) *in emendatis codicibus* and a few lines later in the immediately following section *in emendatis codicibus (intelligo autem Florentinorum Pandectas)*. This, then, is the second source of contamination: in citing the readings he has taken from Bolognini, Alciatus sometimes attributes them to the Florentine manuscript; sometimes to an *antiquus codex* in the singular; sometimes to anonymous *antiqui* or *emendati codices*; sometimes, indeed most times, to no source whatsoever.

If it is hard to imagine a more profound degree of confusion, it is nevertheless reached in our third area of contamination, resulting from the history of Book 2 of the *Praetermissa*, published in the same collection of 1518. The *Dispunctiones* were composed on the basis of Bolognini's notebooks, and to that extent do, for the most part, reflect the readings of the Florentine manuscript, albeit imprecisely and at third hand. But Book 2 of the *Praetermissa*, devoted exclusively to the Digest Greek, does not derive *ex novo* from Bolognini. It is in fact the second edition of a work which started out life three years previously with the self-explanatory title, "A small work in which the Greek is restored throughout the Digest".[6] How Alciatus restored the Greek to some seventy Digest texts in 1515 can be characterised by advancing three propositions. First, the readings he proposes are based almost exclusively on conjecture, unguided by any appeal to manuscript evidence; secondly, these conjectures are all intelligent and plausible; thirdly, the suggested readings are with unfailing regularity completely wrong. Of the seventy or so suggested textual restorations, only a handful actually arrive at the authentic reading preserved in the Florentine manuscript.

Shortly after seeing this work published, Alciatus had Bolognini's notebooks before his eyes. Surveying the full extent of the débâcle, as he himself records in the preface to the second edition, he set about revising his text, and revising it radically. The examination of a few examples of these changes will provide a revealing insight into the character of Alciatus' philology.

6 *Opusculum quo Graecae dictiones fere ubique in Digestis restituuntur.*

First of all it should be noted that in many cases Alciatus simply leaves his original text to stand, tacking on at the end of his treatment some such phrase as, "However, in the Florentine manuscript the reading is completely different, namely X". This procedure may seem absurd – rendering superfluous, as it does, all that had preceded – but at least it has the merit of accuracy. Yet even in this case there is a problem. We might surmise, perhaps, that the added words *in Pandectis* (only once explicitly *in Pandectis Thuscis*) were meant to allude to the Florentine. Yet at the same time he refers to his new sources in other ways, writing once *in aliis codicibus* (D.2.14.7.2), once *in quibusdam codicibus* (D.11.3.1.3), and once *in antiquioribus codicibus* (D.32.70.9). How could any reader know whether these formulations, all in the plural, are to be understood as the equivalent of *in Pandectis*, or rather refer to one of the other *plura exemplaria* he mentioned in the preface to the collection?

Let us turn to a few examples of Alciatus' revisions. In D.1.3.2 the Roman jurist had cited a work of the philosopher Chryssipus bearing the title περὶ νόμου. In his original work Alciatus had conjectured περὶ θεμιστῶν, justifying this reading with the phrase: *ex indiciis veteris scripturae coniectavi*. This last phrase, as with so much of humanist philological vocabulary, is highly ambiguous. Does it mean: I have conjectured from the indications of the old, that is, the true reading – in other words on the basis of the surrounding Latin text? That would surely be a banality: how else would one conjecture the missing Greek word? So does it mean: I have conjectured from the indications of a *vetus scriptura*, that is to say, of a manuscript reading? The phrase *indicia veteris scripturae* would in fact be an apt expression for the primitive attempts to transliterate Greek letters sometimes found in the earliest Digest manuscripts, and this is the natural interpretation of Alciatus' words in the context. At any rate, Alciatus states that he has conjectured – *coniectavi* – on the basis of certain evidence, manuscript or otherwise. Observe, then, what happens to Alciatus' text in the second edition. Alciatus now knows the true reading, περὶ νόμου, deriving ultimately from the Florentine manuscript. But because it is convenient for his existing text, he simply makes a clean excision of the word θεμιστῶν and substitutes the new reading νόμου, leaving the final source allegation, asserting the conjectural origin of the reading, to stand intact.

A further example. In the first edition Alciatus had quoted a conjecture, deriving in fact from Budé, which fits the required meaning of written and unwritten law. The conjecture was wrong, and in the second edition Alciatus was able to substitute the correct reading. So what does he choose this time: *in Pandectis*; or *in antiquis codicibus*; or *in quibusdam codicibus*? No: simply *Ipse malim*, "I myself would prefer", as if, in fact, it were his own conjecture. Nor was it a matter of any concern that the final clause in the chapter was left unchanged: *utrumque convenit*; both readings, the new reading and an alternative reading left in his text, are, it would seem, equally valid.

Finally, we have to note that this process of revision is far from comprehensive. Many of the original conjectures were left to stand without comment. Yet this could not be taken by a contemporary reader as an indication that these were good readings, confirmed by the Florentine, since in some such cases Alciatus simultaneously offered a different reading in another work published in the same collection of 1518. All this amply bears out the picture presented by the *Dispunctiones* themselves. Alciatus oscillates arbitrarily between the citation of the Florentine and anonymous *antiqui codices*. Despite the allusion to *plura exemplaria* in the preface to the work, the plural *codices* is used interchangeably with the singular *codex*. The vaguest of references to a manuscript's age, be it *antiquus*, *antiquior* or *antiquissimus*, are also used interchangeably. No clear demarcation is made between manuscript and conjecture. Usually no source whatever is given, but where sources are cited the result is that sometimes manuscript readings are presented as conjectures, and sometimes conjectures are presented as manuscript readings.

We have, however, not quite reached the nadir. It must be recalled that in the Renaissance manuscripts were in private hands, led a nomadic existence from one owner to the next, and were therefore very difficult to pin down. E J Kenney in his history of the Classical Text takes up the story:[7]

> Since emendation *ingenii ope* ranked below emendation *ex codicum auctoritate*, and since indeed the severer breed of critic, in theory at any rate, altogether rejected conjecture as a legitimate source of improvement to the text, there was a standing temptation for a scholar who wished to gain a respectful hearing for his own ideas to father them on a non-existent MS. To modern ways of thinking this seems curious . . . Nevertheless the phenomenon is amply attested . . . Sometimes it seems as if we have to do with a recognized *façon de parler* . . . a licensed fiction in a conventional and well-understood mode.

About Kenney's conclusion I am not so sure. The humanists stress again and again that such a practice, far from being understood with a nod and a wink, was to be regarded as a gross breach of scholarly *fides*. The persistent

7 *The Classical Text. Aspects of Editing in the Age of the Printed Book* (Sather Classical Lectures 44) (1974) 32–33.

assertion of their own *fides* when citing a manuscript reading, and the equally persistent questioning of the *fides* of their fellow scholars, is such a prominent feature of the writings of the humanists that we must conclude that either they were all paranoid, or the dishonest assertion of manuscript authority was a real, ever-present threat. At any rate, one of the individuals against whom the allegation has been made from the sixteenth century onwards is none other than Andreas Alciatus – who, says Cujas, cites a Digest manuscript the likes of which he had never seen: *qualem nullum viderat unquam.*[8]

Is Cujas right? Space permits just one small piece of evidence drawn from among many others. It concerns a very trivial textual corruption in a text of the Digest title on taxes and tax collectors. The text states:[9]

> The hiring out of the tax contracts, which – but "which" in the wrong case – which the excitement of the bidding (*calor licitantis*) has inflated (*inflauit*) beyond the usual contract price, is to be accepted . . .

The text clearly cannot stand, and Mommsen notes Gebauer's simple solution of emending *quae* to *quam*. Alciatus, however, solves the difficulty by reference to the reading of his personal *volumen antiquissimum*. He writes:[10]

> The text is different in our own more reliable manuscript than in other manuscripts, namely as follows:
> The hiring out of the tax contracts, which has inflated (*inflauit*) the excitement of the bidding (*calores licitantes*) beyond the usual contract price, is to be accepted . . .

Well, this may be grammatically correct – "which" is now the subject – but it seems just a bit incongruous. According to this reading it is the excitement of the bidding which has been inflated beyond the normal contract price; which of course makes no sense. Moreover, it is not the inflation of the *calor*, the excitement, which is legally relevant, but the inflation of the *conductio*, the contract price.

In 1531, Alciatus published a new edition of the *Dispunctiones*. In this edition he takes the opportunity to change not just his own text but, contrary to the usual conventions of scholarship, that of his manuscript as well. Alciatus has come to realise that it was of course the contract price which

8 In his *lecturae* on the Digest title *De verborum obligationibus*, D.45.1.133.

9 D.39.4.9pr: "Locatio vectigalium, quae calor licitantis ultra modum solitae conductionis inflavit, ita demum admittenda est . . ."

10 "Aliter in exemplari nostro fideliori legitur quam in aliis soleat, nimirum his verbis: Locatio vectigalium, quae calor*es* licitant*es* ultra modum solitae conductionis infla*uit*, admittenda est . . ."

was inflated by the excitement of the bidding, and so his manuscript changes accordingly:[11]

> The text is different in our own more reliable manuscript than in other manuscripts, namely as follows:
> The hiring out of the tax contracts, which has been inflated (*inflatur*) beyond the usual contract price by the excitement of the bidding (*calore licitantis*) is to be accepted . . .

What are we to make of this? Well, one may choose to believe that Alciatus had returned to his manuscript only to discover that, despite the pristine clarity he attributes to it, and despite the fact that he was constructing a whole chapter of his work specifically on this reading, he had – somewhat carelessly, it might be thought – misread the manuscript in three places. Or one may believe that Alciatus, like all good criminals, has returned to the scene of the crime.

This, then, is the character of the work which was delivered by the founder of legal humanist philology into the hands of the humanist editors of the Digest. A work further removed from the canons of philology as the term is currently understood it would be hard to imagine. No contemporary editor of the Digest could have begun to reconstruct the sources from which Alciatus had drawn his readings even if he had so desired. But that is precisely the point. No humanist editor of the Digest did so desire, for none cared one whit more about the accurate citation of sources than did Alciatus himself.

C. THE WORKING METHODS OF THE HUMANIST EDITORS

The Digest seems to have fared rather differently from other classical texts in the Renaissance. In the case of Latin literary texts, the corrupting hand of the humanists is often to be discerned even in the fifteenth-century manuscripts. A particularly notorious example is that of Catullus, whose manuscript tradition, to quote F W Hall's *Companion to Classical Texts*, "has suffered greatly from Renaissance interpolators".[12] At the very latest, a humanist editor – or interpolator, to adopt Hall's designation – was charged with seeing the text through the press. Certainly, the prefaces of early editions of the Digest pay lip service to the correction of errors, but, as far as

11 "Aliter in exemplari nostro fideliori legitur quam in aliis soleat, nimirum his verbis: Locatio vectigalium, quae calor*e* licitant*is* ultra modum solitae conductionis inflat*ur*, admittenda est . . ."

12 F W Hall, *A Companion to Classical Texts* (1913) 218.

I can see, the Digest text escaped even the most rudimentary correction. Unusual and hence corrupt Latin words, which had been emended and explained in the classical commentaries of humanist scholars for decades, resurface in the sixteenth-century Digest editions as the same *voces nihili* of the manuscripts. So, in the first half-century of printing, the Digest editions seem to have escaped any form of humanist intervention, being no more than faithful reproductions of the manuscript, or prior edition, which served as printer's copy. Up to 1520, then, the Digest text had been mercifully free from humanist intervention. The waters had not yet been muddied; that was now about to change.

The first edition of the Digest which may be called a humanist edition is that published at Paris by Claude Chevallon in the years 1523–1524.[13] The editor was Ludovicus Blaublommius, a native of Ghent, who worked in the publishing business at Paris from 1520 onwards. The edition (of which there was a reprint five years later in 1528–1529[14]) is in folio, in Gothic type, and includes the Accursian Gloss, so it hardly bears the appearance of any new humanist invention. But it is different from preceding editions in a very important respect: the text has begun to change, and it has begun to change through the insertion of the readings of the humanists, particularly of Budé and Alciatus – and, of course, of the ubiquitous *antiqua exemplaria* which the editor happened to have at his disposal. In the outer margin, beyond the Accursian gloss, we find the beginnings of its successor, the humanist gloss, which was to be given its definitive form later in the century by Dionysius Gothofredus. The pre-Gothofredan glosses, to coin a phrase, here take the form of very short notes by Blaublommius to indicate his intervention in the text and are generally limited to the words, *Vide Alciatum lib. Praetermiss. secundo*, or *Vide Budaeum hic.*

These glosses are, however, a perilous guide to Blaublommius' actual textual intervention. Of course, the Greek passages, here being printed in a Digest edition for the first time, have a high profile and so are generally accompanied by an indication of the source. But even this is not the invariable rule. One interesting case is a text from the Digest title on the praetorian edict *Nautae, Caupones, Stabularii* (D.4.9.1.2), imposing strict liability on such individuals for damage or loss to goods entrusted into their care. The category *nauta*, writes Ulpian, includes the ship's captain, but

13 *Digestorum seu Pandectarum imperatoris Iustiniani prima pars* November 1523. *Secunda pars* May 1524. *Tomus tertius* December 1524.

14 *Quinquaginta librorum Digestorum seu Pandectarum iuris civilis tomus primus (-tertius)* (1528–29).

not a *mesonauta*. The unusual word *mesonauta* is found, in Latin, in the Florentine manuscript; but in Bolognini's notes it is one of those cases which mysteriously turn up in Greek, as μησοναύτης. In *Dispunctiones* III.21 Alciatus writes:[15]

> Ermolao Barbaro interprets *mesonauta* to be the name of a common slave who was stationed in the middle of the ship at the beck and call of all on board, just as by the same rationale those who do the same in a house are called *mediastini*. I would more readily approve this opinion were it not for the fact that in the Florentine manuscript the word is written in Greek as μησοναύτης, with an ἦτα.

The logic is irrefutable; the only problem is that the evidence relied upon is completely spurious. We know that, and we know the source of the error, since we can consult both the Florentine manuscript and Bolognini's notebooks. But Alciatus' contemporaries could do neither. So in the edition of Blaublommius we find the Greek word, or pseudo-Greek word, μησοναύτης promoted to the text of the Digest, without – and this is the crucial point – any accompanying indication of its source. What we have here, then, is not the emendation of the Digest text at the hands of a humanist editor, but its corruption at the hands of a humanist interpolator.

A full check on Blaublommius' use of all the readings proposed by Budé in his *Annotationes in Pandectas* of 1508 comes to the following conclusion: sometimes Blaublommius simply retains the vulgate reading without comment, but this is a minority of cases; sometimes he retains the vulgate reading but records the suggestion of Budé in the margin; sometimes he promotes Budé's reading to the text and notes the fact in his gloss. Finally, and here once again we come to the crux, sometimes he promotes the reading of Budé to the text without any indication of the fact.

If we are tempted to shake our heads in dismay at such cases where Blaublommius simply alters the Digest text without alerting the reader, we must be aware that we are thereby passing judgement on humanist editing as such, as we shall see from the next edition to be considered. This is the humanist edition par excellence, published at Paris in the years 1527–1528.[16] It is an edition of the Digest alone, not a part of the *Corpus Iuris Civilis*, and it is without the Accursian gloss. It is in octavo format, and in Stephanus' beautiful Roman type. Who was the editor of the text? This is unknown, for it has no preface. And more important, there are no marginal notes of any

15 "Interpretatur Hermolaus vilis mancipii nomen esse *mesonautam*, qui in medio navis ad imperia omnium excubet, qua ratione *mediastini* in domo dicuntur; quam sententiam alacrius probarem nisi in Pandectis Florentinis μησοναύτην per ἦτα scriptum esset."

16 *Digestorum seu Pandectarum iuris civilis volumen primum (-quintum)* (1527).

kind. No apparatus, no footnotes, no asterisks: nothing. What is happening to the Digest text, then, is that all these readings of Budé and Alciatus, good and bad, manuscript and conjecture, of the Florentine and so-called *antiqui codices* – in addition, of course, to the readings already concocted in a similar fashion by Blaublommius – are being mixed together and thrown pell-mell into the text without any indication of the fact. Of course, it would be clear that the Greek was new. But what of all those other subtle changes which so affect the meaning of a legal text; Alciatus' suggestions of *coheres* for *heres*, *necnon* for *non*, *non omnino* for *omnino non*, and so on? The Digest text was being subjected to wilful and arbitrary alteration, and the reader had no means of knowing it. This witch's brew of rampant and uncontrollable textual corruption is what is celebrated by historians as humanist philology.

In the year 1529, Alciatus' substantial influence on the editing of the Digest text came to a merciful end. April 1 of that year is the date prominently displayed on the title-page of a work published by the Nuremberg printer, Ioannes Petreius, namely the famous Digest edition of Gregorius Haloander.[17] The modern scholar might indeed be tempted to regard Haloander's edition as an April fool, but his contemporaries were less perturbed by the unrestrained and capricious rewriting of the Digest text which Haloander passes off as a work of textual scholarship. In fact, Haloander's text – the ambiguity of the expression is apt – was to dominate the field for the next quarter century until it was eclipsed by Torelli's edition of 1553. Why Alciatus' influence at this point was already spent can be easily explained. Haloander's major source was precisely the same as Alciatus' had been, namely the notebooks of Bolognini. And whereas Alciatus had treated only a selection of Greek texts, Haloander went systematically through the whole Digest Greek, from *De iustitia et iure* to *De regulis iuris*.

By July of 1529 a copy of Haloander's edition was in the hands of Alciatus.[18] By the end of the following month he could write to Boniface Amerbach that a new edition of the *Dispunctiones* collection was ready.[19] It is in the

17 *Digestorum seu Pandectarum libri quinquaginta . . . editi Norembergae per Gregorium Haloandrum, munificentia ac liberalitate ampliss. ordinis ibidem, anno M.D.XXIX Cal. Apr.* (1529).

18 Alfred Hartmann, Die Amerbachkorrespondenz. III Band (1947) 441–443, letter no 1374, lines 36–38, G L Barni, *Le lettere di Andrea Alciato giureconsulto* (1953) 96–98, letter no 55, lines 38–40 (dated 31 August 1529): "Haloandri editionem vidi iam agitur alter mensis; dono eam mihi dedit Ioannes Panngartner ex Augusta Vindelicorum."

19 Hartmann (n 18) 439–440, letter no 1372, lines 17–18, Barni (n 18) 94–95, letter no 54, lines 16–18 (dated 27 August 1529): "Paradoxis Dispunctionibusque novam adhibui limam, multa in

same month of August 1529 that Alciatus subscribed the new preface to this revised edition (although in the event it was not to be published for another two years).[20] He writes:[21]

> In the *Dispunctiones* I could indeed have restored all those texts in which the Florentine or other old manuscripts differ from the vulgate, which would have been very easy for me, but I preferred to emend only those texts which might cause some legal dubiety, or from which some source of error might arise, lest I seemed to take upon myself the job of a copyist.

Of course, Alciatus had in fact made many textual emendations where no legal issue was at stake. The truth is that in 1529 Alciatus had to relive the painful experience of 1518, the evidence of error and futility once again placed directly before his eyes. This new preface was being written in the wake of Haloander's edition very simply because Alciatus had once again to set about reworking his text, seeking to obliterate the errors, and harmonising his text with the current state of the Digest text. So another wave of emendations was made in the *Praetermissa*, this time on the basis of Haloander's readings. This self-serving exercise repeats the same old story all over again: I prefer X; the Florentine manuscript has Y; *antiqui codices* have Z; not so much citations of sources as hollow literary flourishes. Yet in the end Alciatus was merely wading further into the morass of his own creation. Little did he know that he was standing on precisely the same treacherous sands as when using Bolognini's notebooks fifteen years previously. For, yes, Haloander usually reports the Florentine manuscript; but alas, no, not invariably. In fact there is an admixture of conjectural readings in Haloander's text, and once again no means whatever to discover which is which. To attribute Haloander's readings directly to the Florentine, or to any manuscript, was thus a reckless game of philological roulette.

And, of course, the bullet has to be in the chamber only once for the revolver to fire. Back to the *Praetermissa*, where in one chapter (D.14.3.5.8) Alciatus had reported in the original work of 1515 two conjectural Greek

melius commutavi, quaedam expunxi." Hartmann (n 18) 441–443, letter no 1374, lines 26–27; Barni (n 18) 96–98, letter no 55, lines 27–28; (dated 31 August 1529): "Habeo penes me Paradoxa cum reliquis; emendavi addidique plurima, quaedam subtraxi."

20 *Paradoxorum ad Pratum lib. VI. Dispunctionum lib. IIII. In treis libros Cod. lib. III. De eo quod interest liber unus. Praetermissorum lib. II. Declamatio una. De stip. divisionib. commentariolus. Ex novissima autoris recognitione* . . . (1531).

21 "In *Dispunctionibus* vero omnes omnino locos restituere potuissem, quibus vel Pandectae Florentinae vel alii vetusti codices a vulgatis dissident, idque factu mihi facilimum fuisset, sed malui ea tantum recensere quae probabilem in iure aliquam dubitationem faciebant aut unde errori ansa praestari potuisset, ne viderer etiam librariorum ipsorum munus mihi praeripere."

restorations, one proposed by Budé and one by the Milanese humanist Aurelius Albucius. It is the reading of Albucius, the Greek κτεριστήν, that we find in Haloander's text. By a fine stroke of irony, Haloander's source was with all probability the work of Alciatus himself, for on this occasion he was not in fact reporting the reading of the Florentine, which is completely different. Alciatus nevertheless assumed that this reading, like most of the others printed by Haloander, was that of the Florentine. Hence the gratuitous addition in the 1531 edition of the *Praetermissa* of the words *cui antiqui codices consentiunt* (which is confirmed by ancient manuscripts), a statement which is in fact a complete falsehood.

Another decade was to go by before the game was finally exposed. In 1542 the young Spanish scholar, Antonio Agustín began his collaboration with Lelio Torelli, who was already working on his reproduction in print of the Florentine manuscript. The following year Agustín published the results of his researches on the Florentine in the *Emendationes et Opiniones*.[22] It is in effect a devastating critique of the humanist scholarship of the preceding decades, in particular that of *praeceptor meus*, Alciatus, who had taught Agustín at Bologna for a short time in the year 1537. This doubtless explains why Alciatus is treated so circumspectly in the *Emendationes*; but for those with eyes to see, Agustín's work left no room for doubt. In one simple sentence in Book 3, chapter 3, he provides the clue to understanding the textual quagmire of the preceding thirty years:[23]

> I come now to my master Alciatus, in whose works . . . readings are attributed to the Florentine manuscript which in reality are derived from Bolognini or Haloander.

And pursuing this fundamental insight, Agustín takes us through one case after another in which Alciatus falsely attributes a reading to the Florentine manuscript,[24] whether explicitly identified as such, or attributed anonymously to *emendati* or *antiqui codices*. But one instance stood out in what might otherwise have been excused as a simple misunderstanding, and Agustín does not let it pass. It is a case where Haloander, with his customary nonchalance, had added a Greek word to a Digest text (D.47.18.1.1)

22 *Emendationum et opinionum libri quattuor. Ad Modestinum sive de excusationibus liber singularis. His libris maxima iuris civilis pars ex Florentinis Pandectis emendatur et declaratur* (1543).

23 *Emendationes et Opiniones* III 3 p CXLVII lines 6–10: "Ad praeceptorem meum venio, in cuius libris, quos multos multa eruditione atque elegantia in maximis docendi et respondendi occupationibus scripsit, Tusci libri aut Florentini appellantur nonnunquam Bolognini et Haloandri Digesta."

24 The heading of Book III 3 is *Falso quaedam dici in Tuscis libris esse scripta*.

where there is in fact none in the sixth-century Florentine manuscript. Only this time Alciatus does not simply attribute it to the Florentine, or to *antiqui codices*, but states that it is evidenced by *et antiqui plerique codices et Ethruscae Pandectae*.[25] And that double citation, deliberate yet impossible, gives the game away. Directly citing a manuscript on the basis of a printed text that was believed to represent it, a humanist might of course accidentally attribute a reading to the *Ethruscae Pandectae*; or he might attribute it to *antiqui codices* as a generic expression meaning simply a manuscript reading. What he could not do is attribute it to *plerique codices*, still less to *plerique codices* as well as the Florentine. *Quod nollem fecisset*, comments Agustín,[26] otherwise so reserved in his criticism, on this . . . this what?: deceit, error, confusion, false recollection, carelessness, inaccuracy in the citation of sources? At any rate, since the Greek word in question is not in the Florentine, nor of course in any other *antiqui codices* of the Digest, *plerique* or otherwise, this is one more insight into the perils and pitfalls of humanist philology.

Agustín points forward to the end of our story, which comes with the publication of Torelli's Digest in 1553. This edition is sometimes called a quasi-facsimile, and it is true that Torelli sought, and indeed achieved as far as was reasonably practicable in a sixteenth-century printed edition, to produce a replica in print of the text of the manuscript – including its manifest errors, which he indicated by a specially devised set of symbols and changes of print. It is all a far cry from the founder of legal humanism, with his *Ipse malim*, ubiquitous *antiqui codices* and self-correcting *volumen antiquissimum*. Do we therefore need to revise our negative opinion about humanist textual scholarship? I believe, on the contrary, that it is the Torelli Digest which is a completely exceptional case, due in the end to the chance survival of one extraordinary manuscript. We have to ask ourselves, what would have been the result if the Palazzo Vecchio had burnt down in 1540? The same, I would suggest, as happened in other manuscript traditions: there would have followed three hundred years of *emendatio ope codicum et ingenii* of the *textus receptus*, precisely as in the Digest editions from the 1520s which we have examined, with the added confusion that the readings of the lost Florentine would have continued to be available only through a variety of unreliable and conflicting derivative sources. And that process would have

25 *Παρέργων iuris libri III* . . . (1538). Book I 11: "Dictionem vero Graecam eo modo reponendam et antiqui plerique codices et Etruscae Pandectae nobis indicarunt, cum alii aliter coniectura inani commiscerentur."

26 *Emendationes et Opiniones* IV 16 p CCXLI lines 8–27 at line 15.

been protracted into the nineteenth century, when the manuscripts finally passed into public ownership; a scientific means of dating them was established; a method for determining their relationships invented; and general principles of scholarly precision adopted – until, that is, the birth of philology as the term is currently understood.

D. CONCLUSIONS

So in *The Story of F*, as we might call our tale, we can observe the usual course of classical philology compressed into fifty years rather than three hundred and fifty. In this story it is undoubtedly Alciatus, not Torelli, who presents the typical face of humanist textual scholarship, a fact which raises the question of the very use of the word "philology" in this context. In modern usage the term philology conjures up the world of classical scholarship: the precise collation of manuscripts; the meticulous notation of variants, changes of scribal hand, changes of ink colour, evidence of correction and erasure; the determination of the date and relationship of manuscripts and the construction of a *stemma codicum*; and the presentation of the evidence in an *apparatus criticus*; in short, of painstaking scholarly lives devoted to the minutiae of an ancient text. So when we say that Alciatus was the first jurist to introduce the philological method into the study of the Roman legal sources, we must be clear that we are speaking about humanist philology – in reality a mere parody of philology, if not indeed an oxymoron. In the specific area of the editing of texts, it would surely come nearer the truth to adopt the usage of F W Hall cited above, and, instead of celebrating the scholarly achievements of humanist philologists, recognise the textual depredations of Renaissance interpolators.

PART II
A BREAK WITH THE PAST/CONTEMPORARY CRITIQUES

3 Deconstructing *Iurisdictio*: The Adventures of a Legal Category in the Hands of the Humanist Jurists

Guido Rossi

A. INTRODUCTION

If we were to assess the historical importance of any strand of legal scholarship by its later influence, many great scholars would be utterly marginalised to the benefit of more fortunate ones. This is of course what we do all the time. It is easy. But it is also reassuring: we like to think that time works in a Darwinian sense. We tend to associate the "greatness" of an author with his "payoff", and measure such a "payoff" by its impact on the development of the law. In principle, this of course has its merits. The problem is that we often start with our modern system. Since we look backwards, we measure with hindsight. This way we build a linear, majestic highway connecting past and present. Anything outside it may be safely overlooked, for it does not lead to us. Moreover, in building our highway we can happily revise the past and straighten any curve – after all, when the road bends it goes in the wrong direction. This way, our functional approach leads not just to oversimplifications, but often straight to re-writing history. More than simplifying, it mystifies. As it happens, legal humanism is one of the best examples of all this. There is no doubt that the sixteenth century is the age of legal humanism. Any textbook on European legal history will tell you that.

We teach legal humanists – as we should – because of their alleged profound influence on the law. Perhaps the implied argument is that, if we were to question their actual influence, we might risk having to reconsider whether to teach them at all. And it is very comforting – and easy – to have a nice group of new figures occupying the sixteenth century. Otherwise one should seriously think of teaching the later *ius commune*, a subject which unfortunately lacks grand narratives and so is both difficult and terribly variegated from country to country. Whether those "new figures" were effectively doing what we say they were, is not really the point. They provide us with a superb new chapter, most useful (and timely) to break with Bartolism and make way for the institutional writers, and ultimately natural law.[1]

That the *mos italicus* progressively declined (though at different times in different places) is of course true. What is arguable is whether the advent of legal humanism entailed a scission among jurists between *mos italicus* and *mos gallicus*. What exactly this *mos gallicus* may be is not easy to say. We use this label to group together any heterodoxy in respect of the *mos italicus*, and we move from the draconian principle "*semel-semper*". If a writer does not behave as a Bartolist at any given time, his entire work must be considered part of legal humanism.[2]

As it is well known, the two main elements of legal humanism were history and philology. Legal humanism heralded, among other things, the birth of legal history in the modern sense of the term – namely, the study of the law (mostly Roman) from a historical perspective. But precisely because of this, it was hardly a turning point in legal history. The philological element could have entailed more profound repercussions, since it challenged the very foundations of the *ius commune*. By and large, however, the scope of those repercussions was such as to neutralise them. Strict adherence to ancient texts would have led to conclusions interesting for historians, but untenable for contemporary jurists. Legal history stemmed from legal

1 The link between legal humanism and elegant jurisprudence tends to be less pronounced in most textbooks. This of course seems bizarre, but only at first sight. For elegant jurisprudence was yet another "wrong" bending of the road leading towards the Modern Truth.

2 The opposite is of course also true: we can make sense of the later *mos italicus* as a unitary category only through sweeping generalisations. This has probably nurtured the Bartolists-Humanists divide nearly as much as the *semel-semper* principle. More deeply, it might have even contributed to its very creation.

One of the most recent attempts to explain the interplay between *mos italicus* and *mos gallicus* speaks of "numerous variants and gradations" of the "humanist dimension", and labels the middle ground between Bartolism and legal humanism as "moderate humanism". Beyond this threshold the elegant jurisprudence lies; behind it, we are still in the province of Bartolism. R Lesaffer, *European Legal History* (transl J Arriens) (2009) 353–354.

humanism, but legal historians tend to be innocuous creatures in respect to the development of the law. Further, early legal humanists were often academics in the worst sense of the term, more inclined to quarrels than cooperation. The confusion and variety of different views on what the original text might have been was such that, rather than spreading a single voice, or a polyphonic harmony, it produced a loud cacophonic sound. Or at least this was what coeval jurists perceived.

This contribution will focus on a small example of such legal humanists' "voices" and of their reception among Bartolists, the case of *iurisdictio*. It does not aim at completeness in the least. It is most definitely not an essay on the development of the concept of *iurisdictio* in the sixteenth and early seventeenth centuries, and it lacks any pretence to guide the reader into the intricacies of the subject.[3] The scope is narrower and the purpose more modest: describing the position of some legal humanists on a specific subject, observing the reaction of non-humanist jurists and perhaps glimpsing the ultimate reasons behind their contrast. This is a significant caveat, for the focus of these pages is not on legal humanist theories, but on their immediate impact. Further, such an impact should not be assessed in general terms. The influence of legal humanism on the work of Bartolist lawyers was extremely variegated (to say nothing of the universe behind the terms "non-humanist" and "Bartolist"). Any general account would necessarily result in a broad narration with scant truth in it. Rather, I will focus on a few humanist jurists, mostly of the first half of the sixteenth century, chosen mainly because of their frequent quotation by other non-humanist lawyers on the subject. Also, although the choice of the subject is arbitrary, I believe that the same results could be reached with a different subject. The important point is that the topic is abstract enough to attract legal humanists' attention but not entirely detached from reality, lest it would be ignored by non-humanist jurists. *Iurisdictio* simply fitted the bill. Lastly, although here we are on shakier ground, it offers another advantage, as its "deconstruction" might betray some political intent.

Two last points. The term "*iurisdictio*" refers to the jurisdictional

3 For more exhaustive works on the subject, see first of all the seminal study of M P Gilmore, *Argument from Roman Law in Political Thought, 1200–1600* (1941) esp 77–85, and more recently the important contribution of L Mannori, "Per una 'preistoria' della funzione amministrativa. Cultura giuridica e attività dei pubblici apparati nell'età del tardo diritto comune" (1990) 19 *Quaderni Fiorentini per la Storia del Pensiero Giuridico* 323 esp 345–407. To some extent, despite the somewhat different perspective, the present chapter is meant as a gloss on Mannori's remarkable study.

prerogatives of a judge, not to other subjects (e.g. territorial jurisdiction, state jurisdiction, etc). Second, references to secondary sources are extremely limited. This is intentional. There are many modern excellent works touching on the subject, but very few devoted to it. Several studies mention some of the issues related to our subject while looking at other subjects. Pointing at them might have risked shifting the focus of these pages.

B. ὕβρις: THE ORIGINAL SIN

Early modern public law evolved rapidly. But it did not move away from its medieval framework. Rather, it built on it. The whole administrative structure of the early modern state was still rooted in the medieval concept of *iurisdictio*. In a paradox of history, the modern idea of *iurisdictio* is probably closer to the Roman than the medieval one. It is well known that the medieval concept of *iurisdictio* derives from the conflation of two distinct categories, *iuris-dictio* (to "say" the law) and *iuris-ditio* (the "power" of the law).[4] Of the two concepts, medieval jurists considered that of *iuris-ditio* to be the general one. As such, the general concept of *iurisdictio* did not have a jurisdictional meaning, but it simply meant "authority".[5] In turn, this general *potestas* was divided in two categories: jurisdictional power on the one hand, and any other power (we would say, both administrative and legislative functions) on the other. Jurisdictional power was termed "*iurisdictio simplex*",[6] while the other category was referred to as "*imperium*".[7] *Imperium* was in

4 C Fasolt, *The Limits of History* (2004) 178–185, B Paradisi, "Il pensiero politico dei giuristi medievali", in L Firpo (ed), *Storia delle idee politiche economiche e sociali*, vol II pt 2 (1983) 273–275.

5 Accursius, *Digestum vetus* (1566) vol I *ad* D.2.1.3 col 164 § *Mixtum est*, Bartolus de Saxoferrato, *Super prima et secunda parte Digesti veteris* (1562) *ad* D.2.1.3 p 112 § *Imperium* n 3–4: "qu[a] ero unde dicatur iurisdictio? dicit glossa hic quod dicitur a dictione quod est potestas et iuris quasi iuris potestas . . . nam potestas et iurisdictio idem sunt, ut dixi: et est potestas iuris, ergo est iurisdictio." See also Azo, *Summa codicis* (1563) *ad* C.3.13 § *Quoniam* col 183 n 1: "dicitur autem iurisdictio a ditione (quod est potestas) et iure, quasi dicat, legitima potestas".

6 Bartolus de Saxoferrato (n 5) *ad* D.2.1.1 § *Ius dicentis* n 2 p 107.

7 Ibid: "Ius dicere potest etiam ubi nullum est litigium, ut quando interponitur decretum, super alienatione rerum minorum, vel super transactione alimentorum, quae sunt misti imperii" (*mistus* was a medieval corruption for *mixtus*). It follows that *iudicium dicere* is not coterminous with *ius dicere*. While the former denotes *iurisdictio simplex*, the latter is the expression of *imperium*. See ibid, n 1: "venio ad quod et primo ad ea quae tanguntur in gl. et quaero quare dicit ius dicentis, et non iudicis dicentis? Respond[e]o gl. hoc ideo quia non de omni iudice, sed tantum de eo qui habet merum et mixtum imperium". For this reason Bartolus stresses the importance, in the *Liber Extra*, of the term "*ius dicere*" to designate the chief prerogative of the *iudex*. See ibid, n 4: "nam idem est dicere iudex, quod ius dicens, extra de ver. sig. c. forum [X.5.10: 'iudex dictus quasi ius dicens populo'] quod placet, quia hic sincopatur, quia detrahitur litera: scilicet de

turn separated into *merum* and *mixtum*.[8] The distinction was based on their different aims: *imperium merum* was concerned with public utility; when on the contrary the utility was mainly private, the *imperium* was *mixtum*.[9] Further, *imperium* – both *merum* and *mixtum* – and *iurisdictio simplex* were each subdivided into six levels, so that, for instance, *merum imperium* ranged from the power to enact general laws to that of imposing a modest fine.[10]

This complex system was based on two pillars. First, there was no clear-cut conceptual distinction between *iurisdictio* and *imperium*. They formed a single and unitary category in which jurisdictional prerogatives were but a part of a more general power of government.[11] Secondly, and crucially, the different kinds and degrees of jurisdiction were not to be distinguished according to the functions of the magistrate or the territorial extension of his jurisdiction, but rather according to the personal status of the *iudex*,[12] so that the first and foremost division was that between *iudex nobilis* and *iudex mercenarius*.[13] Unlike the *iudex mercenarius*, the *iudex nobilis* did not need a lawsuit to exercise his jurisdiction. Ultimately, the distinction between *iurisdictio simplex* and *imperium* did not lie in their specific characteristics, but in the status of the *iudex* who exercised them.

medio. Item quia appellatio iudicis refertur ad [iudices] maiores . . . Et ideo dicitur [ius] dicentis, et non iudicis, quia sic placuit sibi." Cf Azo (n 5) *ad* C.3.13 § *Quoniam* n 20 col 187: "quod non dixit officium iudicis, sed officium ius dicentis".

8 Bartolus de Saxoferrato (n 5) *ad* D.2.1.3 § *Imperium* n 4 p 112: "iurisdictio in genere sumpta, dividitur in dua species, scilicet in imperium simpliciter sumptum, et in specie quod est iurisdictio . . . nam potestas et iurisdictio idem sunt, ut dixi: et est potestas iuris, ergo est iurisdictio. Idem de mero et mixtum imperio . . . cui etiam iurisdictio inest, sicut genus inest speciei suae . . . Est ergo iurisdictio genus . . . imperium subdividitur in merum, et mistum. Non enim iurisdictio dividitur in merum et mixtum imperium, sed imperium simpliciter sumptum dividitur in merum et mixtum." See further ibid, nn 7–13 and nn 14–22 pp 112–113, on *merum* and *mixtum imperium* respectively.

9 Ibid, n 6. Cf also ibid, n 15 p 113.

10 Ibid, nn 8–12, 17–22 and 24–26 pp 112–114 (on *imperium merum*, *imperium mixtum* and *iurisdictio simplex* respectively). This sixfold division meant that not even the whole of *iurisdictio* (*simplex*) was entrusted to the *iudex mercenarius*: ibid, n 24 p 113.

11 See the classic works of P N Riesenberg, *Inalienability of Sovereignty in Medieval Political Thought* (1956) 35, and of F Calasso *I glossatori e la teoria della sovranità* (1957) 49.

12 Bartolus de Saxoferrato (n 5) *ad* D.2.1.3 § *Imperium* nn 15–16 p 113.

13 Ibid, *ad* D.2.1.1 § *Ius dicentis* n 12 pp 108–109: "officium nobile est quod per se stat sive hoc iudex suo motu exerceat. sive ad postulationem alterius . . . Quoddam est officium mercenarium quod per se non stat. sed deservit actioni."

C. φθόνος θεῶν: RIGHTFUL CHASTISEMENT

Even from such a short survey it should be clear that the medieval understanding of *iurisdictio* was hardly faithful to the Roman sources. Unsurprisingly enough, the first jurist to insist on the point was Andreas Alciatus (Andrea Alciato, 1492–1550). In the second book of his *Paradoxa*, Alciatus methodically demolished the *ius commune* concept of *iurisdictio*. There is nothing in the sources to justify the idea of *iurisdictio* as a broad and all-encompassing genus. *Merum imperium* hardly entails a general, all-encompassing power. The sources speak of "*merum*" in the restrictive sense of "*solum*" – and not "absolute" and "unbounded", as the civilians would have it. When *imperium* is *merum,* it has no *iurisdictio*. Deprived of any jurisdictional prerogative, *merum imperium* is just the "potestas animadvertendi in facinorosos homines" (D.2.1.3), that is, the power to inflict a punishment.[14] Since Ulpian speaks of a *gladii potestas*, this punishment must refer only to criminal proceedings. Clearly, it has nothing in common with the jurisdictional sphere – *iurisdictio*.[15] Not only, therefore, do extra-jurisdictional powers ("*ditio*") have hardly any similarity at all with *iurisdictio*, but they are not even included in *merum imperium*. Correctly understood, *merum imperium* is but a magistrate's prerogative, not the supreme power reserved to the prince alone.[16] In turn, the sources are quite clear that *mixtum imperium* consists of *bonorum possessio* and of *iudicis dandi licentia*.[17] The entire distinction so dear to civilians between *iudex nobilis* and *mercenarius*, and ultimately between public and private utility, is therefore completely groundless.[18] For instance, condemnation and absolution alike are principally aimed at public

14 Andreas Alciatus, *Paradoxorum ad Pratum libri sex* (1518) lib 2 ch 6 fol 17r: "merum imperium nil aliud esse, quam potestatem gladio animadvertendi in facinorosos homines: et haec definitio cum re definita convertitur: quamobrem iure civili valere eam, negandum non est . . . gladius hic non simpliciter pro telo accipi debet, sed pro quacunque poena, qua ex delicto plectendus sit reus". Cf also ibid, lib 2 ch 7 fol 17v.

15 Ibid, lib 2 ch 8 fol 17v: "imperium aut merum, aut mixtum est. Merum imperium est habere gladii potestatem ad animadvertendum in facinorosos homines. Mixtum est cui etiam iurisdictio inest, quod in danda bonorum possessione consistit. Iurisdictio est etiam iudicis dandi licentia."

16 Ibid, lib 2 ch 6 fol 17r: "si merum imperium nil aliud est, quam potestatem animadvertendi in facinorosos homines habere, certe haec potestas magistratibus tribuitur: quo circa et merum imperium habere dicendum est".

17 Ibid, lib 2 ch 8 fol 17v. Limits of space do not permit forays into the intricacies of the subject and most of all into the manifold interpretations of "iudicis dandi licentia". The issue of *iurisdictio delegata* gave rise to endless and very complex controversies on its meaning and – moreover – scope. Thankfully, however, such controversies did not create new interpretations of *imperium* but rather depended on them. We will return to the point in the conclusion.

18 Ibid, lib 2 ch 7 fol 17v.

utility. But if *merum imperium* had the monopoly of all actions primarily inspired by public utility, then we should conclude that absolution would fall within *merum imperium* too. And this is not what the sources tell us. In short, the whole understanding of the civilians, "who followed Bartolus as a prince of the Legal Republic",[19] was seriously flawed.

Alciatus' *Paradoxa* heralded the offensive. And yet his triumph was partial. Almost by default, among humanist jurists the *pars destruens* of an author's argument was considerably more successful than his *pars construens*. While most legal humanists agreed on what *iurisdictio* and *imperium* were not,[20] no such consensus was reached on what they actually were. The reconstruction proposed by Alciatus was successful mainly in its repudiation of the old scheme, but not in replacing it with a new one.[21]

Having duly deconstructed the civilians' concept of *iurisdictio*, the problem was how to put its pieces together. *Merum imperium* was particularly problematic, and to some extent representative of the legal humanists' approach, as it triggered endless learned disputes. Humanist jurists proved considerably more apt at digging into the texts than building on them. The

19 Ibid, "quem, uti legalis reipublicae principem alii sequuntur".

20 An obvious exception must be made for Ulrichus Zasius (Huldrych Zäsi, 1461–1536). On our subject, Zasius was a strict adherent to the Bartolian orthodoxy, the main addition being solely a more punctual reference to the textual sources than the average civilian. Nowhere did he detach himself from the Bartolian reading of jurisdiction (at the most reporting some variations proposed by Baldus). In his work both definitions and scope of *iurisdictio*, *mixtum* and *merum imperium* are perfectly adhering to the Bartolian *lectura*, together with the distinction between *publica* and *privata utilitas* and between *iudex nobilis* and *mercenarius*, as well as with *delegata iurisdictio*. Zasius' work on *iurisdictio* and *imperium* may be found in his comment to *De iurisdictione omnium iudicum* (*In sequentes ff. veteris titulos lecturae nempe de iustitia et iure, de legibus, de iurisdictione omnium iud.* [1537] pp 101–126), and in his *Paratitla* to the first part of *Digestum vetus* (*In primam Digestorum Partem Paratitla* (1539) *ad* D.2.1 pp 34–39). The first of the two works is particularly detailed on *iurisdictio delegata* (*ad* D.2.1.4–5 pp 111–126), a subject which on the contrary would receive just scant attention in the *Paratitla*. Zasius' work on our subject received great attention – especially from non-humanist jurists. No civilian had any problem in quoting him approvingly or in relying on his interpretation. Zasius was by far the "legal humanist" most frequently quoted by later Bartolists. On Zasius' alleged humanistic approach see S Rowan, *Ulrich Zasius. A Jurist in the German Renaissance, 1461–1535* (1987) 93–96, 105–108 and esp 206–209.

21 Alciatus followed a threefold division based on *actio*, *persecutio* and *accusatio* to explain *iurisdictio*, *mixtum* and *merum imperium* respectively. Alciatus, *De Verborum Significatione Libri Quat[t]uor* (1530) *ad* D.50.16.178.2 § *Actionis* pp 219–220, *ad* D.50.16.9 § *Persecutione* p 109, *ad* D.50.16.197 § *Indicasse* p 232 respectively. See also (but on a smaller extent) his *Paradoxorum ad Pratum libri sex* (n 14) lib 2 ch 10–11 fols 18r-19r. In particular, the least successful element of Alciatus' threefold division was probably the explanation of *mixtum imperium* as *persecutio*, chiefly because it led to an autonomous category rather than to an intermediate one between *iurisdictio* and *merum imperium*. As will become apparent in the next few pages, it was precisely the closeness between *iurisdictio* and *mixtum imperium* that attracted most humanist jurists (and so possibly made Alciatus' scheme less appealing).

main points on which, by and large, many of them tended to agree were two. First, as the *modica coercitio* of *mixtum imperium* is instrumental to *ius dicere*, *iurisdictio* and *mixtum imperium* are deeply related, and can hardly be separated from each other. Second, *merum imperium* is fully separated from *mixtum imperium* and *iurisdictio*. And this was precisely the problem. *Merum imperium* is described in the sources as *animadversio in facinorosos homines*. Hence, most legal humanists considered it as the *executio* of the judgment in criminal cases. But if the *executio* is entrusted to the magistrate with *merum imperium*, and *merum imperium* is wholly detached from *iurisdictio*, it follows that such a magistrate may not have any *cognitio* of the subject matter. In short, the magistrate empowered to give execution to the judgment could not also hear the dispute, and vice versa.

This conclusion was already implicit in one of the first French legal humanists who followed Alciatus, Ioannis Longovallius. But Longovallius did not bring Alciatus' argument to its ultimate conclusion.[22] The honour belongs to Ioannis Gillotus.[23] Gillotus sharply divided the legal proceeding in three phases: *cognitio*, *sententia*, and *executio*. As with Alciatus and Longovallius, and perhaps even more than either of them, in Gillotus *mixtum imperium* encompassed almost any judicial prerogative.[24] While *cognitio* and *sententia* pertain to *iurisdictio* and *mixtum imperium*, *executio* is the province of *merum imperium*. *Executio* is wholly detached from the legal proceeding because it is only concerned with executing the judgment ("sententiae effectus"). Once the decision is rendered, the controversy is over. This way, the magistrate with *mixtum imperium* enjoys full *iurisdictio* over the dispute while at the same time the distinction between *mixtum* and *merum imperium* is maintained.[25]

In Gillotus, the prerogatives of the ordinary (or delegated) judge were

22 Ioannis Longovallius, *Nova et facilis declaratio ad legem imperium ff. de iurisdictione omnium iudicium* (1528). Longovallius' treatise was divided into four parts. The first two were devoted to a lengthy critique of the relevant Bartolist authors. The third, and rather shorter, to an exposition of the correct approach to the subject. The fourth, and longest, to its applications. *Merum imperium* consists of *mera coerc[it]io* (pt 3 fol 20v), whereas in *mixtum imperium* coercion is instrumental to the exercise of *iurisdictio* (ibid, fol 21r). The difference between the two lies therefore in that the *coercitio* of *mixtum imperium* is but a means to a different end, which is *iuris-dictio* in its broad sense (ibid, fol 22r). It follows that the *modica coercitio* of *mixtum imperium* is instrumental to *iurisdictio*, and moreover that *mixtum imperium* and *iurisdictio* form a unitary category, radically opposed to *merum imperium*.

23 Ioannis Gillotus, *De iurisdictione et imperio libri duo* (1538). As this (in all probability, first) edition is extremely rare, I have relied on the more accessible version in Zilettus, *Tractatus universi iuris* (1584) vol III pt 1 fols 2r-18r.

24 Ibid, pt 2 ch 11–14 fols 13r-15r and ch 15 n 3 fol 13r.

25 Ibid, pt 1 ch 16 n 1 fol 8r. Cf ibid, pt 2 ch 19 fol 15r.

consistent with the sources and so surely correct. But the problem remained in respect to the magistrate with *merum imperium*: he would have to execute someone else's judgment without being able to look at it. Lacking any *cognitio,* he would resemble more an executioner than a magistrate. The problem was particularly thorny in case new evidence emerged after the jurisdictional phase. Gillotus sought to solve the problem by restricting the divide between *merum* and *mixtum imperium*. To this end he resorted to the old (civilian) stratagem of dividing a legal category in a broad and general sense and a narrow and specific one. So, Gillotus argued, when specifically referred to criminal cases *merum imperium* is to be understood in its narrow meaning – *merum* as "only": only *imperium*, without any *iurisdictio*.[26] In this sense, *merum imperium* is just *potestas gladii*. Its scope is restricted exclusively to *animadvertere*, which simply means chastisement ("punitionem ipsam significat").[27] As such, in criminal trials *merum imperium* refers exclusively to the *executio* of the decision.[28] Being solely concerned with *executio*, it does not participate in the act of rendering the judgment. For criminal offences, *merum imperium* commences when *iurisdictio* finishes.[29] By contrast, in civil proceedings *merum imperium* may be considered in its broader meaning of *potestas iuris dicendi*. The so-called *lex imperium* (D.2.1.3), concluded Gillotus, is clear in keeping distinct *mixtum* from *merum imperium* so long as the latter means *gladii potestas animadvertendi in facinorosos homines*. But when *merum imperium* does not have such a meaning, the execution of the decision may well be entrusted to the same magistrate that pronounced it.[30]

Insisting on the residual nature of *merum imperium* and on the strict separation of *executio* from *cognitio*, Gillotus reached a deadlock. He was able to solve it only by resorting to some acrobatic interpretations of *merum imperium*, which however remained hardly satisfactory. At least, in the eyes of his fellow legal humanists. An attempt to solve the impasse was made by another (and more famous) French legal humanist, Petrus Loriotus (Pierre Loriot, d c 1568).[31] Loriotus accepted Gillotus' threefold division of *cognitio*, *sententia* and *executio*,[32] but sought to avoid the resulting impasse.

26 Ibid, pt 1 ch 6 n 2 fol 3r.

27 Ibid, pt 1 ch 7 fol 3v and esp ch 8–9 fol 4r-v.

28 Ibid, pt 1 ch 10 n 2 fols 4v-5r, pt 2 ch 3 nn 1–2 fol 7v and ch 5 fol 8v.

29 Ibid, pt 2 ch 5 nn 9–10 fol 8v.

30 Ibid, pt 2 ch 6 n 6 fol 9r-v.

31 Petrus Loriotus, *De iurisdictione et imperio*, in Id. *De Iuris Apicibus, Tractatus* (1545) cols 29–46. Loriotus was probably the only legal humanist to write on the subject in a schematic (and concise) way.

32 Ibid, axiomata 15–16 cols 33–34.

According to Loriotus, *iurisdictio* had to be kept wholly separate from *merum imperium* (which was merely "delictorum coercio"), in accordance with the sources.[33] On the other hand, it was imperative that the magistrate empowered with *executio* (and so with *merum imperium*) could also have *cognitio*, lest it appeared as a mere executioner. Logically, the only way to achieve both things was to relegate *iurisdictio* to the pronouncement of the *sententia*, and to keep it distinct from *cognitio*.[34] Hence, for Loriotus *iurisdictio* had to become only the act of pronouncing the decision, *ius-dicere* in the narrowest possible sense of the term.[35] This way, *merum imperium* and *iurisdictio* would remain separated, but at the same time the magistrate empowered with *executio* could also have *cognitio* of the matter.[36]

Loriotus' scheme was undoubtedly ingenious, but it did not meet with much success among other legal humanists. And this not because his dilemma of *cognitio*, *sententia* and *executio* might resemble the famous river-crossing puzzle with a wolf, a goat, and a cabbage. Rather, because the cure of Loriotus was almost worse than the Bartolian disease. First, *merum imperium* was once again a general *potestas* encompassing the whole criminal jurisdiction.[37] Secondly, Loriotus' *iurisdictio* was even narrower than the Bartolists' *iurisdictio simplex*. Once again, albeit for different reasons, it occupied a very marginal role – in Loriotus, the mere pronouncement of the decision.[38] Lastly, *mixtum imperium* (vaguely defined as "potestas specialiter concessa, cui iurisdictio inest")[39] was not – as we shall see – the main and nearly all-encompassing category of other humanist jurists, but it was relegated to the execution of civil decisions[40] and to non-contentious jurisdiction.[41]

Although of course incorrect, it would be tempting to use the 1540s

33 Ibid, esp axiomata 10, 14–15, 25 cols 32–34 and 36–37.

34 Ibid, axioma 20 col 35: "Adde sanam non esse Gilloti interpretationem, causae cognitionem pro iurisdictione accipientis: cum res separatae sint, et assessor cognitionem habeat, non iurisdictionem: sit qu[a]e cognitio usque ad sententiam dumtaxat, iurisdictio proprie et in sententia est, et in executione." Cf ibid, axioma 25 col 37: "merum purum significat: ut Imperium merum sit pura potestas et separata, non a cognitione (ut Gillotus arbitrabatur) sed a iurisdictione."

35 Ibid, axiomata 1–3 cols 29–30.

36 Ibid, axioma 26 col 37: "non obstat quod in executionibus non admittatur causae cognitio, id enim ex eo fit, quod ante exequutionem [*sic*] iam plena causae cognitio adhibita fuit, sine qua nulla esset exequutio [*sic*]".

37 Ibid, axioma 38 col 41. Cf also axiomata 26 and 38 cols 37 and 41 respectively.

38 Ibid, axioma 38 col 41 ("nihil aliud . . . quam iuris dicendi officium, iure magistratus concessum"). Cf also axiomata 26 and 36–37 cols 37 and 40–41 respectively.

39 Ibid, axioma 31 col 39. Loriotus' difficulty in providing a neat definition of *mixtum imperium* might derive from the complex efforts to disentangle *cognitio* from *sententia*.

40 Ibid, axioma 38 col 41.

41 More specifically: *bonorum possessio, missio in possessionem, restitutio, emancipatio, adoptio, interdicta prohibitoria* and *fideicommissa*: *ibid*, axioma 33 cols 39–40.

to draw a line between earlier and later legal humanist works – both on our subject and, perhaps, beyond it. None of the earlier efforts of humanist jurists to provide a coherent and systematic picture of *iurisdictio* and *imperium* was particularly successful. But they remained the main ones. It was not the difficulty of the task that discouraged later authors. Rather, it was a progressive shift in their interest. From the 1540s their works became increasingly academic and abstract, and the focus progressively more detailed and specific. Each topic underwent a detailed scrutiny according to its adherence to classical sources, legal and non-legal alike. Whether any single sub-topic would fit into the larger picture, it was no longer the point. The more the attention focused on the single classical sources, the less it mattered whether they could underpin abstract and general principles. The door to unbridled historical and philological speculations, already unlocked, now burst open.

With specific reference to our subject, it is with the 1540s that the "deconstruction" of medieval *iurisdictio* lost its character of instrumentality, a means to the end of providing accurate categories more faithful to the sources. The emphasis was progressively more on the analysis of the sources and less on general legal categories. By and large, source analysis became an end to itself. Similarly, the early contrasts among scholars such as Longovallius, Gillotus and Loriotus (each devoting a considerable part of his work to questioning that of the others, Alciatus included) now became fully-fledged academic squabbles on the (allegedly, scarce) learning of the rivals.

In the late 1540s Duarenus, Goveanus and Corasius proposed a new interpretation of *iurisdictio* and *imperium*. Franciscus Duarenus (François Douaren, 1509–1559), accepted the division between *merum imperium* on the one side and *iurisdictio* and *mixtum imperium* on the other, but he offered a new explanation for this, rooted in the jurisdictional prerogatives of different magistrates.[42] The *praetor* only had jurisdiction in private disputes, not in criminal offences. Those were entrusted to the *quaestores*.[43] Shortly thereafter Antonius Goveanus (António de Gouveia, c1505–c1566) published his succinct comment to D.2.1.3.[44] Goveanus agreed with

42 Franciscus Duarenus, *Disputationes anniversariae Liber primus* (1547) ch 53 pp 128–132.

43 Ibid, pp 129–130: "Praetorem Romae creatum fuisse, ut ius diceret in urbe de causis negotiisque privatis, non ut animadverteret in facinorosos homines [. . .] Populus enim, cuius summa potestas erat, quoties animadversio necessaria videbatur, Quaesitores sive Quaestores constituebat, qui adversus facinorosos inquirerent, idque extra ordinem, cum nullo magistratu fungerentur."

44 Antonius Goveanus, *ad Legem III D. Imperium, De iurisdictione omnium iudicium* (1545). I have used the later edition of Goveanus' work edited by van Vaassen, *Antonii Goveani opera iuridica, philologica, philosophica. Ex bibliotheca viri nobilis Gerardi Meerman edidit, vitamque*

Duarenus that *merum imperium* related exclusively to capital punishment and that it belonged to "*caeteri praetores*" – mainly the *quaestores* – and not to the *praetor urbanus*.[45] But in turn Gouveia offered a new interpretation of the division between *iurisdictio, mixtum* and *merum imperium* based on the prerogatives of each magistrate. While it is clear that the *praetor urbanus* lacked *merum imperium* and had both *mixtum imperium* and *iurisdictio*, the *praeses provinciae* enjoyed all three.[46] The treatise of Ioannis Corasius (Jean de Coras, 1512–1572) followed.[47] Although he did not refer explicitly to either Duarenus or Goveanus, Corasius agreed with them on the main points,[48] especially on the division of prerogatives between *praetor* and *quaestor*.[49] The main difference with his two colleagues lay in Corasius' interpretation of *mixtum imperium*. To some extent, Corasius again proposed Gillotus' all-encompassing notion of *mixtum imperium*. Moving from the separation of prerogatives between *praetor* and *quaestor*, Corasius reasoned, Gillotus' shortcomings could be easily avoided. In any matter in which the *praetor* has *cognitio*, he also enjoys *executio*. Although in theory functional to the exercise of *iurisdictio*,[50] in Corasius' analysis *mixtum imperium* stretched beyond the scope of jurisdictional prerogatives. This allowed him to include in *mixtum imperium* also prerogatives more authoritative than strictly jurisdictional in their nature, such as *in integrum restituere*.[51]

In between the publication of these treatises, Eguinarius Baro (François Eguinaire, Baron du Kerlouan, 1495–1550) sent to the press two works on the same subject, triggering one of the harshest disputes among legal humanists. Baro's theory resembled those of other humanist jurists only in the *summa*

auctoris praemisit Iacobus van Vaassen, iurisconsvltvs (1766) pp 3–6. Goveanus' treatise was published in 1545, and so two years before Duarenus'. However, the treatise of Duarenus must have circulated earlier, for Goveanus dedicated his treatise to Duarenus as a comment on his friend's work.

45 Ibid, p 5.

46 Ibid, pp 5–6.

47 Ioannis Corasius, *Miscellaneorum iuris civilis libri sex* (1549) lib 3 *de iurisdictione et imperio* pp 272–280.

48 Specifically: *iurisdictio* and *mixtum imperium* were bound together, and *iurisdictio* was completely separated from *merum imperium*, ibid, nn 1–2 pp 272–273 and n 4 p 275, respectively. On *merum imperium*, see further ibid, n 10 p 277.

49 Ibid, n 5 p 276.

50 Corasius defined *mixtum imperium* as "auctorita[s] et potesta[s] quandam decernendi, dandi, dicendi, addicendi et coercendi, in pecuniariis causis, citra tamen litis controversiae decisionem. Tunc enim esset iurisdictio, quae tamen, ut effectum habeat faciliusque explicari possit, mixto imperio ius dicendi utitur." Ibid, n 15 p 279. Cf also ibid, n 6 p 276.

51 Ibid, nn 17–18 pp 279–280.

divisio between *iurisdictio* and *mixtum imperium* on the one hand, and *imperium merum* on the other.[52] Beyond that, it was *sui generis*. He used the lack of *iurisdictio* so characteristic of *merum imperium* to extend its scope – at the expense of *mixtum imperium*. Thus, for Baro *merum imperium* does not consist solely of *animadversio*. Rather, what lacks *iurisdictio* is to be considered as *merum imperium*, and not as *mixtum*.[53] Further, and moreover, he argued for a twofold notion of *iurisdictio*. In its narrower sense, *iurisdictio* describes the prerogatives of the *iudices pedanei* (whereas the powers of the *praetor* are grouped together as *mixtum imperium*).[54] In its broader meaning, much to the contrary, *iurisdictio* represents jurisdictional power in its entirety. It follows that, in this second and general sense, *iurisdictio* is the genus encompassing also *mixtum imperium*.[55] In this broader meaning, *iurisdictio* resembles more a general power than the limited task of settling a dispute. Looking back at the threefold division between *cognitio*, *sententia* and *executio*, Baro argued that *iurisdictio* encompasses both *sententia* and *executio*, but not really *cognitio* – that is up to the delegated judge.[56] At this juncture, it is hard to see any substantive difference with the old Bartolian "tree of jurisdiction". Indeed, in his apostasy, Baro arrived to speak the unspeakable: as a matter of fact, Bartolus was quite right, though he should have left out *merum imperium*.[57]

52 Eguinarius Baro, *Ad τα πρώτα Digestorum* (1548) tit 1 l 3 fols 67v-68v, Id, *Variarum quaestionum publice tractatarum, ad digesta iuris civilis l. de iurisdictione* (1548) pp 66–67 and 69–70.

53 Id, *Ad τα πρώτα Digestorum* (n 52), tit 1 l 4 fol 68v. An example is the *cautio praetoria*, which according to Baro does not belong to *mixtum* but to *merum imperium* (ibid).

54 Id, *Ad digesta iuris civilis l. de iurisdictione*, p 138.

55 Ibid, p 106, "Iurisdictio enim dicitur generaliter, et cum decernit, et cum iudicat qui iurisdictionem habet: Mistum imperium, quod magis est imperij quam iurisdictionis, species est eius iurisdictionis"; ibid, p 83: "Consequens est igitur ut iurisdictio, quae misto imperio inest, de re privata iurisdictio sit, quae decretis omnibus inesse recte dicitur"; ibid, p 156: "Quisquis habet iurisdictionem, idem hoc quoque imperium habet, de habente generalem iurisdictionem accepit: qualis est Praetor urbanus Romae, et Praeses in provincia". Cf ibid, p 136.

56 Ibid, pp 154–155: "Non enim ius dicit proprie qui decernit iudicium, sed imperat, ut per alium iudicantem, ipse ius dixisse videatur. Nam nec ipsa cognitio causae, iurisdictio est: sed ipsa pronuntiatio, et sententia magistratus, aut eius cui mandavit iurisdictionem: et hoc in civili negotio, quod propria legis actione ordinatur d. l. notionem de verb. sign. [D.50.16.99pr] Deinde ait [Cicero, ad Heren. I.1] de imperio misto. Et hoc quidem imperium ideo mistum dicitur, quia iurisdictioni admistum, et coniunctum est, pertinentque omnino ad officium ius dicentis: adeo ut quisquis habet iurisdictionem, hoc quoque imperium habeat; et qui hoc imperio utitur, ius dicentis officio fungi existimetur." See also ibid, p 161: "Quod vero executionem sententiae, negat extremum esse iurisdictionis, supra a nobis refellitur: ubi ius dici non solum in constituendis iudicijs, et dandis iudicibus, sed in cognoscendo quoque, diiudicando causas privatas, et exequendo dictas iam sententias, ostendimus."

57 Ibid, p 122: "Bartolus iurisdictionem misto imperio inesse, ut genus inest speciei, non male scripsit: sed male tam generaliter accepit iurisdictionem, ut merum quoque imperium complectatur

The answer of Duarenus and Goveanus came at once.[58] What is interesting for our purposes is that both replies went even deeper in their textual analysis than the original treatises, studiously avoiding any general overview. For it was precisely when an author sought to draw general conclusions that his argument detached from the Roman texts – and so became most vulnerable.

Although he wrote his treatise while the controversy between Baro, Duarenus and Goveanus was at its apex, Ludovicus Charondas (Louis Le Caron, 1534–1613) was careful not to take sides – at least openly.[59] Probably, because he did not entirely agree with either of them. As usual, he argued that *iurisdictio* and *merum imperium* should be kept separate,[60] and that

in misti imperij definitione." Cf ibid, p 156. On the contrary, when considered in its narrow sense, for Baro *iurisdictio* was precisely Bartolus' *iurisdictio simplex*: "huius imperij ea particula, quae in cognoscendis, iudicandisque privatis causis, et civilibus versatur, iurisdictio angustissima verbi huius significatione, appellata est" (ibid, p 68, cf also pp 71–72).

58 The structure of the two works against Baro provides an interesting example of different approaches to the refined art of invective. Published in 1549, Duarenus' (short) reply commences with his reconstruction of *iurisdictio* and *imperium*. Each attack on Baro is aimed at strengthening his own theory, so that attack and defence are developed together. Once both are fully laid down, Duarenus focuses on the adversary in a crescendo of abuses (first on his Bartolian sympathies, then quite in general, just in case), *De iurisdictione et imperio apologia Fr. Douareni iur. adv. Eg. Baronem iurisconsultum*, in Id, *Opera Omnia* (1554) n 18 fols 73v-74r and nn 19–20 fol 74r-v respectively). By contrast, in his (remarkably long) *De Iurisdictione libri II, adversus Eguinarium Baronem* (1551) Goveanus neatly separates attack from defence. The first (and shorter) of his two books reports the most salient passages of Baro's work, in order to demolish every single line of it (ibid, pp 1–12). The second (and considerably longer) book (pp 13–46) on the other hand focuses exclusively on Goveanus' own theory (see esp *ad* l 3 [D.2.1.3] pp 23–24). Regrettably, Baro was indelicate enough to die during all this fun, so it fell to his disciple Edward Henryson to answer on his behalf, reaffirming Baro's views and attacking those of his opponents (*Eduardi Henrysonis, Pro Eg. Barone Adversus A. Goveanum de iurisdictione libri II* (1555)).

59 Ludovicus Charondas, *Charondae Iurisconsulti Parisiensis . . . de iurisdictione et imperio libellus* (1553).

60 Charondas accepted wholeheartedly the main tenets of Alciatus' reading and brought them to their ultimate conclusions. The starting point was the *summa divisio* between *merum imperium* and *iurisdictio* (Charondas, *de iurisdictione et imperio libellus* (n 59), nn 3–4 fols 47v-48v). As *merum imperium* is exclusively concerned with *animadversio*, it is excluded from *iurisdictio*. In contrast, and simply enough, *iurisdictio* is *"licentia iuris dicundi"* (ibid, n 5 fol 48v). *Iurisdictio* therefore stretches from the hearing of the controversy to its adjudication (ibid, n 8 fol 51r). It follows that there is no need to neatly separate *cognitio* from *sententia*, for *iurisdictio* and *mixtum imperium* form a unitary and indivisible category (ibid, nn 3–4 fols 47v-48v). Even more, *mixtum imperium* is instrumental to *ius dicere* (ibid, n 20 fol 59r). The old adage that "iurisdictio sine modica coercitione nulla est" does not imply the subordination of *iurisdictio* to *imperium*. Rather, it strengthens the indivisibility of *iurisdictio* and *mixtum imperium* (ibid, n 20 fols 58r-59r). Also, the same principle further separates them from *merum imperium*: the kind of coercion which *merum imperium* requires is structurally different from the "modica coercitio" of *mixtum imperium*. *Missio in possessionem* and *gladii potestas* perfectly represent such a difference (ibid, n 22 fol 60r).

iurisdictio formed a unitary category with *mixtum imperium*.[61] However, unlike Baro, he did not qualify *mixtum imperium* as a species of the genus *iurisdictio*,[62] and unlike Duarenus and Goveanus he ascribed *merum imperium* to the *dictator* – not to the *praeses*.[63] The last point was particularly important: no magistrate holding *merum imperium* (that is, coercive powers) may also have *iurisdictio*.[64] Opting for the *dictator* instead of the *praeses* had its advantages. Ironically, Baro affirmed openly what both Duarenus and Goveanus had prudently left unsaid. So long as we focus on the *praetor urbanus*, then the distinction between *iurisdictio* and *merum imperium* holds. But if we look at the *praeses provinciae*, it is clear that he enjoys both.[65] Systematic expositions and strict adherence to the Roman sources have always proved to be poor bedfellows. Baro was attacked for his Bartolian deviations as much as for his efforts to systematise the unsystematisable.[66] Charondas simply avoided any generalisation, and so escaped much criticism.

Systematisation was dangerous and open to fierce attacks, and increasingly fewer humanist jurists ventured into general categories. But when they did, they moved carefully around the debris of previous intellectual wars. Although somewhat later than the group of legal humanists so far considered, Hugo Donellus (Hugues Doneau, 1527–1591) provides an excellent example of this, and of how attempts at laying out a general structure to our subject were not completely abandoned by authors *lato sensu* considered as legal humanists.[67] Unlike Baro, Donellus' work did not receive harsh critiques. And not just as his comment on *imperium* and *iurisdictio* was

61 Ibid, n 15 fols 55v-56r.

62 Rather – although never openly – Charondas argued for the very opposite. He was adamant that *mixtum imperium* was not just the *modica coercitio* instrumental to the exercise of *iurisdictio*, but the sum of the standard jurisdictional prerogatives: ibid, n 17 fol 56v and esp nn 19–20 fols 57v-59r. While formally distancing himself from Baro (e.g. ibid, n 4 fol 48r-v), substantially Charondas reached similar conclusions. For Charondas, however, the general category was *mixtum imperium* and not, as in Baro, *iurisdictio*. But Charondas was prudent enough not to state as much openly.

63 Ibid, n 14 fol 54r-v.

64 Ibid, n 15 fol 55r-v.

65 Baro, *Ad digesta iuris civilis l. de iurisdictione* (n 52), p 41.

66 Even with regard to the prerogatives of the *praetor*, which in theory encompassed all *mixtum imperium*, Baro had to make an exception for *fideicommissa*, which belonged exclusively to the *consul*. Baro, *Ad τα πρώτα Digestorum* (n 52), tit 1 *ad* l 11 [D 2.1.11] fol 69v.

67 Donellus is a fine example of the plurality of distinct scholarships grouped together under the *mos gallicus* umbrella. Donellus' work was probably the first great systematic re-arrangement of all civil law. In order to include him among legal humanists, it was necessary to add systematisation to the main aims of humanist jurists. As it happens, few things are more remote from legal humanism than systematisation. See also Jakab elsewhere in this volume.

published posthumously.[68] But because Donellus looked exclusively at their application in Roman history – especially the classical period. Nonetheless, it is easy to detect interesting parallels between Donellus and some of the humanist jurists so far mentioned. After the usual definition of *merum imperium*[69] and the statements on the indivisibility of *iurisdictio* and *mixtum imperium*,[70] Donellus argued that, by and large, any form of *imperium* is *executio*.[71] If *iurisdictio* could not be separated from *mixtum imperium*, and *mixtum imperium* is ultimately *executio*, it follows that the magistrate with *iurisdictio* (the *praetor* first of all) has both *cognitio* and *executio*.[72] Further, while *iurisdictio* and *mixtum imperium* may not be separated, the ancillary function of the latter makes *iurisdictio* the principal category among the two.[73] The dichotomy, observed Donellus, is between *iurisdictio* and *merum imperium*. But their structural difference does not necessarily entail their incompatibility: the same magistrate may well have both,[74] as – he argued – is the case of the *praetor*.[75]

Later humanist jurists did not add much to the debate, which progressively became a highly specialised historical discourse on magistrates in ancient Rome. Before this happened, however, the main features of the legal humanistic interpretation of jurisdiction were already neatly defined, and they might be summed up in broad terms. *Merum imperium* was utterly marginalised, largely to the benefit of *mixtum imperium*. The same *mixtum imperium* was increasingly considered as inseparable from *iurisdictio*, for without some degree of coercion *ius dicere non potest*. The distinction

68 Donellus' work on *iurisdictio* and *imperium* was published only in 1596 as part of the seventeenth book of his *Commentarii* by Scipio Gentili. I have, however, opted for Hilliger's edition (*Donellus Enucleatus*, originally published in two volumes, the first in 1611 and the second in 1613, both at Jena) in the neat and carefully edited edition printed at Lucca in between 1762 and 1777.

69 Hugo Donellus, *Opera Omnia* vol IV (1764) lib 17 ch 8 nn 20–1 cols 1142–1149.

70 Ibid, lib 17 ch 8 nn 14–15 cols 1130–1134.

71 Ibid, lib 17 ch 8 n 21 col 1146: "imperium in universum dici exsequendi potestatem, efficiendique, ut ratum sit, quod magistratus statuerit". Cf also ibid, n 15 col 1133.

72 Ibid, lib 17 ch 6 nn 5–7 cols 1087–1090, cf ibid, ch 7 n 7 cols 1103–1105, and nn 15–16 cols 1113–1116.

73 "Sed quia iurisdictio natura prior est, quam imperio adiuncto confirmari oportet, idem, magis imperium iurisdictioni accedere, eique cohaere, et misceri videtur," ibid, lib 17 ch 8 n 14 col 1131. Cf more broadly the whole of cols 1130–1134.

74 "Isto modo et merum imperium dictum, quod alterius rei misturam non habet, solum et per se imperium. Sed nondum id dicimus; quod res est. Nam si id ista infinite et generaliter dicatur, certe falsum sit potestatem animadvertendi in facinorosos esse imperium merum, seu non mistum. Quaecumque enim haec potestas est, coniuncta est cum cognitione," ibid, lib 17 ch 8 n 21 cols 1146–1148.

75 Ibid, ch 8 n 23 col 1151.

between private and public utility was largely rejected,[76] as well as that between *iudex nobilis* and *mercenarius*.[77] As such, the hierarchy among the three components of the Accursian notion of *iurisdictio* was turned entirely upside-down. *Mixtum imperium*, inextricably linked to *iurisdictio*, was now the most important of the three categories, encompassing the vast majority of jurisdictional functions. Beyond this, each legal humanist had different ideas on both definition and scope of the three categories, especially *iurisdictio* and *mixtum imperium*. "Pure" *iurisdictio* was especially tantalising, as well as the issue of which specific prerogatives should fall into *mixtum imperium*, and why.

D. νόστος: THE JOURNEY OF *IURISDICTIO*

In the Euripidean tragedy, the gods had the good sense of intervening one at time. Legal humanism suffered from an overpopulated Olympus. All of a sudden, lawyers were faced with a number of different and mutually contradicting theories, all of which could however claim stronger links with the Roman sources than the traditional *ius commune* one. Whatever the defects of the tradition, the avalanche of new theories had a deeply destabilising effect. In a few decades, the entire subject of *iurisdictio* became extremely confusing. In the words of Ioannis Bologneti (Giovanni Bolognetti, 1506–1575), "such a variety of opinions created a huge confusion in the meaning of the law".[78] Similar comments became so frequent that it would be pointless (and probably impossible) to list them in full.[79]

76 Even those jurists, such as Donellus, who retained it did so within an entirely different framework from the traditional *ius commune* one: ibid, ch 7 n 5 col 1101.

77 While rejecting it in principle, this division often resurfaced among legal humanists, chiefly because of the temptation to identify the *iudex nobilis* with the *praetor*, and the *mercenarius* with the *iudex pedaneus*. But this simply added fuel to the scholarly debate, for it triggered endless disputes on whether the *iurisdictio* of the *praetor* had to be narrowed down to the simple *datio iudicis*, or whether the *praetor* could actually hear the case and pronounce the judgment by himself and, in such a case, whether the *iudex pedaneus* could be said to *ius dicere* at all and, if not, how to define his jurisdictional role.

78 "Ista varietate opinionum causatur confusio magna in intellectu legis", Ioannis Bologneti, *In primam Digesti veteris repetitiones* (1558) *ad* D.2.1.3 n 1 fol 187r.

79 One might even move off a few decades at a time and list the similar complaints he finds published then. So, for instance, about forty years after Bologneti, the extensive commentary of Delrío and de Brosses read, *sub* D.2.1: "Mansit res per se satis aperta incertior quam antea, saepe nimirum litigando veritas amittitur" (Martín Antonio Delrío and Pierre de Brosses, *Ex Miscellaneorum scriptoribus digestorum sive pandectarum iuris civilis interpretatio, index authorum atque Scriptorum miscellaneorum; Index Titulorum Pandectarum*, 2nd edn (1590) *ad* D.2.1 col 74). Again, forty years later, Lindenspür remarked "tam incertae autem hodie sunt de iurisdictione opiniones, variaeque consuetudines ac observantiae, totaeque eius species, quas aut

The later *ius commune* production is typically considered as exceedingly practical-minded and hardly interested in general and theoretical discussions. This is true to some extent. For even the most pragmatically-oriented (or plainly casuistic) lawyers clearly relied on the Bartolian scheme. To give an extreme example, in the 252 pages of his *consilia* devoted to *iurisdictio*, the famed jurist De Luca never once discussed the Bartolian categories. But he always presupposed them.[80]

Commentators had always tested the Bartolian jurisdictional scheme, from Baldus to the very eve of the legal humanist attack.[81] But those discussions always occurred *within* the Accursian gloss, never against it. Now, for the first time, it became vital to defend the very grounds on which the entire jurisdictional framework was built. From the second half of the sixteenth century, when a work touched upon the subject of jurisdiction only in passim it usually adhered to the Bartolian scheme in a few lines and quickly moved on.[82] Other times it simply avoided the whole issue.[83] But when a treatise

usus, aut necessitas, aut quantoque adulatio peperit" (Georg Ludvich Lindenspür, *Dissertatio de successionibus ac mutationibus imperiorum ac familiarum* (1638) p 97 n 2).

80 Giovanni Battista de Luca, *Theatrum Veritatis et Justitiae* lib 3 pt 1, *De jurisdictione et foro competenti* (1691). De Luca is hardly an isolated example: see, e.g., Federico Scotti, *Consilia seu Responsa* (1572) vol I lib 3 resp 13 nn 1 and 3 p 251, vol II lib 6 resp 22 and 38 fols 24v-25r and 39r-40r respectively, and lib 8 resp 5 fols 122r-123v, Marco Antonio Natta, *Consilia* (1588) (1st edn, 1558) vol I cons 82 nn 6–8 fol 64r, vol II cons 405 nn 1–3 fol 107r-v, Giovanni Battista Saminiati, *Controversiae Forenses* (1686) contr 24 n 20 p 306, contr 96 nn 24–26 p 801, contr 99 n 33 p 817.

81 E.g. Filippo Decio, *Commentaria in Digesti Vete[ri] et Cod[ici]* (1567) (1st edn, 1523) *ad* D.2.1.1 § *Ius dicentis* n 10 fol 25r. Possibly one of the last authors who questioned the Bartolian scheme without mentioning the humanist jurists was Gian Girolamo Albani, *Lucubrationes ad Bartolum* (1571) *ad De iurisdictione omn. Iud.*, fols 73r-75v, and *ad summarium in l. imperium*, fol 76r.

82 E.g. Johann Oldendorp, *Loci Communes Iuris Civilis* (1545) § *Iurisdictio* p 173, Marco Bassanello, *Colloquia, seu dialogi* (1553) dialogue 23 pp 55–56, and dialogue 97 p 211, Sebastian Brant, *Titulorum omnium iuris tam civilis quam canonici Expositiones* (1553) *ad* D.2.1.2 *de iurisdictione omnium iudicium* p 16, Bernhard Wurmser, *Practicarum Observationum* (1570) lib 1 *de Iudicibus* n 15 pp 6–7, Hartmannus Hartmann, *Practicarum Observationum* (1570) lib 2 *De Iudiciis* esp n 6 p 177, and n 16 p 183, Dethard Horst, *Synopsis Thesium sive Axiomatum Iuris, ad primam partem Pandectarum seu Digestorum Iuris Civilis Romani* (1583) *ad* D.2.1 nn 1–4, Alessandro Turamini, *Commentarii* (1592) lib 3 ch 2 n 38 p 138, Tiberio Deciani, *Responsorum* (1602) vol IV resp n 40 nn 2–3 p 168v, nn 21–3 fol 170v, and n 47 fol 172v, Giulio Pace, *Synopsis Juris Civilis* (1607) lib 2 n 1 p 15, Id, *Methodica ad Iustinianeum Codicem* (1606) lib 3 tit 13 ch 1 nn 4–6 p 190, ch 2 nn 2–4 p 192, ch 3 nn 23–24 pp 192–193, ch 4 nn 31–32 p 194, Marco Antonio Mureti, *In titulos ad Materiam Iurisdictionis Pertinentes Commentarii* (1615) esp pp 139–140, Ettore Capecelatro, *Selectiorum Consultationum iuris* (1643) lib 1 cons 41 n 9 p 314.

83 This attitude had apparently little to do with the importance of the work or of the author, for it is attested among some of the most celebrated writings as much as in the lesser known ones: e.g. Prospero Farinacci, *Praxis et Theoricae Criminalis* (1634) vol I pt 1 q 7 pp 58–75 (on the subject of the *iudex incompetens*), Marco Antonio Peregrino, *De iurisdictione Ordinaria et Delegata*, in

was devoted (in full or in part) to the subject of jurisdiction, it typically looked at the Bartolian scheme with a significant (humanistic) attention to the sources, in order to defend it.[84]

A particularly vehement apology of the Bartolian categories was that of Hieronymus Muscornius. Muscornius allowed only for minor corrections to the traditional interpretation of the *lex imperium*,[85] which he shielded with many "counter-quotations" from classical sources,[86] as well as with some new interpretations of Latin terms. In particular, he stressed that the verb "animadvertere" is a neuter term, since it just means "vertere animum, atque mentem".[87] As such, it may not be used in a narrow sense. The *animadversio in facinorosos homines* of Ulpian in D.2.1.3, therefore, does not mean that *merum imperium* is confined to the execution of criminal punishments. Rather, and precisely after Bartolus, for Muscornius *merum imperium* is *suprema potestas*.[88]

Muscornius' somewhat drastic attempt was a relatively isolated case.

Id, *Tractatus varii* (1611), Cristopher Cuppener, *Commentarii* (1605) pp 118–119, Erasmo of Chokier, *Tractatus Iurisdictionis Ordinariae in Exemptos* (1624) p 355 n 4.

84 Among the enormous production of the late sixteenth and early seventeenth centuries, see, e.g., Jean Brèche, *Ad titulum pandectarum De Verborum & rerum significatione Commentarii* (1556) *ad* D.50.16.215 § *Potestatis verbo* pp 431–433 esp n 4 p 432–433, Johannes Althusius, *Iuris Romani Libri duo* (1586) lib 1 ch 8 p 18, Pierre Du Faur de Saint-Jorry (Petrus Faber), *ad Tit. de Diversis Regulis Iuris antiqui* [. . .] *Commentarius* (1590) *ad* D.50.17.70 nn 7–10, 14–15, 18–20, 23–27 and 36 pp 179–184, Ludovico Carboni, *Tractatus de legibus* (1599) lib 11 disp 10 pp 497–501, Tobias Paurmeister, *De iurisdictione imperii Romani libri II* (1608) ch 7–9 nn 1 pp 49–56, and esp ch 9 pp 56–67, Orazio Marta, *Tractatus de iurisdictione inter iudicem ecclesiasticum et laicum exercenda* (1609) vol I pt 1 ch 8 nn 1–3 and 5–7 p 19, Marco Antonio Mureti, *In titulos ad Materiam Iurisdictionis Pertinentes* (1615) pp 139–140, Helfrich Ulrich Hunnius, *De iurisdictione tractatus* (1616) esp pt 1 ch 1 nn 1–2, pp 22–25, and ch 2 q 3 pp 70–71, Camillo Borrello, *De Magistratuum edictis* (1621) lib 1 ch 17 nn 24–32 pp 235–237, Hermann Vulteius, *Commentarius at tit. Codicis, qui sunt de iurisdictione et foro competenti* (1630) *ad* C.3.13 nn 4–12 p 10, and n 79 p 48, Jacob Brinkmann, *Dissertatio ad vexatissimam l. de iurisdictione* (1631) thesis 1 nn 2–4, 6–7, 9–10, 16, 25–32. Special mention should also be made of the number of *lexica iuridica* printed between the late sixteenth and the early seventeenth century – often the most representative of the market (and so of the interest of lawyers at large). They typically build on the Bartolian systematisation with significant openings to the new humanist interpretation. See also Maclean elsewhere in this volume.

85 Hieronymus Muscornius, *Tractatus de Iurisdictione atque imperio* (1596). On the Bartolian scheme in general see esp n 12 p 5, and n 18 pp 8–9, on the distinction between private and public utility see nn 63–66, pp 56–68, and nn 78–79, pp 75–76, on the subject of *mixtum imperium* see in particular n 31 pp 21–22, n 145 p 144, nn 149–156 pp 150–156, and nn 158–163 pp 156–161.

86 Ibid, esp nn 4–16 pp 2–7, n 33 p 23, n 36 p 25, n 38 p 28.

87 Ibid, n 44 p 35.

88 Ibid, esp n 31 pp 21–22 and n 38 p 28. Cf also n 36 p 25. The distinction between *cognitio* and *animadversio* is similarly dismissed through the example of the *quaestores*, who enjoyed both: ibid, n 14 p 7.

Especially on *merum imperium*, most jurists tended to agree with legal humanists. "*Merum*" meant "*purum*", not "*summum*", and as such it had to be relegated to criminal disputes.[89] Complete repudiation of legal humanist critiques did not prove successful: some compromises had to be made. Significantly enough, narrowing *merum imperium* to criminal proceedings was the main concession to legal humanism that a jurist as important and representative of the later *ius commune* as Iacobus Menochius (Jacopo Menochio, 1532–1607) could allow. Menochius stated as much at the very beginning of his treatise on *iurisdictio*.[90] Apart from that, however, he fully adhered to the traditional Bartolian scheme,[91] stressing in particular the concept of *imperium* as a unitary category.[92] No matter how Haloander's edition of the Digest would read, for Menochius *iurisdictio* clearly came from *iuris-ditio*, as attested in a number of classical sources, ranging from Cicero to Virgil.[93] Menochius' use of classical texts is revealing of an extremely widespread attitude. On a superficial level, it betrays the effort of many lawyers to pay back legal humanists' attacks in kind.[94] More deeply, however, it attests to the growing interest for a meticulous examination of the sources also among Bartolists (who otherwise would have not felt the need to answer to the humanist jurists' critiques in the first place). If a word or a concept was attested in classical sources, legal and extra-legal alike, it gave weight to the legal argument. Even a Bartolist as orthodox as Muscornius insisted on the importance of interpreting Latin terms according to the sources, not to their modern usage.[95] Thus, behind the curtain of endless

89 E.g. Hunnius, *De iurisdictione tractatus* (n 84) pt 1 ch 1 quaest 4 n 1 pp 39–40, Horst, *Synopsis* (n 82) *ad* D.2.1 n 5 p 48, Althusius, *Iuris Romani Libri duo* (n 84) lib 1 ch 8 p 18, Carboni, *Tractatus de legibus* (n 84) lib 11 disp 10 pp 497–498, Marta, *Tractatus de iurisdictione* (n 84) vol I pt 1 ch 36 nn 10–12 and 25–26 pp 110–111.

90 Iacobus Menochius, *De imperio et iurisdictione commentarii posthumi, duobus libris expositi* (1622) lib 1 ch 1 p 2. See further ch 5 n 4, and esp n 17 pp 53–54. Cf also ch 5 nn 18–20 pp 54–56 (on the scope of *merum imperium* in the Roman sources), ch 15 [q 8] nn 2–3 pp 134–135 (on fines), and ch 16 [q 9] nn 2–6 pp 145–147 (on confiscation).

91 Ibid, lib 1 ch 1 nn 1–3 pp 2–4. In particular, Menochius approved of the twofold Bartolian notion of *iurisdictio* as genus and species (ibid, ch 1 nn 4–9 pp 4–8 and ch 2 nn 1–2 pp 10–11, nn 9–10 pp 15–16, n 23 pp 23–24, ch 3 n 1 p 27, n 5 pp 29–30).

92 Ibid, lib 1 ch 7 n 2 p 85.

93 Ibid, lib 1 ch 2 nn 25–26 pp 24–26.

94 One of the most draconian examples in this direction was the *Lexicon iuridicum* of Sichardus, who went as far as accusing Ulpian of having "usurped" the concept of *iurisdictio* ("Iurisdictionis verbum ab Ulpiano in d. l. imperium [D.2.1.3] stricte et anguste usurpari"), narrowing down a much broader category (i.e that of *iuris-ditio*). Simon Sichardus, *Lexicon iuridicum* (1600) § *imperium* p 437.

95 "Verba quando latine concipiunctur esse semper interpretanda secundum latinos, et non vulgares homines." Muscornius, *Tractatus de Iurisdictione atque imperio* (n 85) n 22 p 11. Muscornius'

debates on the exact meaning of legal terms in the classical sources, there lay practical consequences – not philological appetites.[96] By the eve of the seventeenth century no systematic treatise dealing with jurisdictional issues could avoid long digressions into historical and philological discussions. Unfaithfulness to Roman sources became progressively a clear sign of being plainly wrong. As a consequence, many jurists paid increasing attention to the exact terminology used in Roman sources. Yet, attention to the sources always remained a means, not an end. The end was more practical: grounding current legal issues into *ius commune* categories – and solving them accordingly.[97]

Apart from Menochius and Muscornius, the most important (and quoted) among the treatises seeking to conciliate Bartolism with the main critiques of legal humanism opted for very elaborated schemes. While apparently detaching themselves from the Bartolian orthodoxy, such treatises ultimately aimed at protecting the traditional jurisdictional framework. Among them, mention should be made of at least three: those of Bologneti, Obrecht and Bocerus.

Bologneti divided *iurisdictio* and *imperium* in three different categories (legislative, jurisdictional and equitable),[98] according to their object.[99] Then,

insistence on the correct interpretation of the sources derived from his view of legal humanism as a degeneration of philology applied to the law. In his view, the fallacy of humanist jurists lay in their exasperate attention to the abstract meaning of a word, extrapolated from its broader – and *legal* – context.

96 For example, one such debate focused on the exact meaning of the key-word "animadvertere". In order to prove that *merum imperium* consisted of both *cognitio* and *executio*, Bologneti divided the phrase "animadver[sio] in facinorosos homines" of D.2.1.3 in two parts. *Animadversio* stood for *cognitio*, whereas its application "in facinorosos homines" represented the *executio*. Bologneti, *In primam Digesti veteris repetitiones* (n 78) *ad* D.2.1.3 n 26 fol 190r. In order to achieve the same result with somewhat sounder arguments, Bocerus looked at many classical sources, and concluded that *animadversio* was used both in the sense of *cognoscere* and *coercere*. Henricus Bocerus, *Disputatio de iurisdictione* (1597) n 14 let a-c p 15. Such a conclusion was harshly criticised by Hunnius, *De iurisdictione tractatus* (n 84) pt 1 ch 1 q 3 n 3 pp 31–32, who pointed out that in Roman legal sources (as opposed to extra-legal ones) its meaning was only that of *coercere*.

97 For instance, when commenting on *de in ius vocando* (D.2.1.4) Petrus Costalius (Pierre Coustau) introduced the subject with Duarenus' definition. But then he moved on, perfidly (but lucidly) noting how "nos qui iure pro ratione utimur, opinor, tantam scrupulositatem non servamus" (Costalius, *Ad XXV Libros Priores Pandectarum Adversaria* (1627) p 76).

98 More correctly, *statutaria* ("iurisdictio condendi iura quam ego appello statutariam"), *iuditiaria* ("iurisdictio redendi iura vel ius dicendi seu administrandi iustitiam quam ego appello iuditiariam"), and *gratiosa* ("iurisdictio equitatis statuendi et gratias faciendi et dispensandi quam ego appello gratiosam"). As such, *iurisdictio gratiosa* was somewhat broader than equitable jurisdiction, as it also encompassed pardons. Bologneti, *In primam Digesti veteris repetitiones* (n 78) *ad* D.2.1.3 n 4 fol 177r.

99 Ibid, nn 4–6, and n 10 fols 187v-188r.

he divided the jurisdictional category into *actio* and *persecutio*, *actio* corresponding to (jurisdicitonal) *iurisdictio*, and *persecutio* to (jurisdictional) *imperium*. In turn, and lastly, (jurisdictional) *persecutio* was segmented into *criminalis* and *civilis* after the divide between *merum* and *mixtum imperium*. This way (jurisdictional) *persecutio criminalis* would correspond to *merum imperium*, and (jurisdictional) *persecutio civilis* to *mixtum imperium*.[100] In this new and complex scheme the old Accursian classification became more tenable, as Bologneti was effectively moving elsewhere any segment of medieval *iurisdictio* not attested in the sources.[101] Moreover, Bologneti's scheme could better support the Bartolian division between private and public utility – which he felt was not close enough to the sources – and also that between noble and mercenary judges.[102] For both divisions would now refer only to jurisdictional *iurisdictio* and *imperium* – and not also to the legislative and equitable ones.[103]

Georgius Obrecht (Georg Obrecht, 1547–1612) sought to defend the Accursian notion of *iuris-ditio* by classifying *iurisdictio* as a conceptual category (*notio*), and not – as in Bartolus – a proper power (*potestas*).[104] This way, *iurisdictio* could still be used in its broadest possible meaning but, in accordance with the sources, it was now wholly separated from *imperium* (which on the contrary remained *potestas*).[105] The extreme breadth of the term "*notio*" lent itself perfectly to both meanings in which Bartolus used *iurisdictio*, an all-encompassing genus and a narrow category.[106] In order to further separate *iurisdictio* from *imperium*, Obrecht stressed the closeness between *imperium merum* and *mixtum*, naming them "plenum" and "minus plenum" respectively.[107] Within *mixtum imperium*, Obrecht further distin-

100 Ibid, n 14 fol 188v.

101 Ibid, nn 2 and 8–9 fols 187v-188r, and esp nn 23–24 fol 189v, nn 55–56 fol 196r-v, nn 60–63 fols 197r-198r.

102 Ibid, nn 11–13 fol 188r-v.

103 Ibid, n 15 fol 188v. Having fully explained his new scheme, Bologneti used it to shield the Bartolian classification from the main critiques of humanist jurists, meticulously listed, explained and dismissed one by one: ibid, nn 45–116 fols 194v-208v.

104 Georgius Obrecht, *Disputatio de Iurisdictionis et Imperii Principiis* (1589) thesis 88.

105 Ibid, esp theses 182–185. Specifically, Obrecht defined *imperium* as "the power to give orders, to which one must obey" ("imperium non male definiri videtur, iubendi potestas, cui parere necesse est", ibid, thesis 193).

106 Ibid, thesis 74: "dicitur notio: quia hoc vocabulum generale est, et tam cognitionem, quam iuris dictionem significat." When this *notio* was considered in its broadest meaning, then it encompassed both *imperium* and *iurisdictio* (*simplex*): "latissime considerata definiri potest notio criminalium et civilium causarum, quae vel lege vel iure magistratus competit, et cui interdum imperium cohaeret", ibid, thesis 73, cf also thesis 36.

107 Ibid, theses 223–225.

guished between those prerogatives which were strictly instrumental to the exercise of *iurisdictio* and those which were not.[108]

In comparison with Bologneti's and Obrecht's theories, that of Henricus Bocerus (Heinrich Bocer, 1561–1630) might look disarmingly simple. Bocerus fully accepted the new interpretation of humanist jurists, but divided *iurisdictio* in two kinds – *ordinaria* and *specialis*. *Ordinaria iurisdictio* corresponded to Bartolus' *iurisdictio simplex* together with a few prerogatives traditionally pertaining to *mixtum imperium*,[109] whereas *specialis iurisdictio* grouped all those prerogatives more strictly associated with *coercio* than *cognitio*.[110] We will return to all these theories soon enough.

E. IN LIEU OF A CONCLUSION: *VERITAS VOS LIBERABIT*?

I have said earlier that many non-humanists considered historical and philological debates as important digressions which however were not the ultimate aim of their work. This seems to imply that "proper" humanist jurists on the contrary regarded history and philology as an end to itself. Doubtless, some of them did. But the historian should always look with suspicion at "purely" cultural struggles. The *lex imperium* was the cornerstone of the *ius commune* notion of authority. Deconstructing it, legal humanists attacked the legal foundations of centralised power. Just ten years after Alciatus' *Paradoxa*, the ultimate two consequences of the new approach were clearly outlined by Longovallius, and then shared by most humanist jurists.

First and foremost, *imperium* (be it *merum* or *mixtum*) was hardly the province of political authority. It pertained exclusively to the judge.[111] *Merum imperium* was extremely narrow, just *mera coercio*, and its scope was limited to the execution of criminal judgments.[112] The power to legislate (the highest example of *merum imperium* for the Bartolists) therefore could not be grounded on *merum imperium*.[113] *Mixtum imperium* and *iurisdictio* on

108 Ibid, theses 351–352 and 353–356 respectively.

109 Mainly, *in integrum restituere* and *bonorum possessio*: Bocerus, *Disputatio de iurisdictione* (n 96) n 4 let a-e p 3.

110 "Specialis iurisdictio in iubendo consistere dicitur, quae ad dirimendam civilem controversiam, iubendo et imperando magis quam cognoscendo expeditur", ibid, n 7 p 5. See further ibid, n 6 let a-f pp 4–5, and n 9 let c p 7.

111 Longovallius, *Nova et facilis declaratio* (n 22) pt 3 fol 23v. Cf Gillotus, *De iurisdictione et imperio libri duo* (n 23) pt 2 ch 19 fol 15r.

112 Longovallius, *Nova et facilis declaratio* (n 22) pt 3 fol 20v: "imperium nihil aliud quod coer[ci]tionem et summam potestatem esse existimo".

113 "Meo iudicio non longe abest a veritate, nimirum, statuta condere, legitimare et multa alia non esse imperii, aut iurisdictionis, quia a non habentibus imperium aut iurisdictionem possunt

the other hand were to be interpreted with exclusive regard to the jurisdictional sphere. It followed that the prerogatives ascribed to *mixtum imperium* or *iurisdictio* did not compete to political authorities (first of all the prince), but only to the judges.[114]

Secondly, for our purposes even more importantly, the new approach had profound repercussions on delegated jurisdiction. The Digest was quite clear in that jurisdictional prerogatives pertaining to private controversies could be delegated, whereas any prerogative especially conferred by the law could not.[115] As such, it was not possible to delegate *merum imperium*, whereas *mixtum imperium* (since *iurisdictioni coaeherens*) could be freely delegated.[116] At this point the insistence of most legal humanists on *mixtum imperium* as an all-encompassing category and on the marginality of *merum imperium* may be fully appreciated. The Accursian Gloss interpreted the Roman text as allowing delegation of only *iurisdictio* (*simplex*) and what parts of *mixtum imperium* were instrumental to its exercise.[117] Bartolus' systematisation added weight to this, for an obvious corollary of the basic distinction between *iudex nobilis* and *mercenarius* was that no prerogative belonging to the *nobilis* could be entrusted to the latter.[118] The *magistratus municipales*, therefore, had neither *merum* nor *mixtum imperium*, so that "they could judge only about the lowest cases".[119] By the eve of the sixteenth century, the orthodox position had not changed. It was not possible to delegate to the *magistratus civiles* even those prerogatives which pertained to the *iudex nobilis* for the sake of private utility – let alone

exerceri", ibid, pt 3 fol 23v. Cf Gillotus, *De iurisdictione et imperio libri duo* (n 23) pt 2 ch 20 n 2 fol 15v, and esp ch 21 n 1 fol 16r, Charondas, *de iurisdictione et imperio libellus* (n 59) n 11 and 13–15 fols 53r-56r.

114 Longovallius, *Nova et facilis declaratio* (n 22) pt 3 fol 22v. Cf Loriotus, *De iurisdictione et imperio* (n 31) axioma 4 col 4, Charondas, *de iurisdictione et imperio libellus* (n 59) nn 7–8 and 10, fols 50r-v and 51v-52r respectively.

115 D.1.21.1pr.

116 D.1.21.1.1. On the subject see T Spagnuolo Vigorita, "*Imperium mixtum*. Ulpiano, Alessandro e la giurisdizione procuratoria" (1990) 18 *Index. Quaderni Camerti di Studi Romanistici* 113, esp 125.

117 Accursius, *Digestum vetus* (n 5) *ad* D.2.1.3 § *Mixtum* cols 164–165.

118 Bartolus de Saxoferrato, *Super prima et secunda parte Digesti veteris* (n 5) *ad* D.1.21 § *Quecunque* nn 1–8 pp 101–102, and *ad* D.2.1.3 § *Imperium* n 1 pp 111–112. Bartolus' reading of the Accursian Gloss reduced even more the (already narrow) scope of *iurisdictio delegata*. Now, only the lowest kinds of *imperium* could be delegated to *magistratus municipales*: ibid, § *Imperium* n 12 and nn 21–22 p 113. Not even the whole *iurisdictio simplex* (or rather, those kinds which could be heard by a *iudex mercenarius*: *supra*, note 10) could be delegated, but only the lower groups of its sixfold division: ibid, § *Imperium* nn 25–6 pp 113–114.

119 "Magistratus municipales cognoscunt de vilibus tantum causis", ibid, n 1 p 101.

public.[120] It may be recalled how legal humanists agreed with Alciatus in dismissing the distinction between *iudex nobilis* and *mercenarius* and that between private and public utility, as well as in relegating *merum imperium* to capital punishments. The assimilation of *mixtum imperium* with *iurisdictio* (or rather their inseparability) was the last step towards the full delegability of judicial prerogatives to lower magistrates.[121] Also in this respect it was Longovallius who first brought Alciatus' arguments to their ultimate consequences: unlike *merum*, *mixtum imperium* may be fully delegated.[122] For once, most of legal humanists wholeheartedly agreed.[123]

120 E.g. Jason de Mayno, *Commentaria in primam partem Digesti veteris* (1500) *ad* D.2.1.2 § *Cui iurisdictio* and especially his ponderous *lectura ad* D.2.1.3 § *Imperium*.

121 It is interesting to observe how the same statement of Paul (as reported by Papinian in D.1.21.1.1 – *mixtum imperium* may be delegated so long as it was instrumental to the exercise of *iurisdictio*) was the basis for two completely different interpretations. Of the two, perhaps the Commentators' one was more faithful to the text – though not entirely so. Moving from the Accursian Gloss, they looked at those aspects of *mixtum imperium* strictly instrumental to *iurisdictio simplex*. The obvious conclusion was that only a small part of the prerogatives of *mixtum imperium* could be delegated. Yet, when summing up their conclusions, they detached themselves from the text: the only prerogatives fully delegable were those of the *iudex mercenarius*. By contrast, legal humanists stressed the link between *iurisdictio* and *mixtum imperium* so as to insist on the latter's full delegability. But, apart from Baro, they typically shunned the full assimilation of *iurisdictio* and *mixtum imperium*. As a consequence, they usually jumped to the conclusion that, since *mixtum imperium* contained the *modica coercitio* needed to exercise *iurisdictio*, it was fully delegable. Clearly, this leap forward entirely begged the question: does all *mixtum imperium* consist of *modica coercitio* instrumental to the exercise of *iurisdictio*? The answer was obviously negative. Hence, after having boldly stated that all *mixtum imperium* may be delegated (as *iurisdictioni coaeherens*), they hastily went back a step or two and identified some kinds of *mixtum imperium* totally unrelated to *iurisdictio*, singling them out as exceptions to the rule. A remarkable exception to this *modus operandi*, however, may be found in Donellus. To distinguish between the cases in which jurisdiction on private disputes could be delegated and those in which it could not, Donellus added a third category, an "intermedium genus iurisdictionis", to the usual contentious and non-contentious ones ("contentiosa" and "voluntaria" *iurisdictio*, on whose delegability see his *Commentarii de iure civili* (n 68) lib 17 ch 8 nn 11–12 cols 1128–1129, and ch 10 nn 9–12 cols 1192–1197 respectively). While methodologically important, Donellus' third *genus* was of lesser practical relevance, consisting mainly in *datio tutoris* (ibid, ch 8 n 7 col 1125, n 14 col 1132, and esp ch 9 n 11 cols 1174–1175), and three other somewhat minor prerogatives ("transactio alimentorum testamento relictorum; praediorum minoris alienatio; consilii exercitio", ibid, ch 8 n 17 cols 1136–1137). Having thus excluded those prerogatives of *mixtum imperium* which had no connection with *iurisdictio* and could not therefore be delegated, Donellus then used an implied *argumentum a contrario* so to include in the delegable prerogatives also those with very loose connection with *iurisdictio*, such as *praetoria stipulatio* and *missio in possessionem* (ibid, ch 8 n 11 cols 1128–1129). The point was perhaps worth mentioning in full because it seems to strengthen the centrality of the delegability of *mixtum imperium* in most of the legal humanists mentioned in this essay. Had it been just a peripheral point, they would have probably devoted less attention to it and possibly also avoided structuring their argument in such a dangerous way.

122 Longovallius, *Nova et facilis declaratio* (n 22) pt 4 fols 25v-26r and 30v-32r (on *merum imperium*), and ibid, fols 24v-25r, 26v-27r and 28r-29v (on *mixtum imperium*).

123 Loriotus, *De iurisdictione et imperio* (n 31) axiomata 22 and 24 cols 35–36, and axioma 31,

At first sight, the whole debate might appear hardly relevant to contemporary issues. But if we look slightly beyond the Roman facade, the message was pretty clear. As openly stated by Baro with his usual bluntness, if *iurisdictio* is *basse justice*, *mixtum imperium* is *moyenne justice* and *merum imperium* is *haute justice*, it follows that local judges (*magistratus municipales*) enjoy not only *basse*, but also (and moreover) *moyenne justice*.[124] But in the sixteenth century none of the three categories corresponded perfectly to its Roman equivalent. In particular, *haute justice* was not coterminous with *merum imperium* but it was somewhat broader, encompassing also some prerogatives of Roman *mixtum imperium*. If local magistrates enjoyed *mixtum imperium* in full, then they would also have some prerogatives pertaining to *haute justice*.[125]

If we look back at the main (and most quoted) defences of the Bartolian jurisdictional categories in light of such observations, those apparently abstract (and abstruse) discussions might look quite different. Menochius' insistence on the unity of *imperium*, which could be considered both as species and genus,[126] was aimed at detaching *mixtum imperium* from *iurisdictio*. The more *mixtum imperium* was considered under the genus of *imperium*, the less it would have in common with *iurisdictio*. Far from being a dogmatic digression, Menochius' theory had serious repercussions for the scope of delegated *iurisdictio*. Being two different categories, *mixtum imperium* was not merely instrumental to the exercise of *iurisdictio*. When *iurisdictio* was delegated, therefore, only a few prerogatives pertaining to *mixtum*

col 39, Goveanus, *ad Legem III D. Imperium, De iurisdictione omnium iudicium* (n 44) pp 5–6, and *De Iurisdictione libri II, adversus Eguinarium Baronem* (n 58) pp 23, 29, 40–41 and 44, Charondas, *de iurisdictione et imperio libellus* (n 59) n 18 fol 55r-v, and esp nn 25–26 fol 63r, Donellus, *Commentarii de iure civili* (n 68) lib 17 esp ch 8 n 6 cols 1123–1124. Gillotus went even further, fully equating ordinary judges to higher ones given that they shared the same *potestas iurisdictionis*: Gillotus, *De iurisdictione et imperio libri duo* (n 23) pt 2 ch 18 n 1 fol 14v. By contrast, Baro was somewhat more careful and attentive to the exact scope of D.1.21.1.1: Baro, *Ad digesta iuris civilis l. de iurisdictione* (n 52) p 144. Nonetheless he still overtly argued for the full delegability of *mixtum imperium*: ibid, pp 43, 59, 66, 84, 139, 157, 162, and esp 97–105 and 147–148. More cautious was (as usual) Corasius, who stated as much in a less overt way: Corasius, *de iurisdictione et imperio* (n 47) nn 7–8 p 276.

124 Baro, *Ad digesta iuris civilis l. de iurisdictione* (n 52) p 162. See more broadly also ibid, pp 162–165.

125 Id, *Ad τα πρώτα Digestorum* (n 52) tit 1 fol 71r-v.

126 Menochius, *De imperio et iurisdictione commentarii* (n 90) lib 1 ch 7 n 2 p 85: "Hae opiniones; quae verbis, non sensu differunt, conciliari sic possunt. Mixtum imperium componitur ex Imperio, quod alias, dempta iurisdictione remanet merum, atque ita si consideratur, ut Imperium, sub nomine generis, dicitur simpliciter Imperium: si vero sub nomine speciei, dicitur sublata iurisdictione merum; adiecta autem iurisdictione appellatur mixtum. Et horum sententia mihi etiam probatur."

imperium could accompany it.[127] While studiously avoiding to state as much too openly, Menochius considerably narrowed the powers of the delegated judge in practice.[128] Similarly, Bologneti's division between *actio* and *persecutio* allowed one to distinguish fully *mixtum imperium* from *iurisdictio*.[129] It followed that *mixtum imperium* was not (to borrow a theological term) "consubstantial" with *iurisdictio*: their *substantia* was different, both on a procedural level and on a theoretical one. As such, and crucially, *mixtum imperium* did not follow *iurisdictio*, and when *iurisdictio* was delegated *mixtum imperium* was not.[130] Ultimately, Bologneti's threefold division of both *iurisdictio* and *imperium* (legislative, jurisdictional and equitable) was aimed at structurally preventing any issue on delegation, for the very power to delegate (*potestas delegandi*) did not pertain to judicial *iurisdictio* (*iurisdictio iudiciaria*), but rather to equitable *iurisdictio* (*iurisdictio gratiosa*).[131] Delegating *iurisdictio* was therefore a matter way beyond the reach of ordinary judges.[132] By the same token, the apparently specious classifications

127 Ibid, esp lib 1 ch 24 (q 17) nn 3 and 5–6 pp 180–183.

128 The second – and considerably shorter – book of Menochius' treatise is entirely devoted to the distinction between *ordinaria* and *delegata iurisdictio* (ibid, lib 2 pp 193–214 esp ch 5 pp 201–205 ch 8 pp 209–210 ch 11 p 212 and ch 12 pp 212–214). The approach of Menochius is significantly restrictive on both nature and scope of the powers of the delegated judge (ibid, esp ch 4 [q 4] nn 3–4 and 6 pp 204–205, ch 10 [q 10] p 211, ch 11 [q 11] p 212). And yet he is conspicuously silent on the most debated issue, namely whether *mixtum imperium* may be delegated and, if so, whether it should automatically follow *iurisdictio delegata* (ibid, esp ch 13–15 pp 214–221, the obvious *sedes materiae* for such a discussion). The omission is all the more remarkable for two reasons. First, because Menochius was the only author dealing extensively with the subject to avoid the issue. Secondly, given that the omission itself was just partial, for immediately before he had clearly excluded the delegation of *merum imperium* (ibid, ch 12 [q 12] n 1 pp 213–214), therefore begging the issue when it came to *mixtum imperium*, an omission so remarkable to appear voluntary, all the more given his insistence on the unitary nature of *imperium*.

129 Bologneti, *In primam Digesti veteris repetitiones* (n 78) n 49 fol 195v: "imperium sit iurisdictio quae ex solo motu iudicis vel super persequtionibus [*sic*] expeditur, et verbum persecutionibus ponit differentiam cum iurisdictione quae expeditur solum super actionibus quae sunt ius formatum in iure consistenti." Ibid, n 91 fols 203v-204r: "[mixtum imperium] mixtura consideratur quia ab imperio capit quod ab authoritate dependet, et non fundatur in iure partis principaliter, et a iurisdictione capit quod consistat in causis civilibus. Et ex ista mixtura causantur postea persequtiones [*sic*] quae sunt medium inter actiones et imperium merum."

130 Ibid, n 16 fols 188v-189r, cf also n 91 fol 204r.

131 Ibid, n 32 fol 191r.

132 Ibid, nn 43–44 fols 193v-194v. Cf also n 85 fol 202r. To be safe, Bologneti used the division between *actio* and *persecutio* to prevent the other possible way to broaden the scope of the jurisdiction of lower judges: the appeal. On the subject, the common understanding was that the competence to hear appellate cases depended on the subject matter. As the court of appeal would hear the same controversy discussed before that of first instance, it did not need broader competences. So, if the subject matter fell within the scope of *iurisdictio*, then (at least in principle) the appellate judge did not need *imperium*. To prevent a delegated judge from being entrusted with the appeal, Bologneti looked at the act of appealing (*admissio appellationis*) and

of Obrecht – opposing the *notio* of *iurisdictio* to the *potestas* of *imperium*, stressing the unity of *imperium* and dividing the prerogatives of *mixtum imperium* according to their instrumentality to the exercise of *iurisdictio* – were in fact aimed at detaching *mixtum imperium* from *iurisdictio*, so to narrow as much as possible the prerogatives pertaining to *mixtum imperium* which could be delegated together with *iurisdictio*.[133] Even Bocerus' division between *iurisdictio ordinaria* and *specialis* (or *extraordinaria*) allowed him to keep the vast majority of prerogatives pertaining to *mixtum imperium* away from *iurisdictio*, and therefore to prevent their delegability.[134] In short, far from being convoluted byzantinisms, such re-classifications of the Bartolian scheme were in fact a set of counter-measures to avoid the institutional devolution of *mixtum imperium* to lower judges.

Even if we were to conclude, as any sensible scholar is apparently expected to, that legal humanism was a renaissance of legal culture, selflessly aiming to restore the purity of Roman law for its own sake, some doubts might still linger. Here, we have briefly glimpsed two in particular. First, the effect of those learned observations was potentially of momentous impact. For their target was a stratified system built on the Accursian Gloss and its Bartolian interpretation, a centuries-old system ultimately still stemming from the very trunk which the humanist jurists were trying so industriously to fell. Secondly, and more specifically, many attacks of legal humanists often had a centrifugal purpose, for they targeted the judicial structure of centralised power. Even so, all this remains speculation. It is of course possible that the above debate was a genuine protest led by erudite and accomplished scholars against the great liberties the Bartolists had taken in respect to the Roman texts. And that civilians were just indulging in tedious, useless and abstract speculations – their speciality, after all. Divesting *imperium*

considered it to be beyond the scope of *actio* (i.e. *iurisdictio*) and so within that of *persecutio* (typically, *civilis*), hence requiring *mixtum imperium*. Since lower judges neither had *mixtum imperium* nor could receive it (by delegation), it followed that they could not hear any appeal either. Ibid, esp n 101 fol 206r.

133 Obrecht, *Disputatio de Iurisdictionis et Imperii Principiis* (n 104) theses 227 and 370. Further, the distinction between *notio* and *potestas* allowed Obrecht to insist on the instrumentality of *iurisdictio* to *imperium mixtum* and not vice versa, as most legal humanists held: ibid, thesis 322.

134 Bocerus, *Disputatio de iurisdictione* (n 96) n 3 let b p 3, and n 5 let a-b p 4. Once he had excluded the delegability of the largest part of *mixtum imperium*, Bocerus happily agreed with legal humanists on the instrumentality of *coercitio* to *iurisdictio* and its delegability, in a *crescendo* of lip-service (ibid, esp n 10 let a-b pp 7–8, n 12 let a-f pp 9–12, n 13 let a-g pp 12–14). Among the (many) other authors who did substantially as much see, e.g., Borrello, *De Magistratuum edictis* (n 84) lib 1 ch 1 n 114 pp 26–27, and Vulteius, *Commentarius at tit. Codicis* (n 84) *ad* C.3.13 n 84 p 50, n 91 p 52.

of any legislative and authoritative meaning might appear a harsh attack on a political level, but it may well be a coincidence that the same arguments were pushed to their extreme consequences shortly thereafter by those legal humanists often known as monarchomacs. Similarly, the fact that the largest portion of nearly all humanistic treatises on our subject focused on delegated jurisdiction and implied the effective freedom of lower tribunals from Royal courts could just be an over-analysis. After all, no *Kulturkampf* has ever had political ends.

4 Reassessing the Influence of Medieval Jurisprudence on Jacques Cujas' (1522–1590) Method

Xavier Prévost

A. INTRODUCTION

The fame of Jacques Cujas might make one think that his method is well known. But most research about the French humanist jurisconsult is dated and incomplete.[1] Moreover, they often repeat the same stereotyped presentation of Cujas' method, which tends to implement all the principles of historicist humanism without subtlety. Thus, according to the traditional portrayal, Cujas despised medieval jurisprudence, was not interested in legal practice and only pursued the correction of interpolations. Obviously, there are more nuanced descriptions of his works, but none of them rests on a complete reading of the *Opera omnia*.[2] This is why the method of Jacques Cujas needs to be reassessed.[3]

1 The last monograph, mainly biographical, was published in 1821: J Berriat-Saint-Prix, *Histoire du droit romain suivie de l'histoire de Cujas* (1821).

2 The lack of an overall study about Cujas' work has often been regretted: L Winkel, "CUJAS (*Cujacius*) Jacques", in P Arabeyre, J-L Halpérin and J Krynen (eds), *Dictionnaire historique*

Jacques Cujas[4] was born at Toulouse (in the south of France) in 1522, where he completed his studies. In 1544, after the departure of his master Arnaud Du Ferrier (1506–1585), he left the university to deepen his knowledge in classics. He did not, however, neglect law, and he became lecturer in charge of Justinian's Institutes at the University of Toulouse in 1547. By that time, he had already made the humanist ideas his own, and this had earned him his first praise.

When he did not manage to get a chair of Roman law in Toulouse, he left for Cahors, where he succeeded Antonio de Goveia (1505–1566) as professor in 1554. Less than a year later, Margaret of France (1523–1574), Duchess of Berry, offered Cujas a chair in the renowned University of Bourges, which was then the centre of the reform of legal studies. Cujas had to deal with the opposition of a part of the university. The protesters, led by François Le Douaren (1509–1559), wanted Hugues Doneau (1527–1591) to have the chair. In this context, Cujas resigned himself to leave in 1557. However, after less than two years in the University of Valence, he came back to Bourges in November 1559.

His return was very different from his former professorship at Bourges. He was no longer an unknown jurist: his first books had already begun to establish his repute. In addition, he had multiplied publications during the seven years he spent in Berry. When Margaret of France – who had by then become Duchess of Savoy – called him to teach at Turin in 1566, he was already one of the most renowned jurists in Europe. He stayed less than a year in Italy, where he could not refer to the Florentine manuscript of the Digest, despite a great deal of effort. In September 1567, Cujas was back in Valence, covered with honour and money. Trying not to get involved in the wars of religion, he published a lot, notably his famous *Paratitla* on the Digest and books IX to XIV of the *Observationes et emendationes*.[5]

des juristes français (XIIe–XXe siècle) (2007) 222, J-L Thireau, "La doctrine civiliste avant le Code civil", in A Bernard and Y Poirmeur (eds), *La doctrine juridique* (1993) 13, R Gadave, *Les documents sur l'histoire de l'université de Toulouse et spécialement de sa faculté de droit civil et canonique (1229–1789)* (1910) 68.

3 This chapter sums up one of the main conclusions of my doctoral dissertation devoted to Cujas, which has been published in French under the title *Jacques Cujas (1522–1590), Jurisconsulte humaniste* (2015). I choose the influence of the medieval jurisprudence for this chapter, but my thesis reassesses other questions, such as the historical method of Cujas or his interest in legal practice.

4 For a biographical presentation in English: J Macdonell and E Manson (eds), *Great Jurists of the World* (1914, rep 1997) 83 at 108, C B Schmitt and Q Skinner (eds), *The Cambridge History of Renaissance Philosophy* (1988) 670.

5 About this "work of a lifetime": X Prévost, "Cujas's *Observationes et emendationes*", in S Dauchy,

However, due to a financial conflict, he accepted the offer of the University of Bourges. He came back to Berry in June 1575, after a few months in Paris where the prohibition of teaching civil law had been suspended in his favour. Cujas ended his career at Bourges, where he died on 4 October 1590, celebrated as the greatest jurist of the time. Ten volumes in-folio[6] result from this long and brilliant career, which was devoted to the humanist reform of legal studies.

Humanism appeared at the end of the Middle Ages in Italy, where it first concerned literature and philosophy. But it quickly spread to law during the *quattrocento*, notably thanks to Lorenzo Valla's (c1406–1457) works. This field of humanism extended to France[7] at the beginning of the sixteenth century with Guillaume Budé (1468–1540) and the Milanese Andrea Alciato (1492–1550), who taught at Avignon and Bourges. They had numerous followers, so much so that the new method was called *mos gallicus iuris docendi* (French method of teaching law) in opposition to the *mos italicus*, which described the medieval commentaries of Roman compilations and of canon law. However, legal humanism was not a united movement. If the supporters of the *mos gallicus* shared their main principles, such as the return to the sources, they were divided about their goals.

From the second third of the sixteenth century – the peak of legal humanism and the period in which Cujas was active – two methods clashed, sometimes vehemently. On the one hand, the jurists who were described as systematists tried to discover the ancient Roman law system. In their view, classical Roman law formed a coherent and rationalist system. So, François Connan (1508–1551), Éguiner Baron (c1495–1550), François Le Douaren and above all Hugues Doneau designed an abstract and systematic idea of the law. The systematist jurists aimed to expound the law in a logical order according to a deductive approach, from general to specific. Far from rediscovering the ancient Roman law, they deeply transformed the European

G Martyn, A Musson and H Pihlajamäki (eds), *The Books that made Law in the Western World (thirteenth century-1940)* (forthcoming).

6 The reference edition was due to Charles-Annibal Fabrot: J Cujas, *Opera omnia* (Paris, 1658). It was reprinted three times in Italy in the eighteenth century (Naples, 1722–1727; Naples, 1758; Venice-Modena, 1758–1783). I only refer to those editions. For a precise description of the *Opera omnia* composition, see my thesis: X Prévost, *Jacques Cujas* (n 3) 110 at 133.

7 This chapter focuses on French legal humanism; about other countries, see the other chapters collected in this volume. For an overall view of French legal humanism, see especially J-L Thireau, "Humaniste (Jurisprudence)", in D Alland and S Rials, *Dictionnaire de la culture juridique* (2003) 795 at 800; in English, D R Kelley, "Civil science in the Renaissance: jurisprudence in the French manner" (1981) 2 *History of European Ideas* 261 at 276.

legal orders of modern times.[8] On the other hand, the historicist jurists of legal humanism built their thought around the concept of evolution. Thanks to their knowledge of the ancient sources, they placed Justinian's compilation in its historical context. This approach represented one of the biggest breaks in medieval methods: the humanists thus removed the *Corpus Iuris Civilis* from its timelessness, underlining the different stages of the construction of the legal system. Without a doubt, Cujas was the best representative of this historical method. Nowadays, both his emendations of the texts of the *Corpus Iuris Civilis* and his editions of sources are still sources of reference to modern Romanists.

But the cujacian method is not the epitome of pure theoretical humanism, which would have completely cast out medieval jurisprudence. In that way, Cujas differed notably from François Hotman (1524–1590), whom he is sometimes compared to, described as one of the leaders of anti-Accursianism[9] and anti-Bartolism.[10] Of course, Cujas departed from the medieval approach of legal sources, notably regarding the historical criticism of law, but his method borrows some features from his predecessors.[11] Cujas' position reflects the intellectual freedom of the humanists, who refused to be tied up by authorities. He used the medieval jurisprudence according to his needs, without preconceived ideas.[12] Nevertheless, a detailed analysis of his work shows that the Glossators (B.) and the Commentators (C.) influenced him in different ways.

8 J-L Thireau, "Hugues Doneau et les fondements de la codification moderne" (1997) 26 *Droits, Revue française de théorie, de philosophie et de culture juridiques* 81 at 100, V Piano Mortari, "La sistematica come ideale umanistico dell'opera di Francesco Connano", in *La Storia del diritto nel quadro delle scienze storiche.* Atti del primo congresso internazionale della "Societa italiana di storia del diritto" (1966) 521 at 531.

9 According to C W Westrup, Cujas completely despised the gloss, "Notes sur Cujas", in *Studi in onore di Pietro Bonfante nel XL anno d'insegnamento* vol 3 (1930) 134.

10 For example, F Olivier-Martin: "L'humanisme modifia du tout au tout la tradition bartoliste . . . Le vrai chef du mouvement humaniste fut Cujas . . . Il est ainsi en complète opposition avec le point de vue des bartolistes. Il ne daigne d'ailleurs pas discuter avec eux; comme tous les humanistes, et notamment Rabelais, il se contente de les injurier", *Histoire du droit français des origines à la Révolution* 2nd edn (1951) 430 at 431.

11 "Cujas hat dabei mit des Traditionen den lateinischen Mittelalters nicht gebrochen", H E Troje, "Arbeitshypothesen zum Thema Humanistische Jurisprudenz" (1970) 38 *Tijdschrift voor Rechtsgeschiedenis* 528.

12 The global approach to legal humanism has to be abandoned, cf D J Osler: "Ultimately progress in our understanding of legal humanism – and speculation on its place in the development of modern historical writing – will depend on closely observed studies of the work of individual legal humanists", "Budaeus and Roman law" (1985) 13 *Ius commune (Veröffentlichungen des Max-Planck-Instituts für Europäische Rechtsgeschichte)* 212.

B. THE GENERAL INFLUENCE OF THE GLOSSATORS

Reading Cujas' works proves that all humanists did not break with the medieval techniques completely.[13] For example, the French jurist had himself written glosses. Moreover, this method inspires most of his works (1). Thanks to these medieval foundations, Cujas built his own method, which was neither a simple improved resumption of the gloss nor a total repudiation, but a real intellectual change (2).

(1) A continual resort

The references to the *Great Gloss* in the complete works of Cujas are countless. Accursius (c1182–c1260) is always quoted, especially in the printed lectures of the French jurist. As surprising as it may seem, the *Glossa ordinaria* appears as the working basis of Cujas' lectures. In fact, the return to the sources proclaimed by the humanists also means a return to the sources of jurisprudence. The omnipresence of the gloss filters through in two ways: either a precise analysis, or just a terse reference. The lesson on the *Quaestiones Papiniani* offers numerous examples.

The commentary of Papinianus D.18.1.72pr illustrates the central place of the gloss for the cujacian method very well. After five columns concerning the distinction between pacts and contracts, Cujas notes expressly that he has to study the gloss in order to decide what he thinks is right or wrong.[14] Three columns are then devoted to the *Great Gloss*. Cujas does not just list his agreements and disagreements; he develops his own explanations especially when he disapproves of Accursius. For instance, he contests the tripartite division between the nature, the substance and the accidents of the contract.[15] According to him, if Ulpian uses the word "nature" and Papinian

13 The link between the Glossators and the humanists has already been made by the historiography, sometimes even between Accursius and Cujas: P Dubouchet, *La pensée juridique avant et après le Code civil* (1998) 53, J Gaudemet, "Cujas, Jacques (1520–1590)", in *Encyclopaedia Universalis* vol 25 (2002) 1155. But the question has also been strongly debated: D Maffei, *Gli inizi dell'umanesimo giuridico* (1956) 158 at 161.

14 "Exposui sententiam *hujus legis pacta conventa*; debeo tamen nunc etiam aperire, quae in Glossa Accurs., probenda, vel improbenda sunt", J Cujas, *Commentarii in libros Quaestionum Papiniani*, in idem, *Opera omnia* vol IV (1758–1783) col 230.

15 "Ac primum quidem non probavi, neque probo divisionem Accurs. inter substantialia et naturalia, et accidentalia contractus: nam quae sunt naturalia, substantalia sunt: natura sive substantia emptionis idem est: emptionis substantia constat ex re et pretio; perficitur enim simul ac convenerit inter emptorem et venditorem de pretio: et quae Accurs. vocat naturalia, id est, adminicula, certe accidentalia sunt", ibid.

the expression "substance of the contract", they both refer to the same concept: it is just a difference of vocabulary, not an intellectual divide.[16] In the same commentary, Cujas develops his opposition to the distinction made by Accursius between "nude pacts" and "clothed pacts" in depth.[17] He shows that a pact is necessarily nude, otherwise it is not a pact but a contract. His demonstration multiplies the references to the *Glossa ordinaria*, not only to discuss Accursius' opinion, but also to approve some of his solutions.[18]

Sometimes it is just a simple mention, which highlights the influence of the Glossators. Again, the lecture about the *Quaestiones Papiniani* holds good illustrations. Thus, Cujas notes that he does not study the gloss on Papinianus D.1.5.9.1, because this gloss could be understood by everybody.[19] This assertion means indirectly that the study of the *Glossa ordinaria* is a compulsory step of the lecture. Moreover, Cujas seems to prompt the students to read it. It may be a preparatory work required by the master. For sure, Cujas considers the *Great Gloss* as the intellectual basis of his audience. Thus, the

16 "Haec sunt ex eodem contractu, hoc est, pertinent ad naturam ipsam, et substantiam contractus. Natura contractus est, quo consistit contractus, et sine quo non consistit vel contractus ipse, vel res ipsa, quae contracta est, substantiam dicit Papin. hoc loco, Ulp. naturam in *l. jurisgent. §. idem respondit, de pact.* non est constituenda differentia inter naturam et substantiam. Accurs. dicit, alia esse pacta de naturalibus, alia de substantialibus, quae idem sunt", ibid, col 229.

17 "Non probavi etiam neque probo divisionem pacti nudi, et vestiti: nam omne pactum est nudum, aut sane non est pactum, sed contractus. et vestiri ait Accurs. cohaerentia contractus, aut lege, aut datione rei propriae, vel stipulatione: vestiri cohaerentia, ut si contractui bonae fidei ex continenti pactum adjiciatur: nam non esse nudum pactum, sed vestitum sive coopertum contractu, cui injicitur, quod falsum esse demonstrat *l. 7. §. quinimo, de pact* . . . Pactum autem conventum, et nudum idem est. Pacta igitur, quae transerunt in aliud nomen, quaeque datione aut stipulatione sumpserunt effectum, pactorum principale nomen amiserunt, et contractum assumpserunt, qui tamen nec usquam pacta nuncupatur, licet pactis constitui sint: sunt enim plus quam pacta, sed his pacta inesse dicuntur, sive praecesserint, sive secuta sint. Vera divisio est haec conventionum, alias esse pacta, alias contractus, et coalescere pacta in contractus: falsa haec, nuda alia, alia vestita esse: non est etiam probandum quod ait Acc. pacto ex continenti apposito de augendo vel minuendo pretio, non tolli priorem emptionem: nam hoc proinde est ac si diceres, non licere poenitere ex continenti: ut fundus ille esto emptus decem, imo duodecim, quod est aperte falsum, ut *l. si ita scriptum 67. de hered. inst. l. 21. de manum. test.* Nec obstat lex *non ad ea 88. de cond. et dem* . . . ", ibid, col 230 at 231.

18 "Et pactum illud, quod sequitur ex continenti vel format actionem statim, vel postea, ut Accursius recte docuit duobus exemplis . . . Et post haec Accurs. explicat casus, quibus pacta facta ex continenti non proficiant ad actionem . . . Non est reprobandum quod Accursius ait: si rem tibi dedi sub lege aliqua, quaero an eam rem possum vindicare pacto non impleto? Respondeo, si dedi rem sub conditione, vel modo, qui modus plerumque pro conditione habetur, non impleta conditione mihi competit vindicatio, quia cum res imperfecta fuerit, non videor transtulisse dominium, *l. 1. C. de donat. quae sub modo, l. 3. et 4. et l. cum te, C. de pactis inter empt. et vend.* nec inspicitur solutum fuerit pretium nec ne. Sed si tibi dedi pure, finge, jure emptionis, non jure precarii, non enim transferrem dominium, et convenerit, ut mihi revenderes eandem rem, vindicatio cessat, competunt tantum personales actiones", ibid, col 232.

19 "Prima erit lex 9. *de statu hom.* Omittam quaecunque scripsit Accursius in hanc legem, non quod sint ea contemnenda, sed quod sit vobis in promptu ea legere", ibid, col 731.

French professor exposes his approach at the beginning of his commentary of C.8.13: "I will annotate just a little bit each constitution, unless the wealth of the subject requires it, and I will annotate so much those which Accursius did not observe, badly observed or insufficiently expounded".[20] He justifies the brevity of his comments by the soundness of some glosses and so he refers the students to Accursius. A lot of other examples show that the *Great Gloss* forms the weft of Cujas' lectures on the *Corpus Iuris Civilis*: Accursius and the *Glossa ordinaria* appear in almost all the analyses.

Therefore, it is not surprising that the French humanist regularly defends the works of the Glossators.[21] Numerous superlatives about the gloss run through the *Opera omnia*: "elegantissimum"[22], "verissima"[23], "rectissima et elegantissima"[24]. . . The defence is sometimes more specific about methodological points shared with the Glossators. For instance, considering the concept of cause applied to the codicil, Cujas asserts that "Accursius was not ignorant of all philosophy".[25] The humanist takes the opposite position to some of his contemporaries. This is an obvious criticism of those who reject the whole work of the Glossators, notably due to their alleged ignorance of philosophy. Besides, Cujas does not hesitate to take sides with Accursius against the rest of the jurisprudence, even if he does not share all the solutions of the *Great Gloss*.[26] It is a good example of the nuanced position of

20 "His praemissis tempus est ut perveniamus ad constitutiones hujus tituli. In singulas pauca adnotabo, nisi si forte plura rei propositae ubertas exigat, et ea tantum adnotabo, quae vel Accurs. non observavit, vel male observavit non satis abunde exposuit", J Cujas, *Commentarii in libros Codicis*, in ibid, vol IX col 1114.

21 Even if a part of the historiography has tended to claim that all the humanist jurists stood together against the medieval jurisprudence; for example: D R Kelley, "Legal humanism and the sense of history" (1966) 13 *Studies in the Renaissance* 184 at 190, B Barret-Kriegel, *Les historiens et la monarchie. II- La défaite de l'érudition* (1988) 94.

22 "Scholium Accursii in hoc responso est elegantissimum", J Cujas, *Recitationes ad Modestini Responsorum libros XIX*, in *Opera omnia* vol VI (1758–1783) col 661.

23 "Et verissima sunt quaecunque scripsit Accurs. in hunc §.", J Cujas, *Commentarii in libros Quaestionum Papiniani*, in *Opera omnia* vol IV part 1 (1658) col 620.

24 "Et ut hoc admoneam, quae in eam legem scripsit Accursius, omnia sunt rectissima et elegantissima", J Cujas, *Commentarii in libros Codicis*, in *Opera omnia* vol IX (Naples, 1758) col 457.

25 "Causa, ex qua valent codicilli, est testamentum. Non possunt igitur codicilli esse causa, ex qua valet testamentum. ergo, ut Accurs. notat pertissime, qui omnino Philosophiae non erat ignarus, duae res sibi invicem causae esse non possunt eodem modo . . .", J Cujas, *Commentarii in libros Quaestionum Papiniani*, in *Opera omnia* vol IV part 1 (1658) col 391.

26 "Male autem Joannes et Accursius statuunt contra ea, quae diximus, defensorem ultro interveniente post litem cum reo contestatam, esse condemnandum . . . Quod cum non obtinuerit, aequum est, ut condemnatio recurrat ad eum, qui litem fecit, et contestatus est. Contra, male Doctores omnes Accursium reprehendunt, scribentem hoc loco . . . Haec est sententia Accursii, . . .: quae verissima sententia est", J Cujas, *Commentarii in libros XIX. Responsorum Papiniani*, in *Opera omnia* vol IV (Naples, 1758) col 876.

Cujas: the gloss, as well as each source, has to be examined closely with the techniques of humanist criticism. This applies even to some judgments which seem definitive.

Cujas thus puts Accursius in the first rank of all the legal exegetes, whether Greek or Latin.[27] The expression is surprising from a humanist, but it should be contextualised within the whole work of Cujas. First, the gloss occupies a central position in the *Opera omnia*. Second, this sentence is situated in the third book of the *Observationes et emendationes*, published in 1558. It is one of the first publications of Cujas, who was not yet a renowned jurist, aware of his superiority. If there is no doubt that the French humanist has kept a respectful admiration towards the *Great Gloss* throughout his life, the date of this opinion about Accursius should not be neglected. Third, the context has to be taken into account. This expression relates to a specific gloss, namely the explanation of Modestinus D.31.34.2.[28] Moreover, Cujas immediately limits the significance of his assertion, since he justifies his own commentary by the weakness of the gloss.[29] Though Cujas makes him the head of jurisprudence, Accursius stays fallible. Finally, the defence of the Glossators is not a general agreement of their works, but a continual use which shows that numerous of their interpretations are right.[30] However, the renewed approach of humanism allows Cujas to move away from the word-for-word analysis of the Glossators.

(2) A methodological change

Legal humanism borrows only a few features from the gloss. Significantly, four main stumbling points distinguish Jacques Cujas from the first exegetes of the *Corpus Iuris Civilis*. They characterise the great progress of the "second revival of Roman law", i.e. the consideration of Greek sources, the better command of the language and the search for "classical" Latin, the historical reading of legal texts, and finally the discovery of interpolations and transcription errors.

Thanks to the proliferation of sources, knowledge of Greek deeply alters

27 "Accursius noster, quem ego et Latinis et Graecis omnibus interpretibus juris facile antepono", J Cujas, *Observationum et emendationum libri XXVIII*, in *Opera omnia* vol III (1658) col 71.

28 "At illud tamen pernegatur in *§. Lucia*: ubi Accursius noster, quem ego . . . ", ibid.

29 ". . . antepono, huius rei explicandae gratia tres opiniones adfert, ex quibus postremam ipse verissimam esse iudicio: verum explicatione indiget", ibid.

30 Obviously, Cujas approves of glosses other than those of Accursius, such as some of Bulgarus, Rogerius, Joannes Bassianus, Azo; cf X Prévost, *Jacques Cujas* (n 3) 152 at 153.

the interpretation. On the one hand, Cujas restores and examines the Greek texts of the Justinianic compilations, overlooked by the medieval doctrine. On the other hand, he masters the Byzantine jurisprudence so that he can then confront the Western writings. Because of these shortcomings, interpretations of the Glossators do not always prevail. Among many examples, Cujas says that ignorance of Greek leads Accursius to confer an overbroad scope to Novel 12 about incestuous unions.[31] The glossator applies it to all marriages forbidden by law, while the Greek term used by Justinian's constitution (*ἀθέμιτος*) refers to incest *stricto sensu*. Therefore, the Novel applies only to unions contrary to nature, less numerous than those prohibited by law. The Byzantine jurisprudence also allows for the rejection of some solutions proposed by the Glossators. Despite the confirmation of a gloss of Johannes Bassianus († c1197), Cujas singles out the Greek interpretation of the paragraph Paulus D.17.2.65.5.[32] Described as "rectissima interpretatio", it even surpasses all Latin exegesis.

Jacques Cujas differs also from the method of the Glossators through improved parsing. Thus, our jurist does not hesitate to denounce the errors of the earlier jurisprudence, which distorts the meaning of some texts by its ignorance of the subtleties of the language of the Roman jurists. For instance, in his lecture on the *Quaestiones Papiniani*, he enjoins his pupils to remove one of the glosses on Papinianus D.35.1.73.[33] Indeed, Accursius has

31 "Incestae nuptiae sunt quae natura prohibitae sunt. In *l. 8. et l. sororis, ff. de rit. nupt.* ait, quae moribus, quod idem est, nempe tacito consensu omnium gentium. Confirmat definitionem haec Nov. variis locis: ut cum incestas nuptias naturae contrarias dicit, et bruta quaedam eas conjunctiones abhorrere, et cum jubet ut nos intra naturae fines contineamus, ne contra naturam obnitamur. Male igitur Accursius etiam ad nuptias legibus interdictas hanc Novellam trahit: nam et verbo ἀθέμιτος, quo movetur, illae tantum nuptiae significantur quae sunt naturae contrariae", J Cujas, *Novellarum constitutionum Imp. Justiniani expositio*, in *Opera omnia* vol II (1758–1783) col 915.

32 "Et mirum in modum mihi placet glossa haec verba, *ex tempore*, dempto ultimo commate, quod est ex Joanne. Verum huic exceptioni Proculi mox additur alia exceptio, exceptio exceptionis his verbis, *haec ita accipienda sunt, si nihil de hoc in coeunda societate convenit*, id est, si de hoc, quo de agitur, aliud in coeunda societate conventum non sit, pura, ut etsi vel unius socii interesset societatem non dirimi, etiamsi societatis non interesset ne dirimeretur, si id convenit, si vel unius interesset non dirimi: hoc etiam casu, is, qui renuntiat societati, et cujus interest, ex pacto convento, tenetur actione pro socio. Et ita Graeci rectissime hunc locum interpretantur: Εἰ μὴ ἄρα ἰδικῶς τοῦτο συνεφωνίθη, ὥσε καὶ μὴ βλαπτομένης τῆς κοινωνίασ, εἰ ἐμὲ μόνον συμβῆ ζημιοθῆναι ἐκ τῆσ ἀπαγοροἧσεωσ ἔχειν μετὴν πρὸ σότζιω, id est, *si non specialiter convenerit, ut et si non laederetur societas, si vel mihi noceret renuntiatio societatis, ego haberem actionem pro socio*. Est rectissima interpretatio. Latini perperam omnes. Et ita accipienda haec verba Si non convenerit, ut et intempestive a societate recedere liceat, quasi scilicet tunc liceat etiam intempestive societate abire", J Cujas, *Commentarii in libros LXXVIII. Pauli ad edictum*, in ibid, vol V cols 476–477.

33 "Accursius non intellexit hoc loco linguam Latinam, non intellexit, quid sit *exigere cautionem*, quam Papinianus ait, ab herede fuisse exactam sollicite. Plus est exigere quam agere: nam

not understood the meaning of "exigere cautionem". He assumes that the heir did not take all necessary precautions with regard to the *cautio Muciana* required in this case. Instead, the use of *exigere* by Papinian means that the heir rightly ensured the protection of his interests.

If the grammatical approach is an improvement of the method of the gloss, the fact that history is taken into account is a real breakthrough. The historical analysis of law is indeed one of the main contributions of legal humanism and in particular of Cujas' work. The clarity of the wording used in his commentary of fragments D.50.16.43 at 45 suggests a methodological revolution: "Quod non intellexit Accursius propter ignorantiam juris antiqui".[34] According to the French humanist, the title *De verborum significatione* is not just a legal lexicon. The difference with the exegetical approach of the Glossators is obvious: unlike his predecessors, Cujas seeks to put the fragments of this title in their original context. The method often leads to a very dissimilar interpretation compared to the common opinion of the doctors. The fragment Ulpianus D.50.16.43 illustrates it perfectly. In the Digest, this text extracted from the book LVIII of Ulpian's *Commentary on the edict* defines the word *victus* (provisions). Cujas relates it to its original purpose, i.e. the *res iudicata*. His argument leads him to go back to the XII Tables, but also to make connections with the following fragments, including fragment 48 which concerns the notion of freedom (*solutum*). He contrasts chains to freedom, then he continues with the obligation to provide food (*victus*) to the one who is in chains (*vinctus*), playing on the similarity of the words. Thus, Cujas replaces the text in legal history and can contradict Accursius because of his "ignorance of the ancient law"[35]. For this reason,

exigere est rem, sive cautionem extorquere et exprimere, satis accipere. Et Accursius contra manifesta verba legis ponit quasi certissimum, Titium heredi non cavisse cautionem Mucianam, qui error tolerari non potest, et delenda est Glossa ad verbum actiones", J Cujas, *Commentarii in libros Quæstionum Papiniani*, in ibid, vol IV col 505.

34 J Cujas, *Commentarii in ceteros libros Digestorum*, in ibid, vol VIII col 498.

35 "Lex 43. pertinet ad judicatos et confessos, ad titulos de re judicata et de confessis. De judicatis, et confessis hoc primum cautum fuit lege duodecim tabularum, ut si judicatum non fecissent, id est, si non solvissent, vincti addicerentur creditoribus, deinde ut creditoribus operas darent pro pecunia: tum soluti sunt debitores vinculis et operis, et coguntur aliis rationibus judicato satisfacere, quam servitiis, *l. 12. Cod. oblig. et act.* Sed jus vetus erat, ut vincirentur et necterentur, ad quam partem juris pertinet haec lex, et duae sequentes, et *l. 48.* ut ibi dicam, ubi definit, quis dicatur solutus. Opponitur solutus vincto debitori. At praeterea eadem lege duodecim tabularum cautum fuit, ut debitores addicti creditoribus, si vellent, suo viverent apud creditores, ni suo viverent, creditores, qui eos vinctos haberent, praeberent in dies singulos libras farris singulas, si duo denique non viverent, creditores eos alerent. Quod videtur etiam Praetor subsequutus edicto, et dedisse actionem poenalem in factum in eum creditorem, qui addicto victum non praeberet, cum sit proditum, eum etiam creditorem teneri utili illa actione poenali in factum, si non patiatur judicato victum et stratum inferri, *l. si victum, supr. de re judic.* vel etiam eum

the Glossators have accentuated the leaning of the Digest to give texts a universal (at least timeless) significance. Therefore, the novelty of the humanist method necessarily leads to a questioning of the glosses.

The historical dimension of the humanist approach is also found in the desire to restore the texts to their original purity. Cujas is distinguishable from the previous jurists, since the corrected text differs from that which was interpreted by them: their conclusions are often invalidated by the restored version of the text. Cujas then highlights the obsolescence of those glosses, especially as the *Great Gloss* is the working basis of his lessons. Thus he does for the commentary of Paulus D.10.2.29. Nearly four columns are devoted to the study of the *Glossa ordinaria*, mixing approvals and disapprovals. After confirming several of Accursius' glosses, the analysis on the *verbo obtulerit* is discarded by the French jurist, who corrects the text of Paul as it appears in ancient manuscripts. According to the *Great Gloss*, this section refers to the case of an heir who has partly paid his co-heir. But Cujas shows that it is not a question of division of a deceased's estate, but a comparison with the mortgage action. The mortgage action involves a full payment if the property is not returned. So, the gloss makes a mistake in asserting that a partial payment is sufficient. However, the French humanist does not blame Accursius for this error, because the glossator was misled by the text at his disposal.[36] The emendation of the *Corpus Iuris Civilis* avoids such mistakes.

In view of the methodological differences with the Glossators, the corrections are found throughout the *Opera omnia* and sometimes go with cutting epithets. Several times, Accursius is called "stultus"[37], just as Placentinus'

creditorem teneri actione injuriarum eadem ex causa, qui injuriam mihi facis, si me non sinas uti libertate aliena, aut bonis meis, *l. item apud, §. pen. de injur. l. qui pendentem, de action. empt.* Igitur vel injuriarum actione tenetur, vel poenali illa actione praetoria in factum creditor, qui non patitur victum, aut stratum judicato inferri. Quod non intellexit Accursius propter ignorantiam juris antiqui. Sed addendum est judicato et addicto, dum non solvit, quod in condemnationem deductum est. male additur vulgo, *in carcerem*, potius subaudiendum est, *in nervum*, vel compedes, quibus tenetur vinctus a creditoribus. Igitur vinctus debitor suo vivet, si velit; si nolit, vel si non possit, aletur a creditore invito", ibid.

36 "Quod deinde Accurs. in hac l. notat ad verbum *obtulerit*, scilicet partem pecuniae coheredi; id notat male: debuit dicere obtulerit pecuniam totam creditori agenti hypothecaria: loquitur enim de possessore convento hypothecaria, non de coheredibus agendibus familiae ercisc. de quibus si loqueretur subjiceret, adversus debitorem agentem pigneratitia, non adversus dominum vindicantem: et sane hic error non erat ferendus, nec excidit Accursio: corruptus fuit hoc loco Accurs. nam veteres libri sic legunt: *obtulerit pecuniam, et habet rem.*", J Cujas, *Commentarii in ceteros libros Digestorum*, in ibid, vol VII col 539.

37 For example: "et stultus est Accurs.", J Cujas, *Commentarii in libros Quaestionum Papiniani*, in *Opera omnia* vol IV (1658) col 608; "Et stultus est Accursius", J Cujas, *Commentarii in libros LXXVIII. Pauli ad edictum*, in ibid, vol V col 839.

(c1135–1192) gloss on C.8.13.7.[38] The master of the gloss is even included in the group of bad interpreters of the *Corpus Iuris Civilis* and grouped among the other "half-jurisconsults".[39] Jacques Cujas seems to contradict himself in the same book: how can Accursius be at the same time the head of jurisprudence and a second-class jurist? There is no paradox, because Cujas is not dogmatic. It seems difficult to generalise these opinions: they are not a final judgment about the person, but rather a special assessment on the debated legal point. In this case, the wording shows anyway that only the gloss in question is meant and not all of the work of the glossator. The same point of view could be applied to other terms used about the *Great Gloss*: "ridiculous",[40] Accursius sometimes "talks nonsense"[41] and some of his interpretations are "fantasies".[42]

These criticisms put together artificially increase their virulence. But we must remember that they are spread out over ten volumes and interspersed with praises. Besides, the criticisms are generally much less severe and in principle based on precise legal arguments.[43] Cujas' position is certainly due to his respect for the works of the Glossators, despite the deficiencies of their method. The use of the Commentators has many similarities, which should not obscure their particularities: less quoted by Cujas, they seem to be more criticised.

C. THE MIXED INFLUENCE OF THE COMMENTATORS

Legal humanism was born in response to the drifts of the Commentators of the fifteenth century, who definitely deviated from the texts of the Justinianic compilation. As a backlash, humanists abandoned authorities in order to return to the sources of Roman law, in and outwith the *Corpus Iuris Civilis*.

38 "Ex lege 7. (quam Placentinum perquam stulte scripsit non posse intelligi, dabitque nobis licentiam abeundi)", J Cujas, *Commentarii in libros Codicis*, in ibid, vol IX col 1236.

39 "Sed in hac re Accursius, ceterique semijurisconsulti quobos seipsos erroribus involuunt", J Cujas, *Observationum et emendationum libri XXVIII*, in ibid, vol III col 98.

40 "Ridiculus hoc loco est Accursius . . . Rursus riduculus, quum ait jusjurandum calumniae esse jusjurandum de credulitate, quo verbo plerunque error significatur, et persuasio quaelibet, etiam falsa: riduculus, quum comminiscitur olim jusjurandum calumniae omnibus fuisse remissum . . . Fac igitur, ut totam Glossam Accursii in spongiam tuam adducas", J Cujas, *Commentarii in libros LXXVIII. Pauli ad edictum*, in *Opera omnia* vol V (Naples, 1758) col 45.

41 "Pro quo argumento Accurs. vaticinatur sic Ulp. Ratiocinari", J Cujas, *Observationum et emendationum libri XXVIII*, in ibid, vol III col 226.

42 "Altera constitutio, (in quam, quaecunque scripsit Accursius sunt somnia)", J Cujas, *Commentarii in libros Codicis*, in *Opera omnia* vol IX (1658) col 690.

43 X Prévost, *Jacques Cujas* (n 3) 159 at 162.

Therefore, some humanists do not hesitate to deny any value in medieval jurisprudence.[44] But Cujas does not mingle in the same set as the jurisprudence of the last three centuries. The length of time between Cino da Pistoia's (c1270–c1336) works and Rafaello Fulgosio's (†1427) writings compels one to distinguish them.[45] Due to the interest of their works, the Commentators run through the *Opera omnia*. However, their diversity leads Cujas to opt for an uneven use (1), that gives to the critical analysis its true role (2).

(1) An uneven use

In the writings of Cujas, Bartolus de Saxoferrato (c1314–1357) is clearly distinguished from other jurists of the late Middle Ages. His place proves that Cujas knows the true value of the master of Perugia and that he does not confuse him with the crowd of his followers. The commentary of Paulus D.45.1.2 illustrates how Cujas resorts to Bartolus and it also confirms his absence of dogmatism. The humanist approves some opinions of the commentator, thereby also indirectly reinforcing his own analysis. This is the case for the "very right" interpretation of paragraph 3, about the action against the co-heir of the one who stipulated to give an unspecified slave.[46] The quotations of Bartolus are also used to separate him from the rest of the jurisprudence. Concerning paragraph 2 of the same fragment, Cujas underlines the relevance of the analysis compared to the errors of other exegetes.[47] In contrast, the central place given to Bartolus for the study of this text

44 See the pages of D Maffei about the "svalutazione polemica della scienza giuridica medievale ed esaltazione della metodologia umanistica", *Gli inizi dell'umanesimo giuridico* (1956) 33 at 59.

45 For a synthesis of the diversity of the Commentators, see P Stein, *Roman Law in European History* (1999) 67 at 74.

46 "Idemque est si pro parte sententia judicis absolutio fiat, ut si stipulatior hominis incerti egit pro parte cum uno ex heredibus promissoris et succubuit, quo casu reliqui heredes partem solvendo cujuslibet hominis liberantur: et ita Bart. rectissime accepit *§. si tamen, inf.* quem plerique omnes secuti sunt", J Cujas, *Commentarius ad titulos quosdam Digestorum*, in *Opera omnia* vol I (1758–1783) col 1004. Shortly thereafter Cujas confirms the validity of Bartolus' opinion: "Dictum est homine incerto promisso, vel Sticho aut Pamphilo nihil agere promissorem vel heredes ejus solvendo hominis partem. Exceptiones duae proponuntur in hoc §. quas exposui in §. 1. Et ad secundam pertinet *l. qui hominem, inf. de accept.* Primam recte interpretatur Bartolus", ibid, col 1006.

47 "Nos loquimur de eo, qui egit actione ex stipulatu, ex qua judex personae non praedio sententiam dicit, Servitutem non constituit, quia non potest uni constitui, *§. si fundus*, de eo, qui egit confessoria, qua actione de jure quaeritur, et judex praedio non personae sententiam dicit, nec servitutem constituit, sed eam quae est declarat: et ideo unus ex heredibus agens confessoria, vincit, et vincitur omnibus. Sed aliud est in actione ex stipulatu, quod Bart. intellexit probe. Male haec negantes quidam adstruunt unum ex heredibus servitutem adquirere posse, quod per liberum hominem nobis possessio, et dominium adquiratur", ibid, col 1005 at 1006.

requires highlighting the mistakes made by him. For example, the French humanist chooses the gloss of Accursius on the *verbo coheredes*. Contrary to Bartolus' view, heirs are only obliged in proportion to their share in the estate and not jointly and severally.[48]

The study of Cujas' use of Bartolus requires us to focus on the very atypical commentary of Paulus D.32.89. The thirty columns of this analysis deal with the complicated question of the right of accretion concerning bequests. Two-thirds of the commentary consist of a study item by item of Bartolus' opinion. Cujas tries to consider all the points mentioned by Bartolus. The title of a section shows clearly his approach: "Nunc expendamus ea quae Bartolus in hanc legem adnotavit".[49] It is also reflected in the structure of the commentary, which is very similar to that used by Bartolus.[50] Cujas furthermore specifies this method in the first sentence: first studying the apparently contrary texts, then resolving the legal issues.[51] Concerning the first point, the humanist generally uses the same technique as Bartolus, i.e. casuistry. Furthermore, he confirms – at least partly – some of the medieval solutions.[52] The second point is developed in a very original way in the cujacian works: twenty questions studied successively respond to seventy points identified in Bartolus. Most often Cujas begins by recalling the question raised by the commentator. He then develops his own commentary, which eventually corrects the Italian jurist. There are only few explicit positions, suggesting that Bartolus' views were known to the audience. This confirms the importance of Bartolus in Cujas' method.

48 "Ceterum non tenentur in solidum, quia non tenentur ut opus aliquod faciant, sed ad id quod interest tenentur, vel ad poenam pro parte hereditaria. Et ita Accurs. recte in *ver. coheredes*, Bart. male. Quod tamen qui non prohibuerunt praestiterint, id a coherede qui prohibuit repetent judicio famil. erciscundae, ne ejus facto damnum sentiant, *l. in executione, §. quod si stipulatus, inf. l. inter, §. quod ex facto, sup. famil. erc.* Nec obstat quod dicitur in *l. heredes*, in solidum committi stipulationem, *§. si illa, et §. Cato*", ibid, col 1006.

49 J Cujas, *Recitationes ad titulum De legatis III*, in *Opera omnia* vol X (Naples, 1758) col 1140. The study of Bartolus' position continues to column 1161.

50 Bartolus de Saxoferrato, *Bartoli a Saxoferrato, lucernae iuris, omnia, quæ extant, opera* . . . vol IV (1590) fol 59 at 62.

51 "Bartolus duo facit: Primo ponit oppositiones, dein quaestiones quamplures: si duobus eadem res legetur separatim, re conjuncti sunt, et inter eos est jus accrescendi", J Cujas, *Recitationes ad titulum De legatis III*, in *Opera omnia* vol X (Naples, 1758) col 1140.

52 For example, he approves of Bartolus' use of the analysis of Johannes Bassianus concerning the sixth opposition ("Sexto respicit intellectum quem Joannes dedit, et Bart. sequitur, re tantum conjunctum verbis praeferri, re tantum conjunctum non praeferri re et verbis conjuncto. Itaque Bart. haec, *quod si re*, interpretatur", ibid, col 1142), while he disapproves of the reasoning of the commentators about the next one ("Septimo pertinet ad id quod dicitur inter conjunctos esse jus accrescendi, et obiicit *l. et Proculo 20. lib. 2.* species haec est: . . ., sed Bart. ait, non sunt conjuncti a testore, sed a lege; . . . sed hoc falsum est", ibid).

Apart from Bartolus, Cujas mentions twenty-eight Commentators. These references, far fewer than those to Bartolus, highlight some of the jurists of the late Middle Ages. For instance, Dinus Mugellanus (c1253–1303) has thirty quotations, which are certainly explained by his interest for the *Glossa ordinaria*. Indeed, one of his main works consists in additions to the *Great Gloss*, that obviously interested our humanist. The twelve references to Cino da Pistoia, meanwhile, can partly be linked to his pupil, namely Bartolus. Cujas quotes Cino da Pistoia especially about Justinian's Code, because his main writing is a *Lectura in Codicem*. Thus, the French humanist approves Cino's parallel between the title C.7.58 and the imperial constitution C.4.21.21 as well as his questioning of Accursius' analysis of this text.[53] Thanks to the commentator, Cujas can prove that the *Great Gloss* should not have neglected Martinus Gosia's (†c1157/66) opinion.

The jurists from the school of Orléans[54] are mainly known in an indirect way. In the sixteenth century, the dissemination of their work was still uneven, as evidenced by the publication of some of their writings under Bartolus' name.[55] Thus, Cujas directly picks up some references to Italian disseminators of Orléans thought. In his *paratitla* on C.7.31, he quotes Jacobus de Ravanis' (†1296) view, as mentioned by Cino da Pistoia.[56]

The credence attached to the writings of Alberico da Rosate (c1290–1360) and Baldus de Ubaldis (c1327–1400) probably explains the favour

53 "… , ut ostendi in *tit. si ex fals. instr. etc.* Denique post sententiam, appellatione, vel retractatione non suspensam, non cogitur quasi quis instrumentum iterum producere, potest tamen accusari falsi, et ita recte Cynus conjungit hanc l. cum *d. tit.* rejectis duabus Accursii interpretationibus. Idem etiam Accursius male putat hic jusjurandum de calumnia praestari in causa criminali: paestatur enim ante accusationem falsi ab eo, qui petit instrumentum iterum exhiberi: ergo praestatur nondum coepta criminali causa coram judice civili. At vero nunquam legitur, in criminali causa jusjurandum de calumnia praestari: nam inscriptio sufficit: haec alligat talioni, et calumniam satis coercet, et cohibet, et continet. Haec fuit sententia Martini, a qua male discedit Acc. *l. 1. sup. de jurejur. propt. cal. etc.*", J Cujas, *Commentarii in libros Codicis*, in ibid, vol IX col 291.

54 About the school of Orléans see the thesis of M Bassano, "Dominus domini mei dixit …" *Enseignement du droit et construction d'une identité des juristes et de la science juridique. Le* studium *d'Orléans (c.1230–c.1320)* (2008).

55 This is especially the case of a commentary on the Institutes attributed to Jacobus de Ravanis or Raoul of Harcourt, published in Pavia in 1504 and republished two years later in Milan. About it, see E M Meijers, *Études d'histoire du droit* vol III: *Le droit romain au Moyen Âge*, R Feenstra and H Fischer (eds) (1959) 68, C H Bezemer, *Les répétitions de Jacques de Révigny. Recherches sur la répétition comme forme d'enseignement juridique et comme genre littéraire* (1987) 242.

56 "Specialiter autem mancipatio *sive datio rei, quae fit per aes, et libram praesentibus non minus quam V. testibus civibus Romanis puberibus, et libripende, et interpositis, certis solemnibusque verbis*, quae idem Boetius ex Gajo profert, cujus auctoritate etiam in hanc rem in hoc titulo Cynus utitur ex scriptis, ut ipse fatetur, Jac. Ravennatis", J Cujas, *Paratitla in libros IX. Codicis Justiniani*, in *Opera omnia* vol II (Naples, 1758) col 470.

granted to them by Cujas among jurists of the fourteenth century. The works of Baldus are directly linked to those of his master Bartolus and Cujas' use is quite similar. However, the reference quoted in the study of Gaius D.6.1.24 is notable: the French humanist underlines that for this matter "Baldus's opinion is nowadays usually accepted by the courts".[57] This is a clear indication that Cujas knows judicial practice, contrary to the majority opinion of historiography.

Finally, due to the major methodological differences with humanism,[58] there are only few references to the Bartolists of the fifteenth century. However, Paolo da Castro (c1360–1441) and above all Rafaello Fulgosio are exceptions, because of the number of citations. In the commentary on Julianus D.36.1.26 (25). 3 where Rafaello Fulgosio is quoted along with the *Great Gloss*, a sentence may explain Cujas' interest in the Bartolist. The humanist notes that "no one is more delicate than Fulgosio in order to clear up the contradictions between our laws", even if he does not succeed in that case.[59] Cujas shares with him this will to resolve the internal contradictions of the *Corpus Iuris Civilis*. Thus, in this case, he compensates for the failure

57 ". . . quin etiam uti receptum est, ab initio licere ei simul experiri interd. et rei vindicatione, sicut etiam judex potest simul cognoscere de utroque, de possessione et proprietate, ut Symmachus in Epistolis docet: et generaliter hodie in foro recepta est decisio Baldi in *l. 1. C. de furt.* duo contraria judicia posse cumulari disjunctim: quin olim etiam licuit duo contraria judicia seu diversa cumulare conjunctim; addita tamen protestatione, ex altero tantum judicio suum consequi velle, *l. 1. §. quia autem, quod legat. inf. l. contra, C. de inoffic. test.* et haec est certa interpretatio legis *naturaliter*", J Cujas, *Commentarii ad diversos titulos Digestorum*, in *Opera omnia* vol VII (1758–1783) col 285.

58 See notably the section entitled "La degeneración des 'mos italicus'", in F Carpintero, "'Mos italicus', 'mos gallicus' y el Humanismo racionalista. Una contribución a la historia de la metodología jurídica" (1977) 6 *Ius Commune* 117 at 121.

59 "Videbatur prima specie non valere libertas propter spem fideicommissi, ut *l. heres, et l. seq. §. ult. qui et a quib. manum l. 11. de manumis.* At favore libertatis receptum esse ait, ut libertas servo conservetur, et liberentur heredes filii existente conditione fideicommissi, puta filio decedente sine liberis praestando sorori pretium Stichi: damni nihil faciet, ut recte Fulgosius loquitur, qui pretium feret: et favor quidem est libertatis, si filius non fuerit ignarus fideicommissi, quia videbatur hoc casu propter scientiam filii impedienda libertas, et Stichus ipse omnimodo sorori restituendus. At, si filius fuerit ignarus fideicommissi, recte Accursius notat, nullum esse favorem libertatis: quia et Sticho a filio non manumisso, sed vendito, idem servaretur, propter justam filii ignorantiam, heredes scilicet, liberarentur fideicommissario praestando servi pretium, non etiam omnino absolverentur obligatione fideicommissi: quia, quod notandum, etsi quid fecero per ignorantiam, non debet factum meum alteri nocere . . . Et ex interpretib. idem Fulgos. quo nullus est ingenuus magis in dirimendis controversiis legum juris nostri, non est veritus affirmare, difficile, aut pene impossibile esse iis legib. respondere. Res tamen omnis explicabatur dilucide et vere, si dicas in arbitrio esse fideicommissarii, ut vel summo jure agat cum heredib. heredis scripti, vel humanius, id est, ut vel servum petat sibi restitui omnimodo, quasi non pervenerit ad libertatem, ut in *sup. d. ll.* vel ut aestimatione servi contentus sit, quae humanior sententia est. Hoc confirmat aperte *lex si quis inquilinos, §. 1. de leg. 1*", J Cujas, *Recitationes ad Salvii Juliani libros XC. Digestorum*, in *Opera omnia* vol VI (1758–1783) col 274 at 275.

of Fulgosio. Indeed, if Cujas holds the Commentators in esteem, it is tinged with a regular but measured criticism.

(2) A nuanced criticism

Standard historiography commonly quotes an expression of Cujas, in our view, misleadingly generalising it.[60] Three times in the *Opera omnia*, Cujas uses a phrase to criticise the drifts of the medieval method: he condemns the doctors who "used to be verbose on easy issues, silent on difficult issues, vague on narrow issues", emphasising the verbosity of their analyses.[61] A similar expression appears in the lecture on Paulus D.39.2.18.11.[62] While this text presents no difficulty, the Bartolists developed very long commentaries, while the cujacian exegesis only occupies just over half a column. The French humanist expresses the same criticism towards the canonists in his lecture on book II of the *Liber Extra*.[63] Again, the short analysis of Cujas clearly symbolises the methodological differences between humanism and *mos italicus*. We could also mention the criticisms about Ulpianus D.41.2.12.1. Cujas denounces the "monstrous commentaries" of the Bartolists, while the legal question raised by the text can be "briefly and easily" solved.[64] According to him, his own analysis has "a bigger weight and importance than everything that [the Bartolists] say indiscriminately with thousands of lines on what Bartolus writes about this question in his *repetitio*".[65] Once more, it is noted that the criticisms focus primarily on

60 See especially J Flach, "Cujas, les glossateurs et les bartolistes" (1883) 7 *Nouvelle revue historique de droit français et étranger* 205 at 227, and in English, J Macdonell and E Manson (eds), *Great Jurists of the World* (n 4) 98.

61 ". . . est singulare hoc responsum, meo tamen judicio, in id, cum vim ejus et potestam non bene percipiunt interpretes, inani sermone imprudentia utuntur: sunt verbosi et prolixi more suo, ut solent in re facili esse multi, in difficili muti, in angusta diffusi", J Cujas, *Commentarii in libros XIX. Responsorum Papiniani*, in *Opera omnia* vol IV part 2 (1658) col 214.

62 "Qua de re quantumvis licet facillima et certissima Doctores nostri hic multa, ut solent in re facili saepe multi; in difficili, muti", J Cujas, *Commentarii in libros LXXVIII. Pauli ad edictum*, in ibid, vol V col 689.

63 "Hoc capitulo nullum est in hoc titulo explicatu difficilius; et tamen nullum est, in quod interpretes pauciora scripserint, sunt in rebus facilibus multi, in difficilobus muti", J Cujas, *Recitationes ad Decretalium Gregorii IX. libros II. III. et IV.*, in ibid, vol VI part 3 col 196.

64 "Huic §. nomen dedit jus singulare, quod in eo continetur, et immania, quae in ipsum certatim DD. post Bart. Commentaria conscripserunt, quae nos breviter et facile omnia profligabimus", J Cujas, *Commentarii in ceteros libros Digestorum*, in *Opera omnia* vol VIII (Naples, 1758) col 272.

65 "Et huic quidem quaestioni *h. §.* satis haec abundeque sufficere videntur, quae majoris certe ponderis et momenti, quam quae deblateratis versuum multis millibus in sua repetitione de hac quaestione Bartolus scripsit", ibid, col 273.

the method and, most often, on the legal point studied. As towards the Glossators, these reproaches are based on methodological advances of legal humanism compared to the Commentators.

Thus, their ignorance of Greek is so important that Cujas refuses to mention the medieval interpretation of the fragment Papinianus D.24.3.40, because his "works are not worthy these nits".[66] Thanks to the *Basilica*, he emends the text. Adding a negation disrupts the sense of the fragment and prevents distorting interpretations, which try to justify a wrong solution.

Cujas also criticises Commentators for their occasionally approximate knowledge of Latin. There is another controversial negation in the fragment Scaevola D.22.2.5. In his demonstration, Cujas shows his perfect knowledge of Latin grammar.[67] At first glance, the fragment seems difficult to understand due to a complex construction. But a good Latinist does not see any problem, he just has to rearrange the words to clarify the meaning. It is unnecessary to remove the negation as Bartolus did; Scaevola's reasoning is logical and right, only the structure of the sentence could be confusing.

Consideration for history is another break of legal humanism. For that matter, the few times the Commentators tried to include history into their analyses, they still managed to be wrong. For example, this is what Cujas notes regarding the scope of the first Novel of Justinian.[68]

66 "Quae interpretes de ejus legis sententia scripserunt, non recitabo, nec enim digna sunt opera nostra πάντα μία κόνις. Hoc tantum dico, laborasse eos in loco valde corrupto, quem Graeci nobis conservarunt: namque ex Βασιλικῶν *libris* duobus in locis sub eodem titulo Graecos ita legisse constat. Post dotem datam et nuptias contractas stipulatus est pater sine voluntate filiae, divortio facto dotem dari. Perperam igitur stipulatus est: et tamen, si filia post divortium decesserit, convalescit stipulatio. At si viva filia agat pater ex stipulatu, summovebitur exceptione, si non stipulatus est sine voluntate filiae, argumento *l. 28. §. 1. D. de procurat*", J Cujas, *Observationum et emendationum libri XXVIII*, in *Opera omnia* vol III (1758–1783) col 94.

67 "In nautica pecunia periculi pretium exigitur impleta, seu existente conditione, *l. 4. foenerator, inf. eod.* Ergo in his casibus, ut in nautica exigi debet conditione exsistente. At hic traditur, non exsistente conditione, periculi pretium esse. Bartol. negationem tollit. Dico haec prima verba esse transposita, et lego: *Conditione, quamvis non poenali exsistente. Ut sit sensus: quamvis quod recipio praeter pecuniam, non sit poena, id est, quamvis id non recipiam propter moram, nihilominus tamen id jure recipio, quasi mercedem suscepti periculi.* Exigitur pretium suscepti periculi etiamsi non pro poena exigatur, sed pro quaestu. Secundo movet dubitationem, quod nisi, ut ante emendatum est, legatur, hanc conditionem ocabit poenalem, quae non est poenalis. Nam poena est, quae ob moram infligitur. Usura proprie est foenus, quod ob quaestum instigitur nulla mora intercedente, quae currit statim ex contractu, et haec nunquam dicitur poena. at in hac lege, quod recipitur praeter pecuniam, non recipitur ob moram, sed ob usuram, et periculi mercedem. Ergo usura non est poena. Denique haec conditio est foeneratitia, non pœnalis", J Cujas, *In Digesta notae*, in *Opera omnia* vol X (Naples, 1758) col 463.

68 "Legatorum vero, aut fideicommissorum, aut libertatum praestationem nullo jure refugere possunt. Itaque horum separata ratio est, in quibus tamen ille vult idem jus servari. Et praeterea Novellae constitutiones semper sunt strictius accipiendae, certe nunquam porrigendae ac casus, quorum ratio sit diversa, ut in proposito jam satis ostendi esse diversum: quia tutelam refugio

But Jacques Cujas does not oppose the Commentators systematically. Thus, he does not hesitate to confirm their solutions against those of the Glossators. This is the case about Julianus D.19.1.24pr, which deals with the *capitis minutio* of the usufructuary of a slave who bought land. According to the *Great Gloss*, Julian refers to the *capitis deminutiones maxima* and *media*.[69] Cujas rejects this interpretation thanks to the opinion of three very different Commentators: Jacobus de Ravanis, Alberico da Rosate and Rafaello Fulgosio.[70] The text only concerns the *capitis deminutio minima*. Indeed, Julian gives to the usufructuary the action for the recovery of sums paid but not due (*condictio indebiti*), if the price has been paid after the status change. In the opposite case, the usufructuary has the purchase action (*actio empti*). But, whoever loses his freedom (*capitis deminutio maxima*) cannot act in a court anymore, and whoever loses his citizenship (*capitis deminutio media*) has neither more rights nor property. So, this fragment can only refer to the *capitis deminutio minima*, contrary to Accursius' opinion.

More surprisingly, the Commentators may also triumph over the humanists. Historiographical generalisations about humanism and Cujas collapse: for the same text, the French humanist confirms Bartolus' opinion, while he disputes Alciato's analysis. The value of this example is all the more significant as it concerns a very important field for the humanists, i.e. the correction of the texts of the *Corpus Iuris Civilis*. Cujas only writes two sentences about the *verbo illis vivis* on Scaevola D.28.2.29.6:[71] the first one approves

meo jure, meo privilegio, et jure publico fretus, legatorum, aut similium praestationem nullo jure refugio. In hunc errorem, et illum, et Bartolum, et Doctores omnes primus induxit Jacobus Belvisius summus aretalogus et commentator novellarum", J Cujas, *Commentarii in libros Quaestionum Papiniani*, in *Opera omnia* vol IV (1758–1783) col 928 at 929.

69 "*Minutus*. maxima, vel media, per quas duas finitur usufructus; ut *Instit. de usufruct. §. Finitur*", Accursius, *Corpus iuris civilis Iustinianei, cum commentariis Accursii, scholiis Contii, et D. Gothofredi lucubrationibus ad Accursium* . . . vol I (1627 rep 1966) col 1803.

70 "Sic omnino ponenda heic species est. Nam et minima capitis deminutione hoc jure amittebatur ususfructus ante constitutionem Justiniani, quae est in *l. pen. C. de usufr.* Et ita etiam Jacobus Ravennas, Fulgos. et Albericus sentiunt recte, ponendam esse speciem, reprehenso primo Accursii scholio, primaque glossa, ut loquuntur, quia nec congrua poni potest species in maxima vel media capitis deminutione. Non in maxima, quia nec condictio indebiti, nec ulla alia actio competere potest ei, qui passus est maximam capitis deminutionem, quia servus est. Non item in media capitis deminutione, quam qui passus est, cum sit peregrinus, non civis, omnia ejus bona et jura postea quaesita fiscum sequuntur, *l. 2. C. de bonis proscript* . . . ", J Cujas, *Recitationes ad Salvii Juliani libros XC. Digestorum*, in *Opera omnia* vol VI (1758–1783) col 97.

71 "Probo Bartoli sententiam, ut Scaevola parum ad id animadvertens a singulari transeat ad pluralem: quod et saepissime excidit auctoribus. Nihil hic de pronepote: quod tamen multi tentant his duntaxat verbis moti. Ait, *Post mortem, scilicet avi, nasceretur.* Alciatus emendat, *Post mortem, scilicet qui nasceretur*: quod non probo: cur enim et in *§. prox. sup.* ubi eadem penitus verba sunt, idem non emendat?", J Cujas, *Commentarius ad titulos quosdam Digestorum*, in ibid, vol I col 933.

of the grammatical remark of Bartolus, the second one rejects the emendation suggested by Alciato, who has not understood syntactic structure of the fragment.

We must therefore insist on the pragmatism of our jurist. Retaining only a few sentences of his works, historiography too often includes him in the crowd of the basically anti-Bartolist humanists. However, it is not uncommon to see Cujas share his views with the Commentators, and there is even some praise. The best example is certainly the praise of Paolo da Castro, "quo viro nemo Jurisconsultorum est peritior, nemo doctior".[72] By itself, this sentence symbolises the uniqueness of the French humanist, although its scope should not be generalised. Cujas remains usually more moderate in his compliments to the Commentators.

D. CONCLUSIONS

Finally, it appears that Jacques Cujas tried his whole life to work with discernment: while he criticised the medieval methods, he recognised the qualities of his predecessors.[73] Beyond the methodological issues, we may wonder if it is not by utilitarianism that Cujas moved away from the dogmatism of some of his contemporaries. Indeed, the support of some medieval solutions allows him to reinforce his own interpretations.

72 J Cujas, *Commentarii in libros LXXVIII. Pauli ad edictum*, in *Opera omnia* vol V (Naples, 1758) col 351.

73 A significant comparison is possible with the very interesting conclusions of D J Osler, which relativise the anti-Accursianism and anti-Bartolism of Budé, "Budaeus and Roman law" (n 12) 203 at 206.

5 Redefining *Ius* to Restore Justice: The Centrality of *Ius Gentium* in Humanist Jurisprudence

Susan Longfield Karr

A. INTRODUCTION: WHY REASSESS LEGAL HUMANISM?

"Much, perhaps, too much," in the words of Donald R Kelley, "has been written about legal humanism."[1] Yet, little, indeed, much too little, of this literature has explored conceptions of *ius gentium* (customs in common among all mankind) within humanist jurisprudence (or legal humanism) and its relation to natural law, and especially in relation to *ius* – or right – in both its subjective and objective aspects.[2] As such legal scholars, political

1 D R Kelley, *The Human Measure: Social Thought in the Western Legal Tradition* (1990) 145.

2 There is no exact English equivalent for the Roman legal term *ius*. Depending on the meaning and context within Roman law, in some cases *ius* means right (i.e. *ius* in its subjective aspect), while in others it means law (i.e. *ius* in its objective aspect), but not simply *lex*, insofar as it entails a sense of rightness, or justice, as in the right order of things or the way things ought to be. For three good accounts of the meaning of natural law, *ius*, and *ius gentium* by Roman jurists see P Stein, *Roman Law in European History* (1999), M P Zuckert, "'Bringing philosophy down from the heavens': natural right in Roman law" (1989) 51 *The Review of Politics* 70, and C A Donahue, "*Ius* in the Subjective Sense in Roman Law: Reflections on Villey and Tierney", in D Maffei (eds), *A E Cortese* (2001) 506. For an in-depth discussion of how medieval jurists, canonists and civilians, interpreted *ius*, in both its subjective and objective aspects, see especially B Tierney, *The Idea of Natural Rights: Studies on Natural Rights, Natural Law and Church Law 1150–1625*

theorists and rights scholars alike hold that Renaissance humanists, and early sixteenth-century legal humanists in particular, had nothing substantive to say about these fundamental categories, and therefore, careful attention to their works will yield little, if anything, to our understanding of the history and development of political and legal thought.

This is the case, we are told, because early humanist jurists such as Guillaume Budé (1467–1540) in France, Ulrich Zasius (1461–1536) in Germany, and Andrea Alciati (1492–1550) in France and Italy, turned away from the dominant Scholastic natural law and natural rights discourse of the late-medieval and early modern periods (wherein these categories are central), and turned instead to discussions of the cultivation of civic virtues, civic utility, and procedures for securing the common good.[3] As a consequence of their focus on civil law, they had little interest in – or patience for – abstractions such as natural law, *ius*, or *ius gentium*. Indeed, given their emphasis on civic matters, Richard Tuck concludes that humanist jurists "found it virtually impossible to talk about natural rights, and extremely difficult to talk about rights *tout court*".[4] Likewise, Brian Tierney holds that because "[h]umanist authors emphasized above all the duty to uphold the common good", they were far more concerned with the obligations of subjects and citizens than with conception of rights (natural or otherwise).[5]

James Tully pushes this characterisation one step further, stating that classical, and later Renaissance, humanism essentially "developed in opposition to the universal natural law tradition" insofar as it enabled humanists to turn their attention away from "abstract treatises on natural rights and duties"

(1997), and A Brett, *Liberty, Right, and Nature: Individual Rights in Later Scholastic Thought* (1997).

3 For detailed biographical information on Budé see L Delaruelle, *Études sur l'humanisme Français: Guillaume Budé, les origines, les débuts, les idées maîtresses* (1907), D O McNeil, *Guillaume Budé and Humanism in the Reign of Francis I* (1975), M Monheit, "Guillaume Budé, Andrea Alciato, Pierre de l'Estoile: Renaissance interpreters of Roman law" (1997) 58 *Journal of the History of Ideas* 21, J Plattard, *Guillaume Budé (1468–1540) et les origines de l'humanisme Français* (1966), D R Kelley, "The Science of Philology: Guillaume Budé Begins the Restoration of Roman Law", in D R Kelly, *Foundations of Modern Historical Scholarship: Language, Law and History in the French Renaissance* (1970) 53. For detailed biographical information on Zasius see S W Rowan, *Ulrich Zasius: A Jurist in the German Renaissance, 1461–1535* (1987), R von Stintzing, *Ulrich Zasius: Ein Beitrag zur Geschichte der Rechtswissenschaft im Zeitalter der Reformation* (1857), and H Thieme, *Kaiser Maximilian I. im Leben und in den Werken von Ulrich Zasius* (1963). For detailed biographical information on Alciati see P Viard, *Andrea Alciat; 1492–1550* (1926), R Abbondanza, "Jurisprudence: The Methodology of Andrea Alciato", in E Cochrane (ed), *The Late Italian Renaissance, 1525–1630* (1970) 77, and R Abbondanza, "La Vie et les oeuvres d'Andre Alciat", in *Pédagogues et juristes* (1963) 93.

4 R Tuck, *Natural Rights Theories: Their Origin and Development* (1979) 33.

5 Tierney, *The Idea of Natural Rights* (n 2) 252–253.

in order to establish "a concrete civic liberty in opposition to the abstract freedom of the natural lawyers".[6] Underpinning this indifference to – or even rejection of – natural rights and natural law, so the dominant narrative goes, was the humanists' inability to conceive of freedom as existing outside the confines of civil society. This is the case, Quentin Skinner contends, because "the notion of a state of nature, and the claim that this condition is one of perfect freedom, were assumptions wholly foreign to the Roman and Renaissance texts."[7]

However, that Budé, Zasius, and Alciati were concerned with civil law, civil obligations and civil society did not preclude an interest in – and direct engagement with – conceptions of man's pre-political condition or a "state of nature". Indeed, Budé, Zasius and Alciati each provided an account of the transition from man's natural condition to civil society, wherein they explored the source and moral authority of such universal categories as natural law, natural rights and natural obligations in order to provide legitimisation to and a critique of civil, political and legal authorities within civil society. In other words, for the legal humanists, just as for their predecessors, contemporaries, and those who followed, demarcating the source of and limits of authority – in civil, political and international society – required an explicit engagement with natural law, *ius* and *ius gentium*, in man's pre-political state, which – in the works of Zasius in particular – meets the criteria of what John Locke later defines as "a state of perfect freedom to order their actions, and dispose of their possessions and persons, as they think fit, *within the bounds of the law of nature*, without asking leave, or depending upon the will of any other man", nearly two centuries later.[8] Moreover, this condition of "perfect freedom" not only underlies Zasius' discussion of natural law, *ius* and *ius gentium*, but also informs – and indeed provides the broader context for – his critique of slavery, which stands in turn as a thinly veiled critique of the exercise of arbitrary power by political and legal authorities in civil society.

Nevertheless, if we turn our attention away from the history of political thought to the history of jurisprudence, we find that the latter tends to reinforce the exclusion of early sixteenth-century legal humanism from the scholarship focused on the history and development of rights, and thereby the history and development of fundamental and foundational aspects of

6 J Tully, *Public Philosophy in a New Key* (2008) vol 1, 104–105.
7 Q Skinner, *Liberty Before Liberalism* (1998) 11.
8 J Locke, *Second Treatise of Civil Government* (1689) ch 2 sec 4.

the Western legal tradition.[9] Although there is a vast accumulation of excellent scholarship that demonstrates the role of humanist jurisprudence in the development of Western, European and "national" legal histories, when historians such as Donald R Kelley, Harold Berman and John Witte focus on works by legal humanists, they too tend to concentrate on their definitions and discussions of civic rights, that is, specific privileges, advantages, or immunities formally granted to persons, groups, or corporate bodies by positive or civil laws in society, not their definitions and conceptions of right, in both its subjective and objective aspects that exists prior to – *and indeed transcends* – civil law.[10]

Even in cases when historians of legal humanism proper, such as Douglas Osler, Ian Maclean and Stephen Rowan, or early modern scholars more generally such as John Headley, Annabel Brett and Kathleen Davies, acknowledge that some humanist jurists were in fact interested in and writing about these issues, they do not situate nor examine the implications of these discussions within the broader context of the development of the natural law and natural rights tradition of thought, politics and jurisprudence.[11] As such,

9 Compare, for example, Kelley, *Foundations of Modern Scholarship* (n 3), D R Kelley, "Civil Science in the Renaissance: The Problem of Interpretation", in A Pagden (ed), *The Languages of Political Theory in Early-Modern Europe* (1987) 57, G Kisch, *Erasmus und die Jurisprudenz seiner Zeit: Studien zum humanistischen Rechtsdenken* (1960), D Maffei, *Gli inizi dell'umanesimo giuridico* (1956), R J Schoeck, "Humanism and Jurisprudence", in A Rabil Jr (ed), *Renaissance Humanism: Foundations, Forms, and Legacy* (1988) 310, and H E Troje, *Humanistische Jurisprudenz: Studien zur europäischen Rechtswissenschaft unter dem Einfluss des Humanismus* (1993), with M B Crowe, *The Changing Profile of the Natural Law* (1977), A P d'Entrèves, *Natural Law: An Introduction to Legal Philosophy* (1972), J Finnis, *Natural Law and Natural Rights* (1980), O F von Gierke, E Troeltsch and E Barker, *Natural Law and the Theory of Society, 1500 to 1800* (2001), F Oakley, *Natural Law, Laws of Nature, Natural Rights: Continuity and Discontinuity in the History of Ideas* (2005), M Villey, *Le droit et les droits de l'homme* (1983), M Zuckert, *Natural Rights and the New Republicanism* (1994), Tuck, *Natural Rights Theories* (n 4), Tierney, *The Idea of Natural Rights* (n 2), Q Skinner, *The Foundations of Modern Political Thought* (1978), J G A Pocock, *The Machiavellian Moment: Florentine Political Thought and the Atlantic Republican Tradition* (2003), K Haakonssen, *Natural Law and Moral Philosophy: From Grotius to the Scottish Enlightenment* (1996), Brett, *Liberty, Right, and Nature* (n 2), J Witte Jr, *The Reformation of Rights: Law, Religion, and Human Rights in Early Modern Calvinism* (2007) and J M Headley, *The Europeanization of the World: On the Origins of Human Rights and Democracy* (2008).

10 H J Berman, *Law and Revolution I: The Formation of the Western Legal Tradition* (1983), H J Berman, *Law and Revolution II: The Impact of the Protestant Reformation on the Western Legal Tradition* (2004), A Padoa Schioppa (ed), *Legislation and Justice* (1997), M Bellomo, *The Common Legal Past of Europe* (1995), F Wieacker, *A History of Private Law in Europe with Particular Reference to Germany* (1995), M P Gilmore, *Argument from Roman Law in Political Thought, 1200–1600* (1967), P Vinogradoff, *Roman Law in Medieval Europe*, 2nd edn (1929) and P Koschaker, *Europa und Das Römische Recht* (1953).

11 Brett, *Liberty, Right, Nature* (n 2), A Brett, *Changes of State: Nature and the Limits of the City in Early Modern Natural Law* (2011), K Davies, *Periodization and Sovereignty: How*

early humanist jurists continue to be regarded as insignificant to – and even standing outside – the history and development of an otherwise continuous (sometimes conservative, sometimes progressive) tradition of thought in the West – a tradition that continues to inform contemporary political and legal thought and practice, locally and globally, to this day.

Thus, based on the dominant literature one might well agree that legal humanists had nothing substantive to say about such fundamental categories of political theory and jurisprudence as natural law, *ius* and *ius gentium*. However, given that jurisprudence is fundamentally concerned with – and permeated by – discussions of the source of political and legal authority as well as its limits, it is reasonable to question the dominant literature, and thereby reassess the role of legal humanism in the history and development of political and legal thought focused on natural law, *ius* and *ius gentium*.

B. ULRICH ZASIUS

Turning to the works of Zasius in particular, within his treatises, lectures and orations concerning the foundational principles of law, justice and right, he sets forth an interpretation of jurisprudence wherein a fundamental aspect of legitimate legal and political authority is the recognition of universal rights and obligations within civil society. As such, he held that it is not only necessary for civil laws to protect and enforce universal rights and obligations, but that it was also necessary, and indeed imperative, that those who taught law in the universities, and those who practised, reformed and approved laws beyond them, properly understood the underlying relationship between justice and right (*iustitia et ius*) as expressed in all types of law – natural, customary and civil – over time. Exploring this relationship between justice and right, Zasius turned his attention to the most fundamental definitions of law within the Roman Digest, definitions that had come to structure the interpretations of traditional and Scholastic jurisprudence since its re-discovery in the latter part of the eleventh century. In so doing, Zasius directly engages with customary rights and obligations that exist prior to and extend beyond civil society in the face of the creation of new forms – and the expansion of older forms – of legal and political authority in the early sixteenth century.

Ideas of Feudalism and Secularization Govern the Politics of Time (2008), J M Headley, *The Europeanization of the World* (2008), I Maclean, *Interpretation and Meaning in the Renaissance: The Case of Law* (1992), D J Osler, "Images of legal humanism" (2001) 9 *Surfaces* 101, D J Osler, "The myth of European legal history" (1997) 16 *Rechtshistorisches Journal* 393 and Rowan, *Ulrich Zasius* (n 3).

Zasius was considered by his contemporaries to be one of the greatest German jurists and one of the most brilliant humanists of his time. After being promoted to *Juris Doctor*[12] at the University of Freiburg at the age of 40, Zasius was appointed as a Lecturer of Rhetoric and Poetry at Freiburg in 1500, and later, in 1506, as an Ordinary Professor of Civil Law. In his capacity as law professor, he delivered a daily lecture on the *Corpus Iuris Civilis*, which served as the centrepiece of the academic day.[13] Already well known for his teaching of rhetoric and poetry, his daily lectures on the *Corpus* were well attended by students from across the university, not simply those matriculating in law. As such, Zasius' recitations were aimed at multiple audiences – with different sets of interest and concerns – at once: those studying Roman law informally so as to explore the philosophy and theories that structure and underlie civil law more generally, and those formally studying Roman law so as to draw on the specific principles and procedures found within it as lawyers. Whether studying Roman law informally or formally, after completing their studies with Zasius, many of his students took up positions as jurists, professors, diplomats, bureaucrats and advisers to cities, dukes, princes and electors, and, as such, would play an important administrative role in the on-going process of folding and transforming various customary traditions (written and unwritten) into a single rationalised written legal "tradition", or rule of law, over the course of the sixteenth century, a process accelerated by Maximilian I in 1495 when he called for a systematic reform of legal, economic, social and political structures across the Empire. Beyond his teaching, Zasius continued to practise law, to serve as a legal councillor for the city, and in 1508 he became an imperial councillor to Maximilian I. Moreover, he was well known throughout Germany for his work on the Freiburg *Code*, a model for many other sixteenth-century cities and principalities engaged in the process of codification.[14] Finally, Zasius was known throughout Europe for his positions on controversial legal

12 Zasius only took this degree in Roman law, unlike most of his contemporaries and his students who took the degree of *Juris Utriusque Doctor*, that is in Roman and canon law.

13 For the definitive biography on Zasius see Rowan, *Ulrich Zasius* (n 3).

14 U Zasius, *Neue Stadtrechte und Statuten der Stadt Freiburg im Breisgau* [1520] (1968) and T von Liebenau, *Der Humanist Ulrich Zasius als Stadtschreiber von Baden im Aargau* (1898). For a detailed discussion of this as well as more in-depth biographical information on Zasius see H J Knoche, *Ulrich Zasius und das Freiburger Stadtrecht von 1520* (1957), L A Ricker, *Freiburg: Aus der Geschichte einer Stadt* (1964), Rowan, *Ulrich Zasius* (n 3), Von Stintzing, *Ulrich Zasius* (n 3) and Thieme, *Kaiser Maximilian I.* (n 3). For a discussion of additional works by Zasius, see P G Schmidt, *Humanismus im deutschen Südwesten: biographische Profile* (1993), S W Rowan, *The German Works of Ulrich Zasius* (1977) and U Zasius, *Von Wahrer und Falscher Jurisprudenz: Aus Schriften, Reden, und Briefen, 1507 bis 1526* (1948).

issues,[15] his orations, his lectures, and his published treatises on Roman law – all of which were part of the "canon" of legal thought well into the modern era, and all of which, like his lectures, addressed many audiences at once.

His influence on local, regional, imperial and European legal thought was, in short, expansive, but it was not without contradiction. For example, at the same time that Zasius participated in the extension of the legal, political and economic power of the city of Freiburg over its countryside in writing the *Code*, he rejected the inverse, namely, the expansion of the emperor's power over legal, political and economic structures within Freiburg itself.[16] Further, while using his special position as city councillor to Freiburg and his broader connections with political authorities to secure his position in the university, he also demanded that he be treated as an equal by the rest of the faculty, going so far as to sue them for excluding him from faculty meetings. As a councillor, he extolled the importance of procedures and policies to administer and govern municipal affairs "by the book", while keeping his own "secret book" of the deeds of others to draw on if and when it would suit his own advantage.[17] In short, he wielded personal influence and power at the same time as he criticised others for doing so, and he augmented authority often in the same breadth that he attempted to limit it.

In terms of his legal thought, at the same time as he forcefully attacked the interpretations of Accursius (1182–1260), Bartolus (1313–1357) and Baldus (1327–1400) as well as those who followed them, he effectively legitimised their authority by arriving at some of the same conclusions on a specific point of law, even as he employed different methods.[18] He arrived at the

15 See U Zasius, *Questiones de parvulis Iudaeorum baptisandis* (1508) and *Apologetica defensio contra Ioanne[m] Eckium theologum, super eo quod olim tractauerat, quo loco fides non esset hosti feruanda. Videbis lector Eckium iura ciuilia non perspecte intellexisse. Defensa magni Erasmi assertio, quam in elegantiss. Scholijs super septimo Matthei capite docuit. Experiere lector, quàm omnino periculi plenum sit, in alienam excurrere professionem* (1519).

16 See L A Ricker, *Freiburg: Aus der Geschichte einer Stadt* (1982), Rowan, *Ulrich Zasius* (n 3) and T Scott, *Freiburg and Breisgau: Town-Country Relations in the Age of the Reformation and Peasants' Wars* (1986).

17 Rowan, *Ulrich Zasius* (n 3).

18 For a discussion of Bartolus' and Baldus' legal and political thought and their influence on later jurists – canonists and civilians – see Berman, *Law and Revolution* (n 10), F Maiolo, *Medieval Sovereignty: Marsilius of Padua and Bartolus of Saxoferrato* (2007), G Kisch, *Bartolus und Basel* (1960), C Fasolt, *Limits of History* (2004), Gilmore, *Argument from Roman Law* (n 10) and J Canning, *The Political Thought of Baldus de Ubaldis* (1987). For a discussion of the origins and development of the Scholastic methods see J W Baldwin, *The Scholastic Culture of the Middle Ages, 1000–1300* (1971), N W Gilbert, *Renaissance Concepts of Method* (1960), A S McGrade (ed), *The Cambridge Companion to Medieval Philosophy* (2003), N Kretzmann, A Kenny and J Pinborg (eds), *The Cambridge History of Later Medieval Philosophy: From the Rediscovery*

same conclusion, in part, because rather than rejecting traditional jurisprudence wholesale, Zasius set out to correct misinterpretations within it, to bring jurisprudence and thereby laws back into accordance with justice.[19] In order to correct errors within legal interpretation, rather than overturn it, required a recognition of what was correct as much as it required a knowledge of how and where Scholastic jurists went astray (as he saw it). In order to restore and repair aspects of civil law and civil jurisprudence that needed to be reformed, and to demonstrate how and where it was correct, Zasius combined aspects of the Scholastic and humanist methods in his teaching and interpretation of Roman law. He did so because he held that Roman law reflected aspects of universal jurisprudence.

Perhaps the most notable method that Zasius adopted from Scholastic jurists was the reconciliation – to some extent – of different kinds of law into a single system. Placing Zasius in the context of legal reform, this is not surprising. After all, he and other legal humanists were directly engaged in this process, whether in their capacity as advisers, lawyers, or professors within law faculties. However, Zasius did not attempt to rationalise or systematise the order of the laws, and thereby Law itself, through methods of logical deduction or reconciliation as many of the Scholastic jurists had done. Instead, Zasius historicised the foundational moral principles that he observed ordering the law. These were the foundational principles of moral philosophy: justice and right.[20] Once he defined these basic principles – which he did in the same ways as his legal humanist contemporaries, by using comparative, philological and historical methods – he reconstructed the relationship between natural law, *ius gentium* and civil law according to how these principles came to be expressed in law from its origins. By historicising law and its principles, by treating the law as something that has changed over time, sometimes in accordance with justice and sometimes departing from it, Zasius effectively questioned the formalism of legal interpretation (focused on what the law is) by grounding his interpretations in natural jurisprudence (focusing on what the law should be).

While the historicisation of the law is characteristic of humanist jurisprudence more generally, the historicisation of the moral principles that

of Aristotle to the Disintegration of Scholasticism, 1100–1600 (1982) and L Daston and K Park (eds), *The Cambridge History of Science: Volume 3, Early Modern Science* (2006).

19 S Longfield Karr, *Nature, Self, and History in the Works of Guillaume Budé, Andrea Alciati, and Ulrich Zasius: A Study of the Role of Legal Humanism in Western Natural Law* (2008).

20 U Zasius, "*De iustitia et iure*, lecturae. Udalrici Zasii iureconsulti clarissimi in titulos aliquot digesti veteris commentaria," in *Opera Omnia* (1964 repr), cols 241–269.

underlie it distinguishes Zasius' interpretations. For him the ordering principles of law – *all laws* – consist of self-evident truths (natural law) and principles learned from experience (*ius gentium*). Over time, man comes to understand how the precepts of natural law are embodied in *ius gentium* by instruction as well as by the observation of customs shared among and between peoples, which provides a history not only of the progress of life, but also explains how and why in some cases customs and laws "miss the mark of justice".[21] As such, careful attention to *ius gentium* offers an opportunity to examine the history – and observe the development – of civil society, as well as a means to demonstrate when and how civil laws have been changed for worse and for better over time. Only by careful attention to these changes will it be possible for lawyers and jurists to reform law, and thereby restore justice, rather than continue to perpetuate old or introduce new errors. To understand *ius gentium*, however, requires more than the study of customs and laws over time; it also requires an understanding of universal jurisprudence and thereby justice.

To establish the foundations of universal jurisprudence, it is no surprise that Zasius first turns to natural law, a set of moral precepts that all men know on account of inherent reason. Within his discussion of natural law, he arrives at a definition of *ius gentium*, as customs in common among all mankind, which enables him to provide an explanation for the origins of civil society, and the civil laws that govern it, as well as an account of universal rights and obligations that just civil laws cannot diminish or abrogate, and indeed, must recognise, protect and vindicate in civil society. He provides a critique, in other words, of arbitrary and unlimited authority created by civil law and institutions by turning back to man's natural condition, that is, before civil societies emerged in the first place. In providing his account – or historical narrative – of man's transition from mutual company to civil society, he begins by focusing on innate precepts of preservation and reproduction and, later, moves to a consideration of how man learns additional precepts of natural law through his experience, his observations, as well as through instruction from others (parents, extended family, and the community at large). Within this account, he lays out how natural law precepts came to be expressed in *ius gentium*. To do this Zasius works on two historically subsequent levels. First, he provides an account as to how man comes to structure relations of mutual company prior to civil society; and, second, he provides an explanation as to how and why those same customs

21 Zasius, *De iustitia et Iure* (n 20), lecture, col 265.

and conventions continue to structure relations within civil societies as well as between them. Central to each is an understanding of *ius gentium* as a quality of natural law and as a source of universal rights and obligations, an interpretation that departs fundamentally from traditional jurisprudence at its very foundations.[22]

C. JUSTICE, *IUS*, NATURAL LAW AND *IUS GENTIUM*

Justice, as set out in the first lines of the Roman Digest, is defined in relation to *ius*, as the art of what is good and what is fair.[23] Zasius (like Budé before him) interprets this to mean that in order for law to be just it must meet the criteria of good *and* fair, not simply one or the other.[24] Precisely because Accursius argued that in order for a law to be just it had to be either good or fair, Zasius and his legal humanist contemporaries held that he had committed a grievous error.[25] In Zasius' estimation – as well as Budé and Alciati's – this misunderstanding of such a foundational and fundamental term as *ius* – a term that lies at the heart of Roman and thereby universal jurisprudence – by Accursius and those who followed him stood at the basis of corruptions within civil laws and civil jurisprudence. Thus to begin to restore justice to the latter, required restoring the definition and understanding of the former. Only by restoring the meaning of *ius* (and thereby the understanding) to its original – as the art of what is good and fair, conjoined – would it be possible to reform unjust laws and corrupt institutions within civil society. To effect the latter, however, required more than a rejection of Accursius' definition; it also required a rejection of the reasoning, and thereby method, used to rationalise the split between equity and good in his definition.

To explain this split between good and fair in the law, Accursius invoked an analogy: he argued that just as one could discern the image of the mother through the image of the daughter so too one could one discern justice

22 Zasius, *De iustitia et iure* (n 20), lecture, cols 250–251.

23 D.1.1.1pr.

24 Zasius, *De iustitia et iure* (n 20), *Praefatio*, col 15. This fundamental correction to the *Gloss* by Zasius was based on Budé's assertion that Accursius "separated equity and good in an improper and ignorant fashion". See Budé, *Annotationes* (1508), fol II. Although Alciati also rejected Accursius' understanding of *ius*, he did so implicitly. That is, rather than begin his lecture on the Digest by arguing directly against the Scholastic jurists, Alciati shared Budé's and Zasius' interpretation of *ius* precisely because it was the definition provided in the Digest itself.

25 Accursius, *Digestum vetus sive pandectarum iuris civilis totus primus ex pandectis Florentinis, quae olim Pisanae dicebantur, quod eius fieri potuit, repraesenatus. Commentariis Accursi, & multorum insuper aliorum tam veterum quam neotericorum iurisconsultorum scholiis atque observationibus illustratus* (1566 repr), fol II.

through law.[26] This was possible because any law that met the criteria of being either good or fair had at least a glimmer of justice within it. Zasius rejects Accursius on this point wholesale. Not simply because he held that Accursius misunderstood *ius*, but also because he misunderstood the nature of the relation between *ius* and justice. Indeed, Zasius dismisses Accursius' analogy on the basis that the image of the mother and the image of the daughter are two separate, albeit related, things, whereas justice and *ius* are not: they are one.

Ius then is not simply an aspect of justice it *is* justice: "justice is virtue; however *ius* is the accomplishment of this virtue".[27] Furthermore, according to Zasius, "*ius* is a habit of virtue: since, although it is not in deeds, it is nevertheless sufficient that it has regard to rectitude in habit",[28] therefore just as "justice exists in the uprightness of mind, *ius* comes closer to regulating the activities of men".[29] Although initially formless, justice is given form through actions – "just as a shoe is always in leather, form is always in the substance, thus *ius* was always in justice according to this condition".[30] And further it is justice in action: "Justice is the habit of virtues in abstract form: *ius* is uprightness of action in concrete form."[31]

Moreover, *ius* is not only justice in action, it is also a fundamental attribute of natural law and *ius gentium*. Thus, separating *ius* and justice, arguing that one descended from the other, not only splits *ius* and *iustitia* into two separate – albeit related – things, it also implies that natural law and *ius gentium* are not only separate from *ius*, but also from one another. Yet, for Zasius, they are all different expressions of the same thing: justice. In his *De iustitia et iure* lecture, Zasius engages in a point-by-point interpretation as to the substance of natural law and its relation to *ius* in its objective aspect, that is, justice, which he then follows with an interpretation of how the precepts of natural law are related to one another. In the process, he not only asserts that that the fourth quality of natural law is *ius gentium*, but also suggests that *ius gentium* is related directly to *ius* in its subjective aspect. The pairing, first of natural law and *ius gentium*, and then of *ius gentium* and *ius*, is drawn out more directly – and starkly – by Zasius in his 1518 *Preface* for his *Lucubrationes* or "night musings" written for a broader audience than

26 Zasius, *De iustitia et iure* (n 20), lecture, col 243.
27 Zasius, *De iustitia et iure* (n 20), *Praefatio*, col 15.
28 Ibid, col 14.
29 Ibid.
30 Zasius, *De iustitia et iure* (n 20), lecture, cols 243–244.
31 Zasius, *De iustitia et iure* (n 20), *Praefatio*, col 14.

his lecture.[32] Within his *Lucubrationes* Zasius includes a critique of the traditional understanding of the relation between *ius gentium* and slavery, as well as the relation between slavery and civil laws, which has broader implications for legitimate and illegitimate exercises of authority by rulers in civic society. Pairing together his lecture and his preface, the implications of his discussion become clear, especially in relation to *ius gentium* serving as a criterion for reforming civil institutions, civil laws, and limiting political authority. In order for *ius gentium* to serve as such a criterion, however, Zasius had to establish why it held moral and historical authority.

Zasius opens his 1518 *Preface* with a concise account of the relation between eternal and natural law. In defining – and connecting – the two, Zasius repeats a well-worn tradition. For example, his explanation that natural law extends from external law, a law that directs the impulses and instincts of both animals and man, is in perfect agreement with that held by both Scholastic jurists and theologians. Likewise, that "the kind of natural law that applies to humans participates more truly in the eternal law, namely by intellect and reason"[33] than the natural law that animals follow is also commonplace. Further, his explanation that nothing is "a precept or a rule of right reason . . . unless it is supported by the eternal law"[34] is also typical. However, when Zasius turns his attention away from a description of how eternal law and natural law are related to an explanation of how natural law and *ius gentium* are connected, he departs substantially from the definitions and interpretations of traditional jurisprudence.

Although man knows, according to Zasius, the principles of natural law through reason, it is only through one's interactions with others – i.e. social life – that man is able to understand the "original and common principles" of natural law, or more specifically, the fourth quality of natural law which is *ius gentium*.[35] The difference between knowing what is right and understanding *why* something is right extends from observing the consequences of actions over time, consequences that are observable as a result of living in mutual company (immediate and extended family, with neighbours, and within a broader community). It is precisely because man knows the precepts of natural law innately, but comes to understand them as a result of experience, that *ius gentium* cannot be entirely distinguished from natural law. And thus, according to Zasius:

32 U Zasius, *Lucubrationes*, Preface (1518) 1–3.
33 Ibid, 1.
34 Ibid.
35 Zasius, *De iustitia et iure* (n 20), lecture, col 251.

> From this we conclude, [that] the natural *lex*, or natural *ius*, which is common to all men, is not different in kind from *ius gentium*, but only by a certain adventitious condition. For both *ius gentium* and natural law originate in the first common principles of operative reason, save only that the law of nature proceeds simply and absolutely, but *ius gentium* has come forth through the assistance of discourse and customs.[36]

As Zasius explains in his *De iustitia et iure*, lecture, as it proceeds:

> But not simply through a certain discourse, and it proceeds from accepted customs of peoples: and such operative or practical reasoning produces *ius gentium*, which is not distinct from natural law in its very substance, but in the manner it is produced . . . for this law [*ius gentium*] is produced with a certain kind of discourse, and with a discourse concerning custom [*mores*] concerning those things that happen commonly.[37]

Thus "just as customary practice is not distinguished from various customs and uses, then the law of nature, which is *ius gentium*, should not be distinguished [either]."[38] To emphasise this fundamental break with traditional jurisprudence, Zasius simply asserts that those who do not recognise "the common origin and substance of natural law and *ius gentium* are in error".[39]

Not only has Zasius departed from Accursius, Bartolus and Baldus here, he has also departed from the Romans.[40] By arguing that natural law and *ius gentium* are two expressions of the same thing, Zasius effectively reinterpreted Roman law and in so doing imparted moral authority to *ius gentium* by placing it in direct relation to – and indeed arguing it is an expression of – natural law, which in turn stands as direct expression of justice. Through this reinterpretation the moral authority of *ius gentium*, and its importance, is expanded. For example, if natural law can be used to hold civil laws and civil authorities accountable to a higher criterion justice, and if *ius gentium* is an expression of natural law, then *ius gentium* can likewise be used to hold civil law accountable to justice. Yet, no matter how closely natural law and *ius gentium* are related, some customs and conventions that man learns though his observations, instruction or experiences with others might appear, at first glance, to be in fundamental contradiction with the precepts of natural law, and thereby justice. To address this seeming contradiction, Zasius turns to a well-worn distinction within traditional jurisprudence between primary and secondary *ius gentium*, but explains it through the

36 Zasius, *Lucubrationes* (n 32), Preface, 2.
37 Zasius, *De iustitia et iure* (n 20), lecture, col 250.
38 Zasius, *Lucubrationes* (n 32), Preface, 2.
39 Zasius, *De iustitia et iure* (n 20), lecture, col 250 and *Lucubrationes* (n 32), Preface, 2.
40 Stein, *Roman law* (n 2).

lens of his reinterpretation of *ius gentium* as the fourth quality of natural law.[41]

For Zasius primary *ius gentium* is historically prior to secondary *ius gentium*, in the sense that primary *ius gentium* moderates and structures interactions within communities before the advent of civil society governed by civil laws, whereas secondary *ius gentium* moderates and structures interactions between civil societies under different bodies of civil law. Primary *ius gentium* is also morally superior to secondary *ius gentium*. It guides man's actions toward the pursuit of a universal common good, whereas secondary *ius gentium* reflects man's pursuit of his own good and as such includes things that are "either necessary or useful for the depraved desires of men".[42] As absolutely good, customs extending from primary *ius gentium* include those "that are not inherently bad, such as the sanctity of ambassadors, so that legates may be sacred [inviolate], the protections of guests, contracts, commerce, obligations, property, what is 'mine and thine'".[43] Neither absolutely good nor absolutely bad, the customs that fall under secondary *ius gentium* include boundaries, territories and kingship as well as war, captivity and slavery.[44] While slavery, in particular, may appear to be a direct violation of natural law, Zasius (taking a traditional position here) holds that it is not. It is, rather, a lesser evil in the sense that "Slavery is not good absolutely, but slavery was invented so that captives would not be killed."[45] Further, the customs of primary and secondary *ius gentium* are linked together at their origins, as secondary *ius gentium* also extends from the distinction between "mine and thine". This distinction that demarcates property, boundaries and territories, moreover, extends from natural law and is thereby just. Thus, just as justice and *ius* as well as natural law and *ius gentium* are inherently linked as different expressions of the same thing, so too are primary and secondary *ius gentium*.

All communities and civil societies share conventions and customs of primary and secondary *ius gentium* in common; *ius gentium* stands at the very origins of mutual company and as a result becomes expressed by man's actions over time, including the creation of and living in accordance with civil laws. Thus, careful attention to *ius gentium* enables a properly trained lawyer to observe changes in civil laws over time, for worse and for better,

41 Zasius, *De iustitia et iure* (n 20), lecture, col 252.
42 Zasius, *Lucubrationes* (n 32), Preface, 1–2.
43 Zasius, *De iustitia et iure* (n 20), lecture, cols 250–251.
44 Ibid, 251.
45 Ibid.

because "they [customs and uses] vary according to the progress of life".[46] Again, it is possible for lawyers and jurists to study this "progress of life" because the customs and conventions of *ius gentium*, primary and secondary, are the substance from which civil laws are made. As such, studying the history and development of civil laws and institutions enables one to see how and to what extent they embody or depart from principles that underlie *ius gentium*, and thereby depart from natural law, *ius* and justice.

For example, by studying the entire *Corpus* of Roman law one is able to "observe" the principles that underlie and are encompassed by Roman civil law as a whole. The principles that structure and illuminate the universal jurisprudence within the *Corpus* stand as expressions of primary *ius gentium* and thus they reflect natural law. If one steps back, however, and explores the laws that make up the *Corpus* historically and comparatively it becomes clear that it is not a cohesive or normative body of law. Attention to the disparities between laws within the *Corpus* reveals the "progress of life", man's pursuit of justice over time for worse and for better. Moreover, looking beyond a single community, if one compared the *Corpus* of Roman law with collections of laws from within the Holy Roman Empire, it is possible to observe the principles they share in common. It is also possible, through a comparative history of the development of both to observe how, why and when they diverge from one another. Careful attention to what is shared and what is not, as well as how laws change over time within Rome as well as within the Holy Roman Empire, enables one to see that although there are significant differences within and between bodies of law, the principles that underlie Law as whole – justice and right – are common among all mankind across time and space.

By directing his students and contemporaries to approach the study and interpretation of civil law this way, Zasius offers an interpretation by which his own argument that civil laws emerge from *ius gentium* can be confirmed by the methods and sources associated with the *studia humanitatis*, namely the turn to historical sources and placing them in comparison to observe change over time as well as an emphasis on the fundamental principles the are embodied and expressed by moral philosophy. That is, the methods of interpretation and the interpretation itself stand in a mutually complementary and dependent relation by which Zasius is not only able to ground *ius gentium* in history (existing prior to civil society, over the course of society's development, as well as over the course of the relation between societies),

46 Zasius, *Lucubrationes* (n 32), Preface, 2.

but to argue for its moral authority (linking it directly to natural law, justice and *ius*). His interpretations and the methods that shape them, in other words, not only infuse *ius gentium* with moral authority, they also infuse *ius gentium* with historical authority. Thus, one who understands the relations between the laws, historically and morally, can use *ius gentium* to legitimise and critique broader legal, economic and political reforms as well as to cleanse specific civil laws of errors and corruptions.

D. IUS GENTIUM, RIGHTS, OBLIGATIONS AND CIVIL LAWS

Initially turning to the substance of *ius gentium*, Zasius simply states: "Deduce that that rule, that it is permitted to repel force with force, is found even within animals, and thus has been placed in the first position of natural law . . . and thus that rule is part of natural law and *ius gentium*."[47] This rule – this right to repel force with force – exists on the most basic, foundational and universal level of natural law among men and animals. But, Zasius argues, because man is subject to his self-interest and desires, not all exercises of this right (subjective *ius*) to repel force may be defensive. Moreover, man is prone to act without moderation or considerations of justice. Hence it is difficult to determine whether or not one is exercising force as a matter of defence (justly) or as a matter of offence (unjustly). Complicating matters further, if one exercises force to repel an injury, even if one is justified in doing so, this does not preclude the use of force by another in response, which could soon broaden to include families and neighbours embroiled in cascading violence. Therefore, a judge, a neutral party, is necessary to determine the justness of the exercise of force among and between men, "For the mind having become greatly excited [as a result of injury or insult] and inflamed, does not recognize the law: which is why this entire matter ought to be placed into the judgment of a good man, that is, a just judge."[48] Only a just judge can affect a balance between subjective *ius* (force) and objective *ius* (justice) between those in conflict, as only a third party can make determinations as to whether one's exercise of *ius* against another was justified.

To state that a good man (prior to civil society) or a just judge (in civil society) can make these determinations is one thing; to show why and on

47 Zasius, *De iustitia et iure* (n 20), lecture, col 253. The crucial part of the Digest that Zasius is referring to here is D.43.16.1.27 wherein it states: "Cassius writes that it is permissible to repel force by force, and this right is conferred by nature. From this it appears, he says, that arms may be repelled by arms."

48 Ibid, col 253.

what basis they can do so is quite another. In order to be able to discern a just action from an unjust one, one must understand how and in what ways the right to repel force with force can be deemed morally legitimate. Zasius offers some help by setting forth a number of scenarios in which one would be justified in using force, not only to protect his own life from threat, but also his property, his family, his friends, and even his associates.[49] Linked to this quick succession of morally legitimate uses of violence, Zasius discusses universal obligations that all men share in common, including the obligation (and thereby corresponding right) to come to the aid of another in danger as "naturally it matters that a man is of benefit to a man."[50]

Additional obligations that all men share in common include the fear of God and obedience to one's father.[51] These obligations exist from man's origins and as such pre-date civil laws created to enforce these behaviours in civil society. The obligations associated with promise keeping among men are also universal, and indeed are what make social and civil company possible. Defending one's *patria* or fatherland is also an obligation that all men have.[52] Although it is universally shared it is not timeless, that is, it emerges as a result of the introduction of territorial boundaries and kingship and thus is coextensive with civil society from its creation – as this is an obligation to not only obey one's ruler, but also to defend one's community from external threats. In each case, the right to meet force with force as well as the obligation to come to another's aid – whether it be on the level of the family or on the level of the community or territorial state – are grounded in natural law, are expressed through man's actions, and are reflected in and by *ius gentium*.

Zasius links these universal rights and obligations as essentially two sides of the same coin when he connects the first rule of *ius gentium*, that it is permissible to meet force with force to repel an injury, with an obligation to not resist just, or morally legitimate, punishment. He does not, however, equate one's right to defence to a corresponding right to punish, but rather separates them. In other words, might does not make right for Zasius, nor is unrestrained might just. It is only possible to punish another if "the punishment is not more severe, more aggressive, than what is good and what is fair".[53]

Here, Zasius has effectively split one's right to self-preservation and the

49 Ibid, col 254.
50 Ibid.
51 Ibid.
52 Ibid.
53 Ibid.

power of punishment in such a way as to account for the moral authority of and necessity for a good man or a just judge to make determinations of right (objective and subjective). Further, he also argues that man has an obligation to accept justice, the decision of a good man and a just judge: "If I am attacked justly, it is not permitted to resist."[54] Good men (prior to civil society) and just judges (in civil society), then, not only determine if an exercise of force is legitimate, they also exercise legitimate force when necessary. In both cases, defensive and punitive, it is the limit placed on violence and injury that restores justice. This is central: as only necessary and limited force is in accordance with *ius gentium*, and thereby natural law. This limit on the force that one can exercise against and over another permeates Zasius' discussion of slavery, a discussion that has significant implications for his call for reform, when placed into the broader context of state formation and the crisis of authority that followed the introduction of new civil laws that attempted to diminish and abrogate customary practices, rights and institutions across Germany.

Throughout the early sixteenth century, serfdom intensified in southwest Germany in particular. In response to agrarian crisis, temporal authorities (free cities, manorial lords, regional lords and princes) as well as ecclesiastical authorities reasserted, expanded and centralised their power over the countryside and even over wage-labourers within cities.[55] These authorities instituted restrictions on the freedom of movement and marriage of peasants, curtailed the use of common arable lands and woodlands, and allowed an increase in certain fees and work requirements of the peasants and wage-labourers. These measures resulted in increased resistance – legal and violent. This violent resistance culminated in many respects with the Peasants' Wars of 1524/1525 across Germany. Although there were several instances of rebellion, revolt and outright war by peasants, the urban poor, and even the nobility throughout Germany prior to those associated with the Reformation, those that erupted in the mid-1520s were particularly significant to Zasius.[56] He witnessed the peasants' revolt in Freiburg, which not only led to the cancellation of his lectures, but also posed a significant threat

54 Ibid.

55 For a detailed discussion of how peasants reacted to these changes see P Blickle, *Von der Leibeigenschaft zu den Menschenrechten: eine Geschichte der Freiheit in Deutschland* (2003).

56 See P Blickle, *The Revolution of 1525: The German Peasants' War from a New Perspective* (1981) and P Blickle, *Resistance, Representation, and Community* (1997), T Scott, "Peasant revolts in early modern Germany" (1985) 28 *The Historical Journal* 455 and Scott, *Freiburg and Breisgau: Town-Country Relations in the Age of the Reformation and Peasants' Wars* (n 16).

to his own security: Zasius watched from the second storey of his house as it was being hit by cannon shot.[57]

To what extent Zasius was arguing on behalf of the peasants or the burgers against the clergy, patricians and lords is not as abundantly clear in his works. But it is clear that he was defending customary rights and obligations that extended directly from *ius gentium* that were being changed, corrupted and diminished through the creation of new civil laws. It is in this context that Zasius' discussion of slavery takes on a deeper significance, not only in relation to his departure from Scholastic jurisprudence but also in relation to political and legal authorities within the Empire. Although Zasius uses the term *servus* and follows the definitions of slavery in the Digest, in order to refute Bartolus' interpretation of slavery, he also uses the term *homines proprii*, which is the Latin equivalent of the German *Eigenleute*; *Eigenmenschen*; or *Leibeigene*, or, in other words, unfree peasants or serfs.[58] Indeed, he follows Tacitus' assertion that slavery as the Romans practised it never existed in Germany,[59] indicating that his concern with the Roman category of slavery, just as his discussion of *ius gentium*, natural law and *ius*, goes deeper than pointing out the errors of his Scholastic predecessors.

By placing the definitions of slavery, an institution that extends from secondary *ius gentium*, within the first pages of the Digest, in comparison with those found within Scholastic jurisprudence, especially the opinions of Bartolus, Zasius attempts to demonstrate that although the institution of slavery is common, forms of it change over time and space.[60] Why and to what extent slavery and servitude change over time can be observed by comparing the civil laws and civil practices in different societies throughout history. Indeed, in the case of Germany, a direct correspondence between the Roman legal category of slave and the German unfree peasant, as well as the slaves depicted in select Ancient Greek, Roman and Hebraic texts (below), could not be made. However, there is a category of persons within Roman law that ancient slaves and German unfree peasants might be compared to, namely, Freedmen. The significant aspect here, what makes them comparable, is that Roman Freedmen and the German unfree peasants had access to courts, could enter into contracts and thereby take on obligations, and they could

57 Rowan, *Ulrich Zasius* (n 3), 158.

58 S B Fay, "The Roman Law and the German peasant" (1911) 16 *The American Historical Review* 234.

59 Zasius, *Lucubrationes* (n 32), Preface, 2. See also U Zasius, *Responsa Singularia*, lib I, cap, III col 52.

60 Zasius, *Lucubrationes* (n 32), Preface, 2.

own property. In other words, Roman Freedmen and German unfree peasants could exercise rights and fulfil obligations within civil society precisely because the civil laws did not violate the principles and practices of *ius gentium* by attempting to abrogate or demolish universal rights and obligations.

Here the circularity is quite clear: the civil laws that embody, protect and vindicate the ability for Freedmen and peasants to exercise universal rights and obligations such as promise keeping, self-defence, owning property and participating in civic life, are just because they are in accordance with *ius gentium* and thereby natural law. If, however, civil and political authorities attempt to demolish or abrogate these rights and obligations through the civil laws, they are effectively violating *ius gentium* and natural law. As a condition that extends from secondary *ius gentium*, the institution of slavery does not nullify the rights and obligations that extend from primary *ius gentium*. If it did so, it would not be just. In other words, although a slave's rights and obligations can be limited and diminished on account of his condition, these rights and obligations cannot be annulled altogether. As to do so would be to place him in a condition of complete submission to the power of another, making it impossible to exercise force to repel injury, making it impossible to exercise both his instinct and his right to defend himself in the face of unrestrained and unjust force. If this is the case, the condition of slavery itself becomes morally illegitimate, as it does not preserve the life of a captive so much as place him in a condition that is even more insecure and less stable than war.

Or, on an economic level in relation to serfdom, if civil laws demolish the universal rights and obligations of unfree peasants to the extent to which they are under the total economic and even physical domination of their lord then the impetus for entering into the condition of servitude – tacit or explicit – to gain security and stability is null. Security and stability can only be established if the civil laws that structure and govern such institutions as slavery and servitude do not place one under the complete authority of another. The same goes for civil and political arrangements of protection and power. Although peoples can subject themselves to civil and political authorities, through tacit or explicit contracts and constitutions, they cannot place themselves in a condition of having no stability and security in relation to political and legal authorities in doing so. Thus civil laws and civil institutions that make the conditions of slavery, servitude and subjection increasingly harsh by attempting to abolish customary rights and obligations effectively violate primary and second secondary *ius gentium* as well as natural law. Unjust civil laws, laws that violate universal rights and obligations, create and legitimate unlimited power. Civil laws that enable one to exercise unlimited and absolute power over another, whether it be physical, economic, legal or political, violate the limitation placed on power by the first rule of *ius gentium* and thereby these laws are morally corrupt and stand in need of immediate reform.

Only those who understand the moral and historical relation between justice, *ius*, natural law, *ius gentium* and, finally, civil law would be able to reform corrupt civil laws, and thus bring civil jurisprudence and political authority back into accordance with what it was before unjust laws and institutions were created. Only those who understood the history of the laws in their own society, as well as the history of law in other societies, could restore ancient custom, convention and institutions to their original. This was no esoteric pursuit, or question of semantics, given that the transformation from custom to code, from a predominantly unwritten and varied legal tradition to a written and rationalised one, had the potential to create unlimited and unrestrained power. This power may appear as legitimate according to the letter of civil law, even as it stands in direct conflict with *ius gentium* and thereby natural law, which is all the more reason why, for Zasius, understanding the nature and extent of the errors that stand at the basis of traditional jurisprudence is so important.

E. ABSOLUTE SLAVERY AND ARBITRARY POWER

Traditionally, as a practice and institution that resulted from war, slavery was justified as an institution that provided both peace and security to the slave and the master; slavery was both the result of war and an alternative to it.[61] However, over time as slavery and servitude became increasingly regulated by civil laws, the status of the slave had the potential to be diminished as the power of the master was augmented.[62] This was especially the case when the power of the master, as a legal power, restricted the ability of those under his authority to engage in common practices, like owning property and engaging in trade. In diminishing the legal status of a person in servitude to engage in basic relations (which fall under primary *ius gentium*), the status and power

61 Zasius, *De iustitia et iure* (n 20), lecture, col 267. "For wars are not good, nor slavery, nor captivity; nevertheless with better reason and by way of supposition they may be called just and good, if in fact the will of men has been supposed to be wicked. Therefore slavery is just and good for that reason, [namely] that slaves not be killed; and thus concerning others, just as we say, it is better to lose your clothing than your body [life]."

62 Ibid, col 257.

of the master could become absolute – without limit. This is the position that Zasius adamantly rejects in his 1518 *Preface*, when he argues that the condition of slavery does not place one under the complete domination of another, as Bartolus suggests, nor does *ius gentium* give the master unlimited power; rather it is the "civil law [that] deprives, destroys, and annuls the status of the slave".[63]

To show this, Zasius first turns to the Ancients, whereby he invokes the words of Job to provide evidence that "slaves were able to stand up against their masters by means of legal action, and therefore [slaves] were able to be obligated".[64] Not only were slaves able to enter into contracts, they were also able to inherit property: "Tacitus among the ancient Germans writes, that everywhere it was accepted according to the customs of the people, that slaves were able to acquire goods amongst themselves, and were not much different in this regard than freedmen."[65] Zasius then turns to Greece, drawing from Aristotle who "relates in *Book IV* of the *Politics* that slaves, if they were wealthy by a small amount, could be chosen for administrative civil duties"[66] to show that the status of slaves, and by extension unfree peasants in the German context, was not a status devoid of exercising such basic rights and obligations as defending oneself (by appealing to a good man or just judge), owning property, or fulfilling obligations to promote the common good of the *patria*. Finally, as related in *Exodus*, Zasius continues, "according to *ius gentium* servants/slaves are not able to be destroyed".[67] They are not, in other words, entirely under the physical domination of their masters, even if they are under his power.

Zasius next turns to Rome, to the Digest in order to explain that even there it is acknowledged that "the slave was inherently his own property" and thus "he was able to be obligated by *ius gentium*".[68] With Accursius, Bartolus and Baldus, however, the original meaning was lost. Zasius asserts that they considered the very act of entering into the condition of servitude through *ius gentium* to transform one's status from being one's own property to becoming the property of another. As such, this transition negated any previous obligations and rights that existed prior to entering the condition of slavery. They held this was the case, Zasius argues, because they held

63 Ibid, col 255.
64 Zasius, *Lucubrationes* (n 32), Preface, 2.
65 Ibid.
66 Ibid.
67 Ibid.
68 Ibid.

that "freedom advances from natural law, but domination advances from *ius gentium*".[69] This distinction, this misunderstanding, followed from their misunderstanding of the relation between natural law and *ius gentium*; their misunderstanding of the relation between justice and *ius*; and their misunderstanding of *ius* as the art of what is good and fair, conjoined. The latter makes it possible to hold a contract or condition of servitude that does not limit the power of one in relation to another as just, whereas for Zasius to meet the criteria of being a good (in the sense that the captive is not killed) and fair (in the sense of the slave not being entirely subjected to the force of another) conjoined, force and power must be limited.

Rejecting the interpretation that it is civil law, not *ius gentium*, that creates these limits on power, Zasius argues that "the power of the masters is not restricted from the civil law, although their excessive savagery is kept in check, lest they rage too greatly",[70] but by *ius gentium*: "For since excessive savagery is against natural law even in brute animals, as we said above, therefore it will be more strongly against *ius gentium*, for not in vain is it to be said that 'to be a slave' comes from preserving."[71] Explaining further that "although domination is said to be of *ius gentium*, nevertheless I do not think it is proper to infer from this that the status of the slave is abolished: since the domination of the lord does not require the demolition of the slave".[72]

Moving from violence to law Zasius agrees that the authority of the master over the slave can be held in check by just civil laws. This does not negate his position that it can also be extended by unjust civil laws when they attempt to make the conditions of subjection harsher and harsher as the authority of the superior is increased. Aside from the threat of increased physical power or violence over the slave or servant by the master, which *ius gentium* and civil law attempt to curtail, civil law has the potential to exclude slaves and servants from exercising basic rights and fulfilling basic obligations to others.

For example, if civil laws can obligate a slave, or, rather, an unfree peasant only to his lord and diminish his ability to enter into other obligations as well as trump pre-existing obligations that a peasant may have undertaken before new civil laws were created, then an entire network of common relations – social, economic and political – is threatened. If, in other words, his ability to enter contracts and take on obligations is diminished and violated by increasing the dominion of his lord or master – or whoever has the greatest

69 Ibid: "libertatem naturali iure, dominationem vero ex iure gentium procedere".
70 Zasius, *De iustitia et iure* (n 20), lecture, col 257.
71 Ibid.
72 Zasius, *Lucubrationes* (n 32), Preface, 2.

political, legal and economic power over him – through new civil laws, then it is possible that previous obligations – especially monetary and labour debts – can be changed, or even eradicated, by the increased power of the master. While the master stands to benefit, all others stand to lose what is owed to them by the peasant. If this is done according to a civil law, those who lose have no viable legal means to claim or vindicate their rights to be repaid. Moreover, if a peasant can only be held accountable to and squeezed by one entity – one master – this also diminishes and overturns the authority of long held customs, insofar as old rules of engagement are replaced by new ones; the creation of new civil laws has the potential to augment the power of some at the cost of others. When old rules of conduct are no longer applicable, the stability and security of society as a whole is threatened. It is in this scenario that accepted customs and previous contracts – explicit and implicit – have the potential to give way to arbitrary power.

Further, creating new civil laws to draw an absolute legal boundary around the slave and peasant enables a master or lord to cut off the slave or peasant from the other realms in which he had been previously free to interact. As Peter Blickle shows brilliantly,[73] some peasants responded to these changes by going to court, and successfully argued that although the civil laws changed, their customary rights had not. They did so in some instances with references to contradictions that arose from conflicts in law as different kinds of authorities extended their powers over them. In other instances, they did so by claiming their rights with reference to tacit promises and agreements. In some cases, they were not only able to limit the power that a lord had over them, but even to break free of some obligations altogether on the basis that previous customs, practices and rights, like the freedom of marriage, had been violated or even demolished by the creation of new laws. Likewise, in terms of political subordination, the extension of the political and legal authority over subjects also has the potential to overturn pre-existing freedoms. If civil laws are created to expand the authority of the ruler at the cost of the needs and the security of the ruled by violating common practices, such as trade and commerce, as well as common rights such as the use of courts and the ability to defend oneself, property, family and neighbours from threats, then the relation between ruler and subject is no longer just. Rather it becomes corrupted by the ruler's power, which in turn is able to be augmented further by civil laws, and thus the status of subjects is able to be violated and even diminished altogether.

73 See especially Blickle, *Von der Leibeigenschaft zu den Menschenrechten* (n 55).

However, for Zasius the institutions of slavery, servitude, subjection and subordination as well as the practices that structure and govern these institutions are not in themselves corrupt, as they each extend from *ius gentium*. Rather civil laws that attempt to diminish the status of the subordinate altogether – slave, peasant or subject – are corrupt. Further, civil laws that attempt to augment the authority of master, lord or ruler at the cost of the stability and security of the slave, peasant and subject can make conditions so harsh and limited that they could effectively violate and undermine the original impetus for one to seek security through subordination in the first place. That specific civil laws had overstepped the bounds of propriety by violating *ius gentium* was an indication for Zasius that the law as a whole was in need of adjustment; it was an indication that some attempts to expand legal and political authority in the early sixteenth century had been driven by desire and interests, rather than considerations of justice.

In providing the grounds for his broader argument for the necessity to reform the harshness and severity of civil laws and thereby civil jurisprudence, Zasius' emphasis on the relation between justice and *ius*, natural law and *ius gentium*, as well as between universal rights and obligations carries the weight of, and indeed provides the structure for, his understanding of universal jurisprudence. He does not, however, use this understanding to directly challenge institutions such as slavery, servitude or sovereignty, but rather, in challenging the moral legitimacy of civil laws that attempt to create conditions of unlimited authority, he provides moral authority to these institutions by demarcating their limits. At the same time as he provides a critique of absolute authority, he legitimises authority with reference to the customs of *ius gentium*. In other words, the legitimacy of civil laws and civil authorities extends from how it restrains power – among and between all – as unlimited power violates justice absolutely, whereas limited power serves it.

F. CONCLUSIONS

Five hundred years have come and gone since Zasius offered an alternative interpretation of the principles underpinning Roman law, and by extension universal jurisprudence, to his Scholastic predecessors and contemporaries. Armed with the methods and sources of the *studia humanitatis*, he set out to peel away the misinterpretations and corruptions of Roman law and in the process fundamentally reinterpreted it. Turning away from the glosses and commentaries, to the sources and words of Roman law itself, he called the authority of such luminaries as Accursius, Bartolus and Baldus into question by demonstrating that they had misunderstood fundamental and foundational definitions as laid out in the first title of the Digest, *De iustitia et iure*.

Indeed, he held that at the very foundations of Scholastic jurisprudence stood a grievous error, namely, Accursius' interpretation of *ius*, wherein he split equity and good in his discussion of what criteria a law must meet in order to be just. For Zasius (and his legal humanist contemporaries), this misinterpretation and misunderstanding of *ius* was no mere semantic error: as to misunderstand *ius* was to misunderstand justice (*iustitia*). Rejecting this split between equity and good he reinterpreted *ius* to be "the art of what is good and what is fair, conjoined". He did not stop there: he argued that *ius* was not only the distinguishing characteristic of justice (objective *ius*), but also the distinguishing characteristic of right (subjective *ius*), as well as the crucial link between natural law and *ius gentium*. As such he fundamentally broke with traditional jurisprudence in arguing that *ius gentium* was a form of natural law, and as such stood at the very foundations of civil society. He also departed from traditional jurisprudence – as well as the Romans – when he argued that *ius gentium*, as a record and even source of universal rights and obligations, could be used to hold civil laws and civil authorities to a higher criterion of justice.

In short, by redefining *ius* to restore justice, he not only reinterpreted the law he set out to restore, but also departed significantly from his predecessors and contemporaries by effectively bringing *ius gentium* from the periphery of civil jurisprudence into its centre. Although Zasius was well known and widely read in his own times, and although his works featured in the tradition of historical jurisprudence well into nineteenth and early twentieth centuries, today he remains relatively unknown to modern scholars.[74] Even as modern scholars of legal thought and legal historians are no strangers to the works of Zasius, those concerned with the history and development of natural law and natural rights theories, as well as the history and development of *ius gentium*, have overlooked his contribution to both.

Reassessing legal humanists, especially in light of their discussion of *ius* and *ius gentium*, offers an opportunity to rethink the impact of Zasius (and, by extension, Budé and Alciati) on the history and development of fundamental categories of modern political and legal thought. Rethinking the dominant interpretation that holds that Zasius and other legal humanists

74 See K Davis, *Periodization and Sovereignty* (2008), J H Franklin, *Jean Bodin and the Sixteenth-Century Revolution in the Methodology of Law and History* (1963), Kelley, *Foundations of Modern Scholarship* (n 3), Kelley, *The Human Measure* (n 1) and Skinner, *Foundations* (n 9).

were not concerned with such abstract notions as universal jurisprudence, not only offers an opportunity to rethink legal humanism but also offers scholars – from across the disciplines – engaged with the enormous project of revisiting the history and development of international law an opportunity to rethink aspects of this history. It offers new insights as to the centrality of *ius gentium* to that history within sixteenth-century Europe, especially in terms of reconsidering that the so-called turn to natural law as well as *ius gentium* associated with the Second Scholastic Francisco Vitoria occurs well after Zasius begins lecturing on the first title of the Digest at Freiburg and about a decade after his publication of the 1518 *Preface* to the *Lucubrationes*. At issue here is not a history of reception or the search for the origins of the turn to *ius gentium*, but rather the significance of infusing *ius gentium* with moral and historical authority so as to address local problems within Europe, problems that were emerging as part and parcel of political and legal reforms aimed at rationalising civil authority and jurisprudence.

PART III
LEGAL HUMANISM: A PAN-EUROPEAN METHODOLOGY?

6 Elegant Scholastic Humanism? Arias Piñel's (1515–1563) Critical Revision of *Laesio Enormis*

Wim Decock

A. INTRODUCTION

It is increasingly being recognised that broad tags such as "humanism" and "Scholasticism" fail to do justice to the "hybrid" nature of legal as well as theological sources of the early modern period, certainly in the Iberian world.[1] A case in point are the *Commentarii ad rubricam et legem 2, C. de rescindenda venditione* by the Portuguese jurist Arias Piñel, a successful legal practitioner born in Sesimbra who combined his lawyering activities with a position at the University of Coimbra and later at Salamanca. By submitting C.4.44.2 to thorough philological and historical analysis, Piñel wanted to investigate the

1 This contribution draws on material previously published in W Decock, *Theologians and Contract Law, The Moral Transformation of the Ius commune (c. 1500–1650)* (2013) 566–589.

"true" meaning of *laesio enormis*. Against the gloss and the *communis opinio doctorum*, he claimed that the remedy by virtue of C.4.44.2 was unknown to the Roman jurists before the time of emperors Diocletian and Maximian. In Piñel's view, the irrelevance of lesion to pristine Roman law was obvious from a careful exegesis of various texts in the Digest. Although he expressed the fear that many scholars would bear the "new light of truth" on *laesio enormis* badly, Piñel went further in his critique of traditional legal scholarship by revealing the medieval origins of the allegedly Roman doctrine of objective deceit (*dolus reipsa*) – which was traditionally associated with the teachings on lesion. The mission of the jurist from Sesimbra was to combat anachronistic readings of the Roman sources. He believed that the French humanists did not go far enough in their exercise of contextualising the Roman legal tradition. Piñel wanted to highlight the fundamental difference between the pagan legal culture that had informed the classical Roman jurists, on the one hand, and the new mentality of the *ius commune* as it developed during the Christian Middle Ages, on the other. Having said that, his thinking remained heavily imbued with Christian values. For his defence of justice in exchange he drew heavily on the Scholastic theologians. Moreover, his style of writing sometimes recalls that of the Spanish canonist and theologian Martin de Azpilcueta, one of his former teachers. Eventually, Piñel became an authority himself for "elegant scholastic humanists" such as the Spanish canonist Diego de Covarruvias y Leyva.

B. THE CAREER AND CONVICTIONS OF A HUMANIST JURIST[2]

(1) Combining erudition with practical engagement

In the 1582 edition of the *Corpus Iuris Canonici*, commissioned by pope Gregory XIII, the *correctores Romani* refer to Arias Piñel for further discussion on *laesio enormis*.[3] Arias Piñel (1515–1563) was a humanist jurist from Sesimbra near Lisbon. He ranks among those exceptional Renaissance men who continue to appeal to the modern reader both through depth of knowl-

2 For Piñel's biography this chapter relies on the excellent monograph written by J García Sánchez, *Arias Piñel, Catedrático de Leyes en Coimbra y Salamanca durante el siglo XVI, La rescisión de la compraventa por "laesio enormis"* (2004) 39–143, reviewed by T Wallinga in (2006) 74 *Tijdschrift voor Rechtsgeschiedenis* 185–187.

3 Cf nota *Vide l.2* ad X 3,17,3 (canon *Quum dilecti*) in *Corpus Iuris Canonici* (1582) part 2, col 1123.

edge and liveliness of personality. Piñel appears to have been a successful jurist in his own day. A popular law professor, first at Coimbra (1539–1548 /1556–1559) and later at Salamanca (1559–1563), Piñel alternated legal scholarship with prestigious lawyering activities, serving, for example, as an advocate at the *Casa de Suplicación* in Lisbon.

In light of his own career, it should not come as a surprise that Piñel cites the famous statement that "law schools have the laws shoved down your throat, while the courts make you digest them, since practice is the science of digestion". This expression can be traced back at least to Baldus de Ubaldis (1327–1400),[4] but it became particularly popular in the early modern period. For example, Joost De Damhouder (1507–1581), one of the Low Countries' most influential jurists ever, rebuked those young ambitious lawyers who pleaded before the Council of Flanders or the Great Council of Malines without any knowledge about how those courts worked in practice.[5] In Piñel's own experience, lawyering without a solid theoretical basis is dangerous, but legal scholarship without practical application is ineffective.[6] From classical literature he claims further proof for this insight, citing Pliny the Elder's words that "the real battle takes place on the *forum*, the school is but a harmless kind of thing".

However, if the tremendous erudition displayed by Piñel is anything to go by, for instance in his very praise of legal practice, then we must conclude from this that the humanist ideal which he ultimately aspired to in his life can hardly be attained without some degree of academic learning. In this regard, Piñel's way of thinking is reminiscent of that of the famous Spanish canonist Diego de Covarruvias y Leyva (1512–1577). Covarruvias, too, combined a remarkable passion for humanist learning with a high sensitivity

4 Baldus, *In primam Digesti veteris partem commentaria*, ad D.4.4.38, f 256v, num 35: "Leges in scholis diglutiuntur, in palaciis digeruntur, quia practica est scientia digestiva."

5 J De Damhouder, *Praxis rerum civilium* (1567) cap 96, 182, nr 2: "Nam quamvis saepenumero tales iuvenes sint docti et iurisprudentia plurimum valeant, stylum tamen fori, experientiam, et praxim nondum sunt consecuti, ac procedendi modum non satis tenent, quem quotidiana observatione et usu paulatim tandem assequuntur." On Damhouder, see R Feenstra, "Damhouder", in M Stolleis (ed), *Juristen, Ein biographisches Lexikon, Von der Antike bis zum 20. Jahrhundert* (1995) 152–153. For his seminal contributions to criminal law, see J Monballyu, "La théorie sur la sorcellerie chez Wielant et Damhouder", in F Stevens and D van den Auweele (eds), *Houd voet bij stuk, Xenia iuris historiae G Van Dievoet oblata* (1990) 291.

6 A Piñel, *Commentarii ad rub. et l. 2, C. de rescindenda venditione, cum annotationibus Emanuelis Soarez a Ribiera. Accessit eiusdem argumenti cap. 3 et 4, lib. 2 resolutionum Didaci Covarruviae* (1618), ad l 2, part 2, cap 4, num 2, 152: "Ego autem post longam legendi professionem, postque diligentissimam foro navatam operam, in ea sententia sum, ut theorica sine praxi digestam solidamque iuris cognitionem praestare nequeat, praxisque absque theorica maxime periculosa et manca evadat."

for legal practice. His learned and often highly sophisticated commentaries on the *ius commune* were interspersed with quite personal reflections on legal practice, passionate notes on textual criticism and brilliant quotes from ancient literary sources.

It is this combination of a passion for learning with a remarkable record of practical experience – a combination that is typical of many so-called "humanist jurists" – that we are going to discover as we analyse Piñel's commentary on the *Lex secunda*, that is the second provision of title 44 (*De rescindenda venditione*, on rescission of sale contracts) of the fourth book of the Code. C.4.44.2 famously states that if you or your father have sold a piece of land for a price considerably below its value, it is only human that you either repay the price and get back your land, or that you receive the surplus value, depending on the will of the buyer.[7]

Piñel insists on the necessity of examining the historical and philosophical roots from which the famous *Lex secunda* originated before trying to explain its true meaning. "The arts, like trees, cannot reach high if they are cut off from their roots."[8] In the footsteps of Marcus Tullius Cicero, Piñel was convinced that humanist erudition and a true sense of historical criticism were not just qualities that boost the reputation of a lawyer. They were crucial to the fruitful interpretation of the sacred texts of law in a continuously changing context.[9] A full exploration of Piñel's exposition lies beyond the scope of this chapter.[10] Yet it is worthwhile dwelling for a moment on the following points: his praise of private property and the prohibition against harming fellow human beings.

(2) Praise of the individual against political absolutism

Piñel starts out with a seemingly theoretical investigation on the origin of the sale-purchase contract. It leads him into vast discussions with the Bartolists and the French humanists on subjects that seem to be rather exotic at

7 For further explanation and literature on the subject, please allow me to refer to Decock, *Theologians and Contract Law* (n 1) 529–535.

8 Piñel, *Commentarii* (n 6), ad rubr, part 1, cap 1, 1–2pr: "Artium enim, sicut arborum, altitudo sine radicibus esse non potest, iuxta Ciceronis sententiam." The original expression is slightly different, cf Cicero, *Orator*, 43, 147, in: *Cicéron, L'orateur, Du meilleur genre d'orateurs, Texte établi et traduit par Albert Yon* [Collection des Universités de France] (1964) 53: "Nam omnium magnarum artium sicut arborum altitudo nos delectat, radices stirpesque non item; sed esse illa sine his non potest."

9 See Piñel, *Commentarii* (n 6) 1–65 (65 is wrongly indicated as 63 in the Antwerp 1618 edition).

10 For a more extensive overview of the contents of Piñel's commentary on both the *rubrica* and the *Lex secunda*, see García Sánchez, *Arias Piñel* (n 2) 201–234.

first sight, such as the existence or not of money in the time of the Trojan War. He concludes – in line with traditional teaching – that *emptio venditio* falls under the *ius gentium*. Yet, importantly, Piñel explains why jurists throughout the ages have considered this to be a question worthy of so much debate:[11] "they say that this investigation is useful, because the prince can abolish more easily what falls under the *ius civile* than what falls under *ius naturale*, that is the *ius gentium*".[12] Piñel tries to argue, in this respect, that *ius gentium* and *ius naturale* are synonyms.[13] He cites the Lutheran jurist Johann Oldendorp (c1487–1567) to bolster this opinion, although this reference is probably a little bit dishonest, since Oldendorp was anxious to stress the differences between *ius gentium* and *ius naturale*.[14] If anything, the theoretical difference between natural law and the law of nations resides in the fact that natural law is shared by animals and human beings alike (D.1.1.1–3). So, properly speaking, *ius gentium* and *ius naturale* are only equivalents if *ius naturale* is understood as the *ius naturale* that is proper to the human race.

In any event, Piñel eventually maintains that these distinctions between different types of law are actually superfluous, since all kinds of *ius* must be protected against interference by the prince. Piñel goes to great lengths to combat political absolutism (*absoluta potestas*). In his view, the first kind of harm (*laesio*) that can be done to the citizens is the infringement of their rights by the prince. Moreover, Piñel holds that the prince not only has no right to violate rights that are derived from the *ius gentium*. The prince should in fact never be allowed to violate any transfer of property between citizens, even if their agreement fell under the *ius civile*.[15] Consequently, the traditional distinction between rights deriving from *ius gentium* and rights based on *ius civile* is largely superseded, Piñel claims.

11 Piñel, *Commentarii* (n 6), ad rubr, part 1, cap 1, num 31, 9: "Dicunt enim esse utilem eam inspectionem, quia princeps facilius tollere potest, quae sunt iuris civilis, quam ea, quae sunt iuris naturalis vel gentium."

12 For further explanation, see K Pennington, *The Prince and the Law (1200–1600), Sovereignty and Rights in the Western Legal Tradition* (1993).

13 Piñel, *Commentarii* (n 6), ad rubr, part 1, cap 1, num 18–19, 6.

14 J Oldendorp, *Variae lectiones ad iuris civilis interpretationem* (1546) 16: "Quare cum audis hanc vocem, Ius gentium, non semper exaudiendum est Ius naturale, sed plerumque Ius humanum, ut Livius recte appellat. Neque enim sequitur: Gentes id constituerunt, aut in usum admiserunt: Ergo est ius naturale aut aequum. Imo, saepe iniquissimum est."

15 Piñel, *Commentarii* (n 6) ad rubr, part 1, cap 2, num 1, 10: "Demus enim aliquid acquisitum iure civili, prout ex stipulatione vel alia conventione vel obligatione ex iis quas scribentes dicunt esse iuris civilis, per d. l. ex hoc iure. Certe nulla ratio est, cur princeps auferre possit dominium vel ius quaesitum ex tali conventione iuris civilis, quia in eo laederetur simul lex et ratio naturalis et ius gentium, ut inferius cum Cicerone probabimus."

Mainstream political thought, which defends absolute power, is to be exterminated, according to Piñel, because it is inhumane (*inhumana*).[16] In the meantime, princes should be urged to respect private rights as faithfully as possible. They have only limited power. This is the truth that Piñel finds it necessary to investigate and to explain even if the prince has no superior in his territory. Moreover, he thinks that private individuals have a means of effectively protecting their property against usurpation by the prince – at least if the regime has not turned into a tyranny.

(3) The social nature of man and the do-no-harm principle

The basis of Piñel's diatribe against political absolutism and interference with private property lies in his conception of justice as a kind of do-no-harm principle. This is a principle dictated by natural reason. It is expressed in the legal, the religious, and the philosophical traditions from Classical Antiquity:[17] "Depriving someone of his property or right (*dominium vel ius suum*) clearly is an offence not only against the civil or man-made written law, but also against natural law or the law of nations, and even against the law of God, since harm (*iniuria*) and injustice (*iniustitia*) are inconsistent with each of these bodies of law."

Obviously, Ulpian's definition of justice in D.1.1.1pr fits well into Piñel's conception of justice. In Roman-law terms, justice is the constant and perpetual will to give everybody his right, to do no harm (*neminem laedere*), and to live honestly.[18] Following late medieval jurists such as Baldus and humanists such as François Connan and Guillaume Budé, Piñel repeats that natural reason (*ratio naturalis*) itself dictates that we may do no harm to our neighbours. The text from D.1.1.3 is a positive legal expression of that natural truth. It says that it is nefarious for man to do harm to another man, since nature made us into "relatives" of one another.

In principle, Roman law also contains a prohibition on unjust enrichment. Piñel grants that the prohibition contained in D.12.6.14pr (*ne quis cum aliena iactura locupletetur*) can be seen as an expression of natural

16 Piñel, *Commentarii* (n 6), ad rubr, part 1, cap 2, num 24, 18: "Infertur tandem omnino reijciendam et exterminandam esse inhumanam illam multorum traditionem, cum principi tribuunt plenissimam vel absolutam potestatem, eam ab ordinaria distinguentes, ut ex illa omnia possit, utque facta mentione talis potestatis nulla exceptio obijci valeat."

17 Piñel, *Commentarii* (n 6), ad rubr, part 1, cap 2, num 26, 20: ". . . satis liquere videtur . . . cum alicui dominium vel ius suum aufertur, non tantum ius civile, vel humanum scriptum offendi, sed etiam naturale et gentium, imo et divinum, quibus repugnat iniuria vel iniustitia."

18 D.1.1.1pr-3.

reason (*ratio naturalis*). However, true to the humanist spirit, he denies that the Roman jurists themselves could have meant this to be an expression of the Judaeo-Christian prohibition on stealing. To be sure, parallels between Roman law and Christian theology in regard to the principle of unjust enrichment do exist. After all, both normative systems have been inspired by natural reason. Yet Piñel rejects the idea that Roman jurisprudence was influenced directly by divine law.[19]

To Piñel himself, divine law does matter, of course. *Laesio* inflicted by an absolutist prince or by another citizen goes against the Seventh Commandment not to steal. In reality, Piñel does not cite the Seventh Commandment. He merely refers to *ius divinum* in general. The only Scriptural passages he quotes are the so-called Golden Rule: "Do to others, what you would have them do to you, that is the entire Law and Prophets" (Mt 7:12), and the precept to love your neighbour as yourself (Mt 22:37–39). These prescripts would have been part of Catholic culture in general. Unlike his Protestant counterparts, Piñel would not have felt the need to get involved in profound Biblical exegesis. In fact, he claims that he borrowed the references to these New Testament texts from Augustine's *City of God*.[20]

Contrary to the meagre attention paid to divine law, Piñel is eager to adduce as many authoritative texts as possible from Greek and Roman philosophers to support his views on justice. Aristotle's argument against tyranny serves as a warning that the more power is concentrated in the hands of the rulers, the more likely it is that political stability will be short-lived, since oligarchy and tyranny are the most unstable forms of government.[21] Through Ambrose he quotes the typically Stoic maxim that man is born not only with the aim of becoming useful to himself, but also to others (*homo*

19 For example, he criticises the Ordinary Gloss on D.47.2 (*De furtis*) for interpreting natural law as "divine law" in the Roman text which reads that theft is prohibited as a matter of natural law. According to Piñel, "that interpretation is miles away from the mind of Paul the jurist; in writing this, Paul did not know about the precepts of divine law and sacred Scripture"; cf Piñel, *Commentarii* (n 6), ad rubr, part 1, cap 1, num 21, 7: "Patet errasse glossa in d. l. 1 dum exponit lege naturali, id est, divina. Id enim prorsus a mente iurisconsulti Pauli ibi, qui praecepta divinae legis et sacrae scripturae non cognovit."

20 Piñel undoubtedly refers to Augustinus, *De civitate Dei* (edn CCSL 48) (1955), 19, 14, p 681: "Iam vero quia duo praecipua praecepta, hoc est dilectionem Dei et dilectionem proximi, docet magister Deus, in quibus tria invenit homo quae diligat, Deum, se ipsum et proximum . . ."

21 Aristotle, *Politica* (5th edn, W D Ross) (1957), 5, 12, 1315b11–12, p 187: "καίτοι πασῶν ὀλιγοχρονιώταται τῶν πολιτειῶν εἰσιν ὀλιγαρχία καὶ τυραννίς".

non ut sibi ipsi tantum sed et ut aliis prosit natus).[22] To wrong other people is to violate nature (*naturam violat, qui alteri nocet*).[23]

As is commonly known, patristic social thought, particularly as expressed in Ambrose's *On duties*, is to a very large extent modelled on Cicero's *On duties*. It is hardly surprising, then, to find that Piñel borrows the greatest part of his social views from the famous Roman orator. Accordingly, Piñel regards as one of the most important principles for living in society the universal prohibition on harming another person out of self-interest (*non liceat sui commodi causa nocere alteri*).[24] The do-no-harm principle pertains to natural law. It imposes itself upon all human beings, princes and popes included. It can be regarded as the basis of the *laesio*-interdiction in contractual exchange, in particular.

C. UNHOLY NEW IDEAS: PIÑEL'S CRITICAL INTERPRETATION OF *LAESIO ENORMIS*

(1) The concept of *laesio enormis* is not part of classical Roman law

For the majority of the late medieval jurists, the beginning of Piñel's commentary on the *Lex secunda* would have been shocking.[25]

> Against the gloss and the opinion of all previous writers I strongly believe that the right grounded on C.4.44.2 was issued for the first time only (*nove*) by Emperors Diocletian and Maximian. Consequently, this remedy was entirely unknown by

22 This appears to be a free adaptation of Ambrose, *De officiis*, 1, 28, 132, in *Saint Ambroise, Les devoirs, Livre 1, Texte établi, traduit et annoté par Maurice Testard* [Collection des Universités de France] (1984) vol 1, 158: "Quo in loco aiunt placuisse stoicis quae in terris gignantur, omnia ad usus hominum creari; homines autem hominum causa esse generatos ut ipsi inter se aliis alii prodesse possint."

23 An allusion to Ambrose, *De officiis* (edn Testard), 3, 4, 24, in *Saint Ambroise, Les devoirs, Livres 2–3, Texte établi, traduit et annoté par Maurice Testard* [Collection des Universités de France] (1992) vol 2, 91: "Hinc ergo colligitur quod homo qui secundum naturae formatus est directionem, ut oboediat sibi, nocere non possit alteri; quod, si qui nocet, naturam violet . . . "

24 E.g. Cicero, *De officiis*, 3, 5, 21 (edn Testard, vol 2) 81: "Detrahere igitur alteri aliquid et hominem hominis incommodo suum commodum augere magis est contra naturam quam mors, quam paupertas, quam dolor, quam cetera quae possunt aut corpori accidere aut rebus externis."

25 Piñel, *Commentarii* (n 6), ad l 2, part 1, cap 1, num 3, 66–67: "Ego contra glossam et omnes hucusque scribentes verissimum credo, Diocletianum et Maximianum imperatores, nove hoc ius [C.4.44.2] induxisse, ac proinde iurisconsultis (quorum responsa in libris digestorum habemus) nullatenus hoc remedium cognitum fuisse." Compare his conclusion in loc cit, num 7, 68: "Nemo igitur iuris vel rationis peritus inauditam nostram sententiam reijciendam putabit, cum tot iuribus, totque fundamentis probetur, ut sic contra glossam et omnes hucusque scribentes maneat, ex constitutione hac Diocletiani novum ius inductum fuisse . . . "

> the jurists (whose *responsa* we find in the Digest). May the true sense of many laws be revealed through this insight.

Centuries of reading Roman law in light of Christian principles, or, better still, of doing legal scholarship in search of Roman legal texts giving authoritative support to Christian principles are suddenly being thought of as superseded. Highly indebted to the mentality of Renaissance humanism, Piñel looks for nothing but the true meaning (*verus sensus*) of the Roman texts. He wants to understand them in their original context. He wants to highlight the fundamental difference between the pagan worldview of the classical jurists and the Christian *ius commune* as it developed in the later Middle Ages.

The classical jurists ignored the remedy now associated with C.4.44.2. This is what Piñel infers from the absence of even the slightest reference in other imperial constitutions and in the Digest to this remedy or to a concrete determination of the quantity that constitutes *laesio*. If the remedy for lesion had been as crucially important to the pre-Diocletian Romans as it was to the late medieval jurists, then we could have expected a more elaborate treatment of it in the *Corpus Justinianeum*, according to Piñel.

Moreover, he interprets D.4.4.16.4 (*in pretio emptionis et venditionis naturaliter licet contrahentibus se circumvenire*) as originally constituting a kind of absolute principle of "freedom of contract":[26] "These words do not admit of imaginary afterthoughts and external restrictions by doctors who seek to limit them by virtue of C.4.44.2." The same holds true for D.19.2.22.3 (*in locationibus quoque licet invicem se circumscribere*):[27] "If we love the truth, we cannot interpret these words as admitting of the violent limitations imposed by the doctors."

In Piñel's view, the irrelevance of lesion to original Roman law is obvious from various texts in the Digest. First of all, lesion is not listed as a ground for rescission in *De rescindenda venditione* (D.18.5). Secondly, in obvious cases of lesion the Roman jurists did not provide the *laesus* with a remedy (e.g. D.42.1.15). Thirdly, in his *On duties*, Cicero recounts the story of a sly and wicked vendor called Pythius who tricked Canius.[28] He sold him sterile and absolutely worthless lands by persuading him that these lands were in fact the most fruitful lands. Now Cicero apparently did not think Canius

26 Piñel, *Commentarii* (n 6), ad l 2, part 1, cap 1, num 4, 67: "Quae verba non admittunt commenticias subauditiones, extrariasque restrictiones doctorum ea limitantium ex decisione huius l."

27 Piñel, *Commentarii* (n 6), ad l 2, part 1, cap 1, num 4, 67: "Quae verba (si verum amamus) non admittunt violentam doctorum limitationem."

28 Cicero, *De officiis* (edn Testard, vol 2), 3, 14, 58–60, 100–102.

could have had any other remedy to defend himself except for the *actio de dolo*, even though this was a clear instance of lesion beyond moiety.

(2) The concept of *dolus reipsa* is a late medieval invention

Cicero's story of Pythius and Canius leads Piñel to deconstruct yet another mythical notion that was fabricated in the *ius commune* on the basis of D.45.1.36pr: objective deceit (*dolus re ipsa*). Piñel recognises that he is afraid (*vereor*) that many will badly bear the new light of truth (*novam veritatis lucem*) he is about to shed on the matter, blinded as they are by an inveterate misinterpretation.[29] Yet there is no denying a certain feeling of pride and superiority in his voice as he announces his new exegesis. Perhaps this might explain why his pupil, Manuel Soarez a Ribeira, felt the need to soften the impious impression his master left. He inserted a gloss on *vereor* in what became the standard edition of Piñel's book. In this gloss, he quoted a couple of verses from Horace's *Letters*, expressing the idea that the elderly do not accept criticism against well-known playwrights, either because they think that the right thing is only what pleases them, or because they do not want to admit that what they learned as young boys was false.[30] In this manner, Soarez a Ribeira tries to make clear why Piñel had a legitimate reason to be afraid: people tend to be wary of what is new, because innovation is often detrimental to society.

The upshot of Piñel's argument is that the classical jurists were not concerned with *laesio*, whether big or small, as long as it was not accompanied by *dolus*. In the absence of deceit, they would not consider any deviation from some sort of normal price to be relevant. They had no conception of deceit as something intrinsic to the transaction itself. Only in cases of intentional deceit (*interveniente dolo*) could the quantity of the lesion become relevant. The idea of objective deceit could not possibly have made sense to the classical jurists, since the remedy provided in C.4.44.2 had not yet come

29 Piñel, *Commentarii* (n 6), ad l 2, part 1, cap 1, num 7, 68: "Vereor tamen ne ex tenebris inveterati erroris plures fortasse novam veritatis lucem aegre sustineant."

30 Horace, *Epistulae*, 2, 1, 79–85, in *Horace, Satires, Epistles, and Ars poetica*, with an English translation by H Rushton Fairclough, [Loeb Classical Library, 194], Cambridge Mass/London, pp 402–404: "Attae fabula si dubitem, clament periisse pudorem cuncti pene patres, ea cum reprehedere coner; quae gravis Aesopus, quae doctus Roscius egit, vel quia nil rectum, nisi quod placuit sibi, dicunt, vel quia turpe putant parere minoribus, et quae imberbes didicere, senes perdenda fateri."

into existence.[31] This is a good example of how important the insight of the novelty of the *Lex secunda* is for a correct understanding of the Digest.

The *locus classicus* of the debate on objective deceit was the law: *Si quis cum aliter* (D.45.1.36). In the medieval *ius commune* it was interpreted as containing a distinction between two types of deceit: deceit by tricks (*dolus ex machinatione*) and objective deceit (*dolus reipsa*).[32] Lesion beyond moiety was then deemed to be a species of *dolus reipsa*. However, Piñel reads the law: *Si quis cum aliter* in a completely different way. He does not deny that the text is subdivided into two parts that deal with two different types of deceit. Yet sensitive to the procedural nature of Roman law, he differentiates between deceit at the moment of the conclusion of the contract and deceit that only emerges when the contract becomes the subject of a lawsuit:[33]

> The true sense of D.45.1.36 is that both parts of it deal with a plaintiff who committed deceit. The first part concerns deceit right from the inception of the agreement (*a principio conventionis*). The second part concerns deceit at the moment of the lawsuit (*tempore iudicii*). For that reason, the defendant is equally granted an *exceptio doli* against the deceitful plaintiff in both cases.

Departing from a metaphysical reading of the Latin word "*res*", Piñel rightly gives a much more practically significant meaning to it: "lawsuit". The sentence that was traditionally seen as the foundation of "objective deceit" then simply reads as follows: "the lawsuit itself is affected by deceit" (*ipsa res in se dolum habet*). This new interpretation is illustrated through the following example. Assume that something has been promised or agreed upon in view of a certain reason (*causa*), but that, subsequently, this reason does not come about. There was no deceit at the moment of concluding the contract. Still, the very act of taking the promisor to court would then be deceitful, since the reason that drove the promisor into the contract had not been realised (*causa non secuta*).[34]

31 Piñel, *Commentarii* (n 6), ad l 2, part 1, cap 1, num 7, 68: "Inde etiam eleganter colligitur, cur tantum interveniente dolo iurisconsulti distinxerunt circa quantitatem ... quasi cessante dolo non esset differentia inter magnam vel parvam laesionem."

32 D.45.1.36: "Si quis, cum aliter eum convenisset obligari, aliter per machinationem obligatus est, erit quidem subtilitati iuris obstrictus, sed doli exceptione uti potest; quia enim per dolum obligatus est, competit ei exceptio. Idem est, et si nullus dolus intercessit stipulantis, sed ipsa res in se dolum habet; cum enim quis petat ex ea stipulatione, hoc ipso dolo facit, quod petit."

33 Piñel, *Commentarii* (n 6), ad l 2, part 1, cap 1, num 8, 68: "Verus ergo sensus d.l. est, quod in utraque parte eius parte, agens dolo erat: in prima vero, fuerat dolus a principio conventionis, in secunda tempore iudicii. Ideoque pariter doli exceptio adversus agentem datur."

34 Piñel, *Commentarii* (n 6), ad l 2, part 1, cap 1, num 8, 68–69: "Exemplum autem secundae partis facile colligitur ex l. 1, ff. de condictione sine causa [D.12.7.1], melius vero ex l. 2, § circa, ff.

(3) Imitating and emulating the French humanists

Arias Piñel does not hide the contempt he feels for the *communis opinio*. He deplores that even recent French humanist authors such as Pierre Loriot and Pierre Coustau (Costalius) made the mistake of reading the law: *Si quis cum aliter* and the *Lex secunda* together.[35] Because they did not properly investigate the historical development of C.4.44.2, they ignored the fact that emperors Diocletian and Maximian created a new remedy, which was non-existent in classical jurisprudential literature. Therefore, they also made a futile effort reading *laesio enormis* into D.45.1.36.

As critical as a humanist jurist can be, Piñel concludes that traditional authority failed (*hallucinati sunt*).[36] Originally, Roman law did not care about lesion or some kind of "objective deceit". Only if a case of unequal exchange also involved duress or fraud did the classical jurists grant a remedy. Against this background, Piñel feels disappointed by Charles Du Moulin's harsh assessment of C.4.44.2. How could such a learned man berate Diocletian and Maximian so severely for not giving relief to a lesioned party unless the lesion was beyond moiety?[37] In Piñel's view, it is to the credit of the emperors to have

de doli exceptione [D.44.4.2.3], prout quando aliquid promissum vel conventum fuit ob certam causam postea deficientem. Tunc enim in contractu nulla fraus intervenit. Dolose autem ex eo ageretur, causa non secuta."

35 P Coustau, *Adversaria ex Pandectis Iustiniani* (1554), part 1, ad D.4.4.16, 79: "Et ex par. Idem Pomponius vulgo omnibus in ore est, et iure civili, et pontificio permissum esse contrahentibus se invicem decipere, quod tamen a bono viro alienum est. Plane si deceptio ex dolo veniat, de dolo actio erit, et contractus rescindetur. Idem si dolus in reipsa est, nempe quia deceptio ultra dimidiam iusti pretii intercessit, tunc enim revocari potest [l. si quis cum aliter]. Quod autem hic ad finem [par. nunc videndum] datur potestas quibusdam iudicibus restitutiones dandi, quibusdam adimitur, hodie non est in usu. Iure enim Codicis etiam inferioribus magistratibus hoc competit; est, quod Bartolus hic probat." P Loriot, *Tractatus de pactis*, in *De iuris apicibus tractatus octo, et de iuris arte tractatus viginti* (1555), axiom 91, col 465. For biographical information on Coustau, see V Hayaert, *Mens emblematica et humanisme juridique, Le cas du Pegma cum narrationibus philosophicis de Pierre Coustau (1555)*, [Travaux d'Humanisme et Renaissance, 438] (2008), 27–48. For biographical details about Loriot, see J-L Thireau, sv "Loriot, Pierre", in P Arabeyre, J-L Halpérin and J Krynen (eds), *Dictionnaire historique des juristes français, XIIe–XXe siècle* (2007) 518.

36 Piñel, *Commentarii* (n 6), ad l 2, part 1, cap 1, num 8, 68: "Ego verius puto doctores cum glossa ad verbos iurisconsulti hallucinatos fuisse, nihilque minus iurisconsultum in l. [D.45.1.36] ea sensisse quam de remedio huius l. [C.4.44.2] quod evincitur ex eodem Ulpiano et aliis iurisconsultis in locis supra citatis, dum aperte et indistincte tradunt, laesis in precio nullatenus succurri, nec dolum ex sola laesione censeri."

37 C Du Moulin, *Tractatus commerciorum et usurarum redituumque pecunia constitutorum et monetarum* (1558), num 172, 152–153: "Hic Diocletiano et Maximiano ethnicis visum fuit, satis esse licentiam illam per excessum vel defectum a iusta et vera aequalitate declinandi ad dimidium iusti pretii vel aestimationis, id est ipsius aequalitatis, cohibere, ne ulterius vagari posset. Sed certe haec cohibitio valde disproportionata est, utpote quae proportionem aequalitatis dimidio totius fraudari concedat, et sic inaequalitatem admittit duplae ad subduplam . . . quod est valde

granted relief on the basis of C.4.44.2 in the first place. Rather than being criticised, they should be praised for their sense of equity.[38] Incidentally, it might be remarked that Du Moulin is often seen as a forerunner of liberal commercial ethics. He nevertheless held on to the principles of equality in exchange and just pricing as tightly as the early modern Scholastics.[39]

Another issue on which Piñel disagrees with Du Moulin concerns the interpretation of the famous maxim that it is naturally permitted for contracting parties to try to outwit each other (D.4.4.16.4). True to his humanistic approach, Piñel first of all rejects the medieval jurists' interpretation according to which cheating in sale and lease was allowed as long as the quantity of the harm was moderate. In both the secular and ecclesiastical courts, a remedy was given to the *laesus*, but only if the harm was considerable, that is more than half of the just price (*ultra dimidiam*). Yet, again, this conventional interpretation could not satisfy Piñel's insatiable desire for the truth.

If we want to know the true meaning of D.4.4.16.4 and, by extension, of D.19.2.22.3, we need to free them from the intellectual world in which the medieval jurists lived, according to Piñel. From the classical jurists' perspective, there is no difference between considerable and lesser *laesio*. Moreover, the general terms in which paragraph *Idem Pomponius* is phrased exclude any distinction between lesion beyond and lesion below moiety.[40]

excessivum et a iusta aequalitate et naturali iustitia nimis remotum . . . Hinc durities dictae legis secundae multum placet et opportuna est viris tyrannicis et pleonecticis, qui sciunt et possunt sibi vigilare et cavere ne unquam decipiantur, ut numquam sibi metuant . . ."

38 Piñel, *Commentarii* (n 6), ad l 2, part 1, cap 1, num 22, 72–73: "Ex praedictis infertur contra Molinaeum de commerciis, num. 172 qui hanc legem duram et a tyrannis conditam exclamat, arguens, quod maximam iniquitatem permittat non succurrendo laesis, nisi ultra dimidiam iusti precii. Sed miror virum doctum | et ingeniosum inique et incaute in hanc l. invectum, debuit enim potius ex humanitate et aequitate eam laudare, cum antea nullum remedium laesis dabatur, cessante dolo vel metu vel aetatis privilegio, ut supra probavimus, vel debuit saltem cum omnibus agnoscere, ante hanc legem non fuisse aliam quae laesis magis succurreret, ut sic non magis in hanc quam in alias exclamaret." Pinel then goes on to reprimand Du Moulin for having unrightfully criticised the theologians' understanding of *laesio enormis*.

39 C Du Moulin, *Commentarii in Parisienses consuetudines* (1597) par 33, gl 1 in verb. *Droict de relief*, num 46, 438: " . . . quando de laesione et rescissione agitur, iustum pretium ad tantam pecuniam aestimatur, quantum res iuste valet, non quantum repertum fuit aut reperiri posset . . . Et debet esse aequalitas, et eadem commensuratio inter emptorem et venditorem et eadem iuris summetria."

40 Piñel, *Commentarii* (n 6) ad l 2, part 1, cap 1, num 32, 74–75: "Quae verba [sc. in pretio emptionis et venditionis naturaliter licere contrahentibus se circumvenire] accipiunt glossa et omnes ibi, glossa et omnes hic, glossa et omnes in cap. cum dilectus, et noviores infra citandi, ut tantum referantur ad laesionem citra dimidiam. | Ego autem verissimum puto iurisconsultos in illis verbis indistincte de omni laesione sentire, nec aliquid referre ad mentem iurisconsultorum an laesio modica an maxima sit; tum ex generalitate verborum, quae non admittunt communem restrictionem, tum quia eo tempore incognita erat differentia magnae vel modicae laesionis, de qua agit haec lex, ut supra late probavimus."

No matter whether it is big or small, for the Romans any lesion is irrelevant in regard to the validity of a sale contract. In short, traditional opinion has been misguided by not making the effort to read the different texts from the Digest and the Code in their historical context.

The new interpretation of D.4.4.16.4 suggested by Piñel rests on a reading of the paragraph in its broader textual context. Title 4 of the fourth book of the Digest concerns minors. The law: *In causae cognitione*, in particular, deals with the question whether a minor can be granted other remedies than the extraordinary remedy of restitution (*restitutio in integrum*).[41] According to Piñel, the upshot of the argumentation is that minors cannot appeal to the special remedy of restitution unless the contract they entered into is still valid. Hence, the aim of paragraph *Idem Pomponius* is to determine whether cheating (*circumventio*) invalidates a sale contract or not. If it does, then a minor is granted the ordinary remedies and not restitution.

According to Piñel, what is at stake in D.4.4.16.4 is the availability of the remedy of *restitutio in integrum* for minors (*principaliter agit de concedenda vel neganda restitutione*).[42] Since cheating does not invalidate the contract, the conclusion to paragraph *Idem Pomponius* should be that a minor is granted the remedy of restitution in a contract where buyer and seller have tried to outwit each other. So D.4.4.16.4 is actually about a procedural advantage for minors. The purpose of the argument was not to establish a universal rule of law – rigorous law – that allows buyers and sellers to outwit each other.[43]

Piñel disagrees with Du Moulin in interpreting the meaning of the "natural" permission to cheat. Du Moulin held that it was "naturally permitted" for parties to outwit each other, because they were both willing to turn a

41 D.4.4 (*De minoribus vigintiquinque annis*).16pr: "In causae cognitione etiam hoc versabitur, num forte alia actio possit competere citra in integrum restitutionem. Nam si communi auxilio et mero iure munitus sit, non debet ei tribui extraordinarium auxilium, utputa cum pupillo contractum est sine tutoris auctoritate, nec locupletiorem factus est."

42 Piñel, *Commentarii* (n 6), ad l 2, part 1, cap 1, num 33, 75: "Vides igitur, quod dixi contra omnes, quo ad mentem iurisconsulti ibi, dum principaliter agit de concedenda vel neganda restitutione, nullam esse differentiam inter magnam vel modicam laesionem."

43 Piñel, *Commentarii* (n 6), ad l 2, part 1, cap 1, num 34, 75: "Imo si subtilius mens iurisconsulti expendatur, colliges contra glossam et omnes (quod fortasse mirabile videbitur) verba illa, *licere contrahentibus in precio se circumvenire,* principaliter ibi prolata fuisse in favorem et beneficium laesi, nempe minoris, ut scilicet restitutionem habere posset, quia is est scopus iurisconsulti ibi. Non enim pertinebat ad rubricam nec ad ea quae iurisconsultus ibi tractabat, tradere regulam, vel rigorem illum iuris, ut liceat contrahentibus, in precio se circumvenire. Plane igitur mens iurisconsulti eiusque praecipua decisio id petit, ut non obstante qualibet laesione in precio, contractus valeat, et inde sequatur, minorem restituendum fore."

blind eye to each other's cheating.[44] Piñel rejects this analysis as unrealistic. After profound reflection, Piñel thinks the only correct understanding of "naturally" goes back to the gloss and Thomas Aquinas. Piñel insists that it is dangerous in this context to confound the philosophers' notion of natural law and its juridical meaning. Natural law in the sense of natural equity or the common social bond of love between all men cannot possibly lie behind paragraph *Idem Pomponius*. In this context, the only appropriate meaning of "naturally" is "according to the *ius gentium*".

On account of experience, Piñel argues, people from all nations reasoned that lesion should be permitted (*permittenda*) lest commerce be continually disturbed by too strict an observance of contractual equilibrium.[45] The security of transactions and the stability of the legal system must prevail. Consequently, what may be wrong on an individual basis may become permitted on the level of society as a whole.[46] Piñel draws inspiration from the views of humanists such as François Le Douaren on prescriptive acquisition (*usucapio*). A similar concern for social stability (*tranquilitas reipublicae*) allowed individuals to acquire goods in spite of their bad faith. Interestingly, to support this view, Manuel Soarez a Ribeira adduces Seneca's typically Stoic belief that the Gods care more about the whole than about the individual.[47] Piñel himself referred to Cicero's statement that the salvation of the people is the supreme law.[48] In conclusion,[49]

44 Du Moulin, *Tractatus commerciorum* (n 37), num 182, 161: "Nota quod d. l. 2 non est facta, nisi pro veris et naturalibus contractibus commutativis, in quibus tacito quodam naturali sensu partes sibiipsis modicam laesionem mutuo condonare et indulgere videntur."

45 Piñel, *Commentarii* (n 6), ad l 2, part 1, cap 1, num 39, 76: "Ego aliter ea verba explicanda putabam post rem vero satis consideratam, ita credo sensisse gl. In d. § idem Pomponius ad quem nemo advertit. Exponit enim gl. *naturaliter*, id est *iure gentium*. Intelligo autem, ut secundum exactissimam illam priorem aequitatem naturalem non dicatur licere contrahentibus invicem se in precio nec in alia re circumvenire. Nam secundum eam naturae normam omnes homines cognati et mutua dilectionis lege continere dicuntur . . . Exponitur ergo, *naturaliter*, id est *iure gentium*, quia humana ratione gentiumque et populorum iudicio compertum est, permittendam fuisse eam laesionem in pretio, ne ex nimia aequalitatis observatione commercia turbarentur. Nulla enim conventio securitatem praestaret, nunquam litium finis esset, si ob laesionem in pretio conventa revocarentur."

46 Piñel, *Commentarii* (n 6), ad l 2, part 1, cap 1, num 40, 77: "Unde quo ad universos et pro tranquilitate reipublicae potest favorabile censeri, quod singulis separatum (sic) durum videbitur."

47 Seneca, *De divina providentia*, 3, 1, in *Seneca, Moral Essays*, with an English translation by J W Basore, [Loeb Classical Library, 214], Cambridge Mass/London 1963[3] [=1928], vol 1, 14: ". . . pro universis, quorum maior diis cura quam singulorum est . . .".

48 Cicero, *De legibus*, 3, 3, 8, in *Cicéron, Traité des lois, Texte établi et traduit par G de Plinval, [Collection des Universités de France]*, (1968[2])[=1959], 85: "Salus populi suprema lex esto."

49 Piñel, *Commentarii* (n 6), ad l 2, part. 1, cap 1, num 40, 77: "*Naturaliter* igitur *licere* dixerunt iurisconsulti ex permissione humani iuris seu gentium, secundum quod ad quietem reipublicae magis consentaneum visum est, eam laesionem in precio remittere, et ideo ea non obstante,

The jurists used the expression "naturally allowed" by reason of a permission by human law, i.e. the law of nations, to the extent that it is more conducive to the stability of the republic to condone lesion in the price. As a result, the contract remains valid regardless of the lesion, so that then, in particular, it became necessary to grant restitution as a remedy to minors. That is what Pomponius' fragment is all about.

D. CONCLUDING REMARKS

The humanist flavour of Arias Piñel's legal thought expressed itself through his constant emphasis upon the difference between the original sense of the Roman texts and the meaning that was read into them in subsequent ages. The outrage which Piñel felt at the abuse of the Digest translated itself into scathing remarks about the historical nonsense of the medieval jurists, which sometimes persisted even in contemporary humanist jurisprudence. His philological nature made Piñel fundamentally unhappy with the anachronistic use of Roman legal texts. However, one should not infer from this that Piñel did not share the Scholastic jurists' commitment to adapt legal thinking to the needs of their own, essentially Christian society. Also, his slightly condescending attitude towards the medieval *ius commune* did not prevent him from citing Scholastic authorities such as Thomas Aquinas and Baldus along with the great classical poets and philosophers from Antiquity.

Ironically, Piñel could be considered as a humanist jurist who took the Christian heritage from the Middle Ages more seriously than his Scholastic counterparts. For example, his treatment of the renunciability of the remedy grounded on the *Lex secunda* was deeply influenced by the Christian concern to protect the weak and to promote equity (*aequitas*). While the medieval jurists had recognised that contracting parties had a right to renounce the remedy by virtue of C.4.44.2, Piñel was highly critical of all of those renunciation clauses. Perhaps he was influenced here by the work of Antonio Gómez, a professor of Roman law at the University of Salamanca. Gómez had argued that even the combination of a specific renunciation clause and a donation clause could not deprive the *laesus* of his right to seek support from the *Lex secunda*. He reasoned that the same facility (*facilitas*) with which such a party could become the victim of lesion would be at the basis of his renunciation or donation clause.[50] Piñel took this reasoning a step further.

semper contractus valet, et consequenter restitutio tunc specialiter minoribus necessaria fuit, ad id enim tendit iurisconsultus in d. § ut supra."

50 A Gómez, *Commentarii variaeque resolutiones* (1572), tom 2, cap 2, num 26, 227: "Item adde, quod talis deceptus poterit agere remedio praedictae legis secundae, etiamsi dixerit, quod donat

According to him, even if the lesioned party knew in advance that he was going to suffer lesion, this knowledge did not deprive him of the remedy provided by C.4.44.2. Contrary to the common, medieval opinion, Piñel argued that knowledge does not take away that remedy.

One of the main motivations behind Piñel's attack on the *communis opinio* lay not in his general criticism of the medieval legal tradition, but rather in his loyalty to Christian morality.[51] "The contrary opinion is more true and more decent to Christians."[52] Christian morality urged Piñel to take the possibility of abuse of necessity (*necessitas*) seriously. Knowledge of the true price should not be a ground to relinquish the remedy offered by C.4.44.2, because equity (*aequitas*) lies at the very heart of this constitution.[53] Typical of his practical approach to the interpretation of ancient texts, Piñel also hailed the procedural advantages of this view. In court, the burden of proof now shifted from the *laesus* to the *laedens*. The victim of *laesio enormis* would no longer need to maintain his ignorance, let alone prove it.[54] In other words, Arias Piñel was a jurist with a taste for philological criticism and humanist erudition, but he also showed himself to be sensible to the needs of legal practice, certainly in a Christian society. Conscience required that equity and good faith be observed down to the last detail.[55] In case of conflict, even Piñel's profoundly humanist sense of the pure letter of Roman law must bend before the spirit of equity.

illud quod plus valeret et insuper renunciavit remedio praedictae legis secundae, quia illa verba non debent referri ad magnum pretium, sed ad modicum . . . Item etiam, quia eadem facilitate qua inducitur ad vendendum, inducitur etiam ad ponendum illam clausulam vel aliam similem . . . "

51 For a more profound discussion, see Decock, *Theologians and Contract Law* (n 1) 581–588.

52 Piñel, *Commentarii* (n 6), ad l 2, part 1, cap 2, num 11, 80: "Sed ea scribentium turba nos non deterruit, quin contrarium verius, et Christianis hominibus decentius putemus."

53 Piñel, *Commentarii* (n 6) ad l 2, part 1, cap 2, num 12, 81: "Suadetur etiam ex aequitate, qua lex haec principaliter nititur, quae militat etiam in eo, qui sciebat verum pretium, potuitque ex necessitate vel alia causa moveri. Iuvatur etiam, quia iura saepe succurrunt hominibus dissipantibus bona sua."

54 Piñel, *Commentarii* (n 6), ad l 2, part 1, cap 2, num 16, 81–82: "Infertur similiter necessario, ad praxim et libellum in materia huius legis non esse necessarium articulos vel positiones formare, quod laesio per ignorantiam contigerit . . . Ex quo etiam resultat non solum in processu non oportere probare ignorantiam . . . sed nec eam allegare . . . "

55 Piñel, *Commentarii* (n 6), ad l 2, part 1, cap 1, num 35, 75: "Quae receptior et magis pia traditio satis comprabatur ex iurisconsulto in d. l. iure succursum, 7, § finali, ff. de iure dotali iuncta declaratione superius tradita. Ubi enim exactissime bona fides et aequitas requiritur, prout ibi in causa dotis etiam minor laesio emendari iubetur, quod magis viget in foro conscientiae."

7 The Working Methods of Hugo Grotius: Which Sources Did He Use and How Did He Use Them in His Early Writings on Natural Law Theory?

Martine J van Ittersum

A. INTRODUCTION

This chapter examines the working methods of the Dutch jurist Hugo Grotius (1583–1645), particularly his use and referencing of "sources" in his early works on natural law and natural rights. I will first discuss the methodological issues at stake. I will then say something about Grotius and books in the first two decades of the seventeenth century. Which books did he own? To which libraries did he have access? And, most importantly, what purpose did books serve for Grotius? Which ones did he read from cover to cover and which ones did he use selectively? This, of course, brings us to the issue of Grotius' working methods. How did he gather and process information? How did he construct treatises? What can we say about his use of "sources" in his early works on natural law and natural rights? In answering these questions, I will draw on the research which Peter Borschberg, Jan Waszink, and I have done on Grotius' early works on natural law and natural rights theories, in particular Mss BPL 917, 918 and 922 in Leiden University Library. I will end with a detailed discussion of Grotius' referencing of Thomas Aquinas' *Summa Theologiae* in Ms BPL 917, otherwise known to us as *De Jure Praedae*/Commentary on the Law of Prize and Booty, written by Grotius in 1604–08 at the behest of the Dutch East India Company (VOC). Grotius' own copy of the *Summa Theologiae* is still extant at Lund University Library. It contains lots of underlining. There is much that can be learnt about Grotius' use of "sources" by comparing underlined passages in his copy of the *Summa Theologiae* with his referencing of Aquinas in Ms BPL 917. In my conclusion, I will address the question where we go from here. Will a better understanding of Grotius' working methods afford us new insights into his life and work? Is it important? Why should the "new" intellectual history be preferable to *Ideengeschichte* and *Quellenforschung* old-style?

B. METHODOLOGICAL ISSUES: WHAT IS THE PROBLEM WITH *IDEENGESCHICHTE* AND *QUELLENFORSCHUNG*?

The circulation of knowledge in the early modern world has received much attention in recent years. It has generated truly innovative research in a wide range of disciplines, ranging from book history and the history of science to the history of empire, global history and cultural history. Thanks to large online databases, such as Early Modern Letters On-Line (Oxford), Circulation of Knowledge (Huygens ING in The Hague) and Mapping the Republic of Letters (Stanford), the scholarly communities of early modern Europe can be subjected to network analysis on a grand scale. Ann Blair and Anthony Grafton have shown that a scholar's working methods, particularly his or her strategies for dealing with "information overload", are an essential ingredient in the construction of knowledge. Arguably, this has important implications for the study of legal history, including "legal humanism".

In discussing the methodological issues at stake – not my favourite pastime – I should like to get straight to the heart of the matter. Are legal historians and intellectual historians still wedded – either secretly or not-so-secretly – to the history of ideas as traditionally understood? Do we sufficiently reflect on the implicit assumptions that inform our research agenda? In the case of Grotius, are we still looking – somewhere, anywhere – for the rise of modern international law, for example? At the risk of sounding crude and reductive,

Ideengeschichte can be defined as a conversation among dead white males, aimed a solving present-day problems. This analytical model is problematic on many counts. The Cambridge School of Political Thought has sought to move away from it by recasting the history of ideas as the history of political discourses and languages. The recent emphasis on working methods and circulation of knowledge – approaches pioneered by historians of the book and historians of science – will allow us to move further down this path, and ask new, exciting and far more historically grounded questions.

Ideengeschichte continues to hold many attractions for legal historians, however. Canonical thinkers (usually men, of course) are deemed to have either "invented" important concepts in Western civilisation – sovereignty, the rule of law, rights theories etc – or radically overhauled them, supposedly to create "the modern world". Teleology and anachronism tend to loom large in these narratives. In Grotius' case, it has resulted in endless publications on *De Jure Belli ac Pacis* (1625) and the perceived origins of international law. A case in point is the work of Peter Haggenmacher, who wrote the Grotius entry for the *Oxford Handbook of the History of International Law* (2012). Haggenmacher's magnum opus is his doctoral dissertation, *Grotius et la doctrine de la guerre juste* (1983).[1] It is a classic example of *Ideengeschichte*. Haggenmacher identifies every single medieval author mentioned in *De Jure Belli ac Pacis*, however obscure, and then discusses what Grotius may have learnt from each of these alleged "sources", without ranking them in order of importance, exploring possible connections or disagreements between them, etc, etc. If we may believe Haggenmacher, Grotius' just war theory is taken straight from the greater and lesser minds of the Middle Ages. This understanding of Grotius' life and work is seriously flawed. Haggenmacher never pauses to consider the question (a) whether Grotius actually read any of the alleged "sources" of *De Jure Belli ac Pacis*, (b) how he read them, and (c) why he should have cited or referenced them. Haggenmacher's entire argument is undermined by his inability or unwillingness to consider the working methods of early modern scholars.

Plenty of other Grotius scholars have operated in a similar vein. A fine example is the so-called *editio major* of *De Jure Belli ac Pacis*, edited by Mrs B J A de Kanter-van Hettinga Tromp. Originally published in 1939, it was reissued in 1993 by the late Robert Feenstra, the foremost legal historian of

1 S Peter, D Högger, B Fassbender and A Peters (eds), *The Oxford Handbook of the History of International Law* (Oxford Handbooks in Law)(2012) ch 48. P Haggenmacher, *Grotius et la doctrine de la guerre juste* (1983). In this chapter I will refer to the Dutch version of Henk Nellen's biography of Hugo Grotius. It should be noted that an English translation is also now available.

The Netherlands in the second half of the twentieth century.[2] As Feenstra points out, the *editio major* is a compilation of materials:

- the textual basis is the 1631 edition of *De Jure Belli ac Pacis*, collated with the editions of 1625, 1632 and 1642, 1646;
- yet the critical apparatus is largely copied from P C Molhuysen's edition of *De Jure Belli ac Pacis* (1919), which relies heavily on the 1646 text.

Since, by her own admission, de Kanter-van Hettinga Tromp had no intention of engaging in textual criticism, printing errors remained uncorrected or were re-included (after Molhuysen had corrected them in his 1919 edition!). Both the text and critical apparatus of the *editio major* are reproduced in the 1993 reprint. However, Feenstra sought to purify the critical apparatus by means of "Additional Notes" and added a "List of Sources", in order to specify "the editions we use and refer to in the Additional Notes". In verifying Grotius' references, he tried as much as possible to avail himself of "an edition that Grotius could have used". However, he emphasised in his introduction that "only in very few cases" was it possible to establish "with any degree of certainty which edition Grotius actually used". The only example supplied by Feenstra in his introduction to the 1993 reprint is a faulty reference to Cajetanus' commentary on Aquinas' *Summa Theologiae*, which Grotius probably copied out of the first edition of Vitoria's *Relectiones Theologicae* (1557). Otherwise, Feenstra makes little attempt to identify editions used by Grotius in writing *De Jure Belli ac Pacis*.[3]

As a consequence, the List of Sources can easily lead an unwary reader

2 H Grotius, *De iure belli ac pacis libri tres in quibus ius naturae & gentium: item iuris publici praecipua explicantur* (ed) B J A de Kanter-van Hettinga Tromp (1939) (second, expanded edition with notes by R Feenstra and C A Persenaire 1993) 923–928.

3 H Grotius, *De iure belli ac pacis libri tres* (n 2) 595, 921–945 (particularly n 77 on 940 and n 87 on 941), 949 (n 103a), 1003–1004 (nn 595a, 595b), 1011 (n 670a), 1027–1070, see also R Feenstra, "Quelques remarques sur les sources utilisées par Grotius dans ses travaux de droit naturel" in *The World of Hugo Grotius (1583–1645): Proceedings of the International Colloquium Organized by the Grotius Committee of the Royal Netherlands Academy of Arts and Sciences, Rotterdam, 6–9 April 1983* (1984) 65–81, particularly 65–73. Feenstra points to Grotius' faulty reference to "Caiet 2.2. q. 4 art. 1" in *De Jure Belli ac Pacis* Lib II Cap xxv § v, which should be Cajetanus on Aquinas' *Secunda Secundae* question 40 art 1. According to Feenstra, it suggests that Grotius copied the reference out of the first edition of Vitoria's *Relectiones Theologicae*, published in Lyon in 1557, where the same mistake occurs. In the Additional Notes, Feenstra points out that page numbers supplied by Grotius in the marginal references of *De Jure Belli ac Pacis* allow us to identify editions on two occasions, *De Jure Belli ac Pacis* Lib I Cap IV § xx: reference to Pietro Bizarri, *Senatus populique Genuensis rerum domi forisque gestarum historiae atque annales* (1579) (USTC 401810 and USTC 415043), *De Jure Belli ac Pacis* Lib III Cap IV § xviii: reference to Marcin Kromer, *De origine et rebus gestis Polonorum libri XXX* (1558) (USTC 675238).

astray. For example, the List of Sources includes the 1610 Antwerp edition of the *Opera Omnia* of the Spanish canonist Covarruvias (1512–1577). Yes, it is an edition Grotius could have used while writing *De Jure Belli ac Pacis*. But did he? For Covarruvias' *Practicae Quaestiones* are already referenced in Ms BPL 917 in Leiden University Library, an early work of Grotius on natural law and natural rights. Indeed, references to the *Practicae Quaestiones* are found on folios that can be dated precisely, to 1604–1605. Moreover, Feenstra suggests in his Additional Notes that quite a few references in *De Jure Belli ac Pacis* were copied by Grotius from Ms BPL 917.[4] So the question remains: which edition of Covarruvias did Grotius use? And, more importantly, what can we say about his reading strategies? How carefully did he peruse Covarruvias, and to what purpose? As far as I know, Feenstra never seems to have considered these questions in compiling his massive *Annotationes Novae*. Stranger still, his List of Sources was republished (with a few changes) in the recent Liberty Fund edition of *De Jure Belli ac Pacis* (2005). Transmogrified into the "Bibliography of Postclassical Works Referred to by Grotius", the unwary reader may simply take it to be a list of Grotius' sources.[5] It has all the appearance of authoritative *Quellenforschung*. But what, if anything, does it tell us about Grotius? Should we not investigate his working methods first, before we make any sweeping statements about his alleged "sources"?

C. GROTIUS AND LIBRARIES

Grotius' working methods were shaped to a large extent by the availability of books and other sources of information, certainly at the start of his career. Which books did he own? To which libraries did he have access? And, most importantly, what purpose did books serve for Grotius? Which ones were read from cover to cover, which ones were used selectively? Can we make

4 Grotius, *De iure belli ac pacis libri tres* (n 2) 948 (n 96a-e, 97b-d), 949 (n 97e-f) 1040, H Grotius, *The Rights of War and Peace*, (ed) R Tuck, *Natural Law and Enlightenment Classics*, 3 vols (2005) 1770–1, Leiden University Library, Ms BPL 917 f 12r and f 128v, 129r (reference to "Covarr. *Practicae Quaestiones*, I"), M J van Ittersum, "Dating the manuscript of *De Jure Praedae* (1604–1608): what watermarks, foliation and quire divisions can tell us about Hugo Grotius' development as a natural rights and natural law theorist" (2009) 35 *History of European Ideas* 125.

5 H Grotius, *The Rights of War and Peace* (n 4) 1763–1789. Robert Feenstra briefly discusses second-hand references and quotations in *Mare Liberum* in his Editor's Introduction to the 2009 edition of *Mare Liberum*. See H Grotius, *Mare Liberum, 1609–2009: Original Latin Text and Modern English Translation*, (ed) and annotated by R Feenstra, with a general introduction by J Vervliet (2009) LVI–LIX.

a clear-cut distinction between serious intellectual engagement with texts and mere name-dropping, i.e. listing "authorities" in clusters of references in order to add weight to his argument? Or were there, in fact, many shades of grey in between?

Much can be learned about Grotius' access to books from articles by E J J van der Heijden, P C Molhuysen, E M Meijers, F Dovring, and E Rabbie. The articles of Molhuysen, Meijers and Dovring contain full bibliographical descriptions of books once in Grotius' possession that are still extant in Dutch and Swedish libraries. Largely as a result of his liberal arts education in Leiden, Grotius built up a substantial collection of Greek and Roman authors at an early age. As a student, Grotius may have purchased at least two anthologies of Classical poets: the 1549 edition of *C Julius Hyginus Augustus libertus, Fabularum liber* and the 1589 edition of *Astronomica veterum scripta*, which he used to prepare *Syntagma Arateorum* (1600). His copy of Seneca's *Tragoediae*, a cheap contemporary edition worth ten stivers, is mentioned in a letter to Daniel Heinsius from 1610.[6] Which other books or texts did he own in the first decade of the seventeenth century? Dovring's article mentions Grotius' copy of Emmanuel van Meteren's history of the Dutch Revolt, published in 1603, which is still extant in Lund University Library. Grotius undoubtedly acquired the book with an eye to writing his own *Annales et Historiae*, a history of the Dutch Revolt commissioned by the States of Holland in 1601 and submitted for approval to the States in 1612.[7] In autumn 1604, the Amsterdam directors of the Dutch East India Company (VOC) arranged for Grotius to be sent materials for the *Historica* chapter of Ms BPL 917, including maps of the Indian Ocean and China Sea, verdicts of the Amsterdam Admiralty Court, letters of Dutch captains, and fifteen notarised attestations of Dutch merchants

6 E M Meijers, *Boeken uit de bibliotheek van De Groot in de Universiteitsbibliotheek te Leiden* (1949) (Mededelingen der Koninklijke Nederlandsche Akademie van Wetenschappen, Afdeling Letterkunde, New Series vol 12 no 3) 251–279, F Dovring, *Une Partie de l'Héritage Littéraire de Grotius Retrouvée en Suède* (1949) (Mededelingen der Koninklijke Nederlandsche Akademie van Wetenschappen, Afdeling Letterkunde, New Series vol 12 no 3) 237–249, F Dovring, *Nouvelles Recherches sur la Bibliothèque de Grotius en Suède et en Italie* (1951) (Mededelingen der Koninklijke Nederlandsche Akademie van Wetenschappen, Afdeling Letterkunde, New Series vol 14 no 10) 331–338, E Rabbie, "The History and Reconstruction of Hugo Grotius' Library: A Survey of the Results of Former Studies with an Indication of New Lines of Approach", in E Canone (ed), *Bibliothecae Selectae da Cusano a Leopardi* (1993) 119–137.

7 Lund University Library, Bibl Grotiana . . .. Handskriftsavd Hist Nederl 13. On Grotius' *Annales et Historiae*, see J Waszink, "Your Tacitism or mine? Modern and early-modern conceptions of Tacitus and Tacitism" (2010) 36 *History of European Ideas* 375, J Waszink, "Shifting Tacitisms. Style and composition in Grotius's Annales" (2008) 29 *Grotiana* 85.

and mariners, which were bound together as the "book treating of the cruel, treasonous and hostile procedures of the Portuguese in the East Indies". This particular "book" is still extant at the Dutch National Archives in The Hague. Grotius faithfully reproduced all the evidence received from the VOC directors in chapter 11 of Ms BPL 917. In addition, he borrowed a copy of Vitoria's *Relectiones Theologicae XII*, probably the 1557 Lyon edition, from Amsterdam VOC director Arent ten Grootenhuys. Although this copy is lost – Grotius arranged for it to be returned to its rightful owner in May 1643 – it must have been very well thumbed: Grotius' argument in chapter 12 of Ms BPL 917, published as *Mare Liberum* in 1609, is heavily indebted to Vitoria. As we shall see below, the *Relectiones Theologicae* may also have served Grotius as a kind of reader's guide to Aquinas. It was probably at the time of his writing of Ms BPL 917 that Dom Emmanuel of Portugal gifted him with a splendid four-volume edition of the *Summa Theologiae*, still extant at Lund University Library.[8]

In selecting references and quotations for his early works on natural rights and natural law theory, Grotius could avail himself of a large number of dictionaries, florilegia, and encyclopaedias in his own personal library. So much is clear from the list of books in Grotius' home in Rotterdam, drawn up in March 1620 by Louis Elzevier, a bookseller in The Hague. Perhaps it should be explained here that the Dutch States General convicted Grotius of high treason in May 1619, confiscating all his possessions. Elzevier was engaged by the States General to make an inventory

8 Lund University Library, Bibl Grotiana 4: *Corpus Iuris Canonici*, 3 vols (1569–1570), Dovring, *Une Partie de l'Héritage Littéraire de Grotius Retrouvée en Suède* (n 6) 241, The Hague, Dutch National Archives, Collection 102 (archive H van Zuylen van Nyevelt), inv no 13, Grotius, *De iure belli ac pacis libri tres* (n 2) 940 (n 77), 941 (n 87), 1003–1004 (nn 595a, 595b), *Briefwisseling van Hugo Grotius* ed. P C Molhuysen, B L Meulenbroek and H J M Nellen, 17 vols (The Hague, 1928–2001) vol I, 44–45 and vol 14, 252, 360, 387, 595, W Ph Coolhaas, "Een bron van het historische gedeelte van Hugo de Groot's *De Jure Praedae*" (1965) LXXIX *Bijdragen en Mededelingen van het Historisch Genootschap* 415, P Borschberg, "Grotius Maritime Intra-Asian Trade and the Portuguese Estado da India", in H W Blom (ed), *Property, Piracy and Punishment: Hugo Grotius on War and Booty in De Jure Praedae: Concepts and Contexts* (2009) 32–44, M J van Ittersum, *Profit and Principle: Hugo Grotius, Natural Rights Theories and the Rise of Dutch Power in the East Indies, 1595–1615* (Brill Intellectual History Series) (2006), H Grotius, *Commentary on the Law of Prize and Booty*, transl G L Williams, (ed) M J van Ittersum, *Natural Law and Enlightenment Classics* (2006) xiii–xxvii, 503–556, Van Ittersum, "Dating the manuscript of *De Jure Praedae*" (n 4). Grotius stumbled upon Grootenhuys' copy of Vitoria while tidying up his study in Paris, and immediately contacted his brother in The Hague, Willem de Groot, in order to have it returned to its rightful owner. It will come as no surprise that the Vitoria references in *De Jure Praedae* are all first-hand. According to Elzevier's valuation, the *Summa Theologiae* of Thomas Aquinas was worth twelve Flemish pounds, which made it by far the most expensive book in Grotius' library in 1619.

of Grotius' personal library in Rotterdam and to determine its monetary value as well. According to Elzevier's inventory, Grotius owned a copy of the *Biblotheca Universalis* of Conrad Gessner, a comprehensive listing of all the books of the first century of printing. Other reference works that lined the shelves of Grotius' library were the *Nomenclator* of Hadrianus Junius, an encyclopaedia in eight languages, first published by Christopher Plantin in Antwerp in 1567, and the *Florilegium Ethico-Politicum* of Janus Gruterus, first published in 1610–1612. Arabic, Italian and English dictionaries are also listed in Elzevier's inventory, along with the *Glossarium Graecobarbarum* of Johannes Meursius (1579–1639), the *Dictionarium Linguae Latinae* of Ambrosius Calepinus (c1440–1510), and the *Lexicon sive Dictionarium Graecolatinum* (Geneva 1592) of Robertus Constantinus. With the exception of Meursius' *Glossarium* and the Arabic and English dictionaries, all of these reference works would have been eminently affordable for Grotius at the turn of the seventeenth century, when he was still a young lawyer, without a regular source of income. Elzevier valued the Gessner edition at just ten stivers, while a "very old dictionary" was valued at five stivers. Grotius may also have possessed a substantial number of law textbooks and reference works, including Nikolaus Vigel's *Methodus juris civilis*, Jacques Labitte's *Indices juris varii . . . ad Pandectarum et codicis leges*, the *Paratitla seu synopsis pandectarum iuris civilis* of Johannes Freigius, the *Paratitla* of Matthaeus Wesenbecius, first published in 1566, and, of course, the *Corpus Iuris Canonici*. Again, all these titles were within Grotius' means at the turn of the seventeenth century. Elzevier valued *Methodus juris* at just five stivers, for example. In the case of Freigius' *Paratitla*, we know that Grotius gave it as a present to his younger brother Frans de Groot (1584–1602), who enrolled as a law student at Leiden University in March 1602 and died the following December. After Frans' death, the Freigius edition was returned to Grotius, who probably kept is as a *memento mori*.[9]

9 P Borschberg, *Hugo Grotius' Commentarius in Theses XI: An Early Treatise on Sovereignty, the Just War, and the Legitimacy of the Dutch Revolt* (1994) 60–74, P C Molhuysen, *De bibliotheek van Hugo de Groot in 1618* (Mededeelingen der Koninklijke Nederlandsche Akademie van Wetenschappen Afdeeling Letterkunde, New Series vol 6, no 3) (1943) 6–19 (no 23, 28, 108, 119, 155, 166, 177, 178, 182, 201, 216, 229, 233, 244, 296, 302, 319, 323, 326), Meijers, *Boeken uit de bibliotheek van De Groot in de Universiteitsbibliotheek te Leiden* (n 6) 253, 259, Dovring, *Nouvelles Recherches sur la Bibliothèque de Grotius en Suède et en Italie* (n 6) 8, Dovring, *Une Partie de l'Héritage Littéraire de Grotius Retrouvée en Suède* (n 6) 2, E J J van der Heijden, "De boekerij van Grotius", in (1930) 3 *Grotiana* 18 at 27–35, H Nellen, *Hugo de Groot: Een leven in strijd om de vrede* (2007) 35, 80–81. The Dutch States General convicted Hugo Grotius of high treason and to lifelong imprisonment at Loevestein Castle on 18 May 1619. Johan Halling was appointed as caretaker of Grotius' confiscated possessions on 8 June 1619. At the time of

Other works in Grotius' library in March 1620 would not have been affordable for a young lawyer. Various scholars have noted that the French legal humanists of the sixteenth century (Alciatus, Donellus, etc) are hardly mentioned in the marginalia of Ms BPL 917. The explanation may be a simple one: Grotius may only have acquired their works *after* the manuscript's completion. He purchased a copy of the 1538 edition of Andreas Alciatus' *Iudiciarii Processus Compendium* in 1609, for example.[10] Indeed, quite a few *juridica* present in Grotius' library in March 1620 would have been too expensive for him ten or fifteen years earlier. Allow me to cite from Elzevier's appraisal:

his arrest, Grotius had been living with his wife and children in the official residence of the Pensionary of Rotterdam on Princes' Street. Halling entered the house on 23 March 1620 in order to make a detailed inventory of its contents – furniture, clothing, books, etc. Two members of the Rotterdam town council and a licensed assessor from The Hague were present at these proceedings, which lasted three days. Halling engaged Louis Elzevier, bookseller in The Hague, to value the books in Grotius' possession. A notarial copy of Elzevier's list is extant in the archives of the Dutch States General: it contains 337 titles and their estimated market prices. Grotius' private library made up 30% of the total value of the contents of his house. Van der Heijden provides a transcription of the entire inventory of Grotius' house, including furniture and clothing, along with the valuation of each item. Molhuysen identifies most of the titles on Elzevier's list, which appear only in abbreviated or truncated form in the notarial copy. Gessner's *Bibliotheca universalis* was first published in Zurich in four volumes in 1545–1549. We do not know which edition Grotius possessed. The USTC lists no fewer than twelve Antwerp editions of Hadrianus Junius' *Nomenclator* in the second half of the sixteenth century. Christopher Plantin had the book reprinted twice by his Leiden office in 1585 (USTC 78371 and USTC 340795). We do not know which edition Grotius owned. In a letter addressed to his father, Jan de Groot, on 8 Nov 1624, Grotius requested that both Calepinus' *Dictionarium* and Constantinus' *Lexicon* be sent to him in Paris. See *Briefwisseling van Hugo Grotius*, vol 2, letter no 930 (*http://grotius.huygens.knaw.nl/letters/0930/*). Not all of the dictionaries and reference works in Grotius' library in May 1619 would have been within his means a decade earlier. In March 1620, Elzevier deemed the Arabic dictionary to be worth three guilders, the English dictionary two guilders, and Meursius' *Glossarium* two guilders. Molhuysen may have been mistaken in identifying "*Methodus Juris*" as "*Methodus utriusque juris*", "an often-reprinted incunabula" in Molhuysen's parlance. It is equally possible that "*Methodus juris*" refers to Nikolaus' *Methodus juris civilis*, whereof multiple editions appeared in Lyon and Basel in the second half of the sixteenth century (see USTC 139966, 675833, 678022, 678111, 139966, 141849 & 158014). We do not know which edition Grotius may have owned. Molhuysen was unable to identify the title "*Indices Juris*" found in the list of Grotius' confiscated possessions. He simply labels it as "unknown". The USTC suggests that we are dealing here with Labitte's *Indices juris varii . . . ad Pandectarum et codicis leges*, published in Geneva in 1585 (see USTC 451051). Grotius' copy has not survived. The *Paratitla* of Matthaeus Wesenbeck was first published in Basel in 1566 and reprinted in Basel in 1578 and 1572 two years later (USTC 675408, USTC 675407, and USTC 675404). We do not know which edition Grotius owned. His copy of the 1582 Basel edition of Freigius' *Paratitla* survives in the Library of the University of Uppsala. The title page indicates that Grotius gave this copy of the *Paratitla* as a present to his younger brother Frans de Groot.

10 Dovring, *Une Partie de l'Héritage Littéraire de Grotius Retrouvée en Suède* (n 6) 237, 241, Van der Heijden, "De boekerij van Grotius" (n 9) 18–38, Molhuysen, *De bibliotheek van Hugo de Groot in 1618* (n 9).

Udalricus Zasius, 5 volumes	3 guilders
Jac Cujacius, 4 volumes	5 guilders
Paulus Castrensis' *Lectura in Digesta*	6 guilders
Oceanus Juris, 6 volumes	3 guilders
Jason de Mayno, *Lectura super Digestis*	6 guilders
Bartolus a Saxoferrato, *Commentaria* or *Lectura in Corpus Iuris*	6 guilders
Panormitanus, *Consilia* or *Lectura in Decretales*	2 guilders
Corpus Iuris Civilis	8 guilders

In all probability, Grotius bought the *Corpus Iuris Civilis*, the works of the medieval civilians, and the works of the French legal humanists during his tenure as Advocate Fiscal of Holland (1607–1613) or as Pensionary of Rotterdam (1613–1618). His purchasing power as a magistrate must far have exceeded that of a mere lawyer. In March 1620, Grotius also owned two copies of the *Corpus Iuris Canonici*, one valued at two guilders, the other at one guilder and ten stivers. One of these survives in Lund University Library. It is a three-volume edition, published in Antwerp in 1569–1570. Grotius made his own handwritten indices, thus facilitating easy reference. It is more likely that he would have possessed this standard reference work as a young lawyer than any of the expensive *juridica* listed above.[11]

Could it be argued, however, that Grotius' ownership of printed materials was irrelevant, as long as he had access to the major texts of the Western tradition? Books and manuscripts circulated widely in the Republic of Letters. Even imprisonment at Loevestein Castle in 1619–1621 did not prevent Grotius from borrowing books from his friends, for example. G J Vossius (1577–1649) and Thomas Erpenius (1584–1624) regularly sent the prisoner materials for his philological and theological studies,[12] enabling him to prepare his Stobaeus edition (1623), *Excerpta ex tragoediis et comoediis Graecis* (1626) and his Latin translation of Euripides' *Phoenissae* (1630). Erpenius'

11 Lund University Library, Bibl *Grotiana* 4: *Corpus Iuris Canonici*, 3 vols (1569–1570), Van der Heijden, "De boekerij van Grotius" (n 9) 27–33, Molhuysen, *De bibliotheek van Hugo de Groot in 1618* (n 9) 6–19, Dovring, *Une Partie de l'Héritage Littéraire de Grotius Retrouvée en Suède* (n 6) 238. *Il consolato del mare*, a code of sea laws compiled by order of the Kings of Aragon in the eleventh through thirteenth centuries, was translated into various European languages. Three editions in Italian were published in Venice in the second half of the sixteenth century (see USTC 805285, 805877, 807304). We do not know which edition of *Il consolato del mare* Grotius owned.

12 C S M Rademaker, "Books and Grotius at Loevestein" (1972) 2 *Quaerendo* 2–29, Rabbie, "The History and Reconstruction of Hugo Grotius' Library" (n 6).

plans (never brought to fruition) to compile a polyglot edition of the New Testament induced Grotius to embark on his own *Annotationes*. In October 1620, he could inform Vossius that he had completed his commentaries on the first three Evangelists.[13]

The constant flow of books in and out of Loevestein Castle famously became the means of Grotius' escape. On Monday morning, 22 March 1621, the prisoner stepped into the trunk that was normally used for transporting books, wearing little more than his linen underwear and silk stockings. Unwitting soldiers carried the trunk and its contents to the house of the Daetselaer family in Gorinchem, who served as intermediaries in the exchange of books with Vossius and Erpenius. Once the soldiers were gone, Grotius stepped out of the trunk, donned a bricklayer's outfit (provided by the Daetselaer family) and, thus disguised, managed to flee across the rivers to Antwerp. Despite the hospitable reception in Antwerp, he decided to continue on to Paris, where he would live for most of the remainder of his life. Needless to say, as a scholar and statesman in Paris, Grotius had access to a number of excellent book collections, including that of the Dupuy brothers.[14]

To which libraries did Grotius have access in Holland in the 1600s, though? A young lawyer without a stable source of income could not afford a large book collection of his own. There were two libraries in the vicinity of The Hague that, in principle, would have been adequate for Grotius' needs in the 1600s: Leiden University Library and the book collection of the Court of Holland.[15] The Leiden humanist Janus Dousa (1545–1604), who was also a member of the Board of Overseers of Leiden University, had compiled a list of the 200–odd books in the possession of the Court of Holland in 1594. This list, which survives in the Leiden University Archives, contains the titles of manuscripts and printed works on feudal law and *ius commune*, printed editions of the *Corpus Iuris Civilis* and Decretals, including a glossary of civil and canon law, printed editions of the medieval Commentators on Roman law and canon law, and the works of sixteenth-century legal

13 Rademaker, "Books and Grotius at Loevestein" (n 12) 5–17, Molhuysen, *De bibliotheek van Hugo de Groot in 1618* (n 9) 17, Nellen, *Hugo de Groot* (n 9) 251–257.

14 Nellen, *Hugo de Groot* (n 9) 257–262, 298–316.

15 On the book collection of the Court of Holland at the turn of the seventeenth century, see C L Heesakkers, "Zes viercante witte manden", in J A A M Biemans (ed), *Boeken Verzamelen: Opstellen aangeboden aan Mr J R de Groot bij zijn afscheid als bibliothecaris der Rijksuniversiteit te Leiden* (1983) 182–197, R Feenstra, "Ouvrages de Droit Romain dans les Catalogues des Anciens Pays-Bas Septentrionaux (XIII–XVIe siècle)" (1960) 28 *Tijdschrift voor Rechtsgeschiedenis* 439.

humanists.[16] Andreas Alciatus and Ulrich Zasius are particularly well represented, with at least five publications each.[17] Two works of Franciscus Balduinus are listed: his edition (with commentary) of the Institutes and his "solemnis repetitio" of the Digest title "L. Celsius ff. De usucapionibus".[18] The book collection also contained Jason de Mayno's *Super Prima Parte Codicis*, three works by Baldus de Ubaldis, and at least six commentaries on the Decretals, three of which were authored by popes Boniface, Gregory, and Innocent, respectively.[19] Here, then, was an assortment of law books that would have been worthwhile for Grotius to consult. But did he do so? That seems improbable: the Court of Holland's book collection had been gathering dust in an attic for years when Dousa discovered it by chance and compiled his list in 1594. It is unclear to what extent lawyers who lived and worked in The Hague had access to these materials at the turn of the seventeenth century.

Leiden University Library must have been a far more important source of books for Grotius. He had been trained in the liberal arts at Leiden University from 1594 until 1597. His father had been a member of the University's board of overseers. When Jan de Groot stepped down in 1601, Grotius quietly assumed his father's mantle. In the decade that followed, Grotius was involved in various university appointments, including that of Arminius as professor of theology.[20] Moreover, his move to The Hague in 1600 did not diminish his friendship for Daniel Heinsius (1580–1655),

16 Leiden University Library, Archief van Curatoren, AC101, f 41r-46r.

17 *Alciati in 2 T Ff Juri Civi[lis] Commentarius; Andrea Alciati commentarii in librum pandectarum; Andreae Alciati Paradoxa Juris . . . de primatu petri adversibus Ludderum; Andreae Alciati commentaria de verborum significatione speculum principum ac Justiciae Petry Bellugy; Commentaria Alciati ad rescripta Principum Allexandri ab Alexandro Genialium Dierum; Andrea Alciati commentarii in librum pandectarum; Udalrici Zazy in Usus Feudorum Epitome; Udalrici Zazy in primam partem Digestorum veteris Paratitla; Eiusdem In titulum Institutionum de Actionib; E narratio Eiusdem in titulum digestorum de re judicata lectura; Rhaetoricae ac Dialecticae tractatio Uldalrici Zazy in 8.*

18 *Balduin Eiusdem solemnis repetitio L Celsius ff. De usucapionibus Institutiones Justiniani cum Francisci Balduini Commentis.*

19 *Baldus super 4 et 5 Codicem cum additionibus Alexandri Tartagni et Andreae Barbaciae; Baldi commentum super Feudis; Baldi super Instituta Decretalium in 3 Tomos divisum*
Bonifacius super 6. librum Decretalium
Graegory Papae Decretalium ix compilato bis
Philippi Franchi super 6 librum decretalium
Innocentius Papa super 2,3,4 et 5 decretalium libros
Dominici de Sancto Genimiano super 6 Decretalum
Eiusdem commentaria in Decreta Patrum
Novella Joh Andreae super 3,4,5 Decretalium.

20 Nellen, *Hugo de Groot* (n 9) 39–47, 60–64, 76–77.

a college friend who was appointed Professor of Poetry in 1603. Grotius exchanged quotations, letters, manuscripts, and books with Heinsius on a regular basis. In December 1610, Grotius wrote in reply to a request from Heinsius, that, no, he could not lend him Seneca's *Tragoediae*, since the two copies in his library had been absconded by his two brothers-in-law. Still, he would be happy to send Heinsius his own quick jottings on the *Tragoediae*. On many other occasions, the flow of books, manuscripts, reading notes and quotations went the other way. At Grotius' request, Heinsius oversaw the publication of *Mare Liberum* by Elzevier Publishers in Leiden in spring 1609. Peter Bertius (1565–1629), Master of the *Statencollege* in Leiden (a college for indigent theology students) copied out a draft of Grotius' *Ordinum Pietas* in August 1613 and saw the manuscript through the press. (The French and Latin editions of *Ordinum Pietas* were produced by J Paets in Leiden, printer to the University.) Bertius had been the Assistant Keeper of the University Library in the 1590s, while Heinsius was appointed Keeper in 1607. Both men routinely sent Grotius books from the University Library. Alternatively, Grotius was provided with extracts or strings of quotations. In October 1613, while Grotius was about to complete *Ordinum Pietas*, Bertius sent him quotes from the *Historia ecclesiastica* of Socrates Scholasticus (b 380 AD), from the *Historia ecclesiastica* of Theodoretus (c393–c458 AD), from the Theodosian Code, and from Alciatus' *Lucubrationum in ius civile*, part of the *Opera Omnia*, first published in Basel in 1546–1549. Grotius was a man in a hurry: according to E Rabbie, the modern editor of *Ordinum Pietas*, he may have written the bulk of *Ordinum Pietas* in less than three weeks. No wonder that he employed Bertius as a research assistant, charged with obtaining any information relevant for his treatise.[21]

21 *De Briefwisseling van Hugo Grotius/The Correspondence of Hugo Grotius* (*http://grotius.huygens.knaw.nl/years*) letter no 201 (Grotius to Daniel Heinsius, 8 Dec 1610), letter no 290A (P Bertius to Grotius, 15 Oct 1613) and letter no 291 (Grotius to P Bertius, 19 Oct 1613), H Grotius, *Ordinum Hollandiae ac Westfrisiae Pietas (1613)*, (ed) E Rabbie, *Studies in the History of Christian Thought* (1995) 37–46, M J van Ittersum, "Preparing *Mare Liberum* for the Press: Hugo Grotius' Rewriting of Chapter 12 of *De Jure Praedae* in November-December 1608" (2005–2007) 26–28 *Grotiana* 246, Nellen, *Hugo de Groot* (n 9) 60–129, Rabbie, "The History and Reconstruction of Hugo Grotius' Library" (n 6) 126–130, on Grotius' use of close relatives as research assistants, proof-readers etc, see M J van Ittersum, "Knowledge production in the Dutch Republic: the household academy of Hugo Grotius (1583–1645)" (2011) 72 *Journal of the History of Ideas* 523. Since Bertius sent his letter of 15 Oct 1613 to Grotius' home in Rotterdam, while Grotius was staying in The Hague at that time, not all of the quotes collected by Bertius could be included in the final version of *Ordinum Pietas* before the manuscript went to the printer. Bertius was not the only one who contributed materials to Grotius' *Ordinum Pietas*. As Rabbie points out, Grotius arranged for copies to be made of materials in the archives of the Count of Holland (i.e. an edict of 3 July 1508, regulating labour on Sunday) in March

Oftentimes Grotius must have lacked the time to consult books in person while collecting materials for his publications. His friends in Leiden could help out by providing him with ready-made quotes and excerpts. This was true of his legal scholarship as well. When, in 1615, Grotius prepared a reply to William Welwood's *Abridgement of All Sea-Lawes* (1613), a friend in Leiden, probably Petrus Scriverius (1576–1660), copied out for him various passages relating to the freedom of the seas in Franciscus Balduinus' *Commentarii in libros quattuor Institutionum Iuris Ciuilis*. Grotius may not have owned any works by François Baudouin (1520–1573), a famous sixteenth-century French legal humanist, in the first two decades of the seventeenth century. But the 1583 Lyon edition of Baudouin's Commentary on the Institutes was available in Leiden University Library. The sheet with excerpts –addressed to Grotius in his capacity as Pensionary of Rotterdam – is still extant in Ms BPL 918 in Leiden University Library. The handwriting seems to be that of Petrus Scriverius, another of Grotius' college friends. Scriverius, a scholar of independent means, had studied law in Leiden for a short while in the 1590s, but then joined the select group of students – which included Grotius and Heinsius – tutored by the French philologist Joseph Justus Scaliger (1540–1609). It is unclear whether Grotius explicitly requested the excerpts from Baudouin or whether Scriverius prepared them on his own initiative. Either way, it is doubtful that Scriverius – or Grotius for that matter – read Baudouin cover to cover. A "most copious and useful index" is already advertised on the title page of the 1554 Paris edition of Baudouin's Commentary. In all probability, Scriverius looked up the term "mare liberum" in the index, then went to the pages indicated and copied out the relevant passages for Grotius.[22]

1613, which he subsequently incorporated in *Ordinum Pietas*. It is unclear who was Grotius' assistant on this occasion. Did Grotius have a look at the archives of the Count of Holland himself? Or did he leave it to his assistant's initiative to find and copy materials that could be of use in writing *Ordinum Pietas*? We do not know. See Grotius, *Ordinum Hollandiae ac Westfrisiae Pietas* (ed) Rabbie (above) 228–229, 394.

22 Leiden University Library, Ms BPL 918, f 265–266 (inserted directly behind Grotius' notes on Selden's *Mare Clausum*). The excerpts are *not* in Grotius' hand. They are addressed to "Mijn Heere de Groote, Eerste Raet ende Pensionaris der Stede Roterdam"/Mr Hugo Grotius, First Councillor and Pensionary of the City of Rotterdam". Grotius used these reading notes to prepare his "*Defensio capitis quinti Maris Liberi*" (Leiden University Library, BPL 918, f 238–260), a reply to William Welwood's attack on *Mare Liberum* in *Abridgement of All Sea-Lawes* (1613). Judging by Elzevier's valuation, Grotius did not own a copy of Balduinus' commentary on the Institutes at the time of his arrest in 1619. Yet the Lyon edition of 1583 was available in Leiden University Library. Compare Van der Heijden, "De boekerij van Grotius" (n 9) 27–33, Molhuysen, *De bibliotheek van Hugo de Groot in 1618* (n 9) 6–19 and P Bertius, *Nomenclator: The First Printed Catalogue of Leiden University Library (1595)* (ed) R Breugelmans and

As noted earlier, Grotius' working methods were shaped to a large extent by his access to books and various other sources of information. Let us now take a closer look at the "scholar-at-work". We have already discovered that Grotius received materials for his publications from his family and friends and even from the Dutch East India Company, and that these materials could range from quotations and excerpts to maps and books. What did Grotius do with this large variety of materials? In which ways did he incorporate them into his writings? How did he construct a treatise, in fact? The journey from outline to treatise to printed book was a long one, and included many detours and about-turns. Nor was it Grotius' intention to publish in print everything that he wrote, far from it. Oftentimes, it was a conscious decision to leave materials in manuscripts, and to circulate them only among a small group of scholars and family and friends. All these factors have to be taken into account in evaluating Grotius' working methods.

J J Witkam (1995) folio E1v. The handwriting of the Balduinus notes is possibly that of Petrus Scriverius or, less likely, that of Gerardus Vossius, regent of the States College from 1615 to 1619. (I would like to thank Prof C L Heesakkers for his help and suggestions in identifying the unknown writer of the Balduinus notes.) Compare Leiden University Library, PAP 2 (P Scriverius to Hugo Grotius, 1 June 1622; Grotius addressed as "domino et amico suo aeternum colendo") and BPL 246 (Scriverius to Arnoldus Buchelius, 26 Apr 1621, 27 Sept and 1 Oct 1627), BPL 246 (Vossius to Hugo Grotius, Dec 1615 and Joannes Christenius, XV Kalendae of Jan 1640 (sv); PAP 3 (Vossius to Grotius, 23 Oct 1614 and 16 Sept 1614). The Balduinus notes are definitely *not* in the hand of Daniel Heinsius, head of the University Library (1607–1653), nor in the hand of Petrus Bertius, regent of the States College from 1607 to 1615. Compare Leiden University Library, Vulc 106II (Peter Bertius to B Vulcanius, 25 Feb 1605, and Bertius to Corn Grotius, Apr 1608), BPL 885 (Peter Bertius to "amplissimi viri", Nov 1609), PAP 2 (Daniel Heinsius to Hugo Grotius, 24 Sept 1606 and Heinsius to Grotius, 21 Feb 1611). In summer 1615, Scriverius published a volume of Greek Poetry of Joseph Justus Scaliger, which he dedicated to both Grotius and Heinsius. Grotius thanked Scriverius for the dedication and for sending him a presentation copy in a letter of 23 Sept 1615. See *De Briefwisseling van Hugo Grotius*/The Correspondence of Hugo Grotius (*http://grotius.huygens.knaw.nl/years*) letter no 412A (P Scriverius to Hugo Grotius & Daniel Heinsius, 29 June 1615, i.e. the dedicatory letter in *Jos Scaligeri . . . Poemata Graeca versa ex Lat, Ital et Gall*, Petrus Scriverius publicabat, Leiden 1615, p †2v-[†6r]) and letter no 422 (Grotius to P Scriverius, 23 Sept 1615). On Petrus Scriverius and his friendship with Grotius and Heinsius, see S Langereis, *Geschiedenis als ambacht: Oudheidkunde in de Gouden Eeuw: Arnoldus Buchelius en Petrus Scriverius* (2001) 104–154 and Nellen, *Hugo de Groot* (n 9) 46, 59–63, 105, 235–237, 256–257.

D. GROTIUS' WORKING METHODS

Thanks to the publications of Ann Blair and Anthony Grafton (among others), the working methods of early modern scholars have become a fashionable subject of research in recent years. It is also a subject that resonates far beyond the walls of academia. Blair shows in *Too much to know* (2011) that the problem of information overload which we experience in the West in the twenty-first century can hardly be called new: it already existed in Classical Antiquity, but became acute in Western Europe following the invention of print. The concomitant changes in reading habits and note-taking practices, not to mention the invention of "finding aids" like indexes, tables of contents and bibliographies, have shaped the construction of knowledge in the West into modern times. Grotius' use of various shortcuts in writing his treatises is entirely typical of the working methods of early modern scholars. They had both too little and too much information at their disposal. None of them enjoyed the 24-hour access to texts that, thanks to the internet, we do today in the West. However, the large-scale recovery of classical texts in the Renaissance, the discovery of "new worlds" outside of Europe, and the ever-increasing production of printed texts resulted in information overload in early modern Europe. The closed universe of medieval scholarship, which had relied on just a handful of authoritative texts, was definitely a thing of the past by the seventeenth century. Yet the urge to fill one's writings with quotations from "the authorities" remained undiminished. Grafton has shown that the transition from exclusively text-based knowledge to the construction of knowledge by other means (mathematics, empirical observations, etc) – something we call the Scientific Revolution – was a very slow process in the West. Far into the nineteenth century, referencing the authorities counted for a great deal in constructing an argument. With this in mind, let us now turn to Grotius' working methods.[23]

23 A Blair, *Too Much to Know: Managing Scholarly Information before the Modern Age* (2011), A Blair, "Reading strategies for coping with information overload, ca 1550–1700" (2003) 64 *Journal of the History of Ideas* 11, A Blair, "Annotating and Indexing Natural Philosophy", in M Frasca-Spada and N Jardine (eds), *Books and the Sciences in History* (2000) 69–89, A Blair, "Humanist methods in natural philosophy: the commonplace book" (1992) 53 *Journal of the History of Ideas* 541, A Grafton, *Worlds Made by Words: Scholarship and Community in the Modern West* (2009), A Grafton, *Commerce with the Classics: Ancient Books and Renaissance Readers* (1997), A Grafton, *New Worlds, Ancient Texts: The Power of Tradition and the Shock of Discovery* (1995) and A Grafton, *Defenders of the Text: The Traditions of Scholarship in an Age of Science, 1450–1800* (1994), A Grafton, "Kepler as a reader" (1992) 53 *Journal of the History of Ideas* 561.

In the case of Grotius' early writings on natural law and natural rights, Peter Borschberg was the first to give serious thought to the author's working methods, particularly to his referencing and use of sources. In 1994, Borschberg published his edition of Grotius' *Commentarius in Theses XI*, an autograph manuscript on the legitimacy of the Dutch Revolt, which forms part of Ms BPL 922 in Leiden University Library. Borschberg correctly notes that there is a close connection between *Theses XI* and Ms BPL 917, a manuscript of 163 folios, first published as *De Jure Praedae* (*On the Law of Prize and Booty*) in 1868. Grotius wrote Ms BPL 917 at the behest of the VOC, and substantially revised it at least twice in the period 1604–1608. Chapter 12 of Ms BPL 917 was printed as *Mare Liberum* in April 1609, again at the request of the VOC directors. As I argue in "Dating the Manuscript of *De Jure Praedae*", *Theses XI* seems to be a spin-off of chapter 13 of Ms BPL 917, and should probably be dated to 1607–1609. Borschberg has carefully examined Grotius' working methods and referencing of "sources" in Ms BPL 922. In doing so, he has not just looked at what seem to us finished treatises – *Theses XI*, for example – but also at reading notes, fragments and outlines in Grotius' hand. Ms BPL 922 offers us a unique insight into scholarly working practices in the seventeenth century. Ms BPL 922 is filled with materials that, in one way or another, went into Grotius' thought and writing processes.[24]

Let us start at the beginning. What did Grotius do when he sat down to write? According to Borschberg,

> Grotius commences by preparing a skeleton, often featuring key schematic terms such as theses, propositions, limitations, amplifications, or conclusions. The fragment *De Societate Publica cum Infidelibus/On Public Association with Non-Christians* [in Ms BPL 922] offers one of the most readily visible testimonies of his procedure in its most basic, raw form, while the fragment *De Bello*

24 Borschberg, *Hugo Grotius' Commentarius in Theses XI* (n 9), P Borschberg, "*De Pace*: Ein unveröffentlichtes Fragment von Hugo Grotius über Krieg und Frieden" (1996) 113 *Zeitschrift der Savigny-Stiftung fur Rechtsgeschichte, Romanistische Abteilung* 268, P Borschberg, "*De Societate Publica cum Infidelibus*: Ein Frühwerk von Hugo Grotius" (1998) 115 *Zeitschrift der Savigny-Stiftung fur Rechtsgeschichte, Romanistische Abteilung* 355, P Borschberg, "Hugo Grotius' Theory of Trans-Oceanic Trade Regulation: Revisiting *Mare Liberum* (1609)", IILJ Working Paper (Rev Aug 2006), *History and Theory of International Law Series* (*www.iilj.org*), P Borschberg, "Grotius, the Social Contract and Political Resistance: A Study of the Unpublished Theses LVI", IILJ Working Paper 2006/7, *History and Theory of International Law Series* (*www.iilj.org*), Borschberg "Grotius, Maritime Intra-Asian Trade and the Portuguese Estado da India: Problems, Perspectives and Insights from *De Iure Praedae*", in H W Blom (ed), *Property, Piracy and Punishment* (n 8) 31–60, Van Ittersum, "Dating the manuscript of *De Jure Praedae*" (n 4).

> *ob Libertatem Eligendo/Whether to Choose War or Liberty* [also in Ms BPL 922] exemplifies a subsequent state of the composition. There the running text is divided into three sections that offer premises and three or four conclusions each. But cited and mentioned in this latter fragment and the adjacent notes are only authors of classical antiquity, such as notably Cicero, Tacitus, Lucan, Suetonius, Aristotle and St. Augustine. No medieval or sixteenth century sources are cited in the text, the margins or the notes. In *De Societate Publica cum Infidelibus*, the left-hand side of the paper is left blank (often demarcated by a fold down the middle) which Grotius uses to jot down additional ideas and references. Sometimes he works with pre-prepared notes, but he also evidently amended the manuscript when perusing a new source that he has acquired, taken from his personal library, or also borrowed from family members, friends and libraries.[25]

My own research on Ms BPL 917 suggests that this was the normal way of proceeding for Grotius. Indeed, quite a few of the reading notes found in Ms BPL 922 are closely related to Grotius' reworking of Ms BPL 917.[26]

Borschberg and I are hardly the first researchers to note Grotius' reworking of texts.[27] However, few legal scholars have taken the trouble to study manuscript materials in any great depth. For example, Haggenmacher tends to cite the collotype reproduction of Ms BPL 917, published as part of the Classics of International Law series of the Carnegie Institute in 1950. It is clear from Haggenmacher's publications on Grotius that he has never set eyes on the original manuscript in Leiden University Library. Moreover, his analysis of Grotius' alleged "sources" in *Grotius et la doctrine de la guerre juste* is not based on the collotype reproduction at all. Like quite a few other Grotius scholars, Haggenmacher largely relies on the so-called Hamaker edition of *De Jure Praedae*, first published in 1868, and its English translation, which appeared in 1950.[28] This is problematical. As my compatriot Dr

25 Borschberg, "Grotius, the Social Contract and Political Resistance: A Study of the Unpublished Theses LVI" (n 24) 22–23.

26 See footnote 24 and see also Van Ittersum, "Dating the manuscript of *De Jure Praedae*" (n 4) 128, 131, 135, footnote 38, 143, including footnote 64, 146, including footnote 74.

27 J Kosters, "Het *jus gentium* van Hugo de Groot en diens voorgangers", *Mededeelingen der Nederlandsche Akademie van Wetenschappen, Afdeling Letterkunde*, LVIII, B, 4 (1924) 87, E R Molhuysen-Oppenheim, "Appendix to Fruin's Article", *Bibliotheca Visseriana* (1925) 75–100, P Haggenmacher, "Genèse et signification du concept de 'ius gentium' chez Grotius", *Grotiana*, New Series vol II (1981) 44. Haggenmacher never set eyes on Ms BPL 917 in Leiden University Library. Compare "Genèse et signification du concept de 'ius gentium' chez Grotius" (above) 45, footnote 2.

28 H Grotius, *De Jure Praedae Commentarius*, (ed) H G Hamaker (1868), H Grotius, *Commentary on the Law of Prize and Booty* , 2 vols, *The Classics of International Law*, no 22 (1950) vol I: *A Translation of the Original Manuscript of 1604 by Gwladys L Williams* and vol II: *The Collotype Reproduction*. The translation of Gwladys L Williams was reprinted, with my introduction and my English translations of relevant archival materials, by the Liberty Fund in 2006. See Hugo

Jan Waszink points out, both editions tend to ignore deleted or inserted text in Ms BPL 917, and simply present us with the final version of the text. Nor do these editions identify the layers-upon-layers of references in Ms BPL 917, i.e. references inserted in the manuscript at different times. Since the collotype reproduction is in black-and-white,[29] this makes it difficult for readers to distinguish among layers of text and among layers of marginalia, other than the most obvious insertions, at the top or bottom of a folio page. Consequently, few scholars have hazarded a guess regarding (a) the process of rewriting on Grotius' part, and (b) the approximate dates of the insertions and deletions. Detailed study of Ms BPL 917, particularly the watermarks, quiring and foliation, has shed new light on both issues in recent years. I conclude in "Dating the Manuscript of *De Jure Praedae*" that Ms BPL 917 was initially intended as a presentation copy, written out by Grotius in 1604–1605, but that it was substantially revised at least twice, in January 1607 and November–December 1608. Still, there is a long way to go in decoding the manuscript, particularly the marginal references.[30]

Borschberg's 1994 edition of *Theses XI* includes a detailed discussion of Grotius' use of "sources". According to Borschberg, three categories of sources can be distinguished in *Theses XI*. Sources of the First Category include Francisco de Vitoria's *Relectiones Theologicae XII*, first published in Lyon in 1557, Jean Bodin's *Les Six Livres de la République*, first published in French in 1576, James I's *Trew Law of Free Monarchies*, first published in Edinburgh in 1598, and Thomas Aquinas' *Summa Theologiae*, with the corresponding commentary by Cardinal Cajetan (d 1534). These works are either cited or referred to in the running text of *Theses XI*, and can also be identified in notes and excerpts in Ms BPL 922 related to *Theses XI*. If Borschberg is right, Vitoria, Bodin, James I, Thomas Aquinas and Cajetan

Grotius, *Commentary on the Law of Prize and Booty*, trans by Gwladys L Williams, ed by M J van Ittersum (2006).

29 The pictures used for the collotype edition were probably taken before 1931. See Leiden University Library, BA2 (Bibliotheeksarchief), Correspondentie 1924–1947, Vp – Wa 3, James Brown Scott to F C Wieder (Director of Leiden University Library), 16 Mar 1931, and Leiden University Library, BA2 (Bibliotheeksarchief), Correspondentie 1924–1947, 's Gravenhage, instellingen A–C 3, F C Wieder, Director of Leiden University Library, to Jacob ter Meulen, Director of the Peace Palace Library, 17 Feb 1933.

30 J Waszink, "Using the Works: Remarks on the Text of *De Iure Praedae*", in H W Blom (ed), *Property, Piracy and Punishment* (n 8) 215–245, M J van Ittersum, "The wise man is never merely a private citizen: The Roman *Stoa* in Hugo Grotius' *De Jure Praedae* (1604–1608)" 2010 (36) *History of European Ideas* 1, Van Ittersum, "Dating the manuscript of *De Jure Praedae*" (n 4), Van Ittersum, "Preparing *Mare Liberum* for the Press: Hugo Grotius' Rewriting of Chapter 12 of *De Jure Praedae* in November-December 1608", in *Property, Piracy and Punishment* (above) 246–280.

should be considered Grotius' main intellectual sparring partners in *Theses XI*. It is easy to see why. Question 40, article 1 of the *Secunda Secundae* of Aquinas contains an influential exposition of the theory of the just war, for example. Vitoria could be cited to great effect against Bodin's theory of indivisible sovereignty, and thus be used to justify the Dutch Revolt. If, as Vitoria argued in *De Potestate Civili*, the people or its representatives were at liberty to choose their own constitution, prince or monarch, then the States of Holland had every right to renounce Philip II of Spain as their prince and pursue a just war against him.[31] Before we indulge ourselves again in that wonderful game called "intellectual influences", another note of caution is warranted. Even Sources of the First Category were read selectively by Grotius, and sometimes only read in part. As we shall see below, this is certainly true of Grotius' use of the *Summa Theologiae* in Ms BPL 917. Grotius had no qualms about citing Aquinas second-hand, through Vitoria, for example. An even more egregious case of selective appropriation is Grotius' referencing of *Trew Law of Free Monarchies* in *Theses XI*. Grotius was not proficient in English: if he read texts in English at all, he did so only with great difficulty. Ms BPL 922 contains Grotius' reading notes on *Trew Law of Free Monarchies* and a non-autograph summary of its contents. Borschberg concludes that Grotius never actually read the printed book, but simply relied on a summary prepared for him in Latin.[32] In analysing Grotius' use of sources, we need to be even more careful when it comes to what Borschberg calls Sources of the Second and Third Categories.

Sources of the Second Category are sources either cited or referenced in the running text of *Theses XI*, but not in the notes and excerpts relating to the treatise in Ms BPL 922. In many cases we are dealing with second-hand quotations or references, borrowed from works of contemporary authors. Grotius also seems to have resorted to dictionaries, florilegia, encyclopaedias and other reference works, quite a few of which, as we saw above, were available in his own library. We will return to the topic of second-hand quotations and references in a moment.[33]

31 Borschberg, *Hugo Grotius' Commentarius in Theses XI* (n 9) 43–60, Feenstra, "Quelques remarques sur les sources utilisées par Grotius dans ses travaux de droit naturel" (n 3) 74, A Truyol Serra, "Francisco de Vitoria Y Hugo Grocio" (1984) 111 *Ciencia Tomista* 17. There are twelve mentions of Vitoria in *Theses XI*. He is cited sixty-eight times in *De Jure Praedae* and fifty-six times in *De Jure Belli ac Pacis*.

32 Leiden University Library, Ms BPL 922, f 286 and 292–293, Borschberg, *Hugo Grotius' Commentarius in Theses XI* (n 9) 56–57, on Grotius' inability to read English, see also my "*Mare Liberum* versus The Propriety of the Seas?" (n 22).

33 Borschberg, *Hugo Grotius' Commentarius in Theses XI* (n 9) 60–74.

According to Borschberg, Sources of the Third Category are not mentioned in the running text of *Theses XI*. However, reading notes and excerpts in Ms BPL 922 reveal that Grotius consulted them nevertheless. This category of sources includes, for example, controversial monarchomach justifications of the right to resistance and the Catholic response:

- Theodre Beza's *Du droit des magistrats sur leurs subiets*, first published in Heidelberg and Geneva in 1574
- *Vindiciae contra Tyrannos*, currently attributed to Philippe du Plessis Mornay (1549–1623), but ascribed by Grotius to the French jurisconsult François Hotman
- a reply to Beza by the Italian Jesuit Giovanni Beccaria, entitled *Refutatio cuiusdam libelli sine auctore cui titulus est, de iure magistratuum in subditos*.

In addition, the reading notes in Ms BPL 922 reveal that Grotius was familiar with the *Tractatus de jure et officiis de bellicis et disciplina* (1582) of the jurisconsult Balthasar Ayala (1548–1584), who served as auditor of the Spanish troops in the Low Countries, and with *Controversiae Illustres* of Ferdinando Vazquez de Menchaca (d 1569). This should not surprise us. There are many, many marginal references to Ayala and Vazquez in Ms BPL 917. Both authors are frequently mentioned in the manuscript's running text as well.[34]

This points to an interesting difference between *Theses XI* and Ms BPL 917. While Ayala and Vazquez seem to function in the background in *Theses XI*, they clearly are of major importance for the argument of Ms BPL 917. Moreover, this is explicitly acknowledged in the manuscript's running text and marginalia. It suggests that the distinctions drawn by Borschberg between Sources of the First, Second and Third Categories are not always as clear-cut as he makes them out to be. As we shall see below, even Grotius' references to Sources of the First Category can be vague and ambiguous,

34 Borschberg, *Hugo Grotius' Commentarius in Theses XI* (n 9) 75–89, for Grotius' referencing of Ayala and Vazquez in Ms BPL 917, see below. Giovanni Beccaria is abbreviated as "Becc" in Grotius' reading notes. The *Bayerische Staatsbibliothek* possesses a 1604 edition of Beccaria's *Refutatio cuiusdam libelli sine auctore cui titulus est, de iure magistratuum in subditos, et officio subditorum erga magistratus* (shelfmark Mor 90). It can be viewed digitally at *http://reader.digitale-sammlungen.de/en/fs3/object/display/bsb10595789_00001.html*. Giovanni Beccaria's treatise was, of course, a reply to Theodre Beza's *Du droit des magistrats sur les subiets*, first published in Heidelberg and Geneva in 1574 (see USTC 171 and USTC 61652). The USTC lists a 1580 edition of *Vindiciae contra Tyrannos* (without a place of publication or publisher listed) and a 1599 edition, published in Montbéliard by Jacob Foillet. See USTC USTC 509069 and 110240.

depending on the context. In the case of Grotius' references to Ayala and Vazquez, he seems to have imposed a division of labour on them that can best be described as "good cop, bad cop". Grotius attacked the teachings of Ayala on more than one occasion (on f 53v of Ms BPL 917, for example). Still, he did include Ayala in his grudging praise of the Spanish on f 29r of Ms BPL 917, calling them "a race by no means to be despised in the field of jurisprudence". By contrast, Vazquez was one of Grotius' darlings. The author of *Mare Liberum* (i.e. chapter 12 of Ms BPL 917) explicitly identified Vazquez as "the pride of Spain", and regaled his readers with long, verbatim quotes from *Controversiae Illustres*. Indeed, Grotius paid Vazquez the dubious compliment of copying his references as well. For example, *Mare Liberum* contains two marginal references to Alphonsus de Castro's *De Potestate Legis Poenalis* (first published in Salamanca, 1550), which are both copied from the 1599 edition of *Controversiae Illustres*. In referencing De Castro, this particular edition of *Controversiae Illustres* gives the mistaken page number "572", a printing error dutifully copied by Grotius in Ms BPL 917 and *Mare Liberum*.[35]

35 Leiden University Library, Ms BPL 917:

- marginal references to Ayala on f 23r, 26r, 29r, 33v, 42r (Ayala also mentioned by name in running text), 50r, 53v (Ayala also mentioned by name in running text), 58v (Ayala also mentioned by name in running text), 72v, 73v, 99r, 99v, 135r, 135v
- marginal references to Vazquez on f 4v, 10r, 10v, 11v, 12v, 22r, 23v, 29r, 30a, 32r, 33r, 33v, 36r, 42r (Vazquez mentioned by name in running text), 46r, 53r, 53v, 68v, 98v, 99r, 100v, 108v, 110r, 110v, 115r (Vazquez mentioned by name in running text), 115v, 116r, 128v, 129v, 130r, 130v, 134r, 135r, 135v
- long, verbatim quotes from Vazquez, *Controversiae Illustres*, on f 111r-112r, 112r, 112v-113r.

On f 29r of Ms BPL 917, Grotius included Vitoria, Vazquez and Ayala in his grudging praise for Spanish legal scholars, calling "the Spaniards . . . a race by no means to be despised in the field of jurisprudence" (*Hispanis, quod genus in jurisprudentia minime contemnendum est*). See also Grotius, *Commentary on the Law of Prize and Booty* vol I, 65.

Grotius, *Mare Liberum, 1609–2009* (ed) Feenstra:

- Grotius' marginal references to Ayala: 40, 44
- Grotius' marginal references to Vazquez: 36, 40, 42, 50, 98, 106 138, 140, 142, with long, verbatim quotes from Vazquez, *Controversiae Illustres*, on 110–121
- Grotius' second-hand reference to Alphonsus De Castro: 110–111, 120–121.

For Vazquez as "the pride of Spain", see Grotius, *Mare Liberum, 1609–2009* (ed) Feenstra, pp 108–109.

Controversiae Illustres was reprinted in Geneva in 1599: Ferdinando Vázquez de Menchaca, *Illustrium controversiarum aliarumque usu frequentium*, 2 vols (1599) (USTC 451667 and USTC 451718). According to Feenstra, only this particular edition of *Controversiae Illustres* contains the faulty "p. 572" reference to De Castro, *De Potestate Legis Poenalis*. See Grotius, *Mare Liberum, 1609–2009* (ed) Feenstra 110, Rabbie, "The History and Reconstruction of Hugo Grotius' Library" (n 9) 128–130 and D Beaufort, "Alphonsus a Castro als bron voor Hugo de Groot's Mare Liberum", in *Collectanea Franciscana Neerlandica uitgegeven bij het zevende eeuwfeest van Sint Franciscus, 1226–1926* (1927) 205–218, in particular 209.

Grotius' shameless copying of Vazquez brings us back to the fraud issue of second-hand quotations and references in Grotius' writings. Although more research remains to be done, progress has been made in recent years in investigating this particular aspect of Grotius' working methods. Not surprisingly, Sources of the First Category turn out to have been particularly rich sources of second-hand references and quotations for Grotius. Thus Borschberg points out in his edition of *Theses XI* that a reference to the histories of Suetonius was copied lock, stock and barrel from Bodin's *Six Books on the Commonwealth*. Similarly, Waszink notes that a quote from Hesiod's *Works and Days* in Ms BPL 917 was, in fact, copied from *Stromateis* ("Miscellanies") of Clement of Alexandria. Robert Feenstra identifies in his 2009 edition of *Mare Liberum* a couple of instances of Grotius copying references from Gentili's *De Jure Belli*, Francisco de Vitoria's *De Indis*, and Rodericus Zuarius' *Consilium*.[36] In the case of Gentili, Grotius mined the text of *De Jure Belli* so thoroughly that he ended up copying historical *exempla* as well as references. For example, Grotius declared on f 97r of Ms BPL 917 that various wars had been undertaken for the sake of free trade, including "the Megarean war against the Athenians". The corresponding marginal reference refers to "Diod 11. Plut. Pericle", i.e. the Greek historian Diodorus of Sicily and Plutarch's life of Pericles. Both the historical *exemplum* and the marginal reference were taken straight from Gentili's *De Jure Belli* I, 19 ("De Naturalibus Caussis Belli Inferendi").[37]

Always a man in a hurry, Grotius never lost the habit of incorporating second-hand quotations and references into his writings. There are plenty to be found in *De Jure Belli ac Pacis*. Feenstra has alerted us to references copied from Gentili's *De Jure Belli*, Leonardus Lessius' *De Justitia et Jure* (first published in 1605) and the 1557 Lyon edition of Vitoria's *Relectiones Theologicae*. Jean Barbeyrac (1674–1744), Grotius' most famous eighteenth-century editor, openly commented on second-hand quotations and references in the author index and footnotes of his editions of *De Jure Belli ac*

36 Borschberg, *Hugo Grotius' Commentarius in Theses XI* (n 9) 61–62, Waszink, "Remarks on the Text of *De Iure Praedae*" (30) 221–227, Grotius, *Mare Liberum, 1609–2009* (ed) Feenstra (n 5) LVIII, 27, 29, 31, 35, 41, 75, 77, 79.

37 Ms BPL 917 f 97r, Grotius, *Mare Liberum, 1609–2009* (ed) Feenstra 28 (Feenstra does not seem to realise that Grotius' references to Diodorus of Sicily and Plutarch's life of Pericles were copied from Gentili), Alberico Gentili, *De Jure Belli Libri Tres*, *The Classics of International Law* (1933) vol 1: The Photographic Reproduction of the Edition of 1612, 142 (*De Jure Belli* I, 19 ("De Naturalibus Caussis Belli Inferendi"). Needless to say, Grotius did not use the 1612 edition of Gentili's *De Jure Belli*. He must have used an earlier edition. It was first published in Hanau in 1598. And on this point generally, see Wijffels elsewhere in this volume.

Pacis. A case in point is the "Lycklama (Marcus)" entry in the author index compiled by Barbeyrac: "copied by our author in a citation, wherein he joins two passages of different authors into one" – Grotius had fused quotations from Pliny the Elder's *Natural History* and Marcus Lycklama's *Membranae libri septem* (1608).[38] It was on the basis of revealing errors like these that Barbeyrac could establish that Grotius had taken a Virgil citation and two paraphrases of Livy and Pausanias straight from Gentili's *De Jure Belli*. Barbeyrac realised that Grotius frequently obtained second-hand references and quotations from Bodin as well. To give just one example, the "Amymones among the Cnidians" are referenced in chapter three of *De Jure Belli ac Pacis*, where they are meant to illustrate "a sort of temporary Monarchy", analogous to the dictators in Ancient Rome. Barbeyrac pointed out in his commentary that the correct spelling was "Amnemones" and that the mistake suggested that Grotius had not consulted Plutarch, the original source, but Bodin's *Six Books of the Commonwealth*, where the same misspelling occurred.[39]

It is possible to argue, of course, that it is irrelevant that Grotius quoted the Classics second-hand, on the grounds that, allegedly, he had a deep knowledge of the Classics anyway and simply availed himself of a harmless short-cut while desperately trying to finish a treatise. That may be so. But the fact that he copied *exempla* from Gentili and Bodin suggests that (a) he was more indebted to them than he cared to admit (there is just *one*

38 Tuck, *The Rights of War and Peace* (n 4) vol 3, 1662 and vol 1, 188, footnote 9. An alleged quotation from Pliny the Elder in chapter 2 of *De Jure Belli ac Pacis* consists, in fact, of two different citations strung together: one taken from Pliny the Elder's *Natural History*, the other from the *Membranae libri septem* of the Dutch jurist Marcus Lycklama (1570–1625), who, according to Barbeyrac, "quotes this Passage of Pliny, without specifying the place, and subjoins what here follows in the text of Grotius." *De Jure Belli ac Pacis* contains many more second-hand references and quotations, which can be tracked down by consulting Barbeyrac's index. Compare Tuck, *The Rights of War and Peace* (n 4) vol 3, 1656 ("Baldus" and "Boecler" entries), 1657 ("Cicero" entry), 1658 ("Cujas" entry), 1659 ("Gentili", "Godefroy" and "Faur" entries), 1662 ("Milton" entry), 1663 ("Pausanias" entry).

39 Grotius, *De iure belli ac pacis* (ed) De Kanter-van Hettinga Tromp, with notes by Robert Feenstra (n 2) 1002–1004 (nn 575h-575m, 595a, 595b), R Feensta, *Fata Iuris Romani: Études d' Histoire du Droit* (1974) 343–344 (the references which Grotius copied from Lessius are found in Lessius *De Justitia et Jure* Lib 2, cap 17, dub 5, particularly nos 31–32, and *De Jure Belli ac Pacis* II, ii, 6, i), Tuck, *The Rights of War and Peace* (n 4) vol II, 937, footnote 24 (*Ad Herennium* is the source of an alleged Virgil quote; the erroneous attribution to Virgil is found in Gentili Lib II Cap XXIV), 1060, footnote 21 (Grotius hastily copied some Livy passages from Gentili, *De Jure Belli*, Lib I Cap XXI, and mixed up the references), 1064, footnote 7 (Grotius' unacknowledged paraphrase of Pausanias was taken straight from Gentili, *De Jure Belli*, Lib I Cap XXI), Tuck, *The Rights of War and Peace* (n 4) vol I ,271, footnote 43 (Grotius never looked at Plutarch's *Quaest.Graec* 292, but copied the mistake from Bodin, *Of the Commonwealth*, Lib 1, Cap VIII).

acknowledged reference to Bodin's *Six Books on the Commonwealth* in Ms BPL 917, for example),[40] and that (b) seventeenth-century scholarly debates were conducted within relatively narrow frames of reference. Was it the result of information overload in early modern Europe? Did the flood of editions of classical texts, made possible by the Renaissance and Print Revolution, have the paradoxical effect of inducing scholars to concentrate on a few tried-and-tested *exampla*? Or were the rules of the game slow to change? Was scholarly debate in the seventeenth century still a matter of manipulating a relatively limited number of "authorities", much like it had been in the Middle Ages? Even at the University of Leiden, that fountainhead of "the new philology", *Artes* students like Grotius graduated by means of disputations on Aristotle's works on logics and physics, for example.[41] However radical and startling Grotius' conclusions may have been in *Theses XI* and Ms BPL 917, he reached them through a traditional course of reasoning.

As noted earlier, one of Grotius' copies of the *Corpus Iuris Canonici* – a 1569 edition published by Christopher Plantin in Antwerp – has survived in Lund University Library. The copy is well thumbed and bristles with annotations. Indeed, Grotius constructed his own handwritten indices, using the verso side of a title page and flyleaves and pasteboards. Grotius' indices are very detailed: he must have gone through the materials with a fine-tooth comb and taken notes on nearly every page. It turned this particular copy of the *Corpus Iuris Canonici* into a quick-and-easy reference guide for the Church Fathers and medieval theologians and canon lawyers. It may also have been a one-stop-shop for second-hand quotations and references. A case in point is a marginal reference in *Mare Liberum* to St Augustine's *Quaestiones in Heptateuchum* IV. Feenstra suggests that Grotius copied the marginal reference from Gentili's *De Jure Belli*. He admits, however, that the same reference can also be found in the *Decretum Gratiani*. Who was copying whom here?[42]

40 Leiden University Library, Ms BPL 917 f 45v.

41 Nellen, *Hugo de Groot* (n 9) 46–47.

42 Lund University Library, Bibl Grotiana 4: *Corpus Iuris Canonici*, 3 vols (1569–1570), Molhuysen, *De bibliotheek van Hugo de Groot in 1618* (n 9) 18, Dovring, *Une Partie de l'Héritage Littéraire de Grotius Retrouvée en Suède* (n 6) 2, Van der Heijden, "De boekerij van Grotius" (n 9) 35, Grotius, *Mare Liberum, 1609–2009* (ed) Feenstra (n 5) 29–30, particularly footnote g. I should like to thank Dr Håkan Håkansson, Head of Manuscripts and Special Collections at Lund University Library, for generously providing me with digital pictures of Grotius' handwritten indices in the *Corpus Iuris Canonici*.

E. GROTIUS' REFERENCING OF AQUINAS IN MS BPL 917

As indicated earlier, Grotius' copy of a four-volume edition of the *Summa Theologiae*, published in 1581, is extant at Lund University Library. It contains underlinings, presumably by Grotius, in some parts of Aquinas' text and Cajetan's commentary, but not in others.[43] I had the pleasure of examining this copy in Lund in the summer of 2006, and took the opportunity to check Grotius' references to Aquinas in Ms BPL 917. In some cases, there is a very clear correlation between Aquinas references in Ms BPL 917 and underlined parts in Grotius' own copy of the *Summa Theologiae*. In other cases, there is not. Still, there is a discernible pattern, which tells us much about Grotius' use of "sources".

First it should be noted that Ms BPL 917 is heavily rewritten in parts, particularly in chapters 1–10 and 12. Inserted text is invariably found at the top and bottom of folio-pages, on small scraps of paper,[44] interleaved between the original folios of the manuscript, and, in a few cases, on entirely new, inserted folios.[45] Fortunately, we can clearly distinguish between the original text and the inserts, and, in a number of cases, date inserted text as well, primarily on the basis of the watermarks present in Ms BPL 917 and the manuscripts' quiring and foliation. Grotius copied out the original text of Ms BPL 917 (which is based on an earlier, now lost version, of the treatise) in 1604–1605. We can detect two major rewrites, in January 1607 and November-December 1608, respectively, when Grotius crossed out whole pages of text (but did not destroy them) and recast his argument on entirely new, inserted folios. What about any rewriting done on the original folios of

43 Dovring, *Une Partie de l'Héritage Littéraire de Grotius Retrouvée en Suède* (n 6) 241, University of Lund Library, Bibl Grotiana 16 I, 16 II: 1–2, 16 III: Thomas Aquinas, *Summa Theologiae*, with commentary by Cajetan, 4 vols (1581) vol 1 (*prima pars*), page prior to title page: (in Grotius' hand) *Ex dono Emmanuelis filii Antonio Regis Portugalliae possideo Corpus hoc Thomae Aquinatis* (underneath) Hugo Grotius. Dom Emanuel of Portugal presented Grotius with a four-volume edition of Thomas Aquinas' *Summa Theologiae*, published in 1581. It was by far the most expensive book in Grotius' library in 1619. At that point, its estimated value was twelve Flemish pounds. See Van der Heijden, "De boekerij van Grotius" (n 9) 34 and Molhuysen, *De bibliotheek van Hugo de Groot in 1618* (n 9) 16. Dom Emanuel and Emilia of Nassau married in secret in 1597, against the wishes of Prince Maurice. After a brief spell in Germany, they took up residence in Grotius' hometown of Delft, where the eldest daughter, Maria Belgica, was born in 1599. Emilia of Nassau gave birth to five more daughters and two sons. Only in 1608 could Prince Maurice be persuaded to financially support the destitute couple and their children. Compare *Nieuw Nederlands Biografisch Woordenboek* (ed) P C Molhuysen and P J Blok, 10 vols (1911–1937) vol I 815–816.

44 Leiden University Library, Ms BPL 917 folios 5'a, 11a, 11'a, 11b, 12'a, 30a, 33a, 47a, 50'a, 53a, 53'a, 64'a, 65a, 68a, 75a, 128a, 160a.

45 Leiden University Library, Ms BPL 917, folios 8–9, 18, 39–42, 64–66, 117–118.

the manuscript? It is difficult to date that, of course. In principle, Grotius could have added a reference in the margins or one or more sentences at the top or bottom of folio-pages the day after he had finished copying out the original text or he could have done so almost forty years later in Paris.[46] However, the lack of references to Ms BPL 917 in his correspondence after April 1609 and the dramatic shift in his intellectual and political priorities during the Twelve Years Truce – the conflict between Remonstrants and Gomarists in the Dutch Reformed Church forced him to concentrate on church–state relations – suggest that little rewriting took place in Ms BPL 917 after the publication of *Mare Liberum*. And even if he continued to add references to Ms BPL 917 during his time in Paris – an unstated assumption of the late Robert Feenstra, for example – then we have to ask ourselves the question what the meaning of it might be. Does it show that Grotius continued to care about his juvenilia? Does it suggest that he sought to strengthen the argument of Ms BPL 917 with references to yet more authorities? That is quite possible, of course. But it tells us little, if anything, about how Grotius constructed the argument of Ms BPL 917 in the first place. Authorities are not "sources", not in our twenty-first-century understanding of the term.

Grotius' references to Aquinas in Ms BPL 917 suggest that he read some parts of the *Summa Theologiae* in depth, skimmed over others and may not have read certain parts at all, even though he referenced them in his written work, copying references straight from Vitoria, Vazquez or Gentili. A letter that Grotius sent to Benjamin Aubéry du Maurier, French ambassador in The Hague, in May 1615 is instructive in this respect. The letter contains a list of books that Grotius deemed indispensable for the education of a gentleman. It can hardly come as a surprise that the *Summa Theologiae* was one of Grotius' recommended readings. However, Grotius also claimed in his letter that it was sufficient to "look at/consult" ("inspicere") the *Secunda Secundae*, rather than to read it cover to cover ("perlegere").[47] Did Grotius

46 Grotius' correspondence reveals that he had Ms BPL 917 to hand in his study in Paris in the 1640s. Based on the list of confiscated goods of March 1620, it is commonly assumed that Grotius had Ms BPL 917 at his disposal at Loevestein Castle as well. The Dutch States General did indeed give permission to Grotius' wife to transfer books and manuscripts from Grotius' study in Rotterdam to Loevestein Castle. However, the list of confiscated goods of March 1620 only speaks of "various manuscripts", without identifying their subjects, contents, etc. It is anybody's guess whether (and when) these "various manuscripts" reached Paris after Grotius' escape from Loevestein Castle. I would like to see more evidence for the assumption, common among legal historians, that Grotius regularly consulted Ms BPL 917 while writing *De Jure Belli ac Pacis*.

47 *De Briefwisseling van Hugo Grotius/The Correspondence of Hugo Grotius* (*http://grotius.huygens.knaw.nl/years*), letter no 402 (Hugo Grotius to B Aubéry du Maurier, 13 May 1615).

make selective use of the *Secunda Secundae* himself? The evidence from Ms BPL 917 and Ms BPL 922 suggests that he did indeed.

The Angelic Doctor is mentioned by name on at least four occasions in the original text of Ms BPL 917. On balance, the evidence suggests that Grotius consulted his own copy of the *Secunda Secundae* in all these cases, but that he probably did so after reading Vitoria's *Relectiones XII*. Vitoria, then, was Grotius' readers' guide to Aquinas. Which aspects of the *Secunda Secundae* seem to have been of greatest interest to Grotius? In chapter 13 of Ms BPL 917 ("The Justness of the Case if the War Were Public"), Grotius sought to prove that the Dutch States General – and one of its members in particular, the States of Holland – was fighting a just war against the "tyrant" Philip II of Spain and Portugal. In this context, he mentioned "Thomas" by name on 134v and cited the latter's observation that "the tyrant is seditious, since he feeds his subject people upon discord and civil dissension in order that he himself may rule in greater security."[48] Grotius gave the correct reference (2.2.43, article 2, third point) in the margin of f 134v. The corresponding passage in Grotius' own copy of the *Secunda Secundae* does not contain any underlining, though. The absence of underlining, then, cannot be taken as positive proof that Grotius did *not* read something. However, there is a close correlation between underlining in Grotius' copy of the *Secunda Secundae* and the explicit mention of Aquinas or Cajetan in the original text of Ms BPL 917, along with the inclusion of quotes from the *Secunda Secundae*. As we shall see, Grotius focused in particular on Aquinas' criteria for fighting a just war, which he evaluated through the eyes of Cajetan, and on the question whether "Indians" could be called true owners and true sovereigns, even though they were unbelievers – we can hear distinct echoes here of Vitoria's *Relection on the American Indians*.

Question 40 ("*De Bello*"), article 1, of the *Secunda Secundae*, was one of the most comprehensive and historically influential expositions of the theory of the just war. Grotius referenced it at least seven times in Ms BPL 917 and five times in *Theses XI*.[49] According to Aquinas, for a war to be just, it

48 Leiden University Library, Ms BPL 917, f 134v-135r ("Magis enim tyrannum esse seditiosum, qui in populo sibi subiecto discordias & seditiones nutrit, ut tutius dominari possit"), H Grotius, *De Iure Praedae Commentarius/Commentary on the Law of Prize and Booty*, *Classics of International Law series* no 22 (1950) vol I: *A Translation of the Original Manuscript of 1604 by Gwladys L Williams, with the collaboration of Walter H Zeydel* 299, University of Lund Library, Bibl Grotiana 16 II: 1–2: Aquinas, *Summa Theologiae* vol 3 148–149 = 2.2.42 ("De seditione"), art. 2 *ad tertium* – "Magis autem tyrannus seditiosus est, qui in populo sibi subiecto discordias & seditiones nutrit, ut tutius dominari possit".

49 Leiden University Library, Ms BPL 917, f 14r, 20r, 26r, 48r, 50v-51r, 54v, 135v, Borschberg, *Hugo Grotius' Commentarius in Theses XI* (n 9) 216–217, 238–239, 240–241, 244–245, 262–263.

has to meet three criteria: (a) it has to be declared by the authority of the prince (*auctoritas principis*), (b) it should be waged for a just cause (*causa justa*), and (c) the party declaring a just war must have upright intentions (*recta intentio*), i.e. to advance the peace and common good, while avoiding evil as much as possible. Grotius focused on the first of these criteria in both *Theses XI* and chapter 13 of Ms BPL 917. He sought to extend the meaning of "the authority of the prince" beyond the person of the ruler, and to attribute this competence instead to the "perfect republic" (*respublica perfecta, respublica sibi sufficiens*). In chapter 13 of Ms BPL 917, Grotius endorsed Cajetan's contention that some kings are "kings only in name" – i.e. sovereignty is not vested in one man, but distributed among magistrates and various layers of government. The remark was directed against "proponents of the theory that princes ought to be obeyed absolutely and at all times", meaning Jean Bodin and Balthasar de Ayala. The exact same quote from Cajetan can be found in *Theses XI*.[50] It was taken straight from Cajetan's commentary on Question 40, article 1, which is underlined in Grotius' copy of the *Secunda Secundae*.[51] Cajetan's explication of Aquinas suited Grotius very well: it was an effective weapon against Bodin's theory of indivisible sovereignty and could be marshalled in support of Grotius' contention in both *Theses XI* and chapter 13 of Ms BPL 917 that the Dutch Republic was no rebel state, but fighting a just war against the "tyrant" Philip II of Spain and Portugal.[52]

Grotius focused on the third of Aquinas' criteria for a just war (*recta intentio*) in chapter 9 of Ms BPL 917 ("Concerning the Aims of War"). On f 54v, he referred to the Angelic Doctor by name in the original text and quoted him as saying that "war is waged for the sake of peace, but for the sake of a good peace, not for one that is evil." Which purpose did Aquinas' musings serve in Grotius' argument? A few lines down, the VOC lobbyist cleverly suggested that "this kind of peace" was synonymous with "the repul-

50 Leiden University Library, Ms BPL 917, f 135v, Grotius, *De Iure Praedae Commentarius/ Commentary on the Law of Prize and Booty* vol I at 300, Borschberg, *Hugo Grotius' Commentarius in Theses XI* (n 9) 216–217, University of Lund Library, Bibl Grotiana 16 II: 1–2: Aquinas, *Summa Theologiae* vol 3, 144–147.

51 Leiden University Library, Ms BPL 917, f 135v, Grotius, *De Iure Praedae Commentarius/ Commentary on the Law of Prize and Booty* vol I, 300, Borschberg, *Hugo Grotius' Commentarius in Theses XI* (n 9) 216–217, University of Lund Library, Bibl Grotiana 16 II: 1–2: Aquinas, *Summa Theologiae* vol 3, 144–147, Borschberg, "Grotius, the Social Contract and Political Resistance A Study of the Unpublished Theses LVI", IILJ Working Paper 2006/7 (*History and Theory of International Law Series*) (*www.iilj.org*), footnote 155.

52 Borschberg, *Hugo Grotius' Commentarius in Theses XI* (n 9) 53–56, 58–60, 81–84, 115–135, 206–235, 280–283.

sion of injury" or, what in his view amounted to one and the same thing, "the attainment of rights, not only one's own, but also, at times, the rights of others".[53] Ergo, Jacob van Heemskerck had been engaged in a just war on behalf of the VOC, the States of Holland, the Dutch States General and the King of Johore when he captured the Portuguese carrack *Santa Catarina* in Singapore Straits in February 1603.[54]

Grotius changed tack in his selective reading of Aquinas in chapter 12 of Ms BPL 917 ("The Justness of the Case If the War Were Private"). In this chapter, better known to us as *Mare Liberum*, Grotius sought to prove that his compatriots were at liberty to sail and trade in the East Indies. As various twentieth-century scholars have noted, Vitoria's *Relection on the American Indians* is absolutely fundamental to Grotius' argument here. Indeed, Grotius explicitly acknowledged his debt to Cajetan and Vitoria when he concluded on f 99r that the Portuguese could not forbid the native inhabitants of South-East Asia to trade with the Dutch

> either on the ground that the Pope as lord of the East Indian lands gave away this territory by an unrestricted act of donation, or on the ground that the inhabitants fail to acknowledge the papal dominion; and, indeed, it is also clear that even the Saracens were never despoiled on such grounds.[55]

This clearly echoes Vitoria's arguments against Spanish despoliation of the American Indians. Yet if we look carefully on f 99r, we find even more borrowings from Vitoria. The top left margin of f 99r features a bulky cluster of references, starting with "1 Cor. 5 in fine" (i.e. 1 Corinthians 5) and ending with "Vict. n. 31." When we turn to *Relection on the American Indians* 30–31, we discover that both the example of the Saracens and no less than five references are copied straight from Vitoria. Even the order in which the references appear in Vitoria remained intact when Grotius reproduced them in the top left margin of f 99r:

- I Cor. 5: 12
- Sylvester Prierias, *Summa Sylvestrina*, sv infidelis § 7
- Pope Innocent IV, on the Decretal *Quod Super His* (X.3.34.8)
- Thomas Aquinas, *Summa Theologiae*, II-II qu 66, art 8

53 Grotius, *De Iure Praedae Commentarius/Commentary on the Law of Prize and Booty* vol I, 126.

54 M J van Ittersum, "Hugo Grotius in context: Van Heemskerck's capture of the *Santa Catarina* and its justification in *De Jure Praedae* (1604–1606)" (2003) 31 *Asian Journal of Social Science* 511.

55 Grotius, *De Iure Praedae Commentarius/Commentary on the Law of Prize and Booty* vol I, 223–224.

- Cajetan's commentary on Aquinas, *Summa Theologiae*, II-II qu 66, art 8.[56]

Yet Grotius did not limit himself to playing copycat. He evidently looked up Question 66 ("De furto et rapina") in his own copy of the *Secunda Secundae*: there is underlining in every article of Question 66 and in Cajetan's commentary on articles 2, 3, and 5.[57] Moreover, Cajetan's commentary on article 8 of Question 66 is reproduced in its entirety on folios 99v-100r of Ms BPL 917. Grotius included the lengthy quote – all twenty-nine lines of it – in the manuscript's original text, and explicitly credited the cardinal.[58]

The extent to which Grotius read Aquinas through the eyes of Cajetan also becomes clear when we turn briefly to f 39v of Ms BPL 917. Grotius inserted a marginal reference to Question 64, article 1, of the *Secunda Secundae* "and Cajetan thereon" ("et ibi Cajet."). There is plenty of underlining to be found in Question 64 of Grotius' own copy of the *Secunda Secundae*. But there is no commentary by Cajetan on Question 64, article 1. It was a revealing mistake on Grotius' part. He clearly considered Cajetan's interpretation of Aquinas to be authoritative and definitive. Considering the edition of Aquinas in his possession, it was also logical for

56 Leiden University Library, Ms BPL 917, f 99r, Francisco de Vitoria, *Political Writings* (ed) A Pagden and J Lawrence (Cambridge Texts in the History of Political Thought) (1991) 263–264, see also Grotius, *Mare Liberum, 1609–2009* (ed) Feenstra (n 5) 41.

57 University of Lund Library, Bibl Grotiana 16 II: 1–2: Aquinas, *Summa Theologiae* vol 3 224–230.

58 Leiden University Library, Ms BPL 917, f 99v-100r, University of Lund Library, Bibl Grotiana 16 II: 1–2: Aquinas, *Summa Theologiae* vol 3 229–30 (Cajetan's comments on Thomas 2.2. [quaestio] 66 art 8): "Quidam autem infideles, nec de iure, nec de facto subsunt, secundum temporalem iurisdictionem principibus Christianis: ut si inveniuntur Pagani, qui nunquam imperio Romano subditi fuerunt, terras inhabitantes, in quibus Christiani nunquam fuit nomen. Horumnanque domini, quamvis infideles, legitimi domini sunt, sive regali, sive politico regimine gubernentur: nec sunt propter infidelitatem a dominio suorum privati, quum dominium fit ex iure positivo, & infidelitas ex divino iuro, quod non tollit ius positivum, ut superius in quaestione decima habitum est. Et de his nullam scio legem, quo ad temporalia. Contra hos nullus Rex, nullus Imperator, nec ecclesia Romana potest movere bellum, ad occupandas terras eorum, aut subijciendum eos temporaliter: quia nulla subest causa iusti belli, quum Jesus Christus Rex regum, cui data est omnis potestas in coelis et in terra, miserit ad capiendam possessionem mundi, non milites armatae militiae, sed santos praedicatores, sicut oves inter lupos. Unde nec in testamento veteri, ubi armata manu possessio erat capienda, terrae infidellum indictum lego bellum alicui propter hoc, quod non erant fideles: sed vel quia nolebant dare transitum, vel quia eos offenderant, ut Madianitae: vel ut recuperarent sua divina largitione concessa. Unde gravissime peccaremus si fidem Christi Jesu per hanc viam ampliate contenderemus; nec essemus legitimi domini illorum: sed magna latrocinia committeremus, & teneremur ad restitutionem, utpote iniusti debellatores, aut occupatores. Mittendi essent ad hos praedicatores boni viri, qui verbo & exemplo converterent eos ad Deum; et non qui eos opprimant, spolient, scandalizent, subijciant, & duplo gehennae filios faciant more Pharisaeorum."

him to assume that Cajetan had commented on everything ever written by Aquinas.[59]

Vitoria's *Relectiones XII* served as Grotius' reader's guide to the *Secunda Secundae*. The paragraph directly preceding the lengthy Cajetan quote on folios 99v-100r of Ms BPL 917 testifies to his close reading of Vitoria. On f 99v, Grotius contended that "St. Thomas, the Council of Toledo, Gregory,and practically all of the theologians, canonists and jurists" were in agreement that, even if "barbarians" refuse to accept the Christian faith, "it is still not permissible to make war upon them or to deprive them of their goods merely on these grounds." Grotius was paraphrasing Vitoria's *Relection on the American Indians* § 39, where Vitoria mentioned as his sources "St. Thomas in his ST. II-II.10.8", "Gratian's canon *De Iudaeis*" (Decretum D.45.5), "Consilium IV Toletanum § 56" and yet again "St. Gregory the Great . . . in the canon *Qui sincera*" (Decretum D.45.3). Needless to say, the exact same references to the *Secunda Secundae* and Decretum are also found in the left margin of f 99v. Can it be a coincidence that when we turn to Grotius' copy of the *Secunda Secundae* we find underlining in nearly every article of Question 10 ("De infidelitate in genere")? Vitoria's *Relection on the American Indians*, which Grotius read from cover to cover, evidently spurred him on to make careful study of Question 10 of the *Secunda Secundae*, referenced on folios 98r, 99r, 99v of Ms BPL 917, and Question 66 of the *Secunda Secundae*, referenced on folios 26r, 50r, 55v, 99r of Ms BPL 917.[60] That is not to say that Grotius' referencing of the *Secunda Secundae* was always as closely related to his argument in Ms BPL 917 as we have seen above. If Grotius inserts a marginal reference to the *Secunda Secundae*, but fails to mention Aquinas or Cajetan by name in the original text and/or include a quote from either of them, it usually means that the marginal reference is just there to add weight to his argument, without much in the way of intellectual engagement with the alleged "source".

59 Leiden University Library, Ms BPL 917, f 39v, University of Lund Library, Bibl Grotiana 16 II: 2: Aquinas, *Summa Theologiae* vol 3, 216–222, Grotius, *De Iure Praedae Commentarius/ Commentary on the Law of Prize and Booty* vol I: *A Translation of the Original Manuscript of 1604*, 90.

60 Leiden University Library, Ms BPL 917, f 27r, 50r, 55v, 98r, 99r-v (the reference to Thomas 2.2. [quaestio] 10 art 8 is inserted and crossed out on f 99r), University of Lund Library, Bibl Grotiana 16 II: 2: Aquinas, *Summa Theologiae* vol 3, 36–46, Vitoria, *Political Writings* (ed) Pagden and Lawrence (n 56) 271–272. Feenstra in his edition of *Mare Liberum* identifies the reference to "2.2. qu.10, art. 12" as a mistake, which Grotius copied from Victoria, *De Indis*, I 7. See Grotius, *Mare Liberum, 1609–2009* (ed) Feenstra (n 5) 35. However, there clearly is underlining to be found in Question 10, article 12, of the *Secunda Secundae* in Grotius' copy in Lund University Library.

A case in point is Grotius' referencing of Question 108 ("De Vindicatione") of the *Secunda Secundae* in Ms BPL 917. In principle, Aquinas' pronouncements on the circumstances in which revenge is legitimate would seem to be extremely relevant to Ms BPL 917, a treatise written to justify VOC privateering in the East Indies. Not surprisingly, Grotius' own copy of the *Secunda Secundae* features underlining in Question 108, articles 1 and 4, including Cajetan's commentary on article 1. Marginal references to Question 108 can be found on folios 9r, 15v, 18r, 19r, 39r, 41r and 48v of Ms BPL 917.[61] In a few cases, the relationship between Grotius' argument and Question 108 of the *Secunda Secundae* is clear and straightforward. At other times, it is not. Let me give examples of both. On f 18r – an insert that can be dated between January 1607 and November 1608 – Grotius' analysis of the concept of vengeance and its meaning for Christians is clearly indebted to Question 108. On f 48v, the marginal reference to "Th.2.2.108.art.4" seems to have been put in at a later point in time (we do not know when): it corresponds with the inserted text at the top of the folio-page. Chapter 8 of Ms BPL 917 dealt with the "Forms in Undertaking and Waging War". In this context, Grotius decided to add a clarification at the top of f 48v. He agreed with St Thomas (whom he mentioned explicitly) that "those persons who are essentially possessions and parts, so to speak, of another entity – a description which ought to cover subjects no less than children and slaves – may be penalized in the place of that entity for losses suffered."[62] This conveniently justified indiscriminate VOC attacks on the Portuguese merchant marine, in Atlantic as well as Asian waters. According to Grotius, the VOC was entitled to obtain damages for losses sustained from any subject of Philip III of Spain and Portugal. Citing Aquinas, he argued that all subjects of the latter ruler must be presumed to contribute (by paying taxes, for example) towards his unjust war against the Dutch. Hence they were liable to the payment of damages. However, the connection between Grotius' line of reasoning and Question 108 of the *Secunda Secundae* seems rather tenuous in other places.

61 Leiden University Library, Ms BPL 917, f 9r, 15v, 18r, 19r, 39r, 41r and 48v, University of Lund Library, Bibl Grotiana 16 II: 1–2: Aquinas, *Summa Theologiae* vol 3, 378–380, Van Ittersum, "Hugo Grotius in context: Van Heemskerck's capture of the *Santa Catarina* and its justification in *De Jure Praedae* (1604–1606)" (n 54).

62 Leiden University Library, Ms BPL 917, f 18r, 19r, 48v, Grotius, *De Iure Praedae Commentarius/ Commentary on the Law of Prize and Booty* vol I: *A Translation of the Original Manuscript of 1604,* 108, University of Lund Library, Bibl Grotiana 16 II: 2: Aquinas, *Summa Theologiae* vol 3, 378–380, Van Ittersum, "Dating the manuscript of *De Jure Praedae* (1604–1608)" (n 4). Quite a few marginal references on f 18r, including the references to Questions 72 and 108 of the *Secunda Secundae*, are copied from f 19r, which Grotius deleted in its entirety.

For example, Question 108 of the *Secunda Secundae* is referenced on folios 39r and 41r, both of them inserts, which can be dated between January 1607 and November 1608. Indeed, the references to Question 108 on folios 39r and 41r were copied from, respectively, f 38r, where Grotius deleted the bottom half of the original text, and f 43v, where Grotius deleted the entire folio-page. The marginal reference to Question 108 on f 39r is meant to provide evidence for Grotius' claim that "the most eminent theologians" did not condemn Cicero for placing "vengeance . . . among the manifestations of the natural law". However, the emphasis here is firmly on Cicero and his conceptualisation of "vengeance" in *De Inventione*. Aquinas' views on Cicero in Question 108 are of secondary importance. The marginal reference to Question 108 on f 41r is similarly vague and non-committal. It was entirely typical of Grotius to try to somehow fuse the moral teachings of Christianity with the pagan ethics of the Classical World. Thus he contended on f 41r (in a block of inserted text at the bottom of the folio-page) that "the explanation offered by Plutarch does not differ greatly from the contention of the Scholastics, that we ought to seek vengeance even for our own injuries if they are of such a nature as to redound to the detriment of the Church, that is to say, to the detriment of all good men." Needless to say, Grotius could have made this exact same point without referencing Question 108 of the *Secunda Secundae*. As for Plutarch, he is never so much as mentioned by Aquinas.[63]

Ms BPL 917 contains many more marginal references to the *Summa Theologiae*. In quite a few cases, there is no underlining to be found in corresponding passages in Grotius' own copy of Aquinas. As noted above, the absence of underlining cannot be conclusive proof that Grotius did *not* read something. However, it does suggest a more tenuous connection between

63 Leiden University Library, Ms BPL 917, f 9r, 15v, 39r, 41r, Grotius, *De Iure Praedae Commentarius/Commentary on the Law of Prize and Booty* vol I: *A Translation of the Original Manuscript of 1604*, 17, 34, 89, 94, University of Lund Library, Bibl Grotiana 16 II: 1–2: Aquinas, *Summa Theologiae* vol 3, 378–380, Van Ittersum, "Dating the manuscript of *De Jure Praedae* (1604–1608)" (n 4). Grotius' references to Question 108 of the *Secunda Secundae* on f 9r and f 15v of Ms BPL 917 are equally tenuous. Did Grotius need to reference "Th.2.2.q. 108" on f 9r, simply to piously observe that, "as the Scholastics have maintained, it is not proper for the spirit of the avenger to dwell with pleasure upon any person's ill fortune"? In chapter 3, Grotius considered the question whether there was such a thing as a just war for Christians against Christians. In the context of this larger argument, he had to define the term "Christian", claiming on f 15v that it pertained to "the profession of that name, rather than to the imitation of Christ's life which proves that we are truly Christians". His marginal reference to "Th. 2.2. q. 108 art. 1 ad tertium" was appropriate, in the sense that the corresponding passage in Aquinas emphasised Christian love and charity. However, could Grotius not have made the exact same point without ever mentioning Aquinas?

Grotius' argument in Ms BPL 917 and his "sources", particularly if Aquinas and Cajetan are not quoted or mentioned by name in the manuscript text. In those cases, the *Summa Theologiae* seems to be merely referenced as an "authority", in order to lend weight to the argument. Not coincidentally, marginal references to the *Summa Theologiae* in Ms BPL 917 are oftentimes part of clusters of references, clusters that may, in fact, consist of several layers of references, inserted at different points in time. For example, a marginal reference to Question 109, article 3, of the *Secunda Secundae* is part of a cluster of references at the bottom of f 10r, right next to two blocks of inserted text. The cluster of references also comprises Aristotle's *Politics*, Cicero's *On Duties* and the Digest and Institutes. There is no underlining to be found in Question 109, article 3 ("Utrum veritas sit pars justitiae") in Grotius' own copy of the *Secunda Secundae*. It is unclear how the marginal reference relates to Grotius' larger argument here, except that Aquinas affirms in the "sed contra" of Question 109 that Cicero considered truth to be part of justice ("Tullius ponit veritatem inter partes iustitiae"). However, Grotius hardly needed Aquinas to tell him this: in Ms BPL 917, he cited the relevant passage –"good faith is the foundation of justice" ("fidem esse justitiae fundamentum") – directly from Cicero's *On Duties*.[64]

A big cluster of impressive-looking "authorities" on f 27r of Ms BPL 917 contains a reference to the *Prima Secundae*, Question 47 ("De causa effectiva ira & de eius remediis"), article 1. This Aquinas reference literally threatens to drown in a sea of "authorities", which include the Bible books of Genesis, Proverbs and Psalms, the commentaries on the Digest of Bartolus of Saxoferrato (1313–1357), Jason de Mayno (1435–1519) and Paulus de Castro (d 1441), the commentaries on the Decretals of pope Innocent IV (1195–1254) and Parnormitanus (alias Niccolò Tedeschi, 1386–1445), the *Summa Sylvestrina* of Sylvester Mazzolini de Prierio (1456/1457–1523), the *Epistulae morales ad Lucilium* (*Moral Epistles to Lucilius*) of Seneca the Younger, and, last but not least, the *Commentaria in regulas iuris pontificii* of Dino del Mugello (d 1303). In all probability, this cluster of "authorities" on f 27r was put together in multiple sessions: three references that follow the *Prima Secundae* reference are crossed out, for example. It is doubtful that, in this particular case, Grotius' references to the medieval theologians and jurists are all first-hand: Grotius may well have obtained them

64 Leiden University Library, Ms BPL 917, f 10r, Grotius, *De Iure Praedae Commentarius/ Commentary on the Law of Prize and Booty* vol I: *A Translation of the Original Manuscript of 1604*, 18–19, University of Lund Library, Bibl Grotiana 16 II: 2: Aquinas, *Summa Theologiae* vol 3, 381–382.

from the *Corpus Iuris Canonici* and *Summa Sylvestrina*, for example. The *Prima Secundae* reference on f 27r seems rather curious. The corresponding passage in Grotius' copy of Aquinas contains no underlining. Still, was there at one time a clear relationship between the *Prima Secundae* reference on f 27r and Grotius' claim that "theologians and jurists of no slight authority . . . regard as punishable the negligence of those who have allowed some persons to be injured when they could have prevented such injury"? Did the *Prima Secundae* reference subsequently lose much of its purpose because Grotius continued to add authorities? Ironically, however impressive a cluster of marginal references might look to the reader, it greatly diminishes the importance of each individual reference in the cluster, and frequently obfuscates the relationship with the actual text. Clusters of references tend to take on lives of their own, separate from the author's argument.[65]

In all probability, Grotius inserted marginal references to the *Summa Theologiae* in Ms BPL 917 in multiple sessions, primarily to increase the number of authorities in the manuscript margins. References to the *Prima Secundae* and *Secunda Secundae* tend to be concentrated in the first half of Ms BPL 917, which, not coincidentally, was rewritten most. There is a notable tailing-off of the number of marginal references to Aquinas in the latter half of the manuscript, i.e. the least "worked-up" part of the treatise.[66] Moreover, references to the *Prima Secundae* and *Secunda Secundae* are bunched together: they tend to be found on folio-pages that are physically close to each other, such as folios 5v, 5'a, 6v and 15r-v and 33r-v in the case of *Prima Secundae* references and folios 9r, 10r, 10v, 11r, 11v and folios 14r, 15v, 16v, 17v, 18r, 19r, 20r in the case of *Secunda Secundae* references. This raises

65 Leiden University Library, Ms BPL 917, f 27r, Grotius, *De Iure Praedae Commentarius/ Commentary on the Law of Prize and Booty* vol I: *A Translation of the Original Manuscript of 1604*, 61, University of Lund Library, Bibl Grotiana 16 II: 1: Aquinas, *Summa Theologiae* vol 2, 137–139 and Bibl Grotiana 4, *Corpus Iuris Canonici*, Borschberg, *Hugo Grotius' Commentarius in Theses XI* (n 9) 71–72, 260–261. Grotius referenced the *Summa Sylvestrina* (first published in Rome in 1514) three times in *Theses XI*. He informed his readers in *Theses XI* that he was particularly interested in Sylvester Mazzolini's commentary on the term "bellum", "where he follows the tradition of Hostiensis, Innocent IV and Bartolus". Needless to say, we can also take this to mean that Grotius obtained his references to Hostiensis, Innocent IV and Bartolus from the *Summa Sylvestrina*.

66 Leiden University Library, Ms BPL 917: references to the *Prima Secundae* are to be found on folios 5v, 5'a, 6v, 11r, 15r, 15v, 17v, 27r, 33r, 33v, 35r; references to the *Secunda Secundae* are to be found on folios 9r, 10r, 10v, 11r, 11v, 14r, 15v, 16v, 17v, 18r, 19r, 20r, 26r, 31r, 32r, 33v, 34r, 37v, 39r, 39v, 41r, 47v, 48r, 48v, 50r, 50v, 54v, 55v, 61r, 98r, 99r, 99v, 101r, 121r, 134v, 135v, 139r. On how Ms BPL 917 was put together, see also Van Ittersum, "Dating the manuscript of *De Jure Praedae* (1604–1608)" (n 4), "Preparing *Mare Liberum* for the Press" (n 21), and "The wise man is never merely a private citizen" (n 30).

the question how Grotius went about revising Ms BPL 917. As noted earlier, the original text dates from 1604 to 1605. Grotius crossed out entire folio-pages and inserted completely new ones in January 1607 and November-December 1608, respectively. But what about adding references to margins? When did he do that? Would it have been part of a major effort to rewrite the manuscript text or would it have been done separately? Since inserted folio-pages contain marginal references to Aquinas which were copied lock, stock and barrel from deleted folio-pages, my hunch is that *adding* Aquinas references must have been a separate exercise for Grotius. It probably went like this: he opened up his copy of the *Summa Theologiae* one evening and, leafing through Ms BPL 917, started to insert new references where appropriate. The aim would have been to increase the number of authorities in the treatise's margins, rather than to elucidate an existing argument. When it suited Grotius, even texts from which he had once derived real intellectual sustenance could quickly be turned into "authorities", littering a manuscript's margins and, paradoxically, obscuring the argument. That is exactly what happened when Grotius prepared the second, third and fourth editions of *De Jure Belli ac Pacis*, published in 1631, 1642 and 1646.

F. CONCLUSIONS

An investigation of Grotius' working methods puts paid to various treasured notions of *Ideengeschichte* and *Quellenforschung* old-style.[67] Grotius the Genius – the man who allegedly read every book he ever referenced in *De Jure Belli ac Pacis*, who allegedly engaged with his "sources" in intellectual debates that spanned centuries, if not millennia, and whose supposed aim was to solve the problems of the modern world – turns out to have been non-existent. Grotius the Genius was literally a figment of the imagination of international lawyers in the West in the nineteenth and twentieth centuries. They needed a suitable "front man" for proclaiming the world-historical

67 The research for this chapter was made possible by a sabbatical leave at the Netherlands Institute for Advanced Study (Feb-June 2005), a European Visiting Research Fellowship of the Royal Society of Edinburgh (granted December 2012) and a Visiting Fellowship at Huygens ING in The Hague, a subsidiary of the Royal Dutch Academy of Sciences (July-Aug 2013). I am extremely grateful to Special Collections in Leiden University Library for facilitating my research on Mss BPL 917, 918 and 922, and to Special Collections at Lund University Library for facilitating my research on Grotius' *libri annotati*. I presented my findings at the "Ad Fontes: Reassessing Legal Humanism and Its Claims" international conference at the Edinburgh Law School on 7–8 June 2013. I have profited greatly from the constructive criticism of the conference participants, and from spirited conversations with Professor Henk Nellen at Huygens ING in July 2013.

importance of their own enterprise. When we look closely at the practicalities of scholarship in the seventeenth century, however, we discover the importance of the Republic of Letters: knowledge production was a truly collaborative affair, involving not just other scholars, both nearby and far away, but also relatives and friends, and, of course, printers and booksellers. The exchange of information in various forms and guises was at the heart of the Republic of Letters. We should not assume that canonical texts were at a scholar's disposal 24/7, for example. Grotius may only have purchased the medieval canonists and civilians for his personal library in the second decade of the seventeenth century, for example. The ever-increasing number of printed texts also induced scholars to rely on reference works, encyclopaedias, dictionaries and florilegia as "short-cuts", in order to manage "information overload". Reference works, encyclopaedias, dictionaries and florilegia from the (early) sixteenth century were relatively inexpensive at the turn of the seventeenth century. These must have seemed acceptable substitutes for "the real thing" for young lawyers like Grotius, eager to impress others with his knowledge and erudition, but lacking as yet the means to acquire individual works of famous jurists. That may explain why Ms BPL 917 and Ms BPL 922 in Leiden University Library are deficient in references to the French legal humanists, for example.

We should also keep in mind that the printed book was hardly a scholar's sole source of information. In gathering materials for his writings, Grotius consulted pamphlets, newsletters, maps, the verdicts of Admiralty courts, the resolutions of the Dutch States General and States of Holland, memoranda and notarised statements sent him by the Dutch East India Company, and excerpts and reading notes, either prepared by himself or by others. The excerpts from Balduinus' commentary on the Institutes, still extant in Ms BPL 918 in Leiden University Library, testify to his reliance on research assistants, even in his legal scholarship. If we want to understand the purpose and meaning of Grotius' work, we have to take all his sources of information into account, and not stare ourselves blind on the marginal references in his finished treatises. Moreover, what seems an impressive display of erudition on Grotius' part becomes rather less so when we critically examine his marginal references.

Ms 922 and Ms 917 in Leiden University Library are prime materials for reconstructing Grotius' working methods, precisely because they contain outlines, reading notes and treatises in different states of completion. Our investigation suggests that we should distinguish between sources that Grotius used in drafting his early treatises on natural law and natural rights, and the authorities that he added at a later stage, in so-called clusters of references. *Theses XI* and Ms BPL 917 reveal that the Classics, the *Corpus Iuris Civilis*, the *Corpus Iuris Canonici*, Aquinas' *Summa Theologiae* (with Cajetan's commentary thereon), Vitoria's *Relectiones Theologicae*, Vazquez' *Controversiae Illustres*, Bodin's *Six Books on the Commonwealth*, and, last but not least, Gentili's *De Jure Belli* were of great importance to Grotius' thinking on natural law and natural rights at this point in time. Not surprisingly, these authors are mentioned and quoted by name in Ms BPL 917 and/or *Theses XI*. Moreover, Grotius paid them the dubious compliment of copying their references, without any acknowledgement, of course. This is how Grotius created big, impressive-looking clusters of references in the margins of chapters 1–10 and 12 of Ms BPL 917, which, not coincidentally, are the parts of the manuscript most heavily revised. In multiple sessions, Grotius added layer upon layer of "authorities" in his marginal references, with the aim of adding further weight to his argument. Needless to say, it also served to obscure the true origins of his thinking on natural law and natural rights. To suggest that Grotius engaged in an elaborate, in-depth debate with medieval canonists and civilians, as Haggenmacher and, to a lesser extent, Tierney[68] have done, gives Grotius rather more credit than he is due. In Ms BPL 917 and Ms 922, Grotius' references to the medieval canonists and civilians are largely derived from Vitoria, Vazquez, Gentili, Cajetan and, of course, the *Corpus Iuris Canonici*. To the extent that Grotius was interested in the intricacies of medieval debates on rights, property, and the just war, he looked at these debates through a decidedly sixteenth-century lens. In the case of Aquinas' *Summa Theologiae*, our comparison of Grotius' own copy of the work, extant in Lund University Library, and his references to it in Ms BPL 917 suggests that (a) Vitoria served as a kind of reader's guide to Aquinas and that (b) Cajetan's commentary was accepted unquestioningly as the authoritative interpretation of Aquinas. Grotius' own copy of Aquinas also indicates that he adhered to the reading strategies that he had recommended to Aubéry du Maurier in his letter of May 1615: he read parts of the *Secunda Secundae* in depth and simply skimmed over others. The importance of Question 40 of the *Secunda Secundae* for Grotius' theorising on the just war in Ms BPL 917 can be deduced from the fact that (a) Grotius mentioned Aquinas by name and/or quoted him in the manuscript

68 B Tierney, "Tuck on rights: some medieval problems" (1983) 4 *History of Political Thought* 429–441 and *The Idea of Natural Rights: Studies on Natural Rights, Natural Law, and Church Law 1150–1625*, Emory University Studies in Law and Religion (1997) 316–342.

(in combination with a marginal reference to "Th.2.2.40") and (b) inserted underlining in Question 40 in his own copy of the *Secunda Secundae*, both in Aquinas' text and Cajetan's commentary thereon. However, there are also examples in Ms BPL 917 of Grotius copying marginal references to Aquinas wholesale from Vitoria, or incorporating references to Aquinas into big, impressive-looking clusters of references, making the connection with Grotius' argument rather tenuous. In these cases, Aquinas' usefulness as "authority" clearly trumped his function as "source" for Grotius' thinking on natural rights and natural law. The distinction is not a clear-cut one, of course. But it does serve to underline the fact that for seventeenth-century scholars like Grotius, piling on the "authorities" and manipulating them in support of one's argument was far more important than honestly referencing one's sources. Or is this not so different after all from the "publish or perish" ethic that pervades modern-day academia?

8 Joannes Leunclavius (1541–1594), Civilian and Byzantinist?

Bernard Stolte

A. INTRODUCTION

One of the distinguishing features of legal humanism is the use of Byzantine sources for criticism and illumination of the *Corpus Iuris Civilis*. The sixteenth century saw a gradual increase of the knowledge and accessibility of Greek manuscripts that transmitted these texts, as well as of the number of scholars sharing this interest. Among them, Joannes Leunclavius, as I will argue, occupies a special place. His work on Byzantine sources raises the question whether it was driven by an interest in Roman law or by a fascination with Byzantium. What part did these sources play in Leunclavius' work? Among legal humanists he is probably the best candidate for being a byzantinist. If *he* is not one of that curious breed, who is?

In 1994, some aspects of Leunclavius have been investigated in the *Rechtshistorisches Journal* on the occasion of the quatercentenary of his death.[1] At the time Douglas Osler implied that Leunclavius' interest in Byzantine sources was moved by the same consideration as the other human-

1 The section "Memoria" in (1994) 13 *Rechtshistorisches Journal* 195–243, with contributions by M Th Fögen, D J Osler, K G Pitsakis and B H Stolte, all quoted below.

ists': "one consideration, and one consideration alone: they provided a useful tool for the textual criticism of the basic source of contemporary legal practice in the West, the Latin *Corpus Iuris* of Justinian".[2] Twenty years after the commemoration of 1994, it is time to test that verdict, which goes to the heart of the questions connected with the nature of legal humanism.

B. GENERAL BACKGROUND

The honour for discovering Byzantine legal sources and their potential for textual criticism and exegetical work on Justinian's legislation is due to the legal humanists: *Graeca leguntur*, as the title of Troje's well-known book has it.[3] The presence of Greek is almost a hallmark of work in the humanist tradition, which has contributed enormously to the state of the texts of the Digest, Code and Novels as we read them today in modern critical editions. Part of the reasons for this humanist interest in Byzantium is their awareness of the historical context of Roman law in its Justinianic form, resulting in a return *ad fontes*. Some other aspects of this interest will emerge later on, when I will attempt to provide a fuller explanation of the phenomenon, but let us first take a look at the problem the humanists were grappling with.[4]

That the current texts of Justinian's legislation were not perfect had long been recognised. Medieval jurists were familiar with the famous manuscript of the Digest, the *littera Pisana*, as a possible source for better readings. When in 1406 it was carried off as a prize and became the *littera Florentina*, its accessibility did not improve: it entered the private library of the Medici and permission to inspect it was granted only rarely. Of the *Codex Justinianus* no comparable prestigious manuscript was known. Both texts originally contained Greek passages, which however were being omitted or simply lost in copying and at best represented in the text with "*gr.*" or similar indications. While the medieval jurists contented themselves with this state of affairs, reflected in the so-called *littera Vulgata*, the humanists wished to restore the original glory of the Justinianic texts. Owing to the lack of better manuscripts, either because they were not extant or because they

2 D J Osler, "Homer Dethroned", ibid, 202.

3 H E Troje, *Graeca leguntur. Die Aneignung des byzantinischen Rechts und die Entstehung eines humanistischen Corpus iuris civilis in der Jurisprudenz des 16. Jahrhunderts* (1971).

4 The following paragraphs of this section cover, from a slightly different perspective, the same ground as my "Text and Commentary: Legal Humanism", in K Enenkel and H Nellen (eds), *Neo-Latin Commentaries and the Management of Knowledge in the Late Middle Ages and the Early Modern Period (1400–1700)* [Supplementa Humanistica Lovaniensia XXXIII] (2013) 387.

were inaccessible to them, they often resorted to conjectural emendation, and it is here that Byzantine sources had an important role to play.

Just as all legislation, Justinian's codification and subsequent constitutions had to be explained and taught. Since the emperor had codified Roman law in Latin, whereas the majority of his subjects were Greek-speaking, the new codification had to be translated as well. The result is a mass of translations, paraphrases, summaries and commentaries in Greek, which has reached us mostly in fragments and in indirect transmission. As has been said above, the humanists were the first to discover and study this material, which came within their reach only piecemeal, and to understand that it could be brought to bear on the tradition and interpretation of the Justinianic sources it was based upon.

Although the humanists recognised the value of these first discoveries, philological methods and techniques were still in their infancy and progress was dictated by chance just as much as by effort. It was one thing to unearth Greek texts that appeared to be related to Justinian's legislation, but another to understand what exactly they represented. To compound the problem, these then had to be fitted into a textual tradition that was itself but imperfectly known and hotly debated. It is no wonder that in these conditions the exploitation of the new Greek material led to results that were, to put it mildly, not always satisfactory. It is not just with the benefit of hindsight that we are now able to say this: the humanists themselves were not slow to discover weak points in the argumentation (preferably of their opponents, of course) and were not afraid of severe judgments, as we know from contemporary discussions. An appraisal of the humanist critical effort on the basis of Greek texts can only be fair if we take into account how much the humanists *could* and in fact *did* know, and what exactly they wished to achieve. This holds good for Leunclavius' work as well as for that of any humanist.

C. JOANNES LEUNCLAVIUS (1541–1594)

Although many details remain somewhat obscure, the outline of Leunclavius' biography is clear enough. The main data were collected by Marie Theres Fögen in 1994, to which I refer for particulars.[5] To summarise briefly: he was born in Coesfeld (30 km west of Münster), educated in Wittenberg and

5 M Th Fögen, "Johannes Löwenklau" (1994) 13 *Rechtshistorisches Journal* 197. To the bibliography given there and in the papers by the authors quoted above (n 1) should be added M-P Burtin, "Un apôtre de la tolérance: l'humaniste allemand Johannes Löwenklau, dit Leunclavius (1541–1593?)" (1990) 52 *Bibliothèque d'Humanisme et Renaissance* 561.

Heidelberg, travelled widely, not least to Constantinople, and is known as a prolific translator of Greek historical works, as an historian of the Turkish Sultanate, and as an editor, translator and commentator of Byzantine legal works. It is with the last-mentioned that our concern lies but, as we shall see, we will not be able to neglect his other interests.

As a legal scholar, Leunclavius published three books. The first was, *inter alia*, an edition-cum-translation of the *Synopsis Basilicorum Maior*, the second a Latin translation of the *Collectio Tripartita*. Both were *editiones principes* and were accompanied by a series of notes, which in fact exploited these texts for textual criticism on the *Corpus Iuris Civilis*. A third book appeared posthumously and carried the umbrella title of *Ius graeco-romanum*. It is a miscellany of Byzantine legal texts, some of them *editio princeps* and, in a small number of cases, still the only edition. I propose to deal with these works in some detail, gladly recognising my debt to Troje's *Graeca leguntur* and to the essays in the *Rechtshistorisches Journal* referred to above. As far as I can see, these titles constitute the entire bibliography insofar as Leunclavius' legal work is concerned; the only – but extremely valuable – addition since 1994 is Ludwig Burgmann's detailed biblio-historiographical study of the laws of the Byzantine emperors of 2005.[6] In my opinion, however, there remains ample scope for additions and in some cases I beg to differ. It is especially the larger picture of his work as a humanist scholar that, I believe, is in need of adjustment. To this an attentive reading of his prefaces as well as of some *obiter dicta* in the works themselves could make a contribution.

D. *ECLOGA SIVE SYNOPSIS BASILICORUM* (1575)

Leunclavius' first venture into editing Byzantine legal sources was the publication of the *Synopsis Basilicorum Maior* (SBM), in 1575,[7] on the basis of just one manuscript, which to my knowledge has never been identified and is perhaps no longer extant. The edition, accompanied by a Latin translation, well illustrates the element of chance: he had been given the opportunity

6 L Burgmann, "Die Gesetze der byzantinischen Kaiser" *Fontes Minores* XI (2005) 77, in the author's words a "wissenschaftsgeschichtliche Skizze" (77 n°), which describes in great detail the scholarly effort from the humanist age until the year 2000 in editing *Novellae constitutiones*, Justinianic as well as post-Justinianic; Leunclavius is well represented (esp 88–88, 99, 107, 124, 128–132).

7 *LX librorum* Βασιλικῶν, *id est Vniversi iuris Romani Ecloga sive Synopsis. Item Nouellarum antehac non publicatarum liber* (1575).

to use this one manuscript, supposedly found by Sambucus[8] in Taranto in Southern Italy.[9] Nowadays we know of more than forty, not counting excerpts. The Basilica, promulgated c 900, are a Greek version of the *Corpus Iuris Civilis*, in which a subject is represented by consolidated titles of Digest and Code, followed by the pertinent Novels. The SBM, dating to the middle of the tenth century, is an anthology from the Basilica under key-words that had themselves been arranged alphabetically: thus "sale" is found under the *alpha* of *agorasia*, between *error iuris* (*agnoia tou nomou*) and "land taken from the enemy" (*agroi analèphthentes apo toon polemioon*).[10] The edition has been criticised for rearranging the SBM into the order of the sixty books of the Basilica from which it had been compiled;[11] this was not difficult to accomplish, since the SBM quotes book, title and chapter of the Basilica with the extracts. This palingenesis of the Basilica is itself evidence of the emphasis of Leunclavius' interest: the arrangement of the Basilica provides a more convenient tool for textual criticism of the *Corpus Iuris Civilis* than the SBM with its somewhat haphazard organisation. The reduction of the Basilica to a collection of key-words offers, of course, a clear picture of the state of Byzantine law in the tenth century. We must not forget, however, that in the second half of the sixteenth century the existence of the Basilica was known, but as far as their contents were concerned, scholars must have felt as Tantalus: only fragments were published, mainly by Cuiacius,[12] and a veritable *editio princeps* would not appear until some seventy years later.[13] In the meantime all information was awaited impatiently, and so was Leunclavius' edition. There was even a competitor in the market: Johann Thomas Freigius (1543–1583) was also preparing, or had

8 Johannes Sambucus (1531–1584), physician and historiographer at the Imperial Court in Vienna (see also below, n 23). Sambucus was a great collector of manuscripts, on which see esp H Gerstinger, "Johannes Sambucus als Handschriftensammler", *Festschrift der Nationabibliothek Wien* (1926) 251.

9 Thus Leunclavius in the prooimion. The identification with the present Vindob Jur gr 14 (olim 4), implied by Gerstinger ("J.S. als Handschriftensammler", 326) cannot be correct, since that manuscript contains a *Synopsis Basilicorum Minor*, as already noted by S Perentides, "Recherches sur le texte de la *Synopsis minor*", *Fontes Minores* VI (1984) 219 esp 222–223.

10 For the SBM see N van der Wal and J H A Lokin, *Historiae iuris graeci-romani delineatio. Les sources du droit byzantin de 300 à 1453* (1985) 92–93, 134, Sp N Troianos, *Oi peges tou buzantinou dikaiou*, 3rd augmented edn (2011) 275–278.

11 For examples see Troje, *Graeca leguntur* (n 3) 265 n 92, who is himself much more positive (267).

12 Troje, *Graeca leguntur* (n 3) 255 ff. Cuiacius definitely used Basilica manuscripts for, *inter alia*, his *Observationes et Emendationes*, his commentary on D.27.1–28.6 and, of course, for his Latin translation of the sixtieth book of the Basilica, Βασιλικῶν *liber LX* (1566). See also my "*Graeca Pandectarum in Basilicis*" (2014) IX *Subseciva Groningana* 429.

13 Τῶν Βασιλικῶν βιβλία *LX*. Βασιλικῶν *libri XL in VII tomos divisi* (1647).

prepared, a translation.[14] In fact he accused Leunclavius of having stolen his work, against which the latter wrote a defence, to which I will return later. Let us first take a closer look at the Synopsis edition.

The book published with Eusebius Episcopius in Basel is in fact a composite work. It falls into three parts, as its full title proclaims:

> [1] Of the Sixty Books of the Basilica, that is, of the entire Roman law which had been translated into the Greek language on the authority of Roman emperors, the Ecloga [=Selection] or Synopsis, hitherto lacking, now edited by Joannes Leunclavius from the library of Joannes Sambucus. [2] Furthermore, a book of Novels not published before. [3] Added have been also Annotations of the translator, in which many laws and many passages of the civil law have been restored and emended.

The Synopsis is the first part. Although the title mentions the Novels, there is not a word about them in the prooemium. The reader is not informed that these constitutions are of later Byzantine emperors. This does not transpire until we come to the second part, where a new numeration begins, the first page actually being a new title page:

> New constitutions of ten emperors, together with opinions of some others, from manuscript books now for the first time dug up, cleansed of errors, and "transcribed" [translated, actually] into the Latin language, by Joannes Leunclavius. The reader will find the names of the emperors, with the subjects or "titles" of the novels, appended to the preface.[15]

All this reinforces the impression that the projected book initially did not contain this second part with post-Justinianic constitutions, which have no direct relation to the Justinianic *Corpus Iuris* other than being formally amendments of the Code (*Novellae post Codicem constitutiones/Nearai meta ton Koodika diataxeis*). At the same time it must be pointed out that many of them are in fact transmitted in the manuscripts as an appendix to the *Synopsis Basilicorum Maior*. The third part with Annotations, on the contrary, does bear on the *Corpus Iuris* directly and thus belongs in a sense to the first part, although its pagination is continuous with that of the Novels. These critical notes no doubt were in Leunclavius' mind from the beginning and are mentioned in the first prooemium. The *Annotationes* are in fact a subgenre of a form of expression favoured by the humanists: *Observationes et Emendationes*.

If we wish fully to understand Leunclavius' valuation of Byzantine legal

14 R von Stintzing, "Freigius, Johann Thomas", *Allgemeine Deutsche Biographie* 7 (1878), 341–343 describes his life and work, but does not mention this affair.

15 See also, especially, Burgmann, "Die Gesetze" (n 6) 88–89.

sources, we have to read the two prooemia together, since they express his twofold interest in Byzantium. The first prooemium, to the Synopsis edition, sets out Leunclavius' view of the value of Byzantine sources and enables us to take the measure of his knowledge of that field. He emphasises the value of the Basilica, the last book of which has recently found an excellent translator, whose identity is not disclosed: he is, of course, Cuiacius,[16] who is admonished to publish any other books he may have. He briefly touches on the Annotations and explains how he had proceeded in editing his source, i.e. reconstructing the order of the Basilica. The emphasis of this prooemium is on the *Corpus Iuris Civilis*. The second prooemium, introducing the Novels,[17] sings an entirely different song. Leunclavius is aware of the fact that these are not part of received Roman law and is out to defend their *auctoritas*. These more recent Byzantine emperors, he argues, are *Augusti* of equal right, brothers of the western emperors. The Greeks are intellectually superior to the Occident, and so are their laws, if we compare them to western legislation. They clarify some points of Roman law, remove contradictions, etc. The individual Novels are then presented, and the focus is on a Novel of Nicephorus Phocas (963–969),[18] forbidding the foundation of new monasteries, and on its repeal by Basil II (976–1025).[19] How foolish! A long tirade on the evils of monasticism follows, ending in a quotation from Zosimus in Latin translation:

> The church of the Christians had been occupied by those who are called Monks. These abstain from legitimate marriage, and both in towns and in the country fill colleges with unmarried men, employed neither for war, nor for any other use necessary to the state. All the same, from that time until the present day they have somehow managed to transfer to themselves a large part of the world, and under the pretext of sharing all their goods with the poor, they have, I would almost say, reduced everyone to poverty.

He will not go into detail of other constitutions. But if the *auctoritas* of these emperors does not convince, let their example incite our princes to reform, especially the present heavy taxation of land, which might lead to revolution; the history of Athens and Rome teaches us to what potentially gruesome effect. Also, these Novels are important historical sources. Leunclavius then

16 See above, n 12.

17 It is printed by Burgmann, "Die Gesetze" (n 6), as Anhang II (128–132), and summarised at 89–90.

18 F Dölger, *Regesten der Kaiserurkunden des oströmischen Reiches von 565–1453*, I Teil, 2. Halbband: Regesten von 867–1025, 2nd edn by A E Müller in cooperation with A Beihammer (2003) no 699.

19 Ibid, no 772.

compares himself favourably with Bonefidius, who had given his work the title *Ius orientale*,[20] a scoop of which I suspect Leunclavius was jealous, and gives his sources, in the usual imprecise way.

In the first prooemium, Leunclavius is a straightforward civilian with a humanist perspective: everything that contributes to our understanding of Roman law is worth studying, especially such unknown Byzantine sources, which stem from an intellectually superior culture. In the second prooemium we recognise a Byzantinist, but one with a protestant, reformist agenda. That the two are found between the covers of one and the same book may have been just one of the fortunes of publishing in the sixteenth century, but I would not be surprised if Leunclavius was actually very pleased.

The edition of the Synopsis, for all its idiosyncratic presentation by Leunclavius, remained the only available one until 1869, when Zachariä von Lingenthal published a text that followed the organisation of the manuscripts.[21]

In order to facilitate the use of the edition, Leunclavius provided after the prooemium "an accurate index of the titles of this Ecloga according to the order of the Latin alphabet", followed by "an accurate index of the sixty royal books [=the Basilica], according to the alphabet". The unsuspecting reader might be excused for thinking that the former is an index of the Synopsis, and the latter of the Basilica. In fact, the reverse is the case. The second "index" has been taken from the manuscript of the Synopsis and is a *pinax*, a table that simply lists the contents of the *Synopsis Basilicorum Maior* as it is structured, i.e. according to the key words as they follow one after the other in the Greek alphabet. It is a Greek list and has been duly translated into Latin; we may note the translation of the rubric: ". . . secundum seriem litterarum Graecarum". The first index is an index as we understand the word. It has been compiled by now rearranging the Latin translations of the Greek *pinax* according to the order of the Latin alphabet and referring to page numbers in the edition. It thus provides indirect access to the *Corpus Iuris Civilis*. An example may clarify this. It opens with "De abigeis, p. 517", and if we turn to page 517, we read a fragment from the Basilica, B. 60.25.1 [=D. 47.14.1]. In the SBM this is A 52 (*Peri apelatoon*, note the number 52!), fr 1. In the margin the reader will find the reference to the *Corpus Iuris Civilis*.[22]

20 E Bonefidius, Τοῦ 'Ανατολικοῦ νομίμου, βασιλικοῦ τε καὶ ἀρχιερατικοῦ, βιβλία γ '. *Iuris orientalis libri III* (1573), for which see the detailed presentation by Burgmann, "Die Gesetze" (n 6) 82–88.

21 C E Zachariä von Lingenthal, *Synopsis Basilicorum* = *Jus Graeco-romanum* V (1869), repr in J and P Zepos, *Jus Graecoromanum* (= JGR) V (1931).

22 Here Leunclavius has "l. 1 C. hoc tit.", where "C" should be "D". For the text of the SBM in the edition of Zachariä, see Zepos *JGR* V (n 21) 85.

In the SBM it is, of course, at nearly the beginning of the work, under the first letter, whereas in the Basilica it is almost at the end, in the sixtieth and last book. All this brings out the true intention of the edition, and indeed of publishing Byzantine sources in the first place: in their presentation access to the Byzantine source is subordinate to its exploitation for critical evaluation of the *Corpus Iuris*.

That the edition was a tool, not an end in itself, also transpires from the *Adnotationes*. Their subtitle is illuminating:

> . . . or, brief indications of some passages of the civil law, which either receive some illumination from this Synopsis Basilicorum, or, being corrupt, are restored partly from conjectures, partly from clear proof, or, from their mutilated state, are made whole, while moreover not a few are left that the acute and ingenious reader by himself will be able to rescue[!].

Then follow seventy-nine chapters on the Digest and sixty-five on the Code. The *Adnotationes* are concluded with an Appendix of seven pages, of which more presently.

After the Annotations, on unnumbered pages, there follows a Latin "Index of *res* and *verba* especially noteworthy in the books of the Basilica". At first sight this may come somewhat as a surprise, since it could seem to be a repeat of the already mentioned index, which follows immediately after the prooemium of the edition of the SBM. A closer look, however, reveals its true nature: it is much more detailed, covering thirty-six pages in three columns, in contrast with the first one, which consists of only seven pages in two columns and in larger print. It is a proper index, not just a rearranged *index titulorum* of the Synopsis. Finally, an "Index of *res* and *verba* especially noteworthy in the *Novellae constitutiones* and the *Adnotationes*", with Greek and Latin *voces*, covering little over three pages, again in three columns, brings the volume to a conclusion.

Leunclavius' *Synopsis Basilicorum* demonstrates the two aspects of his scholarship. The SBM and the Annotations belong to the humanist civilian tradition, while the *Novellae Constitutiones* are the work of a byzantinist. The two separate paginations would have emphasised the distinction, if the Annotations had not followed after the Novels and continued the second series of page numbers, a feature that corresponds with the two indices on unnumbered pages at the end. I suspect that all this reflects at least in part how the book has been put together.

The genesis of the book, however, is also connected with the quarrel with Freigius mentioned earlier, and raises questions of authorship and access to a manuscript or manuscripts. The link between Freigius and Leunclavius is the book collector Johannes Sambucus (1531–1584), from whose library, as the title-page proclaims, the manuscript of the Synopsis had come. The letters of Sambucus, edited by Hans Gerstinger,[23] have an interesting story to tell. On 20 January 1569, Sambucus writes to the Basel publisher Episcopius to remind him of his promise to print the Synopsis: "quamprimum te impressurum thesaurum a me tibi datum ingentem". He returns to this in later letters to others. E.g., on 5 January 1573, two years before the actual publication, the subject takes up an entire letter to Samuel Gryneus, "chief-printer" of the House of the Episcopii in Basel: "Basilica mea cum interpretatione sua dudum communicavit Freigius . . .", and a week later, to Hugo Blotius: "Basilica mea graece et latine fere typis sunt absoluta". We learn that Freigius had been involved and the work is claimed to be almost(!) finished. But less than a month later, on 6 February, he implores Theodor Zwinger: ". . . Gryneum et Episcopios meo nomine saluta ac omnibus modis impetra, urge, Basilica mea a Joanne Thoma Freigio versa cum Graecis quamprimum excudant aut saltem ad has nundinas duo prima folia cum epigraphè tamquam specimen deportent, ne mora ista aliqui editionem tam desiderati operis antevertantur. Freigius dudum Episcopiis dedit, . . .". And four days later to the same: "Gryneum quaeso de Basilicis edendis moneto, quorum interpretationem cum graecis Freigius dudum illi tradidit'. Then, finally, on 9 March 1575, in a letter to Crato von Kraftheim (1519–1585): "Episcopius tandem Basilikoon 24 libros ex interpretatione Leonclavii, licet Freigius idem praestiterit, mea causa edidit".[24] There are other mentions, but none of them explain how Leunclavius was able to interfere and claim the work as his own, nor is it clear who actually edited the Greek text or who thought of rearranging it according to the order of the Basilica. Sambucus' fear that someone else might pre-empt the edition indicates the general interest in the world of letters. But an earlier edition requires the availability of other manuscripts. Is it Cuiacius who he is thinking of? Or were other manuscripts known, perhaps a copy of Sambucus' exemplar?

My reading of the affair is that Sambucus had made the manuscript available and asked Freigius to provide a translation and send it to Episcopius in Basel. Episcopius enlisted the help of Leunclavius to edit the Greek text for the press, and Leunclavius apparently was not satisfied with Freigius'

23 H Gerstinger, *Die Briefe des Johannes Sambucus (Zsámboky) 1554–1584. Mit einem Anhang: Die Sambucusbriefe im Kreisarchiv von Trnava von Anton Vantuch* (1968), with information on the names mentioned here.

24 The colophon (on the page where the last index ends) reads: "Basileae, Ex officina Episcopiana, Anno Salutis humanae MDLXXV, Mense Martio".

translation. Freigius, who was in Basel in 1575,[25] understandably was dismayed and gave vent to his feelings, but Sambucus does not seem to have done more than shrugging his shoulders. Leunclavius was able to insert a defence in the form of the Appendix to the *Adnotationes*, where he strongly criticises the translation by Freigius: "The printer showed me a translation of this our Ecloga Basilicorum [=Synopsis], attempted by someone whose name I have decided not to make public on purpose." Obviously this is Freigius, to whom he had already alluded in the prooemium obscurely as *quidam frigidus interpres*. (His humanist friends will have appreciated the word-play and understood the metaphorical meaning of the adjective.)[26] Leunclavius gives a number of examples, intending of course to show the inferiority of Freigius' work. The name is given away in the last line, when Leunclavius quotes Virgil 9,617: *O uere Phrygiae, neque enim Phryges* – note again the malicious word-play on Freigius – meaning so much as "leave the work to real men". Not very nice, but then humanists do not exactly have a reputation for their engaging manners.

Cuiacius certainly read Leunclavius' edition. In fact, in 1579 he devoted chapter 37 of book XVIII of the *Observationes et Emendationes* to "The many mistakes the [recent edition of the] Synopsis has given rise to".[27] We note in passing that Leunclavius is not mentioned by name, just as Leunclavius had not mentioned the name of Cuiacius in the preface of the Synopsis. In typically humanist fashion, however, Cuiacius refers to those "who cannot wait to criticise him who translates most capably before he has edited his own text", to finish with "But enough of these mistakes, and the numerous other ones committed by the same person elsewhere".[28] But whatever the quality of the work and the means employed, it is Leunclavius who may claim the honour of the first, albeit partial, edition of the Basilica.

E. *PARATITLA: COLLECTIO TRIPARTITA* (1593)

Eighteen years after the Synopsis, under the title *Paratitla*,[29] Leunclavius published a translation of the *Collectio Tripartita*, a collection of Greek

25 Thus Stintzing (above, n 14).

26 "indifferent", "feeble", e.g. in Cicero, *Brut*. 48, 178.

27 "Quot erroribus occasionem dederit *Synopsis Basilicorum*".

28 "Sed de his satis, et de aliis ejusdem alias numero multis [sc. erroribus]". The next chapter (XVIII, 38) deals with "another person's mistakes", not with Leunclavius', *pace* Osler, "Homer Dethroned" (n 1) 210.

29 *Paratitlorum libri tres antiqui, ab Io. Leunclauio Latini de Graecis facti. Eiusdem Notatorum libri duo* (1593).

summaries of passages from the *Corpus Iuris Civilis* on religious and ecclesiastical affairs dating to circa 580.[30] It is in itself significant that Leunclavius gave a translation only. In 1575 in the prooemium to the Synopsis, he had deplored the phenomenon of publishing Latin translations without their Greek originals, proudly proclaiming that he, on the advice of Sambucus, had presented the Greek as well.[31] Now he was acting differently, probably not out of choice. The *editio princeps* of the Greek text would not be published until nearly seventy years later, including Leunclavius' translation.[32]

The *prologus* brings out yet another aspect of Leunclavius' views. It takes the form of a letter to Marquard Freher (1565–1614), who three years later would be responsible for Leunclavius' posthumous *Ius graeco-romanum*. First, Leunclavius goes into the word *paratitla*. He explains the word as it traditionally has been understood: "to note at any title of the Digest, information pertinent to that title that is to be found in other titles and places".[33] This is correct for only part of the *Collectio Tripartita*, but it is an aspect he needs for the main thrust of the prologue: he uses it as a peg on which to hang a comprehensive *ratio discendi*, a method to master the contents of the *Corpus Iuris Civilis*. Second, he claims that the fact that this way of learning, this *rectissima et compendiaria via*, was not generally followed, had led to such a chaos:

> . . . that the present age seemed to require a new Justinian for teaching the law and a reform of the courts. This has been the cry of the entire world for a long time now, which proclaims blessed the barbarous tribe of the Turcs, who, without the din of law courts and simply and extrajudicially gives justice to its members, and speedily executes judgement without any means of escape by delay. And all that while they do have a Codex Justinianus in their own language, a fact we are able to testify to as one who has seen those parts with his own eyes, as well as heard things unknown to us westerners . . .[34]

30 N van der Wal and B H Stolte (eds), *Collectio Tripartita. Justinian on Religious and Ecclesiastical Affairs* (1994).

31 *Synopsis*, Prooemium, f *3r.

32 G Voellus and H Justellus, *Bibliotheca iuris canonici veteris* (2 vols with continuous pagination) (1661) II 1217–1478. On the edition see Van der Wal-Stolte, *Collectio Tripartita* (n 30) xliii; Leunclavius' translation accompanied the edition.

33 ". . . quemuis ad titulum adnotare, quae aliis in titulis ac locis illum ad titulum pertinentia reperiantur" (f.):(iiir). Thus also Zachariä von Lingenthal, quoted by H J Scheltema, "Das Kommentarverbot Justinians" (1977) 45 *Tijdschrift voor Rechtsgeschiedenis* 307 (319–324). Scheltema argues rather in favour of "Randscholien", marginal glosses, but see D Simon, "Paratitla Athanasii", *Fontes Minores* VII (1986) 141 esp 141–143. It seems that *paratitlon* has had more than one meaning, indicating now its content, now its outward characteristics.

34 f. [):(vii]r, also referred to by Burtin, "Un apôtre de la tolérance" (n 5) 568. The "Codex Justinianus in their own language" probably is the *Multaqa al-abhur*, a collection of islamic and secular law in Arabic compiled by Ibrahim al-Halabi c1550 at the order of Suleyman the

The cry for a New Justinian had been heard before in humanist circles,[35] but the comparison with the way of administering justice by the Turcs was a novelty. It is the result of a journey to Constantinople undertaken in 1584 in the retinue of the emperor's ambassador to Sultan Murat III. A long sojourn in the former capital of the Byzantine empire enabled him to acquaint himself with the rival and enemy of the Christian empire, a first-hand knowledge that seems to have left him with a certain admiration. It certainly prepared him for writing about the history of the Turcs.[36]

Just as *Adnotationes* had accompanied the Synopsis of 1575, the *Paratitla* are followed by *Notata*, in two books. The first book offers critical notes on the *Corpus Iuris Civilis* based on the *Collectio Tripartita*, the second one is an enlarged and emended edition of the Annotations of 1575 and in part an answer to the critique by Cuiacius of the earlier work.[37] The *Notata* lack a separate preface, but at the beginning of this second book Leunclavius defends his position vis-à-vis Cuiacius and Freigius. The claim of it being an enlarged and emended version is no idle boast: for a start, it is almost twice the size of the *Adnotationes*.

The *Paratitla* together with the first book of the *Notata* provide an excellent demonstration of Leunclavius' working method, since we have not only these, but also the manuscripts he had been able to use, one of which contains annotations in his own hand. For all this I refer to my paper of 1994.[38]

F. *IUS GRAECO-ROMANUM* (1596)

The third and final Byzantine legal work that deserves our attention is the *Ius graeco-romanum*.[39] Leunclavius did not live to see its publication. He had already been trying to find a publisher, as transpires from a letter of 1592: he had offered it to Wechel's heirs,[40] the publisher of his *Paratitla* and

Magnificent. See, for two different approaches, J Schacht, *An Introduction to Islamic Law* (1964) 112–115 and H Hattenauer, *Europäische Rechtsgeschichte*, 4th edn (2004) 507–510.

35 It had been raised by, e.g., G Budaeus, as noted by D Osler, "Budaeus and Roman law" (1985) 13 *Ius Commune* 195 (197–203).

36 *Annales Sultanorum Othmanidarum, a Joanne Gandier dicto Spiegel, interprete Turcico Germanice translati. I. Leunclavius Latine redditos illustravit et auxit, usque ad annum (1588)* (1588) (ed altera 1596); *Historiae Musulmanae Turcorum libri XVIII* (1591).

37 See Osler, "Homer Dethroned" (n 1) 210.

38 B H Stolte, "The Lion's Paws: Observations on Joannes Leunclavius (1541–1594) at Work" (1994) 13 *Rechtshistorisches Journal* 219.

39 *Iuris Graeco-Romani tam canonici quam civilis tomi duo* (1596).

40 On Wechels (De Marne and Aubrey were his sons-in-law and heirs), see R J W Evans, *The Wechel Presses: Humanism and Calvinism in Central Europe 1572–1627* [Past and Present,

his books on Turkish history, but unsuccessfully.[41] It is not clear whether it had already been finished by then. In any case, it was edited from the papers of Leunclavius by Marquardus Freherus, who wrote, by way of a preface, a lengthy and flattering dedication to emperor Rudolph II. The reader will recognise a number of sentences that stem directly from Leunclavius' own prooemia, and it would carry too far to go into this text in detail. Suffice it to say that the problem of the authority of these Greek constitutions is also addressed by Freherus and approached along lines similar to Leunclavius', with some ingenious additions. And he could, of course, not resist the temptation to point out that Leunclavius – and Freherus himself – now had delivered what Cuiacius had promised in 1573, when the French lawyer wrote in so many words that he was preparing an edition of the Novels of Constantine Porhyrogennetus and a great many [other] later Roman emperors.[42]

The first volume contains canon law, the second civil law, and has been analysed recently by Ludwig Burgmann.[43] Most of the *Novellae constitutiones* of 1575 are repeated here.[44] In 1994, the work was briefly summarised by Marie Theres Fögen,[45] and its curious success story in Greece elaborated by Kostas Pitsakis.[46] The two volumes of the *Ius graeco-romanum* contain a number of texts that for many years, indeed centuries, would not be superseded, not least since some "modern" editions are in fact reprints of Leunclavius' texts.

It is worth pointing out that Leunclavius once more showed himself a creative editor. His rearrangement of the *Synopsis* has already been mentioned, but his edition of the Isaurian *Ecloga* in *Ius Graeco-romanum* II, 79–134 as *Liber Leonis et Constantini* is quite a feat in similar vein: to quote Ludwig Burgmann: "Leunclavius has thus compiled from three manuscripts parts of four versions respectively derivatives of the Ecloga."[47] In other words, the text as edited by Leunclavius has never existed. To reproach him for this "falsification", however, would not be entirely fair: it would fail to take into account the limited possibilities and the nature of philology in the

Supplement 2] (1975), I Maclean, "André Wechel at Frankfurt, 1572–1581", in id, *Learning and the Market Place. Essays in the History of the Early Modern Book* (2009) 163.

41 Letter of Leunclavius to Carolus Clusius of 21 November 1592 (old style): Leiden, University Library, ms Vulc 101, facsimile accessible online at: *http://www.library.leiden.edu/special-collections/scaliger-institute/projects/clusius-project.html*

42 Cuiacius, *Observationes et Emendationes* xii, 22 i.f.

43 Burgmann, "Die Gesetze" (n 6) esp 94–98, who also identifies some of the sources.

44 Burgmann, "Die Gesetze" (n 6) 97.

45 "Johannes Löwenklau" (1994) 13 *Rechtshistorisches Journal* 197 (200–201).

46 "Leunclavius Neo-Graecus", ibid, 234–243.

47 L Burgmann, *Ecloga. Das Gesetzbuch Leons III. und Konstantinos' V* (1983) 140–143, esp 141.

humanists' age, and seriously undervalue the increased access to manuscripts in the present age. Only thus has it become possible to distinguish between consciously revised versions and the fortunes of transmission.

G. CONCLUSIONS

What can we infer from this long journey through the three legal works by Joannes Leunclavius, and especially their prefaces? First of all, Leunclavius' own aspirations. He wished to make accessible Byzantine legal texts, in order to provide material for emendation and illumination of the *Corpus Iuris Civilis*. The "Greeks", as he usually calls the Byzantines – here he does not distinguish between the ancient Greeks and their "Eastern-Roman" successors – were culturally and intellectually the superiors of their western neighbours, had provided the Romans with their first laws and later had the advantage of living in an age when the ink of the Roman laws and treatises was not yet dry, so to speak. Here Leunclavius is just one voice in a large humanist choir. Some of it is mere rhetoric, but the principle is sound: Byzantine legal sources may and should be used for that purpose, as they are an independent witness in the transmission of the *Corpus Iuris Civilis*. Many of them date to the first decades of its existence, others build on these same texts. If properly understood, they are valuable for reconstructing missing parts and correcting mistakes in the transmission of the Justinianic texts. The *apparatus criticus* of our modern editions testifies to the results of critical work on this basis. The quality of these results of course depends upon the level of philological, historical and legal insight in both the Byzantine sources themselves and in the *Corpus Iuris Civilis*. The disputes among the humanists, if stripped from their invective, reflect the level of their insight.

So far, there is nothing new or remarkable in the works of Leunclavius, and there is no reason why he should not be considered a civilian. To that extent I agree with Osler's appraisal in 1994.[48] In the second half of the sixteenth century Cuiacius and Leunclavius led the humanist effort, which had started with Politianus a century earlier, to use Byzantine sources for the purpose of illumination, criticism and emendation of the *Corpus Iuris Civilis*. The euphoria had somewhat abated at the end of that century, but the principle of Mommsen's recension of the Digest text is not fundamentally different.[49]

48 "Homer Dethroned" (n 1) esp 210–213.
49 Digesta, ed. maior *Praefatio* lxxiii–lxxvii, esp lxxvi.

But he is also a Byzantinist, and here he is different from, e.g., Cuiacius. The choice of texts demonstrates this. Not only did he produce editions and translations of Byzantine historians, but it also transpires in his choice of the legal texts with which he occupied himself. The *Synopsis Basilicorum*, or rather, the Basilica themselves, and the *Collectio Tripartita* belong to the standard humanist programme, inasmuch as these texts are directly related to the *Corpus Iuris Civilis*. The *Novellae constitutiones* and other texts, especially those collected in the *Ius Graeco-romanum*, lack this direct relation, and the prefaces are witness of the fact that Leunclavius was aware of the difference.

There is, however, more to it than an interest in Byzantium. In my opinion, the remarkable aspect of this wider interest is not so much the interest itself, as the fact that he nevertheless, and almost desperately, tries to maintain the connection with the positive law of his day. This even extends to his work on Ottoman history. He had learnt the language and was respected for his books on the subject. Editions and translations were meant to acquaint his contemporaries with unknown worlds. Indeed, he was not afraid to hold up the Byzantine and Ottoman worlds as a mirror to his own, contemporary Western world.

In most of his work Leunclavius went directly *ad fontes*. Much could be said on his handling of them. The rather bold transformation of the Synopsis into the Basilica and the free-style composition of the Isaurian Ecloga are interesting examples of the way he worked. A detailed analysis of his Adnotationes and Notata, in combination with his translations of both legal and non-legal works, would yield an even clearer picture of Leunclavius as a philologist. But, why *ad fontes*?

The question should be: why to *these* sources? The answer, I would suggest, lies in Leunclavius' person. As has been noted by Burtin,[50] the centre of gravity in Leunclavius' life gradually shifted to a different kind of "humanism", focusing on a "useful" employment of his talents. Intellectual curiosity, certainly, but to a purpose. Demonstrating this shift would require writing his biography. His books and letters, comments by others, etc would yield the picture of a very interesting figure in the sixteenth-century world. The publishing history of his books alone, in a commercially competitive but also theologically sensitive market, would make an interesting subject. As to his three major contributions to Graeco-Roman law, the primary reason for Leunclavius as a civilian undoubtedly was textual criticism of the *Corpus*

50 Burtin, "Un apôtre de la tolérance" (n 5) 569.

Iuris Civilis. If we look at the larger picture, however, trying to encompass Leunclavius as a historian, philologist, indeed humanist, the common denominator of his motives seems to me to be *exemplum*: if not directly applicable, then at least as a lighting beacon on the way to a better world.

9 Brissonius in Context: *De formulis et solennibus populi Romani verbis*

Éva Jakab

A. INTRODUCTION

There is a remarkable drawing, dated 1560–1570, in the collection of the *Hamburgisches Museum für Kunst und Gewerbe*. It depicts – with artful allegories – an eternal dilemma: an aged philosopher stands between two female figures of very different styles and is struggling to choose between them.[1] To his left stands a barefoot, poorly dressed woman holding a money purse in her hand; she is called *Avaritia*. To his right, a nice and richly decorated female stands holding a globe (a symbol of earthly power); she is called *Magnificentia*.[2] The Renaissance painter who produced this drawing drew

1 Already Philostratos' works dealt with the difficult choice between virtuous and vicious life and called it a Herculean decision.

2 Compare E Panofsky, "Der Philosoph auf dem Scheidewege (Ein Beispiel für die Ambivalenz ikonographischer Kennzeichen)", in K Michels and M Warmke (eds), *Erwin Panofskys deutschsprachige Aufsätze* II (1998) 820 at 820–821. The topic, the difficult decision between theoretically possible (but morally strongly diverging) life concepts, was very popular already in

upon an ancient topic and yet gave new meaning to it. A philosopher, educated in the humanist tradition, in reality only had one choice, that of *Magnificentia*: a decision in favour of a rich, wasteful and powerful life.[3] Reputation, fame, influence and wealth were typical and much desired values in humanist circles rooted in a deeply secularised way of thinking.[4] Renaissance and humanism created a new and complex concept of life that had a profound influence both on the arts as well as on the natural and social sciences.[5] Brissonius was born and educated in the stream of these ideas and his life can be considered as the embodiment of humanist values and principles.[6]

He belonged to a great generation of French scholars trained in the humanist tradition. It is commonly accepted that French legal humanism established and developed a new approach to law and legal texts.[7] In the sixteenth century legal humanism criticised and attacked traditional legal science as it had been practised for four centuries across Europe.[8] Leaving the path of the so-called *mos italicus* of the Glossators who focused their attention on Justinian's compilation from the sixth century, the *mos gallicus iuris docendi* preferred a philologically founded historical analysis of legal institutions, which took a broad palette of literary sources into account.[9] For example, Zasius protested against the *Glossa* and other commentaries in a dramatic way: "I have very little [regard for the] jurisprudence of the kind taught by Bartolus and Baldus. For if you disregard their errors not much else remains . . . Barbarism has smothered the pure law like a giant creeper, so much so, indeed, as to become firmly rooted . . . If the jurists had not always adhered so blindly to the authority of the *Glossa* and Bartolus, the

medieval Christian iconography. A good illustration is a graphic in the *Kunstsammlung* of Basel: in the middle of the picture is an elderly man with an angel (*Charitas*) on his left and with an evil (Wasting) on his right side – fighting over his purse (also as a symbol of his soul) that lies before them.

3 About women in the Renaissance see I Maclean, *The Renaissance Notion of Woman* (1980).

4 Panofsky (n 2) 825: "das ewig gültige Paradigma einer antieskethischen Ethik".

5 For the complexity of Renaissance and humanist thinking see J M Kelly, *A Short History of Western Legal Theory* (1992) 165–168, Maclean (n 3) 85–86.

6 Human dignity and freedom became an essential part of humanist thinking, see H Westermann, "Lorenzo Valla: *De libero arbitrio*. Die Freiheit des Menschen im Angesicht Gottes", in R Gröschner et al (eds), *Des Menschen Würde – entdeckt und erfunden im Humanismus der italienischen Renaissance* (2008) 113 at 124–127.

7 D R Kelley, *The Human Measure – Social Thought in the Western Legal Tradition* (1990) 186–190.

8 P Stein, "Legal humanism and legal science" (1986) 54 *The Legal History Review* 297.

9 P Stein, *Roman Law in European History*, 11th edn (2012) 48. There is one trace where French jurists tried to "further enterprise of Italian style, and this was . . . the rationalization of law" – Kelley (n 7) 189–197, D J Osler, *Humanist Philology and Justinian's Digest* (1983), G Kisch, *Studien zur humanistischen Jurisprudenz* (1972) 18–21.

true meaning of the law would now be seen more clearly and in greater purity . . . The only genuine interpreters are those who try to explain the sources themselves."[10] The life and work of Barnabas Brissonius represents these ideas and is an attempt to put these ambitions into practice.

B. BRISSONIUS AND HIS WORK

(1) Life and Death of Barnabas Brissonius

Few facts are known about the private life of Barnabas Brissonius. It is certain that he was born in 1531 and died in 1591. The great humanist jurists such as Cujas (1522–1590), Donellus (1527–1591), Hotman (1524–1590) and Balduinus (1520–1573) were his contemporaries.

His father, François Brisson, lived with the family in Fontenay-le-Comte, in the county of Poitou, and served as *lieutenant particulier* appointed by the king for local administration and justice.[11] Brissonius thought highly of him and was very grateful that he had allowed him to be educated in the humanistic tradition:

> *Semper mihi curae fuit, Pater, iuris civilis scientiam, ad quam ab ineunte paene aetate animi quadam inductione sum delatus, cum optimarum artium studiis coniungere, et adscitis undique ornamentis illustrare.*[12]

Young Brissonius was an accomplished student and soon attended the humanist circles in his home city. Already in his early life he met the famous and powerful André Tiraqueau (1488–1558) who had a considerable influence on his education. It was most likely Tiraqueau who encouraged him to go to Orléans for legal studies.[13] Though he started in Orléans, he soon moved to Bourges and afterwards to Poitiers.

Almost nothing is known of the teachers of the young Brissonius. Already in medieval times Orléans was a famous centre for traditional legal science.[14] On

10 *Zasii Epistolae*, ed J A Riegger, Ulm 1774, P II, Nr VIII, cited by E Wolf, *Grosse Rechtsdenker der Deutschen Geistesgeschichte*, 4th edn (1963) 88 and Stein (n 8) 299. A similar opinion is attested by the non-jurist François Rabelais, compare A Watson, *The Evolution of Western Private Law* Expanded edn (2001) 251.

11 A Sánchez-Gil, *El jurista Barnabé Brisson (1531–1591)* (1995) 11: *Patrem habuit Franciscum Brissonium, virum honestum et divitem, oppidi Fontenaiensis Propraetorem.*

12 *Epistola Dedicatoria ad Patrem suum, Franciscum Brissonium* – from the Notes of Brissonius, Paris, 1556, in the second chapter of his work *Selectarum ex iure civili*.

13 Sánchez-Gil (n 11) 45.

14 R Feenstra, "L'école de droit d'Orléans au treizieme siècle et son rayonnement dans l'Europe médiévale" (1992) 13 *Revue d'histoire des facultés de droit et de la science juridique Paris: Société pour l'histoire des facultés de droit et de la science juridique* 23.

the other hand, the University of Bourges was a bastion of legal humanism, at least since 1529, when Alciatus started his teaching there.[15] Most of the great French humanist lawyers studied in Bourges and almost all of them belonged to Huguenot circles.[16] The University of Poitiers was much younger, founded 1431, but it was considered as an excellent location for teaching *ius commune* and canon law.[17] It is well known that the legal culture in France was split into the "pays de droit écrit" and that of the "droit coutumier".[18] All three universities, frequented by Brissonius, were situated in the territory of "customary law" and counted as famous European centres for legal studies.

Looking at the biographies of the scholars who taught there, Brissonius could have been a pupil of Donellus in Bourges.[19] In 1551, Donellus had obtained his *doctor iuris* degree in Bourges and immediately became professor there. Furthermore, in Bourges Brissonius may have also studied under Duarenus (1509–1559) who was one of the leading representatives of French legal humanism and the teacher of Donellus as well.

As a graduate of Poitiers, Brissonius established a practice as an advocate there. A few years later (1553 or 1556), probably encouraged by Tiraqueau again, he moved to Paris, closer to the Royal Court.[20] And there his star ascended steeply – in a few years he became a respected lawyer and politician. Highly regarded also at the Royal Court, King Charles IX appointed him *avocat général* (1573) to the *Parlement* of Paris. Brissonius was entrusted in 1575 by King Henry III with financial affairs. In 1580 the king made him member of the Crown Council. Some years later, in 1588, Brissonius was elected to be the Sixth President of the Parliament of Paris. Furthermore, he took part in high diplomacy as well. For instance, he was a member of the royal delegation that came to England to ask for Queen Elisabeth's hand. King Henry III charged him also to prepare a French law code, mostly a collection of contemporary customary law. In 1587, Brissonius finished his draft of the *Code Henri* – but it remained just a law book. In creating it, his main purpose seems to have been to unify and consolidate local customary law (*coutumes*).

After a splendid career, Brissonius' life took a tragic turn. At the end of the 1580s the war of religion again escalated in France. The Catholic

15 Kelley (n 7) 189–191.
16 Stein (n 8) 300.
17 H Lange and M Kriechbaum, *Römisches Recht im Mittelalter. Band II Die Kommentatoren* (2007) 946.
18 Lange and Kriechbaum (n 17) 946.
19 Hugues Doneau, 1527–1591, cf Sánchez-Gil (n 11) 45–46.
20 A dedication from July 1556 attests to him being already in Paris.

League revolted and the king and the Royal Court took flight from Paris. The seat of the Parliament of Paris was transferred to Tours by Royal statute. Nonetheless, Brissonius and some of his colleagues (among them also the first president of the Parliament, Achille de Harlay) decided to stay in Paris and tried to negotiate peace with the Catholic League. At first they seemed to succeed; the "Sixteen" appointed Brissonius as the First President of the Parliament. But soon afterwards the revolts turned against him: in 1591 he was accused, arrested and condemned to death. On November 15 of that year, with two other *conseillers*, he was executed.[21]

(2) Works published

During the sixty years of a full life, Brissonius published a considerable oeuvre of scholarly literature – the most important of these being three large volumes on Roman law and a draft French law code.

(1) *Selectarum ex iure civili antiquitatum libri duo* (1556), his first book, published in Paris (and later reprinted in 16 further editions). The second edition came out 1558 in Lyon, containing two further but smaller works of the author: *Ad legem Iuliam de adulteriis liber singularis* and *De solutionibus et liberationibus libri tres*. All later reprints followed the Lyon pattern. It is worth mentioning that the last edition was prepared in 1749 by Trekell in Leiden, under the title *Opera minora varii argumenti*.

(2) *De verborum Quae ad Ius Civile Pertinent Significatione. Libri XIX* (1559), which is also known under the titles *Vocabularium iuris utriusque* or *Lexicon iuris* – it can be considered as the most successful work of Brissonius. It is a detailed legal dictionary, presenting classical legal terminology derived from Justinian's *Corpus Iuris Civilis*. The volume, which fitted the demands both of scholars and lawyers in practice, became a true bestseller. It was reprinted in seventeen editions – the last dating from 1805. In legal scholarship we can find several references to it, up to the nineteenth century. But Brissonius' work *De verborum significatione* was more than a mere dictionary. In the introduction the author summarised the laws of the French kingdom and the elements of Roman law. There is also an overview about marriage and dowry customs of his time. In the Appendix he added the commentaries of François Hotman on French feudal law.[22] This work

21 Being mostly Huguenots, almost the entire French legal humanism movement ended at that time, due to the Massacre of St Bartholomew Day, cf Stein (n 8) 300.

22 One may speculate whether it was a covert way of expressing his support for Hotman's radical Antitribonian views.

of Brissonius had a significant impact on European legal thinking; it is sufficient to mention the fact that even Johann Gottlieb Heineccius revised and corrected an edition of it in 1743, almost two hundred years later, in Halle.
(3) *De formulis et solennibus populi Romani verbis. Libri VIII* (1582/3), an almost complete collection of legal formulas from Roman Italy – it forms the central subject of my chapter. It was reprinted in six editions, the last one dating from 1781, in Leipzig.
(4) *Le Code du Roy Henri III. Roy de France et de Pologne* (1586/7), a law book which Brissonius composed for his king, Henry III. It was a collection of the laws of the whole French Kingdom, an early approach to a codification of the entire legal system. Although never formally enacted, the Code became well known in French legal life: it appeared in ten editions altogether, the last one dating from 1629, Paris. In the sixteenth and seventeenth centuries, its impact upon legal practice seems to have been considerable.
(5) Apart from the "big four", Brissonius published several smaller works, for example an *Observationum divini et humani iuris liber* (Paris 1564), of which the latest edition dates 1697, Gouda; there is also a book *De ritu nuptiarum liber singularis; De iure conubiorum liber alter,* first printed in 1564. As we see, Brissonius was a diligent and fascinating author who made serious efforts to improve legal practice during his time.

The impressive list of his publications just surveyed attests that Brissonius took a strong part in French humanist legal movements in the sixteenth century despite the fact that he was never a professor engaged in teaching, but rather a lawyer engaged in legal practice. Owing to his classical education he possessed an incredibly wide knowledge of ancient sources, literary and legal works as well. Born with a great intellectual curiosity he met the challenge of his time: at a young age he published two significant works: *Selectarum ex iure civili libri* and *De verborum significatione*. Thereafter, he focused on his career at the law courts and at the Royal Court as well and he seems to have become less interested in writing. Later in his life, however, he returned to scholarly work. According to the dating of his two last big volumes (*De formulis et solennibus populi Romani verbis* and *Le Code du Roy Henri III*) one gets the impression that his *De formulis* could have been a result of preparatory works on customary law while planning his *Code Henri*.[23]

23 Customary law played an essential role in humanist theories about setting rules in a society, cf Kelly (n 5) 176–177 and 184–186: a good prince should respect the law and should be bound by the law of his country; law was understood mostly as custom, customary law.

(3) *De formulis et solennibus populi Romani verbis*

In this chapter I intend to deal with some parts from Brissonius' late work *De formulis et solennibus populi Romani verbis*. The titles and contents of the eight books of this hefty volume shape an individual's view on the legal culture of ancient Rome. Modern readers may wonder about the eclectic choice of topics:

Liber primus complectitur Formulas, quae ad rem divinam, precationes, vota, aedium sacrarum et signorum dedicationes, aliaque his cognata et adiuncta, pertinent (221 chapters).
Liber secundus Comitiorum, rogationum, legum et senatusconsultorum, sententiarum in senatu dictarum, eiusque amplissimi ordinis decretorum formulas continet (176 chapters).
Liber tertius Circa edicta, rescripta, mandataque principalia et prudentum responsa versatur (89 chapters).
Liber quartus Militares formulas persequitur (57 chapters).
Liber quintus De formulis iudiciariis agit (231 chapters).
Liber sextus Stipulationum et contractuum formulas comprehendit (199 chapters).
Liber septimus Testamentarias et funebres formulas recenset (190 chapters).
Liber octavus Miscellaneas varii generis formulas (69 chapters).

The eight books summarise the most important subjects in public as well as private law: sacral law, statutes, military law, private procedure, obligations, inheritance law, etc. A brief glimpse at the topics shows that four books (543 chapters) deal with public law, followed by 231 chapters (gathered in one single book) on procedure and three books, altogether with 458 chapters, on private law. It is striking that Brissonius devoted such a big part in his work to private law, more specifically the law of exchange of goods (*inter vivos* and *mortis causa*).

A closer examination of the relation between the single topics reveals further interesting issues – especially if one compares his priorities and groupings with the Justinianic tradition. For the present study, the relation between the law of succession and that of contracts is especially relevant. Brissonius composed only 190 chapters about succession while he dealt with contract formulas in 199 chapters. The *tituli* in the Digest show the opposite: succession (will, legacy, etc) is treated in 352 columns while contract law only in 145 columns.

Table 1:

	Inheritance law	*Contracts*
Brissonius' *De formulis*	190 chapters	199 chapters
Digest	352 columns	145 columns

The considerable disparity attests that in Brissonius' view, the legal practice of contracting seems much more important than that of inheritance. In ancient Rome, one would say, things worked in a different way: the Romans – or at least the wealthy and powerful of Roman society – seem to have been much more interested in the legal practice and state interference (normative regulation) of bequeathing property than in that of everyday commercial life.[24] This striking difference is commonly explained with reference to changing priorities in a changed social environment. Indeed one has to consider also the slightly different approach: Justinian's intention was to establish a law book as a symbol of common identity and ruling power in the Roman Empire of late Antiquity – while Brissonius intended to collect formulas from (and probably for) everyday legal life.

Brissonius speaks of practical considerations as being the main goal of his setting up formulas: the information should serve as a useful guide in legal life. It awakens reminiscences on ancient *topoi*: already Cato and Varro (and according to them, the famous Manilius as well) wanted to help every educated *diligens pater familias* in arranging their public and private affairs.[25] Choosing ante-Justinianic authors for a better understanding and for recovering classical Roman law was a main aim in legal humanism.[26] Furthermore, humanist lawyers stressed that custom and customary law had to be investigated as well as some sort of "law in action" contrasted with the authoritative ruling of the emperor Justinian.[27]

Brissonius stressed an approach that was common among ancient authors but seems surprising to us. Modern scholarship was always rather negligent

24 E Champlin, *Final Judgments. Duty and Emotion in Roman Wills, 200 BC-AD 250* (1991) 27–28.

25 D.1.2.2.39 Pomp 1 sing ench – *Publius Mucius et Brutus et Manilius qui fundaverunt ius civile* – on Roman jurisprudence see N MacCormick, "*De Iurisprudentia*", in J W Cairns and O F Robinson (eds), *Critical Studies in Ancient Law, Comparative Law and Legal History* (2001) 79 at 80. Manilius' *Venalium vendendorum leges* are quoted by Varro rust 2,2,5; 2,1,15; 2,6,3; 2,5,11 and 2,10,5; compare E Jakab, *Praedicere und cavere beim Marktkauf. Sachmängel im griechischen und römischen Recht* (1997) 162.

26 Compare Watson (n 10) 250.

27 Similarly already François Hotman, compare Watson (n 10) 249. Kelly (n 5) 173–174 underlines the idea of humanist lawyers that law should be made by the governed.

in this field. Most scholars dealing with Roman law focus merely on so-called legal sources and leave aside most non-legal authors.[28]

But let's turn to our specific topic, the *liber sextus* of Brissonius' work. The Sixth Book, divided into 199 chapters, offers a unique insight into Roman private law – some main groups can be identified as follows:

Table 2:

Contract type	*Chapters in Brissonius*	*Sum*
Sale	1–63	63
Letting and hiring	64–86	23
Mandate, partnership	87–93	6
Deposit, *commodatum*	94–96	3
Loan, pledge, banking	97–121	25
Marriage and dowry	122–136	15
Servitudes	137–145	9
Precarium, habitation	146–148	3
Donation, *pollicitatio*	149–151	3
Compromise etc	152–157	6
Stipulatio	158–194	37
Variae	195–199	5

The treatment clearly starts with the so-called consensual contracts and continues with obligations founded *re*. In the first 121 chapters, it overturns the order of the *Institutiones* (*obligationes ex contractu*). Dealing with loan, he gathers together all possible legal figures regarding banking and credit. Chapters 97–121 could serve as a good basis for further research on ancient and medieval credit in practice. In the rest, we find a remarkable mixture of topics: Brissonius treats marriage and dowry in detail (reminiscing about his early book from 1564 seems to be one of his favourite topics).[29] Next comes

28 Up to now, there are only a few exceptions to this attitude. For example, the contractual practice as depicted in literary and documentary sources were treated by famous scholars such as Leopold Wenger, Wolfgang Kunkel or Dieter Nörr. Elisabeth Meyer recently studied the remarkable role *tabulae* played in Roman life and belief. However, there is a lack of research even now on testaments, funeral formulas or property related clauses – from a "law in action" perspective.

29 Marriage and family relations were ruled mostly by canon law during this period.

a long section about servitudes – regarding landed property. Together with *precarium* and *habitatio*, it forms a special group of shared property rights. After a short *tractatus* on *donatio* and *pollicitatio* as the main patterns of acquiring ownership gratuitously, he turns to *stipulatio*. Here he sums up a great many legal institutions – in later codification these create a "General part" (personal surety, etc). Such an arrangement, grouping them under the heading of stipulation, was already typical also in the *Institutiones* styled by Gaius or Justinian. Summing up, the short overview shows that Brissonius' real priorities were sale and stipulation – from the whole body of private law. The chapters reveal some sort of numeric significance as well: from the 199 chapters of the *liber sextus* exactly 100 are devoted to sale and stipulation. The major part of contract law deals only with the two main types of contracts, thereby pushing all other types of legally binding agreements into the smaller part (99 chapters).

For a better contextualisation, a brief comparison with the Digest seems to be useful also in this case. One would tend to assume that Brissonius changed the relations and set new standards in contract law. Undoubtedly, in his view sale was the most important of all contracts: sale is the first subject and the one treated in most detail; most likely it was a real challenge in his time. By contrast, Justinian's jurists started with loan and credit transactions, followed by business carried out by agents (mostly slaves). However, a short glimpse proves that the mere relationship between sale contracts and contracts of other types did not change essentially in Brissonius' treatment:

Table 3:

Source	*Sale*	*All other contracts*	*%*
Brissonius	63	199	32
Digest	43	145	30

There are some further considerations about the external structure of Brissonius' work. At first sight, Brissonius seems to have composed his work without any attempt to systematise contract law. Watson argued that most humanist lawyers followed the system of Justinian's *Institutiones* in their works.[30] In this, contracts are grouped under the headings *re*, *verbis*, *litteris*, *consensu*. Obviously it did not really fit Brissonius' conception. Other scholars underlined that there were no really remarkable issues regarding

30 Watson (n 10) 251–252.

systematising in the age of legal humanism.[31] Humanist lawyers focused more on the text and on possible dogmatic connections, and less on method or system in law. Nevertheless, in humanist legal works there are traces of a serious effort to create a new system, independent of that of the "learned law", originating in a deeper logic hidden in ancient sources, especially in non-legal writings, for example in that of Cicero.[32]

In his work *De formulis*, Brissonius broke with the traditional scholarly patterns and tried to create some type of an own, special structure. Was it a selfish approach to establish a partly new system in private law? Was it merely a theoretical experiment, a product of "elegant legal humanism" (removed from the needs of real life), to introduce a new structure (as Donellus did for private law generally)? Or can we assume that he actually tried to sum up the most important legal formulas based on his skills as a lawyer at court? May his intentions have been to serve all colleagues (notaries, advocates, judges) in everyday legal life? Was it probably a structure following the model of law books about "*coutumes*"? Or did it just take over the usual headings used in manuals (for example, for notarial practice) in his time? In my view, Brissonius may have styled his work partly for scholarly usage, partly for legal practice.

(4) Antecedents and patterns

Recent research has shown that there was a remarkably strong impact of Roman law in French legal life since the thirteenth century in relation to drafting legal documents and notarial practice.[33] The most significant evidence came down from Dauphiné or Bourgogne (Franche-Comté). The origins of this unique type of Romanisation (e.g. borrowing contract clauses like eviction etc) can be seen in legal education and in widespread scholarly

31 H E Troje, "Wissenschaftlichkeit und System in der Jurisprudenz des 16. Jahrhunderts", in J Blühdorn and J Ritter (eds), *Philosophie und Rechtswissenschaft* (1969) 63–88, J Schröder, "Die ersten juristischen 'Systematiker'. Ordnungsvorstellungen in der Philosophie und Rechtswissenschaft des 16. Jahrhunderts", in M Kriechbaum (ed), *Festschrift für Sten Gagnér* (1996) 111, J Schröder, *Recht als Wissenschaft. Geschichte der juristischen Methode von Humanismus bis zur historischen Schule (1500–1850)* (2001) 85, 91.

32 Compare Schröder 2001 (n 31) 80, Schröder 1996 (n 31) 129–135 and M Avenarius, "*Neque id sine magna Servii laude* . . . Historisierung der Rechtswissenschaft und Genese von System und Methode bei Donellus" (2006) 74 *The Legal History Review* 61 at 70–71.

33 P Vinogradoff, *Roman Law in Medieval Europe* (1929) 78–89, P Didier, *Le droit romain dans la région dauphinoise, IRMAE V, 4F* (1979) 21, J Bart and M Petitjean, *L'influence du droit romain en Bourgogne et en Franche-Comté (XIIIe–XVe s), IRMAE V, 4E* (1976) 24, J P Lévy, *Le droit romain en Anjou, Bretagne, Poitou, d'après les coutumiers, IRMAE V, 4B* (1976).

literature. There was an active peregrination from Bourgogne to the universities of Padua, Orléans and Montpellier. It was common that legal skills learned at universities (the so-called "gelehrtes Recht" or *ius commune*) were applied (intentionally or subconsciously) in everyday legal life.[34]

From the fourteenth century, more and more collections of customary law appeared in the central and northern provinces of France.[35] Although the authors of these law books made a serious effort to retain and to stress the importance of local customary law, their (Roman-law based) legal education invariably infiltrated the material they worked on. As recent research has shown, in case of controversies they explained local customary law according to Roman legal thinking.[36] Such a rich outcome of collections of local customary law may have encouraged Brissonius to carry on his work *De formulis populi Romani*.

Furthermore, a possible connection between the *ius canonicum* and Brissonius' attempt at collecting legal formulas is also present. In recent years, it has been proved that the Parliament of Paris played an essential role in the secularisation of law in the sixteenth century.[37] Earlier, the influence of canon law on the law of marriage and succession was strong.[38] As mentioned above, Brissonius was repeatedly occupied with such topics in his scholarly work, especially in the middle of his career.

A historical and social contextualisation of Brissonius' oeuvre should also mention the possible influence of a scholar of great impact on the legal theory of his time – Guy Pape (c1402–c1487). Pape created two great collections: the *Consilia Domini Guidonis Pape: consilia singularia [et] quoru[m] materia quotidie i[n] practica in omnib[us] curijs tam ecclesiasticis q[uam] secularib[us] versatur*[39] and the *Decisiones Guidonis Papae, IC et practici celeberrimi . . .* [40] that included court decisions issued by the Parliament of Grenoble. Guy Pape pointed out in his *Decisiones* that the *Libri feudorum* should come into operation only if customary law did not provide any solution

34 H Coing, *Europäisches Privatrecht. Band I. Älteres Gemeines Recht, 1500 bis 1800* (1985) 67–69.

35 Vinogradoff (n 33) 78–79. M Bellomo, *The Common Legal Past of Europe, 1000–1800* (1995) 104–105.

36 Bart and Petitjean (n 33) 28.

37 P Arabeyre, "Le premier recueil méthodique d'ordonnances royales françaises: le *Tractatus ordinationum regiarum* d'Étienne Aufréri (fin XVe – débuit di XVIe siècle)" (2011) 79 *The Legal History Review* 391 at 417–419.

38 Compare Decock elsewhere in this volume.

39 In Princeton University Library there is a print from Lyon 1519.

40 The Princeton University Library collection possesses three examples: one from Lyon 1515, another Frankfurt am Main 1609 and a later from Geneva 1667.

to the case – "*exceptis aliquibus, in quibus consuetudo contraria in hac patria reperitur*". His statement represents the common view of the practical relevance of feudal norms and Roman law in shaping customary law.[41] Indeed, this attitude may have encouraged Brissonius to create his big volume of Roman formulas – for studying ancient antecedents and probably also for using it as a handbook in everyday legal life, especially for designing contract formulas.

(5) Structure and headings – sale formulas

As already stated above, sale is the most elaborate part of the *liber sextus* in Brissonius' survey of obligations. With sale he starts the treatment of contracts, underlining that it is the most important legal act in practice. As we have seen above, he composed his work free from old traditions in systematisation. Also his sixty-three chapters on sale open a new vista, different also from the loose system in the writings of Roman jurists – as it came down in the Digest.[42] It also differs from the style and structure used by the Glossators working with Roman law sources.[43] In the following I try to recover some of his possible ideas.

The sequence of chapters shows some effort at building a new, individual system – according to a logically elaborated *ratio iuris*, which was a common principle in legal humanism.[44] Beginning with sale formulas, Brissonius underlined two main guidelines. Considering these, one arrives at some sort of an individual systematising. On the one hand Brissonius suggested a distinction between selling "*pure*" or "*sub conditione* [*condicione*]" on the other hand a distinction was drawn according to the object of sale: *res mobiles*, *se moventes* and *res soli* (Briss Form VI, 4):

> *Non tantum autem pure, sed & sub condicione venditio contrahi poterat. Cuius rei exempla sumet, qui volet, ex l. 8. §. 1. D. de peric. & commod. rei vend. & l. 7. D. de contrah. empt.45 Nunc quibus legibus & condicionibus tam mobiles, aut se moventes, quam res soli venire solerent, quoad eius fieri poterit, demonstrabo.*

The distinction between contracting "*pure*" or "*sub conditione*" is an old one and it has far-reaching dogmatic and practical consequences.[46] Indeed,

41 Compare Coing (n 34) 70–72 regarding the civil-law countries.

42 Compare J A Crook, *Law and Life in Rome* (1967) 214 – 221.

43 Cf Avenarius (n 32) 61–67, although dealing with Donellus, but comparable.

44 Stein (n 8) 301.

45 D.18.6.8.1 and especially D.18.1.7pr.

46 W Ernst, "Neues zur Gefahrtragung bei *emptio venditio* und *locatio conductio*?" (2004) 121 *Zeitschrift der Savigny Stiftung Romanistische Abteilung* 363 at 373–375.

Brissonius also refers to ancient sources as a foundation for his point. His main distinction between sales with or without a condition is based on Paulus D.18.6.8.1 and Ulpianus D.18.1.7pr. Both texts approach the problem from the aspect of *perfecta emptio*.

Let's have a glimpse at them. The fragment quoted first seems to be a strange one in this context (D.18.6.8.1 Paul 5 Sab):

> Should a sale be made on terms, "be the slave bought, whether or not the ship comes from Asia," Julian is of opinion that the sale is perfect forthwith because it is certain that it has been contracted.

Paul here discussed a contract term, a condition with an ambiguous wording. Collections of sale formulas – like that of Manilius – often mention a condition in a similar style, for example "Est ille servus emptus sive navis ex Asia venerit" – "The slave is bought if the ship arrives from Asia". In this case vendor and purchaser agreed on a sale but inserted an uncertain event as a suspensive condition.

The wording quoted by Paul reminds the reader of a classroom example used to present possible failures. The contracting parties or their scribe/notary seem to have made a mistake in drafting the document; there could have been some sort of uncertainty regarding the content. The condition finally written included both possible versions of the outcome of this uncertain event: if the ship arrives or if it does not. It raised the dogmatic question whether a sale with an invalid condition can be considered valid at all – or whether the entire transaction should be declared invalid. In his decision, Paul referred to an earlier work of Julian. Both jurists tended to regard the sale as valid (perfect) – without a clear argument that an invalid condition results in no condition at all (it should be considered as if it were not written).[47]

Without any doubt the passage quoted by Brissonius deals with an *emptio sub condicione* – but it is obviously not the most trifling text as a foundation for Brissonius' idea. In fact, the ambiguous wording leads to a sale without any condition. Actually D.18.6.8pr Paulus, the fragment located a bit above, would much better meet the requirements in his context:

> It is essential to know when a sale is perfect because we then know who bears the risk in the thing; for once the sale is perfect, the risk is on the purchaser. And if

47 Regarding the legal background see W Ernst, "*Periculum est emptoris*" (1982) 99 *Zeitschrift der Savigny Stiftung Romanistische Abteilung* 216 at 226–237, E Jakab, *Risikomanagement beim Weinkauf. Periculum und Praxis im Imperium Romanum* (2009) 190–193, A Rodger, "*Emptio perfecta* revisited: A study of Digest D.8.6.8.1" (1982) 50 *The Legal History Review* 337.

> the thing sold be identified, what it is, its nature, and quantity, the price be fixed, and the sale be subject to no condition, the sale is perfect. But if it be conditional and the condition not yet satisfied, there is no sale, any more than there would be a stipulation . . .[48]

In scholarly literature this fragment is considered to be the key text for conditional contracts.[49] It is surprising that Brissonius did not quote this one. A brief comparison with the second Digest fragment cited by him, D.18.1.7pr Ulpian, is also telling:

> The sale of a slave "if he shall have settled his accounts to his master's satisfaction" is conditional; now conditional sales become perfect, only when the condition is satisfied.[50]

Obviously, Ulpian here discussed a concrete term from a sale contract: a slave was sold under the condition that he (very likely an *institor*, a manager in his old master's business) should settle all his accounts (regarding all ongoing business) correctly with his former master. The term *arbitrio domini* called the master himself as an arbiter. Ulpian's decision has a direct link to D.18.6.8pr – but not really to D.18.6.8.1 as quoted by Brissonius.

To complete the picture it should be mentioned that two further passages, two generalising articulations of the very principle, are broadly known in the Digest, but neither of them is expressly mentioned by Brissonius. These are rather different texts coming from other institutional environments in the Digest. In one of his works Ulpian stated that "Pacisci contra edictum aedilium omnimodo licet, sive in ipso negotio venditionis gerendo convenisset sive postea."[51] Later on Pomponius stressed simply that "Simplariarum venditionum causa ne sit redhibitio, in usu est."[52] It is rather striking that originally both texts referred to a very special subject in the law of sale, to that of guarantees given or refused by a vendor for latent defects if a slave

48 D.18.6.8pr: *Necessario sciendum est, quando perfecta sit emptio: tunc enim sciemus, cuius periculum sit: nam perfecta emptione periculum ad emptorem respiciet. Et si id quod venierit appareat quid quale quantum sit, sit et pretium, et pure venit, perfecta est emptio: quod si sub condicione res venierit, si quidem defecerit condicio, nulla est emptio, sicuti nec stipulatio . . .* (Watson translation).

49 Jakab (n 47) 190–193 with further quotations.

50 D.18.1.7pr.: *Haec venditio servi "si rationes domini computasset arbitrio" condicionalis est: condicionales autem venditiones tunc perficiuntur, cum impleta fuerit condicio* (with the translation of Watson cited in the text above).

51 D.2.14.31 *Ulpianus libro primo ad edictum aedilium curulium*: "It is quite lawful to make a pact contrary to the edict of the aediles, whether the agreement is made in the course of arranging the sale or afterward." (Watson translation.)

52 D.21.1.48.8 *Pomponius libro vicesimo tertio ad Sabinum*: "It is not our practice to allow rescission in the case of sales where undertakings have been specifically excluded." (Watson.)

was sold.[53] Roman jurists underlined that the vendor's liability for latent defects (according to the edict of the *aediles curules*) is not *ius cogens*. With mutual agreement, the enforcement of market regulations issued by the *aediles* could be excluded at any time. The opposite of a *simplaria venditio* or *pure vendere* is a sale *sub conditione*; the technical word condition (*conditio*, special contract term agreed upon by the parties) was mostly understood as *lex contractus* in Roman jurisprudence.[54]

The second classification mentioned by Brissonius is the distinction between sales of *res mobiles, se moventes* and *res soli.* Where did this distinction come from? Remarkable enough here Brissonius did not refer to a concrete source. Remarkably, traces of such a distinction can be found already in the Digest:

> Labeo writes that the edict of the curule aediles concerns the sales of things immovable as much as of those movable or animate.[55]

Surprisingly, Brissonius here emphasised a certain type of system-building which came down from Byzantine Scholastic theory. It contradicts the common view that legal humanism took a critical approach to Justinianic sources. Humanist scholars consequently tried to improve the "bad Latin" of medieval sources (the Glossators) and return to "classical texts".[56] But here Brissonius based his idea on Byzantine roots. Other texts from the Codex offer even clearer evidence: *In rebus dotalibus sive mobilibus sive immobilibus seu se moventibus, si tamen exstant . . .*[57] and *Ideo per praesentem legem et in Italicis solis rebus, quae immobiles sunt vel esse intelleguntur.*[58]

The first lines in the title D.21.1 present some introductory words to the edict of the *aediles curules* – as it came down from the sixth century. It is common view that this emendation was a product of the *compilatores*, not of Labeo.[59]

It is remarkable that almost the same wording is delivered in a marriage contract from the sixth century (592/3), in Nr 43 of volume IV of the Petra Papyri. The Greek text presents a list of items of the dowry and mentions

53 Compare Jakab (n 25) 186–187.
54 Compare Cato, agr. 146–149.
55 D.21.1.1pr: *Labeo scribit edictum aedilium curulium de venditionibus rerum esse tam earum quae soli sint quam earum quae mobiles aut se moventes . . .* (translation of Watson).
56 Compare, for example, Stein (n 8) 301 and Kelly (n 5) 165–166.
57 C.5.12.30pr *De iure dotium.*
58 C.7.31.1.1 *De usucapione.*
59 The passage has long been considered interpolated, i.e. redone by Justinian's compilers; compare Jakab (n 25) 126.

prágmata kinetá, akíneta kai autokíneta (line 115). It is remarkable that such phrases, at first sight of merely theoretical use, were adopted in contract formulas. More surprisingly, Brissonius chose it as a guideline for a possible system in the law of sale.

Under the heading *res mobiles*, Brissonius grouped the contract formulas concerning slaves (sixteen chapters). Undoubtedly it was the most elaborate subject in Roman jurisprudence – we will return to it soon. Under *res se moventes* he understood domestic animals (sheep, goats, cattle and slaves) and borrowed the formulas from Varro (three chapters). Afterwards he mixed wine, jars, winter pasture and ships. The sale of immovable is summed up in twenty-five chapters. Finally he discussed the *clausula doli*, eviction and personal sureties, closing with the rules of auctions and drafting of *tabulae*.

It is worth mentioning that Brissonius based his main approach – his intention to focus on contract formulas, on everyday practice – on ancient sources. He refers to three honourable authorities, Manilius, Pomponius and Cicero, in particular:[60]

> *Erant namque olim certae rerum vendendarum leges, quas Manilium, quem inter iuris auctores Pomponius noster numerat, civibus suis composuisse*, Cicero lib I de Orat cap 58 *docet.*[61]

Brissonius did not quote Pomponius' text accurately. He actually meant the famous passage at the very beginning of the Digest: *Publius Mucius et Brutus et Manilius qui fundaverunt ius civile.*[62] Here Pomponius sketched a sort of legal history and named the greatest founders of Roman law – among them also Manilius. Near Pomponius, Brissonius mentions a rarely quoted fragment of Cicero *De oratore*. Looking at it more closely, the reference seems badly contextualised: Cicero discusses the virtues of orators and advises them how to compose a speech. Young orators being accused of laziness and negligence of memory – therefore he argues that "nor is there a man among them who, if ever he had to learn some work by heart, would not choose for that purpose the 'Teucer' of Pacuvius rather than Manilius' *Conditions of Sale*."[63] Marcus Pacuvius was a great Roman tragic poet in the second century BC; his plays – among them also the *Teucer* – were founded

60 Similarly, Donellus derived his new system of private law from ancient authors like Cicero and Horace; compare Avenarius (n 32) 70–71.

61 Cic orat 1.58.246.

62 D.1.2.2.39 *Pomp 1 sing ench.*

63 Cic orat 1.58.246: *Nec quisquam est eorum, qui, si iam sit ediscendum sibi aliquid, non Teucrum Pacuvi malit quam Manilianas venalium vendendorum leges ediscere.* (Translation E W Sutton.)

mostly on Greek subjects. Cicero's strange comparison between Pacuvius' tragedy and the sale formulas of Manilius can in no way flatter the great Manilius . . . Quite the opposite: Manilius' *Venalium vendendorum leges* represent here a dry and dull sort of literature, unsuitable for winning attention or admiration in the audience. It is really striking that Brissonius has chosen this very passage as a foundation for his approach – he seems almost mocking his profession with it.

Doubtlessly Cicero's testimony is a clear evidence for the existence of Manilius and his sale formulas – but it is a strange piece of evidence, indeed. In my view there can be two different ways to explain Brissonius' intentions: on the one hand he may have composed his work using a "database", some sort of mechanically collected headwords picked out of ancient sources. In this case he may have quoted Cicero just seeking for passages with the name of Manilius. His choosing Cicero (orat 1.58.246) is surprising as there are several testimonies about the *Venalium vendendorum leges* of Manilius, delivered for example by Varro.[64] On the other hand it can be assumed that Cicero's rather sardonic statement was broadly known in the humanist tradition. Brissonius may have chosen the passage intentionally and a bit showy – because it reminded his readers of a favourite work and a celebrated author from ancient Rome.

(6) His sources

Franciscus Carolus Conradus, the editor of the 1731 edition (which was printed in Halle and Leipzig) listed 103 Latin and Greek authors in his *Index Auctorum* (from Appianus to Zosimus) as ancient sources used by Brissonius. Reading the chapters about sale, one feels impressed with Brissonius' deep knowledge of Latin and Greek authors: Ambrosius,[65] Apuleius, Caesar, Cato, Cicero, Gellius, Herodotus, Horace, Flavius Josephus, Juvenal, Livy, Lucretius, Martial, Ovid, Philostratus, Plautus, Pliny the Elder and Younger, Plutarch, Quintilian, Seneca the Elder and Younger, Suetonius, Tertullian, Tibullus, Valerius Maximus, Varro and Vitruvius.

At first sight, Brissonius seems to make a serious effort to work with ante-Justinian sources, to base his work on literary texts instead of the *Corpus Iuris Civilis* (which was the preliminary source of the Glossators). It seems to fit the general view about the ambitions widely cultivated in legal

64 Compare Varro rust 2.3.5, 2.5.11, 2.7.6.
65 A church father born in Trier who lived c.337–397.

humanism.[66] But, looking closer at each chapter, a slightly different picture emerges. Which sources did Brissonius actually use and which did he miss (from a current point of view)?

A very simple statistical account gives a hint to the relation between literary and legal sources used by Brissonius in the sixty-three chapters of sale formulas:

Table 4:

Ancient sources	*Quoted by Brissonius*	%
Digest	387	66.7
Codex Iustinianus	21	3.6
Institutiones	3	0.5
Literary sources	169	29.1
Literary sources (except auction)	111	19.1
In total	**580**	

As we see, he quotes 387 fragments (66.7%) from the works of classical Roman jurists, as it came down in the Digest. It is clear that he trusted Tribonian enough (in this, he differs from François Hotman[67]) – at least where the Digest text refers expressly to contract drafts. Then follow twenty-one quotations from the *Codex Iustinianus*; with 3.6% it is a weak part, indeed. There he seems to have been extremely critical or cautious. But also the *Institutiones* of Justinian are rather weakly represented with merely three quotations. As to the *Institutiones*, the fact that it is missing does not really matter as it is not a typical source for contract formulas; its main goal was rather to offer an elementary introduction to legal thinking. A similar verdict seems to me convincing about the low representation of the *Codex Iustinianus*. Summing up, there were in total 411 quotations from the *Corpus Iuris*.

On the other side, there is the surprising number of 169 literary (non juristic) sources – surprising in the sense that it does not even amount to one-third of the quotations. The comparison is striking: 66.7% to 29.1%. This result does not seem to justify the common view that legal humanism

66 Stein (n 8) 8 quotes Maffeo Vegio who stated that "if Tribonian had not corrupted the classical texts, there would have been no need for the confused commentaries of Bartolus". Similarly Watson (n 10) 250–251, Kisch (n 9) 26.

67 Cf François Hotman, *Antitribonianus*, written in 1567 but first published in 1603; compare Watson (n 10) 249.

preferred literary sources in order to liberate Roman law from the "falsifications" by Justinian's jurists in the sixth century.

Moreover, a closer look at the chapters will alter even this result and reduce the share of literary texts further. Turning over the pages it is striking that some chapters are based solely on legal sources while others almost entirely on literary ones. A characteristic pattern is the subject of auction: there are five chapters dealing with the formalities of auctions (56 to 60) and they are based almost exclusively on literary texts (fifty-five quotations). If we leave these five chapters out of consideration we get a total of 114 literary quotations to 411 legal ones. It modifies our simple statistics from 66.7% to 19.1%. Indeed, it is a striking result that flies in the face of the common view that humanists preferred pre-Justinianic sources and tried to establish an Antitribonian approach in Roman law.

There is a common view that legal humanism tended to use more Greek sources. Looking at Brissonius' chapters about sale one gets a rather poor result in this respect: from 114 literary texts merely 11 are quoted from Greek authors (not even 10%).

How did Brissonius use ancient sources as a reference? Did he quote correctly or rather superficially? Preparing a reprint of his *liber sextus* it was necessary to check every quotation carefully. It led to the surprising result that 88 of the 114 literary quotations needed corrections. It creates a very bad image indeed. However, a further investigation showed that from this considerable list of errors circa forty (35%) were false references, while forty-eight (42%) were simply references to an old edition differing considerably from modern ones.[68]

The quality of the quotations from the Digest is much better. Here only 25 show some inaccuracy – from a total of 387 (6.4%). Obviously Brissonius worked with good manuscripts or printed editions of the *Corpus Iuris*.[69]

As stated already above, here and there Brissonius also left out important

68 Compare, for example, the checklist of old editions from the sixteenth century under *http://www.ubka.uni-karlsruhe.de/kvk.html* or *www.gallica.bnf.fr* – see as well as H Dondorp and E Schrage, "The Sources of Medieval Learned Law", in J W Cairns and P J du Plessis (eds), *The Creation of the Ius Commune. From Casus to Regula* (2012) 7 at 9–11.

69 It is well known that Politian worked through the *Florentina* (*littera Pisana*) in 1490 and humanist lawyers were very cautious about the quality of the text they used, compare Stein (n 8) 298, Avenarius (n 32) 68, Watson (n 10) 250, Dondorp-Schrage (n 68) 13–5. (Compare also Osler elsewhere in this volume). A good example is also the catalogue of Merton College with its collection of law-books as an illustration of the quality of legal literature that spread all over Europe in the sixteenth century, including the *littera florentina*, Torelli's edition of the Digest, compare A Wijffels, *Late Sixteenth-Century Lists of Law Books at Merton College* (1992) XVI. See also Baston and Maclean elsewhere in this volume.

auctores (like Ulpian or Pomponius) from his collection, even in the opening passages of his *liber sextus*. Looking more closely at his passages, some additional work would be necessary almost in every chapter – based on modern research or databases. Restricting the overview to one sale model, that of slaves, even a quick check points out several lacunae. I give here just some typical examples:

Chapter IV – D. 2,14,31 Ulp.
Chapter VIII – Petron 29, Prop 4,5,50, Suet gramm 4–5, Sen contr 1,2,1,10 and 1,2,5,3, Petron 38,16, in vinculis – D. 21,1,48,3, D. 21,1,17,19, D. 11,47,1
Chapter X – Plin nat 35,200–01, Liv 24,32,28, Mart 2,68,4, Petron 41,1, Sen Epist 47,17,7, Suet Tib 4,2,6, Liv 5,22,1, Liv 24,42,11, Liv 42,63,12, SHA Aurel 7,1,4, Gell 6,4,4–5, Festus p 306M.

In summary, it can be stated that despite the false quotations or missing sources, the importance and relevance of Brissonius' work is not diminished. He carried out a big project, the reconstruction of a great legal culture merely through contract formulas of everyday practice (law in action). His collection opened a new path and it still has the ability to encourage others to continue his work. With this project he stands in the stream of his age: the study of the text as a source of "rare Latin words and of social and political data that threw light on ancient life"[70] was a central topic in legal humanism in the sixteenth century.

(7) A case study

In order to judge the value of Brissonius' work we can hardly do better than consider in some detail his ideas on a few subjects of legal practice. The sale of slaves seems to be the best choice because it represents the largest part of his work. As mentioned above, Brissonius treated sale as the most important contract: sale is the first contract in his *liber sextus* to be dealt with and its treatment is much more detailed than the other contracts.[71] Considering this utmost importance it is rather striking that the chapters of sale focus mostly on the sale of slaves. Was it a mere antiquarian interest of Brissonius? In my view this was not the case – in fact, quite the opposite.

70 Stein (n 8) 298.

71 Sale is treated in sixty-three chapters in total; while *locatio conductio* only in twenty-three and mandate as well as partnership merely in six.

Indeed the sale of slaves was the most elaborated part already in the law of sale of ancient Rome. The sale of slaves and that of land, the two items that really mattered, may have represented the most substantial economic interests in ancient rural societies. The sale of slaves required serious market regulation all over the ancient world, a good example of state interference in the exchange of goods.[72] Considering the central role of contract models for selling slaves, the contract terms established for this topic can be considered as a pattern ripe for generalisation.

Brissonius gave in the chapters V–XVI a comprehensive survey of contract terms conventionally used in sale agreements.[73] He appreciated especially the following legal institutions and legal problems worthy of detailed analysis:

V. IN MANCIPIORUM VENDITIONE *solennes formulae. Stipulatio:* SERVUM SANUM ESSE. *Venules inspici & nudari solebant. Mulierem* PRAEGNANTEM SANAM ESSE, NON *praestabat venditor.*

VI. DE ANIMI VITIIS *quoque* CAVERI *plerumque solebat. Stipulabantur,* SERVUM FUREM, AUT FUGITIVUM NON ESSE, FURTIS NOXISQUE SOLUTUM ESSE, LENONEM NON ESSE.

VII. COMMENDANDI CAUSA *quaenam de servis dicere solerent venditores?*

VIII. TITULUS VENALIBUS SERVIS, *ex Edicto AEdilium Curulium positus.*

IX. *Servorum venditioni lex quandoque dicebatur,* UT PERICULO SUO EMERET EMPTOR.

X. *Quinam* PILEATI, *qui* CORONATI *venum iverint servi? Quid,* SUB CORONA EMERE? *Venales* GYPSATIS PEDIBUS *notabiles.*

XI. MANCIPIORUM *singulorum* NATIONES *indicandae erant. Certus venalibus producendis Romae locus.* PLURES *quandoque* UNA *venibant: quot modis id fieri soleret?*

XII. *Servi* CUM PECULIO *aut* SINE ILLO *venibant, aliisve rebus adiectis.*

XIII. *Mancipia variis sub conditionibus vendita, veluti,* REDHIBENDI INTRA CERTUM TEMPUS, SI DISPLICUISSET, *item,* RATIONUM REDDENDARUM, USUSFRUCTUS, *qui in servo esset, exprimendus erat.*

XIV. *Variae in servorum venditionibus leges dici solitae:* UT EXPORTARENTUR, NE ALIQUO LOCI MORARENTUR; *imo,* NE EXPORTARENTUR.

72 Compare, for example, P Temin, "A market economy in the early Roman Empire" (2001) 91 *Journal of Roman Studies* 169 at 173–179, Jakab (n 25) 61–63, 73–80.

73 For related topics in the Glossa see J Hallebeek, "The Ignorant Seller's Liability for Latent Defects: One *Regula* or Various Sets of Rules?", in J W Cairns and P J du Plessis (eds), *The Creation of the Ius Commune. From Casus to Regula* (2012) 175.

XV. *In venditione mancipiorum, excipi solebat:* NE PROSTITUERENTUR. *Item* MANUS INIECTIO *excipiebatur, si contra legem venditionis quid fieret.*

XVI. *Mancipia quandoque ea lege vendita,* UT MANUMITTERENTUR INTRA CERTUM TEMPUS: *contra quandoque,* NE MANUMITTERENTUR: *aliquando ita,* UT NIHIL EXCIPERETUR.

Modern scholars surveying this list may require some sort of systematisation. In this sense Brissonius' casuistic compilation could be brought under the following headings: guarantee for latent physical or mental defects; implied terms; market regulations (state interference); risk allocation[74] and some of the typical subsidiary clauses.

Approaching the subject from another aspect one may distinguish between legal norms (of whatever kind) and market customs. This leads to the following groupings: (a) law of sale in notary practice – *leges venditionis* (the commonly used terms with enforcement based upon *ius honorarium*, the edicts of the urban praetors and the *aediles curules* with the commentary of Roman jurists, chapters V, VI, VII, VIII, IX, XI). The material can be separated further into two main groups: guarantee (stipulation) based on custom (law in action), chapters V and VI or that based on the edict (partly V and VIII); (b) subsidiary contract terms, commonly used in trade (XII, XIII, XIV, XV, XVI); and (c) mere customs, broadly applied in trade, with some legal consequence (a rather folkloristic part, dealt with in chapter X).

In summary, it can be stated that Brissonius focused on everyday legal practice. His goal was the reconstruction of ancient legal formulas with its most important terms. There are almost no traces of legal theory, of any kind of lawyer's law in his work – he seems to have omitted it intentionally from his treatment. Instead of a normative comprehension, he tries to draw a true picture of custom – the legal culture lived by merchants and proprietors in ancient Rome. As already mentioned above, the investigation of custom, customary law and the emphasis on its priority in relation to statutes was a main aim of legal humanism in the sixteenth century.[75] Brissonius understood and applied these ideas, combining them with the typical humanist interest in the texts, the ancient sources apart the *Glossa*.[76]

Focusing on chapters about slave sales it is striking that his selection is rather eclectic. Some topics are dealt with in an extraordinarily detailed

74 Probably a bit misunderstood by Brissonius, see below.
75 Stein (n 9) 76–79, Kelley (n 7) 192, Vinogradoff (n 33) 75–76.
76 Stein (n 9) 75, Watson (n 10) 250.

manner while others are missing completely. For example, there is no mention of regulations about liability, risk allocation or eviction.[77] Without any doubt, many of the missing points are treated in other chapters focusing on different topics (sale of land, sale of wine, etc).[78] One has the impression that Brissonius considered the contract of sale as a large collection of contractual terms. From these he tried to build a system from a notarial point of view: preparing a concrete deed every scribe or notary is obliged to choose the best and most important ones from the possible set of terms relevant for his actual business. Therefore Brissonius allocated every single term to the very sale model in which it was most essential. In this way he created a rather individual structure for the contract of sale. Just to give some examples: the contractual clauses of eviction can be found in chapters about sale of land while that of risk allocation in chapters about sale of wine.[79]

Assembling the main terms quoted by Brissonius, his view of sale contracts about slaves can be put together as follows:

> *Stipulatur enim emptor,* SANUM ESSE l. 16. §. ult.[80] l. 31. D. de evictionibus.[81]
> *In horum emptione (de pastoribus loquitur) solet peculium accedere: aut si excipietur, stipulatio intercedere,* SANUM EUM ESSE. Ulpianus in l. 14. §. 9. D. de AEdil. Edict.[82]
> *Si venditor nominatim* EXCEPERIT DE ALIQUO MORBO, ET DE CETERO SANUM ESSE DIXERIT, *aut promiserit.* Pomponius in l. 64. §. 1. D. eod.[83]
> EUM HOMINEM, QUO DE AGITUR, FURTIS NOXISQUE SOLUTUM ESSE. ITEM FUGITIVUM NON ESSE, ERRONEM NON ESSE . . . Paulus in l. 3. & l. 11. §. ult.[84]
> FUGITIVUM, ERRONEM NON ESSE . . . FURTIS NOXAQUE SOLUTUS. Cicero lib. III. Officior. c. 17.[85]
> Ulpianus in l. 32. D. de Evictionib.[86] *Si ita quis stipulanti spoponderit,* SANUM ESSE, FUREM NON ESSE, VISPELLONEM NON ESSE, PRAESTARI?
> SERVUM SPECIOSUM, FRUGI, PROBUM, DICTO AUDIENTEM ESSE, l. 43. D. de contr. empt.[87]
> *Quaedam autem ut pluris venderet, adfirmabat venditor, veluti* HOMINEM LITERATUM, *vel* ARTIFICEM ESSE, ALEATOREM NON ESSE, AD STATUAM NUMQUAM

77 Nevertheless, the risk allocation is a question that should be discussed again, below.
78 See, for example, the chapter XX on wine or the chapters XXVI–XXXV on land.
79 This way of thinking is not dissimilar to that of ancient jurists; the titles D.18.1 and D.19.1 give the impression that the *compilatores* of Justinian worked a bit similarly.
80 D.21.2.16.2 Pomponius.
81 D.21.2.31.
82 D.21.1.14.9.
83 D.21.1.64.1.
84 D.21.2.3 and D. 21.2.11.1.
85 Cic. off. 3.17.71.
86 D.21.2.31 – Brissonius quotes erroneously D.21.2.32.
87 D.18.1.43pr.

CONFUGISSE, D. l. 43. de contrahend. empt.[88]
Si venditor hominis, dixit, PECULIUM EUM HABERE DECEM . . . Ulpianus in l. 13. §. 4. D. eod.[89]
UT, NISI PLACUISSET, INTRA PRAEFINITUM TEMPUS REDHIBERETUR, l. 31. §. 22. D. de Aedilic. Edict.[90]
UT EXPORTARENTUR, *vel* UT ITALIA EXPORTARENTUR, l. 2. D. de serv. export.[91]
NE MANCIPIUM PROSTITUERETUR, l. 6. D. de serv. exportand.[92]
UT MANUMITTERENTUR, l. 13. D. de oper. libertor.[93]

A closer study of Brissonius' *formulae* raises a further question: Is his reconstruction complete? Did he find every possible contractual clause quoted in the Digest or in ancient literature? A brief survey shows that Brissonius' impressive collection has some lacunae, too.

In the sixteenth century, the availability of epigraphic sources like wax tablets was rather poor. From the eighteenth century on, excavations brought new evidence about contractual practice that Brissonius could not have considered. Nevertheless, he was able to produce a rather clear and almost complete model of sale formulas and show how they most probably affected everyday practice. It is of utmost interest to compare his reconstruction with sources discovered later on in Campania and in provinces of the Roman Empire.

The Romans used *tabulae*, small wooden tablets as writing material for depicting their contracts. It is a special Roman way of preserving evidence that might have had some sacral roots.[94] What did they look like? Generally, one side of a thin, small wooden tablet (their usual measure was approximately 10 x 15 cm) was slightly deepened and covered with wax (or shellac); the scribe wrote with a metallic switch (called *stylus*) on the waxed surface.[95] It is obvious that this technology was rather imperfect, and could not be trusted to offer infallible proof before court: the wax might have been warmed up and the letters could easily have been erased or "corrected" by someone who did not flinch at forgery. Meanwhile, the notary practice developed two types of *tabulae* to avoid such tricks: the *diptych* and

88 D.18.1.43pr.
89 D.19.1.13, 4.
90 D.21.1.31.22: *Si quid ita venierit, ut, nisi placuerit, intra praefinitum tempus redhibeatur. . .*
91 D.18.7.2.
92 D.18.7.6pr.
93 D.38.1.13pr.
94 See E Meyer, *Legitimacy and Law in the Roman World. Tabulae in Roman Belief and Practice* (2004) 44–63.
95 Compare J G Wolf, *Aus dem neues Pompejanischen Urkundenfund* (2010) 19–20, J G Wolf and J A Crook *Rechtsurkunden in Vulgärlatein aus den Jahren 37–39 n Chr* (1989) 10–14.

triptych. A *diptych* consists of two tablets, a *triptych* of three. In each type the legally relevant text was written on the two interior wax surfaces, then closed by a string and sealed by witnesses. The seals must not have been broken or cut, unless in court.

A considerable collection of such *tabulae* dating in the first century AD came from Campania: from Pompeii, Herculaneum and Puteoli.[96] Furthermore, we possess a few examples of such *tabulae* preserved in provinces like Dacia or Britannia. In general, the Campanian find is the most significant one. Unfortunately there are only a few *tabulae* with sale contracts among them – and almost all in a very poor condition. TPSulp 43 is the best illustration for sale practice on a busy market – as one can assume in Puteoli, in the most frequented harbour of Rome at that time (TPSulp 43, dated August 21, in 38 AD, Tab II pag 3, *graphio, scriptura interior*):[97]

> *[solutum e]sse fugit[i]vom | [err]onem [non] esse [et] cetera | in edicto aed(ilium) cur(ulium) [q]uae huiusque | an[n]i scripta conprehensaque |*[5] *sun[t], recte praestar[i et d]uplam | [p]ecuniam ex form[ula], ita | [u]ti [ad]solet, recte [dar]i stipul(atus) | [e]st T(itus) Vestorius Arpocra mi[n]or | [spo]pondit T(itus) Vestorius Phoenix. |*[10] *Actum Puteol(is) XII k(alendas) Se[p]t(embres), | Se[r(vio) A]sinio Sex(to) Nonio co(n)s(ulibus).*[98]

The first lines of the document are lost: the names of vendor, purchaser or the slave sold are missing, but we do learn that it was a male slave of unknown age. The text as preserved begins with a guarantee for latent defects, physical and mental as well. The vendor promised that the slave did not run away – he is not a runaway (fugitive), not a loiterer on errands or still subject to noxal liability (it means he is free from liability for unlawful damages).[99] In this very document the scribe used a special term generalising the liability for latent defects with a hint to the edict of the *aediles curules*, the magistrates in charge of market regulations (lines 3–5). From line 5 the main body of the stipulation follows: the vendor prom-

96 TH 59, 60, 61 follow the same pattern, see Jakab (n 25) 165–166.

97 Compare G Camodeca, *L'archivio Puteolano dei Sulpicii* (1992, 1999) 117–119.

98 TPSulp 43: . . . to be paid, . . . not to be a fugitive or liable to stray and the other terms written and included in the edict of the *curule aediles* for this year, Titus Vestorius Arpocra minor stipulated that the terms be duly met and that he be duly paid double the sum in keeping with the formula, as is customary, Titus Vestorius Phoenix solemnly promised. Transacted at Puteoli on the 12th day before the Kalends of September under the consuls Servius Asinius and Sextus Nonius (21 Aug 38). Gaius Iulius Senecion, son of Gaius, of the tribe Falerna, Gaius Munnius Rufus, son of Gaius, Aulus Fuficus Donatus, Lucius Pontus Philadelphus, Titus Vestorius Phoenix, Gaius Paccus Felix, Gaius Claudius . . . , Gaius Mateius Primogenus, Gaius Suettius Dama (Translation of Rowe).

99 It is likely that line 1 can be completed with *noxam solutum esse* . . . see below.

ised to take responsibility (*praestari*) for all possible defects ordered by the *aediles*.

Up to this point TPSulp 43 covers almost completely Brissonius' idea of sale contracts. But in lines 5–7 follows a term that is missing in Brissonius' reconstruction: the vendor promised to pay the double sum in a case of eviction.[100] As mentioned above, Brissonius left out eviction here and put all these clauses into the chapters XXV, XXIX, XXXV about the sale of land and especially in chapter LII under the title "*De evictione caveri solebat. Simplae & duplae stipulationes*".

In lines 7–9 of the wax tablet from Puteoli the question and response of the *stipulatio* formula is well preserved, and from it one learns the names of the parties involved: Titus Vestorius Phoenix the vendor and Titus Vestorius Arpocra the purchaser. As usual in Roman documents the dating is placed at the end, the years recorded with the consuls. The agreement was set up in Puteoli and signed by nine seals: the vendor (Tab II pag 4 line 5) and eight further persons witnessed the business, according to the rules of transferring ownership through a formal *mancipatio*.[101]

A wooden tablet from the province Dacia, from a small village called *Kartum* preserved a slave sale in a much better condition (FIRA III Nr 87, Triptych, AD 139, Dacia, *scriptura interior*):

> *Max̣imus Batonis puellam nomine | Passiam, sive ea quo alio nomine est, an|norum circiter p(lus) m(inus) sex, empta sportellaria, emit mancipioque accepit | de Dasio Verzonis Pirusta ex Kavieretio, | (denariis) ducentis quinque. | Eam puellam sanam esse <<a>> furtis noxisque | solutam, fugitivam erronem non esse | praestari : quot si quis eam puellam | partemve quam ex eo quis evicerit | quo minus Maximum Batonis, quove ea res pertinebit, habere possi|dereque recte liceat, tum quanti | ea puella empta est, <tan>tam pecuniam | et alterum tantum dari fide rogavit | Maximus Batonis, fide promisit Dasius | Verzonis Pirusta ex Kavieretio. Proque ea puella, quae s(upra) s(cripta) est, (denarios) ducen|tos quinque accepisse et habere | se dixit Dasius Verzonis a Maximo Batonis.*[102]

100 Double the price paid or double the market value at the time of a future trial.

101 Crook (n 42) 141.

102 FIRA III 87: "Maximus son of Bato has bought and accepted as a *mancipium* a girl by the name of Passia, or if she is (known) by any other name, m(ore or) l(ess) around six years old, having been bought as a foundling, for 205 (denarii), from Dasius son of Verzo, a Pirustian from Kavieretium. It is vouched for that she is a physically sound girl, not charged with theft and damage, is not a runaway (fugitive) or loiterer to errand; but if anyone shall have claimed back this girl or any portion of her, as a result of which it is not legal for Maximus son of Bato or him to whom the affair will be relevant to hold and possess her rightfully, in that case Maximus son of Bato demanded in faith that the exact sum and an equivalent amount be paid. Maximus the son of Bato asked to be given in faith, Dasius son of Verzo a Pirustian from Kavieretium promised in faith. Dasius son of Verzo said that he received and has for this girl, w(ho) i(s) w(ritten) a(bove), 250 denarii from Maximus son of Bato." (Translation of E Meyer.)

A certain Maximus, son of Bato purchased a slave girl called Passia, approximately six years old.[103] The girl may have been abandoned as a baby then found by someone and brought up, probably with the intention of selling her for profit. The vendor is Dasius, son of Verzo, from the tribe of the Pirustanians originating from the village of Kavieretium. The price, agreed and already paid before setting up the present document, amounted to 205 drachmas.[104] The first part of the text summarised the facts, the most important terms of the agreement. The second part includes the guarantee of the vendor for defects and for eviction, according to the same pattern as delivered from Puteoli.[105]

It is really striking how similar these *tabulae* are even though their geographical, legal and cultural environment differed. The first is from the rich harbour of Puteoli, the very heart of Campanian business life from the beginning of the first century AD; the second drawn up a hundred years later in a distant province, Dacia, in a recently established economy and population, in rather poor circumstances. Obviously neither the parties nor the scribes cared about even basic legal capacities like citizenship. The documents focus purely on the main legal consequences derived from the business: transfer of ownership, mutual fulfilment and the only future obligation, the guarantee of the vendor.

Comparing this convincing epigraphic evidence with Brissonius' efforts at recovering sale custom from literary sources it can be stated that he mostly hit the target. Comparing the *triptych* from the second century from the province Dacia with Brissonius' reconstructions, his method can be thoroughly justified. Nevertheless, he seems to have chosen a rather formal, encyclopaedic treatment of the sources. In most cases he just picked out a clause by reason of a headword without thinking of the context and the real meaning of the entire formula.

Although his collection of contract terms could not deliver a complete reconstruction of a sale document, it offers a broad palette of possible clauses. Brissonius opened a new vista on sale practice, showed rare Latin words with special meanings and introduced a fascinating approach to understanding the sources in their social and economic context.

103 Commonly slaves acquired by sale were renamed by their new proprietor; therefore the uncertainty; compare Varro, ling 8.21.

104 W Kunkel, "Epigraphik und Geschichte des römischen Privatrechts", *Vestigia. Beiträge zur Alten Geschichte*, B. 17 (= Akten des VI. Internationalen Kongresses für Griechische und Lateinische Epigraphik) (1972) 193 at 218.

105 Regarding the problem of *peregrini* using a Roman formula, see Jakab (n 25) 168 with further literature.

Finally, some words regarding texts missing from Brissonius' work: a good example is an *epistula* of Horace. Remarkably enough, Brissonius left it out although it may have aptly fitted in his survey.[106] Horace quoted here phrases commonly cried out by slave merchants in market places all over Rome (Hor epist 2.2.4):

> *Flore, bono claroque fidelis amice Neroni,| siquis forte velit puerum tibi venere natum | Tibure vel Gabiis et tecum sic agat: "hic et | candidus et talos a vertice pulcher ad imos | fiet eritque tuus nummorum milibus octo, | verna ministeriis ad nutus aptus erilis, | litterulis Graecis imbutus, idoneus arti | cuilibet: argilla quidvis imitaberis uda; | quin etiam canet indoctum sed dulce bibenti. | multa fidem promissa levant, ubi plenius aequo | laudat venalis qui volt extrudere merces: | res urget me nulla; meo sum pauper in aere. | nemo hoc mangonum faceret tibi; non temere a me | quivis ferret idem. semel hic cessavit et, ut fit, | in scalis altuit metuens pendentis habenae"- | des nummos, excepta nihil te si fuga laedat | ille ferat pretium poenae securus, opinor. | prudens emisti vitiosum, dicta tibi est lex: | insequeris tamen hunc et lite moraris iniqua?*[107]

Horace developed his humorous description in a letter to his friend Florus. He quoted faithfully the wording usual in offers of sale as announced by sellers or by auctioneers. The poet created a pretty set of fictitious *leges venditionis* copying real trading practice: a slave merchant recommends his goods praising a young male slave rather cunningly: telling long tales about his benefits, he tries to hide a basic failure – his being an *erro* or *fugitivus*, a loiterer on errands or a runaway slave.[108] Comparing the poem with legal texts as preserved in the Digest one can immediately notice the close connection.

106 The omission of this text is curious because humanist authors focused mostly on non-legal, literary sources and Horace offers a nice example of it here.

107 Hor epist 2.2.4: "My Florus, loyal friend of great and good Nero, suppose someone by chance should wish to sell you a slave, born at Tibur or Gabii, and should deal with you thus: 'Here's a handsome boy, comely from top to toe; you may take him, to have and to hold, for eight thousand sesterces; home-bred he is, apt for service at his owner's beck, knows a bit of Greek learning, and can master any art; the clay is soft – you will mould it to what you will; moreover, he will sing for you over your cups in a sweet if artless fashion. Too many promises lessen confidence, when a seller who wants to shove off his wares praises them unduly. I am under no constraint; I have slender means, but am not in debt. None of the slave-dealers would give you such a bargain; not everyone would easily get the like from me. Once he played truant, and hid himself, as boys will do, under the stairs, fearing the hanging strap. Give me the sum asked, if his running off, duly noted, does not trouble you': the seller, I take it, would get his price without fear of penalty. You bought him with your eyes open – fault and all; the condition was told you; do you still pursue the seller and annoy him with an unjust suit?" (Translation of H Rushton Fairclough.)

108 Compare W Kudlien, "*Empticius servus*. Bemerkungen zum antiken Sklavenmarkt" (1986) 35 *Historia* 240 at 250, Jakab (n 25) 162–164. On the other hand, P Arzt-Grabner, "'Neither a Truant nor a Fugitive': Some Remarks on the Sale of Slaves in Roman Egypt and Other Provinces", in T Gagos (ed), *Proceedings of the 25th International Congress of Papyrology* (2007) 24 stressed his being a *fugitivus* – in my view both meanings are possible.

The slave being an *erro* was also a relevant fault in market regulations of the *aediles*. Every purchaser had the right to return a slave and claim back his money if he was not informed about this circumstance before concluding the contract.[109] *Praedicere*, giving information in advance – vendors of slaves were obliged to declare every relevant disease or defect, verbally or in written form.[110]

In his *epistula* Horace addressed his friend Florus and sought excuse for his laziness in writing. He argues that he cannot be blamed because he had forewarned Florus that he was a bad correspondent. A previous warning is a real excuse as it is commonly accepted in the slave trade, too. Horace built his metaphor with uncommonly great artfulness and accuracy using phrases commonly cried by merchants.[111]

C. CONCLUSION: BRISSONIUS' *DE FORMULIS* . . . IN CONTEXT

In modern scholarship it is commonly assumed that "elegant legal humanism", especially the French version of it, was only concerned with philological problems of theoretical interest and did not exercise any significant influence on the legal development of Europe.[112] Nevertheless, lawyers educated in humanist tradition were active and creative authorities as judges at French courts and as advisers in preparing legislation. Also Brissonius took a considerable part in legislature and politics of his age. As a practitioner, his scholarly work was rooted not only in legal humanist studies (as attained at the universities of Orléans, Bourges and Poitiers) but also in practical considerations and needs of sixteenth-century French society.

At first sight it seems an antiquarian and selfish idea to collect formulas used in public and private life of ancient Rome. However, this approach originated in an old French tradition. In a great part of France the state of law was governed by custom, customary law. Both in the "*pays de droit écrit*" and in the "*pays de droit coutumier*" custom played a much more important

109 See D.21.1.1.1 Ulp, compare Jakab (n 25) 123.

110 Compare Jakab (n 25) 40–43, 127–129.

111 There is one surprising omission (chapter IX): remarkably enough Brissonius made one real mistake in classifying legal institutions in his works. Reading Plautus he misunderstood the phrase *periculo suo* in a complicated scene. He seems to have considered the phrase *periculo suo* in the sense as it was suggested by Ulpian and Pomponius in some legal decisions, i.e. excluding the warranty for latent physical defects. But in Plautus' comedy the fictitious "business letter" with a mandate to sell a "slave" girl speaks of *mancipatio*, refusing the liability for eviction.

112 Compare, for example, Watson (n 10) 249: the humanists "failed to have much direct influence".

role in the legal system than we are used to in modern times. It is sufficient to mention the famous law-book *Coutumes de Beauvaisis* compiled by Philippe de Remi, sire de Beaumanoir in the thirteenth century which wanted to give "primarily the substance of local custom in his own place – Clermont in Beauvaisis".[113] Beaumanoir set out to depict the customary law of his county under the premise that Roman law or royal statutes are recognised only if they are accepted and applied by local courts. Any legal norm needs an acceptance by French legal custom or jurisprudence.[114]

Such a concept of law leads directly to an overrated estimation of custom.[115] Formulas used in public or private life are clear evidence about the required acceptance. Formulas delivered in ancient literary works or in decisions of Roman lawyers can be considered as first-hand-proofs of legal custom – as a fountain of true, unspoiled sources of a "real", ante-Justinianic Roman law.

It may be worth a deeper investigation to analyse the impact of Brissonius' work in the centuries after his death. Here I can only give some hints concerning its acceptance and popularity. Looking at the publications of Brissonius it is obvious that some of them were printed six or seventeen times in the course of 200 years. The fact that leading German scholar Johann Gottlieb Heineccius devoted himself to a careful revision and correction of the 1743 edition speaks for itself. He knew Brissonius' work; obviously he regarded it highly enough to prepare a new edition. In summary it can be stated that Brissonius' formulas were read and reprinted anew for hundreds of years. The frequent references to later scholars give a hint to his impact as well. It is sufficient to mention such highly estimated names as Ianus Dousa, Gaspar Scioppius, Gebhard Elmenhorstius, Iacobus Gothofredus, Caspar Barthius, Io Henr Boeclerus, Dan Georg Morhofius, Ian Vinc Gravina or Georg Beyerus.

But what about his own age? How did his approaches fit the social and ideological environment of France of the sixteenth century? Legal humanism was part of a greater ideology, of the streams of Renaissance and humanism

113 Vinogradoff (n 33) 81.

114 For a related concept in Scots law compare J W Cairns, "The Moveable Text of Mackenzie: Bibliographical Problems for the Scottish Concept of Institutional Writing", in J W Cairns and O F Robinson (eds), *Critical Studies in Ancient Law, Comparative Law and Legal History* (2001) 235 at 245–246.

115 Compare R C van Caenegem, "Aantekeningen bij het middeleeuwse gewoonterecht" (1996) 64 *The Legal History Review* 97, D Heirbaut, "Who were the makers of customary law in medieval Europe? Some answers on sources about the spokesmen of Flemish feudal courts" (2007) 75 *The Legal History Review* 257 at 266–270.

all across Europe. In this movement, art and science represented a complex view of nature and society borrowing methods from each other. An entire change of approach characterised this epoch which is particularly obvious in art theory: medieval art theory preferred an "imitative art" where a natural object served as a mere "example" or "simile" that was depicted by the painter "according to the image in his soul".[116] But people of the Renaissance believed in the dogma that a work of art is the "direct and faithful representation" of a natural object; the painter was obliged to stress both an "objective correctness" and a "representational correctness".[117] For modern art theory as emphasised by Erwin Panofsky, nature, art and science demonstrated a complex model of thinking with mutual influence at that significant period of European history:

> Art theory, therefore, took an active and most important part in the development of what we know as the natural sciences. From a Renaissance point of view, it is entirely logical for large parts of Leonardo da Vinci's Treatise on Painting to read like a textbook on physics or botany, rather than like a discussion of artistic problems . . . Antonio Pollaiuolo and Leonardo dissected corpses at a period when professional physicians still lectured . . . on the basis of Galen and Avicenna; and Galileo owes more to Leonardo da Vinci than to the learned commentators on Aristotle's Physics. Natural science as we still know it, and art as conceived by the Renaissance can in fact be defined as two parallel attempts at representing the universe in an image based on observation and rationalized by mathematics.[118]

The idea of "representational correctness" may be fulfilled through determining and learning the rules of how to translate natural phenomena into a "language" of a certain art or science.

Reading the works of Barnabas Brissonius one has the impression that two main stages can be distinguished in his oeuvre: his early works followed a pattern he learned in Bourges and Poitiers – tending rather to an "objective correctness". While his later works, also his *De formulis et solennibus verbis populi Romani* presented here, took a different approach. It reminds the reader more of the ideas of "representational correctness", the study of objective phenomena observed in nature or society and a correct depicting of them. In my view, Brissonius was wholly embodied in Renaissance and humanist ideas as those came down plausibly in art theory, too. It is striking that Brissonius followed rather similar patterns in composing his great volume.

116 E Panofsky, *The Codex Huygens and Leonardo da Vinci's Art Theory* (1940) 90 referring to Thomas Aquinas and Master Eckhart.

117 Panofsky (n 116) 91 similarly E Panofsky, *Idea. Ein Beitrag zur Begriffsgeschichte der älteren Kunsttheorie*, 2nd edn (1960) 24, 33, 47–51.

118 Panofsky (n 116) 91.

He tried to captivate a new sight and apply it on legal sources; his method has something in common with the modern "law in action" approach. Without any doubt, it is a method of dealing with casuistic sources from daily life and legal practice which European legal scholarship has lost for a long time.

10 A Lawyer and His Sources: Nicolas Bohier and Legal Practice in Sixteenth-Century France

Jasmin Hepburn

A. INTRODUCTION

The aim of this chapter is to assess the meaning of the term *ius commune* and its relationship with other competing sources of law such as statute and custom in the context of sixteenth-century legal practice in France. This will be achieved through a study of a lawyer, Nicolas Bohier (Nicolaus Boerius) (1469–1539) and his *Consilia*. One of the greater aims of this chapter is to better inform the narratives about humanism specifically and European legal history generally.

Compared to the jurist, the legal practitioner, together with their own written works, have long been overlooked in traditional accounts of legal history. Furthermore, there has been a tendency to generalise in terms of legal humanism and a hastiness to categorise jurists into humanist and "other". Here in particular, the role of the legal practitioner has not been fully considered. In order to establish the extent to which intellectual movements like legal humanism permeated through to legal practice, it is necessary to look at the texts documenting the law in action, and an understanding of the way lawyers interacted with sources. Also, if the concept of the *ius commune* in legal practice is similar to that of the theorists, then this will demonstrate the need for the law in practice, its practitioners and their works, to be held in the same regard as the university jurists and their writings. This has the potential to challenge the traditional narrative of legal humanism and its impact on the *ius commune.*

This will be achieved through a micro-history of Nicolas Bohier and a selection of cases mentioned in his *Consilia*. His citation practices will also be considered with a view to better understanding what and who represented the *ius commune* to the sixteenth-century practitioner. Despite his achievements, Nicolas Bohier, an *avocat*, professor and president of the Bordeaux *Parlement*, has not received much attention in contemporary scholarship. The most complete accounts of his personal life and achievements are to be found in Gerard Guyon's *Le droit bordelais dans tous ses états: Les anciennes coutumes, les juristes et la justice, les institutions de l'Église locale*, where he devotes a detailed chapter to Bohier,[1] and an eighteenth-century work by Georges Calmon, *Avocat General* of the *Cour d'Appel* of Bordeaux.[2] Delivered as a lecture to the *Palais-de-Justice*, Calmon's biography accounts for Bohier's birth, marriage and career but is lacking in its use of authorities and so reliance cannot rest too heavily on this publication. Information can also be found in the introduction to Bohier's *Decisiones Burdegalenses*, provided by Jean Alesme, a *conseiller* at the Bordeaux *Parlement*.[3] However, this brief history is a celebration of Bohier's life and is more of a eulogy than a biography. These works, together with the footnotes of related histories and brief entries in biographical works,[4] are the only accounts of Nicolas Bohier's life currently available.

1 G Guyon, "Un Arrêtiste Bordelais: Nicolas Boerius (1469–1539)", *Annales de la Faculté de Droit, Centre d'études et de recherches d'histoire institutionelle et regionale* (Université de Bordeaux I) 1, (1976) 17.

2 *Le Président Bohier* (Böerius) (1880).

3 *Decisiones Burdegalenses* (1544).

4 Examples of such works include J C F Hoefer, *Nouvelle Biographie Générale depuis les temps les plus reculés, jusqu'à nos jours, avec les renseignements bibliographiques et l'indication des sources à consulter* vol 6 (1852), R J Pothier, *A Treatise on Maritime Contracts of Letting to Hire* (1821) 139.

Bohier was an individual with an illustrious career in the law. He was first and foremost a practitioner, but his role as author and editor goes some way towards suggesting that the traditional firm division between the practising lawyer and the jurist be reconsidered. Works such as the *Consilia* and the *Decisiones* offer much for new enquiries into what kinds of sources and which jurists were deemed authoritative in legal practice, and ultimately enable a clearer understanding of the relationship between the university jurist and the practising lawyer in sixteenth-century France. Any attempt to understand the meaning of the term *ius commune* and its position in relation to competing legal orders such as statute and custom, ought to include reference to these sources.

B. A HISTORY OF NICOLAS BOHIER

Any attempt to consider the legal thought of an individual through their works, must first offer an account of the individual's education and professional history. Only then can a portrait of the legal practitioner's intellectual history be made.

The Bohier name has a long and distinguished history in France.[5] It can be found in many of the prestigious positions of the early modern period, including those held in the Royal Court, the Church and the *Parlement*.[6] Bohier was born in May 1469, in Montpellier, to Jeanne Fornerie and Vincent Bohier.[7] According to Calmon, Bohier's father came from the province of Auvergne and moved to Montpellier to be closer to the University so that he could attend classes there.[8] He married Bohier's mother in the town but died shortly afterwards. It can therefore be assumed that his involvement in his son's upbringing was brief. Indeed, Calmon's account mentions the encouraging devotion of Nicolas' mother in his early education.[9]

5 One of the most famous undoubtedly being Thomas Bohier (c1460–1523). Like Vincent Bohier, Thomas was also born in Auvergne. Married to Katherine de Briçonnet, a French noblewoman and daughter of Guillaume Briçonnet, a French Cardinal. Thomas served as Chamberlain to King Charles VIII of France but is perhaps best known for the construction of the Château de Chenonceau, which would eventually belong to King Francis I, passing to King Henry II, who offered it as a gift to his mistress Diane de Poitiers. See C Chevalier, *Histoire abrégée Château de Chenonceau* (1879). A link between Thomas and Nicolas has not been identified, however the Auvergne link is notable.

6 N L Roelker, *One King, One Faith: The Parlement of Paris and the Religious Reformations of the Sixteenth Century* (1996) 45.

7 G Calmon, *Le Président Bohier* (1880).

8 Calmon (n 7) 7.

9 Calmon (n 7) 7: "sous égide d'une mère tendrement dévouée qui fut son guide et son soutien

Bohier studied law at the university in Montpellier, but would later leave the town and he seems to have visited a number of provinces.[10] He eventually settled in Bourges, the town of his mother Jeanne Fornerie's birth.[11] On 8 July 1499, Bohier married Marie Labourrin.[12] Her Uncle was Guillaume de Cambray, Archbishop of Bourges and once a *conseiller* of the Paris *Parlement*.[13] There is no mention of children in Bohier's will.[14] In his lifetime, Bohier was a jurist, an *avocat*, a *conseiller* in the *Grand Conseil* and President of the regional *parlement* in Bordeaux. He resided in Montpellier, Bourges, Paris and finally Bordeaux, where he died in 1539. Such movement across France would ordinarily appear noteworthy, but, given his range of professional pursuits, it is not extraordinary. This was characteristic of those holding judicial office in late fifteenth- and sixteenth-century France.[15]

Bohier is often referred to as *Vicomte de Pommiers*.[16] This title does not seem to have been hereditary; there is no evidence that any of Bohier's family or close associates held this title before him.[17] Georges Calmon has stated that the title came with land bought by Bohier after his growing success as an *avocat* in Bourges, and shortly before his appointment to the *Grand Conseil* in 1506.[18] It is also possible that the title was given to Bohier as a token of Royal favour. The King himself sought Bohier out for the position of *conseiller*, and so he was clearly held in high regard by the Royal Court.[19] Bohier died in 1539 in Bordeaux. His will revealed his charitable

dans les premiers pas de la vie, il se mit résolument au travail et se prepara par de fortes, études sa l'avenir brillant que son intelligence precoce permettait d'entrevoir".

10 Calmon (n 7) 11.

11 Calmon (n 7) 11.

12 Calmon (n 7) 11.

13 G T de la Thaumassière, *Histoire de Berry* (1689) 81.

14 *Testament du Nicolas Bohier*, dated 20 May 1538. A copy of Bohier's will is available at: *Archives Départementales de la Gironde, Registres d'enregistrement du Parlement de Bordeaux* (1538) B 12 fol 87 to 93.

15 Note that in medieval France the judge was expected to be a native of the town. See A Gouron, *Juristes et droits savants: Bologne et la France médiévale* (2000) 36.

16 He refers to himself as such in his will: *Archives Départementales de la Gironde, Registres d'enregistrement du Parlement de Bordeaux* (1538) B 12 fol 87 to 93. See also P Renouard, *Imprimeurs et Libraires Parisiens du Seizième Siècle: Ouvrage publié d'après les manuscrits de Philippe Renouard* vol 5 (1991) 270.

17 In the *Archives Nationales*, Paris, there are references to *Vicomte de Pommiers*, but the holder of the title was not Bohier. These references also pre-date him so do not preclude him holding this title in his lifetime.

18 Calmon (n 7) 18.

19 On this topic more generally see F Bluche, *L'Ancien Régime: Institutions et Société* (1993).

nature, where he left substantial provision for the *l'Hôpital Saint-André*, and his many books to the *parlement* of Bordeaux.[20]

C. HIS PUBLICATIONS

The increase in litigation during the early modern period caused the printing market to produce more copies of a specific genre of Italian medieval jurisprudence, *Consilia*, and *Decisiones*; practical legal texts that the practising lawyer could utilise.[21] Yet it is the collections of *Annotationes*, *Emendationes*, *Observationes* that have come to be the mark of the humanist and ultimately represent the sixteenth century in contemporary works of legal history. The rise of the public persona of the lawyer would have changed the nature of the law and perhaps further separated it from the university jurist, who appeared removed from the contentious and precarious nature of legal practice.

Those who felt strongly associated with the intellectual movement of humanism, therefore, would have enhanced this demarcation and ultimately created a two-tier legal culture, divided between university teaching and writing, and the physical practice of the law. The rigid periodisation of legal history has caused the sixteenth century to become almost synonymous with legal humanism. Peter Stein has noted: "the scholar could be a humanist but the practitioner had to be a Bartolist".[22] It is this separation of profession and intellectual identity that has resulted in the jurist overshadowing the practitioner. As this chapter will show, this division was perhaps not as pronounced at the time as it is commonly said to have been today. Instead, it is the later post-sixteenth century treatment of legal humanism that has given it, and the Universities, "centre stage"; a theory put forward in much greater detail by Douglas Osler.[23] This is a possible explanation for the overwhelmingly humanist nature affixed to this period of legal history, and the pale figure of the practitioner within it. The roles of the lawyer, the *avocat*, *procurateur*, and their writings, which were not always directly practice-oriented, were dominant ones and central to the narrative of sixteenth-century legal history.

20 See also C B F Boscheron des Portes, *Histoire du Parlement de Bordeaux, depuis sa création jusqu'à sa suppression (1451–1790), Tome Premier (1462–1640)* (1877).

21 D Osler, "Images of legal humanism" (2001) 9 *Surfaces* 101.

22 P Stein, "Legal Humanism and Legal Science", in P Stein, *The Character and Influence of the Roman Civil Law: Historical Essays* (1988) 98.

23 Osler (n 21).

(1) Bohier as author of *Decisiones* and *Consilia*

(1.1) *Decisiones Burdegalenses* (1544)

Bohier's *Decisiones Burdegalenses* is a common type of French law report from the first half of the sixteenth century.[24] It contains a collection of decisions from the *Parlement* of Bordeaux, where Bohier himself was President. Alain Wijffels has observed that the sixteenth century saw those legal authors already steeped in the Italian method further develop other genres of legal literature.[25] The *Decisiones* was one of the more popular genres to emerge. Although initiated during the last centuries of the Middle Ages, the *Decisiones* rose to prominence in the sixteenth century and survived the decline of the Italian method.[26] The importance of this type of work was twofold. First, the *Decisiones* fulfilled a need for consistency in the courts by providing a record of authoritative decisions. It is worth noting here, however, that this take on early modern court reporting is not uniformly accepted: Dolores Freda has argued that the *Decisiones* ought to be thought of more as general case law, than as a binding source.[27] But, whatever their status, it is certain that the *Decisiones* were vital in enabling the *Parlement* of Bordeaux to create a robust representative account of its decision-making practices. Secondly, the law report is likely to have served as, what Wijffels has called, a *locus*: informing the reader of relevant authorities and doctrinal opinions from the literature produced by the Italian method.[28] The success of Bohier's *Decisiones Burdegalenses* is evident from the number of editions published, and its last known printing was in 1665, almost a century after the author's death.

(1.2) *Consilia* (1554)

The earliest known edition of Bohier's *Consilia* was published in 1554. As a source, the *consilia* have been overlooked in legal-historical scholarship, and have seldom been used with any frequency. In his work on Baldus' *consilia*, Jacques Pluss referred to the *consilia* as "untapped sources of inquiry for

24 First published 1544. Edition used here is 1547.

25 A Wijffels, "Early Modern Scholarship on International Law", in A Orakhelashvilli (ed), *Research Handbook on the Theory and History of International Law* (2011) 32.

26 Wijffels (n 25) 32.

27 D Freda, "'Law reporting' in Europe in the early-modern period: two experiences in comparison" (2009) 30 *Journal of Legal History* 263.

28 Wijffels (n 25) 30.

two disciplines, legal history and social history".[29] This is partly owing to the tendency of many legal historians to look more to doctrine than to the law as practised in the courts.[30] The gradual systematisation of the court structure between the fourteenth and seventeenth centuries was just one example of the tendency towards centralisation and the idea of the state. The law, however, could not be so controlled, and so the *consilia* offered a tangible link between the regulated delivery of justice and the free opinion of a jurist; whose opinion although full of diverse sources of law, was thus contained within one document and so offered a single account of the law on a particular issue in that locality. This offer of coherence was an attractive quality of the *consilia*, and as a physical representation of the law as it stood in the early modern period, its value as a legal-historical source is considerable.

Since it, like the *Decisiones*, was published outwith Bohier's own lifetime, one might assume that he did not intend it to be published. However, despite their relative obscurity in contemporary scholarship, the *consilia* were prized publications in their day. Working a century before, but with his work still in demand in Bohier's time, Alexander de Imola achieved considerable success with his *consilia*, producing a work that was allegedly "better than those of other lawyers and superior to his Commentaries; and it was probably on these he founded his reputation".[31]Keen to release his other works for public consumption, it seems strange that Bohier did not attempt this. However, it is likely that the opinions contained within his *consilia* were written during his tenure as President of the *Parlement* at Bordeaux, and so perhaps they were withheld so as to protect his position. Those other *consilia* that have been published were often those of professional jurists, firmly ensconced within their universities, and not the practising lawyer or judge. Yet, the absence of any declaration prohibiting the publication of the *consilia*, together with Bohier's prolific working practices, it seems likely that this was something he may have intended to publish during his lifetime.

29 J A Pluss, "Reading case law historically: a *consilium* of Baldus de Ubaldis on widows and dowries" (1986) 30 *The American Journal of Legal History* 241 at 243.

30 J B Baron, "Interdisciplinary Legal Scholarship as Guilty Pleasure: the Case of Law and Literature", in M Freeman and A D E Lewis (eds), *Law and Literature: Current Legal Issues* vol 2 (1999) 21.

31 P M de Colquhoun, *A Summary of the Roman Civil Law: Illustrated by Commentaries on and Parallels from the Mosaic, Canon, Mohammedan, English, and Foreign Law* (1849) 206.

(2) Bohier: annotator and editor

To better understand Bohier's legal thought through his writings, his role as editor is as revealing as the content of his original scholarship. Bohier's best-known publications, the *Coutumes*, *Decisiones* and *Consilia*, are compilations, and, it seems, written with a practice-oriented purpose in mind. Their contents do reveal a great deal, especially by way of informing us of citation practices, and ultimately form the basis of this chapter. However, it is worth mentioning Bohier's involvement with the publications of others that he selected as noteworthy, to see what this selection can tell us about his legal thought as well as any intellectual and philosophical allegiances he may have had. Bohier's original works were not all published within his lifetime. This is in contrast to those he co-authored or edited which were all released into the public domain during his lifetime. His involvement in the compilation of the latter is therefore more certain.

It is not possible to examine each of those publications that Bohier was involved with here. Instead, his most popular work will be considered in order to identify any intellectual allegiances or professional allegiances Bohier may have had in his role as editor. Achieving success with a great number of editions, Bohier's edited publication of Dynus de Mugello's (1254–1300) works: *Commentaria in regulae iuris pontificii*[32] and *Commentarius mirabilis super titulo de regulis iuris*.[33] An Italian jurist of the thirteenth century, Dynus studied civil law at Bologna, taught at Pistoia and later also at his *alma mater* Bologna, where Cinus de Pistoia was one of his pupils.[34] He is generally believed to have been involved with the compilation of the *Liber Sextus*, on which he also later wrote a commentary.[35]

Many of Bohier's other publishing practices also deal with the canon law, such as his edition of Johannes Andreae's work. Celse-Hugues Descousu (1480–c1540) was also associated with Bohier in a range of publications.[36] Descousu edited Bohier's work on Dynus de Mugello, and a gloss by Etienne Aufreri (c1485–1511) accompanied it.[37] Etienne Aufreri was a

32 The earliest edition of this work that I have found dates from 1551. Bohier is listed as an editor on this work and subsequent editions.

33 Appended to a number of editions of the *De Regulis Iuris* compilation, reportedly first published in 1500, are two of Bohier's *Consilia* (1530 edn).

34 J Canning, *The Political Thought of Baldus de Ubaldis* (1987) 272.

35 M Ascheri, *The Law of Late Medieval Italy (1000–1500)* (2013) 297.

36 In terms of co-edited works and also those editions dedicated to Bohier, such as an edition of the *Stylus Curiae Parlamenti* (1513).

37 This edition is now rare and can be found at the *Bibliothèque municipale de Lyon* (no 126613).

conseiller at the Toulouse *Parlement* and Professor at the University there.[38] Descousu was a *docteur in utroque iuris*, and Professor at the University of Montpellier.[39] He assumed the role of editor on a number of occasions, working together with Bohier on an edition of Dynus de Mugello's work,[40] but he also wrote extensively and published a number of other books. His most notable works include the *Consilia* (published posthumously in 1570),[41] and the *Coutumes de Bourgogne* (1513, 1516).[42] Guillaume du Breuil's *Stylus Curie Parlamenti* was first published in 1330. In 1513, Simon Vincent published the most popular edition of this work in Lyon that was edited by Descousu who dedicated the work to Bohier.

Another of Bohier's edited works, Dynus's *Commentaria*, sees the involvement of Charles Du Moulin (1500–1566). Those editions bearing Du Moulin's name do not appear until after Bohier's death in 1539. It is then highly probable that Du Moulin himself used Bohier's publication to provide his own commentary. Du Moulin studied at Orléans, before becoming an *avocat* before the Paris *parlement*. He then moved to Germany to teach following the French persecution of Protestants, and later was imprisoned in Paris for writing against the Council of Trent. Peter Stein has described Du Moulin as: "the most important exponent of the customs".[43] His main work was the *Commentaria in consuetudines Parisienses* published in 1538, but his *Annotationes ad jus canonicum* (1550) are perhaps most noteworthy here. Du Moulin's position on the canon law was a complex one. His own religious affiliations changed throughout his life, and it was: "one of his points

38 P Arabeyre, J-L Halpérin and J Krynen (eds), *Dictionnaire historique des juristes français (XIIe–XXe siècle)* (2007).

39 G du Breuil, *Stylus Curiae Parlamenti, Nouvelle Edition Critique Publiée avec une introduction et des notes par Felix Aubert* [*Collection de Textes pour servir a l'étude et à l'enseignement de l'histoire*] (1909) LVI. A work discussing the writings of Johann Amberbach mentions Celse-Hugues Descousu in unfavourable terms. In the early sixteenth century it seems that an individual bearing that name was responsible for the theft of some valuable books belonging to the Amberbach family, who had welcomed Descousu into their household for food and discussion. Correspondence charging Descousu with theft and deception offer accounts of this incident. It is not known if this is the same Descousu that is under discussion here, but the dates make it possible and it is therefore an interesting note if it is the same individual. See B C Halporn (ed), *The Correspondence of Johann Amberbach: Early Printing in its Social Context* (2000) 106–110.

40 Dynus, *De regulis Iuris* (1530, 1533, 1535, 1537, 1578, 1583, 1585).

41 Bohier's *Consilia* (1554) was also published posthumously.

42 Interestingly, one of the most complete accounts of Descousu's life can be found in a publication by a "President Bouhier": *Histoire des Commentateurs de la Coutume de Duché de Bourgogne* (1742). Of course, the date reveals that this was not the work of Nicolas Bohier, but it is still worth noting this so as to avoid initial confusion. The author was in fact Jean Bouhier (1673–1746), a *Président à mortier* of the *Parlement de Bourgogne*.

43 P Stein, *Roman Law in European History* (1999) 84.

of departure as well as one of his primary targets. He attacked to plunder it as well as to demolish it. His basic objection was that the canonist standard of judgment was provided not by scripture but by the papal chancery."[44] His involvement in the *Commentaria* was of course to provide an annotated critique of the contents. The precise nature of Du Moulin's affiliation with Bohier is not known, and it is only those editions that appear post-1539 (after Bohier's death) that bear his name. There are also those editions containing notes that were attributed to Du Moulin in publications printed in Lyon that have not been appropriately cited in other copies.[45] A 1533 edition of this work contains the words "*doctorem anonymum*" in its title. This could be a reference to Du Moulin. When his name first appears in 1549 those notes that belonged to the anonymous writer were now expressly attributed to Du Moulin, with a noted absence of the anonymous contributor left out from the title page.[46]

Bohier had an editorial role in other publications such as Joannes Andreae's *Mercuriales domini* (1510). Joannes Andreae (c1275–1348) took his doctorate in canon law between 1296 and 1300 at Bologna was Professor of canon law at the same University by 1303.[47] Andreae had finished his Apparatus to the *Liber Sextus* by 1305 and it was almost automatically accepted as the *Glossa Ordinaria* on the text. Andreae was received well by contemporary canonists. Subsequent commentators on the *Liber Sextus* would use this gloss as a model, and it served as a reference book for lawyers.[48] Bohier's editorship of the 1510 edition[49] of Andreae's *Mercuriales domini* also saw the involvement of Joannes Gradibus and Charles Dumoulin. Joannes Gradibus received his *legibus baccalaureus* from Orléans (1477) and was responsible for a large range of publications including the works of Jason de Mayno, Baldus and Angelus Aretinus.[50] Robert Feenstra has recognised

44 D R Kelley, *Foundations of Modern Historical Scholarship: Language, Law and History in the French Renaissance* (1970) 174.

45 For instance, the Library of Congress collections contain a number of editions of this nature.

46 With thanks to Nathan Dorn, rare books librarian at the Library of Congress Law Library for his assistance with this, in particular the linking of the "*doctorem anonymum*" to Du Moulin.

47 E M Makowski, *Canon Law and Cloistered Women: Periculoso and its Commentators (1298–1545)* (1997) 57.

48 Makowski (n 47) 49, R H Helmholz, "The Bible in the service of the canon law" (1994) 70 *Chicago-Kent Law Review* 1557.

49 Lyon, published by Simon Vincent.

50 Gradibus's involvement can also be seen in many works of jurists at this time, including many of whom Bohier cited: Jason de Mayno, Baldus, Angelus de Aretinus, Alexander Tartagnus, Filippo Decio, to name a few. For a comprehensive list of juristic works where Gradibus was involved, see R Feenstra, "Editions Lyonnaises des *lecturae* de droit civile de Balde", in H Coing, *Ius Commune* (2000) 27, 348–350.

Gradibus' influence as an author of marginal notes and various annotations to the works he was associated with. His name from 1496 onwards often bears the title of *utriusque iuris professeur* or even *consiliarius regis*.[51]

Bohier served as editor for other canon law works: Juan de Torquemada's (c1388–1468) *Commentaria reverendi in Christo Petris* (1519)[52] and *Commentaria super toto decreto* (1519)[53], and Benedetto Barzi's (1350–1410) *Lectura* (1517)[54]. His only editorial work that is not of a canon law nature is his publication of the *Leges Longobardorum* (1512).[55] The fact that nearly all of his editorial works deal with the canon law goes beyond any anecdotal curiosity he may have in relation to Dynus de Mugello. Instead, this is a clear indication that Bohier was acutely interested in the canon law as something worthy of editing and of contemporary commentary. The publication of these works falls within a twenty-year period: the first being in 1500 and the last in 1519. For much of this time, Bohier was a member of the *Grand Conseil*. His original works come later when he is President of the *Bordeaux Parlement*, with the exception of the *Coutumes Biturigium* (1509). It is possible that his position as *conseiller* meant he felt it more appropriate to edit rather than create works that reflected on the practice and operation of the *parlement*. His later works, the *Decisiones* and *Consilia* were most likely compiled while President of the *Parlement*, and are practical works that relate to the decisions of that institution. A notable exception is his collaborative work with Jean Montaigne, *Tracatus Celebris de Auctoritate* (1512). However, it is important to recognise that this work saw Bohier promote and defend the unique position of power that the *Grand Conseil* and its *conseillers* had, and so this is likely to have been tactical.[56]

In terms of his preference for those works of canon law, it is possible that this preference was rooted in a desire to reflect the practical reality of legal practice. The Paris *Parlement*, for example, saw a high number of appeals to its chambers. A sample of appeals heard at the *Parlement* demonstrates that a significant number of these were of a religious nature.[57] It is possible that Bohier was simply wishing to recognise this and provide contemporary editions for reference.

51 Feenstra (n 50) 347.
52 Lyon, published by Simon Vincent.
53 Lyon, published by Simon Vincent.
54 Lyon, co-editor Jean Thierry.
55 Lyon, published by Simon Vincent.
56 See n 97, *Tracatus celebris*, fol 28, 39–40.
57 Série U//419 *Arrêts notables du Parlement de Paris, notes de jurisprudence, consultations, principalement en matière ecclésiastique*, Archives Nationales de Paris.

D. THE *CONSILIA*

The *consilia* have been largely overlooked in legal-historical scholarship.[58] In his work on Baldus' *consilia*, Jacques Pluss referred to the *consilia* as "untapped sources of inquiry for two disciplines, legal history and social history".[59] This is partly owing to the tendency of many legal historians to look more to doctrine than to the law as practised in the courts.[60] *Consilia* reveal the meeting of legal theory and legal practice and show how aspects of medieval Roman law doctrine were applied to the circumstances of a particular case. However, this focus has not moved adequately to the early modern versions, particularly those that were issued in France during the sixteenth century. If the *consilia* have proven illuminating for those investigating the medieval jurists, it stands to reason that the later examples will be similar in their richness.

These later *consilia* enable not only an understanding of the specific law discussed within them, but the meaning of the term *ius commune*, through the citations used by the early modern jurists, and so are deserving of study. The original neglect of the *consilia* as a source of interest can be attributed to two main reasons: a belief that their contents are partisan and so are unreliable as accounts of the law at the time; and, in a practical sense, they are not always easy to work with.[61] This distrust and difficulty is only heightened in the case of the sixteenth-century product, when they were characterised as having increased verbosity. Printed editions of *consilia* also could present problems as a result of the imprecision of typesetters who were not trained in law or who possessed little grasp of the meaning of the texts. Further, such editions could also omit important details that would clarify a text, such as background information on the case.[62]

The sixteenth century was marked by an increased move towards centralisation and the systemisation of the court structure is an example of this. The law, however, was not as controlled and so the value of the *consilia* is clear. Marked by its diverse sources of law, it served to contain them and present

58 Their value has, however, been better realised since the 1990s, with a number of works dealing exclusively with *consilia*: a notable example being Guido Rossi's *Consilium Sapientis Iudiciale*, and the collaborative work, *Legal Consulting in the Civil Law Tradition*, with contributions from Mario Ascheri and Julius Kirshner among others. These studies have tapped into the rich legal and socio-historical resource that is the Italian medieval *consilia*.

59 Pluss (n 29) 241 at 243.

60 Baron (n 30) 33.

61 T Dean, *Crime and Justice in Late Medieval Italy* (2007) 96.

62 Pluss (n 29) 241 at 249.

a single statement of the law on a specific matter in a particular location.[63] The *consilia* as a source offered coherence and a statement of the law as it stood at the time, and also what it can tell us about the kinds of sources used by the author in supporting his arguments. Of course, it is not possible to state with any certainty whether the author physically consulted all cited sources.

Nicolas Bohier's *consilia*[64] offers us many examples of the type of legal reasoning he employed, in particular his handling of competing sources of law. Tammo Wallinga's summary of the *consilia* demonstrates its value as a source in this regard:

> In the *consilia*, the difficult mixture of local statutes and customs is tackled through the techniques of interpretation and argumentation of the Roman lawyers.[65]

Furthermore, it is possible to identify those authorities that Bohier attributed individual points to, or indeed argued against. Such references demonstrate who and what sources Bohier deemed authoritative. Looking to whom and what Bohier cites in his attempts to define *stylus* and custom enable an assessment of possible motivations behind his selection of authorities. In considering the nature of the citations, a few key issues need to be considered. First, it is necessary to ascertain whether there was one main source or set of sources referred to by Bohier. The sources referred to by those jurists in their own works will be noted. The nature of the citations will then be considered, with particular regard to the way in which Bohier referred to these sources and whether any particular motivations for citation can be identified. Then, a concluding assessment of the pattern of citation will be made. Once this has been settled, it is hoped that it will be possible to establish whether the notion of the *ius commune* was doctrinal, or whether traditional accounts of its meaning were right to view it as a loose and abstract body of legal knowledge.[66]

Bohier's *Consilia* contains four cases that deal with the *ius commune*. Of these, two relate to canon-law matters, including an appeal to an arch-

63 For an interesting account of the link between the idea of citizenship and the *consilia*, see P Riesenberg, "Citizenship at Law in Late and Medieval Italy", in *Viator: Mediaeval and Renaissance Studies* vol 5 (1974), 333.

64 I am using the 1554 (Lyon) edition. Digitised version available online via Bavarian State Library.

65 T Wallinga, "The common history of European legal scholarship" (2011) 4 *Erasmus Law Review* 5 at 10.

66 See N Jansen, *The Making of Legal Authority: Non-legislative Codifications in Historical and Comparative Perspective* (2010) 29. And on this matter, see extensively Van Ittersum elsewhere in this volume.

bishop[67] and the age of sub-deacons;[68] and the remaining pair dealt with usufruct[69] and women in private and community offices.[70] Despite containing the fewest number of mentions of the *ius commune*, it contains the case of *consilia* 8, which, it is contended, is of the utmost importance. This particular case considers the authority of and relationship between *stylus*, custom and the *ius commune*. The facts of the case relate to an issue emanating from the canon law; where a judge has condemned an individual in expenses contrary to the *stylus* of a court, and the question of appeal to the archbishop is raised.[71] Recently, Paul du Plessis considered the importance of this case, referring to it as: "a rather important record of the *ius commune* in action".[72] He stressed the need for further study into the relationship between the *ius commune* and the *ius proprium*,[73] and it is hoped that this present work can build upon his findings. The aim is to further demonstrate the value of *consilia* 8, but with an emphasis on the authors and kinds of works cited by Bohier in order to better understand his legal reasoning and the role of the *ius commune* in his decision-making.

This study will consider what are deemed to be the key arguments made by Bohier in *consilia* 8 and have been categorised as follows: a definition of both *stylus* and custom; the essential differences between *stylus* and custom; and the relationship between *stylus*, custom and the *ius commune*. It is hoped that this structure will enable a clear consideration of Bohier's reasoning and his citations. Efforts to identify the date on which printing privilege was granted for Bohier's *consilia* have so far proven fruitless, and the earliest known edition is 1554, some five years after Bohier's death.[74] It is therefore this edition that is being used for the present study.

(1) Defining *stylus* and custom

Bohier's introduction to *stylus* and *consuetudo* rest on provisions in the Codex and Digest: C.8.52.1–2 and D.1.3.32pr-1 respectively. It will be

67 *Cons* 8.19.
68 *Cons* 26.17.
69 *Cons* 46.9.
70 *Cons* 40.125.
71 *Cons* 8, Introduction.
72 P J du Plessis, "A dialogue between legal theory and legal practice – thoughts from the *ius commune*" (2013) 77 *Rabels Zeitschrift* 279 at 386.
73 Ibid at 387.
74 This is the earliest known record found in library catalogues, including La Bibliothèque nationale de France and the Library of Congress, Washington DC. With thanks to Nathan Dorn, curator of rare books in the Library of Congress, Law Library for his assistance in confirming this.

helpful for the discussion to briefly consider these provisions first. C.8.52.1 states that:

> . . . since both the existing custom and the *ratio* (reason) which backed it must be conserved, and the provincial governor must make it his business to see that nothing is done contrary to such ancient custom.[75]

This is followed at C.8.52.2 by a statement establishing limits to legal arguments from custom; essentially that the authority of custom and long-standing usage cannot prevail over reason or statute (*lex*).[76]

D.1.3.32pr opens with a statement that provides in those cases where written statute (*lex*) is lacking, customs (*consuetudines*) and usage (*mos*) ought to be held; but that if what is established by these customs is deficient, then one ought to reason out analogously from these customs; if this reasoning fails then the *ius* that is used in the city of Rome should be applied.[77] The text at D.1.3.32 tries to justify the recourse to custom where statute is lacking on the grounds that the two can be considered as analogous.[78]

Bohier begins his *consilia* by referring to the belief that *stylus*, *consuetudo*, *mos* and *communis observantia* are of the same meaning.[79] Citing evidence for this general position, Bohier draws sources mainly from the doctrinal tradition of the Italian method. However, he quickly challenges this statement of mutuality, and it is worth looking at who he has cited to represent his argument. The selection could be termed a conventional one, including late-medievalists: Petrus de Bellapertica, Cinus de Pistoia, Joannes Faber, Angelus de Perusio, Angelus de Aretino and Bartolus. It is widely known that later medieval Glossators and Commentators looked to D.1.3.32 in

75 (Alexander to Aper, veteran): *nam et consuetudo praecedens et ratio quae consuetudinem suasit custodienda est, et ne quid contra longam consuetudinem fiat, ad sollicitudinem suam revocabit praeses provinciae* (a. 224).

76 (Constantine to Proculus (proconsul Africae)): *Consuetudinis ususque longaevi non vilis auctoritas est, verum non usque adeo sui valitura momento, ut aut rationem vincat aut legem* (a. 319).

77 (Julian, Digest book 84): *De quibus causis scriptis legibus non utimur, id custodiri oportet, quod moribus et consuetudine inductum est: et si qua in re hoc deficeret, tunc quod proximum et consequens ei est: si nec id quidem appareat, tunc ius, quo urbs Roma utitur, servari oportet.* See C Humfress, "Law and Custom Under Rome", in A Rio (ed), *Law, Custom and Justice in Late Antiquity and the Early Middle Ages* (2011) 23 at 27.

78 "For since statutes themselves are only binding because they have been accepted by the judgment of the people, those things which the people have approved without any writing at all will be rightly considered as binding on everyone; what difference does it make whether the people declares its will by vote, or by acts or conducts themselves?" Translation from Humfress (n 77) 28. Original text reads: (Julian, Digest book 84): . . . *nam cum ipsae leges nulla alia ex causa nos teneant, quam quod iudicio populi receptae sunt, merito et ea, quae sine ullo scripto populus probavit, tenebunt omnes* . . .

79 *Cons* 8, pr-1. See du Plessis' account of this.

particular as representing an authoritative and potentially definitive account of the concept of custom.[80] Caroline Humfress in considering the second-century context of the provision suggests that it ought to be approached as "a dynamic, problem-solving text – oriented ultimately towards resolving specific difficulties of legal interpretation that arose during Roman law's expansion from city-state to empire."[81]

With this in mind, let us continue by considering the sixteenth-century use of the provision and its medieval commentaries as cited by Bohier in his *Consilia*.

(1.1) *Stylus quid?*

From the outset of his *consilia*, Bohier offers this description of *stylus*:[82]

. . . est ius non scriptum, ab uno iudice saepius circa sententias & acta iudiciaria introductum sive stylatum . . .	It is unwritten law, often introduced or styled by one judge in relation to [his] decisions and judicial acts . . .

It is worth considering whether Bohier had a particular *stylus* in mind when writing this account. Later in this *consilia*, he makes specific reference to the *stylus Bituricensis* and *stylus de Brolio*.[83] Since the case at hand originated from the canon law, and had been sent to the Bordeaux *Parlement* as a matter of appeal, the *stylus* referred to would be for the ecclesiastical court. It is possible that the particular *stylus Bituricensis* Bohier mentions is the *Stilus Ecclesiasticae jurisdictionis archiepiscopalis primatialis atque patriarchalis Bituricencis*, by Franciscus de Turnone,[84] Archbishop of Bordeaux from 1525 until 1537.[85] It cannot be stated with any accuracy, however, as,

80 M Ryan, "Bartolus of Sassoferrato and Free Cities", *Transactions of the Royal Historical Society* vol 10 (2000) 65 at 67. See also J Hudson, "Customs, Laws and the Interpretation of Mediaeval Law", in P Andersen and M Münster-Swendsen (eds), *Custom: The Development and Use of a Legal Concept in the Middle Ages* (2009) 1–16.

81 Humfress (n 77) at 29. Humfress continues by considering that the very inclusion of ten juristic extracts relating to custom by the Justinianic Digest commissioners perhaps suggests that they too understood how certain juristic arguments "from custom" related specifically to the interpretation (and supplementation) of Roman statute.

82 *Cons* 8, par 2. Thanks to Paul J du Plessis for this translation.

83 *Cons* 8, par 11: "Sed si stylus esset redactus in scriptis, ut est noster stylus Biturice sicut etiam stylus de Brolio in Curia seculari, tunc esset statutum . . ."

84 Francis de Turnone, (1529). Better known examples (but later) include Jean Chenu's *Stylus jurisdictionis ecclesiasticae archiepiscopalis primat et concilio Provinciali in Metropolitana Biturigum civitate habito* (1603). See reference to both Turnone and Chenu: *Catalogue des livres composant la Bibliothèque de la ville de Bordeaux* (1834) 316 at "Chenu" and "Turnone" respectively. Chenu's other notable works include *Recueil de Règlemens Notables* (1614).

85 Jean Chenu documented the successive Archbishops of Bordeaux in his *Archiepiscoporum et episcoporum Galliae Chronologica historia,* (1621): Turnone is listed at p 324.

although Bohier was President of the *Parlement* of Bordeaux at this time,[86] the first edition known of his *consilia* was published only in 1544, meaning the date of the legal opinions contained within it are approximated.[87] In any sense, the case under consideration offers an interesting insight into the role of *stylus* and the relationship between canon and civil judges and the authority of their judgments.

(1.2) *Consilia quid?*

For Bohier, the defining quality of *consuetudo* lies in the nature of its introduction:[88]

Sicut est consuetudo quae tacita voluntate et usu plurium inducitur, [quia] populi vel maioris eiusdem.	Thus *consuetudo* is that which has been introduced through tacit consent and the frequent use of the populace or the larger part of the populace.

Later in the same part of his *consilia*, he continues:

consuetudo tam ex actibus iudiciariis, quam extra iudiciariis interveniente populi consensus, et sic est usus communis . . .	Custom, introduced both through judicial acts and through extra-judicial acts, is the consent of the people, and so it is common usage . . .

This distinction between introduction through popular consent for custom and that of *stylus*'s creation formed the basis of Bohier's rejection to the idea of a shared definition for these sources of law. He was clearly of the opinion that *stylus* and custom were to be understood as two different sources of law because their origins were equally so.

(2) Bohier's citations

To what extent did Bohier take account of the sources he cited? It is clear that he made reference to a number of jurists and their works, and inferences can be made from his citation practices certainly. However, the value of such assessments really rests in the way in which Bohier interacted with the sources he mentions in the text. It needs to be considered whether he

86 Appointed as President of Bordeaux Parlement in 1518 and remained in office until his death in 1539. *Archives Historique du Departement de la Gironde*, available at: *http://archives.gironde.fr/actu/fiche.aso?id_actu=60*.

87 The earliest holding in the Library of Congress is 1554. This particular edition is bound with (preceded by) *Decisiones Burdegalenses* (Lyon 1544).

88 Translation from du Plessis (n 72) 383.

referred to the sources directly; whether they were borrowed; and whether there are any identifiable patterns in the sources he cites in terms of author, geographical origin and type of text (compare Van Ittersum elsewhere in this volume). Further, it is necessary to assess how crucial a role these sources played in Bohier's arguments. By adopting this approach to the juristic references made by the lawyer in his *Consilia*, it is hoped that those occasions where particular points of law were accompanied by a practice of habitual referencing of a particular individual or work will be made clear.

(2.1) Belleperche and Cinus

Bohier begins by citing Pierre de Belleperche and Cinus de Pistoia. Belleperche (Petrus de Bellapertica, d1308)[89] was born at Lucenay, in Bourbon. A student of Jacques Révigny (Jacob de Ravanais d1296),[90] Belleperche had an illustrious career as professor at Toulouse and Orléans, Bishop of Auxerre, and Chancellor of France to King Philip IV for a period.[91] He published a range of works, including commentaries on the Codex, Institutes and *Repetitiones* on the Digest, although Bezemer has contended that his reputation is not as celebrated as it should be, due to "the bad luck of being the Orléans second man, like a junior partner who appears in the slipstream of his senior".[92] Bezemer is referring to Jacques Révigny here as the so-called "senior".

The role of Cinus de Pistoia in Bohier's citations will be examined in greater detail later. For now, however, it is worth noting that the majority of occasions where Belleperche is cited (four times), he is referred to together with Cinus de Pistoia as "*Petric.de Bella Pertic.& Cyn*" or "*Petr.& Cyn.*"; and, incidentally, does not appear to have been cited without Cinus' name alongside his own.[93] Belleperche's commentary on the Codex was widely deemed accessible through Cinus' printed commentary on the same.[94] According to

89 Colquhoun (n 31) 188.
90 Kees Bezemer has remarked that historically (in the 1950s) there has been some confusion over the works of Bélleperche and Révigny; with a lecture on the Codex by Révigny being wrongly classed as belonging to Belleperche. See K Bezemer, *Pierre de Belleperche: Portrait of a Legal Puritan* (2005) 3.
91 J Black, *Absolutism in Renaissance Milan: Plenitude of Power under the Visconti and the Sforza: 1329–1535* (2009) 34.
92 Bezemer (n 90) 5.
93 It is acknowledged that this is a common way of referencing the two.
94 E M Meijers, *Études d'histoire du droit, publiées par R Feenstra et H F W D Fischer Tome III: Le droit romain au Moyen Age. Première Partie: L'enseignement du droit dans trois universités du XIIIe siècle; Histoire des sources* (1959) 120–121.

Bezemer, this is how many would access Belleperche's work, although Cinus' picture of the jurist is: "incomplete, at times even distorted".[95] Perhaps Bohier did too. It is possible that he was viewing the thoughts of Belleperche through that written by Cinus, especially because of the latter's reputation for almost literally reproducing his sources.[96] However thorough Cinus was in his citation, his caution at the start of his *lectura* on the *Codex* reminds us, and Bohier, the perils of such citation borrowing:[97]

Quia omnia nova placent potissime quae sunt utilitate decora: bellissime visum est mihi Cyno Pistoriensi, propter novitates modernorum doctorum super Codice breviter utilia scribere: multis superfluis resecatis	because new things are appreciated most if usefulness is their virtue, it seemed best to me, Cinus of Pistoia, as for the novelties of modern doctors of the Code, to write briefly about such things, leaving out much that is superfluous.

Bezemer urges that this cautionary tale be taken seriously, and it is worth keeping this in mind when referring to Cinus' commentary for the purposes of understanding Bohier's *consilia*.

Bohier cited Cinus often in his *consilia*: four times alongside Belleperche, and separately in two other instances.[98] Joseph Canning referred to Cinus as the "interpreter for Italy" of the early French Commentators, Belleperche and Révigny.[99] A jurist (and poet),[100] Cinus studied law at the University of Bologna for around eight years (until 1300),[101] under Dynus de Mugello, and taught at the Universities of Siena, Florence, Perugia and Naples. His most famous student is Bartolus, whom he taught at Perugia.[102] Bellomo alludes to the jurist's aversion to the *ius proprium*, which he saw as "normally iniquitous and the product of thieves and sharpers".[103] For Cinus, the *ius proprium* was an unsettled and changeable law and the *ius commune* always superior: his view of the so-called system of the *ius commune* unified by the central problem of *aequitas*.[104] Cinus was deeply influenced by the approach

95 Bezemer (n 90) 5. See also Meijers (n 94) 99, 102, 120, and D Maffei, *La "Lectura Super Digesto veteri" di Cino de Pistoia* (1963) 49.
96 Bezemer (n 90) 7.
97 Cinus de Pistoia, at the rubric of C.1.1 (1578).
98 Cited solo in *Cons* 8, par 12, 21.
99 Canning (n 34) 24.
100 Interestingly, he enjoyed a close friendship with fellow Tuscan poet, Dante. On this, see R Hollander, "Dante and Cino da Pistoia" (1992) 110 *Dante Studies* 201.
101 Such was the length of time mandated for a course of this kind, by a statute of 1252.
102 J MacDonell and E Manson (eds), *Great Jurists of the World* vol 1 (1914) 65.
103 M Bellomo, *The Common Legal Past of Europe: 1000–1800* (1995) 189.
104 Bellomo (n 103) 189. On the topic of *aequitas* in the related issue of Milanese absolutism and its sense of the law, see Black (n 91) 191.

of the Orléans school, and his *Lectura in Codicem* was permeated with their ideas.[105]

Bohier cites Cinus' (together with Pierre de Belleperche) commentary on C.8.52.2.[106] Th citation appears to be accurate, with the passage cited in the commentary discussing the origins of custom belonging to popular tacit consent. Most importantly, perhaps, is the express mention and discussion on the topic of *stylus* and how it differs from custom:[107]

stilus est ius quoddam non scriptum usibus introductum ab uno iudice stillatum . . . consuetudo est ius introductus usibus plurium ut a populo . . .	*Stylus* is unwritten law that is introduced by a single judge . . . custom is introduced by the use of many as though a populace . . .

Clearly, Bohier relied on this part of Cinus' commentary. In the first half of this discussion, Cinus refers to the relationship between a secular court and an ecclesiastical *stylus*,[108] very similar to the case in Bohier's *consilia*. Cinus cites Belleperche as authority for the above statements, and it is safe to assume that Bohier did in fact refer to Cinus' *Lectura super Codice* in order to discover Belleperche's opinion on the matter.

(2.2) Angelus de Perusio

Angelus de Perusio (or Ubaldis, 1384–94) is cited alongside Faure and Aretinus with reference to Inst.1.2.9. However, no commentary on the Institutes appears to have been written by Angelus, or at least not one that has survived.[109] Since the 1554 edition of Bohier's *consilia* is the earliest one currently known of or is accessible at least, it is not currently possible to see if this was something that was erroneously printed or omitted by way of comparison with an earlier edition. Indeed, it is likely that this particular edition was in fact the earliest one printed and so all were printed after his death. Assuming so, then this citation is inaccurate, at least in the sense of a direct reference to Angelus' commentary on this part of the Institutes. Instead, it must be referring to the commentary of another jurist who has cited Angelus as authority for the issue at hand, that of the nature of *stylus* and custom.

On the matter of custom, interestingly, reference to Angelus' *super*

105 Black (n 91) 14.

106 Cinus de Pistoia, *Lectura super Codice* (1493).

107 Cinus, *Lectura super Codice* (n 106) note 4.

108 Cinus, *Lectura super Codice* (n 106) note 3: "in curia seculari . . . in ecclesiastica consuetudine usum stilu . . . nec sunt iura scriptu qualiter ista differat inter se".

109 Canning (n 34) 272.

Codice[110] reveals that he did not deal with this topic there either; consideration of *quae sit longa consuetudo* is missed out of his commentary. In such instances, there is normally reference to an alternative work where the issue has already been dealt with in detail, but the edition referred to does not appear to offer this referral. While Angelus did consider this particular section of the Codex in his own *consilia*,[111] it seems even more likely that Bohier was not referring to another work and it was simply erroneously cited, but rather that he read this citation through the work of another.

(2.3) Angelus de Aretinus

Together with Faure and Angelus de Perusio, Aretinus is cited. Aretinus' commentary on the Institutes does reveal a discussion of "*Stylus quid sit, & in quo differat a consuetudine*".[112] Here he makes reference to Cinus and Belleperche's commentary on C.8.52.2 as to the nature of *stylus* and custom and their differences rooted in the issue of consent.[113] Bohier made this citation too. Aretinus' summary of Cinus and Belleperche's opinion bears similarity to that offered by Bohier in his own summary of legal opinion on the matter, but is not a literal reproduction of its wording.

In discussing an earlier question, "*consuetudo quid sit*", Aretinus can be seen citing Bartolus' commentary on *de quibus* (D.1.3.32).[114] Angelus de Perusio is also mentioned. Faure is not cited by Aretinus so although Bohier could have referred to Aretinus for his position on the issue at hand, he would not have been able to use this commentary to take Faure's position. There is of course the possibility that Bohier's familiarity with Faure, given the Montpellier connection alluded to earlier, and his innate knowledge of customary law given his *Consuetudines Biturigum* (which, depending on the date the *consilia* was first written, will have either existed or been being compiled),[115] meant that Bohier would have been well acquainted with Faure's position and so was making a general allusion to his stance on the issue. However, the physical appearance of the citation ("*Ioa.Fab. Angel. de Peru. & Aret.*") suggests it was a deliberate grouping by Bohier that is referring to a citation made elsewhere that includes all three as mentioned.

110 *super Codice* (1490).

111 Most notable being his treatment of *consuetudo* and statute at *cons* 63 in his *Consilia* (1575).

112 Angelus de Aretinus, *In quattuor Institutionum Justiniani libros commentarii* (Lyon) note 6.

113 Aretinus, "*Pet. & Cy. in l.2 C. q. sit lon. Consue.*" (note 6).

114 Aretinus (note 4).

115 Royal privilege was granted for the *Consuetudines Biturigum* in 1509. See E Armstrong, *Before Copyright: The French Book Privilege System, 1498–1526* (2002) 210.

(2.4) Jean Faure

One of Bohier's non-Italian authorities,[116] Jean Faure (Johannes Faber, d1350), is a prominent figure in this *consilia*. Born in Angoulême, Faure was active in legal practice, like Bohier, and turned his hand to writing commentaries, most notably his work on the Institutes.[117] Since Faure taught at Montpellier, where Bohier himself was educated; it has been suggested that these affiliations would have translated into a particular familiarity with his works.[118] At one point in his *consilia*, it is made especially clear that Bohier holds this jurist in high regard, referring to him as the representative voice on a point of law "in Francia".[119] Faure was educated at Orléans, which, in contrast to the school at Bologna, was traditionally characterised by its critical approach to the *Glossa Ordinaria* of Accursius.[120] It seems that Bohier drew from the alumni of this university for his citations in the *consilia*: the most notable, aside from Faure, being Belleperche and Gullielmus de Cuneo.[121] As a jurist of the *ultramontani*, Faure tried to "impart to the customary institutions and political organisations of the time a new vigour and vitality by engrafting therein principles of Roman law."[122] Unsurprisingly, then, his works had a typically practical character.

Bohier cites Faure on some five occasions in this *consilium*.[123] In providing a definition of custom and *stylus*, Bohier refers to "*Ioa.Fab [Angel.de Peru. & Aret.] in d. ex non scripto*". Here he is referring to Inst.1.2.9, *De iure naturali, gentium et civili*. Because of an earlier citation to Faure's work, we know Bohier is citing his *Super Instituta*.[124] A number of editions of this work were published.

116 The other being Petrus de Bellapertica; born in Paris and Professor at Orléans.

117 Colquhoun (n 31) 188. Colquhoun describes Faber's commentary on the Codex as being "remarkable in its terseness" and hostile to those French jurists who at the time were writing in French.

118 Du Plessis (n 72) 383.

119 *Cons* 8, par 18.

120 On Orléans, see K Bezemer, "The School of Orleans as School of Public Administration" (1998) 66 *The Legal History Review* 247–277, and for the education of the legal profession in medieval Europe more generally J A Brundage, *The Medieval Origins of the Legal Profession: Canonists, Civilians and Courts* (2008) 267–348.

121 The most notable is arguably Jacques de Revigny (d1296). There does not appear to be any reference to him in Bohier's *consilia* 8. For an interesting account on Jacques de Revigny, see K Bezemer, *What Jacques Saw: Thirteenth Century France through the Eyes of Jacques de Revigny, Professor of Law at Orleans* (1997).

122 C Phillipson, "The Great Jurists of the World: XVI. Jacques Cujas" (1912) 13 *Journal of the Society of Comparative Legislation* 87 at 88.

123 Bohier, *cons* 8, par 1, 2, 12, 13 and 18.

124 At *cons* 8, *par* 1: "*Ioa. Fab. in ex non scripto. & Ang. Are. ibi Instit. de iure natu. gen. & civi.*"

Faure deals with custom in considerable detail, offering a structured commentary on the matter, divided into six parts:

Primo, circa nomen. Secundo, circa diffinitionem. Tertio, circa introducendi modum. Quarto, circa modum agendi. Quinto, circa modum probandi. Sexto, circa vires.	First, concerning the name. Second, concerning the definition. Third, concerning the mode of introduction. Fourth, concerning the nature of its operation. Fifth, concerning the mode of proof. Sixth, concerning its powers.

If Bohier directly consulted Faure, it is likely that he would have paid the most attention to Faure's first two points. While the second part of Faure's discussion is specifically on defining custom, it is in the first part of his commentary on "*ex non scripto*" that we find a statement on *stylus* and on statute. It is worth noting Faure's provision of two different descriptions for *stylus* and statute, clearly drawing a distinction between the two, something we also see in his commentary on C.8.52.1 in his *Super Codice*.[125] He outlines his position thus:

> *Item differt stylo: quia stylus, proprie dicitur circa illa quae tangent modum ordinandi acta, & sententias, & alias quae scribitur a stylo, quo scribitur, & facit . . . Item differt a statuto: quia illud expresso consensus introducitur, consuetudo tacito . . .*

He cites a range of passages from the Codex and Digest in support of his statement.[126] It is possible that Bohier would have consulted the 1523 edition of the commentary, published in Lyon. The work was edited by Joannes Gradibus, who received his *legum baccalaureus* from Orléans (1477) and was responsible for a range of publications including the works of Jason de Mayno, Baldus and Angelus Aretinus.[127] As mentioned before, Robert

125 Faure's *Super Codice*. Bohier uses Faure's definition of *stylus* as evidence of its origins and form: a product of judicial proceedings. In Faure's commentary on C.8.52.1, he provides this definition of stylus: "stylus 'proprie' est usus circa modum scribendi in iudicio acta, sententias & caetera que possunt modum ordinandi . . ." (Properly speaking *stylus* is the manner of writing used in court decisions, sentences, and other things that can be ordered . . .). He goes on to mention *statuta*, and makes a point of differentiating between it and *stylus*, and their differences with custom: for *statuta*, it is introduced by express consent and custom is introduced tacitly. He is keen to demarcate *stylus* and *statuta* here. As authority for his statement, Faber only makes reference to other parts of the Codex and the Digest, but generally, the commentary on *quae sit longa consuetudo* cites Azo and the Italian canonist, Hostiensis.

126 R Feenstra, "Editions lyonnaises des *lecturae* de droit civile de Balde par Jean de Gradibus, avec un aperçu des autres editions du XVIe siècle" (2000) 27 *Ius Commune* 347.

127 Ibid. Gradibus' involvement can also be seen in many works of jurists at this time, including many of whom Bohier cited: Jason de Mayno, Baldus, Angelus de Aretinus, Alexander Tartagnus, Filippo Decio, to name a few. For a comprehensive list of juristic works where Gradibus was involved, see Feenstra's work noted here at 348–350.

Feenstra has recognised Gradibus' influence as an author of marginal notes and various annotations to the works he was associated with. His name from 1496 onwards often bears the title of *utriusque iuris professeur* or even *consiliarius regis*, and he is referred to in the latter sense in his edition of Faure's commentary.[128]

In the annotations to Faure's work, there is reference to Aretinus, Angelus de Perusio and Cinus and Belleperche. Of course, this shared set of authorities does not necessarily mean that Bohier looked to this and simply copied the citations. For Cinus and Belleperche we know that this is unlikely to have been the case, given his reference to a specific part of the commentary there that is not replicated in the notes in Faure's work. The summary contained in the annotations to Faure's work is in fact very similar to that offered by Bohier on the difference between *stylus* and custom. This is also seen in Aretinus' commentary, but in the body of the text. Is it possible that Bohier referred to the annotations in Faure's work, and these had originally relied on Aretinus' commentary? It would explain why Bohier refers to Angelus in relation to Inst.1.2.9: he was not referring to the jurist's commentary on this part of the Institutes, but rather the citation of Angelus in another's work on it.

This link could be dismissed as overly tenuous, but it is nonetheless a possibility. Of course, it is also possible that Bohier relied on Aretinus for his summary and his citation. Indeed, Aretinus is the only one of the jurists cited in this particular part of Bohier's discussion that cites Bartolus' commentary on *de quibus*; a citation shared by Bohier.[129] However, Bartolus' work on the matter was of course widely known already and he was not cited in a collective fashion like the other jurists were. Also, this does not fully explain the citation's grouping with Faure (who is not mentioned by Aretinus here),[130] and also the striking similarity in the wording of the annotation and of Bohier's own summary is hard to dismiss. It should of course be mentioned here that this theory is somewhat dependent upon Bohier's reference to an edition of Faure's work, which at present cannot be verified.

(2.5) Bartolus de Saxoferrato

Bohier makes reference to Bartolus' commentary on D.1.3.32. This particular section of the Digest stated that:

128 Feenstra (n 126) 347.
129 Aretinus (note 4).
130 An alternative explanation has been offered above in the discussion on Aretinus.

> what ought to be held in those cases where we have no applicable written law is the practice established by customs and usage.[131]

Bartolus de Saxoferrato (d1357) offered the sixteenth-century jurist a concise synthesis of his predecessors' legal opinions. While a characteristic of commentaries generally, Bartolus' approach has been acclaimed as more accessible than others of its time.[132] Bartolus' appeal for this particular *consilia* was in his treatment of the conflict of laws. Bohier is referring to him in this instance as authority for the nature of *stylus* and its introduction through judicial acts.[133] It is possible to interpret this citation as a bid by Bohier to demarcate *stylus* and custom, by using the issue of consent. Bartolus saw that in law-making consent was paramount and could override the will of a superior force. He argued that customary law and statute shared a consensual under-pinning that was rooted in the consent of the people, the former tacit and the latter express, and so did not require superior consent for their authority.[134]

Perhaps Bohier is referring to Bartolus to demonstrate the difference between a law introduced by a single judge and a statute, the latter being expressly approved by the people. In using this opinion, Bohier would have been drawing a distinction between *stylus* and statute, echoing Faure's view, as outlined above.[135] Bohier is stating that *stylus* is neither statute nor custom; referring to Bartolus' legal reasoning to try and demonstrate that *stylus'* nature is not rooted in the same sense of consent, although Bartolus himself does not make specific reference to a *stylus*. It is also likely that Bohier was citing Bartolus as an authoritative statement as to the nature of custom generally. Given that he found a definition akin to his own in Belleperche and Cinus,[136] Bartolus' direct and lengthy consideration of custom and popular consent would have served well as a powerful definition of custom as a source of law. Further, Aretinus' reliance on Bartolus' commentary on *de quibus* was recognised above.[137] Perhaps Bohier was citing Bartolus in a routine sense, one rooted in an awareness of the citation practices of other jurists he deemed authoritative.

131 D.1.3.32 (Watson translation).
132 N E Hatzimihail, "Bartolus and the conflict of laws" (2007) 60 *Revue Hellénique de Droit International* 12.
133 Du Plessis (n 72) 384.
134 Canning (n 34) 96.
135 *Supra* (n 69).
136 *Supra* (n 106).
137 *Supra* (n 112).

Ulrike Müssig has stated that the concept of the nation (of France) was linked to the self-confidence of the parliamentary jurist.[138] This suggests a certain freedom for the jurist who is writing in the context of legal practice. In terms of the law, the sixteenth century has long been characterised by its detachment from the preceding centuries' methods and intellectual approaches to legal sources, namely through the influence of legal humanism. J A Clarence Smith considered the role of Bartolus in sixteenth-century legal writing. He contended that so-called devotees of "pure" Roman law displaced the "Bartolists" in the sixteenth century. He stated:

> "purity" involved the rejection of such concessions to contemporary practice, whether contrary or complementary, as had been operated by the more practical Bartolists. "Pure" Roman law, however, knows nothing directly of the Conflict of Laws; and since this conflict is a fact of life which will not go away by dint of not being thought about, the structure of the rules founded on Bartolo continued to fill the gap.[139]

The so-called gap-filling quality of Bartolus is not convincing. If Bohier is referring to Bartolus in order to handle the competition of laws and to remedy their conflicts, then the reference suggests reliance and it is in this interaction that we see the true definitions of *stylus*, custom, and ultimately of the *ius commune*. Legal humanism, the movement that is so closely tied to sixteenth-century France, did alter the way in which jurists approached Roman law sources, but this is not being debated here. Rather, it is the idea that the value of those sources that had characterised the law prior to the sixteenth century, such as Bartolus, were still being recognised and referred to in relation to the law in action, as embodied in Bohier's *consilia*. Indeed, many humanists of the age did still refer to the likes of Bartolus, and would still adopt, however unconsciously, the commentator-stance on certain topics.[140] This should not be seen as an attempt to categorise Bohier in this way at present, but rather that Bartolus' influence transcended ideological and philosophical barriers that tend to (sometimes superficially) affect jurists

138 Ulrike Müssig, "Superior Courts in early-modern France, England and the Holy Roman Empire", in P Brand and J Getzler (eds), *Judges and Judging in the History of the Common Law and Civil Law: From Antiquity to Modern Times* (2012) 233. See also A Boussuat, "L'idée de la nation et la jurisprudence du Parlement de Paris au XVe siècle" (1950) 204 *Revue Historique* 54.

139 J A Clarence Smith, "Bartolo on the conflict of laws" (1970) 14 *The American Journal of Legal History* 157 at 159.

140 C C Wells, *Law and Citizenship in Early Modern France* (1995) 37. This is true in particular of the practice of citizenship and the issue of legal precedent in France in the fifteenth and sixteenth centuries, which Wells expounds on generally here at 31–57.

and their works. In trying to understand Bohier and the nature of his legal thoughts, this is an important point.

The role of the *ius commune* in Bartolus' commentary on *lex de quibus* is of fundamental importance to the role of this jurist in Bohier's *consilia*. Bartolus' own conception of the *ius commune* can offer an insight into the value of his work for Bohier's own case problem. First, something should be said about what Nikitas Hatzimihail has termed the "Bartolan 'world system'".[141]

(2.6) The Bartolan world

The Bartolan world focused on a world empire – the Roman Empire – constituted by the *populus Romanus* under a secular Emperor and the Pope. Bartolus' chief aim is believed to have been the defence of the nominal authority of the emperor and the unity of the Western Christianity under him and the Pope. Woolf has argued that it is the *ius commune* Bartolus is thinking of in his effort to keep Western Christianity together as *populus Romanus* or when he speaks of the Emperor.[142] Bartolus used the *ius commune* in two main ways. First, in an instrumental sense; where it acts as the "interface" needed to enable his theory of statute and custom to work, by using the *ius commune* not as a positive system of rules that restrict local law, but as an "apparatus" to mediate between them.[143] Secondly, and perhaps most importantly for the purposes of Bohier and his conception of the *ius commune*, is Bartolus' use of it in a conceptual sense. Hatzimihail makes reference to Bartolus' use of "canon-additions from the previous century . . . [including] the distinction of prohibitive statutes into *statuta favorabilia* and *statuta odiosa*".[144] Bartolus effectively sought to reduce the scope of statutes derogating from the *ius commune*: an aim shared with the original Gloss on *cunctos populos* in its bid to protect the Bolognese from the statutes of Modena.[145] Effectively, Bohier's reliance on Bartolus is rooted in this, whether the citation was made with this context in mind. Moreover, it is con-

141 Hatzimihail (n 132) 63.

142 C N S Woolf, *Bartolo of Sassoferrato: 1313–1357: His Position in the History of Medieval Political Thought* (1913) 198.

143 Hatzimihail (n 132) 70. This is not dissimilar to Baldus' approach, where he sees the *ius commune* as a supplementary source for the provisions of local customs and statutes. Joseph Canning has referred to it as providing a suitable standard of law for their interpretation. See Canning (n 34) 149. Further, see J Canning, *Ideas of Power in the Late Middle Ages: 1296–1417* (2011) 147.

144 Hatzimihail (n 132) 70.

145 Ibid.

tended that Bohier's handling of the competing sources of law in his *consilia* bears certain similarities to that of his Italian predecessors. Their similarity rests in both jurists' writing structure.

The definitions of *stylus* and custom form the first contentious part of Bohier's *consilia*. Before putting forward his own position on the matter, Bohier summarises the views of others on the topic in order for comprehensiveness.[146] He makes reference to sources not always immediately containing specific support to the point he is trying to prove, but rather that he is using it to distinguish issues and offer the parameters of the topic he is discussing. Hatzimihail discusses this "art of typology" in relation to Bartolus.[147] Although the very nature of the *consilia* meant that lines of argument and style were more restricted in terms of their length, and we are not offered anywhere near as much in this sense as Bartolus, Bohier still seems to offer the enquirer a background to the topic (although mainly through citing the works of jurists), being sure to account for convergent legal opinions.

Bartolus' own citations on the topic of "de tacito consensu populi", are dominated by references to Bellerpeche, Cinus and Dynus de Mugello. However, Bartolus does not appear to share Bohier's citation from Belleperche and Cinus' *lectura*, despite the majority of citations being drawn from this work.[148]

E. CONFLICT AND COMPETING SOURCES: *STYLUS*, CUSTOM AND *IUS COMMUNE*

(1) The role of the *ius commune* in legal practice

Towards the end of his *consilium*, we see the very essence of Bohier's argument. The rest of the *consilium* has been to set out the position regarding *stylus* and *consuetudo* and the role of the two in legal practice and procedure. Here, Bohier shows the product of this study, and the relationship between the competing sources of law is revealed:[149]

146 This is something that Bohier does later in the *consilia*, in his discussion at *cons* 8, paras 4–5.
147 Hatzimihail (n 132) 46.
148 Bohier's reference: "*Petr.de Bella Pertic. & Cyn. in l.ii.q.iiii.*"
149 *Cons* 8, paras 18–20. Translation from du Plessis (n 72) 385–386.

[1] *Exemplum, lege cautum est, quod in causis iudicialibus non producatur libellus in scriptis, nisi in causis summariis et brevoribus. Et non reperitur expresse determinatum, quae sint causae breviores, nisi secundum quod iudex arbitratus fuerit, modo in curia iudicis est stylus quod in causis 20 solidarum non detur libellus in scriptis, certe hic stylus curiae est in posterum servandus, quia non est contra legem, sed tendit ad declarandum. Secus ubi esset contra legem, quia magistratus et iudices deputati ad ius reddendum, non habent potestatem derogandi legi, seu condendi statutum contra ius commune [ref. to "l.formam C. de of. praefec. praetor."]*

[1] For example, it is stated by law that in legal proceedings a written petition is not to be produced unless in summary or shorter cases. What counts as shorter cases is not found to be expressly determined, unless in accordance with what a judge has decided, namely that in the court of the judge the *stylus* is that in cases to the value of 20 solidi a written petition will not be given, then certainly this *stylus* of the court should be observed in future, since it is not contrary to the law, but aims to clarify it. It is a different matter when the *stylus* is contrary to the law, since a magistrate and judges are deputed to provide the law and they do not have the power to derogate from the law or to claim that a statute is contrary to the *ius commune* [refs].

(2) Bohier's citations

(2.1) C.1.26.2

Bohier makes a direct reference to the Codex here, citing C.1.26.2, *De officio praefectorum praetorio Orientis et Illyrici* (concerning the office of the Praetorian Prefect of the Orient and Illyria), which reads:

Formam a praefecto praetorio datam, et si generalis sit, minime legibus vel constitutionibus contrarium, si nihil postea ex auctoritate mea innovatum est, servari aequum est.

If a rule made by the praetorian prefect is general, and not contrary to the law or constitutions, and no innovation has been subsequently made therein by my authority, it should be treated as valid [emperor Alexander to Restitutulus].

Essentially, C.1.26.2 attests to the qualified authority of the praetorian prefect, whose rules and regulations could not be contrary to the law. The value of this citation is twofold. First, it offers an insight into the way in which Bohier interacted with his sources. It is not yet clear whether this reference was taken from a juristic commentary but, without such a citation, we can assume that he was seeing this reference to the Codex as directly relevant to his argument; namely that a magistrate or judge cannot derogate from the law or to claim that statute is contrary to the *ius commune*. The point he was making was an important one, and it is notable that his reference was to the Roman provision. Secondly, it is interesting as it offers an insight into how Bohier views the magistrate and judge in the sixteenth-century *parlement*.

In a sense, this citation's authority rests on the ability to equate the Roman praetorian *praefect* with the French magistrate or judge, even in the most abstract sense. The praetorian prefect of the East was the second most powerful man in the east, second to the emperor.[150] This observation can be linked to the greater context of sovereignty and authority in early modern France, and perhaps revealing of Bohier's views on this. However, it could also be attributed to a need by Bohier to associate these individuals to provide a necessary ordering to the discussion. Yet, the citation was made on an important point. It is followed by a string of authorities on the next statement concerning the inability to introduce by way of *stylus* something that is contrary to the *ius commune*. This particular point and the reference to C.1.26.2, then, may be rightly viewed as something notable and revealing of Bohier's citation practice and perhaps even his personal motivations for its use; where he saw the authority for this statement on judicial power and how he perceived the hierarchical structure of power and the place of the judge or magistrate.

This practice of equating individuals and procedures of the Imperial Court with those of then contemporary institutions was not unusual between those marked as belonging to both the humanist school and in terms of Scholastic practices. However, the sources referred to in extracting this information varied according to the interpreter. Michael L Monheit spoke of this in respect of Guillaume Budé, Andrea Alciato and Pierre de l'Estoile, in his comparative work on their relationship and interpretation of passages cited from the *Corpus Iuris Civilis* (*CIC*).[151] He recognised the differences between humanist and Scholastic treatment and interpretation, as well as internal conflicts between the former in their approach. Budé, for example, displayed a disdain for the *CIC* and in his treatment of a passage from the Imperial jurist Ulpian (contained in D.1.16.9.1) on the Duties of the Proconsul and Legate. Here he expended little effort on the *CIC* passages (although he did cite them), and instead made reference mainly to sources that were representative of the institutional context within which Ulpian worked, using extra-legal sources.[152] Most importantly for the purposes of

150 T Mommsen, *A History of Rome under the Emperors* (1992) 339.

151 Michael L Monheit, "Guillaume Budé, Andrea Alciato, Pierre de l'Estoile: Renaissance interpreters of Roman law" (1997) 58 *The Journal of the History of Ideas* 21.

152 Monheit (n 151) 24–25.

understanding Bohier's citation practices, it is Bude's equation of procedures at the Imperial Court with those of the French royal courts.[153] This method of interpretation was twofold. First, it was deemed to be more effective to refer to Ulpian in terms of the non-juristic classical sources than work through the various uses of a particular term in the *CIC*. Secondly, it furthered his own ambitions in terms of Royal approval and appointment to a position at Court.[154] As Monheit put it:

> these French practices were a new, quasi-mystical incarnation of those of Imperial Rome, as though there were no gap in culture or indeed in historical causality between the two societies. He [Budé] emphasised the similarity of the Roman and French institutions, despite the varying terminologies used to describe them – hardly a strategy that would take linguistic changes as clues to institutional or cultural ones. Moreover, by his omissions he portrayed Imperial Rome as a society populated by great jurists, but devoid of significant legal thought.[155]

This is compared to his well-known humanist peer, Alciato, who, in his interpretation of this same passage of Ulpian's, displayed a degree of faith in the medieval jurists and the *CIC*; a more harmonious reading than Budé's.[156] This may well be attributable to the difference in the background of the two jurists, who, although both of the humanist tradition, differed in their education. Alciato, for example, was a professional jurist who had studied at Pavia and so, as Monheit recognises, could not have displayed disdain for legal thought in the way in which Budé, who had not completed his formal legal education, did.[157]

This has been mentioned here to demonstrate the existence of other equations made by jurists of the time between their own reality and that of the Romans. Whether Bohier was citing this passage from the Digest directly, or through the work of another, it is still notable and deserves to be mentioned in terms of understanding his citation practices and with regard to the greater aim of this chapter.

153 Monheit (n 151) 26. Budé, *Annotationes* fol LXIIIr, LXIIIv–LXIIIIr.

154 Monheit (n 151) 25–26. Budé dedicated his *Annotationes* to Jean de Ganay (Chancellor of France) and was appointed as Master of Requests to François I in 1522. See D O McNeil, *Guillaume Budé and Humanism in the Reign of Francis I* (1975) 12–14 and 30–31.

155 Monheit (n 151) 27.

156 Monheit (n 151). Note here that we see frequent reference to Bartolus and Accursius, despite his attacks on them. A common humanist approach, it seems. See also Osler elsewhere in this volume.

157 Monheit (n 151) 27.

(2.2) Alexander de Imola

Alexander de Imola (Alessandro Tartagni, 1424–1477) played a key role in this part of Bohier's *consilium*. His *Consilia*, at "*consilio xxxvi*" is cited in support of his statement on the inability of a judge to introduce by way of *stylus* something contrary to the *ius commune*. This work was published extensively, and so here attempts have been made to consult as many editions as possible that were in print during Bohier's lifetime to achieve a certain level of accuracy for control purposes.[158] In this part of his *consilium*, Bohier does not make reference to a particular volume of Tartagni's work, only citing "Alex.in d.consilio xxxvi". Earlier, when referring to Tartagni's *consilia*, he mentions "vol.iii". However, reference to this volume does not offer a *consilium* with relevant content. Instead, it is believed that here Bohier was referring to the second volume of Tartagni's work. Here we find a *consilium* that expressly deals with statute, *stylus* and *ius commune,* outlined at the beginning as: "statutum recipit interpretationem a iure communi";[159] "stilus unius curiae quid inducere possit";[160] and "magistratus deputati ad ius reddendi non habent ptatem [potestatem] derogandi legi vel condendi statutum contra ius commune".[161]

It is likely that Bohier had this third part of Tartagni's *consilium* in mind when citing this source. This discussion reads:

> *Sed ubi esset contra legem quia magistratus deputati ad ius reddendum non habet potestatem derogandi legi seu condendi statuta contra ius commune. [l.formam. C. de offi. Prefec. Preto., l.omnes populi, c.de offi. arcbi.] non possunt ipsi magistratus per stilum inducere aliquid contra ius commune: ita in specie declarant [Belleperche and Cinus in l.ii. in iii col. in versi iii] circa hoc quaeritur cum nos habemus [C. quae sit longa consuetudo, Antonius de Butrio in c. si de consue. in ver.] pro hoc datur differentia inter consuetudinem [et] stilum.*

The similarity between this excerpt and Bohier's own statement in his *consilium* is striking. This is true in terms of both the sources cited and the wording of the passage itself; they are in fact identical and so it is fair to

158 Five different editions were consulted here. Two editions printed 1499 (Venice), two printed in 1492 (Venice) and a 1537 edition (Lyon). Note that a 1488 edition is listed as Alexander de Imola's *consilia*, by Ludovicus Bologninus (1446–1508). For the purposes of this study, the 1537 edition has been most relied upon. Also, it is worth noting here that Joannes de Gradibus was involved in this particular edition.

159 Alexander Tartagni, *Consilia* (1537), *cons* 36, par 8: a statute receives an interpretation by the *iure commune*.

160 *Cons* 36, par 11: what *stylus* the court can induce.

161 *Cons* 36, par 12: magistrate assigned not to derogate from the law or to enforce statute against the *ius commune*.

assume that Bohier has reproduced this part of Tartagni's own *consilium* on the matter. Bohier's statement reads: "Secus ubi esset contra legem, quia magistratus et iudices deputati ad ius reddendum, non habent potestatem derogandi legi, seu condendi statutum contra ius commune".

Looking back to Bohier's preceding statement on the matter of non-derogation from the *ius commune* and the inability to declare a statute contrary to it, it is clear that Bohier copied, almost verbatim, the wording from Tartagni also. This includes his discussion of the "causis summariis et brevoribus" and "in curia iudicis est stylus quod in causis 20 solidarum non detur libellus in scriptis". So it seems this "crux of Bohier's entire exposition",[162] namely that from *consilia* 8, paras 18 to 20, was based on Tartagni's *consilium*.[163]

Now let us turn to the citations. Immediately after this passage reproduced by Bohier, Tartagni refers to C.1.26.2 (*De officio praefectorum praetorio Orientis et Illyrici*). Reference is also made to D.1.1.9 (*omnes populi*), and D.2.2 (*Quod quisque iuris in alterum statuerit, ut ipse eodem iure utatur*) and from the Decretals, ad X.5.7.6 (*de haereticis*)[164] and X.1.23 (*de officio archdiaconi*). Bohier appears only to have cited, and most likely borrowed, C.1.26.2 here in his own *consilium*. There is another familiar citation, however, that follows on from this. Tartagni cites Belleperche and Cinus, and their commentary on C.8.52 (*quae sit longa consuetudo*).[165] We know that Bohier has relied considerably upon this commentary in his *consilia*, and he cites it again at this part of it. Bohier's citation is abbreviated and so appears different from Tartagni's. It is likely, however, that Bohier was borrowing this citation from the latter; a proposition made all the more likely from his practice with other parts of Tartagni's *consilium*.

It is worth mentioning some of the other sources Tartagni cited in this *consilium*, of which Bohier seems to have deemed authoritative. The jurist relied considerably on Antonius de Butrio. The particular parts reproduced by Bohier did not miss out any of the citations to individuals (although some parts of the Digest and Decretal references were not reproduced) and so no conclusions can be drawn here as to whether Bohier did not agree with Tartagni's choice of juristic sources, but although he does himself cite

162 Du Plessis (n 72) 386.

163 This part of Bohier's *consilium* dealt with the method of proving *stylus*: "consuetudo probari debet per turbam, in Francia".

164 J A Hogan discusses this in his *Judicial Advocates and Procurators: An Historical Synopsis & Commentary* (1941) 38.

165 *"Pe. & Cy. in l.ii.in iiii. col. iii "*.

Antonius de Butrio, he is not a dominant authority.[166] However, his reproduction of Tartagni's text and his sources demonstrates that he deemed the jurist authoritative enough for this key part of his *consilium*, and did not feel it important to pay homage to the greater sense of Tartagni's argument or his citation practices, and reproduced without editing. It seems that Tartagni was enough. Of course, the very nature of the *consilia* as a source does limit the opportunity for such things, and cannot be read in the same way as a commentary can, for example.

Is it possible that legal practice altered the way in which an individual used a juristic source; and was one rooted more in necessity, brevity and pragmatism than to any emotive standpoint? In this particular part of his *consilium*, it is fair to assume that he only referred directly to the *consilia* of Tartagni and Decio, and not necessarily to the sources cited therein. Of course, this is not true for the rest of his *consilium*. Yet, it is worthy of mention here, given that he is outlining his general position at this point and even knowingly selecting sources that he feels are most capable of demonstrating his position in an authoritative sense. Moreover, it is possible that those who would refer to Bohier's *consilia*, in an effort to identify the crux of his argument, would look to this end stage of discussion.

(2.3) Filippo Decio

Bohier did, however, insert one of his own citations that do not appear to have been borrowed in this way and here cites another *consilia* as authority for this key part of his case. Bohier cites Filippo Decio's *consilia* in conjunction with Belleperche and Cinus (likely borrowed) and Alexander de Imola. Filippo Decio (Philippus Decius, 1453–1536) was born in Milan, and studied Law at Pavia under Jason de Mayno. Auditor of the Roman *Rota*, and professor of canon law at Padua, Decio had an illustrious career in law.[167] Bohier cited Decio's *consilium* XI earlier in his discussion on the introduction of custom by way of a "*Comitissa aut Ducissa*".[168] This *consilium* deals

166 Antonius de Butrio was cited in those parts of Tartagni's *consilium* that I suspect were most relevant to Bohier. They were cited at par 8 and par 11 by Tartagni, so while not from par 12, which was reproduced by Bohier, they were mentioned in parts that Bohier was likely to have looked at given their content.

167 Note the editing of Decio's work by Gradibus: (Feenstra cited above) See also his treatment of absolute power (of pope or emperor): "Neither the Pope nor the Emperor can overrule natural law or *ius gentium* without cause. . . and for this reason present-day jurists think Angelo (Ubaldis) was wrong when he argued the opposite. . .", Decio on X.1, 2, 7 (*De consitutionibus, c. quae in ecclesiarum*) Decio cites Panormitanus, and Bartolus. (Black (n 91) 30).

168 Bohier, *Cons* 8, par 6.

with a number of points involving *stylus* and statute, and their relationship with *ius commune*.

His citation does not include reference to a specific part of this *consilium*, but a survey of its contents demonstrates that this source held much for him.[169] Let us first consider the issue at hand, namely that a judge may not introduce by way of *stylus* something contrary to the *ius commune*. There does not seem to be specific mention of the role of a judge or magistrate[170] and so no direct treatment like we saw in the case of Tartagni (although this was, as it was shown, copied from there). Instead, there are a number of different parts to this *consilium* that could have been used by Bohier in a general sense. A number of these provisions shall be considered, and although not all of them can be classed as strictly related to the specific part of Bohier's *consilium* under discussion, they are nonetheless important to the overall understanding of the role of the *ius commune*, and to the mind-set of the jurist that Bohier has deemed authoritative.

At the beginning of his *consilium*, Decio addresses the issue of "statutum quod non possit sententia probari per testes, valet".[171] The discussion focuses around the *Statuta Mediolani*, and although it is unlikely that Bohier relied specifically on this part of the work, it is worth mentioning here for a statement made on the *ius commune*. On the question of interpreting statutes, Decio makes this point:

> *Prima quia statuta Mediolani appellant sententiam laudum, seu arbitramentum, unde illa verba, aliquid sententiam, intelliguntur secundum, quod a statutis sententiam appellatur, quia verba statuti debent intelligi, & interpretari secundum quod alia statuta loquuntur. . . ideo potius statutum ab alio statuto recipit interpretationem, quam a iure communi.*[172]

The final part of this excerpt is the most important. Decio seems to state that statutory interpretation, on this occasion, is done by reference to another statute rather than from the *ius commune*. Of course, this does not strictly mean that such an interpretation can be contrary to the *ius commune*, and indeed this would be contrary to a later statement by Decio in this *consilium* that shall be examined shortly.[173] Rather, it offers an insight into the interpretation practices of the time and the way in which the *ius commune* interacted with these other sources of law; moreover, how individuals would

169 Decio, *Cons* 11, par 17.
170 The role of *iudex* is only briefly discussed at *cons* 11, par 2.
171 Decio, *Cons* 11, par 2.
172 Decio, *Cons* 11, par 2.
173 *Cons* 11, par 17.

use these sources, and how this sometimes led to creative interpretative practices. Finally, it shows how one of the roles of the *ius commune*, as a so-called interpretative guide, would not always benefit from primacy, even to statute. Alexander Tartagni is cited here, by Decio, with reference to his *consilium* XXXVI; a citation shared by Bohier.

Decio's treatment of "statuta quod contra iura scripta, non possit allegari consuetudo, qualiter intelligendum" offers a valuable insight into the way in which Decio viewed statute and *consuetudo*. He states: "Confirmatur hoc, quia statutum loquitur de consuetudine, unde cum sit contra ius commune, debet intelligi de consuetudine propria, quae debet esse praescripta [refers to c.fi.de consue.] in ista consuetudine interpretativa, in qua interpretatio non requirit". Essentially, this passage seems to state that since the statute in question speaks to the custom, and that its content is contrary to the *ius commune*, it ought to be understood according to its "custom properties", and not in its statute form. This creative method of interpretation demonstrates the value of custom and the ways in which such approaches to sources of law at this time could overcome the authority of the *ius commune*. It should be stressed that this seems to have been only in those cases where a statute's provisions could be traced to a customary rule, but it is nonetheless an undermining of the authority of the *ius commune*.

Decio deals with the issue of: "Statutum derogans iuri commune, debet quantum potest reduci ad ius commune":[174] discussing when a statute derogates from the *ius commune* and how it ought to be reduced insomuch as possible so as to be in line with the *ius commune*. Under this heading, Decio states:

Quia cum statutum deroget iuri communi, debet quantum potest reduci ad terminos iuris communis.	When statute derogates from the *ius commune*, it should be reduced as much as possible to the boundaries of the *ius commune*.

This particular point is most relevant to the first part of Bohier's statement on the inability of a judge to declare a statute contrary to the *ius commune*, as considered earlier. Although this is not the point to which Bohier is addressing, it is nonetheless worthy of note. It provided a clear statement for this first part of his argument, and so he either deemed it unnecessary to cite specifically in relation to the first point (where he only cited C.1.26.2

174 *Cons* XI pr 17. Editions available during Bohier's lifetime have proven difficult to obtain. The earliest edition held by the Library of Congress is a 1523 edition (Venice) and this has been used here.

and relied wholly on Tartagni) or this reference to Decio's *consilium* XI here is to be taken as authority for all matters under consideration, in this part of Bohier's *consilium*.

Decio deals with the matter of *stylus* under the headings "*Stylus & consuetudo quomodo differant*",[175] and "*Stylus pro forma habetur*".[176] The second of these largely focuses on the problems arising from additions to a *stylus* that appear inconsistent with the rest of its content; it is more a consideration of the *stylus* and its associated problems of form and content. The first, however, discusses the *ius commune*, and it is used as a distinguishing feature between *stylus* and custom; the relationship of each to the *ius commune* differs. Decio's choice of citations should be considered. Here, he cites Antonius de Butrio, Baldus, Bartolus, Angelus de Aretinus, Albericus De Rosate and Alexander de Imola (Tartagni) and his *consilia*.[177] These are individuals who are seen throughout Bohier's *consilium*.

It seems that Bohier's reference to Decio here was made for his general position on statutes, *stylus* and custom, and their relationship with the *ius commune*. It is not known whether Bohier referred directly to Decio's *consilia*, but it is clear that the source offered much to his *consilium* beyond that to which it was specifically referred. Given the very nature of the *consilia* and its inherent restrictions in providing room for facts and indeed citations beyond that which was strictly needed for the case at hand, it may well have been that Bohier's reference to Decio at this stage of his *consilium* was in fuller recognition of his relevance overall, especially given that this point of the discussion was a general statement on the relationship between competing sources of law that had formed the basis of Bohier's argument.

In terms of his preference for those works of canon law, it is possible that this was rooted in a desire to reflect the practical reality of legal practice. The Paris *Parlement*, for example, saw a high number of appeals to its chambers. A sample of appeals heard at the *Parlement* demonstrates that a significant number of these were of a religious nature.[178] It is possible that Bohier was simply wishing to recognise this and provide contemporary editions for reference.

175 Decio, *Cons* 11, pr 11.
176 Decio, *Cons* 11, pr 16.
177 Decio, *Cons* 26 is cited.
178 U//419 *Arrêts notables du Parlement de Paris, notes de jurisprudence, consultations, principalement en matiere ecclesiastique*, Archives Nationales de Paris.

F. CONCLUSIONS

Consilia 8 reveals Bohier's treatment of the competing legal orders of statute, custom and the *ius commune*. This work has sought to analyse the approach of a practitioner to legal texts and how the reading of such documents manifested into practice. The question whether there was a doctrinal meaning attached to the term *ius commune* remains unanswered for now. However, there is a sense of continuity in his legal reasoning and it is possible to detect a pattern of approaches to the sources of law (in particular the *ius commune*), as well as a preference for particular jurists and their works. Jurists from the School of Orléans feature prominently, as do the works of Alexander de Imola and Filippo Decio. There is a tendency by Bohier to apply the *ius commune* in an interpretative sense, relying on it as a constructive aid, to manage competing sources of law such as statute and custom.

The very nature of the *consilia* as a source is an example of the meeting of legal practice with academic advice. University training in Roman law together with the demand for legal expertise in practice would have implications in the wider argument related to legal humanism. "Legal thinking along Roman lines" was in theory promoted by the *consilia*; however, it is likely that the overwhelming motivation for the selection of a source was necessity of practical application, more than any overarching consideration to the juristic school to which the author belonged, or the desire to demonstrate an academic affiliation by the practising lawyer.

11 Humanism and Law in Elizabethan England: The Annotations of Gabriel Harvey

David Ibbetson

A paper on English legal humanism may be, almost by definition, a paper without a subject. If legal humanism is taken in its continental sense described by Douglas Osler, as a concern with the establishment of the true texts of the Justinianic *corpus* and elsewhere, and their interpretation as such, using philological and historical methods, as part of the study of Antiquity, then we would hardly expect there to be very much in England, certainly not in connection with English law. Even if we take a broader approach to humanism, things are not much better. Anyone who takes the trouble to do a Google search on the phrase "English legal humanism" will, at the time this is being written, get hardly a single hit. While none of us would want to treat Google as a definitive index of the world's knowledge, the paucity of references does indicate that it is something of a non-topic. According to one work on humanism in Tudor England, the study of law, like the study of logic, Latin grammar and Aristotelianism, was transformed by the activity of humanist scholars;[1] but the references are to France and Basel, not to England. So far as the modern literature goes, there is nothing there.

It may be that it is not really possible to go much further than John Baker, dealing with the early part of the sixteenth century in his volume in the Oxford History of the Laws of England. Wisely distancing himself from the use of the term "humanism" in favour of a broader idea of Renaissance learning, he makes six points. First, English lawyers did take a historical approach to law, insofar as English lawyers always had to look to the past to identify the law of their own day; and in the sixteenth century they began to print some of the earliest books of the law, dating back to the twelfth and thirteenth

1 J W Binns, "The Humanist Latin Tradition Reassessed", in J Woolfson (ed), *Reassessing Tudor Humanism* (2002) 186, 191 n 32.

centuries. But there is no suggestion that these texts were being edited with a view to the production of an accurate scholarly text, as opposed to simply taking a single corrupt manuscript and printing it. There is nothing to rival the attempts to restore the texts of the civil law. Secondly, the concern for order and system, as found most significantly perhaps in Donellus, has no real parallel in England. There were concerns that English law was disorderly, but very little attempt to try to impose order except perhaps in the field of criminal law. The encyclopaedic work of Sir Edward Coke in the early seventeenth century is anything but ordered and systematic, though there were some attempts to squeeze English law into an institutional framework at this time.[2] Thirdly, those in the van of the new learning on the continent were concerned to spread knowledge through the printing of texts; English law did, of course, get carried on the wave of the printing revolution, but there remained a vibrant manuscript tradition right through the Tudor period. Fourthly, while there was concern for public benefit, the common weal as it is described in the English texts, rather than simple individual advantage, this was if anything a conservative response to economic dynamism and proto-capitalism. Nor can we see a conscious attempt to reshape the law and to improve it. English law knew legislation, of course, and recognised the possibility of improving social conditions; but the legal revolution of the sixteenth century was achieved by internal means rather than external ones. Finally, there was greater interest in equity as opposed to strict law, and while this is something that may genuinely reflect the changes occurring in continental Europe,[3] it can legitimately be doubted whether it had any genuine effect on English law rather than constituting a discourse to a large extent divorced from the law.[4]

That said, the main currents of humanism did not completely pass English law and English lawyers by. We need only think of Lord Chancellor Thomas More in the early part of the century or Lord Keeper Egerton at the end, the former author of *Utopia*, the latter bibliophile and patron of poets; and Cambridge's first Regius Professor of Civil Law took himself to Padua before entering into office so that he could acquaint himself with the new learning. Nor did people we would regard as humanists ignore the law. In the early wave of Henrician humanism the use of the version of French used by lawyers was attacked by writers such as Richard Morison; Thomas Starkey

2 A Watson, "Justinian's Institutes and Some English Counterparts", in P G Stein and A D E Lewis (eds), *Studies in Justinian's Institutes in Memory of J A C Thomas* (1983) 181.
3 D J Ibbetson, "A House Built on Sand: Equity in Early Modern English law", in E Koops and W J Zwalve (eds), *Law & Equity: Approaches in Roman Law and Common Law* (2014) 55.
4 Sir John Baker, *The Oxford History of the Law of England, VI: 1483–1558* (2003) 15–18.

proposed the use of Latin or English rather than French, which was a barbarous language which had no value outside the law, and a language at that which was dishonourable since it was associated with an ignominious conquest by a foreign power. The suggested use of Latin, put into the mouth of Cardinal Pole, was linked to a proposal to replace the English Common law with Roman law, which was better suited to a systematic decision-making that was rule-based and efficient. But if there was any serious movement to replace Law French, it came to nothing.

Among the most interesting of the humanists of the later sixteenth century was the Cambridge scholar Gabriel Harvey.[5] We have the best warrant for calling him a humanist, for he used the term to describe himself. One scholar has referred to him as the "arch-humanist".[6] His practice of signing his name in the books he owned makes it easy for us to identify his own copies, and his practice of reading with pen in hand enables us to trace his thought through his copious marginal notes.[7] By studying his law books, both common law and civil/canon law, we are able to see how one self-styled humanist responded to the law.

Born in nearby Saffron Walden, Harvey matriculated at Christ's College Cambridge in 1566, becoming a Fellow of Pembroke Hall in 1570. He was something of a protégé of Sir Thomas Smith, and in a letter to him in 1573 he sought advice on whether he should follow his inclinations to take up the study of the civil law.[8] This, he wrote,

> I see to be grounded wholly either upon nature, or custom or good decrees, and therefore cannot but be a fruitful and commodious study.[9]

There is no sense of his beginning his study with that critical predisposition which we might associate with humanists: very much the reverse. His real doubt was whether the civil law had any utility,

> . . . by reason that the common law, to speak precisely, is our civil law; and the civil law taketh place only in a few matters and meddleth but with certain cases. And it may be in time also, that the common lawyers will handle the matter so, as I have heard said a great number of them do already go about, that even those few cases too may daily be more and more abridged, and in the end altogether be utterly removed out of England.[10]

5 V Stern, *Gabriel Harvey: His Life, Marginalia and Library* (1979).

6 M Pincombe, *Elizabethan Humanism: Literature and Learning in the Later Sixteenth Century* (2001) 86.

7 G C Moore Smith, *Gabriel Harvey's Marginalia* (1913), reproducing selective marginalia.

8 E J L Scott (ed), *The Letter Book of Gabriel Harvey AD 1573–1580* (1884) 162–165.

9 Ibid, 162–163.

10 Ibid, 164.

Not only is there a positive attitude to the civil law, but even the common law is carried along on this wave of approbation. His approach is that of the (potential) future practitioner, not that of the scholar. It may be that his near-complacency was really the result of a lack of knowledge; he claimed that he had scarcely gone through the first book of Justinian's Institutes and had "run through" Hegendorff, presumably the *Dialectica Legalis* of Christoph Hegendorff, published in 1531.

His interest in becoming a civil lawyer was clearly delayed by his appointment as praelector in rhetoric in Cambridge between 1574 and 1576, but in a letter to Smith which seems to have been written in the latter part of the 1570s he described himself as still having this intention.[11] He regretted that he had still not been able to devote sufficient time to Justinian's Institutes, but said that he was intending to attend the lectures of Thomas Byng, Regius Professor of Civil Law in the University. He may or may not have done so, but in 1578 his move to a fellowship at Trinity Hall, which had been founded specifically for the education of canonists and civilians, suggests that he was serious in his pursuit of a career as a civil lawyer. By now he was referring to himself as a legist. He took his Cambridge LLB in 1584, and his Oxford DCL one year later. At some point he entered Doctors Commons, but he seems never to have built up a practice.

Law was only one of his interests. He is chiefly remembered as a *littérateur* and rhetorician, but had a strong interest in medicine too, and is probably best thought of as a polymath scholar. Hence, when we examine his law books we need to remember that he might be reading them with purely scholarly ends in mind as much as pragmatic ones. This is true in particular of his dabbling in works of English law.[12] This could hardly have been in furtherance of his study of the civil law, and, moreover, there is evidence that he was continuing to look at English law works long after he had started – and probably ceased – to practise from Doctors Commons: in one annotation he refers to John Cowell's *Institutiones Iuris Anglicani*, published in 1605, as well as to Cowell's *Interpreter* "now in hand", which appeared in 1607.[13]

Some dozen legal volumes belonging to Harvey have been identified and examined, covering civil law, common law and legal method:[14]

11 Scott (n 8) 176.
12 Below, 292–294.
13 *Institutions or Principal Grounds of Lawes and Statutes of England*, final blank.
14 Those not listed in the catalogue in Stern, *Gabriel Harvey* (n 5), are marked with an asterisk.

A Alciatus, *De Verborum Significatione* and other works: Bodleian Library Douce A subt 75.

F Duarenus, *De Sacris Ecclesiae Ministeriis* and other works: Trinity College, Cambridge L.12.112.

A Fitzherbert, *Office of Sheriffs*: Library of Congress, available via Early English Books Online.

J T Freigius, *Paratitla seu Synopsis Pandectarum*: Princeton University[15]

J Hopper, *In Veram Iurisprudentiam Isagoges*: British Library C.60.e.14

**Institutions or Principal Grounds of Lawes and Statutes of England*: Library of Congress, available via Early English Books Online

Justinian, *Institutes*: Emmanuel College Cambridge 324.862

T Littleton, *Tenures*: Pierpont Morgan Library W 04 C

*J Mynsinger, *In Tres Libri Secundi Decretalium Titulos, De Probationibus, De Testibus, De Attestationibus et De Fide Instrumentorum Commentarii*: Gonville and Caius College, Cambridge, H.4.31.

J Oldendorp, *Loci Communes Juris Civilis*: British Library Bagford 5991 (fragment)

J Ramus, *Oikonomia seu Dispositio Regularum Utriusque Iuris*, bound with J Foorth, *Synopsis Politica*: Saffron Walden Museum

*N Vigelius, *Iuris Civilis Totius Absolutissima Methodus Universi*: Gonville and Caius College Cambridge H.6.12.

For sure, this was not his complete legal library, for he refers to other books which he owned (such as the two volumes by John Cowell noted above) which have probably not survived. Nonetheless, they give a flavour of his approach to law.

We may divide his manuscript additions to the printed books into three groups. Most simply, there were underlinings. We can deduce very little from these except that he read the part of the book where the underlinings occur with a sufficient degree of concentration to pick out specific words or sentences. Secondly, there are marginal annotations. Many of these are headings simply pointing to the content of the text, perhaps enabling Harvey himself or some other later reader to hit on a particular passage; some are abbreviated summaries of the content of the text, again presumably intended to help a later reader. Others are notes relating to the text but containing something not found there, thereby expanding on the printed text. And substantial passages, especially on the blank pages and endpapers

15 Available at *http://pudl.princeton.edu/objects/47429b415*

at the beginning and end of books, may bear little or no relation to the print, almost as if Harvey used printed books instead of notebooks to record his musings.

Leaving aside Oldendorp's *Loci Communes*, which is too fragmentary to be examined usefully, all of the volumes contain some evidence of Harvey's pen, but the amount and form differ. His copy of Duarenus' *De Sacris Ecclesiae Ministeriis* is bound with the same author's commentaries on the *lex Falcidia* and the Digest title *De Iureiurando*; all were published in Paris in the early 1560s. The binding is later, and the top margins of the first work have been trimmed, at times cutting through Harvey's manuscript notes, but all three works have Harvey's signature on their title pages, so we can have no doubt that he was the owner of all of them. *De Sacris Ecclesiae Ministeriis* has fairly heavy annotations at its start, becoming more intermittent, but the other two works have absolutely nothing. Were it not for the signatures we would probably not identify them as Harvey's at all and assume that the binding together of the three works was down to a later owner. The same is true of his collection of works by Alciatus. Some of the works – the *Paradoxa*, *Dispunctiones* and the commentary on the digest title *Eius quod Interest* – have very little annotation, though sufficient for us to be confident that he had read the books. Others – the *Praetermissa*, *Declamatio* and the commentary *De Verborum Obligationibus* – have nothing at all. The commentary on the penultimate book of the Digest, *De Verborum Significatione*, by contrast, is heavily marked, especially at the beginning, and the same is true of the commentary on imperial rescripts. Harvey's copy of Justinian's Institutes with gloss is surprisingly lightly marked, and that mostly (though not exclusively) on the introductory material on the life of Justinian. We might conclude that he had done little more than dip into it. However, while we know that he had begun his perusal of the Institutes by 1573,[16] this volume was printed at Lyon in 1577 and marked by Harvey as having been purchased in 1579, so it may perhaps be that he had earlier read another copy and simply dipped into this one when his study of the civil law had become more serious. Occasional underlinings in the text, and a signature at the end of the volume with the date March 1579, suggest that the volume did not simply sit on his shelf unopened. At the other extreme are his copy of Hopper's *In Veram Iurisprudentiam Isagoges* and Johann Ramus' *Oikonomia*, which are heavily annotated (more at the beginnings of the works than the ends), and where both have the appearance of having been read and written on twice.

16 Above, 285.

The quantity of annotations in these books probably reflects Harvey's interest. As noted above, he was praelector in rhetoric at Cambridge between 1574 and 1576, and this undoubtedly inclined him towards works of legal dialectic and logic. Already in 1573 he wrote that he had read Hegendorff, by which he almost certainly meant his *Dialectica Legalis*. We do not have this book, but his most heavily annotated legal work, Joachim Hopper's *In Veram Iurisprudentiam Isagoges*, is as much concerned with legal dialectic as it is with law. The prefaces to the several parts of Vigelius' *Iuris Civilis Totius Absolutissima Methodus*, a work which he referred to elsewhere for its approach to logic and method and for its practical reason,[17] are similarly noted, and in Harvey's discursive passages at the beginning and end of the work he specifically refers to their value: it is in these parts of the work that Vigelius explained the reason behind his method of re-ordering the texts of the *Corpus Iuris Civilis* to make them more accessible and comprehensible. Thereby the texts should be better understood, and the advocate in court would more easily be able to find what he needed. The same is true of the first part of Freigius' *Paratitla*, which he elsewhere commended for its logic.[18]

It has been suggested that Harvey's reading and annotating might have been not purely for his own benefit, but designed to produce a composite of the printed text together with his notes and comments.[19] There is some slight evidence of something like collaborative activity in his volume of Alciatus' works; at the end of the volume is the signature *Gabrielis Harveii et amicorum* and the date 1578, pointing squarely to the involvement of others. But this stands alone, and it is unlikely that the practice of underlining would itself have been of any value to a subsequent reader. Moreover, his habit of writing in Latin and lapsing into Greek, Italian or Spanish as well as English from time to time would have presupposed a thoroughly well-educated reader. The predominance of annotation only at the beginning of some volumes points more in the direction of Harvey's starting to read with pen in hand and then putting down the book than towards a deliberate annotation for the benefit of others; this must have been especially so where what was underlined was of peripheral interest to the principal context of the book, as

17 Freigius, second blank, recto and verso; Hopper, [12], [21], 447, 500, 502; Alciatus, final blank; Duarenus, 6.

18 Hopper, [12], [21], 447, 500, 502; *Oikonomia*, 1, 3, 4, 204.

19 L Jardine and W Sherman, "Pragmatic Readers: Knowledge Transactions and Scholarly Services in Late Elizabethan England", in A Fletcher and P Roberts (eds), *Religion, Culture and Society in Early Modern Britain: Essays in Honour of Patrick Collinson* (1994) 102, 113–122.

where he underlines a part of Freigius' discussion of pupillary substitution in the Roman law of succession where it is noted that Raphael Cumanus was said to have heard Baldus lecture.[20] And while sometimes an annotation can elaborate on the text, as where he notes on his copy of Freigius that the jurists of the Sabinian school respected the *ius gentium* in matters of obligations while the Proculians favoured *aequitas*,[21] the note appearing close to where there was a reference to the *ius gentium* in the text, the manuscript addition may bear little relation to the contents of the book: the front and rear blanks of his copy of Hopper, for example, are densely written with notes on food, drink and medicinal herbs, such as that one should drink borage and bugloss for melancholy (something with which modern herbalists would agree), while a good number of the annotations in Ramus' *Oekonomia* are ethical maxims.

Harvey was not merely studying law, but as an intellectual was exploring its underlying idea. He noted its twofold nature, one aspect deriving from *iubendo*, commanding, which was studied through logic and grammar, the other cognate with *iustitia*, justice, referring to its ethical dimension.[22] In the same way, following Alciatus, he noted the opposition between the *verba legis* and the *ratio legis*, the words of the law and the reason of the law; the reason of the law was constant while its words required interpretation.[23] And reason, not merely words, was to be found within Roman law.[24] We have noted above his drawing of the distinction between the Sabinian and Proculian jurists, the former following the *ius gentium*, the latter favouring *aequitas*;[25] his sympathies may have lain with the latter, for he says that positive law should be examined according to the Lesbian rule, a pliable lead ruler capable of measuring curves used by Aristotle as a metaphor for the way in which the law could be adjusted to fit the circumstances of any case.[26] Such a greater concern with equity would align him with the continental lawyers whom we would designate humanists. Harvey might not have used that term himself, but he was aware of the new approach to teaching that was coming from Bourges, noting against Freigius' description of reading for the first year of law study that this was the new method of teaching law.[27]

20 Freigius, 615; the underlining occurs after several hundred pages of virgin text.
21 Freigius, 4.
22 Freigius, 2.
23 Alciatus, 6.
24 Freigius, first blank, 737.
25 Above, note 21.
26 *Nicomachean Ethics*, V.10.
27 Freigius, sig β6.

In line with his humanist inclinations was his tendency towards simplification in the law. He writes of giving primacy to the last two books of the Digest, *De Verborum Significatione* and *De Diversis Regulis Iuris Antiqui*, its "most pregnant" titles, i.e. those that had the greatest potential in the construction of legal argument.[28] His copy of Vigelius' *Methodus*, where the texts of the *Corpus Iuris* were reordered to make it easier to follow the law, has the section on *Regulae Iuris* marked up, while most of the rest of the text of the work is devoid of any annotation. Elsewhere he was to use pregnancy as a term of approbation for legal works and sources of law, typically to refer to other works which could be easily quarried for legal abstractions.[29] Gothofredus' Epitome of the Institutes was "praegnans", the use of Hopper's work was "praegnantissimus".[30] He praised Vigelius' *Repertorium Iuris*, a little book which he said contained the elements of the law and a summary of the *regulae iuris*;[31] we do not know if he owned a copy himself. More generally, he shared Julius Caesar's aspiration of reducing the law to a manageable compass.[32]

Harvey was somewhat ambivalent towards Justinian's Digest. Many things were missing from it, he noted in his copy of Alciatus' *De Verborum Significatione* in 1578,[33] two years later drawing attention in particular to the law relating to divine persons and things.[34] More problematic still was its ordering, which followed no logical principle, although he conceded that it had great value: "the best laws are most precious, even without the best method".[35] Harvey clearly favoured the attempts to reorder the mass of material to make it more comprehensible: hence his repeated praise for Freigius and Vigelius, saying of the latter's method that it was of singular use in the easy understanding of the law for practice as well as for study.[36] Although commentaries were forbidden by Justinian, he observed, paratitles in this form were acceptable, and the proper ordering of the law would replace the work of the Commentators.[37] On the opening blank of his copy of Freigius, too, he sketched out a way of understanding the law along

28 Freigius, 3.
29 Freigius, sig β8, 1, Hopper, 263, 447.
30 Hopper, 447, 263.
31 Hopper, 500.
32 Hopper, preface 4.
33 Alciatus, 268.
34 Hopper, 125.
35 Freigius, second blank.
36 Vigelius, 4.
37 Freigius, sig α8v, 15.

Ramist lines,[38] though this would not have helped him to reorder the substance of Justinian's law.

For all this, Harvey's approach to law was that of a lawyer. In his copy of Freigius – which represents the latest dated notes (1583) in the civilian works we have seen – he criticises Lorenzo Valla for being a mere grammarian and "logodaedalus", tarring Juan Luis Vives with the same brush, dismisses Antonio de Nebrija as a jejune lexicographer, comparing him unfavourably with Accursius, Budé as a philologer and not a solid interpreter of the law, and Hotman as someone more concerned with the form rather than the substance of the law. The jurists he named with approval were those concerned with legal logic and dialectic: Vigelius, Freigius, Vulteius, Bodin, Hegendorff, Cantiuncula, Abel, Oldendorff, Everaerts, and (perhaps surprisingly) Hotman;[39] and already in 1578 he had referred to Hopper and Vigelius as the more capable jurists.[40] In annotations of several of his books he praised works for their practical utility: Vigelius' works of method, Maranta's *Speculum Aureum*, Durandus' *Speculum Judiciale* and Justinian's Institutes with the commentary of Bucherellus.[41] Unlike the legal humanist of caricature he did not reject the writers of the *mos italicus* completely, several times noting the significance of Bartolus,[42] whom he described as the complete legist,[43] and referring to other Italian writers of the thirteenth, fourteenth and fifteenth centuries.[44] In his copy of Ramus' *Oikonomia*, read in 1580, he went as far as to suggest that one should read both laws (i.e. civil and canon) with their glosses together with the works of the most practical – "pragmatic" – doctors, leaving other works for "particular occasions",[45] and in the same year noted both the accumulation of glosses, commentaries and *communes opiniones*, as witnessed by the full (and very valuable) *Repertorium* of Bertachinus,[46] and also the value of glosses and commentaries in clarifying the law, though at the same time noting that the law itself was the best interpreter of the law.[47] Three years later he was perhaps more

38 For his Ramism, Stern, *Gabriel Harvey* (n 5) 21, 29, L Jardine, "Gabriel Harvey: Exemplary Ramist and Pragmatic Humanist" (1986) 70 *Revue des Sciences Philosophiques et Théologiques* 36. He notes that Vulteius and Althusius followed the Ramist method: Freigius, 2.

39 Freigius, sig β8r-v.

40 Accursius, final blank.

41 Freigius, sig β8v, 1, 12, 21, Ramus, 6, 10, 204, Vigelius, 471, final blank.

42 Freigius, 1, 2, Hopper 319, 447, 502, Ramus 6, 204.

43 Ramus, 10.

44 Hopper, 502, Ramus, 204.

45 Ramus, 7.

46 Hopper, 308.

47 Vigelius, 4.

negative, writing of reading the fifty books of the Digest without any gloss or commentary, old or new, and treating glosses as having any value only if they were adamantine, penetrating and sharp;[48] and he observed Justinian's prohibition on producing commentaries on the *Corpus Iuris*.[49]

Throughout his works he underlines legal words or notes them in his margins. Moreover, some of his annotations reveal him to have a knowledge of substantive Roman law. He defines *noxa*, comments on *iusiurandum*, uses the noun quasi-contract ("obligatio ex quasi contractu") where the text which he is noting refers to the Justinianic *obligatio quasi ex contractu*, and opposite a text dealing with *maleficium* he uses the more common *delictum*.[50] *Synallagmata*, he notes, are *ultro citroque obligationes*, echoing Ulpian in a text that can only have been remembered.[51] Revealingly, although the text of his copy of Vigelius' *Methodus* has almost nothing in the way of annotations, he does note the reordering of the title *De Re Militari*, observing that this is not dealt with well elsewhere in Vigelius' works.[52] Similarly, his surviving copy of Justinian's Institutes has occasional underlinings many pages apart, suggesting that the book had been used and not just read (if it had been read at all). There is no reason to question his commitment to both the study and the practice of law. Of all professions, he wrote, it was the most useful, the most powerful, the most wise, the most honourable.[53]

Alongside his study of Roman law, Harvey did not ignore the common law. Indeed, he wrote on the front blank of his copy of the 1560 edition of the *Institutions or Principal Grounds of Laws and Statutes* that a person who was ignorant of the popular books of English law was *idiotikon* (though as a good scholar he did so in a mixture of Latin and Greek). We might have been inclined to dismiss this as the statement of someone who was perhaps musing on pursuing a career as a common lawyer, as he might have been in 1573,[54] were it not for the fact that this note dated from 1584, when he is known to have re-read this work. His copy of Littleton's *Tenures* was the edition of 1581, so must have been obtained then or later; his copy of Fitzherbert's *Office of Sheriffs* is dated 1579 and contains notes of statutes passed in 1585. A note in his volume of Hopper, dating from 1580 at the

48 Freigius, blank before title page, sig α2.
49 Freigius, sig α8v.
50 Hopper, 31, 59, 491, Ramus, 153.
51 Vigelius, 330. The reference is to Ulpian's citation of Labeo in D.50.16.19; Vigelius at this point is dealing with *emptio venditio*.
52 Vigelius, 84–87, giving a reference also to Simon Schard.
53 Freigius, blank before title page.
54 Above, 284.

earliest, lists *Rastell's Termes de la Ley*, the *Institutions*, the *Natura Brevium* and Pulton's *Abridgement of Penal Statutes*, writing that these would constitute a compendious introduction to the common law;[55] it is possible that this marks the beginning of his study of English law. His 1584 note lists the books of English law that he owned: as well as the *Institutions* in which he was writing and Littleton's *Tenures*, there was Perkins' *Profitable Book*, and a *Natura Brevium*, probably an edition of Fitzherbert's work. Although it is not mentioned in this list he probably owned Fitzherbert's *Office of Sheriffs* at this time, and there is a reference to Plowden's *Commentaries*. Later, he noted his acquisition of John Cowell's *Institutiones Iuris Anglicani* and his *Interpreter*.

It is rather doubtful whether we can deduce much from the manuscript markings in his English law books, except that he read them. His Littleton is the most thoroughly marked, with a good deal of underlining together with marginal annotations as a guide to the contents of the work. At the end there is a note that he read it in three days, a task which was *dulcissimum et utilissimum*, and that he re-read it over two days in March 1584. It was a perfect introduction to English feudal law. After this, he wrote, all commentaries on English law would be very easy. Apart from underlinings which show that he had read the work, the *Office of Sheriffs* contains nothing but notes of three statutes of 1585: one on the setting up of the Court of Exchequer Chamber, one on the raising of a subsidy, and one the general pardon of that year. His copy of the *Institutes or Principal Grounds* has, similarly, underlinings, more copious than those in the *Office of Sheriffs*, together with marginal notes like those in his Littleton, providing a guide to the contents of his text. On the blanks at the beginning and end we find a few brief notes on the *Senatusconsultum Macedonianum* in Roman law, a brief quotation from Cicero's *De Legibus* on the custom of Rome, a statement that a Roman *actio iniuriarum* should be sued in an action of trespass or trespass on the case in England. We may guess not only that he was picking up these snippets and noting them down on blank pages that were to hand, but also that he was juxtaposing his knowledge of English and Roman law. He was, of course, not the only person in England to try to place English law in this more intellectual context, and it is conceivable that it was his reading of the *Institutions or Principal Grounds of Laws and Statutes* that encouraged him to do so. The preface to this work bears quoting at some little length:

55 Hopper, 11.

> Demosthenes the renowned orator, defineth law in this wise. The law (saith he) is the thing that all men ought to obey for many skills, but in especially because law is the invention, and also the gift of God, the decrees of prudent men, the chastisement of wilful and unwilful offences, and finally the common surety of a realm, whereby it becometh all men to live, which be conversant in the same. Chrisippus also, an excellent philosopher thus beginneth his book of laws, The law is king of all as well divine as human affairs, the president and controller of things honest and dishonest, the prince, captain and ruler of the just and unjust, and it is of civil creatures as well the commander of what they ought to do as the forbidder what they ought not to do. These authentic sayings of wise men assuredly ought much to inflame us to the knowledge of those things without which we shall be esteemed as no men but as brute and savage beasts.

He goes on to cite the Roman jurist Celsus as saying that the law should not be concerned with the literal interpretation of words, but with their underlying meaning, their "pith and power". The beginning of his text, too, points in the direction of an unfamiliarly classical approach to English law:

> The law is the direction and ministration of justice. And justice is (as the Emperor Justinian saith in his institutions) a constant and permanent will to render unto every person his right and duty.

There is just a hint, perhaps, that the classical approach was unfamiliar to the author of the passage, in translating the Latin as saying that each man should be given his right and duty rather than his right and due, but there is no mistaking the intellectualisation – and Romanisation – of the (supposed) background to the common law. This juxtaposition of Roman and English law was not a simple one-way process for Harvey. At several points in the annotations of his copy of Hopper's *In Veram Iurisprudentiam Isagoges* his sense of the common law comes out. Most clearly, in describing the Roman *transactio*, or compromise of action, where it was essential that something be given in return for dropping a claim, Harvey notes "No agreement or composition without consideration",[56] correctly using the English term in its technical, lawyerly sense. The ease with which he used the term in passing testifies to an understanding of English law which was more than fleeting. Similarly, where the text refers to the revocation of alienations made in bad faith, Harvey's annotation reads "Against fraudulent and covenous conveyances",[57] redolent of the language of the English statute of 1571. Whether this indicates a deeper study of the common law than his books lead us to expect or that as an educated man he had imbibed some of the language of the common law we cannot say.

56 Hopper, 44.
57 Hopper, 95.

The study of one man's habits of reading and annotating do not provide any solid basis for conclusions regarding English legal humanism, especially when that man might have had an interest in common law but was not a common lawyer. They may give us some insight into a humanist's approach to law, but none into a humanist approach. In truth, there was nothing in England to parallel what we have come to call legal humanism in continental Europe. The practical learning of the Inns of Court was too well insulated from the universities, where the new learning might have become established. There was no foundation text of the common law which could be reconstructed by philologists; and while medieval texts were being printed in the later sixteenth century, there was very little evidence of critical engagement with them rather than taking one (probably corrupt) manuscript and printing it. And where there was no foundation text, there were no glosses encumbering it, nothing that could be swept away to recover some underlying purity: discard the Year Books, and there was practically nothing there. What there was had been built up in layers over the previous three or four centuries, and could not simply be dismantled as an excrescence; structurally, English law was completely different from the Roman law which had developed in the medieval universities and was therefore substantially immune from the changes associated with legal humanism.

PART IV
LEGAL HUMANISM AND THE BOOK TRADE

12 The Thesauruses of Otto and Meerman as Publishing Enterprises: Legal Humanism in its Last Phase, 1725–1780

Ian Maclean

A. INTRODUCTION

> Dr Tydeman, who is still an ornament of the university of Leyden, thought it expedient [in 1802] to pronounce and publish an academical oration on the excessive study of the civil law. This is a species of excess which no person, interested in the prosperity of the British universities, need at present anticipate with any painful degree of anxiety; and if too much learning should seem to have made some of our lawyers mad, it must at least be admitted that a very small portion of their learning is drawn from the recondite sources of the Roman jurisprudence. Nothing is indeed more common than to hear them declare their decided opinion as to the utter inutility of such a study.[1]

1 Review of L A Warnkoenig, *Institutiones Juris Romani privati, in usum Praelectionum Academicarum vulgatae, cum introductione in universam jurisprudentiam et studium juris Romani* (1825) in *The Foreign Review, and Continental Miscellany* (1828) 41–42. The reference is to Hendrik Willem Tydeman's *Oratio de eo quod nimium est in studio juris Romani* (1802).

This satirical comment (in a review of one of the early contributions to the nineteenth-century German Historical School of Roman Law) was made almost half a century after the supplement to Gerard Meerman's *Novi thesaurus Juris Civilis et Canonici* (1751–1753; supplement 1780) appeared. It is aimed at English, not Scottish, jurists (the latter being expressly excluded from the accusation in a footnote); but even they had lost interest by this date in purchasing books on the historical study of Roman law, which Meerman's collection of humanist texts, and the earlier *Thesaurus Juris Romani* (1725–1735) associated with the name of Everhard Otto, had vigorously promoted.[2] So for the benefit of whom were these thesauruses produced? My aim here is to address this question by looking at the material facts of their publication and the broader intellectual context of their own time and of what preceded them. This chapter thus combines a study of legal humanism as a genre of legal writing with an examination of the facts surrounding its publication in the form of as multi-volume large-scale enterprises in a commercial, academic, political and ideological context (the United Provinces) that was particularly favourable to it.

B. LEGAL HUMANISM

In 1755, Johannes Fridericus Jugler defined legal humanism ("jurisprudentia elegantior") as "the study of Roman law in very close conjunction with philosophy (primordially that of the Stoics), antiquities, the Greek and Latin language, the art of textual criticism, Roman history and literature."[3] Tydeman offered a more specific account in 1802, including all of the above together with numismatics, the study of the Twelve Tables, ancient legal sects, writings against Justinian, post-Justinian Graeco-Roman law, and the preparation of new editions of the *Corpus Iuris Civilis*.[4] In the eyes of the generation of Otto and Meerman, the first phase of legal humanism began in the early years of the sixteenth century with Guillaume Budé and Andrea Alciato, with whom is also connected the pedagogical phenomenon known as the "mos gallicus iuris civilis docendi", as distinct from the traditional "*mos italicus*". It culminated in the work of Jacques Cujas, who according

2 J W Cairns, "Alexander Cunningham's proposed edition of the Digest: an episode in the history of the Dutch Elegant School of Roman Law" (2001) 69 *Tijdschrift voor Rechtsgeschiedenis* 81 (part A), 307 (part B) at 357.

3 Quoted by D Osler, "*Jurisprudentia elegantior* and the Dutch elegant school" (1996) 23 *Ius Commune* 339.

4 Tydeman (n 1) at 13.

to Meerman generated a "Cuiaciana schola".[5] The so-called Dutch elegant school (which included Arnold Vinnius, Simon van Leeuwen, Ulric Huber, Johannes Voet, Gerard Noodt, van Bynkershoek, Otto and Meerman himself) can be said to represent the last phase. Between these phases there are clusters of scholars mainly active in France: "the Douarens, the Le Contes, the Doneaus, the Baudouins, the Le Carons, the Connans, the Brissons and the Hotmans", in Otto's account;[6] and the Spanish scholars Francisco Ramos del Manzano, José Fernández de Retes, and Juan Suárez de Mendoza of the following century, all of whom Meerman restored to the public eye. This was not seen by either Thesaurus compiler as an unbroken tradition, even if in all generations there were practitioners of legal humanism. Although some clear genealogies can be traced in various universities (in Toulouse, for example, and Salamanca), there is not a neat linear development, as the study of Roman law flourished and declined in different national contexts at different times.[7]

For both compilers, legal humanism was not exclusively associated with ancient languages: Meerman included vernacular works in his survey of juristic scholarship.[8] It had an appeal beyond historians of Roman law qua antiquarians: even the figure who is seen in conventional histories of law as representing the next phase of jurisprudence – Johann Gottlieb Heineccius – wrote a pamphlet in which he stressed the usefulness of legal humanism to students and practitioners.[9] Although there is a clear difference between antiquarian studies of the law and the books produced for practitioners, the common ground of legal semantics, reasoning and interpretation allows both genres to be seen in the light of the other: Meerman's colleague and editor of historical Greek texts David Ruhnken points out that these are less useful for their grasp of history than for their skill at legal explication, and van Bynkershoek allows himself to criticise the great Cujas for being too historical.[10] This indicates that the Dutch elegant school had forensic issues clearly

5 G Meerman, *Novus thesaurus juris civili et canonico* (1751–3) vol 4, 1.

6 E Otto, *Thesaurus Juris Romani*, 2nd edn (1733–5) vol 1, 1.

7 G Meerman, *Conspectus novi thesauri juris civilis et canonici* (1751) at 53–70. D Osler, "Legal humanism", at *http://www.rg.mpg.de/en/forschung/osler-legal-humanism*.

8 Ibid, at 67–68, refers to practical guides to criminal law in national jurisdictions by Pierre Ayrault (1576) and Pierre Bougler (1622).

9 J G Heineccius, "*Praefatio de utilitate Antiquitatum in Jurisprudentia*", in J Perizonius, *Dissertationes septem* (1740). Cairns (n 2) at 353 also points out that scholars such as Johannes Voet, like others practising the *usus modernus pandectarum* who were not antiquarian in orientation, had an interest in the textual work of legal humanists.

10 B Sirks, "Cornelis van Bynkershoek as author and elegant jurist" (2011) 79 *Tijdschrift voor Rechtsgeschiedenis* 229 at 231, 234.

in their focus as well as textual palingenesis, and relied on the appeal of legal humanism to more than a narrow group of legal historians.[11]

Legal humanism was potentially collaborative and cumulative, and one ideal outcome of its efforts would have been a new edition of the *Corpus Iuris Civilis*, as was planned in the early eighteenth century by both Andrew Cunningham and Heinrich Brencmann. Such an edition would present the text palingenetically, use what Meerman calls "limatum iudicium" in choosing *lectiones*, and record in notes the decisions of the editor *ope codicum* and *ope ingenii*.[12] In the case of less ambitious legal-humanistic exercises of a monographical or exegetical kind, two important frontiers had to be marked: that between legal humanism and works intended principally for practitioners, and that between legal humanism and legal pedagogical writing. In the former case, works which addressed legal practice might contain historical material, and be included in the genre for that reason, but that did not apply to the majority of these writings. The latter case was partly complicated by the issue of the use of compendia and the allegation (made in the late seventeenth century in the Netherlands) that law students had a regrettably low level of Latinity which introductions to jurisprudence had to take into account.[13] Meerman explicitly excludes student textbooks from his publishing remit, but it is not clear whether for him texts such as Joannes Schneidewein's Commentary on the Institutes of 1571 (supplemented with additional material supplied after the 1594 edition by three highly respected scholars: Denis Godefroy, Matthäus Wesenbeck and Pieter Cornelis van Brederode) belong in this category.[14] It was published a very great number of times before 1750: One estimate is that it sold between 25,000 and 30,000 copies.[15] Meerman cites other commentaries on the Institutes as belonging to the humanist fold, so his silence in Schneidewein's case is not simply to do with the Institutes being itself an introductory text: it is an implicit judgement on its scholarly credentials.

Similar issues of classification also arose in the eyes of publishers of Latin, for whom law books were an important part of their trade. In Latin legal

11 See, e.g., David Ruhnken's comment that the Greek text of Thalalaeus that he edited had been produced "in gratiam Advocatorum et Procuratorum, qui forum attingere parabant": Meerman (n 7) at 8.

12 Ibid, at 43.

13 M L Hewett (transl and comm), *Ulric Huber (1636–1694). De ratione juris docendi et discendi diatribe per modum dialogi. Nonnullis auctis paralipomenois* (2010) 221–223.

14 Meerman (n 7) at 76, referring to any work that "unice in studiosae juventutis gratiam conscriptus videtur."

15 R Savelli, *Censori e giuristi: storie di libri, di idee e di costumi (secolo XVI–XVII)* (2011) at 309.

writing, clear generic distinctions had emerged by the 1570s: the canonical texts of the law; learned commentaries; *practica* (books aimed at practitioners); manuals and reference works; monographs; polemic; and dissertations. In the estimation of publishers, the texts of the *Corpus Iuris Civilis* and reference works such as *lexica* were clearly profitable, but not to the same degree as *practica*. From the mid-sixteenth century onwards, there were major speculative ventures in Lyon and Venice (both heavily committed to *mos italicus* writings) involving the republication of medieval masters in collections such as the two multi-volume folio compilations known as *Tractatus Tractatuum* (1549, 1584). These appeared alongside successful monographs by modern jurists (Julius Clarus, Josse Damhouder, Giacomo Menochio, Francesco Mantica, Prospero Farinacci, Pedro Barbosa), which continued to appear until the end of the eighteenth century. It is possible to gauge what was profitable in this market from the activities of Geneva printers who issued unauthorised editions on cheaper paper of what they took to be potential bestsellers in all of these sectors. They did not look on works by legal humanists in this way. A few such authors were produced by speculative publishers who aimed at an international market (notably Sebastian Gryphius and Guillaume Rouillé of Lyon, and Thomas Guarin of Basel), but the majority only achieved publication in limited press runs produced by local printers in such places as Orléans, Bourges, Poitiers, Salamanca and Cervera. Of sixteenth-century legal humanists, only Jacques Cujas continued to be reprinted comprehensively after 1600.[16]

C. LAW IN THE BOOK MARKET BEFORE THE THIRTY YEARS WAR

To achieve international publication in a scholarly field in this period, at least two necessary conditions had to be met: promotion by a scholar or rich patron, and adoption by a publisher, who might or might not take on the financial risk of printing. Nearly all books produced at this time were advertised at the twice-yearly Frankfurt Book Fair. This was the largest point of distribution of books in Europe, not only of current but also of past publications, as major publishers kept immense stocks of books in warehouses in the city. The Book Fair catalogues which were issued twice yearly were one means of finding out what was available; there were also the back-lists

16 On law publication in the period before the Thirty Years War, see I Maclean, *Scholarship, Commerce, Religion: The Learned Book in the Age of Confessions, 1560–1630* (2012) at 93.

of publishers known as "nomenclaturae", and other bibliographical tools such as Draudius' massive *Bibliotheca classica* (1610 and 1625), which is separated into disciplines, in which books are grouped by subject. Printer-publishers were not only responsible for the production of this vast reservoir of books; they also helped distribute them by the way in which they settled accounts between themselves. This was principally by *Tauschhandel*, that is, the practice of swapping the same number of printed sheets against printed sheets from other publishers. This meant that for the most part publishers followed the Hansa model of trading (attending fairs themselves, or being represented at them by agents), and relied less on a system of distribution through branches of their own enterprise, or on direct sales to booksellers, other than to those whose scale of purchasing and exchange justified their attendance at the fairs.

Tauschhandel had various important effects. It turned books themselves into currency, and thereby alleviated the perennial cash-flow problems of publishers. They returned home with the books they had acquired by exchange, and offered them for sale themselves, becoming thereby retailers, and at the same time ensuring the transmission of scholarly texts all round Europe. These international publishers were acutely aware of market zones, and the limited degree of control they could exercise over unauthorised reproduction of their most promising titles without seeking the legal protection of expensive privileges in given jurisdictions, such as France or the Holy Roman Empire. They were also aware of potential impediments to free distribution, especially through censorship and ecclesiastical prohibition, and sought as far as possible not to fall prey to these by a variety of means, including the use of false bibliographical addresses and the disguising of an author's name and provenance (the protestant Schneidewein's name, for example, was translated into the Greek sobriquet Oinotomus for the Spanish and Italian markets).[17] Towards the end of this period, publishers increasingly took note of the interests of the growing number of book collectors, and tried to conceive of series of books, which would entice purchasers to continue acquiring works in a specific genre. In this, they were helped by the finding tools that were being produced for the use of purchasers, and they engaged in various other ploys to encourage serious collectors to buy the very latest edition, and thus ensure the expansion of the market.[18]

By the beginning of the seventeenth century, undue optimism in the

17 Savelli (n 15) at 37.

18 On all these points see Maclean (n 16) *passim*.

capacity of this market to expand led to over-production and market saturation. The declarations of the Frankfurt Book Fair trebled between 1593 and 1613, and the vast repositories of unsold books held by the major printer-publishers led in turn to spectacular bankruptcies. These internal factors connected to the operation of the market were exacerbated by a series of external events: local conflicts and plagues that interfered with the free transfer of goods and persons, and most especially the catastrophic Thirty Years War, from the effects of which Frankfurt itself would not recover for many decades. Even the shrewdest and most experienced bookseller-publishers resident in Frankfurt itself fell prey to these negative forces, as the bankruptcy of one such figure, Peter Kopf, in 1633 shows. It was reported at that time that his warehouse was full of unsold and probably unsellable folio editions of legal works, some published in his own name, others acquired through *Tauschhandel*.[19] It took some decades after the 1630s before speculative publishers were again willing to take on large-scale legal publications, and when they did, the market conditions had changed in important ways.

D. THE LATIN TRADE AFTER 1650 AND THE ROLE OF THE NETHERLANDS

By 1650, Frankfurt had declined, and Leipzig – the other great book fair in Germany – was too far to the east to dominate European trade in international books. So it is not surprising that by 1722, Amsterdam had acquired the reputation of being the "bookshop of the world", signalling a translation of the centre of trade in learned books from Germany to the Netherlands.[20] There are many factors that brought about this change. The United Provinces had good roads, and international connections through its ports. It was connected with Iberia through its links with the Southern Netherlands. From the early years of the seventeenth century, it had a well-developed financial market, low interest rates, the legal regulation of commerce, and an international banking system, all of which has earned it the description as "the first modern economy".[21] It benefited from the

19 A Dietz, *Frankfurter Handelsgeschichte* (1970) vol 3, at 82.

20 The description is that of Voltaire: see C Berkvens-Stevelinck, H Bots, P G Hoftijzer and O S Lankhorst (eds), *Le magasin de l'univers: the Dutch Republic as the centre of the European book trade* (1992) at x.

21 J de Vries and A van der Woude, *The First Modern Economy: Success, Failure and Perseverance of the Dutch Economy, 1500–1815* (1997). See also J Luiten van Zanden, "The 'revolt of the early modernists' and the 'first modern economy': an assessment" (2002) 55 *Economic History Review* 619. See also the important article of W D Smith, "The function of commercial centers

flight of Huguenots from France who were involved in the trade of printing, was not hamstrung by excessive regulation at the level of state and guild, and developed various innovations in book manufacture, including the production of very small formats with clear typefaces. In their visits to Frankfurt in the early decades of the seventeenth century, Dutch publishers were the first to resist the system of book-acquisition and sale through *Tauschhandel*,[22] developing instead a credit system through which they dealt with a broad network of bookshops at home and abroad: a network attested by Pieter de Hondt's impressive list of 440 European contacts listed in the *Conspectus* of Meerman's *Novus thesaurus* of 1751. From the early seventeenth century, local booksellers such as Cornelis Claesz of Amsterdam held very extensive stocks, and in their catalogues they encouraged potential purchasers to enquire about works not listed there.[23] Later, booksellers ("bibliopolae") resident in the United Provinces came to act as publisher-financiers, agents for purchase and sale on behalf of others, distributors, and advertisers.[24] Dutch culture was mercantile and polyglot (French, Latin, Dutch, German); it had access through its universities to good scholars who could act as correctors of scholarly editions; there was relative freedom of publication, a degree of religious pluralism and toleration, and a willingness to ignore religious issues in the interests of commerce. As early as 1637, Descartes described it enthusiastically as "a country in which the long period of war has established such good discipline that the armies that are maintained here seem only to serve to ensure that people enjoy the fruits of peace with correspondingly greater security . . . amid a teeming, highly active, great people that shows more interest in its own affairs than curiosity for those of others".[25] The Provinces possessed moreover the requisite range of artisanal trades for printing (compositors,

in the modernization of European capitalism: Amsterdam as an information exchange in the seventeenth century" (1984) 44 *Journal of Economic History* 985.

22 One way in which they undermined *Tauschhandel* was to demand a punitive ratio of exchange (1:3 or 1:4); see N Bachleitner, F M Eybl and E Fischer, *Geschichte des Buchhandels in Österreich* (2000) 68. M Estermann, "Signete und Widmungsbriefe Frankfurter Verleger des späten Jahrhunderts" (2005) 59 *Archiv für Geschichte des Buchwesens* 65 at 90 produces evidence of the persistence of *Tauschhandel* as a practice among German publishers.

23 B van Selm, *Een menighte treffelijcke boecken. Nederlandse boekhandelscatalogi in het begin van de zeventiende eeuw* (1987) at 176.

24 On the new configuration of printers, publishers and booksellers elsewhere in Europe, see Estermann (n 22) at 90.

25 *Discours de la méthode*, 3, AT 6.31: "un pays où la longue durée de la guerre a fait établir de tels ordres, que les armées qu'on y entretient ne semblent servir qu'à faire qu'on y jouisse des fruits de la paix avec d'autant plus de sûreté, . . . parmi la foule d'un grand peuple fort actif, et plus soigneux de ses propres affaires, que curieux de celles d'autrui."

binders, and illustrators), and became in time self-sufficient and competitive in paper production.[26]

At The Hague, Amsterdam and Leiden, the second-hand market in books developed more than in any other place in Europe. By the early years of the seventeenth century, substantial personal libraries were coming up for sale, through which the books that previously had been sought in the warehouses of Frankfurt could be acquired. These were disposed of through auctions, and those desirous of improving their libraries had themselves represented in these cities by purchasing agents. The promoters of the *Thesaurus Juris Romani* and the *Novus thesaurus* – Cornelius van Bynkershoek and Gerard Meerman – relied on rare works acquired in this way by themselves and their collaborators. Their publishers – Johannes vander Linden and Pieter de Hondt – were both active in the auction market of law books (vander Linden, for example, organised the auction of Alexander Cunningham's library in 1730, and de Hondt did the same for the books of Cornelius van Bynkershoek in 1743). One of the reasons that both publishers were willing to risk their own money in the thesauruses they sponsored may well have been their awareness of the interest that would be shown by unsuccessful bidders at auctions in reprints of the rare books they contained. Auctions, as Otto pointed out in the preface to his *Thesaurus*, were a risky and expensive way to buy books.[27] They were regulated by law, and reflected some tight Dutch mercantile practices (one rule specified that books could only be acquired with ready money).[28] The Dutch espoused other new techniques for marketing books, notably sales through subscription. This practice, first developed in England, provided a solution to up-front costs (paper and labour), and came into its own in the late seventeenth century, the era of reference books (large-scale multi-volume publications), for acquisition by those as much interested in displaying their ownership of prestigious

26 On the points made in this paragraph, see de Vries and van der Woude (n 21) at 129, 311, D McKitterick, "Credit, Cash and Customers: Cornelius Crownfield and Anglo-Dutch Trade in the Early Eighteenth Century", in L Hellinga, A Duke, J Harskamp and T Hermans (eds), *The Bookshop of the World: The Role of the Low Countries in the Book-Trade*, 1473–1941 (1999) at 245, P Hoftijzer, " The History of the Book in the Low Countries", in M F Suarez and H R Woudhuysen (eds), *The Oxford Companion to the Book* (2010) vol 1 at 212–215.

27 Otto (n 6) vol 1,1. The notes appended to auction items often confirm this: in The *Viri illustris Friderici Adophi Hansen ab Ehrencron . . . bibliotheca* (1718) at 17, the auctioneer (Abraham de Hondt) noted about item 232 (Augustín's *De nominibus propriis tou Pandektou Florentini*: see below, pp. 313–314), that it was a "lib[er] rar[us] et quantisvis pretii." See also note 53.

28 P de Hondt, *Catalogus bibliothecae Johannis Francisci de Boissy* (1755), verso of title-page: "on avertit le Public, qu'on ne delivrera aucun livre, que contre de l'argent comptant, et non en or".

volumes as in consulting them.[29] In a preface entitled "De vana librorum pompa" to a reprint of Thomas Bartholin's *De libris legendis dissertationes*, published in 1711, Johann Gerhard Meuschen, a Lutheran cleric living in The Hague, lists the vices of those who are active purchasers of learned books of this kind, beginning with their assumption that they will gain cultural credit simply by owning a large number of books, especially ones with nice bindings, without intending to read them, and deploring their unwillingness to let serious scholars have access to their libraries. They may have been vilified here as "vanity" purchasers, but they were essential to the success of ventures such as those of Otto and Meerman, and they played an important part as wholly passive consumers of their Thesauruses. Some of the features of prospectuses for subscription (which was closely regulated by law, as were auctions) reflected this market for scholarly items treated as luxury goods at bargain prices: in the report of the prospectus for vander Linden's *Thesaurus*, the publisher undertook to produce only a limited number of extra copies, and to sell them at twice the price of that paid by subscribers;[30] in the *Conspectus* for Meerman's *Novus thesaurus* (1751) which sets out de Hondt's conditions for subscription, the product is specified as having good paper and fine typeface, a large format with broad margins, a limited press run, and a page recording the names of those who commit themselves to purchasing the work in question (an added sop to their vanity); to all this an attractive title page with a vignette might also be added.[31]

It would be misleading, however, to suggest that these developments were unique to the Netherlands. Auctions took place elsewhere in Europe, and there were notable booksellers active in the production of finding lists for past editions: for example, Simon Paulli's *Bibliotheca juridica* printed in Strasbourg (1671) and the comprehensive *Allgemeines Europäisches Bücher-Lexicon* produced by Theophilus Georgi in Leipzig (1742–58). There was also sporadic engagement in large-scale speculative ventures of legal republication in places such as Lyon, Leipzig and Naples.

29 P J Wallis "Book subscription lists" (1974) 5/29 *The Library* 255.

30 Jean Le Clerc, *Bibliothèque ancienne et moderne* (1723) vol 20 part one, 332. Vander Linden undertook to pay 1,000 francs to the poor of Leiden if he breached this condition.

31 Meerman (n 7) at 77. The same undertaking had been made for the second (Broedelet) edition of Otto's *Thesaurus*: see *Nova acta eruditorum* (Jan 1734) at 47–48.

E. *HISTORIA LITTERARIA*, THE REPUBLIC OF LETTERS AND LEGAL HUMANIST AUTHORS

One of the by-products of humanist scholarship was the celebration of the achievements of humanist scholars themselves. The professions followed suit: lawyers were among the first to produce collections of bio-bibliographies of their predecessors as a way of promoting their discipline. The earliest such work was produced by Giovanni Nevizzano in 1522.[32] In 1679, when Martin Lipenius' *Bibliotheca realis juridica*, the first comprehensive systematic bibliography of law, appeared, there were six entries under the heading "*bibliotheca juridica*", nineteen under the heading "*vitae jurisconsultorum*", and thirty-seven under the heading "*vitae in specie*". By the edition of 1757, the numbers had risen to forty-nine, thirty-eight and 101 respectively: a threefold increase. Many of these volumes were owned and cited by Meerman. This bio-bibliographical genre accompanied a new initiative in the history of scholarship that came to be known as *historia litteraria*, and that was adopted as a mode of teaching in certain German universities. The founding text of this genre is usually said to be Daniel Morhof's *Polyhistor sive de auctorum notitia et rerum commentarii* (1688); it is celebrated in Christoph August Heumann's *Conspectus reipublicae literariae* (1718), and reached its high point in the works of the legal humanist Nicolaus Hieronymus Gundling (*Vollständige Historie der Gelahrheit* 1734–1736) and Johann Andreas Fabricius (*Abriss einer allgemeinen Historie der Gelehrsamkeit*, 3 vols 1752–1754). In these works, accounts were given of the lives and works of individual scholars in both their local and international contexts, and stress was laid on scholarly genealogies of teachers and their disciples, and the ways in which their learned activities meshed with those of others. All this gave rise in turn to an evolutionary version of intellectual history showing the developing systematisation of knowledge and its role as a means of eliminating dogmatism.[33] Legal humanists (of

32 I am indebted to Professor Rodolfo Savelli for this information.

33 M Gierl, "Bestandaufnahme im gelehrten Bereich: zur Entwicklung der '*historia literaria*' im 18. Jahrhundert" in *Denkhorizonte und Handlungsspielräume. Historische Studien für Rudolf Vierhaus zum 70. Geburtstag* (1992) at 53, idem, "Compilation and the Production of Knowledge in the Early German Enlightenment", in H E Bödecker, P H Reill and J Schlumblum (eds), *Wissenschaft als kulturelle Praxis, 1750–1900* (1999) at 70, F Waquet (ed), *Mapping the World of Learning. The Polyhistor of Daniel Georg Morhof* (2000), H Mohnhaupt, "*Historia literaria iuris*: Beispiele juristischer Literaturgeschichten im 18. Jahrhundert", *Max-Planck-Institut für europäische Rechtsgeschichte*, No. 2013–03. There are equivalent movements to *historia literaria* elsewhere in Europe: for example, the eulogies of scholars sponsored by the Académie royale des sciences in Paris after 1699.

whom Gundling was one) were a group specifically associated with the practice.[34]

The rise of the genre was clearly closely related to that of the Republic of Letters, famously described by Pierre Bayle, in his *Dictionnaire historique et critique* of 1696:

> The Republic of Letters is an extremely free state. The only dominion recognized is that of truth and reason; under their auspices, war can be innocently waged on anyone. Friends have to be on their guard against friends, fathers against their children, fathers-in-law against their sons-in-law. Everyone is both sovereign and answerable in law to everyone else . . . Any criticism levelled at a book tends only to show that its author lacks this or that degree of enlightenment; but even with this lack of knowledge, the author can enjoy all the rights and privileges of this society, without his reputation as a man of honour and a good citizen suffering the slightest hurt.[35]

Other commentators went further, and stressed the completely democratic and non-exclusive nature of the Republic, and its transcendence of linguistic, religious and national boundaries.[36] Crucial to its development were the new means of scholarly communication, which replaced the less efficient arrangements that were practised in the Frankfurt Book Fair. This phase of the Republic of Letters came into being shortly after the founding of scholarly journals such as the *Transactions of the Royal Society*, the *Mémoires de l'Académie Royale des Sciences*, the *Acta Eruditorum*, the *Journal des Savants* and the development of newsletters and gazettes such as *Les Nouvelles de la République des Lettres*, the *Bibliothèque ancienne et moderne*, and *the Gazette de Leyde*, in all of which new scholarly works were announced and comprehensively reviewed.[37] By the mid-eighteenth

34 Tydeman (n 1) at 13.

35 P Bayle, *Dictionnaire historique et critique* (1697) sv Catius: "Cette République est un Etat extrêmement libre. On n'y reconnoit que l'empire de la vérité et de la raison ; et sous leurs auspices on fait la guerre innocemment à qui que ce soit. Les amis s'y doivent tenir en garde contre leurs amis, les pères contre leurs enfans, les beaux-pères contre leurs gendres . . . Chacun y est tout ensemble souverain et justiciable de chacun. Les loix de la société n'ont pas fait préjudice à l'indépendance de l'état de nature, par rapport à l'erreur et à l'ignorance : tous les particuliers ont à cet egard le droit de glaive et le peuvent exercer sans en demander la permission à ceux qui gouvernent . . . La critique d'un livre ne tend à montrer qu'un auteur n'a pas tel ou tel degré de lumière : or, il peut, avec ce défaut de science, jouir de tous les droits et de tous les privilèges de la société, sans que sa réputation d'honnête homme et de bon sujet de la République reçoive la moindre attente ; on n'usurpe rien de ce qui dépend de la Majesté de L'Etat en faisant conoître au public les fautes qui sont dans un livre."

36 Vigneul-Marville (pseudonym), *Mélanges d'histoire et de littérature* (1700) vol 2, 60–63.

37 In the *Acta eruditorum* and the *Journal des savants*, the dignity of the study of law was recognised; it was second in the order of disciplines listed (theology being first). Not all jurists thought highly of the publication, however: see Huber (n 13) at 223.

century, journals and monographs on the learned world had proliferated to an astonishing extent: the 1747 edition of Morhof's *Polyhistor* lists no fewer than 784 of them. Much of this activity, which brought academic debate into the public sphere, was centred on the United Provinces, famous for its tolerant regime in this regard. Its influence was felt even in much less liberal regimes such as Spain, where jurists among others quickly learned how to enter into contact with the less repressive North and foster intellectual openness. Among this group are two of the figures who had a major influence on Meerman's *Novus thesaurus*, as we shall see.

The idealistic programmatic descriptions of the Republic of Letters do not mention the prosaic fact that communications in such an international scholarly community needed to be paid for. That of course applies to all legal publication in the era after the Thirty Years War. I have already mentioned the need for both scholarly promoters and financial backers to achieve publication. In theory, it ought to have been relatively easy for legal humanists to find sponsors and achieve wide sales, as they were engaged in an international field of study ("non unius nationis", as Otto put it[38]), written in a universal language; but the evidence shows that such publication as was achieved by living authors tended to be local and limited in press runs, even in developed markets such as that of Germany. One reason for this that has been put forward is the imperfect nature of the Republic of Letters, which was covertly nationalistic.[39] This can be gauged even from the lists of famous legal humanists, which vary from one author to another, and one publication to another.[40] Problems of advertisement and distribution may be another factor.[41]

38 Otto (n 6) vol 1 at 1.

39 M Mulsow, "Practices of unmasking: polyhistors, correspondence, and the birth of dictionaries of pseudonymity in seventeenth-century Germany" (2006) 67 *Journal of the History of Ideas* 219. Christian Heinrich Trotz, a German teaching in Utrecht at the same time as Otto, promoted the work of one legal humanist compatriot (the *Opuscula juridico-philologica* of Christfried Waechtler [1733]) in the introduction to which he expresses his German national pride in the work he is editing, but he also saw the work of one deceased Swiss (Jacques Godefroy in 1736) and one deceased Frenchman (Guillaume Maran in 1741) through the press.

40 Otto (n 6) vol 1, 1 includes Viglius Zuichem in his list (perhaps to flatter his country of adoption); in the many lists that appear in articles in the *Acta eruditorum* (Supplement, vol 8, 1724, at 515), a review of Heineccius' *Antiquitatum Romanarum jurisprudentiam illustrantium syntagma* (1724) article of 1724 (at 515) gives the following somewhat eccentric list of prominent legal humanists: "immortalia nomina Brissonii, Cujacii, Fabrorum [i.e. Pierre et Antoine Favre], Brummeri, Signonii, Spanheimi, Noodtii, Bynkershoekii, Huberi, Schultingii, Thomasii."

41 M H Hoeflich claims that Jacques Godefroy, a Genevan scholar of the early seventeenth century "had little trouble himself (and believed that others would fare as well) in obtaining works from Spain, France, Germany, Italy and the Low Countries": M H Hoeflich, "A seventeenth-century Roman law bibliography: Jacques Godefroy and his *Bibliotheca Juris Civilis Romani*" (1982) 75 *Law Library Journal* 514 at 520. I do not think that this claim is plausible.

Deceased legal humanists fared better in this respect. Everhard Otto pays tribute to the academic figures (the list is not complete) who ensured that their predecessors were reprinted from the sixteenth century onwards: Nicolaus Cisnerus (the edition of François Douaren's works of 1579), Scipione Gentili (Hugues Doneau's *Commentaria*, 1596), Jacobus Lectius (the *Opera Omnia* of François Hotman in 1600), Emond Mérille (those of Antoine Le Conte, in 1616), Charles Annibal Fabrot (the editor of Cujas' ten folio volumes of *Observationes* in 1658), Antoine Marville (Jacques Godefroy's edition of the *Codex Theodosianus* in 1665), and the Neapolitan publisher Bernardino Gessari, who paid for the Naples edition of Mérille's works in 1720.[42] The other producers of works in this list (altogether they represent more than twenty-two stout folios) include members of the elite of late Renaissance humanist publishers (the Wechel presses, Pierre de la Rovière, Eustache Vignon and Jacques Stoer), and the most successful speculative presses of the post Thirty Years War period (Sébastien Cramoisy of Paris, Jean-Antoine Huguetan and Marc-Antoine Ravaud of Lyon). It is striking that, given their scale, these volumes must have been aimed at the same narrow market of rich collectors and institutions as the legal folios produced before the Thirty Years War. It is unlikely that they would have been produced if it were not for the growing practice of collecting books among the elites of Europe. Other legal humanists of the early period also enjoyed republication on a more modest scale, possibly for wider distribution: notably Barnabé Brisson, whose *De formulis et solennibus verbis*, *Selectae ex iure civili antiquitates* and *Opera minora* were printed several times after 1648, and whose legal dictionary (the *De verborum significatione*) appeared singly or with other reference works six times before 1755 (compare Jakab elsewhere in this volume). He is somewhat of an exception in the pantheon of jurists enjoying republication, most other legal humanists being eclipsed by producers of textbook editions such as the already mentioned Institutes of Joannes Schneidewein, and writers of *practica* (Pedro Barbosa, Giacomo Menochio, Francesco Mantica, and Prospero Farinacci).

F. THE *THESAURUS JURIS ROMANI* (1725–1744)

I have referred to Meuschen's dyspeptic essay on the vain pomp of books; it ends on a positive note, by praising those monarchs, grandees and private

42 Otto (n 6) vol 1 at 1. Meerman (n 5) vol 1 ix, vol 2 vii, vol 4 vii recognises on various occasions the importance of Fabrot as a promoter of legal humanism.

collectors who maintain libraries for the most worthy of reasons, and allow scholars to consult their books. Such a figure in The Hague of Meuschen's day was the President of the Supreme Court of Holland, Cornelius van Bynkershoek (1673–1743), a much published legal humanist in his own right, and the sponsor of the *Thesaurus Juris Romani* associated with the name of Everhard Otto. Both these figures promoted the works of others, collected books, and delivered copy to publishers, and as such could almost be seen as honorary members of, the book trade. Van Bynkershoek had three of his monographs published by Joannes vander Linden between 1710 and 1723, and this would have no doubt predisposed him in favour of the publisher, whom Otto and others credited with the initiative that brought about the *Thesaurus*.[43] Van Bynkershoek was also in contact with Everhard Otto (1685–1756), to whom he entrusted the task of acting as corrector (editor and proof-reader) and writing the prefaces. Otto was one of a number of Germans employed as teachers of law in the United Provinces. Since 1720, he had been professor at Utrecht; by that time, he had already published four monographic publications.[44] He was not the only scholarly collaborator: indeed, both Otto's and Meerman's Thesauruses relied on widespread scholarly collaboration. The preface to the first volume also acknowledges the advice of Alexander Cunningham and Heinrich Brencmann, of van Bynkershoek's colleague in the Supreme Court Adolf Visscher (who provided a copy of Antonio Agustín's *De nominibus propriis tou Pandektou Florentini* [1579]), the Leipzig professor Georg Adolf Schuberth (who supplied Joannes Stekius's *Observationes anticriticae juris* [1627]), Abraham Gronovius (the donor of Nicolaus Catharinus's *Observationes et conjecturae* [1660]) and the Frisian advocate Johannes Balk (who edited Petrus Burgius' *Electorum liber* [1585] and Petrus Perrenonius' *Animadversiones et Variae Lectiones Juris Civilis* [1593]). All but Schuberth were listed as subscribers to the *Thesaurus*. In his dedicatory letter to van Bynkershoek, Otto clearly intimates that the other texts came from the dedicatee's own library. How works came eventually to be included or excluded is not discussed in any

43 Van Bynkershoek, *Observationes* (1710), the *Opuscula varii argumenti* (1719) and the *De foro legatorum tam in causa civili quam criminali* (1721). Otto (n 6) vol 1 at 2, Meerman (n 7) 1 attribute the initiative for the publication of the *Thesaurus* to vander Linden.

44 Otto, *De aedilibus coloniarum et municipiorum liber singularis* (1713), *De Diis vialibus plerorumque populorum dissertatio* (1714), *De vita et morte Aemilii Papiniani* (1718), *De perpetua foeminarum tutela* (1719), *Disputatio Juris Canonici … circa electionem pontificis romani* (1721), *Dissertationes juris publici et privati* (1723). For a full bibliography, see M Ahsmann (ed), *Bibliografie van hoogleraren in de rechten aan de Utrechtse Universiteit tot 1811* (1993) nos 204–279.

detail: in the preface to the first volume, Otto simply refers to the three conditions *"raritas"*, *"brevitas"* and *"utilitas."*[45]

Otto writes very warmly of the publisher Joannes vander Linden the Younger, a member of a publishing family that had been active since the 1660s, describing him as a good Latinist, a printer and corrector with the highest standards who was driven by a desire to serve the Republic of Letters.[46] As well as his activity on behalf of van Bynkershoek, he had produced two editions of Gerard Noodt's *Opera* (1713, 1724), the latter in two folio volumes, a translation and edition of the Institutes (1715, 1719), and a number of legal, medical and theological disputations; the *Thesaurus* was however his most extensive undertaking. As far as I can ascertain, no prospectus ("proposition") for vander Linden's *Thesaurus* survives, but there is a full account of it in Jean Leclerc's *Bibliothèque ancienne et moderne* of 1623. The project, the initiative for which is attributed wholly to the publisher, capitalised on the desideratum expressed in the January 1723 issue of the *Acta eruditorum*, where a review of Brencmann's *Historia Pandectarum* expresses the hope that Agustín's *De nominibus propriis tou Pandektou Florentini* (the first entry, and by far the longest text reprinted in the whole *Thesaurus*) would be republished. In Le Clerc's résumé of the prospectus, there is a list of the proposed contents with a separate section naming the desiderata not yet in the hands of the publisher (works by Avellanus, Catherinus, Landius and Steckius). Vander Linden, who acknowledged that he had consulted van Bynkershoek and others about his project, made guarantees about the quality of paper, the detailed conditions relating to financial adjustments if there was variation in the proposed size (three volumes and 6,000 folia), the instalments to be paid, and the timing of the delivery of the volumes, which he undertook to publish only of there were a sufficient number of subscribers.[47] From the instalment of the *Journal des Savants* for April 1724, we learn that the subscription was open in both Holland and Paris.[48]

45 Otto (n 6) vol 1 at 3.

46 Ibid, vol 1 at 5: "is enim operas typographicas non mercenario cuidam, oscitanti et indocto, ut fieri solet, regendas locavit: sed ipse, peritia Latinae linguae satis imbutus, manum admovit operi, immo plusquam manuariam operam praestitit, omnesque diligentiae intendit nervos, ut cum nova forma novum a typis splendorem libri acciperent, iis longe emendatiores in manus lectorum pervenirent".

47 *Bibliothèque ancienne et moderne* 20 (1723) at 325. The criteria of selection include a passage warning against the reprinting of unworthy works of the past simply on the grounds of their rarity, and refers also to the superior survival rate of large volumes, which makes their reprinting less necessary.

48 *Journal des Savants* April 1724 at 255: "on imprime chez Jean vander Linden un livre en 3 vol, in folio intitulé Thesaurus Juris Romani; il contiendra quarante-huit Traités différens, concernant

The list of subscribers (which contain the names of very few French purchasers, in spite of the subscription being made available to them) was printed at the end of the Preface in date order, introduced by a tactful comment pointing out that the titles and dignities of those whose names appeared had not been included to avoid offending those who might feel that their own had been unduly omitted ("neglectis omnibus muneribus et honoribus, ne aliis, quorum dignitates nobis non innotuerunt, aliquid detrahi videatur").[49] This (and other features of the list, such as series of dots representing missing first names, and entries consisting only of initials) tells us that Otto or vander Linden transcribed the real subscription lists set up in Paris and Holland (presumably, at various locations). The absence of details about the subscribers also prevents us from knowing whether the majority of subscribers were indeed the vainglorious non-readers that Meuschen describes, although a comment in the review that appeared in the *Bibliothèque ancienne et moderne* of 1725 suggests that this was indeed the case.[50] We may usefully compare this list to that included in the edition of the Renaissance anatomist Andreas Vesalius's *Opera Omnia*, which also appeared in folio in 1725 (in two volumes), published by the Leiden booksellers Johannes van Vivié and Jan and Herman Verbeek. This list records 199 copies, of which forty-seven went to Dutch booksellers, eighty-eight to Dutch doctors, and thirty-four to other Dutch purchasers. English doctors are the next largest group (fifteen). This may lead us to assume that the Dutch subscribers to Otto's *Thesaurus* were in the main involved with the legal profession, confirming the claim made in 1690 by the Jena jurist Adrian Beier that scholarly books were written in collusion with publishers who financed them, and purchased by the scholarly community alone, although not exclusively for scholarly purposes.[51]

le droit Romain, la plupart de divers Auteurs. On a souscrit pour cet ouvrage en Hollande et à Paris."

49 This problem probably arose from the fact that Otto had before him the original lists with the signatures (not all of them legible or complete) of the subscribers.

50 *Bibliothèque ancienne et moderne* 23 (1725) at 327: "Depuis les Grands Recueuils des Antiquitez Romaines et Greques, publiez par Mrs. *Graevius et Gronovius*, eurent le succès, que l'on sait, et sur tout depuis peu de tems en çà; il s'est fait de diverses entreprises sembables, dont on a bien auguré. Jamais on n'a tant publié de Recueuils en Hollande, qu'on a fait dans l'espace de peu d'Années. ... Si l'on demande ; si cela vient de ce, qu'il y a plus de gens qui étudient qu'autrefois? je crois, que la plûpart répondront, que cela vient plûtôt de ce, que plus de gens font des Bibliotheques, qu'on ne faisoit auparavant ... Il n'étoit pas facile d'executer ce Projet, à cause du mépris, que les Praticiens faisoient de la meilleure Critique, et de l'ancienne Jurisprudence Romaine, que l'on n'employe guere au Barreau, à présent. "

51 *Kurtzer Bericht/ von der nützlichen und fürtrefflichen Buch-handung und deroselben Privilegien* (1690) 5–6: "Die Wahren [des Buch-Händlers] sind von und vor niemand als Gelehrten ... Der Buch-Händler allein ist der Gelehrten eigentlicher Abnehmer."

Otto's subscription list reveals that of 401 copies accounted for (all on the same grade of paper), 168 went to booksellers mainly in Germany and the Low Countries. The rest of the subscribers were (to judge by their names) from the Netherlands, apart from three Scots, four Germans and four Italians. It is not clear whether the copies acquired by booksellers were on a sale-and-return basis;[52] if so, then the publication was a very speculative affair. Sixteen months later, the *Journal des Savants* (Dec 1726, p, 726) records that volumes 1 and 2 had appeared, volume 3 was well advanced, and there would be a further volume which would include Jacobus Constantinaeus's *Enodationes* (1627), Henricus a Suerin's *Repetitae lectiones* (1585), the *Opuscula* of Scipione Gentili (1588), those of his brother Alberico Gentili, and similar works by François Baudouin and others. In the event, not all of these were included (the fact that Alberico's works had been published in 1720 at Naples by Giovanni Gravier probably led to their not being printed again; and it is possible that vander Linden got wind of Nicolaus Hieronymus Gundling's imminent reprinting of Baudouin's works, which appeared in Leipzig and Halle between 1726 and 1730).[53]

In the preface to the first volume, Otto begins by linking the *Thesaurus* to the history of legal humanism from Budé to Cujas. He next pays tribute to those who as promoters of dead scholars kept their works alive by editing them (see above, p. 312). He also discusses the genre of thesaurus itself, first in the context of much earlier legal productions, naming the eighteen folio volumes produced by Francesco Ziletti of Venice known as the *Tractatus tractatuum* (1584), and the eight volumes of *Repetitiones* produced by Pompeius Limpius (1608). Much closer to home, and to his own time, however, were the massive antiquarian enterprises, the twelve folio volumes of Roman antiquities (1694–1699), thirteen of Greek antiquities (1697–1702), and fourteen of Italian antiquities (1704–1725), all known as thesauruses, edited variously by Joannes Georgius Graevius, Jacobus Gronovius and Pieter Burman, and produced by the successful but unpopular Leiden publisher Pieter van der Aa.[54] This is the publishing model, where Ziletti is the juristic precedent; but there is a difference in both cases

52 See P Hoftijzer, "The Leiden bookseller Pieter van der Aa (1659–1733) and the international book trade", in Berkvens-Stevelinck et al (n 20) 169 at 176.

53 Christian Thomasius had issued a letter in 1689 in which he declared that he was preparing an edition of Baudouin's work, but this had come to nothing: *Ad fautores jurisprudentiae atque historiae epistola . . . de nova editione quam parat operum Francisci Balduini* (1689).

54 See Hoftijzer (n 52) 169–184. Otto also mentions Janus Gruter's *Lampas sive fax artium liberalium* (1602–1634).

with vander Linden's enterprise. Whereas the other thesauruses could be described as aspiring to adequate coverage of the subject, that is not the case with Otto's *Thesaurus*, which looks much more like a gap-filling enterprise for those collectors who had acquired a library of readily available works by legal humanists, and sought the rare items that they or their agents had not been able to acquire. In the 1775 supplement to Martin Lipenius' standard analytical bibliography of law, this fact is recognised by the categorisation of Otto and Meerman not under "thesaurus" but under "opera et opuscula".[55]

Otto was employed to ensure that the technical legal material appeared in a correct form, that the chosen texts were reproduced without the typographical and other errors of earlier editions, and introduced with the normal biographical facts about authors that the practice of *historia litteraria* required. Here he rebelled somewhat, averring that fastidious concentration on the details of the lives of less well-known scholars did not contribute anything to the understanding of their works, and could in any case be readily found in other biographical compilations such as those by Paul Freher, Henning Witte, and Antoine Teissier.[56] On the other hand, while recognising how difficult and delicate the role of a critic was, he undertook to provide a detailed review of the contents of the works, pointing out problems, omissions, and mistakes.[57] His comments on Agustín's *De nominibus propriis tou Pandektou Florentini* – a book so rare and expensive that collectors such as Alexander Cunningham had been only able to buy it for his rich clients, but not acquire for himself until after its

55 It is pertinent to note that in B G Struvius' *Bibliotheca iuris selecta*, ed C G Buder (1756) at 389–390, the predecessor of these Thesauruses is said not to be the *Tractatus Tractatuum*, as Otto suggests, but the six united works of legal humanism published as *Novarum declarationum et variorum lectionum, resolutionumque iuris libri XXII*, part-edited by Alexander Albertonius, and published by Johannes Gymnicus of Cologne in 1576 (with later editions in 1585 and 1609).

56 There is an implicit criticism of the practices of *historia litteraria* here, which may be found in other sectors of the academic world: see A Grafton, "The world of the Polyhistors: humanism and encyclopedism" (1985) 18 *Central European History* 31, H Zedelmaier, "*Cogitationes de studio litterario*: Johann Lorenz Mosheims Kritik der *Historia Litteraria*", in M Mulsow (ed), *Johann Lorenz Mosheim 1693–1755: Theologie im Spannungsfeld von Philosophie, Philologie und Geschichte* (1997) at 34.

57 Otto (n 6) vol 1 at 6: "Proxime nunc foret, de singulis Auctoribus, unde domo fuerint, quando et ubi vixerunt, qua industria, quibusque subsidiis, ad eos scribendos sese accinxerunt, quae munera in Republica sustinuerint, et quid de singulis habendum sit, dissererem; nisi plerorumque nomina vix unquam fando audita, prorsus in obscure laterent; ceterorum vero vitae in Freheri, Witteni, Teisseri, aliorumque Biographorum scriptis, omnium manibus tererentur. Erat Hebraeorum paroemia: fatuitatis esse respicere dolium, non id quod est in dolio; jamque sat multos invasit stadium supervacuas minutias in historia litteraria tractandi, quibus operose nihil agunt, nec doctiores fiunt, sed molestiores."

republication in the *Thesaurus*[58] – take up most of the space of the preface, which is written in a self-consciously humanist style, with plentiful use of literary allusions and quotations. His assessment of the authors chosen by van Bynkershoek follows the unforgiving rules of the Republic of Letters to which I have already alluded: he describes one (Carolus Selvaghus) as "indignus ille olim Mureti in cathedra Romani nunc Augustini successor, barbarismis et soloecismis refertus, succo vero omni et sanguine destitutus", and in another case (Nicolaus Catharinus), he quotes at the author's expense Gilles Ménage's use of a cruel epigram of Martial about books ("sunt bona, sunt quaedam mediocria, sunt mala plura").[59] At the end of the preface to volume three, he included a request to his readers for a number of works that the publisher wanted to locate: Philippus Berterius' *Pithanon diatribae duae* (1613); Marquard Freher's *Sulpitius* (1608) Fridericus Lindenbrog's *Commentarius* (1618) and Edmond Mérille's *De jure accrescendi* (1603). In all these cases, he was successful, but he failed to locate copies of Antonio Agustín's *Jurisconsultorum enchiridion* and his *De perfecto jurisconsulto*, both not attested as printed works.[60]

The subscription list suggests a limited, mainly local, success, but it was enough to warrant the four volumes being reprinted (vander Linden having died by this time) by Jan Broedelet in Otto's Utrecht in 1733–1735, with a fifth volume added by Otto himself. Broedelet (active between 1728 and 1771), was from a publishing dynasty. His list was made up of works in French, Latin and Dutch, including Dupin's very extensive *Nouvelle bibliographie des auteurs ecclesiastiques* (1631–1645). The *Thesaurus* seems to have been a new style of undertaking for him. The *Acta eruditorum* of January 1734 refers to the enterprise, sets out the contents of the as yet to be published fifth volume, the price and conditions of the subscription, and where it can be signed up for ("the same booksellers as for the first edition"). The article in the *Acta* records the fact that most of the works of the fifth volume came from van Bynkershoek's library as before. Otto's acknowledgements also show to what degree the enterprise was collaborative. For their

58 Cairns (n 2) at 345. The cost of a copy before the republication in the *Thesaurus* was reported by a Dutch Jurist in a letter written to the Leipzig Publisher Thomas Fritsch in about 1720 to be 300 florins (in the sale of Cunningham's library in 1730, it had fallen to 32 florins): see G C J J van den Bergh, *Die holländische elegante Schule: ein Beitrag zur Geschichte von Humanismus und Rechtswissenschaft in den Niederlanden 1500–1800* (2002) at 126 note 78.

59 Otto (n 6) vol 1 at 42, ibid, at 44.

60 Otto (n 6) vol 3 xxviii. In one instance, he may have been misled by the subtitle to Andreas Schott's *Laudatio funebris v.c. Antonii Augustini Archiepiscopi Tarraconensis in qua de vita scriptisque disseritur: de perfecto item Jurisconsulto et Episcopo* (1586).

help in providing copy Johann van Nispen, Wilhelm Blancardus, Didericus Schagen, Johannes Hermannus Schminckius, Jacobus Philippus d'Orville, Johannes van de Water and Isaac Sweerts are named. Otto also thanks Egbertus Cotius for compiling the Index to the *Thesaurus* (an instrument promised at the end of the third volume). This consists, together with a list of contents to the four volumes, of three sections: an "Index locorum juris, quae in IV tomis Thesauri . . . illustrantur, explicantur, emendantur"; an "Index auctorum veterum, quae in IV tomis Thesauri . . . illustrantur, explicantur, emendantur"; and an "Index locorum, quae in Praefationibus IV tomis Thesauri praemissis, illustrantur explicantur, emendantur." It is striking that Otto's critical assessments of *lectiones* in his prefaces have been listed as well as those of his chosen authors. Otto also records that he had hoped to publish two texts he had not been able to locate: Henricus Ernstius's *Catholica Juris* (1634), and Eduardo Caldeira's *Variae lectiones* (1595). He made it known that if he were given access to them, he would leave out two other texts (by Antoine Guibert Costanus [1557] and Guillaume Ranchin [1597]); a fact picked up later by Meerman in his *Conspectus* of 1751, who was able to find the Caldeira and include it in his own compilation.[61] How Otto reached this comparative judgement is not clear. A subscription list was printed in Broedelet's first volume, consisting of 351 copies, 13 of which were on large paper; 230 of these went to booksellers, mainly in the Netherlands and Germany. As before, the titles and dignities of those listed were omitted.

It is beyond the scope of this chapter to give an accurate analysis of the contents of the five volumes of the *Thesaurus* by date and national affiliation. This would in any case not be easy for various reasons: the authors can be associated either with their country of birth and education or that of their adoption, the works reprinted can be dated according to when they were composed or their first appearance in print, and there is no clear criterion for establishing what counts as a single work, given the significant number of miscellanea with titles such as "Opuscula". For the purposes of this chapter, an impressionistic survey will suffice. In Struvius and Buder's *Bibliotheca iuris selecta* of 1756, the compilation is said to consist of eighty-five separate items. Over half of these date from before 1600, and more than two-thirds before 1650. Thirty-five are by French authors, ten by Italians, ten by Germans and six by Spanish, the remaining coming from Burgundy, Switzerland, the United Provinces and the Southern Netherlands. Otto makes no claim in his prefaces about privileging any past school of legal

61 Meerman (n 7) at 19.

humanism: it is striking, however, that the largest single group of his texts comes from pre-1600 France.

The final edition of the *Thesaurus* appeared in Basel in 1741–1744, from the presses of another member of a publishing dynasty, Johann Ludwig Brandmüller. He had been active as a publisher since the 1710s. He was a specialist in large-scale multi-volume productions of histories and reference works, including the histories of Jacques-August de Thou and the *Dictionnaire critique et historique* of Pierre Bayle, nearly all of which were unauthorised editions of works published elsewhere, probably for distribution in Switzerland and Southern Germany.[62] Brandmüller was a successful and hardheaded speculative publisher, and seems not to have relied on a subscription. He was asked in 1739 by the local professor of law in Basel, Johann Rudolf Iselin, to produce a sixth volume with a new range of texts, which he refused to do, perhaps because he recognised that the market was saturated.[63] He took the unusual step for this Basel publishing house of advertising it at the Leipzig Spring Book Fair.[64] Gerard Meerman records that his edition was very sloppily produced, contrasting his edition implicitly with those produced by the two Dutch publishers who had higher scholarly standards and a genuine wish to serve the Republic of Letters.

G. THE *NOVUS THESAURUS* AND ITS SUPPLEMENT (1751–1780)

I come finally to the compilations of the Leiden graduate and Pensionary of Rotterdam Gerard Meerman (1722–1771), who, like Otto, had considerable experience of publishing before he undertook the *Novus thesaurus*.[65] He was an active book collector in his own right (attested by the *Bibliotheca Meermanniana* of 1824, the auction catalogue of his library and that of his son). He was also a bibliophile and book historian: in 1765, he produced a

62 The market zone may be inferred from the absence of engagement with the hugely influential Leipzig fair: see J Goldfriedrich, *Geschichte des deutschen Buchhandels vom Westfälischen Frieden bis zum Beginn der klassischen Litteraturperiode (1648–1740)* vol 2 (1908) at 336.

63 Meerman (n 7) at 3. Evidence of Brandmüller's hard commercial approach is to be found in the complaints brought against him by other publishers: see H J Koppitz, *Die kaiserlichen Druckprivilegien im Haus-, Hof-, und Staatsarchiv Wien* (2008) at 73 and 163.

64 *Catalogus universalis, oder Verzeichniss derer Bücher, welche in der Franfurther und Leipziger Oster-Mess des ietzigen 1742 Jahres entweder gantz neu gedruckt, oder sonsten verbessert, wieder aufgeleget worden sind* . . . (1742), sig c3v.

65 *Diatriba antiquario-juridica inauguralis, exhibens nonnullas de rebus mancipi, et nec mancipi, earumque mancipatione conjecturas* (1741), *Specimen calculi fluxionalis* (1742), *Specimen animadversionum criticarum in Caii jurisconsulti Institutiones* (1742).

commercially very successful account of the origins of printing. This confirms the connection between a sophisticated knowledge of the contemporary international book market, bibliography and *historia litteraria* (which can be traced in other figures, such as Nicolás Antonio, a Spanish jurist who also produced a comprehensive bio-bibliography of Iberian writers).[66] Various factors prompted Meerman to undertake his compilation: an extensive group of collaborators of various kinds; Otto's earlier successful *Thesaurus*; and the publication at Lyon in 1735 of Juan Puga y Feijoo's *Tractatus academici sive opera omnia posthuma*, a Spanish author whom he admired. The two most important collaborators, both jurists and members of the pre-Enlightenment movement in Spain, were Gregorio Mayans y Siscar of Valencia (1699–1781), who had retired from directing the Spanish Royal Library in 1739, and José Finestres y Monsalvo of the University of Cervara (1688–1777), who were generous with their advice and with gifts from their collections of books and manuscripts. In the Netherlands, he benefited from the scholarship of two Germans, David Ruhnken and Wilhelm Otto Reitz, whose editions of Byzantine Greek legal texts he was to publish. He was helped by a number of other jurists, including Johann Rudolf Iselin of Basel, Johann van Nispen of Leiden, Johann Michael van Langendonck, a court official in Louvain, and Cornelius Henricus de Wael, an advocate in The Hague, from whom he gained access to a very important collection of rare Iberian legal books and manuscripts once owned by the Danish diplomat Fridericus Adolphus Hansen von Ehrencron, sold by auction in The Hague by Pieter de Hondt's father in 1718 (Meerman himself subsequently obtained some volumes of this collection). Meerman also records his gratitude to a number of figures in libraries particularly rich in holdings of legal humanism (one such being Ruhnken, who exploited the resources of Leiden's university library). Father Louis Fabre of the *Bibliotheca Proustelliana* in Orléans allowed him to reproduce items from the collection of Guillaume Prousteau, a major book collector whose library was bequeathed for open access to all, and entrusted to the Maurists of Orléans.[67] Meerman also acknowledges l'abbé Claude Sallier who was director of the Royal library in Paris, Gottfried van Swieten, a diplomat from Vienna and son of the Librarian of its Imperial Library whom he would later succeed, the quondam Spanish Royal librarian Mayans

66 Antonio, *Bibiotheca hispana* (1672). Meerman makes frequent reference to this, and publishes one of Antonio's (The *De exilio*) in the third volume of his *Novus thesaurus*.

67 See the *Bibliotheca Prustelliana, sive catalogus librorum bibliothecae [...] Guillelmi Prousteau* (1721). Meerman published Prousteau's *Recitationes ad legem 23 contractus, D de Regulis Juris* in the third volume of the *Novus thesaurus*.

y Siscar, through whom he learned about the resources of the Escurial, and the Portuguese bibliophilic family, the Counts de Vimieiro. This group of collaborators helped him establish his list of desiderata, and he also used the finding tools listed in the bibliography of Lipenius, many of which he possessed, together with the other bibliographical and literary tools such as those by Matthieu Mattaire and Jean-Pierre Niceron to identify other works he hoped to publish.[68] He also appealed to his readers to suggest yet others. The *Conspectus* reveals Meerman's awareness of contemporary Dutch and German jurists. These include the Germans Johann Gottlieb Heineccius (1681–1741), a legal humanist better known for his natural law theories, and Christian Heinrich Trotz (1703–1773), a colleague of Otto at the University of Utrecht, and an active promoter of past legal humanists, including Jacques Godefroy, Guillaume Maran and Christfried Waechtler.[69]

Meerman's publisher was Peter de Hondt, who like vander Linden belonged to a publishing dynasty: he was active from 1720 until his death in 1763. He produced at his own expense a lavish *Conspectus* for Meerman's *Novus thesaurus* in 1751, in the confidence that the compilation would attract purchasers from both the humanist and practitioner communities: he himself avers in the Conditions of subscription which are published in the *Conspectus* that "as [Otto's] Thesaurus found in the course of time so many purchasers that three editions appeared, and for that reason, many copies of this new Thesaurus could have been published without any risk ('*absque ullo periculo*') the bookseller has allowed himself to declare piously and emphatically that he has ordered not more than 825 standard copies and 100 large paper copies to be printed." He probably arrived at these figures from a consideration of the subscription lists of 1725 and 1733, and the fact that Brandmüller's edition would have accounted for even more sales.

The *Conspectus* would itself have been expensive to produce, as it is more than eighty pages long; it contains the list of 440 booksellers acting as de Hondt's agents in European countries (including Brandmüller, whom Meerman accuses of sloppiness in the *Conspectus*: clearly the Swiss publisher's hope of gain led him to ignore the insult). It is of note that this list far exceeds the places of subscription available for the purchasers of Otto's volumes (just Paris and a number of Dutch cities). It closes with a three-page catalogue of de Hondt's publications, all of which are in French. They

68 Matthieu Mattaire, *Annales typographici* 9 vols (1719–1741), Jean-Pierre Niceron, *Mémoires pour servir à l'histoire des hommes illustres dans la république des lettres*, 43 vols (1729–1741). Meerman also refers to Draudius' much older *Bibliotheca classica* (n 7) 76.

69 See note 30, above.

include one book by a protestant theologian and another about the Catholic province of Brabant; the same indifference to confessional allegiance is found in Brandmüller's publications, and indicates how the commercial aspect of publishing is by the eighteenth century no longer inflected by partisan religious issues.

The *Conspectus* begins with a general introduction by Meerman, followed by paragraphs on each of the works to be reprinted, a list of desiderata, and concludes with a survey nation by nation of legal humanists up to 1750, a large number of whom are judged to be deficient in one way or another. The price for the five planned volumes was set at ten florins for the standard and fifteen florins for the deluxe copy per volume, with 1,000 printed sheets being the overall expected length (i.e. 4,000 pages in folio); and the subscribers were promised that their names would appear in the second volume (*Conditiones* VIII). Condition VI set a formula for the adjustment of price if the eventual volumes exceeded or failed to reach 1,000 folia; in the event, the seven (not five) volumes consisted in 1,440 folia (or 5,760 pages) and the price was adjusted to seventy-two and 108 florins. This expansion of the project is a feature the *Novus thesaurus* shares with many subscription sales at this time (and even with their modern analogues).

The subscription list did not appear until the end of the seventh and last volume, and contains, unlike Otto's list, full details of the subscribers. Two hundred and twenty-five standard copies are listed, and fifteen large paper copies: fifty-six of these went to booksellers (not all of them de Hondt's agents). It is significant that among the booksellers in the subscription list there is no representative from Iberia or Italy, although they figure in the list of agents: this part of the world clearly had not espoused the Dutch forms of book salesmanship. I have found no other subscription lists in any of the copies of the *Novus thesaurus* I have consulted, so it looks safe to conclude that the venture was not a resounding success. This is confirmed by the fact that in 1769, when Meerman issued a new *Conspectus* for the supplement to his compilation, there were unsold copies of the seven volumes in the hands of a Leiden bookseller called Theodor Haack, whose father (also a bookseller) is named in the subscription list of 1753. But it seems also to be the case that it was not seen as a commercial failure. The press run of the supplement advertised in 1769, to which I shall return shortly, is identical to that of the *Novus thesaurus* (825 copies on ordinary, 100 on large paper), perhaps to ensure that complete sets of all eight volumes could be made up. Meerman comments that there was no need to print fewer copies of the supplement in view of the number of subscribers of the *Novus thesaurus*, which suggests that there had been a reasonable sale of the compilation to non-subscribers. The *Novus thesaurus* was not advertised at the Leipzig Book Fair, but an account of at least two of its volumes did appear in one running annual bibliography of law books, August Gottlieb Jenichen's *Allerneueste Nachrichten von juristischen Büchern, academischen Abhandlungen, Deductionen und Verordnungen grosser Herren*, which provided a translation into German of Meerman's Latin prefaces.[70]

The title-page specifies that the contents are drawn from Meerman's own library (which the *Conspectus* shows to be not altogether true), that the field of the compilation now covers both manuscript and printed works of civil and canon law mainly by Spanish and French authors, and that the chosen texts all use classical literature, antiquities, coins and monuments to emend, explain and illustrate the texts discussed. Like the Broedelet edition of Otto's compilation, there is a vignette on the title page, which is the mark of a bibliophilic enterprise, that is to say, one attractive to purchasers more interested in the appearance and quality of the printing than the contents themselves. The vignette portrays Tribonian and a scribe standing in front of the seated emperor Justinian, holding a volume with the motto "sparsas colligit undique leges". Translated into the terms of Meerman's dedication to William Charles, Prince of Orange, the supplicants become Meerman himself and Peter de Hondt, the "sparsas leges" the rare works of the compilation, and the imperial figure the Stadhouder: the parallel being drawn could thus be construed as an egregious case of self-flattery, as well as flattery to the Prince of Orange.

Meerman's prefaces differ from those of Otto in various ways. They are much shorter, and written in less ostentatiously humanist Latin: there are no abstruse idioms or recondite quotations and allusions. Meerman takes his duties as a practitioner of *historia litteraria* very seriously, and continues to undertake research into the lives of his chosen authors even after the moment they appear in their allotted place in the compilation; several volumes carry addenda relating purely to their biographies, and in the last volume, there are four full pages of such additions. The book historian Meerman gives very full bibliographical descriptions of printed texts, which are almost wholly lacking in Otto. He does not engage in a detailed critique of the contents of the books he reprints, but he and at least one of his collaborators are willing to record strongly negative judgements about

70 *Allerneuste Nachrichten* (1752–1753) at 608–629 (review of vol 3 of the *Novus thesaurus*) and 687–694 (review of vol 5).

them, exercising the same privilege of the Republic of Letters that Otto had exercised. The most striking example of this is found in *Conspectus*, in which there is a letter by Finestres y a Monsalvo attributed only to "doctus Hispanus" (his name is revealed in the preface to volume seven), in which the Spanish jurist is highly critical of much contemporary Spanish legal scholarship, referring to it as "stuffed with meaningless words and pure [scholarly] trickery".[71]

As well as the prefaces to the volumes, the *Conspectus* reveals the principles by which Meerman included or excluded the texts he considered for publication. In it, Meerman undertakes to publish forty-four works, and lists a further twenty as desiderata which he will publish if someone will come forward with copy (which they did: he managed to find eleven of this list, including two works by the Scot Edward Henryson). He allowed himself to change his mind about eight of the works he undertook to publish if he could locate them, and the last part of the preface to volume seven set out his reasons for excluding them. He is faithful to the principles of the Republic of Letters, and does not exclude or privilege any national group, but does adjust his plans according to the state of the book market, in that he chooses not to print works available through other reliable editions; he expressly says that German legal scholarship and the Dutch elegant school fall into this category.[72] He is very harsh on plagiarism, prolixity (for which he implicitly criticises his friend Finestres) and he dismisses most of what he calls "farragines", or works of mixed quality. As for genres, he sets aside works that are wholly introductory and pedagogical, compendia (about which there was a debate just before his time), and material designed only for use by practitioners.[73] He initially thought of including a work which treats its subject "novo perjucundo dicendi genere" (Franciscus de Petris' *Festivarum lectionum libri III* [1622]), but decides eventually that it is not weighty enough.[74] His principles for inclusion are based on the best practices of legal humanism (information about the history of ancient languages; use of numismatics and inscriptions), and on rarity. This may arise in the case

71 Meerman (n 7) 58–59: "inanibus logis et tricis meris subfarcinati"; see also Meerman (n 5) vol 3 v (on Sengeberus: a repeat of Otto's criticism, followed by a defence of the author).

72 Meerman names only two German legal humanists in the *Conspectus* (n 7) (at 68): Uldaricus Zazius of Freiburg and Joachimus Stephanus of Greifswald. For other names, see Johann Salomon Brunquellus, *Historia iuris Romano-Germanici*, 2nd edn (1730) sig 5xv and 385–412. See also P Stein, *Roman Law in European History* (1999) at 104–105.

73 See above note 13 and Meerman (n 7) 14 (exclusion of "unice in gratiam studiosae juventutis digesta"); Meerman (n 5) vol 5 ii (exclusion of works "ad praxin forensem unice accommodata").

74 Ibid, vol 7 sig *2v.

of genres such as lecture notes which were rarely printed, and from short press runs (as in the case of self-financed publication), from publication in places that were not linked to international distribution networks, and the academic context in which a work was produced which might have hindered its advertisement and distribution (as was the case in the second half of the seventeenth century in France, where legal humanism had lost its place of honour in the scholarly world).[75] In the best traditions of *historia litteraria* and the Republic of Letters, he is particularly keen to recover the unpublished remains of great legal humanists, and engages in great efforts to locate these. He is particularly keen to find their annotated copies of parts of the *Corpus Iuris Civilis*, with mixed success: he found some of Jacques de La Lande's work through a clerical relative, but could not locate Pierre Pithou's annotations on Cujas. About twelve of the eighty or so items deal with canon law, but I could find no place where Meerman justifies or discusses their inclusion, simply noting that the five massive volumes of Emanuel Gonzalez Tellez's *Commentaria perpetua in singulos textus quinque librorum Decretalium Gregorii IX* (1715) had dispensed him from having to consider the claims of many canonists.[76]

It is easier in Meerman's case than in Otto's to give an analysis of at least one aspect of the contents of his compilation, as he provides the requisite bibliographical information. Forty-two items are from France, and twenty-two from Spain;[77] nineteen pre-date 1600, twenty-six fall between 1600 and 1650, and twenty-three in the period 1650 to 1700. Only three of the items were written after that date. Four authors are represented by manuscript transcriptions, and there are two substantial editions of Byzantine Greek texts. This confirms the claim made on the title page. If there is an absence to be noted, it is that of Italian scholars (only one is included in the seven volumes).

Meerman's involvement with the reprinting of legal humanism did not end in 1753. Thirteen years later, he was the promoter of Jakob van Vaassen's edition of the sixteenth-century scholar Antonio Gouveia's *Opera juridica, philologica, philosophica* from books in his own library, together with materials he obtained from Gregorio Mayans y Siscar. Meerman assisted Vaassen by using his contacts to make enquiries on behalf of the editor about holdings in the great libraries of Europe. Vaassen specifically

75 Ibid, vol 4 ii.

76 Meerman (n 7) 56.

77 The title page gives priority to Spanish over French authors, in spite of the numerical ascendancy of the latter.

links this publication to other editions of legal humanists: those of Antonio Agustín (in Lucca) and the Gentili brothers (in Naples). These appeared at about the same time, suggesting an international degree of optimism about sales of legal humanism among publishers, even at this relatively late date.

Meerman himself then planned a Supplement to his own *Thesaurus* with Nicolas van Daalen (the publisher at The Hague to whom he had turned after the death of Pieter de Hondt), for which a *Conspectus* appeared in 1769, which was also printed in the *Journal des Savants* of February 1770. The major work to be included in the supplement was the edition of the *Promptuarium* or *Manuale legum* of Constantinus Harmenopulus. This was mentioned as a desideratum in the preface to volume seven of the *Novus thesaurus*, and had been edited by Wilhelm Otto Reitz, who died before being able to find a publisher; his son Karl Konrad Reitz would see this text through the press, and was responsible also for the Index to all eight volumes of the *Novus thesaurus*, which Meerman saw as an indispensable tool, just as Otto had done for his compilation. Only one of the other nine works to be included (Samuel Fermat's *Dissertationes*) had been listed among the desiderata in the *Conspectus* of 1751. There is only one text whose original edition appeared before 1600. Four appeared before 1700, and the remaining four thereafter. There are three texts by French, five by Dutch and two by German authors. The same wide range of European agent-booksellers was available to take subscriptions, which, Meerman announced, would remain open until 1 June 1770. An undertaking was made to publish the compilation within two years of that date. In fact, it did not appear until 1780, eight years after Meerman's death. The preface contains the literary history of the authors; *The Monthly Review or literary journal* of 1783 reported on the publication, and cautiously declared that because of the edition of Harmenopulus, "it must naturally be considered as a valuable publication by those who have a taste for the study of ancient jurisprudence" (probably implying that these would not be very numerous among the English readers of the Review).

H. CONCLUDING REMARKS

As publishing enterprises, these Thesauruses reflect the fate of all learned books after the Thirty Years War. The market for such products was a somewhat self-regarding one; learned books were written in collusion with the publishers who financed them, and purchased by the relevant sector of the scholarly community.[78] A certain proportion of this community bought books only for show; without their purchasing, and that of book collectors and institutional libraries, it is difficult to see how the market could have sustained itself. Works like the Thesauruses were clearly aimed at both these constituencies of purchasers.[79] Such compilations were not welcomed by serious collectors of rare books. George Turnbull of Aberdeen wrote indignantly to a correspondent in 1730 that Otto's compilation "has much diminished the value of a law library . . . gathered from all parts of the world with great care."[80] By publishing rare and neglected items, Otto and Meerman were supplying a complex market which served both bibliophiles and scholarly collectors.

When the two Thesauruses entered in their turn the second-hand market for books through catalogues and auctions, they seem not to have accrued value in the passing of time.[81] By using the subscription system, their publishers were guaranteed a degree of profit and protection from loss if the publication overran its allotted number of pages and volumes, but this system was eventually to harm the constituency of serious collectors and institutional libraries that it was designed to attract. To take one example: by the early years of the nineteenth century, the Library of All Souls College Oxford had exhausted its buying funds by making too many open-ended commitments to subscription purchasing in which it had been engaged since the 1760s, and had to desist from new purchases.[82] The publishing history of these works does not therefore support the view that the subjects they treat were seen as a vibrant part of the market by publishers. They saw that it delivered reasonable profits, as did reference books, and that the subsidy or guarantee provided by a subscription list could protect them against bad losses. The Thesauruses aspired to international sales, but the evidence of the subscription lists suggests that sales outside the Netherlands and Germany were sparse. We may contrast this state of affairs with that which obtained before the Thirty Years War, when there seems to have

78 *Kurtzer Bericht/ von der nützlichen und fürtrefflichen Buch-handung und deroselben Privilegien* (1690) 5–6: "Die Wahren [des Buch-Händlers] sind von und vor niemand als Gelehrten . . . Der Buch-Händler allein ist der Gelehrten eigentlicher Abnehmer."

79 Their bibliophilic qualities are stressed in Guillaume-François de Bure's *Bibliographie instructive ou traité de la connoissance des livres rares et singuliers : volume de la jurisprudence et des sciences et arts* (1764) 87–107.

80 Cairns (n 2) 327. See also above, note 53.

81 Georgi, *Allgemeines Europäisches Bücher-Lexicon* vol 4, 209 (Otto's *Thesaurus*, estimated at 45 Thaler). Meerman is not quoted, even in the 1758 edition.

82 E Craster, *The History of All Souls College Library* (ed) E F Jacob (1971) 86–92.

been almost unlimited optimism about the commercial viability of legal tomes.

In respect of Otto and Meerman's Thesauruses, most historians of law would not demur from them being seen as evidence of the adage that the owl of Minerva flies at dusk. They certainly helped recover scholarly works, especially from France and Spain, and brought dignity to authors who had been languishing in obscurity. Indeed, in one sense, they are almost as much about the history of scholarship as about legal humanism. Of course, they also contributed to the accumulation of insights into the historical text of the *Corpus Iuris Civilis*, especially through their comprehensive Indexes, which allowed subsequent scholars to refer efficiently to these massive enterprises. They threw light on the general historical context of Roman law, and helped disseminate the Byzantine Greek authors who provided new information about the later reception and meaning of canonical texts. Through their supra-national approach, they contributed to the spread of Enlightenment in Europe; or rather, emanating as they did from the United Provinces and from wide scholarly collaboration, they provided examples of critical thinking in the spirit of the Republic of Letters. But they did not perpetuate legal humanism itself, paradoxically because of the same critical spirit, which subjected the assumed pre-eminence of Roman legal rationality to searching scrutiny. It might almost be said that the open-minded approach of legal humanists damaged the very object that they were committed to protect (and may have done so from the very beginning of the movement).[83] Legal humanism was succeeded by new jurisprudential movements influenced by modes of thinking derived from the philosophical developments of the seventeenth century. When English libraries decided to strengthen their continental holdings, they did not look to Otto and Meerman but to Heineccius' *Elementa juris naturae et gentium* (Halle 1737) and its like.[84]

I began this chapter with the report in the *Monthly Review* that Civil Law

83 J H Franklin, *Jean Bodin and the Sixteenth-Century Revolution in the Methodology of Law and History* (1963) (on the rise of general jurisprudential reasoning out of legal humanism, in relation to figures such as Hotman and Baudouin).

84 All Souls College, Library Minute book, for 15 February 1765: "agreed . . . that Dr Bever be empowered to purchase such modern writers on the Ius Gentium and Civil Law as shall be necessary to complete the collections in that Branch, viz. van Bynkershoek, Heineccius, etc. etc. etc." The *De formulis* of Brisson "in the last edition" were acquired by order of the minute of 7 September 1767; the works of Gerard Noodt by order of the minute of 7 April 1777. The Thesauruses of Otto and Meerman were not purchased (Otto was donated later to the College; a copy was also donated to St John's College). The only college in Oxford to own a copy of Meerman's *Novus thesaurus* (Queen's) acquired it through an adventitious bequest of money in the 1840s.

(and more specifically legal humanism) had lost reputation to the extent that by 1802 one of the young luminaries of legal studies in the Low Countries felt able to give an inaugural lecture arguing that too much was being made of it. Tydeman did not, as the reviewer in the *Monthly Review* suggests, argue that the knowledge of Greek and Roman languages, histories and antiquities had no role to play in legal education. Indeed, his inaugural lecture at the Gymnasium Illustre in Deventer defended the value of legal humanist knowledge, but subordinated it to the practical aims of teaching that characterised the approach of that establishment, for which the core of jurisprudence lay in its responsibility to civil society, and its dispensing of justice and equity through legal reasoning.[85] The justification of studying Roman law, claims Tydeman, is that it is a privileged example of this mode of jurisprudence, but it is not the only one. In the following year (1803), Tydeman moved to Franeker, a Calvinist University with a long history of classical scholarship and historical research, in which Ulric Huber, the defender of legal humanism in the 1680s, had taught.[86] Tydeman adapted his inaugural lecture to his audience, and the oration was entitled *De jure Romano Justinianeo, per benignam Dei providentiam, ad salutem generis humani opportune instaurato*, with which Otto and Meerman would have been wholeheartedly in accord. But in Deventer, he had allowed himself, in the thesis which forms the first part of his oration, to refer to the "sterile erudition" of legal humanists, and to accuse them of being time-wasting "grammarians, antiquarians, historians and literati" rather than jurists, of whose name and honour they were unworthy.[87] Although Otto and Meerman might have found his more moderate concluding remarks about the scholarship that they professed almost acceptable, they clearly could not have agreed with this damning judgement on what they did. It remains an open question whether their detour into philology and history led them too far from the proper concerns of their profession.

85 A A M de Haan, "Geschiedenis van het wijsgerig onderwijs te Deventer", in H W Blom, H A Krop and M R Wielema (eds), *Deventer denkers: De geschiedenis van het wijsgerig onderwijs te Deventer* (1993) 29–122. See Jakab elsewhere in this volume.

86 Huber (13) 221–223. Christian Heinrich Trotz (see above, p. 322) was a professor of law there in Meerman's time.

87 Tydeman (n 1) 13–14.

APPENDIX

The contents of the *Thesaurus Juris Romani* (1725–1726, 1735), the *Novus Thesaurus Juris Civilis et Canonico* (1751–1753) and the *Supplementum Novi Thesauri* (1780)

This is a short title list, with identification of the editions used insofar as this is possible. Otto records very few bibliographical details of the works in the prefaces to the *Thesaurus Juris Romani* (hereafter TJR): these have been supplied where possible from the Auction Catalogue of Cornelius van Bynkershoek's library (*Catalogus bibliothecae . . . Corn. Van Bynkershoek, quae . . . publice destrahenda est per Petrum de Hondt*, The Hague, 1743), which is said by Otto to be the source of many of the items reprinted (here indicated in square brackets by B followed by the format [fol, 4, 8, 12] and the number in the catalogue, in which the various formats for all subjects are listed serially). Where Otto acknowledges a source other than Bynkershoek, this is mentioned. It has been assumed that the text used as copy was not destroyed by the compositor, as was frequently the case, and that the reprinted books were replaced in van Bynkershoek's library. In some cases, he seems subsequently to have acquired copies of texts that he borrowed for inclusion in the publication of the TJR. In all, about half the items can be confidently attributed to van Bynkershoek's library, but the number may be higher, if the auction catalogue (as is not infrequently the case in this sort of publication) failed to list all the items in the *Sammelbände* on sale. Where it is known that the reprinted text was borrowed for the purpose of reproduction by Otto, this fact and the borrower's name (if known) are included in brackets. The forms of authors' and publishers' names (whether vernacular or Latin) are those most frequently found in modern library catalogues, and are recorded in the nominative case. I have followed the itemisation of the various contents pages of the TJR, even where a sequence of works by the same author is to be found in a single publication. For the *Novus Thesaurus Juris Civilis et Canonico* (1751–1753: hereafter NTJ) and the *Supplementum Novi Thesauri* (1780: hereafter SNT), the identification of the texts poses almost no problems, as full bibliographical details are given in the Conspectuses and Prefaces.

Taken together, this tripartite collection of the works of legal humanists does not constitute a definitive thesaurus (there is hardly anything from the Dutch elegant school, for example). It reveals rather what were thought to be important gaps in the materials readily available (the principle "raritas").

Both Otto and Meerman give summary lists of the authors who might be considered classic (see above, pp. 312, 301). Their two Thesauruses exclude some worthy materials that were deemed too long (the principle "brevitas"), and some that were too exclusively historical (the principle "utilitas"). In Meerman's case, the Thesaurus is the result of a survey of all writers who discuss ancient jurisprudence after the generation of Budé, Alciato and Zazius. If his judgements are to be believed, it reveals a dearth of legal humanism in Italy, and relatively few legal humanists working in Germany (which is not to say that some very distinguished legal humanists of German extraction were not active in the United Provinces: see above, p. 313). Where Meerman has acknowledged borrowings, I have recorded this; as in the case of Otto, they reveal that the Thesauruses are more the result of collaboration than might at first appear to be the case. **MS** indicates previously unpublished material, including additions to commentaries and to monographs by others. Meerman made a point of obtaining MS notes from famous scholars: a practice which complicates simple bibliographical description. I have not expanded the abbreviated references to books, titles and laws of the *Corpus Iuris Civilis*, as this bibliography is intended for specialists in the field. Most editions have been identified through *http://hpb.cerl.org*, which failing, Google. The bibliographical details of the contents of the TJR, the NTJ and the SNT are listed here in turn.

***Thesaurus Juris Romani*, volume 1**

1 Antonius Augustinus, *De nominibus propriis Pandectarum*, Tarragona, Philippus Mey, 1579, fol. [TJR 1.3 declares that it was borrowed from Adolphus Visscher; TJR 1.7 records the bibliographical details of this book].

2 Carolus Selvaghus, *De origine, ethymo et praestantia Pandectarum [. . .] recitationes solemnes*, Rome, Franciscus Moneta, 1658, 4to

3 Jacobus Lectius, *De vita et scriptis Aemilii Papiniani, seu de officio prudentum oratio*, Geneva, Johannes Le Preux, 1594, 8vo [B 8.264]

4 --- *De vita et scriptis Domitii Ulpiani orationes duae*, in *Orationes*, Geneva, Petrus de la Rovière, 1615, 8vo [B 8.387]

5 --- A*d Aemilium Macrum de publicis iudiciis*, Lyon, Franciscus Faber, 1597, 8vo [B 8.264]

6 --- *Ad Modestinum de Poenis*, [Geneva], Johannes Le Preux, 1592, 8vo

7 Jean Chifflet, *Apologetica dissertatio de Iuris utriusque architectis, Iustiniano, Triboniano, Gratiano et S. Raymundo*, Antwerp, Balthasar Moretus, 1651, 4to [B 4.208]

8 Gabriel Trivorius, *Observatio apologetica ad inscriptionem orationis ad Antecessores Digestis Iustiniani propositae, adversus quosdam Iurisconsultos et Procopii anecdota*, Paris, Sebastianus Cramoisy, 1631, 4to [B 4.212]

9 Petrus Burgius, *Electorum Liber, quo varios Iuris locos illustrandi, conciliandi et sanandi ratio tentatur*, Paris, Guillielmus Bichonus, 1585, 4to [B 4.244: TJR 1. 3 records that this text was edited for the volume by Johannes Balk]

10 Christophorus Colerus, *Parerga ad varios Pandectarum et Institutionum locos, obiter etiam varii Scriptores emendantur, aut nove explicantur*, Nuremberg, Paulus Kaufmannus, 1607, 8vo [B 8.558]

11 Gabriel Vallius, *Libri singulares ad L. Gallus 29 D. de Lib et posthum.; L. unic. C. de Sentent. quae pro eo quod etc.; L. in Quartam 91 D. ad L. Falcid.; L. Filium quem 14 C. Famil. hercisc.*, Poitiers, Julianus Thoreau, 1617, 8vo [B 8.361]

12 Petrus Avellanus, *Restitutiones locorum aliquot bonorum auctorum*, Poitiers, Enguilbertus Marnesius, 1541, 8vo

13 Nicolaus Catharinus, *Observationum et coniecturarum liber*, Bourges, Joannes Christo, 1661–1662, 8vo [TJR 1.3 records that this was borrowed from Abrahamus Gronovius]

14 Joannes Stekius, *Observationes anticriticae Iuris*, Basel, Johannes Jacobus Genathius, 1627, 4to [TJR 1.3 records that this was borrowed from Adolphus Schuberth]

15 Detlev Langebekius, *In leges aliquot perdifficiles et nondum satis intellectas novae annotationes*, ed Joachimus Cluten, Frankfurt, Petrus Musculus and Rupertus Pistorius, 1609, 8vo [The editor is named in TJR 1.44]

16 Petrus Perrenonius, *Animadversionum et variorum lectionum Iuris Civilis libri duo*, Cologne, Gosvinus Cholinus, 1593, 8vo [8.315 ; TJR 1.3 records that this text was edited for the volume by Johannes Balk]

17 Georgius Conradus Crusius, *Ex variis observationibus, quae ad Jus Civile pertinent, diatribe*, Leiden, Cornelius Driehuysen, 1669, 4to [B 4.291]

18 --- *Dissertatio ex Ulpiani lib. IV ad Edictum, de Pactis et conventionibus*, Leiden, Cornelius Driehuysen, 1669, 4to [B 4.291]

19 Ludovicus Charondas, *Peithanōn sive verisimilium libri,* Paris, Joannes Foucherius 1552, 8vo [B 8.345]

20 --- *Ad tit. D. de Verbor. obligat. scholia*, Paris, Joannes Foucherius 1552, 8vo [B 8.345]

21 --- *De iurisdictione et imperio libellus*, Paris, Joannes Foucherius 1552, 8vo [B 8.345]

22 Marquardus Freherus, *Verisimilium libri duo, in queis varia Juris Civilis loca nove explicantur, emendantur, illustrantur, etc.*, ed Joannes Bosch, Nuremberg, Simon Halbmaier, 1629, 4to [B 4.391] [The editor is named in TJR 1.44]

***Thesaurus Juris Romani*, volume 2**

1 Gulielmus Fornerius, *Selectionum libri III*, Orléans, Eligius Gibierius, 1566, 4to [B 4.240]

2 Radulphus Fornerius, *Rerum quotidianarum libri sex*, Paris, Ambrosius et Hieronymus Drouart, 1606, 8vo [B 8.336]

3 Josephus Nerius, *Analectorum libri duo, in quibus praeter ea quae ad Ius pertinent varia historica, et quaedam in tacito illustrantur, emendantur*, Perugia, Marcus Naccarinus, 1619, 8vo

4 Ferandus Adduensis, *Explicationum libri duo quorum primus in Pandectas; secundus in alias Iuris Ciuilis partes*, Lyon, haeredes Sebastiani Gryphii, 1560, 8vo [B 8.370]

5 Ludovicus Vitalis, *Variarum lectionum libri duo*, Turin, Franciscus Dulcis and Martin Cravotus, 1619, 8vo

6 Franciscus de Roye, *Dissertatio triplex: ad L. Transfugam 51 D. de Aquir. rer. domin. ; ad L. Unicam C. de Athletis; ad L. 4 D. de Usur. et fruct.*, Orléans, Aegidius Hotot, 1651, 8vo

7 Christophorus. Riccius, *Vindicarum Iuris praemessa, adversus novatorum affanias et corruptelas*, Danzig, Georg Rhete [sold through Leiden, Bonaventura and Abraham Elzevier, 1633], 4to [B 4.290]

8 Franciscus Marsius Gordonius, *Praetermissorum Iuris Civilis liber, in quibus legum antiqua et recepta lectio, contra omnium interpretum emendationes, defenditur*, Paris, Samuel Celerius, 1632, 4to [B 4.225]

9 Valentinus Guilielmus Forsterus, *Observationum succisivarum libri duo*, Wittenberg, Clemens Bergerus, 1609, 8vo [B 8.417]

10 --- *Interpres sive de interpretatione Iuris libri duo*, Wittenberg, Clemens Bergerus, 1613, 8vo

11 Desiderius Heraldus, *De rerum iudicatarum auctoritate libri duo*, Paris, Olivier de Varennes, 1640, 8vo [B 8.335]

12 --- *Observationum et emendationum liber unus*, Paris, Olivier de Varennes, 1640, 8vo [B 8.335]

13 Hieronymus Elenus, *Exercitationum ad Ius Civile libri tres, quorum primus continet de ratione studii Iuris orationes tres, secundus locorum*

quorundam Iuris novas explicationes et legum antinomias, Antwerp, Christophorus Plantinus, 1576, 8vo

14 Gilbertus Regius, *Enantiophanōn Iuris Civilis libri duo*, Hanau, Guilielmus Antonius, 1598, 8vo [B 8.334]

15 Nicolaus Sudorius, *Disputationum civilium liber*, Paris, Fredericus Morellus, 1578, 4to [B 4.243]

16 Joannes Mercerius, *Opiniorum et observationum libri duo*, Bourges, Petrus Bouchierius, 1573, 8vo [B 8.327] **or** Hanau, Guilielmus Antonius, 1598, 8vo [B 8.334]

***Thesaurus Juris Romani*, volume 3**

1 Jacobus Gothofredus, *Fontes IV. Iuris Civilis*, Geneva, Joannes Antonius and Samuel de Tournes, 1653, 4to [B 4.259]

2 --- *Animadversionum Iuris Civilis liber*, Geneva, Jacobus Chouetus, 1628, 4to [B 4.258]

3 --- *De cenotaphio deque diversis super religione Ulpiani et Martiani sententiis diatriba*, issued with *Libanii oratio pro templis gentilium non excindendis*, [Geneva], Pierre Chouët **or** Pierre Aubert, 1634, 4to [B 4.258]

4 Paganinus Gaudentius, *Expositionum juridicarum libri duo*, Florence, ex typographia Sermartelliana, 1631, 8vo

5 Gregorius Lopez Madera, *Animadversionum Iuris Civilis liber singularis*, Turin, haeredes Nicolai Bevilaquae, 1586, 4to **or**: Cologne, Johannes Gymnicus, 1594, 8vo

6 Pardulphus Prateius, *Jurisprudentiae mediae libri IV*, Lyon, Gulielmus Rovillius, 1561, 8vo

7 Emundus Merillius, *Ad libros II. Quaestionum Callistrati commentarius* [**MS**: B 8.265]

8 Osius Aurelius, *Dispunctor ad Merillium, de variantibus Cuiacii interpretationibus*, Orléans, Aegidius Hotot, 1642, 8vo [B 8.286]

9 Guilielmus Barclaius, *In titulos Pandectarum de Rebus creditis et de Jurejurando commentarii*, Paris, Franciscus Huby, 1605, 8vo [B 8.368]

10 Marcus Vertranius Maurus, *De jure liberorum liber singularis*, Lyon, Joannes Tornaesius et Gulielmus Gazaeus, 1558, 4to [B 4.269]

11 Carolus Hannibal Fabrotus, *Ad titulum Codicis Theodosiani de Paganis, sacrificiis et templis notas*, Paris, Sebastianus Cramoisy, 1618, 4to [B 4.251]

12 --- *Exercitationes XII*, Paris, Mathurinus Du Puis, 1639, 4to

13 --- *Replicatio adversus Cl. Salmasium, in qua mutuum alienationem*

esse ostenditur ; item de dominio dotis, et de conditione tractatur, Paris, Sebastianus and Gabriel Cramoisy, 1647, 4to [B 4.252]

14 Constantius Landus, *Enarrationes [. . .]*, Piacenza, Joannes Maria Simoneta, 1549, fol.

15 Joannes Leunclavius, *[. . .] Notatorum libri duo*, Frankfurt, haeredes Andreae Wecheli, 1593, 8vo [B 8.339]

16 Henricus Brencmannus, *Lex Remmia, sive de Legis Remmiae exitu liber singularis [. . .] Dissertatio de fatis calumniatorum sub imperatoribus*, s.l. [dedication dated 1726]

17 Carolus Labbaeus, *Veteres glossae verborum Juris, quae passim in Basilicis reperiuntur*, Paris, Adrianus Beys, 1606, 8vo [B 8.261]: *accesserunt ipsis glossis additiones ex libro MS. Praeterea Jos. Scaligeri et aliorum doctorum virorum emendationes, denique notae Antonii Schultingii*, **MS**

***Thesaurus Juris Romani*, volume 4**. This was completed after Otto's call in *Thesaurus Juris Romani* 3.xxviii for certain works to be provided by others as copy. The items are marked "borrowed" in this list.

1 Henricus a Suerin, *Repetitarum Lectionum Juris Civilis liber*, Basel, Conradus Waldkirch, 1586, 8vo

2 --- *Quaestionum de usufructu accrescendo, liber unus*, Basel, Conradus Waldkirch, 1585, 8vo

3 Marcus Antonius Muretus, *Observationum Juris liber singularis*, Augsburg, Hans Schultes, 1600, 8vo

4 --- *Commentarius de origine et progressu Juris Romani [. . .]* [i.e. *Tractatus aureus de iurisdictione et imperio*], Frankfurt, Johannes Ludovicus Bitschius, 1603, 8vo [B 8.563]

5 Theodorus Marcilius, *Legis XII. Tabularum collecta et interpretamentum*, Paris, Stephanus Prevosteau, 1600, 8vo [B 8.373]

6 Adrianus Pulvaeus, *Ad Legem Atiniam: sive de rei furtivae prohibita usucapione liber singularis*, Paris, Vincentius Sertenas, 1558, 8vo

7 Fridericus Lindenbrogius, *Commentarius in L. unic. C. si quis Imperator maledixerit. Et L. 8. T. 1. Lib. 2. Legum Wisigothorum, de non criminando principe, notae breviores*, Hamburg, Paulus Langius, 1608, 8vo [borrowed]

8 Marquardus Freherus, *Sulpicius, sive de aequitate commentarius, ad L. I. C. de Legibus*, Frankfurt, Theodorus and Joannes Israel de Bry, 1608, 4to [borrowed]

9 Pardulphus Prateius, *Jurisprudentia vetus, sive Draconis et Solonis, nec*

non Romuli Romanorum Regis, ac XII. Tabularum Leges collectae interpretataeque, Lyon, Gulielmus Rovillius, 1559, 8vo

10 Jacobus Constantinaeus, *Subtilium emendationum sive elucidationum libri duo*, Coutances, Johannes le Cartel, 1627, 8vo [borrowed]

11 Franciscus Zoannettus, *Restitutionum ad libros L. Digestor. liber singularis*, in *Opera*, Marburg, Paulus Egenolphus, 1600, 4to [B 4.392]

12 Thomas Papillonius, *Tractatus de directis heredum substitutionibus*, Paris, Pierre Durand, 1616, 8vo

13 --- *De jure accrescendi libellus*, Leiden, David Lopes de Haro, 1640, 12mo

14 Philippus Berterius, *Diatribe duae, quibus Civilis Imperii Romani notitia et Ecclesiae politia illustrantur*, Toulouse, vidua Jacobi Colomerii and Raymondus Colomerius, 1608, 4to [B 4.210]

15 Petrus Pantoja de Aiala, *Commentaria ad Tit. D.et C. de Aleatoribus*, Madrid, Petrus Tazo, 1625, 4to

16 Caesar Costa, *Variarum ambiguitatum Juris libri tres*, Naples, Horatius Salvianus, 1573, 4to

17 Scipio Gentilis, *Parergorum ad Pandectas libri duo*, Frankfurt, Nicolaus Bassaeus, 1588, 8vo

18 --- *Originum liber singularis*, Frankfurt, Nicolaus Bassaeus, 1588, 8vo

19 Antonius Augustinus, *Emendationum et opinionum libri IV [. . .] Ad Modestinum, sive de excusationibus liber singularis*, Lyon, Antonius de Harsy, 1591, 8vo [B 8.258]

20 --- *L. Aelii Taurelli, ad Gallum et Legem Velleam ad Catonem et Paullum de Militiis ex casu*, Lyon, Antonius de Harsy, 1574, 8vo [B 8.259]

21 Franciscus Husmanus, *Paradoxa ad Legem Falcidiam*, Paris, Arnoldus Sittart, 1584, 4to

22 Emundus Merillius, *Obscurorum, seu de jure accrescendi et coniunctionis, liber singularis*, Troyes, Jean Griffard, 1603, 8vo

***Thesaurus Juris Romani*, volume 5**

1 Hieronymus Groslotius, *De usucapionibus [. . .] In nobilissimam Pauli jureconsulti L. lecta, quae est sub titulo .ff. Si certum petatur*, Paris, Joannes Lodoicus Tiletanus, 1538, 4to

2 [Marius Arcadis and] Petrus Aldobrandini, *Interpretatio L. I. C. de Edendo*, Lyon, Sebastianus Gryphius, 1543, 8vo [B 8.380]

3 Jacobus Curtius, *Eikastōn, id est coniecturalium libri VI*, Antwerp, Joannes Stellsius, 1550, 8vo: *Tomus secundus*, Louvain, Petrus a Colonia, 1554, 8vo [B 8.323–4]

4 Antonius Guibertus Costanus, *Quaestionum Juris memorabilium liber*, Hanau, Guilielmus Antonius, 1598, 8vo [B 8.325]

5 Pardulfus Prateius, *Ad Tit. Instit. de Officio iudicis*; *Veteres populi Romani Leges [cum adiectionibus Everardi Ottonis]*; both works in Prateius' *Lexicon juris civilis*, of which there are many editions [Lyon, Guilielmus Rovillus, 1567, 1574; Venice, Hieronymus Scotus, 1572; Frankfurt, Sigismundus Feyerabendius, 1576; Cologne, Johannes Gymnicus, 1583, all fol.] and **MS**

6 --- *Ad Legem Iuliam de Fundo dotali*, in *De dote tractatus*, Frankfurt, Sigismundus Feyerabendius, 1586, fol, pp. 669–696

7 Antonius Lescurius, Julius Pacius, Joannes Mercerius, Franciscus Davydargenteus et Marquardus Freherus, *In L. frater a fratre XXXVIII. D. de Condictione indebiti commentarii*, Hanau, Guilielmus Antonius, 1599, 8vo: this edition contains also a commentary by Henricus a Suerin, and lacks a commentary by Franciscus Davydargenteus

8 Petrus Grangianus, *Paradoxa Juris Civilis*, Lyon, Alexander Marsilius, 1581, 8vo [B 8.310]

9 Elbertus Leoninus, *Praelectiones in Tit. C. de Jure emphyteutico*, Frankfurt, Wolfgang Richter, 1606, 4to [B 4.471]; *http://hpb.cerl.org* records this as 16mo

10 Claude Chifflet, *De substitutionibus*; *De portionibus legitimis*; *De Jure fideicommissorum libri IV*; *De secundo capite Legis Aquilae disquisitio*, Lyon, Joanna Jacobus Junta, 1584, 8vo [B 8.362] The works are listed separately on Otto's contents page

11 Guilielmus Ranchinus, *Variarum lectionum libri III*, Paris, Hadrianus Perier, 1597, 8vo [B 8.333]

12 Joannes Solorzanus, *De parricidii crimine*, in *De Indiarum jure*, Lyon, Laurens Anisson, 1672, fol [B fol.303]

13 Jacobus Leschasserius, *De vocabulis ad geographiam Juris Romani pertinentibus*, Frankfurt, no name of publisher, 1619, 8vo

14 Henricus Ernstius, *Variarum observationum libri duo*, Amsterdam, Joannes Janssonius, 1636, 12mo

15 Josephus Fernandez de Retes, *Ad tit. D. de Interdictis et relegatis*, Valladolid, Typographia regia, 1643, 4to; **or** Lyon, Philippus Borde, Laurens Arnaud, and Claudius Rigaud, 1660, 4to

16 Benedictus a Iesu Christo, *Novae veteres vindiciae dignitatis et auctoritatis Juris Civilis*, Lyon, Claudius Prost, 1664, 4to **or** Venice, Joannes Petrus Brigonc, 1665, 4to

17 Justus Zinzerlingus, *Opinationes variorum de vero intellectu*

[ad] L. 5. D. de Nautico foenore, Lyon, Joannes Anard, 1614, 8vo [B 8.386]

18 Tussanus de la Rue, *Amoenae Juris observationes*, Paris, Guillaume Saugrain, 1697, 8vo

19 Joannes Koolius, *ad Legem Ateriam Tarpeiam de Multis*, Utrecht, Franciscus Halma, 1698, 4to

20 Everardus Otto, *De vita et scriptis Servii Sulpicii, liber singularis; Alfenus Varus, ab iniuriis veterum et recentiorum liberatus*, Utrecht, Joannes Broedelet, 8vo [B 8.477] The two works are listed separately

***Novus Thesaurus Juris*, volume 1**

1 Henricus Stephanus, *Juris Civilis fontes et rivi*, [Geneva], Henricus Stephanus, 1580, 8vo

2 Michael Psellus, *Synopsis Legum, versibus iambis et politicis, Graece edita, adiecta Latina interpretatione et notis Francisci Bosqueti, itemque observationibus Corn. Sibenii*, Paris, Joannes Camusat, 1632, 8vo [ed Archbald Maclaine]

3 Valerius Probus, *Libellus de interpretandis Romanorum litteris, ex MSS codicibus auctus et notis illustratus a Henrico Ernstio*, Copenhagen, Georgius Holstius, 1647, 4to: with Fredericus Lindenbrogius, *Observationes* from Valerius Probus, *De notis Romanorum interpretandis libellus*, Leiden, Andreas Cloquius, 1599, 8vo

4 Flavius Franciscus de Hauteserre a Salvaison, *Notae et animadversiones ad indiculos ecclesiasticorum canonum Fulgentii Ferrandi et Cresconii Afri*, Poitiers, Julianus Thoreau, 1630, 4to: with Petrus Franciscus Chiffletius, *Notae in Fulgentii Ferrandi [. . .] Opera*, Dijon, Petrus Pallot, 1649, 4to

5 Alexander Politus a Sancto Sigismundo, *De patria in testamentis condendis potestate libri quatuor*, Florence, Jacopo de Guiducci and Sancti Franchi, 1712, 4to

6 Ioannes Filleau, *Tractatus singularis de comitibus consistorianis, ad Tit. 10 Lib. XII Cod.*, Paris, Gervasius Alliot, 1652, 4to

7 Pierre Pithou, *Excerpta ex adversariis*, in *Divers opuscules tirez des memoires de M. Antoine Loisel*, ed Claude Joly, Paris, veuve Jean Guillemot and Jean Guignard, 1652, 4to, pp. 293–344

8 Antoine Loisel, *La vie de Publicus Rutilius Rufus*, in *Divers opuscules tirez des memoires de M. Antoine Loisel*, pp. 161–174

9 Nicolaus Rigaltius, (1) *De Lege venditioni dicta observatio duplex, ad Leg. Curabit praeses 5 Cod. de Actio. Empti [. . .]* (2) *De modo proposito*

foenori observatio ad constitutionem regiam anni 1643, Paris, Simon Belgrand and Jean Laurent, 1644–1645, 4to [(1) borrowed from Johan van Nispen; (2) ed Gregorius Mayansius]

10 Athanasius Otyeza et Olando, *Paralipomenon et electorum Juris Civilis, selectarum antiquitatumque tomus I*, Valladolid, Antonius de Rueda, 1646, fol

11 Janus a Costa, *Commentarii seu praelectiones ad Tit. Dig. de Servitutibus; Ad quatuor Tit. Codicis, ex delictis defunctorum in quantum heredes conveniantur, de constituta pecunia, de probationibus, et de testibus*, **MS** [borrowed from Johan van Nispen]

***Novus Thesaurus Juris*, volume 2**

1 Joannes Suarez de Mendoza, *Commentarii ad Legem Aquiliam*, Salamanca, Hyacinthus Tabernier, 1640, 4to

2 Antonius de Quintanaduegnas et Villegas, *De jurisdictione et imperio libri duo*, Madrid, Ludovicus Sanchez, 1598, 4to

3 Franciscus Calletus, *Commentarius ad Titulum de evictionibus 45 Lib. VIII. Cod.*, Poitiers, Julianus Thoreau, 1627, 8vo

4 Nicolaus Fernandez de Castro, *Aquaeductus novae et antiquae Romae, praelectio extemporanea ad Theodosium et Valentinianum, in Leg. ad reparationem 7. Cod. de Aquaeductu Lib. XI*, Salamanca, Didacus de Cassio, 1640, 4to

5 --- *Exterminium Gladiatorum, sive praelectio solemnis ad Flav. Constantinum in L. unica C. de Gladiatorib. penit. toll. lib. XI.*, Valladolid, Antonius Vasquez, 1643, 4to

6 Joannes Altamiranus et Velazquez, *In priores XIII. Libros ex XX Quæst. Q. Cervidii Scaevolae Commentarius*, Cervera, Emmanuel Ibarra, 1739, 4to

7 Thomas Papillonius, *Commentarii in quatuor priores Titulos Libri primi Digestorum*, Paris, Petrus Durand, 1624, 8vo

8 Johannes Philippus Dattus, *De venditione liberorum diatriba, occasione Legis 2. Cod. de Patrib. qui fil. Distrax*, Ulm, Georgius Wilhelmus Kuhnius, 1700, 8vo

9 Petrus Anderanus, *De privilegiis creditorum Commentarius*, Antwerp, Johannes Bellerus, 1560, 8vo

10 Petrus de Abaunza, *Ad Titulum 15. de Sagittariis Libro V. Decretalium praelectio*, Seville, Ludovicus Estupinnan, 1627, 4to

***Novus Thesaurus Juris*, volume 3**

1 Thalelaeus, Theodorus, Stephanus, Cyrillus [aliorumque auctorum Graecorum], *Commentarii in Tit. D. et Cod. de Postulando sive de Advocatis, Gr. et Lat.*, ed and comm David Ruhnkenius **MS**

2 Nicolaus Antonius, *De exilio, sive de exilii poena antiqua et nova, exulumque conditione et juribus libri tres, cum additionibus postumis auctoris quam plurimis, nunc primum editis*, Antwerp, Jacobus Meursius, 1659, and **MS**

3 Gulielmus Ranchinus, *Tractatus de successione ab intestato*, Lyon, Fratres de Gabiano, 1594, 8vo

4 --- *Edictum Perpetuum Salvii Juliani restitutum*, Paris, Hadrianus Perier, 1597, 8vo

5 Joannes Matthaeus Magnus, *Rationum et differentiarum Juris Civilis libri duo: prior de actionibus arbitrariis, alter de eo, quod interest*, Angers, Joannes Hernault, 1602, 8vo

6 Guilielmus Dyemenus, *Tractatus de formulis quibusdam copulatis et disiunctis, ad Salvii Juliani nobilissim. locum ex libro eius singulari de Ambiguitatibus (in Leg. 13. s. 2. et seqq. Dig. de Rebus dubiis)*, Louvain, Joannes Masius, 1606, 4to [borrowed from Johan Michael van Langendonck]

7 Joannes le Gendre, *Episcopale judicium adversus calumnias Jac. Gothofredi acerrime descensum, nec non ab omni falsi suspicione plenissime vindicatum*, Paris, Lamberti Rouland filius, 1695, 4to

8 Polycarpus Sengeberus, *Disceptatio de mutuo, adversus Claudii Salmasii novum dogma*, Paris, vidua Mathurini du Puis, 1646, 8vo [borrowed from Nicolaus Hopfius]

9 Josephus ab Exea et Descartin, *Recitatio solennis ad Leg. unicam Cod. de Palatiis et domibus dominicis Lib. XI*, Zaragoza, Didacus Dormer, 1655, 4to

10 Eduardus Henryson, *Commentatio ad Tit. 10. Lib. II. Instit. de Testament. ordinandis*, Paris, Michael Vascovanus, 1556, 8vo [borrowed from Johan Michael van Langendonck]

11 --- *pro Eguin. Barone adversus Ant. Goveanum de jurisdictione libri duo*, Paris, Vincentius Sertenas, 1555, 8vo [borrowed from Cornelius Henricus de Wael]

12 Guillaume Prousteau, *Recitationes ad Leg. 83. Contractus, Pand. de Regul. Jur.*, Orléans, Claudius Borde and vidua Jacobi Borde, 1684, 4to

13 Eduardus Caldera, *De Erroribus pragmaticorum libri quatuor, totidemque variarum lectionum*, Madrid, Cosmo Delgado, 1610, fol

14 Paganinus Gaudentius, *De Justinianei Seculi moribus nonnullis partes duae. Accedit de lege, quae feminas a successione repellit, exercitatio*, Florence, Amator Massa, 1637–1638, 4to [another ed Strasbourg, Fridericus Spoor, 1654, 8vo]

***Novus Thesaurus Juris*, volume 4**

Joannes d'Avezan, *Opera iuridica omnia*:

1 --- *Contractuum liber*, Orléans, vidua Aegidii Hotot and Aegidius Hotot, 1644, 4to

2 --- *Contractuum liber alter, plures tractatus continens*, Paris, Petrus Lamy, 1659, 4to

3 --- *Servitutum liber*, Orléans, Maria Paris and Aegidius Hotot, 1660, 4to

4 --- *Liber de Censuris Ecclesiasticis, cum dissertatione de pontificia et regia potestate. Continentur etiam in hoc opera, 1. Tract. de excommunicatione. 2. Tractatus de depositione, et suspensione. 3. Tractatus de interdicto*, Orléans, vidua Aegidius Hotot, 1654, 4to

5 --- *Liber de renunciationibus, sive resignationibus, et pensionibus beneficiorum ecclesiasticorum, deque portione congrua et competenti ex eorum reditibus Vicariis perpetuis assignanda*, Orléans, Claudius and Jacobus Borde, 1658, 4to

6 --- *De sponsalibus et matrimoniis*, Paris, Edmundus Martinus, 1661, 4to

7 --- *Dissertatio patronatus Juris pontifici*, Paris, Dionysius Langlois, 1666, 4to

Jacobus de La Lande, *Opera ad Jus Civile Romanum et Canonicum quae extant* :

8 --- *Exercitationes utriusque Juris ad Titulum de Aetate, qualitate, et ordine praesciendorum apud Gregorium IX. cum brevi Tractatu de nuptiis clericorum vetitis, aut permissis, et ad Titulum de Liberis praeteritis vel exheredatis Cod.*, Orléans, vidua Aegidii Hotot, 1654, 4to

9 --- *Praelectiones in Titulum de Decimis, Primitii, et Oblationibus, lib. 3. Decretalium Gregorii IX*, Orléans, Claudius and Jacobus Borde, 1661, 4to

10 --- *Juris dissertatio de ingressu in secretaria judicum, et cum his considendi societate, viris honoratis competente, de honorariis dignitatibus*, Orléans, Franciscus Hotot, 1674, 4to

11 --- *Traité du Ban et Arrière-Ban*, Orléans, François Hotot, 1675, 4to

12 --- *Juris dissertatio ad Novellam Imperatoris Justiniani CXXX. cuius argumentum est de transitu militum, eorumque annona, et de metatis,*

Gallice, du passage, des etapes, et logemens des gens de guerre, Orléans, François Hotot, 1679, 4to

13 Carolus Hannibal Fabrotus, *Praelectio in Titulum Decretalium Greg. IX de Vita et honestate clericorum*, Paris, Augustin Courbé, 1651, 4to

14 Johannes Petrus de Maurize, *Juris Canonici selecta, et eorum quae ad usum Fori Gallicani pertinent, brevis comprehensio, seu summa*: with Carolus Annibal Fabrotus, *Recitationes in quosdam Titulos Decretalium Gregorii IX. a G[ulielmo] F[abroto] studioso eius nunc primum editae*, Paris, Gervasius Clouzier, 1659, 4to

15 Vincentius Cabotius, *Variarum juris publici et privati disputationum libri duo*, Paris, Claudius de Monstroeil and Joannes Richerus, 1598, 8vo

16 Claudius David, *Velitatio legalis, ad Proöemium, duosque priores Titulos Lib. I Instit.*, Paris, Abel l'Angelier, 1584, 8vo

17 Petrus Beloius, *Variorum Juris Civilis libri quatuor [. . .] disputationes de successionibus ab intestato, de jure pignorationum vel marquae, et de compensationibus*, Paris, Gervasius Mallot, 1583, 8vo

18 Franciscus Broëus, *Analogia Juris ad vestem, qua Juris Naturalis, Gentium et Civilis species illustrantur*, Paris, Claudius Cramoisy, 1623, 8vo

19 *Parallela legis et nummi, quibus triplex Juris species, Naturalis, Gentium, et Civilis philologice exponitur*, Paris, Mathurinus du Puis, 1633, 8vo

20 Joannes Broëus, *Nuptiae jurisprudentiae et philologiae*, Paris, Dionysius Langlaeus, 1651, 4to

***Novus Thesaurus Juris*, volume 5**

1 *Basilicorum libri quatuor, IL. L. LI. LII. ex Codica Manuscripto Regiae Bibliothecae Parisiensis*, ed, trans and comm Guilelmus Otto Reitz, **MS**

2 Thalelaeus, Theodorus, Stephanus, Cyrillus, aliorumque auctorum Graecorum, *Commentarii in Titulum D. et Cod. de Procuratoribus et Defensoribus, Gr. et Lat.*, ed and comm David Ruhnkenius, **MS**

3 Franciscus Ramos del Manzano, *Ad Leges Juliam et Papiam, et quae ex libris jurisconsultorum fragmenta ad illas inseribuntur, commentarii et reliquationes*, Madrid, Typographia Imperialis, 1678, fol

--- *Accedunt dissertationes duae extemporales, prior ad Titum Gaium de Usufructu municipibus legato in L o. Dig. de Usufr. Leg. altera de Domesticis et protectoribus ad L. 2. Cod. de Excusat. mun., his omnibus praemissa est auctoris vita, scriptore Gregorio Mayansio, nunc primum edita*, **MS**

4 --- *Schediasma de Concubinis, earumque tum similitudine, tum differentia a legitimis uxoribus*, in Ferdinand Arias de Mesa, *Variarum juris resolutionum et interpretationum libri III*, Geneva, Samuel Chouët, 1658, 4to [according to NTJ 5.1]

5 Emanuel Soarez a Ribiera, *Observationum juris liber*, Lyon, Claudius Servanius, 1562, 8vo

***Novus Thesaurus Juris*, volume 6**

1 Josephus Fernandez de Retes, *Epitaphia illustrata, sive solennis publica relectio ad L. 6. Cod. de religios. et sumpt. fun.*, Salamanca, Franciscus a Roales, 1644, 4to

2 --- *Opusculorum libri quatuor, quorum primus est totus varius miscellaneusque, et ex nova plerumque observatione; secundus De contractibus incertis, et actionibus, quae ex illis competent, et de pactis in continenti adiectis; tertius, Commentarius ad Librum sing. Quaestionum Scaeuolae; quartus et ultimus notas uberiores continent ad notas Claudii praefixas libris Responsorum et Digestorum eiusdem Scaevolae*, Salamanca, Didacus de Cossio, 1650, fol

3 --- *Opusculorum alii libri quatuor*, Salamanca, Josephus Gomez de los Cubos, 1658, fol

4 --- *Titulos de Bonor. poss. contra tabulas, de Legatis praestandis, et inofficioso testamento scolastica adversaria*, Salamanca, Antonius a Cossio, 1663, 4to

5 --- *Ad Leges, Edicta, et Constitutiones, quibus prohibita usucapio, selectio succisiva. Acced. ad Leges Attiniam, Plautiam, Juliamque de Vi, et repetundarum academica seriata selectio*, Salamanca, Sebastianus Perez, 1663, 4to

6 --- *De donationibus academica relectio*, Salamanca, Antonius a Cossio, 1666, 4to

7 --- *De donationibus inter virum et uxorem liber singularis*, Salamanca, Antonio a Cossio, s.d., 4to

8 Petrus Martresius. *Ad L. veteribus D. de pactis: in aliquot auctorum locos notae*, Paris, Guilielmus Morelius, Jacobus Kerver, and Vincentius Sertenas, 1550 [or 1551], 8vo

9 Gabriel de Gast, *Disp. de actione arbitraria ad L. centum Capuae D. de Eo, quod cert. loc.*, Orléans, Eligius Gibierius, 1576, 4to

10 --- *Commentarii in duos Titt., Cod. de impub. et al. substit.: De sententiis, quae pro eo, quod interest, proferuntur,* Orléans, Eligius Gibierius, 1578, 4to

11 Nicolaus Catharinus, *Observationum et coniectur. libri quatuor*, Bourges, Joannes Christo, 1660–1661, 8vo [made available through the Bibliotheca Pruselliana in Orléans]
12 Foppius ab Aezema, *Dissertationum ex Iure Civili libri duo*, Helmstedt, Jacobus Lucius, 1607, 4to
13 Henricus Ernstius, *Breviores annotationes in librum primum Digestorum*, Copenhagen, Henricus Crusius, 1646, 4to

***Novus Thesaurus Juris*, volume 7**

Franciscus Ramos del Manzano, *Praelectiones variae academicae nunc primum editae* [some purchased from the Ehrencron sale of 1718 by Cornelius Henricus de Wael, and then borrowed; some provided by Gregorius Mayansius]:
1 --- *De privilegiis rei rustica collectanea, sive in pragmaticam Eborensem in savorem agricolarum emissam A[nno] 1619 recitationes solemnes*, **MS**
2 --- *Ad Tit. C. de Apochis publicis commentatio methodica*, **MS**
3 --- *Ad Tit. C. de Nauticularibus breves et dilucidae enarrationes*, **MS**
4 --- *Ad Tit. D. de Justitoria actione commentarius adversarius*, **MS**
5 --- *Ad Leg. I. s. ult. D. Depositi academica commentatio*, **MS**
6 --- *Ad Tit. Dig. de Servitutibus commentarius*, **MS**
7 --- *Ad Leg. Frater a fratre 38. Dig. de Condictione indebiti breves et dilucidae recitationes*, **MS**
8 --- *Ad Tit. Dig. de Acquirenda vel amittenda possessione recitationes nov-antiquae, cum appendice*, **MS**
9 --- *Ad Tit. Dig. de Re iudicata curae secundae*, **MS**
10 --- *Ad Tit. Dig. de Verb. Obligat. recitationes academicae*, **MS**
11 --- *De venditione liberi hominis ad L. 23. D. De liberal. caus.*, **MS**
12 --- *Praelectio ad L.. 25. Dig. de Act. rer. amotr.*, **MS**
13 --- *Commentar. ad Scaevolam in L. Gallus 29. Dig. de Lib. et posthumis*, **MS**
14 --- *Commentar. ad Ulpianum L. 83. Dig. de Adquir. vel omit. heredit.*, **MS**
15 --- *Praelectiones ad Titulos de Legatis et fideicommissis*, **MS**
16 --- *Ad Tit. Dig. de Vulg. et pupil. subst. praelectiones*, **MS**

Josephus Fernandez de Retes, *Tractatus varii Academici nunc primum editi*:
17 --- *Repetita praelectio ad Tit. Dig. de Verbor. obligat.*, **MS**
18 --- *Ad Tit Dig. de Adquir. vel amitt. poss. praelectio academica*, **MS**

19 --- *De interdictis et remediis possessoriis etc. scholastica relectio*, **MS**

20 --- *Ad Tit. Dig. de Re iudicata novi tractatus academici*, **MS**

21 --- *Subcisiua selectio ad L. 50. Dig. de Legatis secundo*, **MS**

22 --- *Ad L. 83. D. de Verb. oblig. nov-antiqua praelectio*, **MS**

23 --- *De dividuis et individuis obligationibus commentarius repetitae praelectiones academicae*, **MS**

24 --- *De fideicommissis perpetuo familae elicitis academica commentatio*, **MS**

25 Doctor Nieto, *Tractatus academicus de praelegatis, nunc primum editus*, **MS**

26 Gerardus Meerman, *Specimen animadversionum criticarum in Caii aucti Institutione: accedit earumdem Caii Institutionum summarium a Petro Aegidio Antverpiensi primum publici juris factum anno 1517*, Paris, Sebastianus Jorey, 1748, 8vo

27 Iulius Paulus, *Sententiae cum notis Petri Fabri: Animadversionibus in notas Iacobi Cuiacii, nunc primum editis*, **MS**

28 *Ulpiani Regularum fragmenta, cum notis Petri Fabri, quibus suas adiecit Gerardus Meerman*, **MS**

29 Gabriel Catianus, *De eo quod interest, syntagma*, Lyon, Sebastianus Gryphius, 1542, 4to

30 Tatius Alpinus, *Epistola ad Wolphgangum Hungerum de furto per lancem et licium concepto*, Basel, Joannes Oporinus, 1545, 4to: with Vitus Amerbachius, *Epistola ad Andr. Alciatum de furto per lancem et licium concepto*, Basel, Joannes Oporinus, 1549, 8vo [information provided by Joannes Rudolphus Iselin of Basel]

31 Guilelmus Barclaius and Joannes Matthaeus Magnus, *Comm. ad Tit. Dig. de iurisd.*, ed Mauricius Calloët, Angers, Antonius Hernault, 1604, 8vo [made available through the Bibliotheca Prustelliana in Orléans]

32 Franciscus de Hauteserre a Salvaison, *Exercitationes ad Tit. Decretal. de Aetate, qualitate, et ordine praeficiendorum*, Paris, Petrus Lamy, 1635, 4to [made available through the Bibliotheca Prustelliana in Orléans]

33 Osius Aurelius, *Pactum renunciationis, sive diss. de pacto dotalibus instrumentis adiecto, ne puella, quam cognatus elocat patri vel cognato succedat*, Orléans, Maria Paris, 1644, 4to

Supplementum Novi Thesauri

1 Constantinus Harmenopulus, *Promptuarium Juris*, trans and ed Gulielmus Otto Reitzius, **MS**

2 Petrus Poncet, *Tractatus de jure municipali, quo ea, quae ad cives,*

municipes, et incolas, muneraque et privilegia eorum, nec non et quae ad civitates et municipia spectant, fusius tractantur, Lyon, Joannes Lertout, 1625, 8vo

3 J D P [Franciscus de Roye?], *Quaestio utrum secundum allegata et probata, ut aiunt, iudicare debeat, an secundum conscientiam*, **MS Angers**

4 Samuel Fermat, *Dissertationes tres, quorum prima est de re militari, seu de quibusdam legibus Romanis ad utramque militiam, sacram scilicet ac profanam, pertinentibus; secunda de authoritate Homeri apud jurisconsultos, tertia de historia naturali*, Toulouse, Joannes Peck, 1680, 8vo

5 Cornelius van Eck, *Dissertatio de septem damnatis legibus Pandectarum, seu crucibus jurisconsultorum*, Leiden, Abrahamus Elzevier, 1682, 4to

6 --- *Disputatio de quota litis*, respondente George Ernst a Gerssdorff, Utrecht, Franciscus Halma, 1698, 4to

7 Petrus Tronchin, *Disputatio de variis capitibus juris*, Franeker, Johannes Gyzelaar, 1694, 4to

8 Adrianus van der Hoop, *Disputatio de iis, qui antiquitus apud Romanos de criminibus judicarunt*, Leiden, Samuel Luchtmans, 1723, 4to

9 Augustus Florens Rivinus, *Dissertatio de poena gladii ex legibus Romanis*, Leipzig, Immanuel Titius, 1727, 4to

10 Johannes Fridericus Christius, *Historia legis Scatiniae (de crimine nefando latae) antiquorum codicum testimoniis emendatis, illustrandis passim distincta*, Halle, Johannes Christianus Krebs, 1727, 4to

13 Humanist Books and Lawyers' Libraries in Early Eighteenth-Century Scotland: Charles Areskine of Alva's Library

Karen G Baston

I. LAW TEXTS AS PART OF A LIVING LEGAL SYSTEM: CONVERSATIONS AND TOOLS
   (1) Conversations with the dead
   (2) Tools of the trade
J. CONCLUSIONS: BOOKWORMS AND MOTHS

A. INTRODUCTION: CHARLES ARESKINE OF ALVA

Charles Areskine of Alva, Lord Tinwald (1680–1763) was a leading figure of the Scottish legal establishment in the early eighteenth century. He was a teacher and professor, the first Regius Professor of the Law of Nature and Nations at Edinburgh, before he changed tack and became an advocate in 1711. His legal career lasted more than fifty years. He was appointed Solicitor General in 1725, then Lord Advocate in 1737. He was elected to the Bench as Lord Tinwald in 1744 and he became Lord Justice Clerk in 1748. Areskine was later praised as

> . . . an eminent lawyer and judge, but likewise a polite scholar, and an elegant speaker and writer . . . This gentleman was possessed of excellent talents, which were improved by culture, and set off to great advantage by a graceful persuasive eloquence in a strain peculiarly his own.[1]

Areskine's professional success and the income he derived from his estates enabled him to collect a large library of books. From 1731 until his death, Areskine kept a catalogue of his growing collection. This library catalogue, and many of his books,[2] survives in the National Library of Scotland,[3] giving the opportunity for an exploration of the books collected and used by an eminent Scottish lawyer of the first half of the eighteenth century.

Areskine was the product of a humanist education in Scotland, one enhanced by his legal studies in the Netherlands. The books Areskine collected show evidence of his interest in humanism, his need for legal sources in practice, and the changes in Scots law during his lifetime. His pursuit of these academic activities allowed him to achieve professional and social success in the world of early Enlightenment Scotland.

1 J Ramsay of Ochtertyre, *Scotland and Scotsmen in the Eighteenth Century*, (ed) A Allardyce, vol 1 (1888) 100–101.

2 Books included in Areskine's library catalogue are referred to throughout by the places where they appear in the catalogue. The catalogue divides the books by size (folio, quarto, and octavo et infra) and by type (legal or miscellaneous).

3 National Library of Scotland (NLS) MS 3283.

B. SCOTTISH EDUCATION AND SCHOLARLY TRAVEL

(1) Humanism and early modern Scottish education

Humanism, the idea of being educated in subjects beyond the studies needed to pursue professions, was an innovation of the European Renaissance. Fifteenth-century Italian universities developed a programme of education around the "teacher of the *studia humanitatis*, who based his course . . . on grammar and rhetoric, poetry and history, and the ethical writings of classical Antiquity".[4] Humanist scholars focused their attentions on "recovering and reviving ancient knowledge and ancient eloquence, ancient purity of diction and ancient techniques of argument"[5] while studying and translating Greek and Latin texts. University teachers and scholars embraced the humanist approach and it spread across Europe.

After the Reformation, Scottish educators created a Protestant system of education with a goal of developing a reformed society of godly people.[6] A key figure was Andrew Melville (1545–1622). Melville's continental studies included attending the law lectures of the humanist François Baudouin in Paris.[7] He returned to Scotland in 1574 and began to implement a programme of educational reform along humanist lines. Melville's ideal curriculum included reading Aristotle in the original Greek, studying the "new humanist subjects such as history and sacred chronology", learning ancient languages, and basic logic and philosophy.[8] Because Scotland had not experienced a "great rejection of Aristotle or the medieval intellectual heritage",[9] Melville's reforms, although soon rejected,[10] did not represent radical change in the educational system. Instead, "there was a gradual incorporation into this tradition of the Renaissance focus on *ad fontes* study of classical texts, and some limited . . . engagement with sixteenth-century humanist reforms in logic and rhetoric".[11] The arts curriculum was well established by the first half of the seventeenth century when visitors from the Church of

4 J B Trapp, "The Humanist Book", in L Hellinga and J B Trapp (eds), *The Cambridge History of the Book in Britain*, 3: *1400–1557* (1999) 285–315 at 285.

5 Trapp (n 4) at 285.

6 S J Reid, *Humanism and Calvinism: Andrew Melville and the Universities of Scotland, 1560–1625* (2011) 1.

7 Reid (n 6) 61.

8 Reid (n 6) 49.

9 Reid (n 6) 270.

10 Reid (n 6) 233.

11 Reid (n 6) 270.

Scotland General Assembly toured the universities to inspect their academic arrangements. The universities accepted their recommended course, which included Greek, logic, Aristotle's logic, physics and *De anima*, ethics, metaphysics, geometry, and physics.[12]

As this was much the same curriculum that he studied at St Andrews from 1694 to 1699, Charles Areskine must have had a good knowledge of Aristotelian philosophy and some skill in logic and mathematics by the time he took his master's degree. Areskine's Greek was certainly good enough for him to prepare a translation and interpretation of a Pindaric Ode as part of his public debate and trial when he successfully applied to be a regent at Edinburgh in 1701.[13] As a regent, Areskine taught the recommended curriculum and added his own interest in Newtonian science to his lectures.

Two notebooks kept by his students from his time as a regent survive, and along with the printed theses he wrote for his students to defend, these show the topics Areskine discussed during his lectures. Dictates taken down by Patrick Wilkie in 1703 include notes on lectures on ethics, pneumatics, physics, and philosophy. They also include a manuscript copy of the *Theses philosophicae*.[14] Nicholas Montgomery's notes, also of 1703, record lectures on mathematics and physics.[15] The Scottish arts curriculum was not static and Areskine's *Theses philosophicae* of 1704 focus on Newtonian theory.[16]

Regents had presided over the four-year programme of their students' university educations for centuries and Areskine was one of the last. The Principal of the University of Edinburgh, William Carstares, was inspired by the Dutch professorial system, which featured specialised instructors for each subject. He favoured removing Edinburgh's regents and appointing professors. Areskine quickly obtained a place in the new structure as the first Regius Professor of the Law of Nature and Nations in 1707. He donated two works of classical history to the university library then requested leave

12 C Shepherd, "A National System of University Education in Seventeenth Century Scotland", in J J Carter and D J Withrington (eds), *Scottish Universities: Distinctiveness and Diversity* (1992) 26–33 at 26.

13 A Dalzel, *History of the University of Edinburgh from its Foundation*, 2: *History* (1862) 273. This may or may have not been a feat of academic prowess since Pindar's Odes vary considerably in difficulty. I am grateful to Ernest Metzger for this observation.

14 P Wilkie, "Lecture notes, 1703", NLS MS Adv.20.7.1.

15 N Montgomery, "Annotationes ad Johannis Cleridi Physicam. Dictatae a. Magistro Carolo Areskino in Academia Edinburgensi" (1703), EUL, Centre for Research Collections MS Dc.7.98.

16 C Areskine, *Theses philosophicae, quas, auspice summo numine, generosi aliquot & ingenui juvenes universitatis Jacobi Regis Edinburgenae alumni, hac vice cum laurea emittendi, eruditorum examini subjicient, ad 12. diem Maii, H. Lq. S.* (1704).

to travel to the Netherlands to study his new subject. He was granted two to three years' leave to travel abroad before taking up his post.[17]

(2) Scholarly travel

The *peregrinatio academica* was a long-established tradition in Western Europe by the early eighteenth century. Students seeking educations for the professions, especially medicine and law, travelled to centres of learning to study with specialist professors or to take degrees. Their destinations changed over time as political situations demanded or as new centres featured the attraction of influential and popular professors. Students could matriculate at most continental universities regardless of their religious affiliations. By the time Areskine embarked on his *peregrinatio academica* in 1708, France had given way to the Netherlands as the preferred destination for Scottish students. Scottish students appreciated the tolerant attitude to religion and the quality of instruction they found there.[18] Scottish exiles, including Viscount Stair and John Erskine of Carnock, had spent time in the Netherlands in the 1680s: this strengthened trade links and eased financial transactions between the nations. When he matriculated at Leyden on 2 February 1708 as "Carolus Areskin, *Scoto-Britannus*",[19] Areskine was one Scot amongst many: Scottish academic travel to Leyden reached a peak between 1681 and 1730,[20] and nearly 60% of them studied law.[21]

C. LEARNING LAW IN THE LOW COUNTRIES

(1) Arts and law

Legal scholars in the Netherlands expected an education which included a thorough study of the texts of the *Corpus Iuris Civilis*. History and philology helped scholars understand the Institutes, Digest, Code, and Novels of

17 J W Cairns, "The origins of the Edinburgh Law School: the Union of 1707 and the Regius Chair" (2007) 11 *Edinburgh Law Review* 300 at 333–334.

18 J W Cairns, "'Importing our Lawyers from Holland': Netherlands' Influence on Scots Law and Lawyers in the Eighteenth Century", in G G Simpson (ed), *Scotland and the Low Countries* (1996) 136 at 144.

19 E Peacock (ed), *Index to English speaking students who have graduated at Leyden University* (1883) 4.

20 E Mijers, "Scottish Students in the Netherlands, 1680–1730", in A Grosjean and S Murdoch (eds), *Scottish Communities in the Early Modern Period* (2005) at 305–306.

21 The rest studied arts, medicine, and theology: Mijers (n 20) at 313.

Justinian in their proper contexts. Legal scholars also studied the techniques of eloquence that they would need to plead in court and used mathematics as a basis for the structured forms they would need in practice.[22] For scholars of Areskine's generation, the Low Countries offered an appealing "late humanistic culture . . . based on the study of the classics and the ancient world, including the historical and philological study of Roman law".[23]

Ulrick Huber, a former judge in the court of Friesland and a prolific author of legal works, was professor of law at Franeker from 1682.[24] His *De ratione juris docendi & discendi diatribe per modum dialogi nonnullis aucta paralipomenois* of 1688 set out his ideas about what he expected from students and the knowledge and skills they would gain when they studied with him. Huber believed that a student of law should have a strong background in general studies before starting his law course. For Huber the potential legal scholar:

> should first work to learn literature and the arts tolerably well, for without them jurisprudence cannot be effectively understood. By literature I understand Latin and Greek literature, the former should be learned more precisely and thoroughly, the latter in such a way that the writings of the ancients can be handled clearly and rationally at least with the help of a translation.[25]

A student who had done this groundwork could progress to his first year of legal studies. These would include not law, but instead logic, ethics, and history. Huber said that he:

> . . . would like my first year student to attend lectures on logic and ethics, commit to memory a *compendium* of universal history and see to it that he understands Suetonius clearly and fully. For in Suetonius most things relating to Roman and juridical antiquities present themselves to be understood in an easy and historic order . . . Meanwhile, in his spare time progress must be made with reading other writers of ancient history, and also in composing, not only by reading but also by imitating the eloquence of ancient writers . . . there will be no lack of those who, in the same year, can master the basics of physics and mathematics then, when the study of law if begun in the second year, I do not think that the new law student should so devote himself to the law alone, that he abandons his initial studies in the humanities and literature and considers that they do not concern him any longer.[26]

22 Cairns (n 18) at 138.

23 J W Cairns, "Legal Theory", in A Broadie (ed), *The Cambridge Companion to the Scottish Enlightenment* (2003) 222 at 235.

24 R Feenstra, M Ahsmann and T Veen, *Bibliografie van hoogleraren in de rechten aan de Franeker Universiteit tot 1811* (2003) 47.

25 U Huber, *De ratione juris docendi & discendi diatribe per modum dialogi nonnullis aucta paralipomenois*, transl M L Hewett (2010) 51.

26 Huber (n 25) 52–53. Areskine owned works by Suetonius.

Only after this first year, could the law student "attend lectures on the Institutes of Justinian and then continue with reading the elements of the whole subject".[27] The "next year ought to be spent on the *Pandects*" since Huber:

> found that the most important factor of all in my practice and programmes is the following: namely that those students who, in the three years, which are occupied with the *Institutes* and the *Pandects*, spend their spare time in reading ancient writers, and hence are already acquainted with their subject, are students who can select and refer to the appropriate texts all the material for illustrating the Roman law which they find in philosophy, rhetoric, history and the poets.[28]

The university education that Scottish students received in Scotland before they set off for their legal educations prepared them for their legal studies abroad. They were well equipped to undertake the studies that Huber indicated.

(2) Legal textbooks at Leyden

Areskine's library list of 1731 suggests that he purchased textbooks in the Low Countries. It is likely that Areskine studied with one or more of the Leyden professors who were in post during his educational tour of 1708 to 1711. These were Johannes Voet (1647–1713), Philippus Reinhardus Vitriarius (1647–1720), Antonius Matthaeus III (1635–1710), and Gerard Noodt (1647–1725).[29] Areskine's library contained books by all of them.

Voet's textbook, *Commentarius ad Pandectas*[30] "dominated the market completely".[31] In it, Voet explained Roman legal principles and considered their application in modern use. Voet saw law as both a science and an art: it could be applied creatively.[32] In the eighteenth century, especially when Areskine was a practitioner, Voet's influence was "clearly discernable in the

27 Huber (n 25) 52.

28 Huber (n 25) 54–55.

29 Cairns (n 18) at 145. Cairns has discussed the books Areskine may have acquired as a student. Cairns (n 17) at 334–339.

30 Folio 38: *Johannis Voet jcti & antecessoris in Academiâ Lugduno-Batavâ Commentarius ad Pandectas: In quo praeter Romani juris principia ac controversias illustriores, jus etiam hodiernum, & praecipuae fori quaestiones excutiuntur* (1707). Areskine's copy, containing his bookplate, is now in the Advocates Library (B.1.1). Areskine may have acquired his copy after he returned to Scotland. He was not the first owner since an inscription on the title page reads "Leydon [sic] Septbe 17th 1710" and the owner of 1710's name has been removed.

31 G C J J van den Bergh, *The Life and Work of Gerard Noodt (1647–1725): Dutch Legal Scholarship between Humanism and Enlightenment* (1988) 263.

32 J W Wessels, *History of Roman-Dutch Law* (1908; repr 2005) 320–321.

judgements of the Scottish Courts".[33] Voet's "Commentary" was "a very cleverly made and practically useful synthesis of Roman law as it applied in Holland"[34] and his *Compendium juris juxta seriem Pandectarum*[35] was "known to generations of students".[36] John Clerk of Penicuik, who studied with Voet for a year, recalled that "he kept close to his own Compend on the Institutes and Pandects".[37] From Vitriarius,[38] the German born scholar of public law who related his studies to natural law, Areskine had *Institutiones juris naturae et gentium*[39] and *Institutiones juris publici Romano-Germanici selectae*.[40] However, Areskine could not have had the second of these at the time of his Leyden visit since his copy was in an edition of 1714. Vitriarius was popular with Scots law students.[41] Clerk thought he was "certainly one of the greatest lawyers in the world" and noted that he had "a particular kindness especially to Scotsmen".[42]

The "elegant" scholar Noodt did not use a textbook for his civil law courses. Areskine had Noodt's study of usury, *De foenore et usuris*,[43] which explored its subject within its historical and comparative legal contexts,[44] his

33 R Feenstra and C J D Waal, *Seventeenth-century Leyden Law Professors and Their Influence on the Development of the Civil Law: A Study of Bronchorst, Vinnius and Voet* (1975) 85. Voet (1647–1713) was professor of civil law at Leyden from 1683 to 1713. J Clerk, *Memoirs of the Life of Sir John Clerk of Penicuik, Baronet Baron of the Exchequer extracted by himself from his Own Journals, 1676–1755*, ed J M Gray (1892) 14–15.

34 Van den Bergh (n 31) 94.

35 Octavo 253: J Voet, *Johannis Voet . . .Compendium Juris juxta seriem Pandectarum, adjectis differentiis juris civilis et canonici: ut et definitionibus ac divisionibus praecipuis secundum institutionum titulos* (1688). Areskine's copy, which contains his bookplate, is now in the NLS (Alva.151).

36 Cairns (n 18) 137.

37 Clerk (n 33) 15.

38 Cairns (n 18) at 136–137. Vitriarius (1647–1720) was professor of law at Leyden from 1682 to 1719. M Ahsmann and R Feenstra, *Bibliografie van hoogleraren in de rechten aan de Leidse universiteit tot 1811*(1984) 320.

39 Octavo 14: P R Vitriarius, *Institutiones juris naturae et gentium in usum Serenissimi Principis Christiani Ludovici Marchionis Brandenburgici . . . ad methodum Hugo Grotii* (1692). Areskine's copy is now in the NLS (Alva.262).

40 Octavo 301: P R Vitriarius, *Institutiones juris publici Romano-Germanici selectae . . . Editio nova prioribus omnibus correctior. Accesserunt Aurea Bulla, Instrumenta Pacis Westphalicae, Suecicum & Gallicum, Capitulationes Josephi I. & Caroli VI* (1714). Areskine's copy is now in the NLS (Alva.263). It contains his son James Erskine, Lord Alva's bookplate.

41 Cairns (n 17) at 335.

42 K van Strien and M Ahsmann, "Scottish law students in Leiden at the end of the seventeenth century: the correspondence of John Clerk, 1694–1697" (1992) 19 *LIAS* [Sources and Documents relating to the Early Modern History of Ideas] 271 at 319, 322.

43 Quarto 75: G Noodt, *De foenore et usuris libri tres* (1698).

44 Van den Bergh (n 31) 181–191.

De forma emendandi doli mali,[45] which examined ancient contract law,[46] and his *Opera varia*,[47] which included his humanistic monographs *De jurisdictione et imperio libri II* and *Ad legem Aquiliam liber singularis* on Roman public law and compensation for losses respectively.[48] Since Vitriarius and Noodt both offered a *Collegium Grotianum* when he was at Leyden,[49] it is possible that Areskine studied with both of them. Matthaeus III meanwhile was a humanist who shared Noodt's interests[50] and Areskine had his *Miscellaneae exercitationes, adversus Abrahamum a Wesel*.[51]

(3) An academic social network

Travelling legal scholars derived benefits beyond knowledge. They acquired a unique polish from the reading and learning they did abroad. Clerk declared that

> I think every man who has studied here at Leiden should at his return enter advocate, if it were only to let people see he has spent his time to the purpose, whether they have any expectation of either employment or preferment or not.[52]

Training to be an advocate therefore increased intellectual and social opportunities for legal scholars. Not only did it help students to qualify for professions, travel also fostered their feeling of belonging to an international community of scholars. Travelling was an effective means of increasing networking and the Republic of Letters was continuously refreshed with young scholars.[53]

Scots legal scholars shared this sense of community and they remained in contact with the continental professors long after they completed their studies. Charles Binning, who studied at Utrecht from 1695 until 1697, sent a copy of his advocate's theses to his professor Cornelis van Eck after his admission to the Faculty in 1698. Over the next few years Binning regularly

45 Quarto 73: G Noodt, *De forma emendandi doli mali, in contrahendis negotiis admissi, apud veteres, liber* (1709).
46 Van den Bergh (n 31) 244–252.
47 Quarto 72: G Noodt, *Opera varia. Quibus continentur Probabilium juris civilis libri IV. De jurisdictione et imperio libri II. Ad legem Aquiliam liber singularis* (1705).
48 Van den Bergh (n 31) 167–181.
49 Van den Bergh (n 31) 271.
50 Van den Bergh (n 31) 98.
51 Octavo 149: *Miscellaneae exercitationes, adversus Abrahamum a Wesel* (1678).
52 K van Strien and M Ahsmann, "Scottish law students at Leiden at the end of the seventeenth century: the correspondence of John Clerk, 1694–1697" (1993) 20 *LIAS* 1 at 32.
53 T J Schlereth, *The Cosmopolitan Ideal in Enlightenment Thought: Its Form and Function in the Ideas of Franklin, Hume, and Voltaire, 1694–1790* (1977) 2–5.

wrote to van Eck requesting information and advice about legal matters and sharing news about common acquaintances. Although his letters to Binning do not survive, it is clear that van Eck replied to his former student.[54] John Clerk wrote to his friend the Leyden medical professor Herman Boerhaave many years after his return to Scotland. Clerk was, by the time of his letter, a Baron of the Exchequer who had inherited the family estate at Penicuik. His letter describes his scholarly arrangements in his home, including his library, since he hoped to entice Boerhaave to Scotland for an intellectual visit.[55] When they travelled abroad, future Scottish advocates gained a shared an experience of a "polite, gentlemanly, scholarly" education.[56]

(4) Book collecting abroad

Scottish and other legal scholars bought books as an integral part of their studies. At the time when travelling students enjoyed the opportunities for legal education on offer at its universities, the Netherlands was also the centre of book production and trade[57] which had a "virtual monopoly on the Latin trade" with the "most popular books [being] compendia and other textbooks by Leiden and Utrecht professors, the classics and books on languages and applied mathematics".[58]

Book buying was so important to Leyden's academic community that the daily lecture programme was suspended on the days book auctions were held there.[59] In 1636 the university "stipulated that small-scale auctions were only allowed at times when there were no lectures, and larger ones

54 C Binning to C van Eck, "Letters", 30 Apr 1698, 10 Apr 1699, 7 Aug 1699, 25 Nov 1699, 20 Aug 1700, UB Utrecht HS 1000 7B3. Binning's letters to van Eck and some insights on van Eck's surprisingly humanist teaching will be the subjects of a forthcoming article by K Baston and J W Cairns.

55 J Clerk, "Description of the estate and old house at Penicuik, in a letter from the Baron to Boerhaave", transl T Graves Law, in J M Gray (ed), *Memoirs of the life of Sir John Clerk of Penicuik, Baronet, Baron of the Exchequer, extracted by himself from his own journals, 1676–1755* (1892) 237.

56 Cairns (n 18) 138.

57 R van Vliet, "Print and Public in Europe, 1600–1800", in S Eliot and J Rose (eds), *A Companion to the History of the Book* (2007) 247 at 248–249. For the book trade between Scotland and the Low Countries in the sixteenth and seventeenth centuries, see A J Mann, *The Scottish Book Trade, 1500–1720: Print Commerce and Print Control in Early Modern Scotland: An Historiographical Survey of the Early Modern Book in Scotland* (2000) 67–93. Compare Maclean elsewhere in this volume.

58 E Mijers, "The Scottish-Dutch trade", in S W Brown and W McDougall (eds), *The Edinburgh History of the Book in Scotland, 2: Enlightenment and Expansion: 1707–1800* (2012) 203 at 204.

59 Van den Bergh (n 31) 95.

only during vacations".[60] Between 1677 and 1708 an average of twenty-five auctions occurred in Leyden every year.[61] The presence of the university at Leyden ensured a steady supply of second-hand books.[62] The town attracted Dutch and French booksellers.[63] Leyden booksellers also established themselves as importers of books and libraries from other places.[64] Booksellers advertised their sales in newspapers and provided catalogues which they ensured were widely available. As many as 27,500 book catalogues were produced in Holland between 1599 and 1800.[65]

Scottish students purchased books they were unable to obtain at home. Most of the "Scottish-Dutch trade . . . relied more on private contacts than on commercial exchange".[66] Clerk, for example, tried to fulfil his uncle David Forbes' commissions "if it be possible" by buying books at auctions and "send[ing] them home with mine".[67] Despite the undoubted demand for books from aristocrats and members of the professions, politics could interfere with book importation into Britain on occasion until 1714.[68] Dutch universities recognised the importance of book buying for their students and scholars were encouraged and expected to attend auctions. John Erskine of Carnock attended auctions at Leyden and Utrecht and had to "put up" his "books and other things"[69] as he travelled throughout the Low Countries as a student and political exile in the 1680s.[70] By 1696, after nearly two years abroad, Clerk's library was well developed. He had "near 400 guilders worth [of books], which are all choice books and few or none to be got in Scotland".[71]

60 O S Lankhorst, "Dutch Book Auctions in the Seventeenth and Eighteenth Centuries", in R Myers, M Harris and G Mandelbrote (eds), *Under the Hammer: Book Auctions since the Seventeenth Century* (2001) 65 at 69.

61 L Cruz, "The secrets of success: microinventions and bookselling in the seventeenth-century Netherlands" (2007) 10 *Book History* 1 at 21.

62 Cruz (n 61) at 22.

63 Mijers (n 20) at 323.

64 Cruz (n 61) at 4.

65 Lankhorst (n 60) at 68. For examples see "Book Sales Catalogues of the Dutch Republic, 1599–1800", available at *http://bsc.idcpublishers.info/*.

66 Mijers (n 58) at 205.

67 Strien and Ahsmann (n 52) at 57.

68 G Barber, "Book Imports and Exports in the Eighteenth Century", in R Myers and M Harris (eds), *Sale and Distribution of Books from 1700* (1982) 77 at 90.

69 J Erskine, *Journal of the Hon. John Erskine of Carnock, 1683–1687*, (ed) W MacLeod (1893) 113.

70 Erskine (n 69) 110, 177, 178.

71 Strien and Ahsmann (n 52) at 28.

D. BUYING LEARNED BOOKS IN BRITAIN

(1) London

Learned books were widely available in Britain and British collectors did not need to make repeated continental visits to complete their libraries. Some continental sellers recognised the importance of the British market and expanded their businesses to include shops in London. Some of these sellers concentrated their efforts on the "Latin trade", that is, scholarly books. David Mortier, a Dutch bookseller, had established himself in London by 1698. After a sojourn in Holland from 1709 to 1719 when he took over his brother's part of the family business, Mortier was back in London by 1720. From 1702, he printed catalogues that featured his selections of used books, new foreign books, and maps and prints. All of his stock was printed or sourced in Holland.[72] Areskine had at least three books from the Mortier concern, all published in Amsterdam.[73] He also owned books from other foreign booksellers based in London including the French Huguenot booksellers Paul and Isaac Vaillant[74] and the Dutchman Pierre Gosse.[75] These foreign sellers used their continental connections, often members of their families, to supply books from Holland and France.[76] They managed sales and auctions on both sides of the Channel[77] and they were able to supply the books their cosmopolitan clientele demanded.

Booksellers made their sale catalogues available at book shops and in coffee houses where learned gentlemen met to discuss the latest publications and compare their book desiderata. Areskine regularly visited London

72 K Swift, "Dutch Penetration of the London Market for Books, c 1690–1730", in C Berkvens-Stevelinck et al (eds), in *Le magasin de l'univers: the Dutch Republic as the Centre of the European Book Trade: Papers Presented at the International Colloquium, held at Wassenaar, 5–7 July 1990* (1992) 265 at 268–270.

73 Miscellaneous quarto 12: J Le Clerc, *Historia ecclesiastica duorum primorum a Christo nato saeculorum, e veteribus monumentis depromta* (1716), Miscellaneous octavo 58: A-N Amelot de La Houssaie, *Histoire du gouvernement de Venise* (1695) and Miscellaneous octavo 221: P Desmaizeaux, *Scaligerana, Thuana, Perroniana, Pithoeana, et Colomesiana. Ou remarques historiques, critiques, morales, & litteraires* (1740).

74 Miscellaneous quarto 73: A Johnstoun, *Arturi Johnstoni Psalmi Davidici cum argumentis et notis, juxta editionem in usum serenissimi principis* (1741) and Miscellaneous octavo 27: A Cunningham, *Alexandri Cuningamii Animadversiones, in Richardi Bentleii notas et emendationes ad Q. Horatium Flaccum*, (ed) A Cunningham and R Bentley (1721 [probably printed at The Hague]).

75 Miscellaneous octavo 44: R Rapin, *Oeuvres* (1725).

76 Swift (n 72) 270.

77 Swift (n 72) 277.

from the 1720s to the 1740s as a Westminster MP. He also acted in appeal cases before the House of Lords. He would have had easy access to London's bookshops.

(2) Edinburgh

Booksellers in Scotland also realised that their well-travelled customers wanted books from other sources and took pains to import them. The printer and bookseller Robert Freebairn advertised an auction of "A Parcel of Books, Lately imported from England, and Holland . . . to be sold at this Shop below the Trone-Church on 22 January 1734".[78] It is not known if Areskine attended this sale, but his Edinburgh townhouse in Mylne's Square was directly opposite the Tron Kirk, and it is possible that Areskine looked at the stock on offer or indeed attended the auction. He was certainly at others. He bought books at the Sir Alexander of Pitmedden sale of 1720 and this is verified by the interleaved clerk's copy of its catalogue which survives in the National Library of Scotland[79] as well as the presence of the books he bought on the day which appear in his 1731 list.

Perhaps because of the close links between the Low Countries and the Scottish book trade and because Scottish customers were used to the idea, auctions were popular in Scotland.[80] The earliest surviving Scottish book auction catalogue is dated 1686 – a sale of the Edinburgh bookseller John Reid's stock.[81] Few Scottish auction catalogues survive but sales were advertised in newspapers such as *The Scots Courant* and the *Edinburgh Gazette*[82] and catalogues of the "curious and valuable books" were available at the many bookshops that lined Edinburgh's High Street. Customers who had been abroad would have recognised the procedures as well as the opportunity to collect quality books at good prices. In auctions of law libraries,

78 R Freebairn, *A parcel of books, lately imported from England and Holland, by Mr Robert Freebairn, To be sold by auction at his shop below the Trone-Church, upon Tuesday the twenty second day of January, 1734* (1733).

79 NLS MS 3802: Interleaved clerk's copy with buyer's names and prices of *A catalogue of valuable books, in several languages and faculties, viz. divinity, law, medicine, history, philosophy, mathematicks, with several of the best editions of the classicks, a curious collection of pamphlets and controversies, & c being the library which belong'd to Sir Alexander Seaton of Pitmedden, Baronet, lately deceased. To be sold by way of auction on Munday the 11 Day of January 1720* (1719).

80 M C T Simpson, "'Every one is sure to get something for his money': a 1712 book lottery and auction in Edinburgh" (2010) 5 *Journal of the Edinburgh Bibliographical Society* 36.

81 Simpson (n 80) at 36.

82 Simpson (n 80) at 36.

buyers could take advantage of the chance to augment their collections of foreign legal texts brought to Scotland by a previous generation of travelling scholars.

E. ARESKINE'S BOOKS: HUMANISM AND LEGAL HISTORY

(1) Traditional legal history

Book collecting was an important part of Areskine's intellectual life. Well over half of the books in his library catalogue were related to law and legal studies. These brought together varied legal traditions that were relevant to their early eighteenth-century owner. Many of them came from the humanist educational tradition of which Areskine was a product. A brief survey of the modern historiography of legal history helps put them into context.

By the fifteenth century, Justinian's codification of law had acquired a range of commentaries, glosses, and other medieval interpretations. Jurists of the humanistic persuasion decided that these once useful apparatus were strangling the original texts. The approaches of adding explanations and interpretations used by medieval Glossators and Commentators continued to be used, especially in Italy, but a new way of studying the sources of Roman law developed alongside them. Jurists worked to determine the interrelationships between the *ius commune*, the civilian tradition, and their local customary laws across early modern Europe.

Some legal scholars eagerly took up the humanist approach. Legal humanists worked to edit, amend, and annotate Justinian's texts while studying and interpreting classical legal writings.[83] They approached the material they found with questions medieval jurists had not asked. They "wanted to know about the authority of the text, how accurate it was [and] what were the fact-situations that lay behind the writings of classical jurists".[84] They hoped to discover the original meanings of Justinian's texts by considering these questions.[85]

Franz Wieacker's *A History of Private Law in Europe*, has dominated legal history since its publication in 1952. Wieacker created a compelling narrative of the history of legal evolution that divided jurists into categories and that divided legal authors into competing schools of scholars. These

83 Van den Bergh (n 31) 113.
84 P Stein, *Roman Law in European History* (1999; rep 2009) 75.
85 Stein (n 84) 77.

legal scholars then engaged with ideological and methodological controversies as law progressed to a state of codified perfection in the nineteenth century. Wieacker's model was based on the schools of legal history that had developed in nineteenth-century Germany and he used it to look back at earlier times.[86] Since modern legal historians were often at loggerheads, so too must their juristic ancestors have been. For Wieacker, humanism represented a break with earlier schools of scholarship which gradually gained a dominant influence over legal science.[87] Wieacker's heroic legal humanists felt a connection with the ancient world, attacked other forms of legal scholarship, and worked to reconstruct the sources of ancient law. They would eventually "triumph" over rival scholars.[88]

Wieacker offered an outline of legal history in which he identified "four great shifts in European legal thinking" and matched these to "epochs in the history of German private law".[89] In his model, legal science developed in the twelfth to fourteenth centuries and was then diffused "throughout the whole of Europe between the thirteenth and sixteenth centuries". The seventeenth and eighteenth centuries saw the "rise and dominance of the modern law of nature", while the nineteenth was characterised by the "historical school and positivism". Finally, the twentieth century witnessed the "collapse of positivism" and legal crisis.[90]

(2) Challenges to the traditional legal history narrative

Wieacker's influential outline became what Douglas Osler has described as the "syllabus of the class of European history".[91] It has influenced generations of scholars and has provided the foundation for legal history textbooks across Europe.[92] The book's reissue in 1995 showed its enduring popularity.[93] But there are serious problems with Wieacker's narrative and these, as Osler has pointed out, can in part be examined by studying the histories of book publishing and of libraries. Osler criticised Wieacker for failing to

86 F Wieacker, *A History of Private Law in Europe: With Particular Reference to Germany*, transl by Tony Weir (1995) 1.
87 Wieacker (n 86) 60–63.
88 Wieacker (n 86) 63–65.
89 Wieacker (n 86) 7.
90 Wieacker (n 86) 7.
91 D J Osler, "The myth of European legal history" (1997) 16 *Rechtshistorisches Journal* 393.
92 Osler (n 91) at 393.
93 R Zimmermann, "Foreword", in F Wieacker, *A History of Private Law in Europe: With Particular Reference to Germany*, transl T Weir (1995) v–xiii at x.

recognise basic historical and geographical facts in his study. His overemphasis on the achievements of Protestant northern European legal humanists distorted the overall picture and gave a selective version of history, a narrative of progress which neglected Spain, which dominated Europe throughout the sixteenth and seventeenth centuries, and England, which created a unique legal system despite being "completely . . . integrated in the economic, political and intellectual history of Europe".[94]

Klaus Luig describes the development of written forms of law as a four-stage interrelated process. First, the study of Roman law throughout the Middle Ages provided the basis of the *ius commune* of Europe. The second stage saw jurists trying to reconcile differences between Roman law and their local law. Local statutes and customs were blended with Roman law to create relevant systems. In the third stage these "particular legal systems were commented upon and described separately from the *ius commune*". The fourth stage saw the emergence of national legal systems as objects of study in their own right. Roman law was "no longer the central topic of European legal science" and Latin was replaced by works in vernacular languages as jurists discussed "the indigenous legal sources of statutory law and decisions of the courts".[95] All of this activity ensured a steady supply of book publication at every stage.[96]

But, and in contrast to Wieacker, Luig's "four stages of the reception and assimilation of Roman law and the development of national legal systems did not occur in a straightforward chronological order".[97] The legal literature of the four stages existed concurrently.[98] Roman law remained as an international focus of study and its works were "frequently reprinted in almost all European countries".[99] Manlio Bellomo emphasises that "the various movements – legal humanism, Italian Bartolism, 'practical jurisprudence', German *Usus Modernus Pandectarum*, the 'Seconda Scholastica' – were all European in scope and were present everywhere".[100] This juristic activity encouraged book production across Europe.

94 Osler (n 91) 397–402, quotation at 401.
95 K Luig, "The institutes of national law in the seventeenth and eighteenth centuries" (1972) new ser 17 *Juridical Review* 193 at 194–195.
96 For a description of the various types of publications available to Renaissance legal scholars – many of which were present in Areskine's eighteenth-century library – see I Maclean, *Interpretation and Meaning in the Renaissance: The Case of Law* (1992) 30–34.
97 Luig (n 95) at 197–198.
98 Luig (n 95) at 198.
99 Luig (n 95) at 198.
100 M Bellomo, *The Common Legal Past of Europe, 1000–1800*, transl L G Cochrane (1995) 224.

Humanism's appearance in the fifteenth century did not eliminate other methods of intellectual endeavour and humanists did not shut themselves off from contemporary concerns. It was, as Randall Lesaffer describes, at first a "fairly marginal movement" and even as it developed it "did not propose its own comprehensive worldview".[101] The humanist impulse developed Western civilisation in significant ways but it did not replace the Scholasticism of the Middle Ages. Humanism encouraged critical and comparative approaches to authoritative ancient texts and to different cultures. It broke down Christian religious assumptions and it promoted the development of the individual.[102] Humanism acted in tandem with other ways of looking at the world and, while they might have indulged in attacks on their intellectual rivals, individual scholars were likely to use multiple methodologies. Wieacker admitted that his definition of early humanism suffered from "instability". Hence the fourteenth century jurist Cino da Pistoia "protested against juristic method on humanist grounds" but "was himself one of the great Commentators".[103]

(3) Areskine and the legal history narrative

Areskine, an early modern practising lawyer with an academic interest in the sources of law, had no inkling of Wieacker's twentieth-century construct. Areskine's legal texts came from many different early modern "schools" and the make-up of his collection challenges the traditional legal history narrative. Areskine bought his books not as an expression of his membership of a specific school of legal scholarship but as a practising and scholarly lawyer of the first half of the eighteenth century. His books show his interest in what was later dubbed "legal humanism" but are not limited to this tradition. His collection shows his concern for comparative law and includes not only notable editions of the *Corpus Iuris Civilis* but also collections of customary law from across Europe.

Areskine collected, read, and used his books in practice. Any of his books, including those by classical authors and early modern humanists, had potential as a source for constructing legal arguments. A more relevant metaphor for Areskine's law is captured by Reinhard Zimmermann who describes

101 R Lesaffer, *European Legal History: A Cultural and Political Perspective*, transl by J Arriens (2009) 346. See also Osler (n 91) at 404.

102 Lesaffer (n 101) 346–349.

103 Wieacker (n 86) 63. See also Wim Decock's contribution on "Elegant scholastic humanism?" in this volume for this tension.

the development of legal thinking as a "tapestry of many different shades and nuances" in which "the various strands of tradition were very closely interwoven".[104]

F. EARLY MODERN LAW BOOKS

Law books were produced in large numbers throughout the early modern period. Students, teachers, and practitioners all required legal texts. Popular books could be frequently reprinted in different printed centres across Europe. The Spanish jurist Antonio Gómez's *Commentariorum variarumque resolutionum juris civilis communis et regii tomi tres*, for example, appeared eighteen times in six cities between 1562 and 1631.[105] Areskine had the version printed at Geneva in 1631.[106] The format of choice for lawyers was the folio, which was ideal for display on a university lectern or on the shelves of a practitioner's consultation room.[107] Scottish booksellers imported folio books from England and the Continent since they "were not so commonly printed in Scotland".[108]

Printers and investors recognised the importance of the market for legal books and

> [as] well as standard texts and their glosses . . . entrepreneurial publishers saw to it that the monuments of medieval jurisprudence in various genres (criminal law, *consilia* and decisions, specialist books on evidence and interpretation) remained in print. They actively pursued living authors for their writings, especially in the area of practical law, and set about printing them in their own market zones (or reprinting them if they had first been published elsewhere).[109]

Many of the products of this sixteenth- and seventeenth-century activity came to rest in Areskine's eighteenth-century library.

Although the Scottish printing industry developed, book buyers continued to demand stock from abroad.[110] Scottish buyers of humanist texts, both legal and miscellaneous, relied on imports until the mid-eighteenth century.

104 R Zimmermann, *Roman Law, Contemporary Law, European Law: The Civilian Tradition Today* (2001) 160.

105 I Maclean, *Scholarship, Commerce, Religion: The Learned Book in the Age of Confessions, 1560–1630* (2012) 65.

106 Folio 39: *Commentariorum variarumque resolutionum juris civilis, communis, et regii tomi tres: primus, Vltimarum voluntatum materiam continent; secundus, Contractuum; tertius Delictorum* (1631).

107 Maclean (n 105) 64, 277 n 87.

108 Mann (n 57) 226–227.

109 Maclean (n 105) 65.

110 Mann (n 57) 228.

In 1756, the Foulis brothers of Glasgow, printers to the university there, published their celebrated edition of Homer's *Iliad*. This was followed by the *Odyssey* in 1757. These featured "accurate and legible texts, supported by well-cast and designed founts".[111] Areskine, however, owned copies of Homer produced in Geneva and Amsterdam.[112]

G. HUMANIST LAW BOOKS

(1) Legal humanists

The publication of the *Florentina* in the Torelli edition of 1553 marked a turning point in humanist legal scholarship. Unlike earlier humanist scholars who had worked to remove glosses and commentaries or who had sought to "improve the quality of their texts",[113] Lelio and Francesco Torelli, in collaboration with Antonio Augustín, worked directly from the manuscript preserved in Florence, the earliest known copy of the Digest. Their edition of the *Florentina* recreated as closely as possible the original spelling in the manuscript and they stressed that their only interventions were to correct obvious errors and to add minor punctuation. They also provided a list of their few emendations. Early modern scholars greatly admired the editorial integrity of the project and the resulting publication provided a model for other humanist publishing endeavours.[114]

(2) "*Bibliotheca juris civilis Romani*"

Some of the books early modern legal book buyers acquired contained bibliographic information. One of the foremost of these was by Jacques Godefroy (1587–1652), an internationally renowned humanist scholar, whose "*Bibliotheca juris civilis Romani*", the second part of his *Manuale iuris*, listed a range of books and provided bibliographical guidance for scholars of Roman law: this would retain its usefulness for nearly a cen-

111 I Beavan and W McDougall, "The Scottish Book Trade", in M F Suarez and M L Turner (eds), *The Cambridge History of the Book in Britain vol. 5: 1695–1830* (2009) 352 at 359.

112 Miscellaneous octavo 155: *Homeri poemata duo, Ilias et Odyssea sive Ulyssea. Ejusdem Batrachomyomachia, Hymni et Epigrammata, cum latina interpretatione ad verbum. Adjecta sunt etiam Coluthi de raptu Helenae et Tryphiodori de Ilii excidio poemata* (1604). Areskine had another copy of the *Odyssey* at Miscellaneous octavo 156: *Odyssea* (1707).

113 Stein (n 84) 77.

114 B Richardson, *Print Culture in Renaissance Italy: The Editor and the Vernacular Text, 1470–1600* (2004) 130–131.

tury.[115] M H Hoeflich has pointed out the importance of this work as a resource for the history of the publication of Roman law texts in the sixteenth and seventeenth centuries. It was one of the earliest bibliographies of Roman law books and commentaries on them, it showcases the humanist approach to legal scholarship, and its frequent reissue meant it was widely available to scholars and jurists.[116]

In addition to his two copies of his *Manuale iuris*, Areskine had many of Godefroy's other works including his edition of the *Codex Theodosianus*,[117] his other studies of pre-Justinianic law,[118] his books on civil law,[119] and his discourses on legal history.[120] The books Godefroy recommended in his "*Bibliotheca*" had informed his own research projects and he had many of the books in his own library.[121]

Areskine's 1731 manuscript list includes the seventh or eighth and the ninth editions of Godefroy's *Manuale iuris*.[122] Areskine's copy of the ninth

115 M H Hoeflich, "A seventeenth century Roman law bibliography: Jacques Godefroy and his '*Bibliotheca juris civilis Romani*'"(1982) 75 *Law Library Journal* 514 at 517–518.

116 Hoeflich (n 115) at 518.

117 Folio 8: *Codex Theodosianus cum perpetuis commentariis Iacobi Gothofredi . . . praemittuntur chronologia accuratior, cum chronico historico, & prolegomena . . . opus posthumum . . . recognitum & ordinatum ad vsum Codicis Iustinianei, opera et studio Antonii Maruillii* (1665). This was his study of the Theodosian Code of 438, a collection of imperial enactments which were the "first official codification of the law". G Mousourakis, *The Historical and Institutional Context of Roman Law* (2003) 381.

118 Quarto 118: *De Cenotaphio: deq[ue] diuersis, super eius religione, Ulpiani & Marciani sententiis, diatriba* (1634) bound with *Libanii Antiocheni pro Templis Gentilium non Exscindendis, ad Theodosium M. Imp. Oratio . . . /nunc primùm edita à Iacobo Gothofredo . . . notisq[ue] illustrata. Gr. & Lat.* (1634). Quarto 119: *Iac. Gothofredi . . . Orationes politice tres: puta, I. Ulpianus: seu, De maiestate principis Romani legibus soluta. II. Iulianus: seu, De arcanis Iuliani Imp. artibus, ad profligandam religionem Christianam. III. Ahaica: seu, de causis interitus Reipublicae Achaeorum* (1634) bound with *Iac. Gothofredi . . . De imperio maris déque iure naufragii colligendi, hypomnēma ex iure Romano, ad legem Axiōsis seu legem Deprecatio, 9, Digestis [sic] de L. Rhodia de Iactu* (1637) and *Iacobi Gothofredi . . . De Famosis Latronibus Investigandis, dissertatio ad L. Si Barsatoram 13. Cod. de Fideiussoribus* (1652). Quarto 121: *Iacobi Gothofredi ic. Opuscula varia; iuridica, politica, historica, critica: Quae ab authore, dum in viuis erat, edita, deinde ab eodem recognita & aucta, nunc denuo post eius obitum in vnum collecta, locupletiora ac emendatiora prodeunt* (1654).

119 Quarto 117: *Iacobi Gothofredi ic. Animadversionum iuris civilis liber: pro vero nonnullarum legum intellectu: & genuinâ earundem lectione. Ad antecessores Bituricenses* (1628). Quarto 122: *Q. Sept. Florentis Tertulliani Ad nationes: libri duo: hactenus inediti* (1625). Quarto 169: *Iacobi Gothofredi IC. v. cos. nouus in titulum Pandectarum de diuersis regulis iuris antiqui, commentarius. Quo id potissimum variis modis agitur* (1652).

120 Quarto 120: *Iacobi Gothofredi ic. Opuscula varia; iuridica, politica, historica, critica: Quae ab authore, dum in viuis erat, edita, deinde ab eodem recognita & aucta, nunc denuo post eius obitum in vnum collecta, locupletiora ac emendatiora prodeunt* (1654).

121 Hoeflich (n 115) at 526.

122 The author is misidentified as "Gothofredi (Dion:)". There are two dates given at the entry for Octavo 172 so it is not possible to know exactly which edition Areskine had.

edition, dated 1676 and published in Leyden, survives in the National Library of Scotland.[123] Although there are no notations or other marks in the book which might indicate that Areskine used the "*Bibliotheca*" as a buying guide, there are so many matches between the recommended list and Areskine's catalogue that they are probably not coincidental.

Legal humanists, as their propaganda repeatedly reminds their readers, looked at the sources of Roman law to determine what the *Corpus Iuris Civilis* actually said instead of relying on medieval explications of ancient texts. Key to the process was a revival of Greek learning in the West, which was inspired by the fall of Justinian's one-time capital Constantinople in 1453 (see Stolte elsewhere in this volume). Scholars who could read Greek arrived in the West and scholars of both Greek and of classical Latin turned their attention to the *Corpus Iuris Civilis*. Godefroy cited only humanist editions of the *Corpus Iuris Civilis* in his "*Bibliotheca*".[124] In "*Historia, seu progressus Juris Civilis Romani*", which precedes the "*Bibliotheca*" in *Manuale iuris*, Godefroy listed scholars he admired because he thought that they had personally studied the *Florentine Pandects*. These included a roll call of humanist scholars from across Europe including Guillaume Budé, Andrea Alciati, Gregor Haloander, Antonio Agustín, Lelio Torelli, Henricus Zoesius, Wiggle van Aytta, and Jacques Cujas.[125] Areskine had works by all of these in his library and some of his books were the editions that Godefroy recommended.

Godefroy praised Gregor Haloander's edition of the Digest published in 1529 and 1531[126] for its use of the Florentine manuscript and its attempt at restoring the original text.[127] Godefroy also mentioned Louis Russard and François Duaren's notes on the *Corpus Iuris Civilis* published in 1567.[128]

123 Octavo 173: *I. Gothofredi Manuale iuris, sev parva juris mysteria: ubi quatuor sequentia continentur. Juris civilis Romani I. Historia. II. Bibliotheca. III. Florilegium sententiarum juris politicarum, & communium notionum, ex corpore Justinianeo desumptarum. IV. Series librorum & titulorum in Digestis & in Codice* (1676). NLS Alva.143 with Areskine's bookplate.

124 Hoeflich (n 115) at 525.

125 Godefroy (n 120) at 40. See Douglas Osler's contribution to this volume for Alciati's questionable methodology, Haloander's text tampering, and the differences between humanist and modern philology.

126 Quarto 3: *Digestorum seu Pandectarum libri quinquaginta* (1529). Folio 18: *Nearōn Ioustinianou basileōs, tōn en tō nun heuriskomenōn, kai hōs heuriskontai, biblion . . . Nouellarum constitutionum Dn. Iustiniani principis, quae exstant, et vt exstant, volumen. Appositi sunt item canones sanctorũ Apostolorũ per Clementem in unũ congesti. Gregorio Haloandro interprete* (1531). For Haloander's unreliability, see Osler (n 125) and elsewhere in this volume.

127 Hoeflich (n 115) at 525; Godefroy (n 123) at 69, 73.

128 Octavo 2: *Ius ciuile manuscriptorum librorum ope, summa diligentia et integerrima fide infinitis locis emendatum, et perpetuis notis illustratum; L. Russardo . . . auctore: consilio tamen &*

Godefroy preferred editions of the *Florentina* for which their editors claimed to have worked directly from the manuscript so his inclusion of the 1553 edition of the *Florentine Pandects* published by Lelio and Francesco Torelli[129] is unsurprising. Louis Le Caron's edition of the *Corpus Iuris Civilis* published in 1575[130] is listed without any comment.[131] His father, Denis Godefroy's edition was the best available version.[132] Although he did not have an edition of Denis Godefroy's *Corpus Iuris Civilis* of the same year in the recommended edition, Areskine had three other editions of the work, which were published in 1589,[133] 1628,[134] and 1705.[135]

Areskine's catalogue also has matches in author, title, publication, and date with Godefroy for works by Agustín,[136] whom Godefroy admired as an accurate editor of pre-classical legal texts,[137] and by François Baudouin[138] and Scipio Gentili.[139] Areskine seems to have substituted alternate versions when the specific editions recommended in the "*Bibliotheca*" were not available, in one example Areskine has the Paris edition of 1584 of Agustín's *De*

auctoritate Fran. Duareni . . . qui summaria in Pandectas præscripsit, Nouellasque constitutiones ad optimum Græcum exemplar collatas, antiquę integritati restituit (1567).

129 Hoeflich (n 115) at 525. Godefroy did not have his own copy. It was already a rare and expensive book. Hoeflich (n 115) at 526. Folio 1: Justinian I, Emperor of the East & L Taurellus, *Digestorum seu Pandectarum libri quinquaginta ex Florentinis Pandectis repraesentati* (1553).

130 Folio 164: *Dn. sacratissimi principis Iustiniani pp. a. Iuris enucleati ex omni vetere iure collecti Digestorum seu Pandectarum libri quinquaginta: Cum breuissimis doctissimorum quorundam Iurisconsultorum annotationibus in margine adscriptis, quibus plerique loci vel restituuntur, vel diligentiùs explicantur* (1575).

131 Hoeflich (n 115) at 526.

132 Hoeflich (n 115) at 526.

133 Octavo 1: *Corpvs Ivris Civilis/ 2, Codicis Dn. Iustiniani libri XII* (1589).

134 Folio 167: *Corpus iuris ciuilis quo ius uniuersum Iustinianeum comprehenditur: Pandectis, ad Florentinum . . ., Codice . . ./cum notis repetitae quintùm praelectionis Dionysii Gothofredi* (1628).

135 Quarto 1: *Corpus juris civilis Romani, in quatuor partes distinctum /Dionysio Gothofredo, jc. authore, cum appendice, seu auctario eorum, quae prioribus hujus formae editionibus defuerunt, atque indicibus singulari cura revisis ac locupletatis. Singulorum contenta syllabus praefationi praemissus monstrabit* (1705).

136 Octavo 22: *Antonii Augustini iurecos. Emendationum, & opinionu[m] lib. IIII: Eiusdem ad modestinum, siue de excus. Liber singularis. Item, Laelij Taurelli, ad Gallum, & legum Velleam, ad Catonem, & Paulum, de militiis excasu. Omnia quidem secundum Pand. Flo. Editionem* (1560) and Octavo 23: *Antonii Augustini iurecos. Emendationum, & opinionu[m] lib. IIII: Eiusdem ad modestinum, siue de excus. Liber singularis. Item, Laelij Taurelli, ad Gallum, & legum Velleam, ad Catonem, & Paulum, de militiis excasu. Omnia quidem secundum Pand. Flo. Editionem* (1560).

137 Hoeflich (n 115) at 522.

138 Octavo 80: *Fran. Balduinus . . . ad leges de iure civili, Voconiam, Falcidiam, Iuliam Papiam Poppaeam, Rhodiam, Aquiliam* (1559) and *Francisci Balduini . . . Iustinianus, sive, de iure novo, commentariorum libri III* (1560).

139 Octavo 57: *Scipion. Gentilis iuriscos. de bonis maternis, et de secundis nuptiis, libri duo* (1606).

legibus et senatusconsultis liber[140] instead of the recommended Rome edition of 1583. Even if he did not acquire every book Godefroy mentioned, Areskine certainly shared his preference for works which demonstrated a humanist approach to the legal scholarship that Justinian's laws attracted.

(3) Areskine as a legal humanist

Areskine's library contained multiple versions of the *Corpus Iuris Civilis* and its component parts. This shows that Areskine was certainly interested in obtaining editions of the *Corpus Iuris Civilis* which had been created by humanists. These included books that were familiar to serious scholars of legal humanism such as the Torelli edition of the *Florentine Pandects*, Haloander's editions of the *Corpus Iuris Civilis* mentioned above and Charles Annibal Fabrot's *Basilikon libri LX*.[141] But this is not enough to assign him membership in an intellectual "school". While he appreciated humanist scholarship, Areskine did not limit his book collecting to texts published by humanists. Nor did he limit his selections of works by legal humanists to their editions and commentaries on the *Corpus Iuris Civilis*. His collection is much richer and more varied and offers a challenge to the standard narrative of legal history, which overemphasises the importance of the humanists and their works.

H. HUMANISM IN EIGHTEENTH-CENTURY SCOTLAND

The humanist tradition came to be challenged in the early eighteenth century. One of its major critics was Jean Le Clerc, an author Areskine had lectured on during his time as a regent. Le Clerc and others judged that humanism had failed because its translation exercises had been carried out by inadequate scholars using questionable methodologies and because its publications had not provided enough historical context for their work to be

140 Folio 58: *Antonij Augustini Archiepiscopi Tarraconensis De legibus et senatusconsultis liber: adiunctis legum antiquarum & senatusconsultorum fragmentis, cum notis Fulvij Vrsini, multò quam antea emendatius, additis etiam locorum quorundam notis, cum duobus indicibus locupletissimis. Adiectus est Iusti Lipsij libellus de legibus regijs & X. viralibus* (1584). Areskine's copy, containing his bookplate, is now in the Advocates Library (Alva Collection, 1).

141 Folio 207: *Tōn Basilikōn biblia LX = Basilikōn libri LX: in VII. tomos divisi Carolvs Annibal Fabrotvs antecessorum Antecessorum Aquisextiensium decanus Latinè vertit, & Græcè edidit* (1647). For these see J W Cairns, "Alexander Cunningham's proposed edition of the Digest: an episode in the history of the Dutch elegant school of Roman law (parts I–II)" (2001) 69 *Tijdschrift voor Rechtsgeschiedenis* 81, 307 at 344–345.

understood.[142] The humanist tradition had also failed to make its learning relevant and accessible to the educated lay reader.[143] The polite learning of the Enlightenment offered a fresh approach by encouraging scholars to look at texts anew and to offer fresh comments and interpretations.[144] By 1688, periodicals such as the *Journal des Sçavans*, *Acta Eruditorum*, and the *London Gazette*[145] were stocked by the Advocates Library in Edinburgh. The presence of these polite publications demonstrates the advocates' gentlemanly interests in the arts, sciences, and current events.

The integrated approach to polite learning was not new for legal scholars, especially those connected with "elegant" jurisprudence, who had been looking at texts critically and composing commentaries since the seventeenth century.[146] Although they shared humanistic concerns about the proper use of language and the use of rhetoric, these jurists also put law into historical context. In the Scottish context, meanwhile, humanistic and enlightened themes co-existed. As humanism's traditions and concepts took on new meanings during the eighteenth century,[147] there was a tension between the types of learning that Scottish *literati* were able to resolve. Their humanist educations allowed them to process learned material and they shared, explained, and discussed knowledge in the sociable world of the Enlightenment.

I. LAW TEXTS AS PART OF A LIVING LEGAL SYSTEM: CONVERSATIONS AND TOOLS

Books were part of a living legal system for Areskine and his contemporaries. Practising lawyers did not need texts full of arcane knowledge or springboards for exploring linguistic or historical problems: they needed sources used to support contemporary legal arguments. Scottish lawyers' "Informations" and other types of written pleadings presented to the court,[148] were peppered

142 J I Israel, *Enlightenment Contested: Philosophy, Modernity, and the Emancipation of Man, 1670–1752* (2008) 414–415.

143 Israel (n 142) 416.

144 Israel (n 142) 415.

145 J M Pinkerton, *The Minute Book of the Faculty of Advocates*, vol 1: *1661–1712* (1976) 84.

146 The traditions of glossing and commenting on legal texts were, of course, long standing and had been practised since the Middle Ages.

147 J W Cairns, "The Formation of the Scottish Legal Mind in the Eighteenth Century: Themes of Humanism and Enlightenment in the Admission of Advocates", in N MacCormick and P Birks (eds), *The Legal Mind: Essays for Tony Honoré* (1986) 253 at 258.

148 For these see A Stewart, 'The Session Papers in the Advocates Library", in H MacQueen (ed), *Miscellany Four by Various Authors* (Stair Society 2002) 199–223.

with references to such authorities as Justinian's Digest, the *lex Rhodia*, classical authors, and natural law texts such as those of Grotius and Pufendorf.

(1) Conversations with the dead

The dead could help construct modern arguments via their written works. Early modern scholars could perceive themselves as directly linked to the ancients and with more recent authors. René Descartes noted, in his *Discours de la méthode*,[149] that reading an old book offered the chance to have a conversation with its author.[150] This was an ancient idea and Descartes may have been inspired by such a "conversation" with Seneca whose letters (one describing his conversations with books when ill and bedridden) were published in France in the same year as Descartes' *Discours*.[151] In his *De la sagesse*, Pierre Charron described two types of educational experience:[152] benefits could come from conversations with both the living and the dead.[153] Both Descartes and Charron echoed ideas of Renaissance humanists and their relationship with ancient writers: ancient authors came from a different place and time but "despite their acknowledged otherness [could] speak powerfully to modern concerns".[154] Linked with this idea of conversation was the modern's place for engaging in the activity. This was "the study or the library, in which the lone reader embarks upon a dialogue with the books and the authors" read.[155]

The implication is that if he wanted to know what an ancient such as Cicero, Livy or Seneca, a humanist such as Buchanan, Craig, or Henryson, or a natural law theorist such as Grotius or Pufendorf thought about a legal or historical matter, an early modern reader could ask him for opinions via their writings. The freshly translated and well-produced books created by humanists in the sixteenth and seventeenth centuries allowed later scholars an improved conversation with classical and modern luminaries. Scottish

149 Miscellaneous quarto 53: R Descartes, *Discours de la méthode : pour bien conduire sa raison, & chercher la verité dans les sciences; Plus La dioptrique; Les meteores; Et La geometrie. Qui sont des essais de cete méthode* (1637). The copy listed in Arskine's library catalogue has the bookplate of his son, James Erskine and is now in the Special Collections of the Stanford University Libraries. See also Maclean elsewhere in this volume.

150 R Goulbourne, "Conversations with the dead in early modern France" (2013) 108 *Modern Language Review* 90 at 91.

151 Goulbourne (n 150) 93–94.

152 Miscellaneous octavo 80: P Charron, *De la sagesse trois livres* (1662).

153 Goulbourne (n 150) at 95–96.

154 Goulbourne (n 150) at 95.

155 Goulbourne (n 150) at 94.

lawyers regularly cited classical authors in their Session Papers. It is not fanciful to suggest that this support for modern legal arguments from respected ancient authors came from lawyers actively interrogating their libraries to add authority to their legal arguments.

(2) Tools of trade

The fictional lawyer Paulus Pleydell's assertion that he relied on his books to succeed in his profession bears this out. Lawyers needed more than legal textbooks if they were to do their work well. In Sir Walter Scott's *Guy Mannering*, Mannering visits Pleydell's library which features "the best editions of the best authors". Pleydell calls these his "tools of trade" and goes on to explain that a "lawyer without history or literature is a mechanic, a mere working mason; if he possesses some knowledge of these he may call himself an architect".[156]

Areskine could have claimed the title: his *Information for the East India Company of Holland, of the Chamber of Zealand* of 24 March 1729 is a thirty-five-page-long display of legal knowledge. Areskine's examination of the right to the ownership of goods which survived a shipwreck includes references to civil law and interpretations of it as well as comparing the customary laws of Burgundy, England, the Hanse Towns, Holland, and Scotland.[157] Given the closeness in date between the initiation of his library catalogue and the case, many of the sources he cites were available to him on his library shelves when he prepared this case. This "Information" provides evidence for the practical character of Areskine's collection.

On page 23 of this "Information", Areskine says:

> It would be an endless labour, to run thorow the whole Authorities upon this Point which are almost innumerable, and is to be seen in the most common Books in the Hands of Lawiers; and therefore 'tis believed it may be taken for a settled Point, without troubling the honourable Judge with further upon this Branch of the Argument.[158]

"Information for the East India Company of Holland" shows that Areskine used his private library for reference in his legal practice and it demonstrates the practical nature of his collection for him as lawyer. Furthermore, his

156 W Scott, *Guy Mannering; or The Astrologer*, 4th edn, vol 2 (1817) 290.
157 C Areskine, *Information for Appollonius Lampsints, Hieronymus Joseph Boudaen, Johan Steengragt, and Peter van Hoorn, Lords and Directors of the Honourable East India Company of Holland* (1729).
158 Areskine (n 157) 23.

comment shows that he expected his legal colleagues would have, or at least have access to, similar books: they would be known to his fellow practitioners in the eighteenth century without the need to cite them specifically.

In addition to their private collections, Areskine and other Edinburgh advocates had access to an important source of books in the form of the Advocates Library. The Minute Book of the Faculty of Advocates recorded on 25 March 1682 that the advocates planned to "taike one two or three rowmes to keep ther bookes in" and to "print a programme giving notice to all persons who have any law books or others to sell, that they send catalogues of the volumes and editions therof" to them.[159] The recently elected Dean of Faculty, Sir George Mackenzie of Rosehaugh "and any quorum of his councill" were "to consider what bookes are fit to be baught".[160]

By 1711, the year Areskine became an advocate, John Spotiswoode reported in his *Form of process* that the advocates had developed the Advocates Library to such an extent that it was "already the best in *North-Britain*, & in Process of time, may come to be the best in the Isle . . . by reason of the *Number*, & *Goodness of the Books*, for the *Advocats* bestow yearly very liberally that way, and their Stock . . . is dayly increasing".[161] Spotiswoode also noted that the advocates were remaining true to Mackenzie's vision of creating a law collection for lawyers and that, although "Men are of different Geniuses" and "the Library may be furnished with the *Best Books* in all Sciences", they favoured those "which have a Tendance towards *Knowledge of the Law*".[162]

Areskine's "Miscellaneous" texts also follow the recommendations for forming a legal collection that Mackenzie outlined in his inaugural oration of 1689 celebrating the foundation of the Advocates Library. As well as being one of the founders of the advocates' collection in Edinburgh, Mackenzie was a prolific scholar and legal professional, nominated "Historia, Critica, & Rhetorica" as "Jurisprudentiae inservientia"[163] and therefore necessary

159 Pinkerton (n 145) 59.

160 Pinkerton (n 145) 59.

161 J Spotiswood, *The form of process, before the Lords of Council and Session, observed in advocations, ordinary actions, suspensions* (1711) xlv. Areskine had a copy listed at Octavo 280.

162 Spotiswood (n 161) xlv.

163 G Mackenzie, *Oratio Inauguralis habita Edenburgi Id. Mar. 1689. A Dom. Georgio Mackenzeo, De structura bibliothecae purè juridicae, et hinc De vario in jure scribendi genere* (1689) 24. For a translation see G Mackenzie, "*Oratio inauguralis*" in *Oratio inauguralis in aperienda jurisconsultorum bibliotheca*, transl J H Loudon (1989) 46–86. For the early development of the library and its collection see B Hillyard, "The Formation of the Library, 1682–1729", in P Cadell and A Matheson (eds), *For the Encouragement of Learning: Scotland's National Library, 1689–1989* (1989) 23–66.

elements in a legal collection. Areskine's library included texts related to all three of these attendant disciplines. Areskine collected the works of classical authors such as Cicero, Tacitus, and Virgil, histories of various nations, and collections of essays and speeches. The divisions in the collection are not always clear and the two basic categories of law and miscellaneous seem quite fluid. What is certain, however, is that Areskine's library went beyond the books he needed to understand and serve the law. If his legal library showed his knowledge of the law, his engagement with legal humanism and continental law, and his abilities as a lawyer, Areskine's miscellaneous books demonstrated his taste, his familiarity with philosophical ideas and debates, his interest in and involvement with the desire to "improve" the nation via scientific progress, and his interest in the study of its history.

J. CONCLUSION: BOOKWORMS AND MOTHS

The techniques and methods of legal humanism helped develop new books of Scots law. Viscount Stair, Mackenzie, Lord Bankton, John Erskine of Carnock, and Baron David Hume all cited earlier and foreign sources in their important works but Scots law increasingly relied on its own voice and character. Scottish jurists and lawyers came to depend less on the civilian tradition and humanistic interest in the Latin and Greek texts of law faded in favour of case law and natural law as the Scottish legal system developed throughout the eighteenth century. By the mid-nineteenth century the style of law that had been practised by Areskine was no longer viable and the books he had used took on an antiquarian aspect. Lawyers of Areskine's generation of Scottish lawyers came to be seen as:

> honest, able worms that burrowed away their lives amid the parchment, the print, and the moths of Voet and Heineccius, of Stair and [John] Erskine, of the Ius Feudale and the Pandects . . . From 1850 Vinnius and the Corpus Juris vanished into obscurity. When dragged by the erudite from their hiding places they are now greeted with a sneer! . . . Lawyers would now as soon as dream of trying to revive a mummy as of reverting to such archaic models of pleading.[164]

Humanism gave way to Enlightenment in Scotland. There was still a place for classical learning but a new curriculum at the universities with specialist

164 J Crabb Watt, *John Inglis, Lord Justice-General of Scotland: A Memoir* (1893) 54–55. Watt regretted the loss of written pleadings enforced by the Court of Session Act of 1850 and admired (at 54) the "Many tomes of recondite lore, classified and ranged along the gallery of the Law Room [in the Advocates Library] . . . accordingly monumental of the erudition, the patience, and the industry of three centuries of the Scottish bar".

professors and new subjects, including the law of nature and nations, and modern sources of Scots law became increasingly important as the century progressed. Areskine's library bears witness to the change that occurred in the eighteenth century as lawyers' "training came to privilege learning in natural law . . . over an older legal humanism".[165]

165 Cairns (n 23) at 222.

Postscript

Paul J du Plessis

The chapters contained in this volume have been arranged in a specific order with a view to reassessing larger claims about legal humanism. As such, it is not merely an edited collection loosely arranged around a central theme. Rather, it is an attempt to initiate further discussion about legal humanism and its role in the narrative of European legal history in a structured and systematic way.

The four parts of this volume deal with certain fundamental questions. In the first part, "Defining legal humanism", Olser and Wijffels outline some of the main problems in identifying and defining legal humanism as a movement in the narrative of European legal history. Their contributions show that there is little scholarly consensus on the essential features of legal humanist scholarship and consequently also on the convenient classification of a jurist as a "legal humanist" or "other", characteristic of earlier works on European legal history.

This uncertainty about method and classification foregrounds the next part, "A break with the past/contemporary critiques". It is a well-established and often-repeated *topos* in earlier scholarship on European legal history that legal humanism represented a break with the legal method of the Bartolists. While the latter were seemingly applying Roman law to the contemporary problems of the day, the former were preoccupied with seemingly ephemeral issues of textual criticism and philological analysis, thereby contributing to the "historicising" of Roman law. This fundamental question is addressed here. In this section, the contributions of Prévost, Rossi and Longfield Karr collectively demonstrate two important points. First, that the break with the past was in fact not a break at all. Rather, humanist scholars continued to engage with medieval legal scholarship in a profound, albeit selective manner. In doing so, they were not above criticising the medieval lawyers for their failings. More importantly, however, as Rossi and Longfield Karr show, the legal humanists' preoccupation with seemingly trivial matters of textual analysis was directly aimed at contemporary concerns. Using history and philosophy, they launched a devastating critique against problems connected with the emerging idea of the nation state such as sources of power, government corruption and the absence of good governance.

These insights lead on to the next part, "Legal humanism: a pan-European methodology?". The aim of this part of the volume is to establish the impact of legal humanism across Europe by focusing on a number of micro-histories covering Spain, France, Germany, Portugal, the Netherlands and England. These micro-histories raise a number of important points. The first of these is the use of sources. Decock, Van Ittersum and Hepburn investigate the sources used by legal humanists when compiling their own works. In doing so, they reflect on issues such as the use of *compendia* to create impressive lists of references, the acknowledging of sources "borrowed" from elsewhere and the working methods of jurists in the early modern period. Hepburn also draws a number of important conclusions about the relationship between legal theory and legal practice. The second theme emerging from this section is the methodologies employed by legal humanists. As Jakab, Stolte and Ibbetson show, the philological methods employed by the jurists of this period do not always stand up to modern scientific scrutiny. This rather important conclusion hints at the large amount of work that still needs to be done on the "humanist" reconstructions of Greek and Roman texts, most notably in relation to the Byzantine sources (Stolte) and in applying the insights of the humanists to further modern understanding of "law in action" (Jakab).

The final part of this volume, "Legal humanism and the book trade", reflects on the importance of printing and the dissemination of legal literature in Europe during this period. Maclean investigates the importance of the Dutch Republic and its printing presses in the spread of humanist ideas across Europe, while Baston ends with a fascinating account of the importance of the printed books to Scottish advocates in the eighteenth century and the way in which the connection with the Dutch Republic allowed for the substantial infiltration of humanist ideas in Scots law.

So what does this all amount to? As many scholars of European history have pointed out, this period (whatever one may choose to call it) is a particularly unsettled time in the history of Europe. Four main currents dominate it, namely the Renaissance, the Reformation, the Counter-Reformation and the discovery of the "New World". Each of these events, in turn, generated much political, economic and social upheaval. One may legitimately enquire why, amid such uncertainty, the jurists of Europe chose to reflect back upon the history of their shared legal heritage as the way forward. The answer to this question requires further investigation. Preliminary thoughts suggest that it may be related to the humanist understanding of the function of history as the provider of *exempla* both good and bad from which contemporaries could choose. This essentially Roman understanding of the purpose of history would not be incompatible with the endeavours of the humanists.

It would be very easy to conclude this book with a barbed comment aimed at one of the authors of the general surveys of European legal history currently dominating the market. But such a comment would be unfair. After all, European legal history is a relatively young discipline and, until now, authors of such surveys had little to work with apart from sweeping grand narratives often produced for ideological reasons. It would also not be in keeping with the spirit of this series. I will therefore end on the following note. For those who maintain that the humanists are somehow to blame for the demise of Roman law by virtue of their "irrelevant" historical and philological analyses, I call upon Cicero, in many ways the poster-child of the Renaissance, to answer them as follows: "Nullius autem agricolae cultu stirps tam diuturna quam poetae versu seminari potest." (*De Legibus* 1.1.)

Index

EU Authorised Representative:
Easy Access System Europe Mustamäe tee 50, 10621 Tallinn, Estonia
gpsr.requests@easproject.com

Printed and bound by CPI Group (UK) Ltd, Croydon, CR0 4YY
29/09/2026
02224987-0008